THE LAW OF CORPORATE
INSOLVENCY IN SCOTLAND

AUSTRALIA
Law Book Co.
Sydney

CANADA and USA
Carswell
Toronto

HONG KONG
Sweet & Maxwell Asia

NEW ZEALAND
Brookers
Wellington

SINGAPORE and MALAYSIA
Sweet & Maxwell Asia
Singapore and Kuala Lumpur

THE LAW OF CORPORATE INSOLVENCY IN SCOTLAND

THIRD EDITION

John St Clair, Advocate in the
Government Legal Service of Scotland

and

The Hon. Lord Drummond Young

THOMSON

™

W. GREEN

Published in 2004 by
W. Green & Son Ltd
21 Alva Street
Edinburgh EH2 4PS

www.wgreen.thomson.com

Typeset by LBJ Typesetting Ltd of Kingsclere
Printed and bound in Great Britain by
TJ International Ltd, Padstow Cornwall

No natural forests were destroyed to make this product;
only farmed timber was used and replanted

A CIP catalogue record for this book is available from
the British Library.

ISBN 0414 01508 8

9 780414 015081

To David, Andrew, Kirstin, Alice and Anna

PREFACE

Since the second edition of our book, the landscape of corporate insolvency law in Scotland has been changed by the Human Rights Act 1998, the Scotland Act 1998 and by a significant amount of legislation emanating from Brussels. Finally the Enterprise Act 2002 has effectively abolished receivership in Scotland with administration now the chosen regime of corporate rescue. We have attempted to bring all these developments together in what, we hope, is an accessible textbook, which also discusses the sometimes controversial considerations that have driven some of the many changes.

We have received help and encouragement from many friends and colleagues for which we are very grateful. We would like to thank in particular Craig French of the Scottish Executive and Iain Talman of Biggart Baillie, solicitors, for their valuable input to the chapter on employment and pensions, and Donna Mackenzie Skene of Aberdeen University for kindly reading our chapter on the international dimensions of corporate insolvency law and giving us some very constructive suggestions. We are, of course, responsible for the text.

The law is stated as at March 1, 2004.

John St Clair
James Drummond Young

CONTENTS

PART 1

The History and Context of Scottish Insolvency Law

PART 2

Various Insolvency Regimes

PART 3

Effect of Insolvency

PART 4

Securities and Special Creditor Rights

PART 5

Procedure and Practice

PART 6

The International Dimension

TABLE OF CASES

TABLE OF STATUTES

TABLE OF STATUTORY INSTRUMENTS

THE HISTORY AND CONTEXT OF SCOTTISH CORPORATE INSOLVENCY LAW

CHAPTER 1

HISTORICAL BACKGROUND

Recent developments

With the coming into force of the insolvency provisions of the **1–01** Enterprise Act 2002 on September 15, 2003, the law of corporate insolvency has undergone its most radical overhaul since the Insolvency Act 1986 enacted recommendations of the committee chaired by Sir Kenneth Cork.[1] In the intervening years a country's laws of corporate insolvency have been recognised as of key importance to the proper and efficient working of a modern capitalist economy—as much part of a country's infrastructure as its roads, railways and airports. On their own a new set of laws will not transform a lawless and corrupt state, but they are a necessary condition for this transformation along with good corporate governance and a morality that values honesty, integrity and work. This importance is now almost universally recognised. The World Bank in April 2001 published *Principles and Guidelines for Effective Insolvency and Creditor Rights Systems*.[2] The *Principles and Guidelines* are being used in a series of experimental country assessments in connection with the program to develop *Reports on the Observance of Standards and Codes* (ROSC), using a common template based on the principles.[3] The United Kingdom has announced that it is to submit its insolvency laws, including those of Scotland, to a World Bank audit based on the *Principles and Guidelines*. It is the first major industrialised country to submit its laws to such an audit. Work starts in 2004 and is expected to take 12 to 18 months.

The big idea that has taken place in the intervening years since the Cork reforms is the concept of corporate rescue, which his report largely introduced to UK corporate insolvency law. Focus on this aspect of insolvency law has become established across the industrialised world.[4]

---

[1] Cmnd. 8558 (1982).

[2] This document is to be found on the World Bank website (*www.worldbank.org*).

[3] The World Bank is also collaborating with UNCITRAL and other institutions to develop a more elaborate set of implementational guidelines based on the principles.

[4] Examples are Chap.11 in the United States, the administration proceeding in the United Kingdom, the *redressement judiciare* in France, the examinership in Ireland, the extraordinary administration for large enterprises in Italy, judicial management in Singapore, commercial reorganization in Canada, voluntary administration and deed of company arrangement in Australia, the aptly named legislation in India for "sick" companies, and recent equivalent procedures in Belgium, the Czech Republic, Finland, Germany, Russia, the Slovak Republic, Sweden, Thailand, and many others. Nearly all these systems were created in the past 20 years, with only a few earlier examples, such as

However, the feature that most impresses about recent developments is how enormously complex corporate insolvency law has become—and the World Bank in *Principles and Guidelines* warns of the dangers of this, driving up transaction costs and impairing transparency. For example under the pressure of globalisation the complex area of cross border insolvency law has developed rapidly with initiatives from Europe and elsewhere.[5] Also, domestically there has been a growth industry in special insolvency regimes confined to a narrow class of firms like public-private partnerships, railway companies etc.,[6] where there is a public interest in an activity continuing. (Insurance companies for obvious reasons always had a special insolvency regime designed to ensure that assets held on behalf of policy holders were not in-mixed with assets of the company and the insurance business itself was handed over in an ordered state to another insurer if the firm went bust.[7]) Thirdly—and most complex of all—to protect the integrity of the financial markets and exchanges, deep inroads were made by Part VII of the Companies Act 1989 into the general law of insolvency to allow netting and charges to be effective within the markets before the general law operates. First were "market contracts",[8] followed by fixed and floating charges securing "money market" (currency exchange) contracts,[9] system-charges taken by settlement banks to secure obligations arising from uncertified securities,[10] and awaited are the Financial Collateral Arrangements (No.2) Regulations 2003, which implement the European Parliament and Council Directive 2002/47/EC on financial collateral arrangements which disapply some of the general insolvency laws on formalities of instruments in relation to financial collateral arrangements.[11] Yet, despite the growth in quantity and complexity of the regulation, public confidence in the United Kingdom in the integrity of the financial markets has been severely damaged by the misselling of pensions and endowment mortgages, and faith in auditors has been dented by the role of Arthur Anderson in the collapse of Enron.

Format of chapter

This chapter gives a brief history of corporate insolvency law in Scotland down to and including the Cork reforms enshrined in the

---

the Spanish Suspension of Payments of 1922 and the Japanese Corporate Rehabilitation Law of 1952, the latter influenced by the US Chandler Act of 1938 (Source *Principles and Guidelines*).

[5] See Chap.22.

[6] See para.5–07.

[7] See the Insurance Companies Act 1982 (now repealed) and the Financial Services and Markets Act 2000. Insurance companies are now regulated by the Financial Services Authority. The provisions governing winding up in Scotland are contained in the Insurers (Winding Up) (Scotland) Rules 2001 (SI 2001/4040 (S.21)) made under s.379 of the Financial Services and Markets Act 2000, which supplement the Insolvency (Scotland) Rules 1986 in relation to the winding up of insurers in Scotland, revoking, and re-making with modifications, the Insurance Companies (Winding up) (Scotland) Rules 1986; see also the Insurers (Reorganisation and Winding Up) Regulations 2003 (SI 2003/ 1102).

[8] Companies Act 1989, Pt VII; Financial Markets and Insolvency Regulations 1991 (SI 1991/880).

[9] Financial Markets and Insolvency (Money Market) Regulations 1995 (SI 1995/2094).

[10] Financial Markets and Insolvency Regulations 1996 (SI 1996/1449). This and SI 1995/2049 amend Pt VII of the Companies Act 1989.

[11] SI 2003/3226, effective December 26, 2003. It revoked SI 2003/3112 before it came into force. See also para.3–01.

Insolvency Act 1986 and attendant legislation. The background to the Enterprise Act reforms is given in the chapters covering the various subjects.

Early history

Until the nineteenth century Companies Acts, there were two ways by which companies were brought into existence: (a) by Act of the Scottish and then the United Kingdom Parliament or by Royal Charter (or its equivalent, *viz.* letters patent from the Sovereign); and (b) by private association. There was no procedure for the registration of companies, which is the modern procedure.   **1–02**

(1) Act of Parliament and Royal Charter

Until the growth of trade in the eighteenth century, most commercial activity was carried on by individual merchants or by partnerships. There were, however, certain areas of national concern where the investment of a large amount of capital was necessary, such as foreign trade and banking. When companies were set up for these purposes they were usually incorporated either under Act of Parliament or under Royal Charter. Transferability and transmissibility of the shares (*i.e.* they could be sold or bequeathed) were accepted necessary conditions of their corporate personality. As regards limitation of liability—at all events after 1707—it was not even thought competent for the Crown to incorporate by charter except with limited liability since a charter providing for unlimited liability would have been *ultra vires* of the royal prerogative without the consent of Parliament. Companies incorporated by Act of Parliament or Royal Charter were also usually given a legally enforceable monopoly, which was seen as a necessary protection for the shareholders.

The Darien Company and the Bank of Scotland, for example, were incorporated by Acts of the Scots Parliament in 1695. The Darien was incorporated for the purpose of trading with Africa and the Indies and setting up a Scottish colony in Panama. It has been estimated that as much as one-third of Scottish savings were invested in it. Its total failure, including 2,000 lives lost, was a national disaster and convinced many of the economic necessity of a merger of Scotland and England.[12] The Bank of Scotland, on the other hand, has survived to this day. The Royal Bank of Scotland had an Act of Incorporation in 1719 followed by

---

[12] In 1707 one of the last acts of the Scottish Parliament, as it sat on to wind up its affairs after the Treaty of Union with England, was to recommend William Paterson to Queen Anne for his "good service" in helping to draft the trade and finance articles of the Treaty of Union and calculate the Equivalent. Paterson was the founder of the Bank of England—adopted by the English Parliament in 1694–and inventor of the English national debt. He was also architect of the Darien scheme. The Equivalent was a key financial inducement in the Treaty—£398,085 10s.—which was to be paid by England to Scotland as a one-off capital compensation payment for the part of the Scottish revenue to be appropriated to service the English national debt. First priority claim on the Equivalent after currency adjustment was payment in full of the £250,000 invested in the Darien Company with accrued interest at five per cent.

a Royal Charter in 1727, and also still survives as an independent company. Both these banks had transferability, transmissibility and limited liability from the beginning, although without statutory monopoly.

(2) Voluntary associations

1–03   Appreciation of the advantages attaching to trading as joint stock companies, with official management and interests freely transferable, as exemplified by the statutory and chartered corporations, led to attempts in England and Scotland to achieve the same results by voluntary association—with differing results in the two Kingdoms.

English law recognised no half-way house between full incorporation under statute or charter and a loose association of individuals. There was no such thing in England as the legal personality of a partnership, as distinct from its component members[13] let alone a non-statutory joint stock company with limited liability. Even holding an organisation out to be a company was illegal, and a creditor could immediately go against any member of the partnership or association for debt and without first constituting the debt against the partnership.

In Scotland, in contrast, where a partnership had legal personality, a debt had to be first constituted against the partnership, and if the partnership's assets could not satisfy the debt, the creditor could then go against the partners.

The fact that in England joint stock companies were not recognised in law, like the chartered companies with limited liability, meant that subscribers to shares in unincorporated joint stock companies became immediately liable for the total debts of these companies. Despite their illegality and unlimited liability in England, however, there was a rush of joint stock companies and a mania of speculation, fraudulent prospectuses and crashed companies at the beginning of the eighteenth century. This led to the Bubble Act 1720. Its preamble described what had been going on: "Whereas in many cases, undertakers or subscribers have presumed to act as if they were corporate bodies, and have pretended to make their shares transferable or assignable without legal authority, either by Act of Parliament, or Charter from the Crown." It enacted that all such undertakings or attempts were to be deemed "illegal" and "void", and put down as "common and public nuisances".

Although the Bubble Act extended to Scotland, joint stock companies continued to flourish. The Act seems to have been pled only twice in the Scottish courts. In the case of the "Masons of Lanark"[14] it was pled, but the court disposed of the questions raised without reference to the Act. In *MacAndrew v Robertson*,[15] it was held that the Act did not apply to a company—although it was managed by directors and had shares which were transferable on certain conditions.

---

[13] See Sir William Holdsworth, *History of English Law* (3rd ed.), vols 8 and 15.
[14] (1730) Mor. 14555.
[15] (1828) 6 S. 950.

Both the Royal Bank of Scotland and the British Linen Company, which was incorporated by letters patent in 1746, seem to have been preceded by some form of joint stock company. Probably the fact that a partnership had legal personality in Scotland served as a useful model for the development by the common law of the legal personality of the joint stock company. The Act of 1825,[16] which coincided with the virtual repeal of the Bubble Act[17] in that year, vouched for their success. It stated that the practice had prevailed in Scotland of instituting societies having joint stocks with shares either transferable or conditionally transferable for the "purpose of carrying on banking and other commercial concerns, many of which had transacted business for a number of years, to the great advantage of that country". (A parliamentary return printed in the following year lists no fewer than 32 unchartered Scottish banks.) Joint stock companies, engaged in activities other than banking, were also common.

Arran Fishing Company and *Douglas Bank* cases

Arran Fishing Company case

A good example of the typical Scottish joint stock company of the **1–04** period was probably the Arran Fishing Company whose affairs were brought out in the case of *Stevenson & Co v MacNair* in 1757.[18] The Arran Fishing Company had been formed by 40 people in order to advance the fishing trade at the mouth of the Clyde and in the Western Isles. Each subscriber paid £50 making a total stock of £2,000. The trade was to be carried on by directors mentioned in the deed of association, with one clause giving the directors the power "to give such orders and directions concerning the stock and employment of the whole of the company's affairs as to them should seem meet which should be binding on the partners to the extent of their respective subscriptions until such orders or directions should be altered by general meeting . . . provided, nevertheless, that nothing herein contained shall be understood to import a power to the directors to compel any partner or subscriber to pay or contribute any more money to the stock than the sum by him subscribed".

In the case the pursuers, Stevenson and Company of the Rope Work at Port Glasgow who had supplied £72 worth of ropes, brought a case, not against the company or the partners in general, but against two or three partners who were monied men, "being advised that each and all of the partners were liable conjunctly and severally". The defence was: (1) that all the partners, or at least the directors representing the partners, should have been called as defenders; and (2) that the directors could not, by contracting debt, subject to liability any of the partners beyond the funds severally subscribed by them; and (3) that the defenders, having paid into the company the whole sum subscribed by them, were not further liable.

---

[16] 6 Geo. 4, c.131.
[17] 6 Geo. 4, c.91.
[18] Mor. 14560 and 14467; Kam Sel No 135; 5 Brown Sup. 340; and Bell's *Commentaries*, ii, 517 and 518.

The court waived giving judgment on the second defence but upheld the defenders on the first defence on the grounds that all parties having an interest were not called into the field or, in the words of the Lord President, "that in all societies, there is no bringing the partners into Court without calling either the managers or the whole partners". The second defence in relation to the limiting of liability came up in front of the court again a month later. The Lord Ordinary did not uphold the second defence but found the defenders liable, conjunctly and severally. The whole court, however, unanimously altered the Lord Ordinary's judgment and, according to Kames, sustained the defence upon the following grounds:

> "There is an obvious difference between the present case and that of a company trading without reference to a stock. In the latter case, each partner must be liable in solidum for the company's debts, for there is nothing here to limit the credit, and if the partner be liable at all, he must be liable in solidum. In the present case, the managers are liable for the debts they contract, and each partner is liable to make good his subscription. But upon what medium can he be made further liable? Not upon the common law, for he has neither contracted the debt nor given authority to contract beyond his stock. The very meaning of confining the trade by a joint stock is that each should be liable for his subscription and no further . . . with respect to equity, Grotius justly observes (1.2,c ii s 13) 'that it is not expedient to make partners further liable, because it would deter everyone from entering into a trading company'. To show the inexpediency and even absurdity of making each partner liable for the whole debts of a company, having a joint stock, consider only the Whale Fishing Company composed of a vast number of partners for the subscription of £35 each. According to the interlocutor pronounced by the Lord Ordinary, any one partner loaded with the whole debts of the company might be crushed to atoms in a moment."

For many years, the *Arran Fishing Company* case was regarded as fixing the law in favour of limited liability in the case of joint stock companies. Professor Bell, in his treatment of joint stock companies in the *Commentaries*, accepted the view as sound in law.[19] Adam Smith, writing 20 years later, regarded each partner "being bound only for his share", as one of the characteristic features of the joint stock company in Scotland.[20]

Douglas Bank case

The judgment in the *Arran Fishing Company* case, however, was not followed when the question came before the court again in 1778 by the failure of the Douglas Bank.[21] The matter was complicated by the fact that the question was at the instance of the company, which called upon

---

[19] Bell (5th ed., 1826), ii, 628.
[20] *Wealth of Nations*, Book V, Chap.i, Pt 3; (Bohn's ed.), ii, 261.
[21] *Douglas, Heron & Co v Alexander Hair* (1778) Mor. 14605.

certain members to furnish contributions for the liquidation of the banking indebtedness of the concern in excess of their subscription; that the company, while trading indifferently as the "Douglas Bank" and the "Ayr Bank" was really carried on under the social name of "Douglas, Heron and Company"; and that it was possible to regard the provision in the deed as to contribution of a certain amount of capital as merely providing for the original contribution of the partners and not as the subscription of a certain defined amount to the stock. The *Arran Fishing Company* case does not seem to have been considered by the court which held the partners, who were sued personally, jointly and severally, liable to pay the further sums called for by the company.

Pressure for reform

From the date of the *Douglas Bank* case until 1856 the fact of unlimited **1–05** liability of members of joint stock companies seems to have been accepted as a matter of course. Each shareholder was liable for the whole debts of a company. Sir Walter Scott was ruined by the failure of Ballantynes' in 1825. The Mercantile Law Commission in their report in 1854 accepted unlimited liability as a fact without question.[22] The growing necessities, however, of a rapidly developing trade and the example of foreign nations at length created a pressure in favour of reform and the introduction of limited liability in the modern sense, although the Mercantile Law Commission in 1854 recommended against its introduction. The matter came to Parliament as a Bill for Limitation of Liability and was passed by large majorities in 1855. Limited liability did not extend to Scotland until the following year.

Limited Liability Act of 1855

The Limited Liability Act, passed on August 18, 1855,[23] introduced **1–06** limited liability by the very simple measure of limiting the liability of a shareholder upon execution against him (in default of the company) to the portion of his shares not paid up, and providing that execution should only issue against a shareholder by leave of the court in which action or proceeding had been brought.[24] Lord Palmerston said in discussing the measure in committee:

> "My own opinion is—and no one denies it—that these Bills are of the utmost interest and importance . . . I will say in a few words that I consider that this contest lies between the few and the many. It is just one of those instances in which, I won't say the prejudices, but in which the opinions of the few are to be set against the interests of the great bulk of the community. There is nothing, I am persuaded, that would tend more to the general advantage of the public and the setting free of capitals, as these Bills propose to do,

---

[22] 1854 Report, *Lord Curriehill's Memorandum*, p.11 of appendices.
[23] 18 & 19 Vict., c.133.
[24] s.8.

that they may be turned to profitable employment. The present law prevents that being done. There is consequently a great quantity of small capital locked up which if these Bills were passed might be employed for the benefit of those who possess them, and also for the advantage of the community at large."[25]

The Bill as originally drafted applied only to companies having a nominal capital of £50,000 divided into shares of a nominal value of not less than £25 each. The capital requirement was reduced when the Bill passed into law. The main ground of opposition to limited liability was that it would be a "rogues' charter", enabling Victorian "bandit" firms to defraud creditors. The original high capital requirement had been an attempt to deny the privilege of limited liability to the small business sector, where the fraudulent abuse of limited liability at the expense of creditors was most to be expected, and indeed has been prevalent, until the present day. However, the counter-argument that this restriction would make the privilege of limited liability even worse—a rich man's charter—won the day.

Companies Acts 1856 and 1862/winding up

1–07   The principle of limited liability was extended to Scotland by the Companies Act 1856,[26] which first introduced companies constituted in the modern manner by memorandum and articles of association. However, it was the Companies Act 1862 which really laid down the foundations upon which all modern legislation relating to companies has been built. It introduced the concept of the company with limited liability available upon complying with the statutory formality of registration. It also provided a modern regime for dealing with a company which became insolvent. Briefly it provided:

(1) a company might be wound up voluntarily whenever the members had resolved that the company could not, by reason of its liabilities, continue in business and that it was advisable to wind up. The liquidator in such a voluntary winding up was appointed by the members and its proceedings were conducted without any representation on the part of the creditors (a distinction was not made, nor was it to be made for another 67 years until the 1929 Act, between the concept of the members' (solvent) liquidation and the creditors' (insolvent) liquidation);

(2) if the company had resolved to be wound up voluntarily, the court might make an order directing that the voluntary winding up should continue, "but subject to such supervision of the Court, and with such liberty for creditors, contributories, or others to apply to the Court, and generally upon such terms and subject to such conditions as the Court thinks just";

(3) a company might be wound up by the court in certain circumstances, such as the company was "unable to pay its

---

[25] *Hansard*, Vol. 139, ser.3, cols 1389, 1390.
[26] 19 & 20 Vict., c.47.

debts"; a company was "deemed to be unable to pay its debts" in three particular cases:

  (a) whenever a creditor served on the company at its registered office a written demand requiring the company to pay any sum due, and the company had, for the space of three weeks, "neglected to pay such sum, or to secure or compound for the same to the reasonable satisfaction of the creditor";
  (b) whenever an execution on a judgment obtained by a creditor against the company had been returned unsatisfied in whole or in part;
  (c) whenever it was proved to the satisfaction of the court that the company was unable to pay its debts.

Where the company was wound up by the court, the person appointed to assist the court and to administer the proceedings, was called an "official liquidator". There was also power, where an order for the winding up of a company subject to supervision of the court was subsequently superseded by an order directing the company to be wound up compulsorily, to appoint the voluntary liquidator to be official liquidator. Not all companies registered with limited liability. Apart from the chartered banks which had limited liability, the other banks[27] took the view that unlimited liability was good for public confidence. The City of Glasgow Bank was in that position when it collapsed in 1878. Its liabilities stood at £12,400,000[28] with assets of £7,200,000. Advances stood at 132.7 per cent of deposits. The shareholders, in addition to the loss of their paid up capital, had to find another £4,400,000. Calls totalling £2,750 per shareholder were made. Only 254 of the 1,819 shareholders avoided bankruptcy, although depositors were eventually paid. All the directors were charged in the High Court in Edinburgh—a Glasgow jury being thought too biased—of fraudulently uttering false balance sheets. They were all found guilty and imprisoned.

It is still not compulsory for companies to register with limited liability; unlimited liability companies are still registered notwithstanding the City of Glasgow Bank disaster. There is provision in Part V of the Insolvency Act 1986 for the winding up of unregistered companies and in terms of s.226(2) of that Act, a contributory is liable for all the debts of the company including winding-up expenses.

---

[27] Like Lloyd's of London today, or the bodies who control the provision of accounting and legal services and deny their members the full benefits of incorporation with limited liability which those providing banking services enjoy. Lloyd's is now detracting from its unlimited liability in the face of staggering underwriting losses, spread unevenly among its members. In the case of the leading accounting firms and legal firms, which are structured so that the partners are not only more numerous, but collectively more highly paid than the boards of any UK listed company, it is thought that the risks of unlimited liability are becoming too great. The exposure of Price Waterhouse, Ernst and Young and Allen and Overy arising out of the collapse of BCCI runs potentially to thousands of millions of dollars. Since the second edition of this book warned of the risks to the big accountancy firms of unlimited liability Arthur Anderson has collapsed as a result of the Enron scandal.

[28] These figures should be multiplied by about 50+ times to achieve today's values.

Floating charges and receivers

1–08   The Scottish common law never managed to invent a "floating charge". A floating charge is a legal instrument which gives security over corporeal moveable property (*i.e.* physical assets). In common law this is contrary to the principle of Scottish law that security over such property cannot be created without delivery of the property. The floating charge came to Scotland from England where it was devised by the Court of Chancery in the 1860s. Its three principal characteristics were as follows:

(1) it is a charge on a class of assets of a company specified in the charge both present and future;

(2) those assets are of a kind which, in the ordinary course of business of a company, would be changing from time to time; and

(3) it is contemplated that, until some step is taken by or on behalf of those interested in the charge, the company may carry on its business in the ordinary way, and dispose of all or any of those assets in the ordinary course of business.

The floating charge as devised by the English Court of Chancery was, therefore, an equitable charge on present and future assets. It was quickly adopted by the English financial community because it gave an easy security upon the entire undertaking of the borrowing company, thus conferring maximum security upon the lender, while at the same time permitting the borrowing company complete freedom to deal with and dispose of its assets in the ordinary course of business. Recognition of the usefulness of the floating charge as a financial instrument led to it being introduced to Scotland by statute, by the Companies (Floating Charges) (Scotland) Act 1961. Soon, however, it was recognised that the reform introduced by floating charges would not succeed unless the English idea of receivership, a mechanism for enforcing a security, was also transplanted.[29] Scotland had no institution of a receiver or any office of "official receiver". Without the appointment of a "receiver", the only way the holder of a floating charge could enforce his security was to petition for the winding up of the company. Receivers were accordingly introduced to Scotland by the Companies (Floating Charges and Receivers) (Scotland) Act 1972. There is still no office of "official receiver" in Scotland, although the Accountant in Bankruptcy performs some of the functions of that officer.

Cork reforms

1–09   The need for law reform of the insolvency laws had been recognised for many years before Cork. The Scottish Law Commission published major reports dealing with the Scottish law of insolvency.[30] However,

---

[29] See Scottish Law Commission Report, Cmnd 4336 (1970), para.38.
[30] Memo. No.16 on *Insolvency, Bankruptcy and Liquidation in Scotland* in 1971; and *Report on Bankruptcy and Related Aspects of Insolvency and Liquidation* in 1982 (Scot. Law Com. No. 68).

the impetus came from Europe. In England an advisory committee was appointed in 1973 under Sir Kenneth Cork to report on the implications of the draft EEC Bankruptcy Convention. This committee reported in 1976.[31] The committee highlighted the need for reform of the domestic insolvency laws. Subsequently the Secretary of State for Trade and Industry announced the setting up of a review committee in October 1976 on insolvency law and practice.[32] The committee again was established in January 1977, again under the chairmanship of Sir Kenneth Cork. Its remit was nothing short of a total review of all aspects of personal and corporate insolvency. Its terms of reference were:

(1) to review the law and practice relating to insolvency, bankruptcy, liquidation and receivership in England and Wales and to consider what reforms were necessary or desirable;

(2) to examine the possibility of formulating a comprehensive insolvency system and the extent to which existing procedures might, with advantage, be harmonised and integrated;

(3) to suggest possible less formal procedures as alternatives to bankruptcy and company winding-up proceedings in appropriate circumstances; and

(4) to make recommendations.

The committee considered representations from Scottish bodies and issued their final report in June 1982.[33]

Recommendations of Scottish Law Commission

The Scottish Law Commission dealt mostly with personal insolvency. **1–10** Where they dealt with corporate insolvency, such as in their recommendations with regard to (a) gratuitous alienations and (b) unfair preferences, the recommendations were largely acted upon. A further main recommendation, that, where possible, the law in relation to bankruptcy and liquidation should be harmonised, was also followed to a large extent. However, the way it was done was in the view of the authors misconceived.[34] Although personal and corporate insolvency share features, and although corporate insolvency grew out of bankruptcy, the considerations that inform policy are so different that it is better to treat them as discreet areas of the law in their own right. Harmonisation was sensibly achieved in following the list in items (1) to (5) with similar provisions in the Insolvency Act 1986 and the Bankruptcy (Scotland) Act 1985. But for some unknown reason, in relation to items (6) to (12) were applied to liquidations by the Insolvency (Scotland) Rules 1986, so that unlike the position in England bankruptcy and corporate insolvency law are woven together[35]:

(1) Unfair preferences—harmonised by s.36 of the Bankruptcy (Scotland) Act 1985 and s.243 of the Insolvency Act 1986.

---

[31] Cmnd 6602 (1976).
[32] *Hansard*, H.C. Deb., Vol. 918 (Oct. 1976), written answer no.20.
[33] Cmnd 8558 (1982).
[34] See para.3–01.
[35] For further discussion see para.3–01 at n.2.

(2) Gratuitous alienations—harmonised by s.34 of the Bankruptcy (Scotland) Act 1985 and s.242 of the Insolvency Act 1986.

(3) Effects of diligence—harmonised by s.37(1) to (6) of the Bankruptcy (Scotland) Act 1985 and s.185(1)(a) of the Insolvency Act 1986.

(4) Management and realisation of assets—harmonised by s.39(3), (4), (7) and (8) of the Bankruptcy (Scotland) Act 1985 and s.185(1)(b) of the Insolvency Act 1986.

(5) Preferential debts—broadly harmonised by Schedule 6 to the Insolvency Act 1986 which lists the preferential debts in winding up and Schedule 3 to the Bankruptcy (Scotland) Act of 1985 which lists preferential debts in bankruptcy.

(6) Criminal offence in relation to producing false claims or evidence—s.22(5) and (10) of the Bankruptcy (Scotland) Act 1985.

(7) Further evidence in relation to claims—s.48(5), (6) and (8), together with ss.44(2) and (3) and 47(1) as applied by those sections of the Bankruptcy (Scotland) Act 1985.

(8) Adjudication of claims—s.49 of the Bankruptcy (Scotland) Act 1985.

(9) Entitlement to vote and draw dividend—s.50 of the Bankruptcy (Scotland) Act 1985.

(10) Liabilities and rights of co-obligants—s.60 of the Bankruptcy (Scotland) Act 1985.

(11) Determination of amount of creditor's claim—Schedule 1, except paras 2, 4, and 6, to the Bankruptcy (Scotland) Act 1985.

(12) Accounting periods, taxation of accounts, unclaimed dividends—ss.52, 53 and 58 of the Bankruptcy (Scotland) Act 1985.

Cork Committee recommendations

1–11   The Cork Committee Report contained "numerous recommendations, and many of them radical and far reaching", to use its own words. Its most radical recommendations were:

(1) 10 per cent fund

1–12   The Cork Committee pointed out that there was widespread dissatisfaction with the way that holders of floating charges were often in a position to attach for the holder of the floating charge the whole assets of a company, leaving no surplus funds for ordinary creditors. This also deterred ordinary creditors from participating in the winding up. The committee accordingly recommended that a fund equal to 10 per cent of the net realisations of assets subject to a floating charge should be made available for distribution among the ordinary creditors. This recommendation was not accepted by the Government or passed by Parliament, although it has been taken up in the Enterprise Act reforms.[36]

(2) Crown preference

1–13   The Cork Committee approved the comments of Lord Anderson in the Scottish case of *Admiralty v Blair's Trustee*, 1916 S.C. at 248. Lord Anderson had expressed the view that it was unjust that the Crown

---

[36] See para.19–25.

should have preference in insolvency for its debts at the expense of the individual creditor. Lord Anderson rejected the principle of Crown preference for the following reasons:

> "In the first place, because the principle is inequitable. In the case of *Palmer* Lord Macnaughten justifies the doctrine on the ground that its assertion results in the benefit of the general community (that is, the general body of taxpayers) although at the expense of the individual. I should have thought this was a reason for condemning the principle. Why should individuals be made to suffer for the general good, especially in a case like the present, where the general is infinitesimal but the individual loss substantial? In the second place, this alleged prerogative is hostile to the general policy of the Bankruptcy Acts, which aim at equal treatment of all creditors in the matter of the distribution of the estates of a bankrupt."

The Cork Committee proposed the abolition of Crown preference in relation to unpaid tax. The Government resisted efforts to cut down the Crown's privileged position as a preferential creditor for unpaid tax, but Parliament overrode the Government's proposals and amended the Bill so as to eliminate Crown preference in respect of taxes assessed upon the company directly as taxpayer to the Inland Revenue.[37] The Cork Committee also proposed the abolition of VAT preference, which the Scottish Law Commission had also proposed in its recommendations in relation to bankruptcy (see para.15.8 of the 1982 Report). This recommendation was not accepted, but Parliament again overrode the Government and reduced the preferential treatment of VAT to that attributable within a six-month period as opposed to a 12-month period for other debts due to Customs and Excise. Seventeen years later the Enterprise Act 2002 the abolition of crown preferences has been carried to completion.

(3) Local rates

Both the Cork Committee and the Scottish Law Commission recommended the abolition of preference for local rates. This was rejected by the Government but passed by Parliament.[38]   **1–14**

(4) Company administrators

The Cork Committee was of the view that, where there was no floating charge giving a receiver power to take charge of an ailing company, in a significant number of cases companies had been forced into liquidation, and potentially viable businesses capable of being rescued have been closed down for want of a floating charge under which a receiver and manager could have been appointed. Accordingly the Cork Committee proposed a new insolvency procedure known as "administration order procedure" which would enable the management of a failed or failing company to be placed under the control of an   **1–15**

---

[37] See Insolvency Act 1986, Sch.6.
[38] *ibid.*, Sch.6.

administrator for a period of time with a view to securing the survival of as much of the company as could be saved, or alternatively, the most orderly and advantageous realisation of its assets as could be achieved. This recommendation contained in Chap.9 of the Cork Report was accepted by the Government and was made law in ss.8 to 27 of the Insolvency Act 1986. The Enterprise Act now builds on the Cork reforms, making administration the primary rehabilitation regime, with administrative receivership more or less abolished.

(5) Voluntary arrangements

1–16   The Cork Committee was of the view that the arrangements available whereby a company would be able to effect an arrangement with its creditors were defective. The system was cumbersome and it was difficult to get the requisite majorities of votes of the creditors in order to bind them all. The Cork Committee proposed a procedure whereby a company would be able to effect formal and binding arrangements with its creditors subject only to a majority vote of the creditors without any need for any sanction of the court. This proposal, contained in Chap.7 of the Cork Report, was accepted in part by the Government and made law by ss.1 to 7 of the Insolvency Act 1986.

(6) Delinquent directors

1–17   The Cork Committee was concerned at the fraud and other abuses widespread on company insolvency by directors, managers and liquidators, and made recommendations in this regard including the disqualification of delinquent directors and their being made personally liable for the debts of insolvent companies under certain circumstances. These proposals, contained in Chap.45 of the report, were adopted by the Government with modification and made law in the Company Directors Disqualification Act 1986.

(7) Insolvency practitioners

1–18   The Cork Committee thought that there should be public control of who could act as insolvency practitioners and that they should have professional qualifications and experience as a condition of being allowed to act. The detailed proposals contained in Chap.15 of the report were largely adopted by the government with only members of recognised bodies, or specially authorised persons, allowed to act as insolvency practitioners in terms of ss.388 to 394 of the Insolvency Act 1986.

CHAPTER 2

THE DEFINING OBJECTIVES OF CORPORATE INSOLVENCY LAW

Introduction

The primary objective of corporate insolvency law is to provide an **2–01** orderly mechanism to restructure companies which have become financially non-viable either because they are unable to pay their debts as they become due, or because their balance sheet is sufficiently weakened as to pose a question mark on their financial viability.[1] If the company has an obviously temporary cash flow problem, this may be overcome by the company securing additional borrowings. Similarly a weakened balance sheet may be restored to health by a rights issue or by additional long-term funding arrangements. Liquidity problems may also be overcome by creditors agreeing to waive some or all of their debts or to accept equity in the company in return for debt. None of these types of arrangement need involve the courts but are determined by market forces. It is only in situations where market forces have not delivered the necessary financial rehabilitation that companies find themselves in the insolvency courts.[2]

Where the market has clearly signalled that it is not prepared to back a company further, the classical theory is that the function of the insolvency courts is to restructure the company by winding it up in an orderly manner. This does not mean that the company does not have valuable assets, or an economically viable business. It just means that the financial structure of the company at that stage cannot be sustained. An obvious example of such a type of situation would be the Channel Tunnel, which is a very valuable cash generative asset, but is held by a company, which for historic reasons, has a difficult to service debt burden. The winding up process frees businesses to find financially sounder new owners and often more competent new managers. Secondly, where businesses are genuinely economically no longer viable, it

---

[1] In terms of s.123(2) of the Insolvency Act 1986, a company is deemed unable to pay its debts if it is proved to the satisfaction of the court that the value of the company's assets is less than the amount of its liabilities, taking into account its contingent and prospective liabilities. "Liabilities" is a much broader term than "debts", and would include claims arising in contract or in delict or by way of restitution (see *Re a Debtor (No.17 of 1966)* [1967] Ch. 590).

[2] Many such companies, of course, go into creditors' voluntary winding up which largely bypasses the insolvency courts, or are dissolved by being struck off the Register under s.652 of the Companies Act 1985 without having gone through any insolvency regime.

facilitates the break-up of these businesses and thereby the reallocation of their assets—including human assets—to potentially more productive use. This reallocation of resources often from sunset to sunrise industries is at the heart of the capitalist dynamic in a competitive and enterprise driven economy.[3] The classical statement of how this dynamic works was made in the following terms in 1942 by the Austrian economist, Joseph Schumpeter:

> "The first thing to go is the traditional conception of the *modus operandi* of competition. Economists are at long last emerging from the stage in which price competition was all they saw. As soon as quality competition and sales effort are admitted into the sacred precincts of theory, the price variable is ousted from its dominant position. However, it is still competition within a rigid pattern of invariant conditions, methods of production and forms of industrial organisation in particular, that practically monopolises attention. But in capitalist reality as distinguished from its textbook picture, it is not that kind of competition which counts but the competition from the new commodity, the new technology, the new source of supply, the new type of organisation (the largest-scale unit of control for instance)—competition which commands a decisive cost or quality advantage and which strikes not at the margins of the profits and the output of the existing firms but at their foundations and their lives. This kind of competition is as much more effective than the other as a bombardment is in comparison with forcing a door, and so much more important that it becomes a matter of comparative indifference whether competition in the ordinary sense functions more or less promptly; the powerful lever that in the long run expands output and brings down prices is in any case made of other stuff."[4]

"Rescue" culture

2-02   Although liquidation is the defining purpose of corporate insolvency law, there is now greater emphasis on what is now known as the "rescue culture"—a phrase which is now incorporated into our jurisprudence.[5] The new approach in Britain came from evidence to the Insolvency Law Review Committee (the Cork Committee) and from the Committee's Report *Insolvency Law and Practice*.[6] The introduction of the administration procedure in the 1986 Insolvency Act was based on the premise that the market was not working perfectly and was failing to support companies that were potentially both financially and econom-

---

[3] The Treaty of Rome commits Member States of the EC including the UK to capitalism, albeit a capitalism fettered by a framework of duties imposed on the Member States by the Treaty of Rome and by the social and economic rights that are derived by the citizens of the EC from the Treaty of Rome.

[4] Joseph Schumpeter, *Capitalism, Socialism and Democracy* (Harper, New York, 1975) (originally published 1942), pp.84–85.

[5] See the speech of Lord Browne-Wilkinson in *Powdrill v Watson* [1995] 2 A.C. 394 at 442, 445, 446.

[6] Cmmd. 8558 (1982).

ically viable. Again, recognising the imperfect working of the financial markets, the Bank of England in 1990 initiated discussions with the London banking associations designed to set a framework for multi-bank support for companies in distress. The bank was concerned with the growing problems of companies in financial difficulty, the prevalence of cross-default clauses and the lack of bank support for customers facing financial difficulties. Principles were informally agreed by the London banking community and are now embodied in informal arrangements known as the "London Approach". Basically the banks have informally agreed not to act precipitously in appointing a receiver and to act collectively with other creditors to see if a company can be given financial support. The Bank of England itself is sometimes prepared to act as an honest broker. The London Approach is primarily directed at large, multi-banked companies, and is not of concern to intermediate sized or small companies.

The level of intervention in pursuit of a rescue culture will vary from country to country. In the United States it has been stated that "the fundamental purpose of reorganisation is to prevent a debtor from going into liquidation, with the attendant loss of jobs and possible misuse of economic resources".[7] This approach tends to favour shareholders at the expense of creditors and to protect incompetent managers from being replaced.[8] Civil law jurisdictions also tend to place high emphasis on workers' rights and the importance of preserving the enterprise, especially in France,[9] although Government paternalism in the EC is of course subject to the rules against State aid.[10] The UK law in contrast is much more weighted in favour of creditors' rights, self help and the use of contractual remedies. Although the Cork Committee believed that an aim of a good modern insolvency law was "to provide means for the preservation of viable commercial enterprises capable of making a useful contribution to the economic life of the country",[11] the committee emphasised that society had no interest in the preservation or rehabilitation of the company as such,[12] although it might have a legitimate concern in the preservation of the commercial enterprise.[13]

---

[7] *NLRB v Bildisco & Bildisco*, 465 US 513, 528 (1983), quoting the views of Congress, HR Rep. No.95–595, p.220 (1977). Further useful discussion is also to be found in G. Dal Pont and L. Griggs, "A Principled Justification for Business Rescue Laws: A Comparative Perspective Part (I)", International Insolvency Review, 4 (1995) at 189; and Pt (II), International Insolvency Review, 5 (1996), at 47–79.

[8] This last effect is possible because Chap.11 leaves the incumbent management in place, unlike an administration or liquidation when the company is in the hands largely of outside management.

[9] See Axel Flessner, "Philosophy of Business Bankruptcy Law: an international overview" in *Current Developments in International and Comparative Corporate Insolvency Law* (ed. Jacob S. Ziegel), p.22.

[10] The rules applicable to State aids are to be found on: *http://europa.eu.int/comm/competition/state_aid/legislation/*.

[11] Report of the Cork Review Committee, *Insolvency Law and Practice*, para.198.

[12] During the passage of the Enterprise Act 2002, this point was conceded by the Government but is not properly reflected in the Act—see discussion in para.5–16.

[13] See *Insolvency Law of Practice*, para.193. For further discussion of the philosophy and objectives of insolvency law, see *Orderly and Effective Insolvency proceedings: Key Issues* (Legal Department, International Monetary Fund, May 1999); Roy Goode, *Principles of Corporate Insolvency Law* (2nd ed., Sweet & Maxwell, 1997), Chap.2; and the *Report of the G-22 Working Group on International Financial Prices* (Oct. 1998), s2.5.

Stakeholders in corporate insolvency

2–03　　Although the Schumpeter model of "creative destruction" may be the big picture of what is going on in a capitalist system, with the majority of reorganisations ending in the failure of liquidation,[14] most jurisdictions recognise in differing degrees that parties other than trade creditors may have a stake in the survival, at least in the short or medium term, of the company or the enterprise. Included normally among these stakeholders would be the employees of the enterprise and the local community where the enterprise is situated, as well as governments with their interest in the tax base of the company and their concern to manage economic change in such a way as to avoid excessive economic dislocations with high attendant social costs. Some jurisdictions also choose to privilege some creditors above others, such as employees' entitlements, or claims by the state itself. In determining the appropriate level of judicial intervention to protect the interests of various stakeholders (usually at the expense of ordinary trade creditors), the state has to make political and social choices, which may vary from country to country and from time to time. For example, in one country, stamping out corruption and corporate fraud may be of supreme importance at a particular conjuncture in its history. In another, keeping employment up in a deep economic downturn may be the priority.

　　Sometimes in the face of extraordinary economic forces, industrial transition has had to be managed by administrative bodies specially designed to effect the orderly liquidation or quasi liquidation of whole swathes of a country's industries. This happened in May 1990 in Germany with the creation by specific purpose legislation of a body commonly known as the *Treuhandanstalt*, tasked with smoothing the economic reunification of the two Germanies. The legislation was enacted to deal with the state enterprise sector of the former East Germany. Under that legislation, administrative processes were employed to restructure individual state enterprises to the point where they might be privatised. For state enterprises that could not be privatised, the legislation provided for a liquidation process, which involved a gradual and orderly sale of their assets and, in some cases, their businesses (or part of them). This was administratively processed and overseen by the *Treuhandanstalt*. Many of these state enterprises had an excess of liabilities over assets, which, under normal circumstances, would have required them to be liquidated under the normal insolvency process. To avoid this (and to ensure a better result) a consultative bargaining process was employed with creditors of these state enterprises. The aim of this process was to reach agreement with creditors on the reduction of their claims to a level equal to the proceeds of the sale of the assets of the enterprises, but not as low as that might be occasioned by a formal bankruptcy process. This was largely achieved by endeavouring to keep the business of the enterprises, operational, and by selling them at going concern values.[15]

---

[14] See Working Group Paper 10 (Debtor-Creditor Regimes) of the World Bank Insolvency Initiative (Washington D.C., Sept. 14–15, 1999), at para.26: *http://www4.worldbank.org/ legal/insolvency_ini/WG10–paper.htm*.

[15] See *"Building Effective Insolvency Systems"*: *"Rehabilitation"*, Paper of Working Group 6 of the World Bank Insolvency Initiative (Sept. 14–15, 1999), which discusses the main principles and priorities of any rehabilitation model: *http://www4.worldbank.org/legal/ insolvency_ini/WG6–paper1.htm*.

Creditors as stakeholders

An important group of stakeholders in a corporate insolvency are the **2–04** creditors of the company. In shaping its corporate insolvency laws, the state has to balance the interests of the other stakeholders with the interests of the creditors. The state has also to balance the interests of the creditors among themselves. The political objectives may only be achieved by a machinery which is orderly and is seen to be reasonably equitable. The weight given to each group of stakeholders can fluctuate in the course of an insolvency with more of an emphasis on the interests of the employees and the preservation of the business in the course of an administration, whereas once the company is in liquidation the emphasis normally switches more to the interests of the creditors.

An underlying assumption of most systems of insolvency law is that the interests of individual creditors must give way to the collective interests of the general body of creditors. A disorderly scramble by creditors to seize the assets of a company is assumed to be contrary to the organisation of the company's affairs for the benefit of creditors as a whole. This collective interest is considered best achieved through a collective debt collection procedure, with an ascertainment of the company's liabilities, a realisation of assets and a distribution of proceeds as a dividend among the creditors in a laid down order of priority.

A particular question in relation to the ranking of creditors' claims is whether the general law should intervene to disturb the debt arrangements which the company has with individual creditors. On one argument the proper function of insolvency law is to translate pre-insolvency assets and liabilities into the insolvency forum with minimal dislocation.[16] This argument has certain attractions. First, the granting of credit is not mandatory. It is based on express or implied contract. Secondly, the granting of credit is not an isolated act but is usually part of a calculation. So, for example, the creditor can offload the risk of insolvency by insuring the debt, by discounting or factoring the debt, by insisting on a post-dated letter of credit confirmed by a bank of status or on some other security, or by writing the risk of a bad or slow debt into the price of the goods or services using a risk factor produced by a credit rating agency.

This model of a scientific approach to the granting of credit faces two problems in particular. First, any credit rating set by organisations like Standard and Poor is based on historical information and cannot predict economic sea changes of the type described by Schumpeter. Secondly, not all players in the market place have equal bargaining power, or are privy to the same level of economic information. It may be that custom demands the giving of credit and the various methods of offloading risk are not available to certain groups of creditors. These factors have suggested that the state should intervene and in the event of insolvency

[16] Jackson, "Translating Assets and Liabilities to the Bankruptcy Forum", 14 Journal of Legal Studies 73 (1985).

interfere with the rights of the various creditors as contractually set up. Part of the thinking behind such interference has been a desire to strengthen the collective aspect of corporate insolvency law. The idea is to bind in and engage as many creditors as possible in the insolvency machinery. This engagement helps those policing the insolvency laws for fraud and wrongdoing. It also may give otherwise dispossessed ordinary creditors a stake in the outcome of the insolvency process, and also a perception that the insolvency machinery tempers the credit terms available in the original marketplace with a degree of equity.

An example of the above type of thinking is contained in the Enterprise Act 2002, which upsets the previous insolvency ranking based purely on contract, and sets aside for ordinary creditors a percentage of funds which would otherwise go to holders of floating charges.[17] Creditors of a business to a degree do have an interest in the salvage of the business, in so far as a rehabilitated company with a business may continue to give them trade (and so this continuing trading relationship makes up for any money written off). However, such an outcome can be very speculative, with new managers using new suppliers. By giving a set aside percentage of funds to ordinary creditors, a more concrete benefit is accorded. Ordinary creditors also thus have more of an incentive to co-operate with liquidators and provide them with information about the pre-liquidation state of affairs of the company, so that a full and proper financial inquest on a company may be carried out by the liquidator, and liability for their conduct pinned on corrupt or negligent management, and slack or complicit auditors.[18] The aim of tying of ordinary creditors into these public interest functions of liquidators informed the thinking of the Cork Committee in proposing that, on winding up, 10 per cent in value of assets, subject to a floating charge, should be required to be surrendered to form a fund available for distribution among unsecured creditors. This proposal proved too controversial at the time and was not adopted. Its adoption now in the Enterprise Act 2002, and at double the level of fund originally proposed by the Cork Committee, is a tribute to the clarity and far thinking of the original promoter of the idea, Professor Roy Goode.[19]

---

[17] See the Insolvency Act 1986 (Prescribed Part) Order 2003 (SI 2003/2097). Basically in terms of that Order, 50% of all funds under £10,000, which otherwise would be available to holders of floating charges, have to be set aside for ordinary creditors, as well as 20% of funds above that level up to limit of £600,000 (see chapter on administrations).

[18] In the UK liquidators may bring civil actions for damages against negligent directors, auditors and regulators, as well as report delinquent directors to the DTI for potential disqualification (see Chap.8). The prospect of negligence and fraud being brought to book through liquidation is meant to act as a deterrence to fraud, and make directors alert to their exposure for negligence. The liquidation process should therefore perhaps properly be seen as primarily designed to restructure failed companies but with the important secondary objective of helping maintain standards of probity in healthy companies. This second feature is built into all OECD insolvency models.

[19] See Roy Goode, *"Is the Law Too Favourable to Secured Creditors"* (1983–1984) 8 Can. Bus. L.J. at 67. The Cork Committee appears to have been unaware of the origin of the proposal.

CHAPTER 3

THE SCOTLAND ACT 1998 AND THE HUMAN RIGHTS ACT 1998

Introduction

The Scotland Act 1998 was a major constitutional measure which **3–01** altered the government of the United Kingdom. This is reflected first, in the fact that, apart from s.25, the whole Act applies throughout the United Kingdom (s.131). Also, not only the Union with England Act 1707 (Scot c.7) but also the Union with Scotland Act 1706 (6 Anne c.11) has effect subject to the Scotland Act 1998 (s.37). Secondly, ss.29(2)(d) and 57(2) of the Scotland Act 1998 put it beyond the power of the Scottish Parliament to legislate, and of a member of the Scottish Executive to act, in a way that is incompatible with any of the Convention rights.

This integration of Convention rights into the constitutional settlement of the Scotland Act 1998 means that, whenever a member of the Scottish Executive does an act which is incompatible with Convention rights, the result produced by all the relevant legislation is not just that this act is unlawful under s.6(1) of the Human Rights Act 1998. That would be the position if the Scotland Act 1998 did not apply. When s.57(2) is taken into account, however, the result is that, so far as his act is incompatible with Convention rights, the member of the Executive is doing something which he has no power to do: his "act" is, to that extent, merely a purported act and is invalid, a nullity.[1] This *vires* constraint on the Scottish Parliament and on the Scottish Executive means that care has to be exercised to avoid acts or actions that are incompatible with Convention rights, resulting in the radical consequence of nullity (which is tempered only to a limited extent by the powers of the courts and tribunals under s.102 of the Scotland Act 1998 to vary or suspend some of the effects of a nullity resulting from an incompatibility with Convention rights).

In legislating on insolvency matters the Scottish Parliament faces a second minefield as regards competence. The relevant provision in relation to corporate insolvency is Head C2 of Schedule 5 to the Scotland Act 1998, effected by s.29 of that Act. Reserved in relation to business associations are—

"(a) the modes of, the grounds for and the generally legal effect of winding up, and the persons who may initiate winding up,

---

[1] *HM Advocate v R* [2003] 2 W.L.R. 317 at 357 and 360, *per* Lord Rodger of Earlsferry.

(b) liability to contribute to assets on winding up,
(c) powers of courts in relation to proceedings for winding up, other than the power to sist proceedings,
(d) arrangements with creditors, and
(e) procedures giving protection from creditors.

Preferred or preferential debts for the purposes of the Bankruptcy (Scotland) Act 1985, the Insolvency Act 1986, and any other enactment relating to the sequestration of the estate of any person or to the winding up of business associations, the preference of such debts against other such debts and the extent of their preference over other types of debt.
Regulation of insolvency practitioners.
Co-operation of insolvency courts."

Exceptions to the reservation in relation to business associations are:

"(a) the process of winding up, including the person having responsibility for the conduct of winding up or any part of it, and his conduct of it or of that part,
(b) the effect of winding up on diligence, and
(c) avoidance and adjustment of prior transactions on winding up.

Floating charges and receivers, except in relation to preferential debts, regulation of insolvency practitioners and co-operation of insolvency courts."

What the reservation tried to do was to keep within a UK legislative framework the main aspects of insolvency law in relation to companies and corporations. Procedural law in relation to the insolvency of companies was to be devolved, as was the law of bankruptcy in Scotland. It might be said that there was a fundamental flaw in this approach in that there was no easy dividing line between substantive corporate insolvency law and procedural corporate insolvency law. Neither was there a clear-cut legislation boundary between bankruptcy law and company insolvency law. In both England and Wales, and Scotland, corporate insolvency law grew out of bankruptcy law. This historical evolution is apparent from the fact that both the Insolvency Act 1986 and the Insolvency (Scotland) Rules 1986 apply the Bankruptcy (Scotland) Act 1985 to windings up. Section 169(2) of the Insolvency Act 1986 explicitly states that in a winding up by the court in Scotland, the liquidator has (subject to the rules) the same powers as a trustee on a bankrupt estate.[2]

The artificial divide in Head C2 of Schedule 5 to the Scotland Act 1998 in relation to corporate insolvency has proved unsustainable. The

---

[2] S.112(1) of the Insolvency Act 1986 allows this power to be extended to a liquidator in a voluntary winding up. The difficulty and absurdity of this way of formulating corporate insolvency law from bankruptcy law in England was brought out forcibly by Vinelott J. in *Re Berkeley Securities* [1980] 3 All E.R. 513 at 526–529.

Scottish Parliament accordingly through a "Sewel motion", consented to Westminster legislating in the Enterprise Act 2002 to abolish receiverships in Scotland except for limited purposes, although this could have been largely effected by the Scottish Parliament.[3] Similarly implementation of the EC Regulation on insolvency proceedings was done by the Secretary of State (and not Scottish Ministers) using powers under s.2(2) of the European Communities Act 1972.[4] A similar use of s.2(2) of that Act was also made in implementing Directive 2002/47/EC of the European Parliament and of the Council of June 6, 2002 on financial collateral arrangements (implemented December 26, 2003 by SI 2003/3226 (see para.1–01, n.11)).[5]

The Human Rights Act 1998 and liquidations

It is thought by the authors that the Human Rights Act 1998 will **3–02** apply to liquidations and other insolvency proceedings.[6] There is no question that a company, although an artificial person, is able to avail itself of the rights set out in the Convention.[7] If a public authority acts in

---

[3] By a convention devised by the Labour Peer, Lord Sewel, the Scottish Parliament must consent to Westminster legislating in a devolved area, although Westminster obviously has the legal powers to do so if it so wishes, the Scottish Parliament being after all a creature of a Westminster statute. The motion of the Scottish Parliament debated on April 17, 2002 was in the following sparse terms: "That the Parliament agrees that provisions in the Enterprise Bill which relate to the devolved matter of receivership should be considered by the UK Parliament."

[4] Council Regulation (EC) No.1346/2000 of May 29, 2000. Although an instrument under s.2(2) of the European Communities Act 1972 can and usually does amend primary legislation, a Sewel motion in the Scottish Parliament is not required for such an instrument based, it is supposed, on the fictitious premise that legislation made under s.2(2) of the European Communities Act 1972 is subordinate legislation.

[5] This important Directive to a large extent removes certain types of financial arrangements from the usual law relating to company securities and insolvency law. The Directive applies to Financial Collateral Arrangements ("FCAs"). In basic terms an FCA is an arrangement under which one party (the collateral provider) provides collateral (cash or securities) to the collateral taker, as security against the fulfilment of financial obligations, which are owed to the collateral taker. There are two different types of FCA covered by the Directive: (a) The collateral taker may receive title to the collateral at the time that the arrangement is entered into and be obliged to return it if the financial obligations which it is securing are met—this is a *title transfer* FCA; (b)
Alternatively the collateral taker may take security over the collateral which he can enforce to take possession of or dispose of the collateral if the relevant financial obligations are not met—a *security* FCA.
The basis for adopting a Directive on Financial Collateral was that there was too much legal uncertainty faced by participants in the financial markets regarding the enforceability of cross-border collateral arrangements. There has been an increasing use of cross-border collateral by market participants to reduce their credit risk and this use of collateral has been impeded by differences in the various jurisdictions of the EU. Participants in the EU market who use collateral arrangements face 15 different regimes as regards perfection requirements procedures a collateral taker must follow to ensure the rights to the collateral are good against third parties including a liquidator in the event of insolvency.

[6] Useful articles are: W. Trower, *"Bringing Human Rights Home to the Insolvency Practitioner"* (2000) 13 Insolvency Intelligence 41–43, 52–53; Simmons & Smith; "The Human Rights Act 1998: The Practical Impact on Insolvency" (2000) 16 I.L. & P. 167c. Gearty & Davies, *Insolvency Practice and the Human Rights Act 1998*, (Jordans, Bristol, 2000) and N. Pike [2001] Insolvency Lawyer 25–31.

[7] See *Observer Limited and Guardian Newspapers Limited v United Kingdom* (1991) A 216, para.49; *Yarrow v United Kingdom* No. 9266/81, 30 D.R. 155 (1983). This case is referred to in Dignan, *"Company Law and the Human Rights Act 1998: interesting times"* (2000) 21 Co. Law 151; and *County Properties Limited v The Scottish Ministers (ex Div)*, 2001 S.L.T. 1125.

contravention of s.6 of the Human Rights Act 1998, a person aggrieved may be granted relief in accordance with s.8 of that Act. Included in terms of s.6(3)(b) of that Act as a public authority is any person whose functions are of a public nature. It is thought that liquidators of companies in compulsory liquidation and administrators appointed since the Enterprise Act 2002 came into force, who are officers of the court, would be regarded as public authorities when carrying out functions which can be seen as being of a public nature. Also, voluntary liquidators may be regarded as public authorities, even though they are not officers of the court, when they carry out functions of a public nature such as when they have to report to the Secretary of State for Trade and Industry under s.7 of the Company Directors' Disqualification Act 1986, should they arrive at the view in the course of their investigations of an insolvent company, that a director is not fit to be involved in the management of a company.

Effect of Convention on Corporate Insolvency Law/Obtaining of Evidence

3–03   It has been held that a decision is not required to comply with Art.6 of the European Convention on Human Rights if any appeal to or review by a court is conducted before a judicial body which has full jurisdiction to examine all questions of fact and law. Although the decisions of liquidators are subject to the control of the court under s.167(3) of the Insolvency Act 1986, and aggrieved persons may apply to the court for determination of questions under s.112(1) of that Act, it is not clear whether the provisions of Art.6 of the Convention are satisfied. The problem is that the court is reluctant to interfere with decisions of liquidators unless the decision of the liquidator is such that no reasonable liquidator, properly instructed and advised,[8] could in the circumstances arrive at it.[9] In the case of *Mitchell v Buckingham International plc*[10] it was held that this approach was limited to where liquidators were exercising their administrative powers to realise assets. In the light of these approaches, it is suggested that insolvency practitioners may have to be more careful in relation to decisions which have a determinative effect on the substantive rights of third parties. The court may also have to be prepared to look more closely at decisions and their underlying basis, rather than confining the approach to deciding whether the decision was within a discretion. In each case the court will have to weigh up what is at stake in the proceedings against the overall fairness of the decision making process.[11] In making the balancing decision and interpreting the Insolvency Act 1986 or the Companies Act 1985 in the light of the Human Rights Act 1998, it should be borne in mind that convention rights may in certain circumstances be justifiably infringed. These are where the interference is:

---

[8] Re Edennote Ltd [1996] B.C.C. 718 at 722; [1996] 2 B.C.L.C. 389 at 394, CA.
[9] See *Re Hans Place Ltd* [1992] B.C.C. 737; *Re Greenhaven Motors Ltd* [1997] B.C.C. 547; *Re Edennote Ltd*, above; *Hamilton v Official Receiver* [1998] B.P.I.R. 602.
[10] [1998] 2 B.C.L.C. 369.
[11] See Trower, *"Bringing Human Rights Home to the Insolvency Practitioners—Pt 2"* (2000) 13 Insolvency Intelligence 51.

(a) lawful;
(b) it serves a legitimate purpose;
(c) it is necessary in a democratic society; and
(d) it is not discriminatory.[12]

Section 219 of the Insolvency Act 1986, as originally enacted, allowed an answer given by a person to a question put to him in the exercise of the powers conferred by s.218(5) to be used in evidence against him in criminal proceedings. The jurisprudence of the Human Rights Act 1998 and that of the European Court of Human Rights in relation to the use of compelled evidence has led to s.219 of the Insolvency Act 1986 being qualified by amendments introduced by s.11 of the Insolvency Act 2000, which inserted subss (2A) and (2B) into s.219. The amendments came into effect from April 2, 2001.[13] The effect of the new provisions is that evidence which has been obtained under the powers conferred by s.218(5) may not be adduced in evidence in criminal proceedings in which the person concerned is the accused, unless evidence relating to it is adduced, or a question relating to it is asked in the proceedings by or on behalf of the accused. The decision therefore belongs to the accused whether to relinquish the protection provided by s.219(2A) of the Insolvency Act 1986.[14] Section 11 of the Insolvency Act 2000 was enacted largely in the light of the judgment of the European Court of Human Rights in the case of *Saunders v United Kingdom* (the "Saunders" case).[15] Prior to the enactment of the Human Rights Act 1998, the interface between the traditional freedom from self-incrimination right and the right to a fair trial under Art.6 of the Convention was the main area of focus of human rights law in corporate insolvency. The Human Rights Act 1998 is not retroactive, and accordingly the convictions of the defendants in the "Guinness Affair" could not be quashed, even if the European Court of Human Rights subsequently ruled that use of evidence obtained by the prosecution from inspectors using powers under the Companies Act 1985 was in infringement of Art.6 of the European Convention on Human Rights, because at the time s.434(5) expressly made admissible by statute in force at the time of the trial.[16]

As part of their investigatory remit liquidators need to obtain information about companies that are being wound up.[17] Two types of examination may be set in motion during a liquidation: public and private under respectively ss.133 and 236 of the Insolvency Act 1986. The development of the law (prior to the enactment of s.11 of the Insolvency Act 2000)

---

[12] *De Freitas v Permanent Secretary of the Ministry of Agriculture, Fisheries, Land and Housing* [1998] 3 W.L.R. 675.

[13] SI 2001/766.

[14] The protection of s.219(2A) of the Insolvency Act 1986 does not extend to false statements made on oath otherwise than in judicial proceedings, or made otherwise than on oath: see s.44(1) or (2) of the Criminal Law (Consolidation) (Scotland) Act 1995.

[15] [1997] E.H.R.R. 313; [1998] 1 B.C.L.C. 362; [1997] B.C.C. 872.

[16] *R. v Lyons* [2002] B.C.C. 968.

[17] *Re Arrows Ltd (No.4)* [1994] B.C.C. 641 at 643, *per* Lord Browne-Wilkinson H.L.

was driven by the "Saunders" case, and the litigation arising out of the insolvency of Maxwell Communications.[18]

Effect of Convention on the Law of Inhibitions and Arrestments in Scotland

Inhibitions on the dependence

3–04   The ready availability of inhibition on the dependence has been the subject of repeated criticism by writers on Scots law since at least 1822, including recently the criticism of the Scottish Law Commission in its report published in March 1998, *Report on Diligence on the Dependence and Admiralty Arrestments*, which drew in part on valuable work done by Professor Maher in his article, "Diligence on the Dependence: Principles for Reform", 1996 J.R. 188. In the case of *Karl Construction Ltd v Palisade Properties plc*[19] the use of inhibition on the dependence in the circumstances of that case was challenged as contrary to Art.1 of the First Protocol to the European Convention on Human Rights. It was submitted that inhibition on the dependence involved a restriction on the use of property. It was necessary for the court to consider the aim that was being pursued by a restriction on the use of property, and consider whether a fair balance was struck between that aim and the property owner's rights. Although it was legitimate for a state to make available to a creditor pursuing a well-founded claim a mechanism whereby the debtor may be prevented from seeking to avoid payment of a just debt by illegitimate means, it was argued that such a mechanism must strike a fair balance between that end and the right of the proprietor to use and enjoy his property. It was further argued that in considering whether such a fair balance was struck, the availability of compensation for unjustified use of the restriction was relevant.

In his judgment, Lord Drummond Young, reviewing the relevant jurisprudence at length and considering models in other jurisdictions, took the view that automatic inhibition on the dependence was incompatible with the defender's convention rights. Instead, inhibition on the dependence could only be granted if a specific justification is put forward for the grant, and the court is satisfied that the pursuer has a *prima facie* case. The main weaknesses in the historical use of inhibition on the dependence was that it was disproportionate, if an objective justification for its use was not put forward and compensation for wrongful use was only available in restricted circumstances. Lord Drummond Young was careful to point out in that case[20] that, despite

---

[18] The treatment of the fascinating history of these scandals and how the courts developed the law in relation to the public interest and the individual's interest in non-incrimination is not within the scope of this work. For a treatment of these developments the best treatment is in Chaps 22 and 27 of *The Law of Insolvency*, by Ian Fletcher (2002, Sweet & Maxwell) and authorities cited therein, and *McPherson's Law of Company Liquidation*, by Andrew Keay (2001, Sweet & Maxwell, London) at paras 15.14–15.48.

[19] 2002 S.L.T. at 312.

[20] *Karl Construction Ltd v Palisade Properties plc*, 2002 S.L.T. (OH) at pp.327 and 328; see also the judgment of Lord Drummond-Young in *Barry D Trentham Ltd v Lawfield Investments Ltd*, 2002 S.L.T. (OH) at 1094 where an inhibition on the dependence was confirmed in a case where there was a significant risk of the defender's insolvency.

his judgment, he believed that inhibition on the dependence would continue to be widely available. It would be a sufficient justification for use of inhibition on the dependence that the pursuer could demonstrate a substantial risk of the defender's practical insolvency, in the sense that the defender appeared to be unable to pay debts as they fell due. In cases where a pursuer had sued for a liquid debt which had been the subject of a demand for payment, and either there was no obvious defence to the claim or the pursuer was able to aver that he was not aware of any possible basis of defence, the court would be justified in drawing the inference that there was a substantial risk of practical insolvency from the defender's failure to pay. In such cases, inhibition on the dependence would normally be available.

Arrestments on the dependence

The approach of Lord Drummond Young in relation to inhibitions on the dependence has been followed by the Inner House in relation to arrestments on the dependence in the case of *The Advocate General for Scotland for and on behalf of the Commissioners of Inland Revenue v Maureen Taylor*.[21] According to the court the essential mischief which had to be addressed was that diligence of arrestment on the dependence prior to their judgment was available as of right, irrespective of whether the pursuer's claim was well founded in fact or in law, and without any judicial assessment of the validity or otherwise or the strength or weakness of that claim. What was required to cure the current mischief and to bring the law on the obtaining of diligence within Art.1 of the First Protocol, was that the grant of warrant should in essence be a judicial act. That did not mean that in every case there must be a hearing in court before a judge. It did, however, mean that an application was made to the court for a warrant and that such an application was judicially considered before it is granted.

Human Rights Act 1998 is not retroactive

Human Rights Act 1998 is not retroactive. This was clearly decided by the House of Lords (overturning the Court of Appeal) in *Wilson v First County Trust Ltd (No.2)*.[22] This means that, for example, inhibitions granted prior to that Act coming into force are valid, as well as follow-on proceedings post that Act coming into force, even if an inhibition granted in the same circumstances post that date would be invalid as ECHR incompatible.[23]

Other areas of corporate insolvency law, where Convention rights might impact

At this stage it is not possible to flesh out the detail of how the Human Rights Act 1998 will impact on the law of corporate insolvency in Scotland. Most cases are not as clear cut as the decision of Lord **3–05**

---

[21] 2003 S.L.T. 1340.
[22] [2004] 1 A.C. 816; [2003] 3 W.L.R. 568.
[23] See *Amalgamated Roofing and Building Co v Wilkie*, 2004 S.C.L.R. 267 (OH).

Drummond Young in the case of *Karl Construction Ltd v Palisade Properties plc*[24] or *The Advocate General for Scotland for and on behalf of the Commissioners of Inland Revenue v Maureen Taylor*.[25] However, a further area of concern in relation to a potential incompatibility with Convention rights, again Art.1 of the First Protocol to the Convention, is perhaps likely to be gratuitous alienations at common law and under the provisions of s.242 of the Insolvency Act 1986. The problem with the way gratuitous alienations have been traditionally treated in Scotland is that the transaction at undervalue is quashed (reduced), with the result that the asset that has been obtained at undervalue reverts to the company and the purchaser is left with an ordinary unsecured claim against the company in liquidation. The gratuitous alienation may be innocent. Accordingly if, for example, a house valued at a £1m was bought for £800,000, the house would revert to the company and the purchaser would be left with a claim for £800,000 against the company in liquidation. The effect of this mechanism is commonly to deprive the purchaser of the whole purchase price, in that he may as an ordinary creditor receive nothing out of the liquidation. It is suggested that this is an unjustified and disproportionate remedy. Section 242(4) of the Insolvency Act 1986 provides that, on a challenge being brought under subs.(1) of that section, "the court shall grant decree of reduction or for such restoration of property to the company's assets or other redress as may be appropriate". The problem is that the courts have held in Scotland that reduction was the principal remedy if applicable.[26]

In contrast to the Scottish position the comparable position in s.238 of the Insolvency Act 1986 in relation to England and Wales requires the court to make such order as it thinks fit for restoring the position to what it would have been if the company had not entered into the transaction.[27] Without prejudice to the generality of the power conferred on the court by s.238(3) the court may (subject to s.241(2)) make any of seven types of order specified in s.241(1) of the Insolvency Act 1986. Included in that list are orders permitting proof of debt by a person affected by the order. This position, though applicable to transactions at an undervalue as well as to preferences, is directed mainly to the latter. In the case of transactions at an undervalue the justice of the case will usually require a condition of repayment by the company (through its liquidator or administrator) of any sum received in exchange for property ordered to be reconveyed to the company; thus avoiding the mischief in Scotland of the transferee having to rank as an ordinary creditor for the purchase price paid. The Scottish mischief is well stated by Professor Roy Goode:

> "To require the transferee to return to the company property transferred at an undervalue while leaving him to prove in competi-

---

[24] A useful attempt at listing areas where recalibration might be required is in *Human Rights and Insolvency in English Law* by Gillian Benning (a paper for the Cayman Islands Human Rights Conference Sept. 10/14, 2001; *www.humanrightstoday.ky/papers/benningparsons.pdf*).

[25] 2003 S.L.T. 1340.

[26] *Short's Tr. v Chung*, 1991 S.L.T. 472; see also *Cay's Tr. v Cay*, 1998 S.C.L.R. (IH) 456.

[27] S.238(3) of the Insolvency Act 1986.

tion with other creditors for the amount of the price he originally paid would not only be extremely harsh but would provide an uncovenanted windfall for the general body of creditors, for if the transaction had never been made in the first place the company would not have received the price."[28]

It is thought that the necessary change in the law to end the mischief would not need legislative change, since the relevant legislation[29] is wide enough to be reinterpreted in a way that is compatible with Convention rights.

---

[28] R. Goode, *The Principles of Corporate Insolvency Law* (2nd ed., 1997, Sweet & Maxwell Ltd, London) at p.382.

[29] S.242 of the Insolvency Act 1986 (and also s.34 of the Bankruptcy (Scotland) Act 1985 in relation to personal insolvency).

VARIOUS INSOLVENCY REGIMES

CHAPTER 4

INSOLVENT LIQUIDATIONS

Introduction

There are procedural differences between the way a creditors' voluntary **4–01**
winding up and a winding up by the court are conducted. However, it
is thought by the authors that the general law in relation to insolvent
liquidations in Scotland forms a unity (as opposed to two systems that
share features), and that the reader will understand the general law
better if the general law is given primary place. The procedural
differences are brought out in the text, but given secondary place.

The chapter is divided into *six* parts:

- Part I describes the legal effects of winding up.
- Part II describes the appointment, removal, resignation and
  release of the liquidator.
- Part III describes the title, status and functions of the liquidator.
- Part IV describes the duties and powers of the liquidator.
- Part V describes the back-up powers of the court, which the
  liquidator may call to assistance.
- Part VI describes the various stages in the liquidation not
  already covered.

PART I

LEGAL EFFECTS OF WINDING UP

Date of commencement of winding up

Winding up commences at the time of the passing of the resolution **4–02**
for winding up,[1] or in the case of a winding up by the court (where
there has been no resolution for winding up), at the time of the
presentation of the petition to the court for winding up.[2] In the case of a
voluntary winding up, the date of commencement may not be varied.[3]
When an order for winding up is made on more than one petition, the

---

[1] Insolvency Act 1986, ss.86 and 129(1).
[2] *ibid.*, s.129(2).
[3] *Re Norditrack (UK) Ltd* [2001] 1 W.L.R. 343; [2002] 1 All E.R. 369.

order and therefore the commencement of the winding up dates from the earliest.[4]

Effect of winding up on carrying on of business

4–03   The resolution for a creditors' voluntary winding up or a winding-up order does not affect the corporate state and corporate powers of the company, which continue until the company is dissolved.[5] However, articles of association which are inconsistent with the winding-up provisions of the statutes cease to operate; for example an article restricting the right of the company to make calls,[6] or an article giving rights inconsistent with the reconstruction facility contained in s.110 of the Insolvency Act 1986.[7]

When winding up commences, the company must cease to carry on its business[8] in the case of a creditors' voluntary winding up, except that the company may carry on its business so far as the carrying on of the business may be required for a beneficial winding up.[9] There is no statutory right of a company being compulsorily wound up to carry on its business, even if required for its beneficial winding up. However, the court or the liquidation committee has the discretion to sanction the company to carry on the business of the company so far as may be necessary for its beneficial winding up.[10] Because winding up is deemed to commence from the date of the presentation of the petition, a company in provisional liquidation could not carry on business without the sanction of the court or the liquidation committee. In relation to the powers of a provisional liquidator, it is suggested that the high-water mark of a provisional liquidator's powers would be if he had the same powers as the liquidator.[11]

In order to satisfy the test whether the carrying on of the business is "necessary" or "required" for the beneficial winding up, the question is not one of preferred options, but rather whether there is a "mercantile necessity" that its business is carried on; which would not include carrying on business with the hope that prospects might improve, or be determined by whether a majority of creditors is in favour or not.[12] However, where the liquidator has the requisite authority, it is sufficient that he bona fide and reasonably believes that the carrying on of the business is necessary for the beneficial winding up of the company.[13] The liquidator must not carry on business with a view to reconstructing the company,[14] although he may in order to sell it as a going concern.

---

[4] *Re Filby Bros (Provender) Ltd* [1958] 2 All E.R. 458, 460.
[5] Insolvency Act 1986, s.87(2) and *Smith v Lord Advocate*, 1978 S.C. 259 at 271.
[6] *Newton v Anglo-Australian Investment Co's Debenture-holders* [1895] A.C. 244.
[7] *Payne v Cork* [1900] 1 Ch. 308.
[8] Insolvency Act 1986, s.87(1).
[9] *ibid.*, s.87(1).
[10] *ibid.*, s.167(1)(a) and Sch.4, para.5.
[11] See *Re ABC Coupler and Engineering Co Ltd (No 3)* [1970] 1 W.L.R. 702.
[12] *Liquidator of Burntisland Oil Co Ltd v Dawson* (1892) 20 R. 180.
[13] *Re Great Eastern Electric Co Ltd* [1941] 1 Ch. 241.
[14] *Re Wreck Recovery Co* (1880) 15 Ch. D. 353.

He does not have the powers of an administrator[15] or a Scottish receiver[16] to set up subsidiaries and hive down the business to them, which is a form of reconstruction. It will often be a difficult matter to determine whether the carrying on of the business is necessary. There will often be no guarantee that the proposal will be beneficial, but rather it will be a question of assessing whether the prospects of success with their beneficial results make the proposal a business necessity. For example, authority was granted to a liquidator to carry on the business, when the property of a company in liquidation consisted of a hall, let for public entertainments, and it was expedient to delay its sale until the time of the year when such property could be sold to best advantage.[17] Because, however, the corporate state and powers continue, a business could not be continued which was *ultra vires* the objects of the company. Hence a limited duration company could not be carried on in business beyond its set span. The advice, in doubt, should be to ask the court even if the liquidation committee approves.

Effect of winding up on receiver carrying on business

A receiver may carry on the business attached by a floating charge.[18] **4–04** Until a resolution to wind up or a winding-up order is made, the receiver may carry on the business of the company in the name of the company (all commercial documentation must give notification that the company is in receivership).[19]

The law governing the receiver's rights to carry on the business after a winding up is not easily understandable. At best the liquidator may only carry on business for the "beneficial winding up" of the company. The logical presumption would therefore suggest that, if the company in liquidation is restricted in carrying on its business, its deemed agent, "a receiver", would also be restricted. Statute, nevertheless, appears to have cut across the logical presumption. By statute a floating charge attaches the company's assets on crystallisation at winding up,[20] and if a receiver is appointed he has the power to carry on the business of the company which is covered by the floating charge.[21] He may enforce the security and exercise all the powers listed in Sch.2 to the Insolvency Act 1986,[22] provided they are not inconsistent with the terms of the floating charge, and in this his rights take precedence to those of the liquidator.[23] The holder of the floating charge, however, is under no obligation to appoint a receiver and he can leave it to the liquidator to secure his rights.[24]

---

[15] New Sch.B1 to the Insolvency Act 1986.
[16] Sch.2 to the Insolvency Act 1986.
[17] *Liquidator of Victoria Public Buildings Co* (1893) 30 S.L.R. 386.
[18] Insolvency Act 1986, s.55(2), Sch.2, para.14.
[19] *ibid.*, s.64(1).
[20] Companies Act 1985, s.463.
[21] Insolvency Act 1986, s.55(2), Sch.2, para.14.
[22] *ibid.*, s.55(2).
[23] *Manley, Petr*, 1985 S.L.T. 42.
[24] *Libertas-Kommerz GmbH Appellants*, 1978 S.L.T. 222.

Effect of winding up on company's property

4–05   Unlike vesting in a bankruptcy, the company's property does not vest in the liquidator by statute. He takes no new or independent title to the property unlike a trustee in bankruptcy,[25] although an order may be sought, vesting the property of the company in the liquidator.[26]

Effect of winding up on directors' powers

4–06   In a creditors' voluntary winding up, all the powers of the directors in relation to the business ceases on the appointment of a liquidator, except so far as the liquidation committee (or, if there is no such committee, the creditors) sanctions their continuance.[27] Similarly in a compulsory winding up the directors' powers to act on behalf of the company cease on a winding-up order,[28] or on the appointment of a provisional liquidator if there is an appointment of a provisional liquidator prior to the winding up order.[29] Unlike the position in a creditors' voluntary winding up, there is no power in a compulsory winding up for the directors' powers to be continued.[30] The directors retain certain residuary powers including the right to appeal against a winding-up order,[31] and have certain duties imposed upon them in relation to the winding up.[32] The directors will also still exercise powers they may have vested in them as trustees of the company's pension scheme.[33] The authors consider that the appointment of a liquidator or the making of a winding up order does not cause the directors to cease to hold office, and that they will continue to be directors unless and until they formally resign. There is provision that in a voluntary winding up, the powers of the directors may be continued.[34] This implies that the directors stay in office. The usual pattern of the Insolvency Act, would be that a s.112 application would be to the court for any powers available in a compulsory liquidation, to be also available in a voluntary liquidation. There is a presumption that both regimes, in principle can be conducted in the

---

[25] *Gray's Trs v Benhar Coal Co Ltd* (1881) 9 R. 225; *Clark v West Calder Oil Co* (1882) 9 R. 1017; *Queensland Mercantile and Agency Co Ltd v Australasian Investment Co Ltd* (1888) 15 R. 935 at 939.

[26] The power to vest the property in the liquidator in a winding up by the court may be sought under s.145 of the Insolvency Act 1986; the power to vest in the liquidator could be sought under s.112(2) of the Insolvency Act 1986 in the case of a creditors' voluntary winding up. The authors know of no case in which these provisions have been used in Scotland.

[27] Insolvency Act 1986, s.103.

[28] *Fowler v Broad's Patent Night Light Co* [1893] 1 Ch. 724.

[29] *Re Mawcon Ltd* [1969] 1 W.L.R. 78 at 82.

[30] *Re Farrow's Bank Ltd* [1921] 2 Ch. 164.

[31] *Re Union Accident Insurance Co Ltd* [1972] 1 All E.R. 1105 at 1113, *per* Plowman J. In saying that the directors had the residuary power to appeal against a winding-up order, he added that a good test of the extent of directors' residuary powers was to inquire whether the power which the board is said to have lost is one which can be said to have been assumed by the liquidator.

[32] Production of a statement of affairs under s.99(1) of the Insolvency Act 1986 in the case of a creditors' voluntary winding up and under s.131(3) in the case of a compulsory winding up.

[33] *Smith, etc, Petrs*, 1969 S.L.T. (Notes) 94.

[34] S.102 of the Insolvency Act 1986.

same manner. In England there is case law to the effect that the office of directors does not terminate on liquidation.[35] Similarly, in relation to compulsory windings up, it was decided in the case of *Madrid Bank Ltd v Bayle*,[36] that directors could be made to answer interrogatories in their capacity as officers of the company even after the liquidator had been appointed, and that there was nothing in the legislation making the persons concerned cease to be directors. Australian cases have held that the making of a winding up order does not remove the directors.[37] The authors' view is reinforced by the provisions in the Enterprise Act 2002,[38] which provides for there to be an administration, although liquidation has been entered into. The legal mechanics of this innovative procedure is not spelt out in the legislation.[39] However, if the directors were meant to cease to hold office, it is thought that some provision for reinstating the directors would have been spelt out in para.38 of new Schedule B1 to the Insolvency Act 1986.

In relation to creditors' windings up,[40] the powers of directors are severely limited between the date of the commencement of the winding up (*i.e.* the date of passing of the resolution to wind up), where no liquidator has been appointed or nominated, until the nomination or appointment of the liquidator. In terms of s.114 of the Insolvency Act 1986 (acting partly on the recommendations of the Cork Committee), statute intervened to regulate the conduct of the company's affairs in this period and restrict the former unfettered powers of the directors to act during this period since unscrupulous behaviour had not been uncommon. (Indeed the Cork Committee had gone so far as to recommend that a provisional liquidator should take over immediately upon the passing of the resolution of the board of directors; entailing that the directors find a qualified person willing to act as a provisional liquidator before the passing of the resolution.) In terms of s.114(2) of the Insolvency Act 1986, the powers of the directors may not be exercised during that period except for the purposes of summoning the creditors' meeting and making out the Statement of Affairs in terms of sections 98 and 99 of the Insolvency Act 1986. The directors are, however, allowed to dispose of perishable goods and other goods, where the value is likely to diminish if they are not immediately disposed of.[41] They may also do other things which are necessary for the protection of the company's assets.[42] The present linguistic formula, "to do all such things as may be necessary for the protection of the company's assets", does not specify what precisely this power means, and is very difficult to

---

[35] *Midland Counties District Bank Ltd v Attwood* [1905] 1 CH. 357.

[36] [1866] L.R. 2 Q.B. 37.

[37] *Austral Brick Co Pty Ltd v Falgat Constructions Pty Ltd* [1990] 8 A.C.L.C. 1011; *McAusland v DFC of T* [1994] 12 A.C.L.C. 78; *Re Pollnow* [1994] 12 A.C.L.C. 88. In contrast, see *A.G. v Blumenthal* 1961 (4) S.A. 313 (T) (a South African case); there is also the view taken in the English case of *Measures Brothers Ltd v Measures* [1910] 2 Ch. 248 that on a court winding up a company, the appointment of the directors terminate automatically.

[38] Para.38 of new Sch.B1 to the Insolvency Act 1986.

[39] See para.5–17.

[40] See the Insolvency Act 1986, Sch.11, para.4.

[41] *ibid.*, s.114(3)(a).

[42] *ibid.*, s.114(3)(b).

construe. It is not clear whether this means "doing everything necessary to ensure that the balance sheet is in the healthiest possible state at the date of the appointment of the liquidator" or is specifically confined to doing things analogous to "disposing of perishable goods and other goods the value of which is likely to diminish". It is suggested that this power must be read narrowly. Otherwise, it totally detracts from the purpose of the section. Accordingly, it is suggested that it means "to take what legal steps are necessary or other immediate measures necessary to preserve assets", and has nothing to do with trading—which would also involve liabilities—or any other type of conduct involving the carrying on of the business.[43]

Effect of winding up on contracts other than employment contracts

4–07   Apart from contracts of employment which are in a special category,[44] or unless there is an express term of the contract that a liquidation should constitute an event of default or breach, contracts are not terminated by liquidation. The liquidator has the option of adopting[45] any contract beneficial to the company (independently of his decision in respect of any other contract), or of terminating it and allowing a ranking for damages.[46] It is necessary for the liquidator to intimate within a reasonable time (which depends on the nature of the contract) whether he intends to adopt the contract; otherwise he will be held to have abandoned the intention to proceed with it.[47] It will be a question of circumstance what the period will be during which the intention must be made clear. There is no statutory grace period.[48] If the company through the liquidator decides to occupy a property beneficially after the winding up, rates will be payable as an expense of the winding up.[49] Utilities may not now refuse to supply services to a company in liquidation until paid arrears (although they may require the liquidator to guarantee payment in respect of services to the company in liquidation).[50]

Building and engineering contracts frequently make express provision for forfeiture of materials and plant in the event of failure by the contractor to implement the contract, or even for the deemed vesting of plant and materials in the employer as soon as they are delivered to site.

---

[43] It is to be noted that a similar provision in the Bankruptcy (Scotland) Act 1985, s.39(6) is concerned with the preservation of the market value of assets.

[44] See Chap.11.

[45] "Adopt" means to refrain from repudiating; *per* MacPherson J., *Re Diesel's & Components Pty Ltd* (1985) 9 A.C.L.R. at 827.

[46] *Grey's Trs v Benhar Coal Co* (1881) 9 R. 225; *Commercial Bank of Scotland v Pattison's Trs* (1891) 18 R. 476; *Asphaltic Limestone Concrete Co Ltd v Glasgow Corporation*, 1907 S.C. 463; *Clyde Marine Insurance Co v Renwick*, 1974 S.C. 113; *Turnbull v Liquidator of Scottish County Investment Co*, 1939 S.C. 5; *Smith v Lord Advocate*, 1978 S.C. 259.

[47] *Crown Estate Commissioners v Liquidators of Highland Engineering Ltd*, 1975 S.L.T. 58.

[48] Insolvency Act 1986, s.57(5) provides for a statutory grace period of 14 days in employment contracts in receiverships.

[49] *Re National Arms Ammunition Co* (1885) 28 Ch. D. 474; *Re Blazer Fire Lighter Ltd* [1895] 1 Ch. 402; *Re Nolton Business Centres Ltd* [1996] B.C.C. 500.

[50] Insolvency Act 1986, s.233.

The validity of such clauses must be determined by the general principles of Scots law relating to the transfer of moveable property; for this purpose, the underlying commercial reality of the clause must be examined carefully. It is thought that clauses which purport to vest plant in the employer are invalid, on the basis that the commercial reality of such a clause can only be security; possession of the contractor's plant will not normally be transferred from the contractor to the employer, and thus the security will be invalid. Clauses which purport to vest materials on site in the employer are likely to be valid, since transfer of property in the materials accords with the commercial reality of a building contract. There seems to be no reason why the general rules applicable to sale of goods should not apply to such cases. It has been held in England that, if a building contract is terminated owing to the insolvency of the contractor, a clause purporting to forfeit materials and plant is invalid in a question with the liquidator.[51] It is thought that the same reasoning should apply in Scotland. The liquidator may not adopt contracts which are not in the interests of the creditors and members, where these contracts are not legally enforceable but binding only in honour.[52] If, however, the liquidator had the authority to carry on the business of the company, it might be argued that the honouring of non-legally enforceable obligations was a legitimate aspect of the carrying on of the business.[53] The liquidator may ratify, on behalf of the company as agent of the company, acts which are invalid, which the company in general meeting could have ratified.[54]

Effect of winding up on contracts of employment

The effect of winding up on contracts of employment is dealt with in Chap.11. **4–08**

Effect of winding-up on pending actions

At any time after the presentation of a winding-up petition, and before a winding-up order has been made, if there is any action or proceeding against the company pending, the company or any creditor or contributory may apply to the court having jurisdiction to wind up the company to restrain the proceedings, and the court then has a discretion to stay, sist or restrain the proceedings on such terms as it thinks fit.[55] If, however, the action or proceeding against the company is in the High Court or the Court of Appeal in England and Wales or Northern Ireland, the application has to be made to the court in which the action or proceeding is pending.[56] If, after a winding-up petition has been presented, but before a winding-up order has been made, a **4–09**

---

[51] *Ex p. Baxter* (1884) 26 Ch. D. 510. On the matters discussed in this paragraph, see Chap.11.

[52] *Clyde Marine Insurance Co v Renwick*, 1924 S.C. 113.

[53] *ibid.*

[54] *Alexander Ward and Co Ltd v Sam Yang Navigation Co Ltd*, 1975 S.C. (H.L.) 27.

[55] Insolvency Act 1986, s.126(1)(b).

[56] *ibid.*, s.126(1)(a).

provisional liquidator is appointed, no action or proceeding may be proceeded with or commenced against the company or its property except by leave of the court and subject to such terms as the court may impose.[57] This rule applies also from the time that a winding-up order is made.[58] Leave of the court is not required to counter-claim against a company in liquidation if the counter-claim is for less than the amount sued for by the company.[59] In the case of a company registered under s.680 of the Companies Act, no action or proceeding may be commenced or proceeded with against the company or its property and any contributory of the company, in respect of any debt of the company, except by leave of the court, and subject to such terms as the court may impose.[60] Where a petition or application for leave to proceed with an action or proceeding against a company which has been wound up is unopposed and is granted by the court, the cost of the petition or application must, unless the court otherwise directs, be added to the amount of the petitioner's or applicant's claim against the company.[61] These provisions do not affect any action taken by an investment exchange or clearing house recognised under the Financial Services Act 1986 for the purposes of its default proceedings.[62] If property (other than land) is held by a recognised investment exchange or recognised clearing house as margin in relation to market contracts, or is subject to a market charge, no diligence or execution or other legal process for the enforcement of any judgment or order may be commenced or continued without the consent of the investment exchange or clearing house in question (in the case of property provided as cover for margin), or of the person in whose favour the charge was granted (in the case of a market charge).[63]

In order to avoid loss to parties who deal with the company after it has gone into liquidation, s.188 of the Insolvency Act 1986 imposes a requirement that every invoice, order for goods or business letter issued by or on behalf of the company or the liquidator after the winding-up order has been made must contain a statement that the company is in liquidation. A criminal penalty in the form of a fine is imposed upon the company and any of its officers, or the liquidator, who knowingly and wilfully authorise or permit default in respect of this requirement.

Effect of winding up in relation to stamp duty

4–10   In the case of a winding-up by the court, or of a creditors' voluntary winding up of a company registered in Scotland, various documents are by statute exempt from stamp duty. They include conveyances relating solely to property which forms part of the company's assets, but only property which, after the execution of the conveyance, remains the company's property for the benefit of its creditors.[64]

---

[57] Insolvency Act 1986, s.130(2).
[58] *ibid.*
[59] *G.&A. Hotels Ltd v THB Marketing Services Ltd*, 1983 S.L.T. 497.
[60] Insolvency Act 1986, s.130(3).
[61] *ibid.*, s.199.
[62] Companies Act 1989, s.161(4).
[63] *ibid.*, s.180(1).
[64] Insolvency Act 1986, s.190(3); "conveyance" in terms of the sub-section in this context comprises several categories of legal instruments.

Effect of winding up on dispositions of property

Section 127 of the Insolvency Act 1986 provides that, in a winding up **4–11** by the court, any disposition of the company's property, and any transfer of shares, or alteration in the status of the company's members, made after the commencement of the winding up is, unless the court otherwise orders, void. Because winding up is deemed to commence on the presentation of the petition on which the winding-up order was made, unless the company was already in voluntary liquidation at the time of the petition, in which case the winding up is deemed to commence on the passing of the resolution for voluntary winding up,[65] dispositions of the company's property are blocked from the date of the presentation of the petition. The purpose of the provision being back-dated is to prevent the dissipation of the company's assets while the hearing of the petition is pending. The provision catches all dispositions, whether preferences or bona fide business transactions. Except where there is a provisional liquidator, who has been given powers by the court, it is important that the company obtain authority from the court to enable it to continue trading while there is a hearing of the petition. After a liquidator is appointed he is given powers under s.167 of the Insolvency Act 1986 which would appear to remove the need for separate permission under s.127 of that Act. It is also thought that a receiver in Scotland would not need to make an application under the section.[66] Property comprised in a standard security may be sold by the holder of the security following the procedures laid down in the Conveyancing and Feudal Reform (Scotland) Act 1970.[67] In the case of an insolvent company it is necessary for the applicant to satisfy the court that the proposed transaction would be beneficial to the company.[68] A shareholder may make an application.[69] The granting of a floating charge has been held in Scotland to be a disposition of the company's property for the purposes of the predecessor of s.127 of the Insolvency Act 1986.[70] In such a situation the disposition would be void, but it may be validated.[71] It has been held in England that a disposition in implementation of a contract would not require leave under s.127 of the Insolvency Act 1986.[72] It is thought that a right of set-off would not be covered by s.127. Similarly, assets held by a company are not its property to the extent of any security interest it has given over them in favour of a creditor. The principles upon which a court would grant applications for the validation of dispositions is discussed in detail in the English case of *Re Gray's Inn Construction Co Ltd*.[73] The fundamental principle informing the court in the exercise of its discretion is that it

---

[65] Insolvency Act 1986, s.129.
[66] *Manley*, 1985 S.L.T. 42.
[67] Conveyancing and Feudal Reform (Scotland) Act 1970, s.24(1).
[68] *Re AI Levy (Holdings) Ltd* [1964] Ch. 19; [1963] 2 All E.R. 556; *Re Burton and Deakin Ltd* [1977] 1 All E.R. 631; and *Re Webb Electrical Ltd* [1988] B.C.L.C. 382; 4 B.C.C. 230.
[69] *Re Argentum Reductions (UK) Ltd* [1975] 1 All E.R. 608.
[70] *Site Preparations Ltd v Buchan Developments Co Ltd*, 1983 S.L.T. 317.
[71] *Re Park Ward & Co Ltd* [1926] Ch. 828.
[72] *Re French's (Wine Bar)* [1987] B.C.L.C. 499.
[73] [1980] 1 All E.R. 814; for what is a company's property, see Chap.12; R.M. Goode, *Legal Problems of Credit and Security* (2nd ed., 1988) p.35.

will not validate any transaction which would result in pre-liquidation creditors being paid in full at the expense of other creditors who will only receive dividends, unless to do so will benefit the unsecured creditors as a whole.[74] This principle is very much in keeping with the philosophy informing the Enterprise Act 2002, in which the interests of all the creditors collectively is one of the overriding emphasis of that Act in the area of insolvency.

PART II

APPOINTMENT, REMOVAL, RESIGNATION AND RELEASE OF LIQUIDATORS

Presentation of petition

4–12 Where a company is insolvent, a winding-up petition is usually presented by:

  (a) the company[75];
  (b) the directors[76];
  (c) a creditor or creditors (including any contingent or prospective creditor or creditors)[77]; and
  (d) a contributory or contributories.[78]

Petition by the directors

4–13 In *Re Instrumentation Electrical Services Ltd*[79] it had been suggested that a winding-up petition had to be supported by all the directors. This is probably not the case given the judgment in *Re Equiticorp International plc*, which concerned the same position in relation to the presenting of a winding-up petition, and it was held that it was sufficient that the petition had been approved by a resolution of the directors.[80] A guarantor of a debt of a company is a contingent creditor and is entitled to petition.[81]

Petition by creditor or creditors

4–14 A petition may be presented by a contingent or prospective creditor.[82] "Contingent creditor" means a creditor in respect of a debt which will only become due in an event which may or may not occur, and

---

[74] This is a complicated area of the law. See *Bank of Ireland v Hollicourt (Contracts) Ltd* [2000] B.C.C. 1210; *Coutts & Co. v Stock* [2000] 2 All E.R. 56; and *Re Tain Construction Ltd, Rose v AIB Group UK plc* [2003] All E.R. (D.) 1991 (Jun.), Ch. D.

[75] Insolvency Act 1986, s.124(1). Where the company has already gone into voluntary liquidation, it is competent for the liquidator to present the petition. Cf *Re Zoedone Co* [1884] 53 L.J. Ch. 465. Where the company is in administration, or if an administrative receiver has been appointed, the office holder is entitled to present a petition for the winding-up of a company in terms of para.21 of Sch.1 to the Insolvency Act 1986.

[76] Insolvency Act 1986, s.124(1). Cf *Re Emmadart Ltd* [1979] Ch. 540, which held that the directors were not entitled to present a petition in the name of the company without the sanction of a general meeting. The need for the sanction of a general meeting is no longer necessary in terms of the Insolvency Act 1986, s.124(1).

[77] Insolvency Act 1986, s.124(1).

[78] Insolvency Act 1986, s.124(1).

[79] [1988] B.C.L.C. 550, 4 B.C.C. 301.

[80] [1989] B.C.L.C. 597; [1989] 1 W.L.R. 1010.

[81] *Re Dollar Land Holdings plc* [1993] B.C.C. 823.

[82] Insolvency Act 1986, s.124(1).

"prospective creditor", means a creditor in respect of a debt which will certainly become due in the future, either on some date which has already been determined or some date determinable by reference to future events.[83] If there is a genuine doubt that there is a bona fide dispute, the court would normally sist the petition to allow the petitioners to constitute their debt.[84] Where a petitioner is found not to be entitled to present the petition, the court may sist as petitioner in the place of the original petitioner any other creditor or contributory who is entitled, in the opinion of the court, to present a petition.[85] If the alleged contingent debt is disputed by the company in good faith, the petition would normally be dismissed.[86] It is provided in s.125(1) that a petition shall not be dismissed merely because there appear to be no assets(or none available for unsecured creditors). There may be other important considerations such as the need to investigate irregularities.[87]

Petition by a contributory

The right of a contributory to petition for a winding up is limited in **4–15** that, except where the ground of the petition is that the number of members is reduced below two, the shares in respect of which the petitioner is a contributory, or some of them, must either have been originally allotted to the petitioner, or have been held by him, and registered in his name, for at least six months during the 18 months before the commencement of the winding up, or have devolved on the petitioner through the death of a former holder.[88] This provision is designed to prevent an outsider from acquiring shares simply in order to have the company wound up by the court. The expression "contributory" includes an allottee whose name does not appear on the register. However, if there is a genuine dispute as to the validity of the allotment, the petitioner must first establish the validity of the allotment before proceeding with the petition.[89] If a petitioner is found not entitled to present a petition (and in certain other circumstances specified in Rules of Court) the court may sist as petitioner in place of the original petitioner, any creditor or contributory whom the court is of the opinion is entitled to present a petition.[90] In addition to the above restrictions, a contributory whose shares are fully paid up will not be permitted to proceed with a petition unless he can show that he has a tangible interest in the relief sought. This would normally mean that there were assets available for distribution to the shareholders. In the case of *Re*

---

[83] *Walter L. Jacob & Co Ltd v Financial Intermediaries, Managers and Brokers Regulatory Association* 1988 S.C.L.R. 184, Sh. Ct; *Stonegate Securities Ltd v Gregory* [1980] Ch. 576.

[84] *Landauer & Co v WH Alexander & Co Ltd*, 1919 S.C. 492.

[85] Rule of Court of Session 74.24 (SI 1994/1443(S.69))); Act of Sederunt (Sheriff Court Company Insolvency Rules) 1986 (SI 1986/2297), r.21.

[86] *Re Fitness Centre (South East) Ltd* [1986] B.C.L.C. 518; *Re a Company (No 003028 of 1987)* [1988] B.C.L.C. 282, 3 B.C.C. 575.

[87] *Bell Group Finance (Pty) Ltd (in liquidation) v Bell Group(UK) Holdings Ltd* [1996] B.C.C. 505.

[88] Insolvency Act 1986, s.124(2).

[89] *Re JN2 Ltd* [1977] 3 All E.R. 1104; [1978] 1 W.L.R. 183.

[90] Rule of Court of Session 74.24 (SI 1994/1443 (S.69))); Act of Sederunt (Sheriff Court Company Insolvency Rules) 1986 (SI 1986/2297), r.21.

Commercial and Industrial Insulations Ltd,[91] Hoffmann J. stated the principle:

> "The rule in the case of a contributory's petition is that no order may be made for a winding-up unless the contributory has shown what Jessel MR in *Re Rica Gold Washing Co* [1879] 11 Ch D 36 at 43 called 'a tangible interest'. That usually means that there will be a surplus for distribution on a winding-up, although that is not the only instance of a tangible interest and other examples were given by Oliver J in *Re Chesterfield Catering Co Ltd* [1976] 3 All ER 294, [1977] Ch 373. In this case, however, it does not appear to me that the evidence shows that in his capacity as a contributory the petitioner would have any tangible interest in the event of a winding-up. It was argued that there is an exception to this rule in a case in which the petitioner's inability to prove his tangible interest is due to the company's own default in providing him with information to which as a member he is entitled. The way in which that proposition is put by Oliver J in the *Re Chesterfield Catering Co Ltd* case is that the petition will not in that event be regarded as demurrable[92] on the ground of the petitioner's lack of *locus standi*. This, if I may say so, seems to me to be commonsense, because it would obviously be unjust to the petitioner to have his petition struck out *in limine* because he was unable to allege a surplus on a winding-up on account of wrongfully being deprived of access to the necessary information. The position is, I think, different once the petition has come to be heard. By that time the petitioner will have been able to take advantage of procedural mechanisms available for obtaining information needed to support his case."[93]

The most recent Scottish case also suggested that a contributory is entitled to bring a petition for winding up only if both the statutory requirements in s.124 of the Insolvency Act 1986 are met and he has an interest in the outcome of the liquidation, *i.e.* there must be a likelihood of a surplus of assets from which he could draw a dividend.[94] It is not sufficient to establish title and interest to petition for a winding up merely to have an action for damages against the company since that does not establish the petitioner as a contingent or prospective creditors.[95] It has been suggested that a shareholder will be able to petition

---

[91] [1986] B.C.L.C. 191.

[92] Demurrable means "dismissible".

[93] See also *Re Martin Coulter Enterprises Ltd* [1988] B.C.L.C. 12, 4 B.C.C. 212.

[94] *O'Connor v Atlantis Fisheries Ltd*, 1988 S.C.L.R. 401. Although this case probably reflects the law in Scotland, it highlights the narrow view of "interest" taken in Scotland. At the stage of the petition for the winding up, it may not be knowable whether there may be actions under ss.212, 213 or 214 of the Insolvency Act 1986, and hence eventually a surplus in which the contributories might participate. Secondly, contributories have often non-financial real interests in finding out through the liquidation process the causes of the insolvency, and having the actions of those responsible put under scrutiny, with those responsible if necessary sued or prosecuted. Of course, in such a situation he would be entitled to bring an action on the "just and equitable" ground also, but the "unable to pay its debts" ground might be simpler for him to prove. In doubt the petition should list both grounds, especially because it would be easier relevantly to aver material in a "just and equitable" ground which could enable the petitioner to recover documents.

[95] *Walter Jacob & Co Ltd v The Financial Intermediaries Managers and Brokers Regulatory Association*, 1998 S.C.L.R. 184.

for winding up on the ground that the company is unable to pay its debts, if his shares are partly paid up and his financial interest lies in procuring that the company's affairs are wound up before his liability to contribute is increased by further losses.

Appointment of liquidators

(1) Creditors' voluntary winding up

The creditors and members at their respective meetings in a creditors'   **4–16** voluntary winding up may each nominate a liquidator, but the nomination of the creditors will prevail, subject only to a successful application to the court by any director, member or creditor within seven days after the date of the nomination challenging the appointment.[96] On a successful challenge the court may then appoint the members' nominee jointly, or replace the creditors' nominee with some other person.[97] During the interval between the members' nomination and the creditors', the members' nominee's powers are restricted.[98]

(2) Compulsory winding up

The procedure is similar in a winding-up by the court except that the   **4–17** court appoints a liquidator (to be known as an interim liquidator) when it makes a winding-up order.[99] The interim liquidator then summons meetings of members and creditors for the purpose of choosing the liquidator.[1] These meetings are known respectively as "the first meeting of contributories" and "the first meeting of creditors", and jointly as "the first meeting in the liquidation", and any such meetings of creditors or contributories must be summoned for a date not later than 42 days after the date of the winding-up order, unless approved by the court.[2] The meetings (with creditors having precedence) then choose the liquidator.[3] As in the case of creditors' voluntary windings up, there is a right of challenge in court within seven days of nomination, by creditors and contributories, where meetings are held and different persons are nominated.[4] The directors do not have the right of challenge since their powers cease on the winding-up order.[5]

Grounds of challenge to appointment of liquidators

There are various grounds of challenge open when a decision of the   **4–18** meetings are challenged under ss.100(3) and 139(4) of the Insolvency Act 1986. In practice now, however, the latitude of discretion in appoint-

---

[96] Insolvency Act 1986, s.100(3). (See also para.4–90—for a case of a members' voluntary winding up converted to a creditors' voluntary winding up.)

[97] *ibid.,* s.100(3).

[98] See para.4–47.

[99] *ibid.,* s.138(1) and (2).

[1] *ibid.,* s.138(3) and (4).

[2] R.4.12(2) and (2A) of the Insolvency (Scotland) Rules 1986 as amended by para.14 of the Schedule to the Insolvency (Scotland) Amendment Rules 1987.

[3] Insolvency Act 1986, s.139(3).

[4] *ibid.,* s.139(4).

[5] *ibid.,* s.103.

ments is circumscribed by the fact that liquidators must be qualified "insolvency practitioners"[6] and challenges are likely to be less frequent. Where a firm of insolvency practitioners is appointed liquidator, or provisional liquidator, it is important to check that there is not a conflict of interest within the firm, although it has been held that there was no conflict of interest in the case of a firm of insolvency practitioners who had been appointed to act as provisional liquidators of one company, the associates of whose controlling shareholder controlled other companies in respect of which the same firm had been appointed in England as receivers by the court.[7]

Although it is not illegal to appoint a liquidator who is not resident in Scotland, he must normally be resident in Scotland unless there are strong grounds for departing from that practice.[8] However, persons resident in England have been appointed liquidators where there was a strong reason, for example, to enable contracts beneficial to the company to be continued.[9] A former director may also be appointed liquidator but probably only where he is not the sole liquidator.[10] This is because the court attaches particular importance to the office holder being independent and being seen to be independent of the persons he may have to investigate. In *Re Corbenstoke Ltd (No 2)*[11] Harman J. discussed the possibility of a director acting as a liquidator. He observed:

> "In my view, it is most unlikely that a director could ever be a proper liquidator of a company. I do not say it is totally impossible, but it must be a matter of the rarest occurrence because inevitably a director will have responsibility for the affairs of the company even if, as is said to be the case, this company were a non-trading company operating through a web of subsidiaries and sub-subsidiaries. In such a case the liquidator is bound to investigate the attitudes and actions of the director in controlling the subsidiaries of the company, and it cannot be right that the same person should both be liquidator and director."

Any objection to an appointment should be of "a tangible and definite nature".[12] Normally the wishes of the creditors will be followed but this is not binding, so that in the case *of Matthew Wishart, Petr*[13] both the company and the creditors sought a joint liquidator in addition to the then current liquidator, but the court refused because of the small size of the company, seeing no reason "why there should be two horses in a one horse concern". The court will appoint an additional liquidator or additional liquidators in matters of complexity.[14] Where joint liquidators

[6] Insolvency Act 1986, ss.388 and 390.
[7] *Re Arrows Ltd* [1992] B.C.C. 121.
[8] *Baberton Development Syndicate Ltd* (1898) 24 R.654.
[9] *Liquidators of Bruce Peebles & Co Ltd v Shiells*, 1908 S.C. 692.
[10] *ibid.*
[11] (1989) 5 B.C.C. 767; [1990] B.C.L.C. 60.
[12] *Anderson & Sons v Broughty Ferry Picture House*, 1917 S.C. 622.
[13] 1908 S.C. 690.
[14] *Liquidator of Ecudorian Association v Fox* (1906) 14 S.L.T. 47.

are appointed, the appointment or nomination must contain a clear indication whether the joint office holders must act together, or whether one or more can do any act on their own authority.[15] Following the policy, however, of trying to give effect to the wishes of the creditors in appointing liquidators, the court has confirmed the appointment of an auditor as liquidator because he was knowledgeable of the affairs of the company, and has replaced a managing director as liquidator with a neutral liquidator where the other liquidator was also well versed in the affairs of the company.[16]

It is thought that these decisions would not be followed today and that the court would require a much greater degree of independence. In the Australian case of *Re Capital Management Securities Ltd*[17] the court refused leave for an auditor to act as liquidator. McLelland J. stated:

> "Mere grounds of convenience and the improbability of any wrong-doing having occurred which may be discovered by a liquidator seem to me to be elements which are likely to be present in many cases, and are not the kind of matters which should induce the Court to depart from the legislative policy that normally a liquidator should be, and be seen to be, entirely independent of the pre-liquidation activities of the company."

In another Australian case, *Attalex Pty Ltd v Brian Cassiday Electrical Industries Pty Ltd*[18] the court ordered the appointment of an independent liquidator where there was a good balance of convenience arguments in favour of the appointment of the same person who had already acted as provisional liquidator. What swayed the court was the fact that a partner of the provisional liquidator had advised in relation to the affairs of the company and a possible scheme of arrangement in connection with which the company had commenced the winding-up proceedings. There was no adverse reflection either on the partner or the provisional liquidator. However, McLelland J. observed that "[t]he question at issue really amounts to how much weight should be given in the circumstances to a liquidator's being seen to be completely detached from those associated with the company whose conduct he will be under an obligation to investigate."

This stricter modern approach is also taken in relation to conflicting interests and duties of liquidators. There is a specific need to avoid conflicting duties and interests. The case of *Re Corbenstoke Ltd (No.2)*[19] gives a good illustration of the type of conflicts of interest and duty which can arise. That was an application for the removal of a liquidator. The liquidator was also acting as trustee in bankruptcy for an individual's estate. The statement of affairs of the bankrupt had claimed ownership of 99 per cent of the share capital issued by the company. In

---

[15] Insolvency Act 1986, s.231.
[16] *Argylls v Ritchie & Whiteman*, 1914 S.C. 915.
[17] [1986] 4 A.C.L.C. 157.
[18] [1984] 2 A.C.L.C. 654.
[19] (1989) 5 B.C.C. 767; [1990] B.C.L.C. 60.

order to protect that interest the liquidator had appointed himself as a director of the company and had held that office for a few weeks. For a short period he had even been the sole director of the company. In the capacity as trustee in bankruptcy he then claimed to be a creditor of the company by virtue of subrogation following discharge of guarantee liabilities. As a result of his activities in relation to another company, the liquidator was also a debtor of Corbenstoke Ltd. In commenting on the affidavit in support of the application for removal Harman J. observed:

> "The affidavit goes on to set out the grounds for removing [the liquidator] as liquidator; first, that he was a director of the company before it went into liquidation; secondly, that he claimed to be a creditor; thirdly, that he appears to be a debtor; and fourthly—a quite separate matter—grounds of his previous conduct.
>
> As counsel puts the matter to me, there are really two separate categories of grounds: first, that [the liquidator] is in a position where his duty, and not necessarily his interest, but his other duty in a different capacity, are in inevitable conflict. So far as it is alleged that he is a debtor of the company, it is also a matter where his duty as liquidator and his personal interest as debtor must be in conflict. It is the oldest rule of all in equity that a man should not place himself in a position where his duty and his interest conflict, without the fullest disclosure of the conflict and the approval of his continuing to hold that position despite the conflict. It is a proposition which applies across many fields to anyone holding a fiduciary office. Here the office of liquidator is well set out by Swinfen Eady J in *Re Charterland Goldfields Ltd* (1909) 26 TLR 132, and it is plain that a liquidator, although not strictly speaking a trustee, is nonetheless a fiduciary, holding an office with statutory duties analogous to the duties of a trustee to his beneficiaries being the duties of a liquidator to his creditors."

A particular problem in relation to conflict of duty arises where an insolvency practitioner deals with the liquidation of a group of companies. That this is an appropriate course in the right circumstances is recognised in the Secretary of State's "code of conduct" in relation to insolvency practitioners. It states:

> "In certain circumstances there will be an advantage, seen and agreed by creditors, for all the companies in a group, or otherwise associated, to be administered by one insolvency practitioner; but such prospect of economy should not hold sway where there is any suggestion that the affairs of individual companies within such a 'group' have been dealt with oppressively to the advantage of others."

Although there are statements suggesting a very strict test,[20] the Court of Appeal in England in *Re Esal (Commodities) Ltd*[21] suggested that,

---

[20] See comments of Harman J. in *Re Corbenstoke Ltd (No.2)*, above; *Re P Turner (Wilsden) Ltd* [1987] B.C.L.C. 149; *Re Bi-Print Ltd* [1989] 2 Insolvency Intelligence 76; *Re GK Pty Ltd* [1983] 1 A.C.L.C. 848.

[21] (1988) 4 B.C.C. 475; [1989] B.C.L.C. 59.

provided insolvency practitioners behaved sensibly, such appointments were not to be ruled out. Dillon L.J. stated:

"Of course there are possible conflicts of interest. It is unnecessary to go into them in detail, but one of the more obvious is that in an insolvency situation the subsidiary will have its own creditors whose claims will have to be met. Sometimes the creditor will include the parent company or the subsidiary next up the line. Sometimes the interests of the parent company or subsidiary next up the line will merely be an interest as shareholder which ranks behind the creditors of the subsidiary. But these sorts of potential conflicts do not in practice give rise to any serious difficulty because they are well known to the experienced insolvency practitioners."

Provisional liquidators

(1) Appointment

The court has power to appoint a "provisional" liquidator at any time **4–19** before the first appointment of a liquidator.[22] This applies in a winding up by the court only.[23] (The "provisional" liquidator should not be confused with the "interim" liquidator, which is the name given to the liquidator appointed by the court in a winding up when the winding-up order is given.[24] He is called an "interim" liquidator to cover a situation where, after the meetings of the company's contributories and creditors, somebody different from the interim liquidator is selected to be liquidator, and who then replaces the interim liquidator as liquidator.[25])

The petition for winding up usually contains an application for the appointment of a provisional liquidator. The application for the appointment of a provisional liquidator may be made by the petitioner in the winding up or by a creditor of the company, or by a contributory or by the company itself or by any person who would be entitled to present a petition for the winding up.[26] It is usual practice for the application to be granted, unless the petition is opposed on grounds which appear substantial. The appointment of a provisional liquidator is not a first step in the winding up of the company, but rather a holding operation pending the decision whether or not to wind up.[27] In considering whether to make an appointment the court is primarily concerned to maintain the status quo in the affairs of the company and to avoid prejudice to parties.[28] In an English case it was stated[29]: "[n]ow the provisional liquidator's appointment is not only provisional, but contingent in this sense, that it operates to protect the property for an equal

---

[22] Insolvency Act 1986, s.135(3).
[23] *ibid.*, s.135(1).
[24] *ibid.*, s.138(2).
[25] *ibid.*, s.139(3).
[26] Insolvency (Scotland) Rules 1986, r.4.1.
[27] *Teague, Petr,* 1985 S.L.T. 469.
[28] *Levy v Napier,* 1962 S.L.T. 264.
[29] *Re Dry Docks Corporation of London* (1888) 39 Ch. D. 306 at 314, *per* Fry LJ on appeal.

distribution only in the event of an order for compulsory winding up being made; and if no such order is made, then his appointment ought not to interfere with the rights of third persons."

(2) Powers and duties of provisional liquidators

4–20   Subsections 135(4) and (5) of the Insolvency Act 1986 merely state that the provisional liquidator shall carry out such functions as the court may confer on him, and that the powers of the provisional liquidator may be limited by the order appointing him. How the second provision should be properly interpreted has been the subject of some discussion in Scotland.[30] The better view is that express powers should be sought.[31] He has the statutory power to require a statement of affairs to be produced.[32] Also, because winding up commences at the presentation of the petition[33] and he has been appointed liquidator provisionally,[34] he has, in principle, the normal powers of a liquidator in a compulsory winding up. However, the view that the provisional liquidator's powers are restricted and that express powers should be sought is given extra backing by s.135(4), which requires him to have express "functions" conferred by the court. What powers he should have will depend on what functions are conferred, *i.e.* which will be necessary for the carrying out of the functions. It is the usual practice to ask in the winding-up petition for the powers in Pt II of Sch.4 to the 1986 Act, but others may be added as appropriate.

The provisional liquidator has a duty to notify his appointment to the Registrar of Companies, to the Accountant in Bankruptcy, to the company, and to any receiver that there is over any part of the property of the company.[35] He is also under a duty to advertise his appointment according to any directions laid down by the court.[36] If he considers that advertisement would be harmful or otherwise not appropriate, he should apply to the court for an order dispensing with the advertisement.[37] His main duty, however, as stated above, is to preserve the status quo and to avoid prejudice to the parties. He is therefore not really there to "liquidate" the company as a liquidator proper, and perhaps would be better named a "caretaker". One could not, after all, talk about a "provisional executioner".[38]

---

[30] See McBryde, "The Powers of Provisional Liquidators", 1977 S.L.T. (News) 145.

[31] *Lochore and Capledraw Cannel Coal Co Ltd* (1889) 16 R. 556; *Wilsons (Glasgow and Trinidad) Ltd (in Liquidation)* 1912 2 S.L.T. 330; *Drummond Wood Ltd,* December 7, 1971, unreported.

[32] Insolvency Act 1986, s.131(1). See also Chap.18 on accounting law and practice.

[33] *ibid.,* s.129(2).

[34] *ibid.,* s.135(1).

[35] Insolvency (Scotland) Rules 1986, r.4.2(1), as amended by SI 1999/1820.

[36] *ibid.,* r.4.2(2).

[37] *International Factors Ltd v Ves Voltech Engineering Services Ltd,* 1994 S.L.T. (Sh. Ct.) 40; 1993 S.C.L.R. 906.

[38] In the case of *Re Hawk Insurance C. Ltd* [2001] B.C.C. 57 at 78, the provisional liquidator is described as a "liquidator whom the court appoints to act provisionally". However, that was a classic case of the provisional liquidator acting as a caretaker. The case concerned an application of an insurance company in provisional liquidation for

As in the case of a winding-up order, where there has been an order to appoint a provisional liquidator, no action or proceeding may be proceeded with or commenced against the company or its property, except by leave of the court and subject to what terms the court may impose.[39] If a provisional liquidator becomes the liquidator he does not need to be formally discharged from the office of provisional liquidator.[40]

(3) Remuneration of provisional liquidators

The remuneration of the provisional liquidator is fixed by the court.[41] **4–21** If a winding-up order is not made, his remuneration is to be paid out of the assets of the company, and where a winding-up order is made as an expense of the liquidation.[42] Although the remuneration and expenses of the provisional liquidator are, if a winding up order is not made, to be met out of the property of the company, it is nevertheless open to the court to make an order as to expenses to the effect that these charges are to be borne ultimately by any other party as it thinks fit.[43] If no winding-up order is made he may retain out of the company's property such sums or property as are or may be required for meeting his remuneration and expenses.[44]

(4) Release of provisional liquidator

The provisional liquidator gets his release[45] on an application by him **4–22** to the court from such time as the court may determine.[46]

Appointment of special manager

The liquidator may now apply to the court for the appointment of a **4–23** "special manager" under s.177 of the Insolvency Act 1986, when it appears to him that the nature of the company's business or property, or

---

sanction of a scheme of arrangement under s.425 of the Companies Act 1985 and for the conferring on the provisional liquidator of powers to compromise claims in terms of the scheme. The company did not go into liquidation; rather the provisional liquidator acted as caretaker and company doctor. The case is interesting in clearing s.425 schemes as ECHR compliant. Another case of the provisional liquidator engaged in company rescue and not liquidation (with the encouragement of the courts) was *Smith v UIC Insurance Co. Ltd.* [2001] B.C.C. 11 at 22, in which Judge Dean Q.C. stated that, in the case, the provisional liquidator had powers conferred on him "for the purposes of producing a resolution of the company's financial problems in the context of the complex financial and commercial interests which inevitably are raised by the event of the insolvency of a reinsurance company with international connections". These two cases concerned insurance companies where administration was not available at that time, which may now be the preferred route.

[39] Insolvency Act 1986, s.130(2).
[40] *Brown v Dickson*, 1995 S.L.T. 345. (See also paras 4–03, 4–06 and 4–08 for effect of appointment of provisional liquidator on directors' powers, carrying on of business and contracts of employment.)
[41] Insolvency (Scotland) Rules 1986, r.4.5(1).
[42] *ibid.*, r.4.5(3).
[43] *RBM Graham (as liquidator of John Tullis & Son) plc v John Tullis & Son (Plastics) Ltd*, 1991 S.C.L.R. 832.
[44] *ibid.*, r.4.5(3)(a) and (4) as inserted by para.10 of the Schedule to the Insolvency (Scotland) Amendment Rules 1987.
[45] For release see para.4–29.
[46] Insolvency Act 1986, s.174(5).

the interests of the company's creditors or contributories or members generally, require the appointment of another person to manage the company's business or property, and the special manager may be granted any of the powers of a liquidator. This procedure is used only in the case of large or complicated companies. The liquidator must support any application for a special manager with a report giving the reasons for the appointment and include the estimate of the value of the assets in respect of which the special manager is to be appointed. The special manager's appointment must be for a specific duration, or until a certain occurrence, or be made subject to renewal. His remuneration, and his areas of competence, are to be fixed by the court.[47] There is no requirement for the special manager to be a "qualified insolvency practitioner". The traditional way the court met the need for special managers was by the appointment of joint liquidators from persons knowledgeable in a business. Because, however, liquidators must be "qualified insolvency practitioners" it is not open to the court or creditors to appoint an expert in the field who is not qualified as an insolvency practitioner. Only the liquidator may make the application under s.177 of the Insolvency Act 1986 whereas, in relation to the appointment of liquidators, creditors and contributories may. In a case where the Secretary of State had brought a public interest winding up petition against a company, which was dismissed, the company had to bear the costs of the provisional liquidator and the special manager appointed prior to the dismissal.[48]

Removal of liquidator

4–24   The liquidator may be removed on an application to the court or by the resolution of the creditors.

(1) Application to court

4–25   In terms of s.108 of the Insolvency Act 1986, the court may on cause shown remove a liquidator and appoint another. This power is additional to the power to remove on a successful challenge made within seven days of nomination.[49] Only someone with an interest in the outcome of the liquidation may petition, and so in an insolvent liquidation a contributory may not petition.[50] Where a person has refused to act as a liquidator he is not held to have been validly appointed and an action of removal is not necessary.[51] Even if a majority of creditors wants a liquidator removed, "cause" must be shown.[52] Misconduct does not need to be established, but it is necessary to show that it is in the best interests of the liquidation.[53] Conflict of interest is a

---

[47] Insolvency (Scotland) Rules 1986, r.4.69(5).
[48] *Re Walter L Jacob & Co Ltd* [1987] 3 B.C.C. 532.
[49] See para.4–16.
[50] *Re Corbenstoke Ltd (No.2)* [1989] 5 B.C.C. 767; see also the important Privy Council case of *Deloitte Touche A.G. v Johnson* [1999] B.C.C. 992.
[51] *Charles, Petr*, 1963 S.C. 1.
[52] *Ker, Petr* (1897) 5 S.L.T. 126.
[53] *McKnight & Co v Montgomery Ltd* (1892) 19 R. 501; *Gaunt's Exrs v Liqrs of Mancha Syndicate Capital Ltd* (1907) 14 S.L.T. 675.

reason for the removal of a liquidator.[54] The appointment of a receiver as liquidator has been successfully challenged.[55] It is generally undesirable that the same person should be both receiver and liquidator.

The Insolvency Act 1986 makes the appointment of a liquidator a matter for the members and creditors if they so choose.[56] At one time it was at the discretion of the court to decide who was to be liquidator in a compulsory winding up, but little of this survives. However, it will still be open to any director, member or creditor in a voluntary winding up, or any member or creditor in a compulsory winding up, to appeal against the exercise of the court's discretion where they have judicially challenged an appointment within seven days under ss.100(3) and 139(4) of the Insolvency Act 1986. However, where a judge has exercised his discretion in appointing or confirming a liquidator with the material facts before him, the decision will not be reviewable, unless it can be shown that there are circumstances affecting the personal character or honesty of the liquidator, or that there was something improper in the appointment.[57] If a judge has removed a liquidator, and an appeal is taken against the interlocutor removing him, that interlocutor is suspended and the liquidator may still act.[58] Although there are provisions in terms of s.162(2) and (3) of the Insolvency Act 1986 for certain orders made by the Vacation Judge[59] to be given effect until the Inner House (Appeal Court) has disposed of the matter, the position in *Levy, Petitioner*[60] is the more usual position. Accordingly, where an unsuitable liquidator is using the appeal process to delay loss of powers, the position is not wholly satisfactory.

(2) Creditors' resolution

A liquidator may be removed (but not a provisional liquidator[61]) by **4–26** resolution of the creditors at a meeting of creditors specially summoned for that purpose under s.171(2)(b) of the Insolvency Act 1986 (in the case of a creditors' winding up), and under s.172(2) of the Insolvency Act 1986 (in the case of a winding up by the court). A meeting must be summoned by the liquidator for this purpose, if he is requested to do so by creditors representing not less than one quarter in value of the creditors.[62] In the case of a liquidator who has been appointed by the court under s.108 of the Insolvency Act 1986 in a creditors' voluntary winding up (*i.e.* on a vacancy or after a successful removal application) there is a requisite percentage required of at least half in value for summoning a meeting for the removal of the liquidator.[63] The requisite majority to remove is a majority in value of creditors voting.[64]

---

[54] *Monkland Iron Co v Dun* (1886) 14 R. 242; *Lysons v Liquidator of the Miraflores Gold Syndicate* (1895) 22 R. 605.

[55] *Re Karamelli & Barnett Ltd* [1917] 1 Ch. 203.

[56] Insolvency Act 1986, ss.100(2) and 139(3).

[57] *Steel Scaffolding Co v Buckleys Ltd*, 1935 S.C. 617.

[58] *Levy, Petr*, 1938 S.C. 46.

[59] Those listed in the Insolvency Act 1986, Sch.3, Pt II.

[60] 1938 S.C. 46.

[61] Insolvency Act 1986, s.172(2).

[62] Insolvency (Scotland) Rules 1986, r.4.23(1).

[63] Insolvency Act 1986, s.171(3)(b).

[64] Insolvency (Scotland) Rules 1986, r.7.12(1).

Resignation of liquidator

(1) Resignation of liquidator

4–27　　The liquidator may resign only because of ill health or because a joint liquidator is no longer required, or because he intends to cease practising as an insolvency practitioner, or there has been some conflict of interest or change of personal circumstances which precludes or makes impracticable by him the further discharge by him of the duties of the liquidator.[65] If a liquidator resigns, in a creditors' voluntary winding up, the creditors may fill the vacancy.[66] In a compulsory winding up by the court, the court fills the vacancy.[67] Before resigning his office, the liquidator must call a meeting of the creditors for the purpose of receiving his resignation. The notice summoning the meeting must draw attention to the law in relation to his being granted a "release".[68] The notice must also be accompanied by an account of the liquidator's administration of the winding up, including a summary of his receipts and payments.[69] The meeting may accept the liquidator's resignation. If it is accepted, it is effective from the date that the creditors' meeting determine.[70] If the resignation is accepted, the liquidator must then send a notice of his resignation to the Accountant in Bankruptcy and also to the court in a compulsory winding up on a Form 4.15 (Scot).[71] If the liquidator's resignation is not accepted, the court may, on the liquidator's application, make an order giving him leave to resign.[72]

(2) Vacation of office

4–28　　If the liquidator does not resign, he "vacates" office after the final meeting of creditors as soon as he has sent notice to the Accountant in Bankruptcy, and also to the court in a compulsory winding up.[73] Where a liquidator vacates office by, for example, automatically vacating office through loss of his practising certificate, he still has sufficient interest to apply to the court under s.108(1) of the Insolvency Act 1986 to have some other person including a colleague appointed in his stead.[74]

Release of liquidator

4–29　　A release is a "discharge" which discharges the liquidator from all liability in respect of both his acts and omissions in the winding up.[75] He is still, however, potentially liable under s.212 of the Insolvency Act 1986.[76] The procedure is for the liquidator, on resignation, removal, or

---

[65] Insolvency (Scotland) Rules 1986, r.4.28(3).
[66] Insolvency Act 1986, s.104.
[67] *ibid.*, s.108(1).
[68] Insolvency (Scotland) Rules 1986, r.4.28(2).
[69] *ibid.*, r.4.28(2).
[70] *ibid.*, r.4.29(2) and (7).
[71] Insolvency Act 1986, ss.171(6) and 172(6); Insolvency (Scotland) Rules 1986, r.4.29.
[72] *ibid.*, r.4.30.
[73] Insolvency Act 1986, ss.171(6) and 172(8).
[74] *Re AJ Adams (Builders) Ltd* [1991] B.C.C. 62.
[75] Insolvency Act 1986, ss.173(4) and 174(6).
[76] Summary remedy against delinquent directors, liquidators, etc., see Chap.8.

vacation of office, first to seek a release from the creditors and, if he is not granted release by the creditors, to apply to the Accountant of Court for his discharge using a Form 4.12 (Scot).[77] The procedure works as follows:

(1) Removal

When creditors' meetings are summoned for the purpose of removing **4–30** a liquidator, the notice summoning the meeting must draw attention to section 174 of the Insolvency Act 1986, which entitles the meetings summoned for that purpose either to resolve against or for the liquidator's "release".[78] If the creditors do not resolve to "release" the liquidator he is not released unless he applies to the Accountant of Court and the Accountant of Court gives him a release.

(2) Resignation

The notice summoning the meeting to consider a liquidator's resigna- **4–31** tion must refer to the discretion of creditors in giving a release in the same way as a notice summoning a meeting for his removal.[79] It may either resolve against or for his release and, if he is not granted a release, he is not released unless the Accountant of Court grants it.

(3) Winding up

The final statutory meeting in a compulsory winding up and in a **4–32** creditors' winding up may also release or resolve against releasing the liquidator. There is no provision in the legislation however for the notice summoning the final meeting to draw this to the attention of the creditors.

PART III

TITLE, STATUS AND FUNCTIONS OF LIQUIDATOR

Title of liquidator

The liquidator of a company in Scotland should be styled "the **4–33** liquidator", formerly called "the official liquidator".[80] The liquidator must be an individual.[81]

Liquidator required to be insolvency practitioner

The liquidator must be a "qualified insolvency practitioner"[82] as **4–34** defined by s.390(2) of the Insolvency Act 1986. A provisional liquidator also must be a "qualified insolvency practitioner", as must an admin-

---

[77] Insolvency (Scotland) Rules 1986, r.4.29(4) applying r.4.25(2) and (3); r.4.25(2) and (3); r.4.31(6), as applied to creditors' voluntary windings up, applying r.4.25(2) and (3) of the Insolvency (Scotland) Rules 1986; Insolvency Act 1986, ss.173(2)(b) and 174(4)(b).
[78] Insolvency (Scotland) Rules 1986, r.4.23; Insolvency Act 1986, s.174(4)(a) and (b).
[79] Insolvency (Scotland) Rules 1986, r.4.28(2).
[80] Insolvency Act 1986, s.163(a).
[81] *ibid.*, s.390(1).
[82] *ibid.*, s.230(3).

istrator, administrative receiver, and a supervisor under a voluntary arrangement.[83] In order to qualify as an insolvency practitioner an individual must be authorised to do so by virtue of membership of a duly recognised professional body and be permitted so to act by the rules of that body, or hold authorisations so to act granted by the Secretary of State or another competent authority.[84] The Secretary of State may declare a body to be a recognised professional body for the purpose of the recognition of insolvency practitioners if it is a body which regulates the practice of a profession and maintains and enforces rules for securing that such of its members as are permitted, by or under the rules to act as insolvency practitioners, are fit and proper persons so to act, and meet acceptable requirements as to education and practical training and experience.[85] The Insolvency Practitioners Regulations 1990[86] lay down certain prescribed requirements in relation to the practical training and experience that the recognised professional bodies will be expected to demand of their members. Given the different legal practice in Scotland, the Law Society of Scotland does not require any particular number of cases to be handled or hours spent on insolvency business in any particular period prior to the time of application for a certificate. The recognised professional bodies at present are the Law Society of Scotland, the Institute of Chartered Accountants of Scotland, the Insolvency Practitioners Association, the Law Society, the Institute of Chartered Accountants in England and Wales, the Institute of Chartered Accountants in Ireland and the Chartered Association of Certified Accountants.[87] In addition a practitioner may apply direct to the Secretary of State or, in relation to a case of any description specified in directions given by the Secretary of State, to the body or person so specified in relation to cases of that description, for an authorisation under s.392 of the Insolvency Act 1986. The Secretary of State or body concerned is referred to as the "competent authority". The application must be made in such manner as the competent authority may direct and must contain or be accompanied by such information as the authority may reasonably require and must be accompanied by a prescribed fee. Authorisations are granted subject to a maximum duration of three years.[88] There is also a procedure for an appeal to the Insolvency Practitioners' Tribunal under s.397 of the Insolvency Act 1986.

Nobody, other than insolvency practitioners, is allowed to act as liquidator, as well as be a liquidator. The requirement of entrusting the insolvency procedures to qualified insolvency practitioners was affirmed by Hoffmann J. in the English case of *Re Ipcon Fashions Ltd*.[89] That case was concerned with an application under s.6 of the Company Directors Disqualification Act 1986, in which it was sought to disqualify a director

---

[83] Insolvency Act 1986, s.388(1).
[84] *ibid.*, s.390(2)(a) and (b).
[85] *ibid.*, s.391(1) and (2).
[86] SI 1990/439 as amended by SI 1993/221 and SI 2002/2710.
[87] Insolvency Practitioners (Recognised Professional Bodies) Order 1986 (SI 1986/1764).
[88] Insolvency Practitioners Regulations 1990, reg.10.
[89] (1989) 5 B.C.C. 773.

on the ground of unfitness. The director had stated before the official receiver's examiner that, at a time when the company was already insolvent, he had decided to "wind down the company's affairs with a view to paying all creditors". Hoffmann J. observed that:

> "[The director] suggested that he was in effect acting as a liquidator at lower rates than a professional liquidator would have charged. But the law, for good reason, requires a liquidator to be an independent and qualified insolvency practitioner and I do not think [the director] was entitled to take into his own hands the liquidation of an insolvent company."

Making over of assets to employees

It was formerly the case that a company might be prevented from **4–35** making *ex gratia* payments to employees after the cessation or sale of its trade on the ground that such payments were not for the benefit of the company and hence were *ultra vires* or, more strictly, an abuse of power.[90] The position was changed by the Companies Act 1980, the provisions of which were re-enacted in s.187 of the Insolvency Act 1986 and s.719 of the Companies Act 1985. Section 719 of the Companies Act 1985 empowers a company to make provision for the benefit of its employees or former employees of the company or its subsidiaries in connection with the cessation of the whole or part of the undertaking of the company or a subsidiary, or its transfer to any other person,[91] whether or not the exercise is in the best interests of the company.[92] The section provides that, on the winding up of a company, whether by the court or voluntarily, the liquidator may make any payment which, before the commencement of the winding up, the company decided to make under s.719 of the Companies Act 1985. In addition, the power to make provision for employees or former employees conferred by s.719 may be exercised by the liquidator after the commencement of winding-up, provided that:

(1) the company's liabilities have first been fully satisfied and provision has been made for the expenses of the winding-up;
(2) the exercise of the power has been sanctioned by the appropriate resolution of the company; and
(3) any other requirement applicable to the exercise of the power by the company has been met.

The required resolution referred to in (2) above is an ordinary resolution of the company or, if a memorandum or articles require the exercise of the powers to be sanctioned by a resolution requiring more than a simple majority, with the sanction of a resolution of that description.[93] These provisions will only be relevant in a case where there is supervening solvency in the liquidation.

---

[90] *Gibson's Executor v Gibson*, 1978 S.C. 197; 1980 S.L.T. 2; applying *Parke v Daily News Ltd* [1962] Ch. 927 [1962] 2 All E.R. 929.
[91] Companies Act 1985, s.719(1).
[92] *ibid.*, s.719(2).
[93] *ibid.*, s.719(3)(a), (c).

Status of liquidator

4–36   Lord Fraser stated that the exact status of the liquidator was in some doubt.[94] In most liquidations the question of the status of the liquidator is of academic interest only, but it can be important in some contexts such as in taxation questions, standards of care and probity, etc.[95]

(1) Agent of creditors/members

4–37   The liquidator has been described as an agent of the creditors but is so only in the sense that he represents the creditors through the company[96]; he is not the agent of the members, so that in the case of an overpayment by the liquidator to members through an error in law the liquidator could not rely on any agency to seek return of the money.[97]

(2) Trustee of creditors

4–38   The liquidator has been described as a trustee for the creditors. Thus Lord Selbourne said: "[t]he hand which receives the calls necessarily receives them as a statutory trustee for the equal and rateable payment of all the creditors".[98] It cannot be inferred from that decision that all the results follow which would follow if the liquidator were a trustee in the full sense. Although relying on the trustee concept, he has been held bound to disclose to the general body of creditors a report he had obtained on the possibility of an application under s.322(1) of the Companies Act 1948,[99] and it has been confirmed by the House of Lords that, in the context of a taxing statute, when a company enters insolvent liquidation it ceases to be the "beneficial" owner of its assets.[1]

(3) Agent and administrator of company

4–39   The liquidator is primarily the agent and administrator of the company.[2] As agent he acts as an administrator.[3] Lord President Emslie described the multifaceted nature of the liquidator's status in the case of *Smith v Lord Advocate*[4]:

> "I have not forgotten either that, in the particular circumstances of the many cases cited by counsel for the liquidator, a liquidator has been described in many ways, e g a paid agent for the Court, an Officer of the Court, an agent or administrator for the creditors and contributories. None of these cases decides, however, that he may not in, for example, the matter of completion of a company contract,

---

[94] *Taylor v Wilson's Trs*, 1974 S.L.T. 298.
[95] There is an enormous English case law on this subject: see, for example, B.H. McPherson *The Law of Company Liquidations* (5th ed., 2001) at paras 8.22–8.25.
[96] *Waterhouse v Jamieson* (1870) 8 M. (HL) 88.
[97] *Taylor v Wilson's Trs*, 1975 S.C. 146.
[98] *Re Black & Co's Case* (1872) 8 Ch. App. 254 at 262 (CA).
[99] *Liqr of Upper Clyde Shipbuilders*, 1975 S.L.T. 38; the law is changed in emphasis by r.7.27 of the Insolvency (Scotland) Rules 1986.
[1] *Ayerst v C & K (Construction) Ltd* [1975] 3 W.L.R. 16 (HL).
[2] Insolvency Act 1986, ss.165(3), 167(1) and Sch.4.
[3] *Smith v Lord Advocate*, 1978 S.C. 259.
[4] 1978 S.C. 259 at 273.

be regarded as acting as a manager, for and on behalf of the company itself. The liquidator is an official with many characteristics and he may, in certain circumstances, quite properly attract one or more of the descriptions which have been applied to him. There is nevertheless nothing inconsistent between his answering to such descriptions in appropriate circumstances and his possession of the character of manager and administrator of the company's affairs, and of a person acting for and on behalf of the company in the matter of the completion of company contracts. In such circumstances he may also, at the same time, have the character of a person with certain statutory obligations of a fiduciary character, or of an officer of the Court or, indeed, of an administrator or agent for the benefit of creditors and contributories."

(4) Fiduciary status

A liquidator, as Lord Emslie stated, occupies a fiduciary position.[5] He **4–40** must not make a secret profit,[6] or allow conflicts of interest to continue. Any transaction entered into by an associate may be set aside by the court at the instance of any interested party and the liquidator ordered by the court to compensate the company for any loss occasioned. Such transaction may not be set aside if sanctioned by the court, or if it is shown to the court's satisfaction that the transaction was for value *and* that it was entered into by the liquidator without knowing or having any reason to suppose that the person concerned was an associate.[7] The same type of action for misfeasance, breach of trust, etc. may be brought against him as against a director under s.212 of the Insolvency Act 1986, and he can be ordered to pay an appropriate sum to the company's assets. An action seeking such an order may be brought by a creditor or contributory,[8] except that a contributory needs leave of the court but need not benefit from any order the court might grant.[9]

(5) Officer of court

Liquidators in a compulsory winding up are also "officers of the **4–41** court"[10] and can be appointed by the court in a creditors' winding up. This jurisdiction may have implications in relation to judicial review in Scotland.[11]

(6) Liquidator's standard of care

The liquidator must exercise a degree of care and skill appropriate to **4–42** the circumstances; so that, for example, although he is not an insurer he must show the degree of skill appropriate to the task he has assumed, and by assuming, held himself out as possessing.[12] When, however, he

---

[5] See also *Lamey v Winram*, 1987 S.L.T. 635.
[6] *Silkstone and Haigh Moor Coal Co v Edey* [1900] 1 Ch. 167.
[7] Insolvency (Scotland) Rules 1986, r.4.38.
[8] Insolvency Act 1986, s.212(3).
[9] *ibid.*, s.212(4).
[10] *Millar* (1890) 18 R. 179.
[11] See para.4–47.
[12] *Re Home and Colonial Insurance Co* [1930] 1 Ch. 102, 125 and 133.

does a specific act after seeking and obtaining the approval of the court he cannot be held liable in negligence.[13] Also the option which the liquidator has of applying to the court to appoint a "special manager", means that he can avoid getting into the hot water of taking on responsibilities beyond him. This option, it is thought, will impose a duty to exercise such care in the appointment of a special manager in a situation that every reasonable liquidator would apply.

(7) Personal liability of liquidator on contracts

4–43   The liquidator does not incur personal liability when entering into contracts on behalf of the company.[14] He may engage on behalf of the company and warrant that the company's assets are sufficient to cover the contract, but does not need to do this.[15] He should be able to avoid personal liability not only by changing all commercial documentation to show that the company is in liquidation (as required under s.188 of the Insolvency Act 1986), but also by signing as "liquidator" of the particular company. Where the liquidator grants a disposition, he incurs liability in practice by granting certain warranties.[16] In litigation expenses have been awarded against liquidators on the ground that liquidators of a company (like trustees who defend actions in a representative capacity) personally warrant the sufficiency of the funds in their hands, and are personally liable for expenses.[17] A company when it litigates may be asked to find caution for expenses in terms of s.726(2) of the Companies Act 1985, but because a liquidator is person-ally liable, caution will not be required if there is no suggestion that he would be unable to honour the obligation.[18] The liquidator has a right of relief out of the funds[19] except where the funds are insufficient, or the action is caused by his personal blame-worthiness and the decree finds him personally liable.[20]

Those who contract with a liquidator acting for and on behalf of a company in the carrying on of a company's business are entitled to full satisfaction before any question of the ranking of the creditors at the date of the winding up comes to be decided.[21]

Functions of liquidator

4–44   The Insolvency Act 1986 uses several expressions to denote the functions of a liquidator in an insolvent liquidation. For example:

---

[13] *Highland Engineering Ltd v Anderson,* 1979 S.L.T. 122.

[14] *County Council of Lanarkshire v Brown* (1905) 12 S.L.T. 700.

[15] See *Smith v Lord Advocate,* 1978 S.C. 259.

[16] *Liqr of Style & Mantle Ltd v Price's Tailors Ltd,* 1934 S.C. 548.

[17] *Sinclair v Thurso Pavement Syndicate* (1903) 11 S.L.T. 364; *Liquidator of the Consolidated Copper Co of Canada v Peddie* (1877) 5 R. 393; *Aitken* (1898) 5 S.L.T. 374.

[18] *Stewart v Steel,* 1987 S.L.T. (Sh.Ct) 60.

[19] *Smith v Lord Advocate,* 1978 SC 259 at 273, *per* Lord President Emslie.

[20] *Kilmarnock Theatre Co v Buchanan,* 1911 S.C. 607; and *Liquidator of the Nairn Public Hall Co Ltd,* 1946 S.C. 395.

[21] *Smith v Lord Advocate,* 1978 S.C. 259 at 273, *per* Lord Emslie; Insolvency (Scotland) Rules 1986, r.4.67(1)(a).

(a) the liquidator in a creditors' voluntary winding up is described by s.100(1) as: "liquidator for the purpose of winding up the company's affairs and distributing its assets";

(b) s.130(4) states: "[a]n order for winding up a company operates in favour of all the creditors and all of the contributories of the company as if made on the joint petition of a creditor and contributory"; and

(c) s.143(1) states: "[t]he functions of a liquidator of a company which is being wound up by the court are to secure that the assets of the company are got in, realised and distributed to the company's creditors, and, if there is a surplus, to the persons entitled to it".

Legal cases make quite clear what these expressions taken together mean. Liquidators are administrators of the company's assets with the management of the company vesting in them.[22] "They are administrators for the purpose of dividing the estate among the creditors of the company, and if there is any balance, for dividing it among the contributories. But if the estate is insolvent, then the sole purpose for which the liquidators administer is to distribute it amongst the various creditors of the company according to their rights as creditors."[23]

Caution

Section 390(3)(b) of the Insolvency Act 1986 and regs 11 and 12 of the **4–45** Insolvency Practitioners Regulations 1990[24] require an insolvency practitioner to have a bond of caution which complies with the requirements in Pt I of Sch.2 to the Regulations. Such caution must be for at least £250,000. The practitioner is required to submit to his authorising body a monthly bordereau containing particulars of every appointment accepted, any increase in specific penalty and any release or discharge (or a statement that there are no such relevant particulars for the month). The bordereau containing entries relating to the proceedings is to be retained in the Sederunt Book. There is no requirement to file the bordereau (rather details of caution) with the Registrar.

A person who appoints an insolvency practitioner to any office must satisfy himself that the person appointed has caution, in terms of r.7.28(1) of the Insolvency (Scotland) Rules 1986. The liquidation committee is, in any event, under a duty to review the amount of caution from time to time, in terms of r.7.28(2). Rule 7.28(3) provides that the expense of caution is an expense of the liquidation. Rules 4.3 and 4.4 make specific provision for caution of a provisional liquidator, and for his failure to find or maintain caution.

---

[22] *Smith v Lord Advocate*, 1978 S.C. 259.
[23] *Clark v West Calder Oil Co* (1882) 9 R. 1017; see Lord President Inglis at 1025 and Lord Shand at 1030.
[24] SI 1990/439 as amended by SI 1993/221 and SI 2002/2710.

PART IV

DUTIES AND POWERS OF THE LIQUIDATOR

DUTIES OF LIQUIDATOR

4-46 **(1) Duty to take control of the company's assets,** which will involve examining persons who have been involved with the company, including examination of witnesses and obtaining orders, where necessary, for the company's property in the wrong hands to be delivered back;

(2) Duty to make out a list of the company's creditors and contributories, which is to enable the liquidator to assess the liabilities of the company and to pay debts owed to creditors as far as the company's assets allow, and to pay the contributories is there is any surplus, the contributories also being creditors (although subordinated creditors) of the company;

(3) Duty to realise the assets of the company, *i.e.* to "liquidate" the assets of the company in order to pay the creditors and contributories. Included among assets will not only be the fixed assets, current assets, *e.g.* receivables, stock, etc., but any other uncalled capital of the company, *i.e.* claims against contributories where they become liable as debtors of the company for issued but not fully paid up shares;

(4) Duty to discharge the debts of the company according to law, which involves paying the creditors their debts or a part of their debts as "dividends" out of the assets of the company in accordance with the "ranking" rules laid down by law; and

(5) Duty to pay any surplus after payment of the creditors of the company to the contributories in their capacity as subordinated creditors of the company.

POWERS OF LIQUIDATOR

4-47 Liquidators are given by law a formidable battery of powers to enable them to perform the duties given to them by law. Although liquidators appointed in a creditors' voluntary winding up are not "officers of the court"—if the liquidator is appointed by the creditors and not by the court, all liquidators have powers which go beyond the powers which a company itself, if not in liquidation or any other private organisation, would have. They can require evidence in relation to claims. They are entitled to access to documents relating to the business in the hands of third parties. They can require delivery of title deeds of the company even if they are subject to a lien. They "adjudicate" claims. They must be drawn from a pool of authorised "insolvency practitioners". This jurisdiction will make them subject to judicial review in Scotland where no appeal is available.

Liquidators have *two* classes of powers:

(1) Ordinary powers, by which is meant powers which all liquidators have for which no further authority is necessary before they use them.

(2) Extraordinary powers, by which is meant those special powers which liquidators obtain only with the sanction of the court or the liquidation committee[25] or sometimes only with the sanction of the court. Sanction may be granted retrospectively.[26]

There is no difference between the "ordinary powers" and the "extraordinary powers" exercisable by the liquidator in an insolvent liquidation whether it is a creditors' voluntary winding up or a compulsory winding up, except in relation to two of the powers listed as "ordinary powers"[27] which require sanction in the case of compulsory winding up, and certain powers (note (k)) which are exercised by the liquidator in a creditors' winding up but by the court in a compulsory winding up. In a creditors' voluntary winding up none of the powers may be exercised by the liquidator if he has been appointed by the members, except with the sanction of the court, prior to the creditors confirming the liquidator at their meeting, except the taking custody and control of property, disposing of perishable goods and protecting assets.[28]

(1) Ordinary powers of a liquidator

(a) Sale of assets

The liquidator has the power, without the sanction of the court or the **4–48** liquidation committee, to sell any of the company's property by public auction or private contract, with power to transfer the whole of it to any person or to sell the same in parcels.[29] This power, with power to execute deeds includes the power to sell in any fashion any of the company's property—heritable or moveable—with power to convey heritage. A disposition is given in the name of the company with the consent of the liquidator.[30] The liquidator may not sell a lease which contains a covenant against assignation without the landlord's consent. He may accept consideration for a sale other than cash.[31]

The liquidator is entitled to sell heritable property, even if there is a security over the heritable property, if he is able to obtain a price high enough to discharge every security over the property.[32]

---

[25] For liquidation committee see paras 20–05 to 20–100.
[26] *Re Associated Travel Leisure and Services Ltd* [1978] 2 All E.R. 273.
[27] Notes (n) and (o) and marked by asterisks**.
[28] Insolvency Act 1986, s.166(2).
[29] *ibid.*, ss.165 and 167 and Sch.4, para.6.
[30] For the liquidator's personal liability on a disposition see para.4–43.
[31] *Agra and Masterman's Bank* (1866) L.R. 12 Eq. 509.
[32] Insolvency Act 1986, s.169(2); and Bankruptcy (Scotland) Act 1985, s.39(4) as applied to liquidations by r.4.22(5) of the Insolvency (Scotland) Rules 1986 amended as above, but subject to the modifications in r.4.16(2) and any other necessary modifications.

Where the liquidator has intimated to the secured creditor that he intends to sell, the creditor is precluded from taking any steps to enforce his security; but equally where a creditor has intimated to the liquidator that the creditor intends to commence the procedure for sale of that part of the property covered by his security, the liquidator may not commence the procedure for the sale of that part secured by the creditor.[33] If there is any failure to comply with any requirement in relation to the procedure described above, the validity of the title of any purchaser of the heritable property shall not be challengeable on that ground.[34] If there is any doubt as to the propriety of a sale, such as in relation to a member of the liquidation committee, the liquidator should seek the sanction of the court.[35]

(b) Execution of deeds

4–49 The liquidator has the power, without the sanction of the court or the liquidation committee, to do all acts and execute, in the name and on behalf of the company, all deeds, receipts and other documents and for that purpose to use, when necessary, the company's seal.[36] (If there are joint liquidators the need for counter-signature will depend on determination at appointment.[37])

(c) Claiming in bankruptcy

4–50 The liquidator has the power, without the sanction of the court or the liquidation committee, to prove, rank and claim in the bankruptcy, insolvency or sequestration of any contributory for any balance against his estate, and to receive dividends in the bankruptcy, insolvency or sequestration in respect of that balance, as a separate debt due from the bankrupt or insolvent, and rateably with the other separate creditors.[38]

(d) Drawing of bills

4–51 The liquidator has the power, without the sanction of the court or the liquidation committee, to draw, accept, make and indorse any bill of exchange or promissory note in the name and on behalf of the company, with the same effect with respect to the company's liability as if the bill or note had been drawn, accepted, made or indorsed by or on behalf of the company in the course of its business.[39] The liquidator must be careful to state on any bill: "For and on behalf of [*name of company*] [*signature*] liquidator". He may be personally liable if he merely signs "[*signature*] liquidator".[40]

---

[33] Insolvency Act 1986, s.169(2); and Bankruptcy (Scotland) Act 1985, s.39(4) as applied to liquidations by r.4.22(5) of the Insolvency (Scotland) Rules 1986 amended as above, but subject to the modifications in r.4.16(2) and any other necessary modifications.

[34] Insolvency Act 1986, s.169(2); and Bankruptcy (Scotland) Act 1985, s.39(7) as applied to liquidations by r.4.22(5) of the Insolvency (Scotland) Rules 1986 amended as above, but subject to the modifications in r.4.16(2) and any other necessary modifications.

[35] *Dowling v Lord Advocate*, 1963 S.L.T. 28.

[36] Insolvency Act 1986, ss.165, 167, Sch.4, para.7.

[37] *ibid.*, s.231.

[38] *ibid.*, ss.165 and 167 and Sch.4, para.8.

[39] *ibid.*, ss.165 and 167 and Sch.4, para.9.

[40] See the Bills of Exchange Act 1882, s.26(1); see *Rolfe Lubel & Co v Keith* [1979] 1 All E.R. 860.

(e) Mortgaging assets

The liquidator has the power, without the sanction of the court or **4–52** the liquidation committee, to raise on the security of the assets of the company any money requisite.[41] The liquidator may not grant a security in priority to any existing secured creditors except with consent or if they are personally barred.[42] Obligations incurred have priority (even if not secured) out of the assets of the company.[43]

(f) Acting as executor to a contributor

The liquidator has the power, without the sanction of the court or **4–53** liquidation committee, to take out in his official name confirmation or letters of administration to any deceased contributory and to do in his official name any other act necessary for obtaining payment of any money due from a contributory or his estate which cannot conveniently be done in the name of the company. In all such cases the money due is deemed, for the purpose of enabling the liquidator to take out the confirmation or letters of administration or recover the money, to be due to the liquidator himself.[44]

(g) Appointment of agent

The liquidator has the power, without the sanction of the court or **4–54** liquidation committee, to appoint an agent to do any business which the liquidator is unable to do himself.[45] He must exercise his discretion personally,[46] and in Australia was held not entitled to appoint an agent to effect a compromise of a debt owing to the company,[47] or to give a general authority to his accountants to act as his agents for the purposes of the liquidation and all accounting matters.[48] He may employ a solicitor and pay for legal services but they may not be paid for before taxation by the auditor,[49] and in the case of a compulsory winding up the liquidator must give notice to the liquidation committee that he is employing a solicitor.[50] Law agents must not do any of the liquidator's job and may only be employed specially where legal work is necessary,[51] and the liquidator's fee will be reduced by the court if a law agent has done the liquidator's work.[52]

(h) Power to require evidence from persons in relation to claims

The liquidator has the power, without the sanction of the court or the **4–55** liquidation committee, to require any creditor who has submitted a claim to produce further evidence, or require any other person who he

---

[41] Insolvency Act 1986, ss.165, 167, Sch.4, para.10.
[42] *Re Regent's Canal Ironworks Co, ex p. Grissell* (1875) 3 Ch. D. 411.
[43] Insolvency Act 1986, s.115.
[44] *ibid.*, ss.165 and 167 and Sch.4, para.11.
[45] *ibid.*, ss.165 and 167 and Sch.4, para.12.
[46] *The Scotch Granite Co* (1868) 17 L.T. 533.
[47] *Rendall v Conroy* (1897) 8 Q.L.J. 89.
[48] *The Timberland LHS* (1979) A.C.L.R. 259.
[49] Insolvency Act 1986, s.169(2) and Bankruptcy (Scotland) Act 1985, s.53(2) as applied to liquidations by r 4.68(1) of the Insolvency (Scotland) Rules 1986.
[50] Insolvency Act 1986, s.167(2)(b).
[51] *Leith and East Coast Steam Shipping Co (in Liquidation)*, 1911 S.L.T. 371.
[52] *A.B. & Co Ltd (in Liquidation)*, 1929 S.L.T. 24.

believes can produce evidence, to produce the evidence. If they fail to comply, or delay, he may apply to the court for an order for private examination before the court. The court may make an order requiring the creditor or any other person to attend for private examination before it on a date at least eight and not more than 16 days after the order, at a time specified in the order, and the examination should be on oath. The liquidator may have a solicitor or advocate to represent him or he may appear himself.[53]

(i) Power of access to documents in the hands of third parties

4–56   The liquidator is entitled, without the sanction of the court or liquidation committee, to access to all the documents relating to the assets of the business or financial affairs of the company sent by or on behalf of the company to a third party and which are in that third party's hands. He is entitled to make copies of these documents. If the liquidator meets with obstruction he may apply to the court for an order ordering any person to cease obstructing him.[54] It is easier in court to get a negative interim interdict order than an interim positive order so that mechanically an order forbidding persons "obstructing" would be easier to obtain than an order for access.

(j) Power to require delivery of title deeds of company

4–57   The liquidator may, without the sanction of the court or the liquidation committee, require to have delivered to him any title deed or other document of the company even where there is a right of lien claimed over the title deed or document. The title deed holder keeps any preference as holder of the lien.[55]

(k) Settling list of contributions, making calls

4–58   In a creditors' voluntary winding up, the liquidator has the power (without the sanction of the court or the liquidation committee) and the duty to settle the list of contributories, make calls, and summon general meetings of the company and pay the company's debts and adjust the rights of the contributories among themselves.[56] In a winding up by the court, the court settles the list of contributories,[57] makes calls,[58] adjusts rights,[59] and causes assets to be realised and debts discharged.[60] In a creditors' voluntary winding up the powers may only be exercised with the sanction of the court prior to the first creditor's meeting.[61]

---

[53] Insolvency Act 1986, s.169(2) and Bankruptcy (Scotland) Act 1985, ss.48(5), (6) and (8), 44(2), (3) and 47(1) as applied to liquidations by r.4.16(1) of the Insolvency (Scotland) Rules 1986.

[54] Insolvency (Scotland) Rules 1986, r.4.22(2) and (3) as inserted by para.18 of the Schedule to the Insolvency (Scotland) Amendment Rules 1987.

[55] Insolvency (Scotland) Rules 1986, r.4.22(4) as inserted by para.18 of the Schedule to the Insolvency (Scotland) Amendment Rules 1987.

[56] Insolvency Act 1986, s.165(4) and (5).

[57] *ibid.*, s.148(1).

[58] *ibid.*, s.150(1).

[59] *ibid.*, s.154.

[60] *ibid.*, s.148(1).

[61] *ibid.*, s.166(2).

(l) Adjudication of claims

The liquidator has power, without the sanction of the court or **4–59** liquidation committee, to adjudicate on claims, but the adjudication may be appealed by any claimant or by any creditor.[62] The determining of the amount of a claim is governed by paras 1, 3 and 5 of Sch.1 to the Bankruptcy (Scotland) Act 1985.[63]

(m) Payment of dividends

The liquidator has the power, without the sanction of the court or **4–60** liquidation committee (and the duty, if the funds of the company's estate are sufficient after making allowance for future contingencies), to pay a dividend out of the estate of the company to the creditors in respect of each 26–week accounting period.[64] If the liquidator is not ready to pay a dividend in respect of an accounting period, or he considers it would be inappropriate to pay a dividend because the expense of doing so would be disproportionate to the amount of the dividend, he may postpone the payment to a date which must be not later than the time for making of the dividend in respect of the next accounting period.[65] Where the liquidator considers that it would be expedient he is entitled to shorten the accounting period, with the consent of the liquidation committee, to end on the date agreed, and the next accounting period should run from the end of that shortened period.[66] Where an appeal is taken against the acceptance or rejection of a creditor's claim, the liquidator has power to set aside an amount sufficient to cover the claim if the determination on appeal was that the claim should be accepted.[67] Where late claims are put in for dividends, the liquidator has power to pay dividends to which a creditor would have been entitled.[68] The liquidator is not entitled to pay a dividend to the creditors until his accounts are audited, his outlays and remuneration fixed, and a scheme of division prepared. This will usually mean that payment of the dividend will be eight weeks after the end of the accounting period, but this period is postponed if the liquidator or any creditor appeals against a determination by the liquidation committee or court determining the amount of outlays and remuneration payable to the liquidator; in which case the dividend may not be paid until the appeal is determined.[69] Where a creditor's claim is adjusted upwards or downwards, the liquidator may adjust any dividend upwards or down-

---

[62] Insolvency Act 1986, s.169(2); and Bankruptcy (Scotland) Act 1985, s.49, as applied to liquidations by r.4.16(1) of the Insolvency (Scotland) Rules 1986.

[63] Insolvency (Scotland) Rules 1986, r.4.16(1).

[64] Insolvency Act 1986, s.169(2) and Bankruptcy (Scotland) Act 1985, s.52(3) as applied to liquidations by r.4.68(1) of the Insolvency (Scotland) Rules 1986.

[65] *ibid.*, s.169(2) and Bankruptcy (Scotland) Act 1985, s.52(2) as applied to liquidations by r.4.68(1) of the Insolvency (Scotland) Rules 1986.

[66] *ibid.*, s.169(2) and Bankruptcy (Scotland) Act 1985, s.52(6) as applied to liquidations by r.4.68(1) of the Insolvency (Scotland) Rules 1986.

[67] *ibid.*, s.169(2) and Bankruptcy (Scotland) Act 1985, s.52(7) as applied to liquidations by r.4.68(1) and (2) of the Insolvency (Scotland) Rules 1986.

[68] *ibid.*, s.169(2) and Bankruptcy (Scotland) Act 1985, s.52(9) as applied to liquidations by r.4.68(1) of the Insolvency (Scotland) Rules 1986.

[69] *ibid.*, s.169(2) and Bankruptcy (Scotland) Act 1985, s.52 as applied to liquidations by r.4.68 of the Insolvency (Scotland) Rules 1986.

wards, or require the creditor to repay any part of any dividend already paid.[70]

Unclaimed dividends and unapplied or undistributable balances must be lodged by the liquidator in a Scottish bank on deposit receipt in the name of the Accountant of Court, and the deposit receipt sent to the Accountant of Court.[71] Any person producing evidence of his right may apply to the Accountant of Court to receive a dividend from the money so deposited if the application is made not later than seven years after the date of the deposit.[72]

(n) Power to engage in legal proceedings

4–61 The liquidator in a creditors' voluntary winding up (but not in a winding up by the court) may, without the sanction of the court or liquidation committee, bring or defend any action or other legal proceedings in the name and on behalf of the company.[73] There is an exceptional category of actions, namely actions under ss.213 (fraudulent trading), 214 (wrongful trading) , 242 (gratuitous alienations) and 243 (unfair preferences) of the Insolvency Act 1986, as amended by s.253 of the Enterprise Act 2002, which require sanction in both types of winding up.

Unless proceedings are under s.145(2) of the Insolvency Act 1986, under which the liquidator may sue in his own name after an order has been made under s.145(1) of the Insolvency Act 1986 vesting property in him personally (a virtual dead letter), a liquidator sues in the name of the company.[74] If sanction is not obtained from the court or liquidation committee the competency of the action is not affected.[75] Before an action has been raised by a third party, a liquidator is entitled to ask the court in a compulsory winding up (as an officer of the court) for himself to be substituted for the original pursuer where the pursuer was a trustee in bankruptcy.[76]

(o) Carrying on business

4–62 The liquidator has the power, in a creditors' voluntary winding up, to carry on the business of the company so far as may be necessary for its beneficial winding up.[77] In the case of a compulsory winding up the liquidator only has the power to carry on the business of the company so far as may be necessary for its beneficial winding up with the sanction of the court or the liquidation committee.[78]

---

[70] Insolvency Act 1986, s.169(2) and Bankruptcy (Scotland) Act 1985, s.53(9) as applied to liquidations by r.4.68(1) of the Insolvency (Scotland) Rules 1986.

[71] *ibid.*, s.193(2).

[72] Bankruptcy (Scotland) Act 1985, s.58(1) as applied to liquidation by r.4.68(1) of the Insolvency (Scotland) Rules 1986.

[73] Insolvency Act 1986, ss.165, 167, Sch.4, para.4.

[74] *Munro v Hutchison* (1896) 3 S.L.T. 268.

[75] *Stewart v Gardner, etc* 1933 S.L.T. (Sh. Ct) 11.

[76] *Millar* (1890) 18 R. 179.

[77] Insolvency Act 1986, s.165, Sch.4, para.5.

[78] *ibid.*, s.167 and Sch.4, para.5.

(p) Ancillary powers

The liquidator has the power, without the sanction of the court or the **4–63** liquidation committee, to do all other things as may be necessary for winding up the company's affairs and distributing its assets in addition to the powers listed.[79]

(2) Extraordinary powers of a liquidator

The liquidator of a company has the following extraordinary powers, **4–64** *i.e.* powers only exercisable with the sanction of the court or the liquidation committee, or sometimes only with the sanction of the court:

(a) Distribution of estate

The liquidator is entitled to pay the expenses of the liquidation as **4–65** defined in r.4.67 at any time, and the preferred debts at any time but only with the consent of the liquidation committee or the court.[80]

(b) Payment of a class of creditors in full

The liquidator has the power, with the sanction of the court or the **4–66** liquidation committee, to pay any class of creditors in full.[81]

(c) Compromises and arrangements with creditors

The liquidator has the power, with the sanction of the court or the **4–67** liquidation committee, to make any compromise or arrangement with creditors or persons claiming to be creditors, or having or alleging themselves to have any claim (present or future, certain or contingent, ascertained or sounding only in damages) against the company, or whereby the company may be rendered liable.[82]

(d) Compromises with debtors

The liquidator has the power, with the sanction of the court or the liquidation committee to compromise, on such terms as may be agreed:

> (i) all calls and liabilities to calls, all debts and liabilities capable of resulting in debts, and all claims (present or future, certain or contingent, ascertained or sounding only hi damages) subsisting or supposed to subsist between the company and the contributory or alleged contributory or other debtor or person apprehending liability to the company; and
>
> (ii) all questions in any way relating to or affecting the assets or the winding up of the company, and take any security for the discharge of any such call, debt, liability or claim and give a complete discharge in respect thereof.[83]

---

[79] Insolvency Act 1986, ss.165 and 167 and Sch.4, para.13.
[80] *ibid.*, s.169(2) and Bankruptcy (Scotland) Act 1985, s.52(4) as applied to liquidations by r.4.68(1) and (2) of the Insolvency (Scotland) Rules 1986.
[81] *ibid.*, ss.165, 167 and Bankruptcy (Scotland) Act 1985, s.52(6) and Sch.4, para.1.
[82] *ibid.*, ss.165 and 167 and Sch.4, para.2.
[83] *ibid.*, ss.55, 165 and 167, and Sch.4, para.3.

A compromise entered into with one contributory does not discharge his transferor from liability as another contributory. They do not stand to each other in the relation of principal and guarantor.[84] The liquidator cannot be forced to compromise a call,[85] and a discharge got by designedly false statements or intentional misrepresentations may be reduced (legally quashed) by the court.[86] The fact that the liquidator may compromise debts and liabilities of the company with the sanction of the liquidation committee is a very strong reason for having a liquidation committee. Otherwise the valuable right to compromise would require the sanction of the court.

Section 65(1) of the Bankruptcy (Scotland) Act 1985 states:

"(1) The permanent trustee may (but if there are commissioners only with the consent of the commissioners, the creditors or the court)—

(a) refer to arbitration any claim or question of whatever nature which may arise in the course of the sequestration; or

(b) make a compromise with regard to any claim of whatever nature made against or on behalf of the sequestrated estate

and the decree arbitral or compromise shall be binding on the creditors and the debtor."

Given the terms of s.65(1) of the Bankruptcy (Scotland) Act 1985 and the powers of the liquidator referred to above, it is competent in Scotland if the liquidator in a liquidation, or liquidator in liquidations agrees, and the trustee in a sequestration agrees, that the court or the liquidation committee and commissioners in the sequestration sanction that the liquidation or liquidations and the sequestration proceed jointly to the effect that a single scheme of division should be prepared. This would normally be sought where the assets in a liquidation and personal assets were so intermingled that this would be the most expeditious solution.[87]

(e) Sales for shares

4–68   The liquidator has the power, with the sanction of the court or the liquidation committee, to sell or transfer the whole or part of the company's business or property in return for shares, policies or other interests in the company to which the business is being transferred.[88]

---

[84] *Nevill's Case* (1870) 6 Ch. App. 43; *Hudson's Case* (1871) L.R. Eq. 1.

[85] *Tennent v City of Glasgow Bank* (1879) 6 R. 972.

[86] *Liquidators of City of Glasgow Bank v Assets Co* (1883) 10 R. 676 at 678.

[87] *Peter Cranbourne Taylor, the Official Liquidator of George Morris (Hotels) Ltd*, Note in the liquidation of, Court of Session, June 5, 1991, *per* Lord Osborne, unreported, affirming *Juba Property Company Ltd*, Note in, 17 January 1978, *per* Lord Kincraig. See also *Thurso Building Society* 2001 (O.H.) S.L.T. 797, in which the court reviewed the circumstances under which a judicial factor might be appointed by the court and explained the power of such a factor to bring legal proceedings.

[88] Insolvency Act 1986, s.110(1) and (2), as modified by SI 2001/1090, Sch.5, para.15.

This power is expressly written into the Insolvency Act 1986 in the case of a creditors' voluntary winding-up.[89] The liquidator probably also has this power with the sanction of the court in a compulsory winding-up.[90]

PART V

BACK-UP POWERS OF THE COURT

The court has the following powers in both compulsory windings up **4–69** and creditors' voluntary windings up. Usually the court is given the powers in a compulsory winding up but it may exercise these powers in a creditors' voluntary winding up on the application of the liquidator or any contributory or creditor under s.112(1) of the Insolvency Act 1986 provided it is convinced that the exercise of the power is just and beneficial.

Public examination of officers in a compulsory winding up

The liquidator in a compulsory winding up[91] may apply at any time to **4–70** the court for the public examination of any person who has been an officer of the company, or has acted as liquidator or administrator or receiver of its property, or has been concerned with its promotion, formation or its management. In addition the liquidator, if requested by creditors representing one-half in value of the company's liabilities, or by the contributories representing three-quarters in value, is under a duty to make an application to the court.[92] When the liquidator makes the application, it is mandatory for the court to direct that a public examination of the person to whom the application relates takes place.[93]

This obligation on the court to grant an order for a public examination when the liquidator makes an application, is to be contrasted to an application for a private examination, where the court has discretion whether to grant it. A further distinction between a "public examination" and a "private examination" is that an order for a public examination may be made on the persons whether or not they are British subjects and whether or not they are within the jurisdiction of the Scottish court, whereas a private examination is thought to be competent only where the person to be examined is subject to the jurisdiction of the Scottish court. In *Seagull Manufacturing Co Ltd*[94] Mummery J. explained the reasoning behind his decision as follows:

---

[89] *ibid.*, s.110(1).

[90] *ibid.*, s.167(1)(b) and Sch.4, para.13; *see Re Agra and Masterman's Bank* (1866) L.R. 12 Eq. 509 and *Re Cambrian Mining Co* (1882) L.T. 114. It is suggested that Lord Romilly was wrong in the case of *Re London and Exchange Bank* (1867) 16 L.T. 340 to suggest that this type of sale could not be effected in a compulsory liquidation. It cannot be intended that the court has less power than liquidators.

[91] Insolvency Act 1986, s.133(1).

[92] *ibid.*, s.133(2).

[93] *ibid.*, s.133(3).

[94] [1991] W.L.R. 307.

"The provisions for private examinations are different from the provisions of section 133 in two important respects. First, the power of the court to summon persons to appear before it for private examination extends to a very much wider class of persons than the court's power in the case of a public examination. The power to summon for a private examination applies not only to any officer of the company (or to the bankrupt) but also to any person who may have in his possession any property of the company (or of the bankrupt) or who may be indebted to the company (or the bankrupt). It even extends to any person who may be able to give information to the court concerning the company (or the bankrupt) and the relevant dealings, affairs and property.

As was observed by Dillon LJ in *In re Tucker* [1990] Ch 148, 156G, if the words 'any person' are given their natural meaning in the private examination provisions they 'cover any person of any nationality in any part of the world'. The very width of the class of person specified in the private examination provisions in the bankruptcy legislation was an important factor leading the court to the conclusion that the relevant class of persons must be limited by the territoriality principle and therefore confined to persons in England at the relevant time who could be served with a summons of the English court in England.

By way of contrast, the power of the court to order public examination under section 133 is confined to a restricted class of persons who have voluntarily concerned themselves in a specified capacity in the affairs of the company which is being wound up, ie as officer, liquidator, administrator, receiver or manager, or as participant in the promotion, formation or management of the company.

The second important difference between the provisions for public examination and for private examination is that the latter contain express provisions (namely section 237(3) in the case of a company and section 367(3) in the case of a bankrupt) which, in the words of Dillon LJ in *In re Tucker*, 'conclusively' and 'inevitably' connote that if the person in question is not in England he is not liable to be brought before the English court. By way of contrast, such a provision is conspicuously absent from both section 133 and the provisions for its enforcement in section 134."

After there has been an order made for a public examination, the court must appoint the day for the public examination and make a direction that the person named in the application must attend on that day and be publicly examined as to the promotion, formation or management of the company or as to the conduct of its business and affairs or his conduct of dealings in relation to the company.[95] At the public examination questions may be asked by the liquidator, any special manager, any

---

[95] Insolvency Act 1986, s.133(3).

creditor who has submitted a claim in the winding up, and any contributory of the company.[96] Unless the court has made an order differently, the liquidator must give at least 14 days notice of the time and place of the examination to those who are entitled to ask questions as described above and he may, if he thinks fit, advertise the public examination in newspapers circulating in the area of the principal place of business of the company.[97] It is important, however, that no advertisement must appear in a newspaper before at least seven days have elapsed from the date when the person to be examined was served with the order of the court.[98] This provision allows the person to be examined the opportunity to appeal against an order, although it is difficult to see what grounds are open because it is mandatory once the application is made. An appeal would have the effect of postponing the evil day of the examination because the appeal would recall the order. Alternatively, at the stage at which the application is made, it might be open to the person whose examination was sought to seek reduction of the application and interim suspension of it. A possible ground of challenge, for example, could be that this was improper persecution. Although the Cork Committee[99] suggested that one of the justifying reasons in favour of public examination was for it to act as a sanction or deterrent, this was not written into the legislation. Accordingly it could be argued that a liquidator was misdirecting himself if the application is not for a liquidation purpose, but is extraneous to the beneficial winding up, i.e. it is aimed *only* at punishing directors by putting them in a public pillory. A quasi-penal use of the section could also run into ECHR problems.

Those creditors or contributories requesting the liquidator to ask the court for a public examination (where he has not of his own initiative asked for the public examination) must give a list to the liquidator of all the creditors or contributories wanting the public examination and specify the name of the person to be examined and what relationship he had to the company, and the reasons why his examination is requested.[1] They must also deposit with the liquidator such sum as the liquidator may determine to be appropriate by way of the expenses of the hearing of a public examination.[2] When a liquidator gets a request to make an application to the court for a public examination, he must make the application within 28 days of receiving the request or apply to the court for an order relieving him of the obligation to make the application if he is of the opinion that the request is an unreasonable one in the circumstances.[3] The liquidator may make an application for an order relieving him of the obligation to apply *ex parte*.[4] If the court makes an order relieving him of the liability to make an application, he must give notice of the order straight away to the requisitionists who have asked

---

[96] Insolvency Act 1986, s.133(4).
[97] Insolvency (Scotland) Rules 1986, r.4.74.
[98] *ibid.*, r.4.74.
[99] Cork Committee Report, paras 653–657.
[1] Insolvency (Scotland) Rules 1986, r.4.75.
[2] *ibid.*, r.4.75(3).
[3] *ibid.*, r.4.74(5).
[4] *ibid.*, r.4.75(6).

him to make the application.[5] Alternatively, if the court does not relieve him of the liability to make the application, he must make the application forthwith on the conclusion of the hearing of the application for a relieving order.

The legislation does not lay down rules in Scotland as to how the public examination should be conducted. The legislation allows questioners to ask questions in relation to the dealings with the company with which the person to be examined was concerned.[6] The court may make an order directing what questions might be put to the person to be examined to keep the questions within the scope of what are lawful questions in the circumstances of the case.[7] There is authority that the proper conduct of a public examination in an individual sequestration is for the trustee to question the bankrupt, and creditors can then ask any questions which they think necessary to supplement the trustee's questions but may not cross-examine the bankrupt on claims of other creditors.[8] However, it is suggested that the public examination of an officer of a company is so wide-ranging in its scope that it is not possible to lay down rules in advance for how an examination should be conducted. It is suggested that, apart from the restrictions mentioned above, there should be no restriction on the questions or number of questions which those attending may ask or on the duration of the public examination. It is suggested that questions to the person to be examined are directed through the chairman. The Insolvency Act 1986 and the Insolvency (Scotland) Rules 1986 do not seem to impose any duty on the person to be examined to answer questions.[9] One of the aims of the public examination will of course, incidentally, have been obtained even if no questions are answered. It will still have acted as a public pillory to assuage public anger. The issue of whether questions must be answered, and if so on what basis, is not thought to be closed by the absence of a specific duty in terms of the Insolvency (Scotland) Rules 1986, but may be inferred by implication from the terms of s.47(3) of the Bankruptcy (Scotland) Act 1985. This issue is problematic in relation to the answering of questions in both a public and private examination, and is not properly settled in law. (The question of whether answers obtained by compulsion by inspectors appointed to investigate someone following a report under s.218 may be used in criminal proceedings, is discussed in para.3–03).

---

[5] Insolvency (Scotland) Rules 1986, r.4.75(6).

[6] Insolvency Act 1986, s.133(3).

[7] *Jacks' Tr v Jacks' Trs*, 1910 S.C. 34.

[8] *Delvoitte v Baillie's Trs* (1887) 5 R. 143 at 144.

[9] See, in contrast, the Bankruptcy (Scotland) Act 1985, s.47(3), which states, "the debtor or the relevant person shall be required to answer any questions relating to the debtor's assets, his dealings with them or his conduct in relation to his business or financial affairs and shall not be excused from answering any such questions on the ground that the answer may incriminate or tend to incriminate him or on the ground of confidentiality", the Bankruptcy (Scotland) Act 1856, s.91, which states: "the bankrupt and such other persons shall answer all questions relating to the affairs of the bankrupt", and the English rule, which states: "The examinee shall at the hearing be examined on oath; and he shall answer all such questions as the court may put, or allow to be put to him", r.4.215 of the Insolvency Rules 1986.

No privilege against self-incrimination at public examination

The Court of Appeal in the case of *Bishopsgate Investment Management Ltd v Maxwell*[10] stated that in a public examination conducted under s.133 of the Insolvency Act 1986, in the case of a compulsory winding up, or under s.112 of that Act in the case of a voluntary winding up, there was no privilege against self-incrimination. Dillon L.J., going into all the authorities, concluded that Parliament must have exercised its undoubted capacity to abrogate the privilege against self-incrimination. This decision was followed by the same approach in the House of Lords in the case of R v Director of the Serious Fraud Office, ex p. Smith,[11] in which the SFO was found entitled to require a person to attend and answer questions on pain of conviction of an offence under the Criminal Justice Act 1987, although the person had already been charged with other criminal offences pertaining to the subject matter of the questioning.

Power to order private examination in a compulsory winding up

The court may, on the application of the liquidator, summon to appear before it any officer of the company, any person known or suspected to have in his possession any property of the company or supposed to be indebted to the company, or any person whom the court thinks capable of giving information concerning the promotion, formation, business, dealings, affairs or property of the company.[12] The court may require any of these people to submit an affidavit to the court containing an account of their dealings with the company or to produce any books, papers or other records in their possession or under their control relating to the company or generally about their dealings with the company.[13] The court has power to issue a warrant for the arrest of someone who fails to appear in front of it without reasonable cause or looks like absconding and for the seizure of any books, records, money or goods in that person's possession, and the person may be kept in custody.[14] If it appears to the court that any person has in his possession any property of the company, the court may, on the application of the liquidator, order that person to deliver the property to the liquidator, or, if it appears to the court that the person is indebted to the company the court may order the person to pay the money to the liquidator.[15] The court is unlikely, unless there has been a miscarriage of justice, to upset on appeal an order to appear in front of the court for examination,[16] or unless the application is oppressive.[17] An order for a private examination may be obtained by the liquidator, a creditor or contributory, but the court has a discretion whether to make the order or not, although

4–71

---

[10] [1992] B.C.C. 214; [1992] 2 All E.R. 856.
[11] [1993] A.C. 1; [1992] 3 W.L.R. 66.
[12] Insolvency Act 1986, s.236(2).
[13] *ibid.*, s.236(3).
[14] *ibid.*, s.236(4), (5) and (6).
[15] *ibid.*, s.237(1) and (2).
[16] *Re Joseph Hargreaves* [1900] 1 Ch. 347.
[17] *Heiron's Case* (1880) 15 Ch. D. 139.

weight will be given to the views of the liquidator who is closely acquainted with the company's affairs.[18] Strangers to the company may be examined if they are capable of giving useful information, and this includes those with information coming into existence after the company ceased active trading. Although the court may refuse disclosure of privileged materials.[19] An order authorising messengers-at-arms to search for and recover books, and if necessary to open lock-fast places, is competent.[20]

The procedure in Scotland involves the citation of the individual concerned to appear for examination on oath before the insolvency judge.[21] He may be required to bring all documents in his custody as specified in the note for such examination. He may be represented by counsel and re-examined by him to explain his evidence but his counsel may not attend when other witnesses are examined.[22] It is a private examination. Rule 9.4 of the Insolvency Rules 1986 lays down the procedure for a private examination of the officer of a company in England, including the requirement that he must answer the questions. As in the case of a public examination of an officer of the company, etc. there is no statutory provision in Scotland in relation to whether the person being privately examined must answer questions, and if so on what basis.

Public and private examination in a creditors' voluntary winding up

(a) Public examination

4-72   Although the Insolvency Act 1986 does not give the liquidator in a creditors' voluntary winding up any express power to apply to the court for a public examination which the court must grant, he has the power, as does any contributory or creditor, to apply to the court to exercise all or any of the powers which the court might exercise if the company were being wound up by the court.[23] The object of that section is to leave the company, its contributories and creditors, if possible, to settle their affairs without coming to the court for a compulsory order, but to provide them under this section with the means of access to the court in the voluntary winding up, just as in a compulsory winding up.[24] The court has discountenanced any distinction between the jurisdiction in a voluntary winding up and a winding up under a compulsory order.[25] In the case of a compulsory winding up, the court has the power to order a public examination and has no discretion in the matter if there is an application from a liquidator. It is thought that the application by the liquidator in a compulsory liquidation is a formal requirement in

---

[18] *Re Maville Hose* [1939] Ch. 32.
[19] *Re Highgate Traders Ltd* [1984] B.C.L.C. 151.
[20] *Ken v Hughes*, 1970 S.C. 380.
[21] *ibid., Welch*, 1930 S.N. 112.
[22] *Liquidators of Larkhall Collieries* (1905) 13 S.L.T. 752.
[23] Insolvency Act 1986, s.112(1).
[24] *Rance's Case* (1870) 6 Ch. App. 104, 115.
[25] *Black and Co's Case* (1872) 8 Ch. App. 254.

relation to the court exercising its jurisdiction, although there is no Scottish authority on this.[26] The application is not a condition precedent for the existence of the jurisdiction. Accordingly, it is thought that an application may also be made in a creditors' voluntary winding up. However, unlike the case of an application under s.133(2) of the Insolvency Act 1986, the granting of the application is not mandatory, but rather the court must be satisfied that the exercise of the power will be "just and beneficial".[27] In a creditors' voluntary winding up, because the liquidator is not bound by the statutory obligation to make an application for a public examination when requested by the liquidation committee as a compulsory liquidator is, it will be a matter for the liquidator's discretion whether he makes an application under s.112(1) for an order that a person be publicly examined.[28]

(b) Private examination

It is thought that the liquidator in a creditors' voluntary winding up **4–73** may apply for an order under s.112 of the Insolvency Act 1986 for a private examination of an officer of the company, etc. on the same arguments as above in relation to a public examination. This proposition was affirmed in England by the Court of Appeal in *Re Bishopsgate Investment Management Ltd (in prov liq) v Maxwell*.[29] In the words of Dillon L.J.:

> "It should be noted, however, that though s 270 of the 1948 Act and its predecessors applied in terms only in winding up by the court and only on provision of a further report by the Official Receiver, it was held by Wynn-Parry J in *Re Campbell Coverings Ltd (No 2)* [1954] 1 All ER 222, [1954] Ch 225, following a suggestion of Evershed MR in *Re Campbell Coverings Ltd* [1953] 2 All ER 74 at 78, [1953] Ch 488 at 497, with which Denning LJ had concurred, that public examination was available in a voluntary liquidation because s 307 of the 1948 Act enabled the court, on the application of the liquidator or any contributory or creditor of a company in voluntary liquidation, to exercise all or any of the powers which the court might exercise if the company were being wound up by the court. Section 112 of the Insolvency Act 1986 is in the same terms as s 307."[30]

Accordingly ss.133 and 236 should be seen as covering both compulsory and voluntary insolvent windings up.

Exercise of the court's discretion in ordering a private examination

It has been noted above that where there is an application for an order **4–74** under s.133 of the Insolvency Act 1986, it is mandatory that the court make such an order. Where a liquidator is requested by one-half, in

---

[26] English authorities are *Re Campbell Coverings Ltd (No. 2)* [1954] Ch. 225; *Re Bishopsgate Investment Management Ltd., Mower Group Newspapers plc v Maxwell* [1993] Ch. 1 at 24, 46 (CA).

[27] Insolvency Act 1986, s.112(2); see *Re Gold Co* (1879) 12 Ch. D. 77 and *Heiron's Case* (1880) 15 Ch. D. 139.

[28] Sch.1 to the Insolvency (Scotland) Rules 1986 states that Chap.11 does not apply in a creditors' winding up but relates only to an order under s.133(4); not under s.112 of the Insolvency Act 1986.

[29] [1992] B.C.C. 214; [1992] 2 All E.R. 856.

[30] *ibid.*, at 870.

value, of the company's creditors, or three-quarters, in value, of the company's contributories, the liquidator shall make an application unless the court directs otherwise. Accordingly in that situation the court has a discretion as to whether to veto an application for a public examination. In contrast there is always a discretion where there is an application for a private examination under s.236 of the Insolvency Act 1986. Section 236 entitles administrators and administrative receivers equally with liquidators to seek a private examination involving the production of documents and oral examination. In the case of *Cloverbay Limited (Joint Administrators) v Bank of Credit and Commerce International SA*,[31] the English Court of Appeal reviewed the previous authorities on the court's exercise of discretion. In the course of his judgment Sir Nicholas Browne-Wilkinson V-C, set out how the court should exercise its discretion in relation to both the production of documents, and oral examination.

Soon afterwards, the guidelines were reviewed and elaborated by the Court of Appeal,and the House of Lords in the case of *Re British and Commonwealth Holdings plc (No.2)*.[32] Ralph Gibson L.J. in the Court of Appeal set out seven principles which were clearly established by the jurisprudence, the principles later being endorsed by the House of Lords. They were:

(1) the discretion conferred on the court by s.236(2) is an unfettered and general one;

(2) that discretion nevertheless involves balancing the requirements of the office holder against possible oppression to the person from whom information is sought;

(3) the power conferred by the section is an extraordinary one whose existence is due to the fact that the office holder usually comes as a stranger to the relevant event;

(4) the power can be used not merely to obtain general information but to discover facts and documents related to contemplated claims, whether proceedings have been started or not, against the proposed witness or someone connected with him;

(5) the power is directed to enabling the court to help the office holder to complete his function as effectively and with as much expedition as possible, and to discover with as little expense and as much ease as possible, the facts surrounding any possible claim;

(6) great weight is to be given to the views of the office holder, who will have detailed knowledge of what problems exist and what information he needs;

(7) matters relevant to the balancing exercise will include that —

(a) the case against a former officer will usually be stronger, since he owes both a fiduciary duty to the company and a duty under s.235 of the Act to assist the office holder;

---

[31] [1991] B.C.L.C. 135.

[32] [1992] Ch. 342 (Court of Appeal) and [1993] A.C. 426 (H. of L.). For cases where documents are situated in foreign jurisdictions see *Re Mid East Trading Ltd* [1997] ALL E.R. 481 and *Re Bank of Credit and Commerce International SA, Morris v Bank of America National Trust and Savings Association* [1997] B.C.C. 561.

(b) to ask a third party to expose himself, to liability involves an element of oppression;

(c) an order for oral examination is more likely to be oppressive than one to produce documents;

(d) to require a person suspected of wrongdoing to prove the case against himself on oath prior to proceedings being brought, is oppressive.

The Court of Appeal and the House of Lords in that case dropped the idea of Sir Nicholas Browne-Wilkinson that the purpose of s.236 was to enable the officeholder to get sufficient information to reconstitute the state of knowledge that the company should possess. If there is no prima facie evidence of a substantial case against a relevant person, which would bring a real prospect of money for creditors, such an examination would not normally be ordered.[33] Also such private examination could not be used for the ulterior motive of getting information to help with litigation against another party.[34] A person is entitled to be heard before a private examination is ordered as a general rule.[35]

The Court of Appeal considered again recently the factors in deciding whether to order private examination of directors of a company under s.236 of the Insolvency Act 1986 on the application of its liquidators in circumstances where the liquidators had already commenced proceedings against directors. In the case of *Re RBG Resources plc; Shierson v Raspog*,[36] according to the Court of Appeal it was common ground that the power to order private examination under s.236 of the Insolvency Act 1986 should be read together with s.235, which placed a duty on directors to co-operate with insolvency officeholders. Although s.235 contained a mandatory obligation on a director to give information reasonably required, the court had a clear discretion whether to order a private examination under s.236. Parliament must have intended that the court retained a discretion to refuse to make an order under s.236, although the fact that the proposed examinee is or was a director obliged under s.235 to give information reasonably required, would be likely to be a powerful factor in favour of making the order. The court, in exercising its discretion to order examination, had to conduct a balancing exercise in which the fact that the intended examinee was a director made for a stronger case for ordering examination than where he was a third party, but the oppression in ordering examination of a person against whom proceedings had been or were to be brought weighed in the scales the other way. It was oppressive to require a defendant accused of serious wrongdoing to provide what amounted to pre-trial depositions and to prove the case against himself on oath. Oppression might, however, outweigh the liquidator's legitimate requirements. However there was a critical difference between an application for an order under s.236 to seek an advantage in litigation

---

[33] *Re Adlards Motor Group Holdings Ltd* [1990] B.C.L.C. 68.
[34] *Re Sasea Finance Ltd* [1998] 1 B.C.L.C. 559.
[35] *Re Maxwell Communications Corporation plc Homan v Vogel* [1994] B.C.C.; *Re PFTZM Ltd (in liquidation)* [1995] B.C.C. 280.
[36] [2002] B.C.C. 1005.

and an application for examination required in order to enable the liquidator to fulfil his general duties as liquidator to reconstitute, investigate and understand the company's affairs and to get in its assets. A s.236 order should be granted where the legitimate requirements of a liquidator to obtain speedy information from those who ran the company and other relevant considerations outweighed any oppression to the directors.

Only officeholder may make applications for examination

4–75   Until the passing of the Insolvency Act 1986, it had been thought that a contributory had *locus standi* to ask the court for an examination under the statutory predecessors of ss.133 and 236 of the Insolvency Act 1986.[37] However, the terms of ss.133 and 236 of the Insolvency Act 1986 would seem to preclude anyone other than an officeholder making the application.

Power to order company officer to attend meetings

4–76   The court has power to order any officer of the company to attend any meeting of creditors or contributories or liquidation committee for the purpose of giving information as to the trade, dealings, affairs or property of the company.[38] The court may control what questions are to be asked at such a public examination.[39]

Power to order arrest of a contributory

4–77   The court has the power to arrest a contributory who appears about to abscond.[40]

Power to order inspection of books by creditors

4–78   The court may at any time give creditors and contributories the right to inspect the company's books and papers.[41] This facility is not open to persons other than creditors and contributories. A stranger to the company may not obtain an order to inspect the register of members after commencement of the winding up.[42] These books of the company are not to be confused with the sederunt book of the liquidation. The power to allow inspection of the company's books under s.155 should be exercised for the benefit of those interested in the liquidation, and not to assist actions by individual shareholders against directors[43] or to

---

[37] *Re Silkstone & Dodworth Coal and Iron Co, Whitworth's Case* [1881] 19 Ch. D. 118; *Re Embassy Art Products Ltd* [1988] B.C.L.C. 1.
[38] Insolvency Act 1986, s.157.
[39] *London and Globe Finance Corporation v Basil Montgomery* (1902) 18 T.L.R. 661.
[40] Insolvency Act 1986, s.158.
[41] *ibid.*, s.155(1).
[42] *Re Ken Coalfields Syndicate Ltd* [1890] 1 Q.B. 754.
[43] *Re North Brazilian Sugar Factories* (1887) 37 Ch. D. 84.

assist creditors in obtaining information to pursue a scheme to terminate the liquidation and reconstruct the company.[44]

Power of rescission of contracts by the court

The court may, on the application of a person who is either benefited **4–79** or burdened by a contract with the company in liquidation, make an order rescinding the contract on such terms as to payment by or to either party of damages for the non-performance of the contract, or otherwise as the court thinks just.[45] If damages are payable under an order to the person, they rank as a debt in the winding up.[46] Where there are several unconnected contracts between some person and the company, it does not follow that, because one or more may be rescinded, all of them will be rescinded.[47]

This provision was extended to Scotland for the first time by the Insolvency Act 1986. The statutory code of disclaimer in England was not introduced to Scotland. The Scottish Law Commission was of the opinion that the existing Scottish common law has much the same effect as the statute law in England and there had been no complaints.[48] The provision, however, would allow the rescission of a contract where, for example, a liquidator had inadvertently adopted a contract by not repudiating it within the time that a court would have thought reasonable.

The Companies Act 1989 excludes these rights of rescission arising under the Insolvency Act 1986 and the common law from application to certain contracts of person engaged in financial markets. It provides that s.186 of the Insolvency Act 1986 and the rule of law in Scotland corresponding to s.178 of the Insolvency Act 1986 (Disclaimer of Unprofitable Contracts and Onerous Property in England and Wales) do not apply to a market contract or a contract effected by a recognised investment exchange or clearing house for the purpose of realising property provided as a margin in relation to market contracts.[49] It also provides that, where action has been taken by a recognised investment exchange or clearing house against a company under its default rules, a liquidator of that company is bound by any market contract or other such contract as mentioned above, notwithstanding the rule of law in liquidations corresponding to the provisions in s.42 of the Bankruptcy (Scotland) Act 1985 concerning deemed refusal to adopt contracts (s.164(2) of the Companies Act 1989[50]).

Power to order delivery of property to liquidator

Where *any* person has in his possession or control any property, **4–80** books, papers or records to which the company appears to be entitled, the court may require that person to pay, deliver, convey, surrender or

---

[44] *Halden v Liquidator of SCottish Heritable Security Co Ltd* (1887) 14 R. 633.
[45] Insolvency Act 1986, s.186(1).
[46] *ibid.*, s.186(2).
[47] *Re Castle* [1917] 2 K.B. 725.
[48] Scot. Law Commission Memo. No. 16, p.146.
[49] Companies Act 1989, s.164(1).
[50] ''Recognised'' means recognised under the Financial Services Act 1986.

transfer the property, books, papers or records to the provisional liquidator or liquidator.[51] This important power only became available in 1986.[52] Previously the power was available only against a contributory, trustee, receiver, banker, agent or officer of the company.[53] This provision applies to property which the company was entitled to have conveyed to it under contract, and the policy of the section is that, in the winding up of insolvent companies, the representative of the creditors is to be put into immediate possession of the property to which the company has a substantial right.[54] Where the liquidator seizes or disposes of any property which is not the property of the company, and at the time of seizure or disposal believes, and has "reasonable grounds" for believing, that he is entitled to seize or dispose of that property, the liquidator is not liable except where loss is caused by the liquidator's negligence.[55] "Reasonable grounds for believing" would cover general reasonable grounds and where a court order had been made.[56] Where property has been seized or disposed of, the liquidator has a lien on the property, or the proceeds of its sale, for expenses which would be incurred in connection with the seizure or disposal.[57]

Appointment of special manager

4–81   In the case of a provisional liquidation or a liquidation, the court has the power, on the application of the liquidator, to appoint a special manager.[58]

Rectification of the register

4–82   The court has power, in a compulsory winding up, to rectify the register of members of the company.[59] The liquidator, or any contributory or creditor, may apply to the court to have the register rectified in a voluntary winding up[60]; the power is that given by s.359 of the Companies Act 1985 which continues after a winding up.

Power of court to cure defects in procedure

4–83   In all windings up, of all types, and in administrations and receiverships the court now has a broad power to remedy and cure defects. This power now does not need to be exercised through the equitable jurisdiction of the Court of Session but may be exercised by a judge, either in the Court of Session or in the sheriff court, who is dealing with

---

[51] Insolvency Act 1986, s.234(2).
[52] *ibid.*, Sch.11, para.4(2).
[53] Companies Act 1985, s.551.
[54] *Dunlop v Donald* (1893) 21 R. 125 at 133.
[55] Insolvency Act 1986, s.234(3), (4)(a).
[56] *ibid.*, s.234(3)(b).
[57] *ibid.*, s.234(4)(b).
[58] *ibid.*, s.177.
[59] *ibid.*, s.148(1).
[60] *ibid.*, s.112(1).

the insolvency proceedings. This power is in addition to the equitable jurisdiction of the Court of Session, which can be a call of last resort.[61]

General power to determine questions

There is a general power of the court to determine any question in a **4–84** voluntary liquidation given by s.112 of the Insolvency Act 1986 which invokes the powers exercisable by the court in a winding-up by the court.[62] In the case of *Leith and East Coast Steam Shipping Co (in Liquidation)*,[63] Lord Johnston speaking for the First Division stated: "I think expense could often be saved by liquidators requesting the Lord Ordinary to grant them an interview to arrange matters incidental to the liquidation, without presenting formal notes." Section 112 does not empower the court to allow the liquidator to carry out *ultra vires* transactions.[64] The test to be applied is whether in all the circumstances of the case it is just to make an order under the section.[65]

PART VI

STAGES IN INSOLVENT LIQUIDATIONS

Differences between voluntary and compulsory winding up

A voluntary winding up commences by a different procedure from a **4–85** compulsory winding up. Briefly, in a creditors' voluntary winding up, or a members' voluntary winding up converted to a creditors' voluntary winding up, the liquidation is a non-judicial affair. It is largely in the hands of the members, creditors and their nominee, the liquidator. It is initiated by the board of directors calling a meeting of the members of the company at which a resolution is proposed to wind up the company. If this is passed, a creditors' meeting is called at which the creditors have the right to nominate a liquidator. In contrast, a compulsory winding up is initiated by a petition to the court asking the court compulsorily to wind up a company. Thereafter the court appoints a liquidator, who barring challenges, is the choice of the creditors if they so choose. From the stage of the appointment of the liquidator, the procedure in a creditors' voluntary winding up and a liquidation by the court is very similar. The main differences are that:

(1) as already described in Part IV a liquidator in a creditors' voluntary winding up and a liquidator in a compulsory winding up have slightly different powers;
(2) certain functions in a voluntary winding up are carried out by the liquidator whereas in a compulsory winding up they are

[61] The power is given by r.7.32(1) of the Insolvency (Scotland) Rules 1986, applying the Bankruptcy (Scotland) Act 1985, s.63 to insolvency proceedings.
[62] *Black & Co's Case* (1872) 8 Ch. App. 254.
[63] 1911 1 S.L.T. 371 at 373.
[64] *Re Salisbury Railway and Market House Co Ltd* [1969] 1 Ch. 349.
[65] *R-R Realisations Ltd (formerly Rolls-Royce Ltd)* [1980] 1 ALL E.R. 1019.

legally done by the court (although in fact the court is really making the orders on the initiative of the liquidator). These functions are to settle the list of contributories,[66] to make calls,[67] to adjust rights between contributories,[68] and cause assets to be realised and debts discharged[69];

(3) there are different reporting requirements in the two types of liquidation. In a liquidation by the court the liquidator has to report to the court;

(4) only registered companies may be voluntarily wound up, whereas a whole range of types of company may be wound up by the court; and

(5) a creditors' voluntary winding up may proceed if the directors are unable to make a statement of solvency in relation to the company, or in a members' voluntary winding up the liquidator finds that the company is insolvent, whereas in a compulsory winding up the legal position is much more complex. There are other grounds for winding up a company by the court (some of which directly relate to solvency, others indirectly and others not at all).

Because most of the differences in the two types of liquidation are at the initial stage it is proposed to treat separately the initial stage of a creditors' voluntary winding up and the initial stage of a compulsory winding up but thereafter to treat the two together.

1. COMMENCEMENT OF CREDITORS' VOLUNTARY WINDING UP

Directors' duties

4–86   The first steps in putting a company into creditors' voluntary liquidation are taken by the directors. Under normal procedure they do the following:

- Call a meeting of the company, *i.e.* the members, for the purpose of:
    - (a) putting the company into liquidation;
    - (b) nominating a liquidator; and
    - (c) nominating the members' appointees on the liquidation committee.[70]
- Call a meeting of the creditors for the purpose of:
    - (a) nominating a liquidator[71]; and
    - (b) nominating the creditors' representatives on the liquidation committee.[72]

---

[66] Insolvency Act 1986, s.148(1).
[67] *ibid.*, s.150(1).
[68] *ibid.*, s.154.
[69] *ibid.*, s.148(1).
[70] *ibid.*, ss.98(1)(a), 100(1) and 101(2).
[71] *ibid.*, s.100(1).
[72] *ibid.*, s.101(1).

- Prepare a statement of the company's affairs for laying before the creditors' meeting.[73]
- Appoint one of their members to preside at the creditors' meeting,[74] although the proceedings are not invalidated if no director attends.[75]

Meeting of members

The business of the meeting of members is as follows: **4–87**

(1) It passes either a special resolution that the company be wound up voluntarily[76]; or an extraordinary resolution to the effect that the company cannot, by reason of its liabilities, continue in business, and that it is advisable to wind it up.[77]
(2) It nominates, by ordinary resolution, the liquidator.[78] As has been seen, if the meeting of creditors nominates a different person as liquidator, the creditors' nomination will prevail.[79]
(3) In addition the meeting may nominate up to five persons to act on the liquidation committee appointed by the creditors.[80]

The creditors' meeting

The company has a duty to do the following: **4–88**

(1) it must summon a meeting of its creditors for a day not later than the 14th day after the day on which there is to be held the company meeting at which the resolution for a voluntary winding up is to be proposed;
(2) it must have the notices of the creditors' meeting sent by post to the creditors not less than seven days before the day on which that meeting is to be held; and
(3) it must have notice of the creditors' meeting advertised once in the *Edinburgh Gazette* and once in at least two newspapers circulating in the relevant locality (that is to say the locality in which the company's principal place of business in Great Britain was situated in the six months immediately preceding the day on which the notices are sent summoning the meeting of the company).[81]

Business of creditors' meeting

At the creditors' meeting the following business is conducted: **4–89**

---

[73] Insolvency Act 1986, s.99(1).
[74] *ibid.*, s.99(1)(c).
[75] *The Salcombe Hotel Development Co Ltd* [1991] B.C.L.C. 44.
[76] Insolvency Act 1986, s.84(1)(b).
[77] *ibid.*, s.84(1)(c).
[78] *ibid.*, s.100(1).
[79] See para.4–16.
[80] Insolvency Act 1986, s.101(2). (See Chap.20.)
[81] *ibid.*, s.98(1).

(1) *Statement of affairs*—the directors of the company are obliged to make out a statement of affairs and lay the statement of affairs before the creditors' meeting.

(2) *Nomination of liquidator*—the creditors may nominate a person to be liquidator for the purpose of winding up the company's affairs and distributing its assets.[82]

(3) *Liquidation committee*—the creditors at the first meeting or at any subsequent meeting may, if they think fit, appoint a liquidation committee of not more than five persons.[83]

The chairman of the meeting is one of the directors who must be appointed by the directors to attend the meeting and to preside at it.[84]

Members' voluntary winding up converted to creditors' voluntary winding up

4–90   The Insolvency Act 1986 makes an important change in the law in relation to voluntary windings up where there is insolvency. Under the law applicable to windings up commenced before December 29, 1986, one had an insolvent voluntary winding up in two sets of circumstances:

(1) a creditors' voluntary winding up (as described above);

(2) a members' voluntary winding up, with the liquidator finding supervening insolvency.

In the second set of circumstances where there was a members' voluntary winding up and the liquidator formed the opinion that the company would not be able to pay its debts in full, he was obliged to summon a meeting of the creditors and lay before the meeting a statement of the company's assets and liabilities.[85] If the winding up continued for more than one year the liquidator had to summon a general meeting of the company and a meeting of the creditors at the end of the first year from the commencement of the winding up, and of each succeeding year, or at the first convenient date within three months from the end of the year (or a longer period allowed by the Secretary of State) and lay before the meetings an account of his acts and dealings and of the conduct of the winding up during the preceding year.[86] He also had to call a final meeting of the company and its creditors.[87]

Although the liquidator had the obligation under the law applicable to windings up commenced before December 29, 1986, to summon these creditors' meetings *as if*, in terms of s.586, of the Companies Act 1985,

---

[82] Insolvency Act 1986, s.100(1).
[83] *ibid.*, s.101(1).
[84] *ibid.*, s.99(1)(c).
[85] Companies Act 1985, s.583(1).
[86] *ibid.*, ss.594 and 586.
[87] *ibid.*, ss.595 and 586.

the members' voluntary winding up were a creditors' voluntary winding up, the winding up legally stayed a members' voluntary winding
up. Accordingly the power of appointing a liquidator and fixing his
remuneration remained with the members.[88] Also there was no statutory
authority to enable the appointment of a committee of inspection.[89]

Law applicable to windings up commenced after December 29, 1986

The Insolvency Act 1986 brings the law up-to-date and makes it more **4–91**
rational. A voluntary winding up under the supervision of the court in
terms of s.606 of the Companies Act 1985 is abolished.[90] Where there
now is a members' voluntary winding up and the liquidator forms the
opinion that the company is insolvent, then the members' voluntary
winding up is converted to a creditors' voluntary winding up.[91] The
creditors may now appoint the liquidator,[92] with the right for a director,
member or creditor to apply to the court in relation to who should be
liquidator, where there are different nominations.[93] These creditors may
also now appoint a liquidation committee.[94] The above results are clear
when ss.96, 97(2) and 102 of the Insolvency Act 1986 are read together,
although the logic and the English are convoluted.

The only differences now between a creditors' voluntary winding up
and a members' voluntary winding up which has been converted into a
creditors' voluntary winding up are:

(1) Meeting of creditors

In the case of a converted winding up the liquidator summons a **4–92**
meeting of the creditors which is to be not later than 28 days after the
day he formed the opinion that the company was insolvent.[95] In the case
of a creditors' voluntary winding up, the company summons a meeting
of its creditors, which should be not later than 14 days after the day on
which was held the company meeting at which voluntary winding up
was proposed.[96]

(2) Statement of affairs

In a converted winding up the liquidator makes out a statement of **4–93**
affairs, lays the statement before the creditors' meeting and attends and
presides at the meeting.[97] In a creditors' voluntary winding up the

---

[88] Companies Act 1985, ss.579 and 580.
[89] *ibid.*, ss.487 and 590.
[90] Although this procedure is technically competent in relation to voluntary windings up
started before December 29, 1986, it was virtually extinct as a procedure and as far back as
1962 the Jenkins Committee had recommended its abolition.
[91] Insolvency Act 1986, s.96.
[92] *ibid.*, s.100(1) and (2).
[93] *ibid.*, s.100(3).
[94] *ibid.*, s.101(1).
[95] *ibid.*, s.95(2)(a).
[96] *ibid.*, s.98(1)(a).
[97] *ibid.*, s.95(3).

directors make out a statement of affairs, have the statement of affairs laid before the creditors' meeting and appoint one of their number to preside at the meeting.[98] In a converted voluntary winding up, the statement of affairs is to be verified by affidavit of the liquidator,[99] whereas in a creditors' voluntary winding up the statement of affairs is verified by affidavit of some or all of the directors.[1]

(3) Information to creditors

4-94   In the case of a converted winding up, the liquidator must furnish the creditors, free of charge, with information concerning the affairs of the company as they may reasonably require.[2] In a creditors' voluntary winding up, the notice sent to the creditors must state *either* the name and address of a person qualified to act as an insolvency practitioner who in the period up to the date of the meeting can give them information as to the company's affairs that they may reasonably require *or* allow them an inspection of the creditors' list in a place within the locality of the company's principal place of business on two business days prior to the day of the creditors' meeting.[3]

2. COMMENCEMENT OF COMPULSORY LIQUIDATION

4-95   The Scottish courts have a wide jurisdiction in both (1) The types of company which may be wound up; and (2) The grounds of winding up.

(1) Types of company which may be wound up

4-96   Subject to the provisions of the EC. Regulation on Insolvency Proceedings[4] the following types of companies may be wound up under the Insolvency Act 1986[5]:

(a) Registered companies

4-97   Any company registered in Scotland may be wound up.[6] The Court of Session has jurisdiction to wind up any company registered in Scotland and certain unregistered companies.[7] The sheriff court has jurisdiction concurrently with the Court of Session to wind up any company whose registered office is situated within the sheriffdom, provided that the company's share capital paid up or credited as paid up does not exceed £120,000.[8] The sheriff court may not wind up a company limited by guarantee or an unlimited company.[9]

---

[98] Insolvency Act 1986, s.99(1).

[99] *ibid.*, s.95(4).

[1] *ibid.*, s.99(2).

[2] *ibid.*, s.95(2)(d).

[3] *ibid.*, s.98(2).

[4] See Chap.22.

[5] See Council Regulation (E.C.) 1346/2000 and SI 2003/2109.

[6] Insolvency Act 1986, s.120(1); for the definition of company see the Insolvency Act 1986, s.251, and the Companies Act 1985, s.735.

[7] See para.22–05.

[8] Insolvency Act 1986, s.120(3).

[9] *Pearce, Petr*, 1991 S.C.L.R. 861. There would seem to be no good reason why the Sheriff Court should not be given jurisdiction in the case of companies limited by guarantee, subject to an amount of the guarantee, preferably the same amount as the paid up share capital limit.

(b) Unregistered companies

Unregistered companies, as defined by s.220 of the Insolvency Act **4–98** 1986, may be wound up. That includes any association and any company. The essential feature of a company is that there are mutual obligations or liabilities among the membership.[10] Railway companies incorporated by Act of Parliament are excluded[11] whether or not they are dissolved or have ceased to carry on business (s.221(5)(a)). Included in the category of unregistered companies have been trustee savings banks, building societies not registered under the building societies legislation,[12] life assurance companies,[13] friendly societies,[14] companies incorporated by Royal Charter[15] and companies incorporated by Special Act.[16]

(c) Companies incorporated under certain statutes

Companies and organisations incorporated under certain Acts may be **4–99** wound up, *e.g.* building societies under ss.88 to 90 of the Building Societies Act 1986, industrial and provident societies under s.55 of the Industrial and Provident Societies Act 1965, but not trade unions.[17]

(d) Insurance companies

Insurance companies carrying on business within the United King- **4–100** dom may be wound up, but not under the Insolvency Act 1986. Insurance companies are treated in a different legal way from other companies. Insurance companies are now regulated by the Financial Services Authority, and the provisions governing winding up in Scotland are contained in the Insurers (Winding Up) (Scotland) Rules 2001[18] made under s.379 of the Financial Services and Markets Act 2000. Insurance companies may not be wound up voluntarily without the consent of the Financial Services Authority.[19] The authors know of no insurance company that has been wound up in Scotland in recent times, so the law is wholly statutory.[20] Also the Insurers (Reorganisation and Winding Up) Regulations 2003[21] implement the Directive of the Parliament and the Council on the reorganisation and winding up of insurance undertakings (2001/17/EC) for all UK insurers except Lloyd's, and provide that as from April 20, 2003, no winding up proceedings or voluntary arrangements in respect of EEA insurers can be undertaken in the UK except in the circumstances permitted by the

---

[10] *Caledonian Employees Benevolent Society*, 1928 S.C. 633.
[11] Insolvency Act 1986, s.220(1)(a).
[12] *Smith's Trs v Inline and Fullerton Property and Investment Building Society* (1903) 6 F. 99; *Re Ilfracombe Permanent Mutual Benefit Building Society* [1901] 1 Ch. 102.
[13] *Re Great Britain Mutual Life Assurance Society* (1880) 16 Ch. D. 246.
[14] *Canavan, Petrs*, 1929 S.L.T. 636 10; *Re Oriental Bank Corporation* (1884) 54 L.J. Ch. 481.
[15] *Re Oriental Bank Corporation* (1884) 54 L.J. Ch. 481.
[16] *Re South London Fish Market Co* (1888) 39 Ch. D. 324; *Re Bradford Navigation Co* (1870) L.R. 10 Eq. 331.
[17] See the Trade Union and Labour Relations (Consolidation) Act 1992.
[18] SI 2001/4040 (S.21).
[19] S.366(1) of the Financial Services and Markets Act 2000.
[20] In December 2003 a Dalkeith insurance company called Tribune went into liquidation.
[21] SI 2003/1102.

Regulations. EEA reorganisation and winding up proceedings are to be recognised in the UK.[22]

(e) Foreign and oversea companies carrying on business in Scotland

4–101   Companies incorporated outside Great Britain carrying on business in Scotland may be wound up, even if already being wound up under an order of a foreign court.[23]

(2) Grounds for a compulsory winding up

4–102   The Scottish courts have *five* main grounds for winding up registered and unregistered companies. They are:

(a) technical reasons;
(b) just and equitable grounds;
(c) special resolution;
(d) insolvency; and
(e) prejudice to a floating charge.

The first three grounds are dealt with very briefly by way of elucidation because they do not relate to insolvency.

(a) Technical reasons

4–103   In the case of registered companies, they may be wound up for technical reasons, for example, in the case of a public limited company, where it has not been issued with a certificate under s.117 of the Companies Act 1985 (public company share capital requirements),[24] or that it has not commenced its business within a year from its incorporation or suspends its business for a whole year,[25] or that the number of its members is reduced below two.[26]

(b) Just and equitable

4–104   In the case of registered and unregistered companies the court may wind up the company if the court is of the opinion that it is just and equitable that the company should be wound up.[27] The expression "just and equitable" covers an unrestricted number of circumstances.[28] Winding-up orders have been made on the grounds that the substratum of the company had gone (the substratum is the main object for which the company is formed),[29] that the company was a bubble[30] and that

---

[22] See para.21–12.
[23] Insolvency Act 1986, s.225; *Marshall* (1895) 22 R 697; *Re Compania Merabello San Nicolas SA* [1973] Ch 75; *Re Allobrogia Steamship Corporation* [1982] Ch 43; for the criteria for winding up foreign companies, see Chap.22; and the comments of Sir Richard Scott V.-C. in the Court of Appeal in *Banco Nacional de Cuba v Cosmos Trading Corp.* [2000] 1 B.C.L.C. 813 at 816–817.
[24] Insolvency Act 1986, s.122(1)(b).
[25] *ibid.*, s.122(1)(d).
[26] *ibid.*, s.122(1)(e), as amended by SI 1992/1699, Sched. 1, para. 8..
[27] *ibid.*, ss.122(1)(g) and 221(5)(c).
[28] *Ebrahami v Westbourne Galleries Ltd* [1973] A.C. 360, *per* Lord Wilberforce at 379.
[29] *Re Suburban Hotel Co* (1867) 2 Ch. App. 737, approved in *Galbraith v Menu Shipping Co*, 1947 S.C. 466.
[30] *Re London and County Coal Co* (1867) L.R. 3 Eq. 355.

there was complete deadlock.[31] The "just and equitable" ground has relevance in relation to the law of insolvency only in a situation where a business is unsuccessful and, although not yet insolvent, would become insolvent. A winding-up order on "just and equitable" grounds may be granted where the requisite majority for a special resolution for voluntary winding up is not obtainable.[32]

(c) Special resolution to wind up

The company may be wound up compulsorily if it passes a special **4–105** resolution resolving that the company be wound up by the court.[33] This is not common because it is more likely that a company will be wound up voluntarily than that a special resolution seeking compulsory winding up will be passed, but it is used from time to time.

(d) Insolvency

Both registered[34] and unregistered[35] companies may be compulsorily **4–106** wound up if they are unable to pay their debts. This is the most common basis for compulsory winding up.

There are statutory provisions under which a creditor or member may legally prove that the company is unable to pay its debts.

Creditor's demand notice. First, a company is deemed to be unable to pay its debts if a creditor (by assignation or otherwise) to whom the company is indebted in a sum exceeding £750 then due has served on the company, by leaving at the company's registered office, a written demand (using Form 4.1 (Scot) as substituted by SI 2003/2109) requiring the company to pay the sum so due and the company has for three weeks thereafter neglected to pay the sum or to secure or compound for it to the reasonable satisfaction of the creditor.[36] A winding-up order may be resisted if the company finds caution for the amount of the claim on the basis that the debt is disputed.[37] Alternatively the amount of the claim may be consigned to court.[38] It is a defence to a winding-up petition that the debt is secured in the hands of the creditor.[39] The procedure envisages the creditor being able to point to a debt of a specified sum that cannot be seriously questioned as to its existence or quantum.[40] The debt must be "then due", which means "presently payable".[41] The formal demand it is thought may not be made by fax

---

[31] *Re Expanded Plugs Ltd* [1965] 1 W.L.R. 514.
[32] *Pirie v Stewart* (1904) 6 F. 847.
[33] Insolvency Act 1986, s.122(1)(a).
[34] *ibid.*, s.122(1)(f).
[35] *ibid.*, s.221(5)(b).
[36] *ibid.*, s.123(1)(a) and s.222(1); in the case of an unregistered company the letter should be left at its principal place of business, or by delivering to the secretary or some director, manager or principal officer of the company or otherwise as the court might direct.
[37] *Pollok v Gaeta Pioneer Mining Co Ltd*, 1907 S.C. 182.
[38] *Cunninghame v Walkinshaw Oil Co* (1886) 14 R. 87.
[39] *Commercial Bank of Scotland Ltd v Lanark Oil Co Ltd* (1886) 14 R. 147.
[40] *Re a Company (No 003729 of 1982)* [1984] B.C.L.C. 323.
[41] *Re Bryant Investment Co Ltd* [1974] 2 All E.R. 683.

although the position in England may be different.[42] The period of omission to pay the money demanded is probably 21 clear days from the date of service.[43] If a sum larger than the sum due is demanded, this may not imply a demand for the lesser sum. *In Re A Company*[44] Nourse J. described a demand as "a solemn document with potentially serious consequences". He said that in that case "the discrepancy between the figures of £161,000 and £83,000 is so enormous that I am by no means certain that the telex-demand for £160,000 could be relied on as a statutory demand for the lesser sum".

The statutory demand must be delivered at the debtor company's registered office by a person duly authorised by the creditor to do so.[45]

It is normal practice to have the statutory demand delivered by an officer of the court, but this is not necessary in Scotland.[46]

Expiry of charge. A second mode of proof of "inability to pay debts" is if the *induciae* of a charge (the time limit on the statutory demand notice) for payment on an extract decree or an extract registered bond, or an extract registered protest, have expired without payment being made.[47] There is no financial limit on this provision.[48]

Unable to pay debts as they fall due. A third method of proof is to prove to the satisfaction of the court that the company is unable to pay its debts as they fall due.[49] This may be demonstrated in a number of ways, *e.g.* a company dishonouring acceptances[50] or the company has admitted that it has no assets,[51] or no good defence to an action has been put forward.[52]

As noted above in the case of *Pollok v Gaeta Pioneer Mining Co Ltd*[53] a winding-up petition will be refused if the debt is disputed. In the case *of Blue Star Security Services (Scotland) Ltd v Drake & Scull (Scotland) Ltd*[54] a

---

[42] Insolvency Rules 1986 (England) rr.4.5 and 4.6; *Re a Company* [1985] B.C.L.C. 37. The demand must nevertheless be in the form prescribed, *i.e.* Form 4.1 (Scot): see s.123(1)(a) and r 7.30.

[43] This seems the case from the wording of Form 4.1 (Scot) and s.123(1)(a) of the Insolvency Act 1986 which supersedes the case of *Neil McLeod and Sons, Petrs*, 1967 S.L.T. 46.

[44] [1985] B.C.L.C. 37 at 41 and 43.

[45] r.7.21(3) of the Insolvency (Scotland) Rules 1986; *Craig v Iona Hotels Ltd*, 1988 S.C.L.R. 130, Sh. Ct: see in contrast *Re A Company (Number 008790 of 1990)* [1991] B.C.L.C. 561, where a demand was sent by registered post and delivery was not disputed at the registered office and it was held that that was sufficient for the purposes of the section.

[46] *Lord Advocate v Blairwest Investment Ltd*, 1989 S.C.L.R. 352; 1989 S.L.T. (Sh. Ct) 97: *Lord Advocate v Traprain Ltd*, 1989 S.L.T. (Sh. Ct) 99.

[47] Insolvency Act 1986, ss.123(1)(c), 224(1)(b).

[48] *Speirs & Co v Central Building Co Ltd*, 1911 S.C. 330.

[49] Insolvency Act 1986, ss.123(1)(e), 224(1)(d).

[50] *Re Globe New Patent Iron and Steel Co* (1875) L.R. 20 Eq. 337; *Gandy*, 1912 2 S.L.T. 276.

[51] *Re Flagstaff Silver Mining Co of Utah* (1875) L.R. 20 Eq. 268.

[52] *Stephen v Scottish Banking Co* (1884) 21 S.L.R. 764.

[53] 1907 S.C. 182.

[54] 1992 G.W.D. 15–844.

creditor petitioned for the winding-up of a debtor, claiming that invoices in respect of security services remained unpaid. The sheriff refused warrant to cite on the ground that, the debtor company having a claim against the creditor in respect of items stolen from their premises, there was insufficient evidence that the debt was undisputed and therefore that the debtor company was unable or unwilling to pay. On appeal, it was held by the Sheriff Principal that the correspondence indicated the debtor's continuing failure to pay despite pressure from the creditor. Accordingly the debtor's claim did not, strictly speaking, bring the creditor's debt into dispute, and in any event not to more than the value of the debtor's claim, which the creditor had excluded in his petition from the amount said to be due.[55] It has been held in England that, where a cheque in payment of a debt has been dishonoured, and the cheque has been re-presented, the creditor is not allowed to petition for winding up of the debtor company if he has first re-presented the cheque. In the case of *Re A Company (No 001259 of 1991), ex p. Medialite Ltd*[56] Harman J. held that the re-presenting of a cheque amounted to a suspension of a presenter's right to sue. While the cheque was in the clearing it had to constitute a conditional payment which, if the cheque is honoured, would amount to a payment as from the date of presentation. The inability to pay debts is not related to the solvency of the company. Where a creditor's debt is clearly established, the creditor has a right to present a winding up petition, even though it appears that the company is solvent because the persistent non-payment of the debt suggests that the company is unable to pay its debts.[57]

Although the serving of a statutory demand is a useful ground whereby an unpaid creditor who may have no detailed knowledge of the debtor company's financial state of affairs, can force the company either to settle the debt in question or, be deemed to be "unable to pay its debts" so that it may be wound up on the creditor's petition, the drawback of a statutory demand is that the debtor company has three weeks from the date of the service of the demand in which it can comply with it. During that intervening period, the assets remaining to the company may be dissipated in a final attempt by the directors to keep the company in business, and by the holders of floating charges who may take steps to crystallise their floating charges and secure assets solely for the payment of their debts. A final drawback is that, if the company eventually is put into liquidation, the commencement of the

---

[55] See in England the case of *Re FSA Business Software Ltd* [1990] B.C.L.C. 825, in which the Chancery Division held that where there was a counterclaim in respect of the debt on which a winding-up petition was founded, the court had a discretion to be exercised on all the facts to dismiss the petition or make a winding-up order. In that case, on the facts, failure to make a winding-up order would mean that the petitioning company would be kept out of its money to which it was undoubtedly entitled for a long period of time and the debtor company might eventually fail in its counterclaim. In addition the debtor company would have seven days in which to pay the petitioning creditor's debt were a winding-up order made, and accordingly in the light of those considerations, it was proper that a winding-up order be made.

[56] [1991] B.C.L.C. 594.

[57] *Re Globe New Patent Iron & Steel Co* (1875) L.R. 20 Eq. 337; *Cornhill Insurance Improvement Services Ltd* [1986] B.C.L.C. 26.

winding up is deemed to be at the date of the presentation of the winding-up petition, and not at the date of the service of the statutory demand.[58] Hence the petition of the creditor founding on the statutory demand may be too late to achieve his object.

These considerations have suggested to creditors to refrain from using the statutory demand method and to seek the more direct route using s.123(1)(e) of the Insolvency Act 1986, whereby the mere fact of a company having failed to pay a debt as and when it was due is treated by the court as a sufficient indication that the company is unable to pay its debts. All the creditor has to do is to present a winding-up petition averring that the company is indebted to the petitioner for an amount which is more than the minimum amount which would have entitled the creditor to serve the statutory demand; that the debtor company has not suggested in any way that the debt is disputed; and that the company is accordingly unable to pay its debts and the winding-up petition should be granted. The propriety of this approach has been approved in England by the Court of Appeal in the case of *Taylors Industrial Flooring Ltd v M & H Plant Hire (Manchester) Ltd*.[59] In that case Taylors were indebted to the company for an aggregate amount of almost £10,000 which was owing at the date when the winding-up petition was presented. It was averred that the company had been given full notice of the debt, and that the company had given no notification of any dispute in connection with the invoices. The court held that there was no requirement that a creditor must serve a statutory demand before presenting a winding-up petition, and that if a debt is due from a company and it is not disputed, the failure of the debtor company to pay is evidence of an inability on the part of the company to pay its debts. Dillon L.J., who gave the leading judgment, was careful to confirm that where a company disputes a debt it must establish a substantial ground for doing so in order to avoid the winding-up petition being successful. Further endorsing what Dillon L.J. said and almost encouraging this ground of winding up, Staughton L.J. stated:

> "I entirely agree with everything that has been said by Dillon LJ. Many people today seem to think that they are lawfully entitled to delay paying their debts when they fall due or beyond the agreed period of credit, if there is one. Alternatively they may think that no remedy is in practice available to the creditor if they do delay payment. There is a greater degree of truth in the second belief than the first. Legal remedies are in themselves slow and expensive. A creditor will often tolerate late payment, rather than incur further expense. But this can cause great hardship to honest traders, particularly those engaged in small businesses recently started. Anything which the law can do to discourage such behaviour in my view should be done.
>
> In my judgment *M & H Plant Hire (Manchester) Ltd* had allowed quite enough gratuitous time for payment to the company when

---

[58] Insolvency Act 1986, s.129(2).
[59] [1990] B.C.L.C. 216.

they presented their petition. Indeed, they would have been justified, like Lord Clive, in being astonished at their own moderation."

In determining whether a company is unable to pay its debts, only debts which are due and payable are to be taken into account. Existing debts payable in the future, prospective debts and contingent liabilities must be ignored. In the case of *Re European Life Assurance Co*[60] a petition sought the winding up of an insurance company under s.80 of the Companies Act 1862 on the ground of its inability to pay its debts. It was not disputed that the company was paying its debts as they fell due but it was argued that this was achieved only by using current premium income to pay past liabilities and that the company would be unable to meet substantial future claims. The contention was rejected. Sir W M James V.-C. stated:

"I take it that the court has nothing whatever to do with any question of future liabilities, that it has nothing whatever to do with the question of the probability whether any business which the company may carry on tomorrow or hereafter will be profitable or unprofitable. That is a matter for those who may choose to be the customers of the company and for the shareholders to consider. I have to look at the case simply with reference to the solvency or insolvency of the company, and in doing that I have to deal with the company exactly as it stood on the date to which the evidence relates—viz., the 31st of December, 1868 which I assume to represent substantially the state in which the company stands now. I must take it as if all the business which the company ever intended to do was then done, as if its business were confined to its existing contracts, and as if it did not mean to enter into one single fresh contract or do anything more."

Debts even if they are technically due, may be ignored where there is no evidence that the creditors are requiring repayment.[61] If that were not the case, most banks would be insolvent, because they operate on the basis that at any particular time not all the depositors would demand repayment. Even if it is proved that the company is unable to pay its debts, it is thought that in Scotland the court has a discretion whether to grant the winding-up order. Outside factors, such as the prospect of additional finance for the company which has a deficiency of assets, may be taken into account when the judge is exercising his discretion as to whether to grant a winding-up petition.[62]

Balance sheet test. A fourth mode of proof of inability to pay its debts is if it is proved to the satisfaction of the court that the value of the company's assets is less than the amount of its liabilities, taking into account its contingent and prospective liabilities.[63] The law underwent a

---

[60] (1869) L.R. 9 Eq. 122.
[61] *Re Capital Annuities Ltd* [1978] 3 All E.R. 704.
[62] *Byblos Bank SAL v Al-Khudhairy* (1986) 2 B.C.C. 99 at 549, *per* Nicholls L.J.
[63] Insolvency Act 1986, ss.123(2), 224(2).

major reform with the Insolvency Act 1986. Previously the appropriate section read "if it is proved to the satisfaction of the court that the company is unable to pay its debts, and, in determining whether a company is unable to pay its debts, the court shall take into account the contingent and prospective liabilities of the company".[64] That provision was interpreted in England to mean "unable to pay debts in full as they fell due", which is the third statutory mode of proof now. In Scotland, however, the courts on occasion ordered winding up on the basis of a company's balance sheet alone, where it disclosed large deficiencies of both total assets and current assets. The case of *Re A Company (No 007694 of 1983)*[65] decided the interpretation of the previous wording in England, but its detailed analysis elucidates how the present wording should be read. Winding up was sought on the ground, *inter alia*, that when contingent and prospective liabilities of the company were taken into account it was insolvent in balance sheet terms. Nourse J. stated:

"In the present case I have come to the conclusion that the test has not quite been satisfied on the facts which are before me. Although the company has ever since March 1982 been paying the petitioner only at the last possible moment, I think that, on the evidence, the company is just able to pay its debts as they fall due. If, on the other hand, the company pursued the same course of conduct any longer, it might very well be that the court would take the opposite view.

That is the first part of section 233(b). That is not an end of the matter, because I must now consider the second part, which required me to take into account the contingent and prospective liabilities of the company. Counsel for the petitioner submits, correctly, that every time the company borrows money from somebody else to pay off the petitioner or the supporting creditor, or whoever, that borrowing increases its prospective liabilities, because it incurs a further debt prospectively due to the lender. Counsel says that if I take into account the contingent and prospective liabilities of the company, it is clearly insolvent in balance sheet terms. So indeed it is if I treat the loans made by the associated companies as loans which are currently repayable. However what I am required to do is to 'take into account' the contingent and prospective liabilities. That cannot mean that I must simply add them up and strike a balance against assets. In regard to prospective liabilities I must principally consider whether, and if so when, they are likely to become present liabilities. As to that, I have evidence from a director of the company, to the effect that there is no question of those loans being withdrawn. He has exhibited four loan agreements under which the loans are expressed not to be repayable until 30th June 1985. He adds that, although all of them bear interest, interest has so far been waived by the lenders and that they intend to continue to waive it. It seems to me, on the basis of that evidence, that if I take account of the prospective liabilities, I must approach the company's financial position on the footing that

---

[64] Companies Act 1948, s.223(d) and Companies Act 1985, s.518(1)(e).
[65] [1986] B.C.L.C. 261.

those loans will not be called in until 30th June 1985, and possibly until later.

"In those circumstances, I am in the end satisfied that the petitioner has not established that the company is unable to pay its debts even taking into account its contingent and prospective liabilities."

The yardstick is now radically different. It is no longer necessary to prove to the satisfaction of the court that the company is unable to pay its debts which is a *cash flow* or *liquidity* test. It is *deemed* unable to pay its debts provided the statutory test is satisfied. The test is whether the value of the company's assets is less than the amount of its liabilities. That is a *balance sheet* test.

Contingent liabilities

There is a problem in determining the level of a provision for a **4–107** contingent liability. One approach is to argue that if there is more than a 50/50 chance of the contingency occurring, there should be a provision for the full amount of the liability discounted to take account of its futurity. Following this approach, a contingent liability with an 80 per cent chance of accrual would not be discounted for the 20 per cent chance that it would not accrue, whilst a liability with a 50 per cent chance of accrual would be discarded altogether. Another method is to value the contingent liability at the percentage of the likelihood of its occurrence, so that where there was an 80 per cent likelihood of the liability occurring, the provision would be 80 per cent of the full liability discounted to reflect its present value. Following the latter approach, a contingent liability with a 10 per cent chance of accrual would be estimated at the present value of 10 per cent of the full liability. The prevailing accounting practice is to value the contingency in full (less any discount for futurity) if it will probably occur and is capable of valuation and disregard it altogether in other cases.[66] It is thought that the second approach should be the legal approach. The cost of removing a contingent liability from a balance sheet will be roughly the amount of the contingent liability divided by the chances of it occurring. By that formula it would cost roughly £20 to remove from any balance sheet a contingent debt of £100 where there was a one in five chance of the debt being payable.

Liabilities to be taken into account

The Insolvency Act 1986 employs two distinct formulations as to the **4–108** liabilities to be taken into account in applying the balance sheet test:

(1) All liabilities, taking into account contingent and prospective liabilities

This is the formulation used in the provisions relating to winding up,[67] **4–109** administration,[68] in England the avoidance of challengeable transactions[69]

---

[66] SSAP No 18.
[67] Insolvency Act 1986, s.123(2).
[68] *ibid.*, s.8(1).
[69] *ibid.*, ss.240(2), 245(4), applying s.123.

and in Scotland gratuitous alienations.[70] However, the expenses of a winding-up are not included.

(2) Debts and other liabilities and expenses of winding up

4–110   This is the definition of "insolvent liquidation" which relates to wrongful trading[71] and the disqualification of directors.[72] It includes contingent or prospective liabilities.[73]

It is thought that normal accounting practice will be followed in "taking into account" contingent and prospective liabilities on the balance sheet, *i.e.* a provision if prudence requires it for a contingent liability, and, perhaps, under certain circumstances, long term non-interest bearing loans discounted to reflect the net present liability.

Valuation of assets on a "going concern basis"

4–111   Although the provisions of s.123 of the Insolvency Act 1986 are consistent with s.214 of that Act, apart from the inclusion in s.214 of expenses of the winding up as a liability to be taken into account, it is not clear on what basis assets should be valued, *i.e.* whether on a "break up" basis or on a "going concern" basis. It is thought that they should be valued on a "break up" basis for the purposes of s.214.[74] For the purposes of that section the director is to look to see what the position would be in a liquidation and to assess what the balance sheet would be. For the purposes of that section, going into a non-insolvent liquidation would not constitute "wrongful trading". For the purposes of s.123 of the Insolvency Act 1986, the balance sheet is to be struck at the date of the hearing of the petition. That is not a prospective test. The question is what the value of the company's assets is as at that date, which is before the company has gone into liquidation, and on the basis of the balance sheet struck at that date, the decision is made whether the company should go into liquidation. SSAP No.17 on *Accounting for Post Balance Sheet Events*[75] distinguished "adjusting events" from "non-adjusting events". Paragraph 8 of SSAP No.17 provided: "[s]ome events occurring after the balance sheet date, such as a deterioration in the operating results and in the financial position, may indicate a need to consider whether it is appropriate to use the going concern concept in the preparation of financial statements. Consequently these may fall to be treated as adjusting events."

Paragraph 22 of the Appendix to SSAP No.17 made it clear that this adjustment is to be made whether the application of the going concern basis becomes inappropriate as a result of events which provide additional evidence of conditions existing at the balance sheet date or

---

[70] *ibid.*, s.142(4)(a) read with s.382(3).
[71] *ibid.*, s.214(6).
[72] Company Directors Disqualification Act 1986.
[73] Insolvency Act 1986, s.382(3).
[74] See para.8–13.
[75] This was the SSAP in force at the time of the passing of the Insolvency Act 1986. It is now superseded by FRED 27, *Events after the Balance Sheet Date*.

solely as a result of post balance sheet date events not related to such conditions. Because the balance is struck at the date of the hearing of the petition, there can be no question of post balance sheet events requiring the adjustment. It might be argued that the bringing of the petition itself could adversely affect the status of the company, and hence introduce a distress element in the sale of its assets, even if the company did not go into liquidation. While this might be the case, where there were a number of winding-up petitions brought, and the company lost credibility in the market place, it is thought that a court would reject this argument. The first ground for rejection would be that the dismissal of the petition on the basis that the company was solvent, should restore the credit-worthiness and status of the company. Secondly, it would be inequitable if a winding-up petition itself was allowed to interfere with what is meant to be an objective test. If the court had to hold hearings on the adverse effect of the winding-up petition on the status of the company, these hearings would further undermine the company's status.

The thinking of s.123 is consistent with the "wrongful trading" provisions of s.214 of the Insolvency Act 1986, under which directors may be personally liable where they do not take all reasonable steps to minimise the potential loss to a company's creditors when there is no reasonable prospect that the company will avoid going into insolvent liquidation, *i.e.* into liquidation when its assets are insufficient for the payment of its debts and other liabilities and the expenses of the winding up. One route, under the 'wrongful trading' provision, by which a director avoids liability is by minimising the loss to creditors through ceasing to trade and liquidating the company. The alternative method, is that new equity is put into the company to cover its debts. The threat of a winding-up order may be what Parliament had in mind as a way of compelling shareholders and backers of companies to ensure that companies are properly capitalised.

(e) Prejudice to floating charge holder

In Scotland a company which the Court of Session has jurisdiction to wind up may be wound up by the court if there was a floating charge over property comprised in the company's property and undertaking, and the court is satisfied that the security of the creditor entitled to the benefit of the floating charge is in jeopardy.[76] A creditor's security is deemed by law to be in jeopardy if the court is satisfied that events have occurred or are about to occur which render it unreasonable in the creditor's interests that the company should retain power to dispose of the property which is subject to the floating charge.[77] This provision has survived from the period when a floating charge holder could not appoint a receiver in Scotland. **4–112**

3. Creditors' Voluntary Winding Up Made Compulsory Winding Up

The fact that a creditors' voluntary winding up has commenced does not **4–113**

---

[76] Insolvency Act 1986, ss.122(2), 221(7).
[77] *ibid.*, ss.122(2) and 221(7).

bar a creditor or contributory applying to the court to have the company compulsorily wound up, although, in the case of an application to the court by a contributory, the court would have to be satisfied that the rights of the contributories would be prejudiced by a voluntary winding up.[78]

In deciding the matter, the court may have regard to the wishes of the creditors or contributories and, if it thinks fit, summon meetings of the creditors or contributories to ascertain their wishes, and in assessing these wishes regard, in the case of the creditors, is had to the value of the creditors' debt and, in the case of the contributories, regard is had to the number of votes conferred on each contributory by the Companies Act or the Articles.[79] Where there is a creditors' petition, the wishes of the company or its members will not result in the petition being refused.[80] Where creditors differ as to whether there should be a compulsory winding up, the court will normally have regard to the wishes of the majority in value of the creditors.[81] Even if the creditors in favour of a continuation of the voluntary liquidation are a minority in value, the court may refuse a compulsory order if there appears to be no advantage to creditors in making one,[82] such as if the voluntary liquidation was almost completed and a compulsory order would only add to the expense.

As in deciding on schemes of arrangement, the court must have regard to the general principles of fairness and commercial morality. The court may also take into account not only the value of the debts but the possible or probable motive of creditors in making their choice. Thus creditors who are also shareholders or connected with the former management may have less weight given to their view than those who have no interest except in their capacity as creditors. In the case of *Re Palmer Marine Surveys*[83] Hoffman J., using these principles, held that "a judicial exercise of discretion should not leave substantial independent creditors with a strong and legitimate sense of grievance".[84]

4. Stopping Liquidation Proceedings Once Commenced

4–114   The court may, at any time after an order for winding up, make an order sisting the proceedings either altogether or for a limited time, if it is proved to the satisfaction of the court that all proceedings in the winding up ought to be sisted.[85] The liquidator or any contributory or creditor may make a similar application in the case of a voluntary

---

[78] Insolvency Act 1986, s.116.
[79] *ibid.*, s.195.
[80] *MacDonnell's Trs v Oregonian Railway Co* (1884) 11 R. 912.
[81] *Pattisons Ltd v Kinnear* (1899) 1 F. 551; *Elsmie and Son v Tomatin Spey District Distillery* (1906) 8 F. 434.
[82] *Re Medisco Equipment Ltd* [1983] B.C.L.C. 305.
[83] [1986] B.C.L.C. 111.
[84] See also Hoffmann J.'s remarks in *Re Lowestoft Traffic Services Ltd* [1986] B.C.L.C. 81.
[85] Insolvency Act 1986, s.147(1).

winding up.[86] The sist will not be granted if this will have the effect of benefiting the directors but not the creditors.[87] Also, a sist will not normally be granted in the absence of firm and acceptable proposals for satisfying all creditors and in the absence of consent from, or arrangements binding, the liquidator and all members.[88] The criteria for what are acceptable proposals are strict. In the case of *Re Lowston Ltd*,[89] Harman J. stated the level of detailed assurances that a court would require before it allowed a stay of proceedings. He stated:

> "In my view, the test I have to apply is still that laid down by the first Buckley J in *Re Telescriptor Syndicate Limited* [1903] 2 Ch 174 that the court has to be satisfied that it is right to stay the winding-up proceedings, and, if there be matters as to which the court has doubts, it should not so stay. Megarry J was of the same view in *Re Calgary & Edmonton Land Co Ltd* [1975] 1 All ER 1046, [1975] 1 WLR 355. I have to be satisfied that it is proper to allow this company with this history to re-emerge back as an unencumbered company able to trade and carry on business.
>
> In my view, the fact that there is a claimant who has a disputed debt against it does not in any way mean that the present winding up ought to remain on foot. The winding-up order was made upon a basis which has proved to have been false. . . . It may turn out to be correct but that will require substantial litigation. . . . In those circumstances it seems to me I must look at the history of this company and see whether there are any shady practices or unattractive incidents which would disable the applicants from having the company restored to their hands. In the *Telescriptor* case there were dealings which were of an extremely curious nature which led Buckley J . . . to refuse to restore the company to the register in that state.
>
> The position today is quite different. I am offered . . . undertakings by both applicants who are creditors and contributories that they will procure that the company will file all necessary statutory accounts and returns within 3 months of the making of this order and will submit them to the relevant inspector of taxes. That means inevitably that a whole series of procedural steps which appear to have been omitted, such as the fixing of an accounting reference date, the appointment of auditors, the preparation of accounts, the audit of the accounts, etc, will all have to be conducted and, since the undertakings are given by the two applicants personally, they will be personally at risk if they are not complied with, which may involve them in financing those matters."

The court was also offered assurances that the creditor undertook to be postponed to other creditors, which gave proper protection for present and putative future creditors of the company.

---

[86] Insolvency Act 1986, s.112(1).
[87] *Re F Burrows (Leeds) (in Liquidation)* (1982) 126 SJ 227.
[88] *Re Calgary & Edmonton Land Co Ltd* [1975] 1 WLR 355.
[89] [1991] B.C.L.C. 570.

5. Settling of List of Contributories

Procedure

4–115　　In a creditors' voluntary winding up the liquidator settles the list of contributories,[90] and in a winding up by the court this is done by the court.[91] What happens is the list is prepared by the liquidator and submitted to the court by way of a note in the petition. The court will normally order intimation to all persons on the list allowing seven days (eight days in the sheriff court) for answers to be lodged. The list is then settled by the court after disposing of any objections which may be lodged. If it appears to the court or to the liquidator that there is no uncalled capital or that there is to be no surplus for members, the liquidator or the court may dispense with the settling of the list of contributories.[92] The sort of case in which the court could properly dispense with the settlement of a list of contributories is likely, in an insolvent liquidation, to be a case where there is a small number of shareholders and the company is clearly insolvent, when it is possible to establish that the position is perfectly clear without going through the rules relating to the settlement of the list. In the case of a large company with a large number of shares widely held by a large number of shareholders, the settlement of the list should not be dispensed with.[93]

Definition of "contributory"

4–116　　Contributories are members or former members of the company who are:

> (1) as *debtors* of the company, liable for "debts" of the company. "Debts" in the case of a company registered with limited liability entails liability to the amount of any unpaid capital on their shares.[94] "Debts" in the case of a company not registered with limited liability entails liability for all the debts of the company including the expenses of the winding up.[95] "Debts" in the case of a company limited by guarantee entails liability of the contributory to the extent of his guarantee unless the company has a share capital in which case the member would be liable for the amount of his non-paid up share capital[96]; and
>
> (2) as *creditors* of the company, entitled, in an insolvent liquidation, to share in any surplus which turns out to be available to shareholders after the payment of other creditors. (Where there is a surplus and some contributories cannot be found, the whole surplus falls to be distributed to the known contributories.[97])

---

[90] Insolvency Act 1986, s.165(4).
[91] *ibid.*, s.148(1).
[92] *ibid.*, ss.148(2) and 165(4)(a).
[93] *Re Paragon Holdings Ltd* [1961] 2 All ER 41.
[94] Insolvency Act 1986, s.74(1), (2)(d).
[95] *ibid.*, ss.74(1) and 226.
[96] *ibid.*, s.74(3).
[97] Joint Liquidators of Automatic Tools Ltd, Noters, February 1, 2000 (Outer House) (Unreported).

The liability of past members is restricted to those who have been members within one year from the commencement of the winding up, and only then when existing members are unable to pay the debts due by them. A past member is not liable to contribute in respect of any debt or liability of the company contracted after he has ceased to be a member.[98] It is perhaps thought unfair that past members should be liable, but the thinking is clear that if one assigns or transfers an onerous obligation, there should be some residual surety that the assignor is good for his money—at least for a year—although strictly the relationship is not that of surety but a primary obligation.

In terms of s.74(2)(f) of the Insolvency Act 1986, where a company is being wound up, a sum due to any member of the company (in his character of a member) by way of dividends, profits or otherwise is deemed to be a debt of the company, payable to that member in a case of competition between himself and any other creditor not a member of the company, but any such sum may be taken into account for the purpose of the final adjustment of the rights of the contributories among themselves. It has been held in Scotland that dividends declared but unpaid may be converted into loans. In the case of *Liquidator of Wilsons (Glasgow and Trinidad Ltd) v Wilson's Trs*[99] the court considered s.123(1)(vii) of the Companies (Consolidation) Act 1908, which was the statutory predecessor of s.74(2)(f) of the Insolvency Act 1986. In that case a member of the company, Mr Wilson, maintained with the company a "cash account current" which at its inception recorded the purchase price paid by the company for the purchase of a business and, as well, the issues of shares in the company to Mr Wilson. Thereafter for some years there were various debts and credits in the account of a miscellaneous nature including dividends carried to the credit of the account on Wilson's instructions. Balances were regularly struck and interest was paid. The company had the benefit of the balances for the purposes of its business. The ultimate balance was, in the liquidator's view, made up of unpaid dividends. In rejecting the liquidator's contention, Lord Cullen stated:

> "On a consideration of the nature of the account and the dealings with it I am unable to agree with the liquidator's view. The account extends over a considerable period of years. It is a miscellaneous account. To Mr Wilson's credit there were carried not only dividends payable by the company but also dividends received by him from other companies and miscellaneous receipts. On the other side there were debited a series of miscellaneous payments made from it on Mr Wilson's behalf. On credit balances interest at 6 per cent was allowed and credited by the company to Mr Wilson. In short, the company would seem, *quoad* this account, to have acted as bankers for Mr Wilson. It is conceded that if the company had paid over such dividends to Mr Wilson and he had immediately paid the same back in order that it should be credited to him in the account

---

[98] Insolvency Act 1986, s.74(2).
[99] 1915 1 S.L.T. 424.

current the view taken by the liquidators would not have applied. I do not think that the absence of this circuity of dealing should affect the result. The account current, as is conceded, was a *bona fide* account, and not a mere makeshift resorted to in order to obviate actual payment of the company dividends to Mr Wilson. The true view in law, as it seems to me, is that when sums payable as dividends to Mr Wilson were credited to the account current they did not thereafter retain the character of unpaid dividends, but were sums of money lent by Mr Wilson to the company, bearing interest at 6 per cent, while not drawn out on his behalf."

In that case there was no suggestion that any express or implied agreement had to be shown in order to effect a change in the character of debt. The judge appears to have been influenced by such considerations as—(a) the account was a miscellaneous account extending over many years; (b) interest was payable on the recurring balances; (c) its inception was due to the purchase price of the business being carried there; (d) the company acted in the way of a banker; (e) the account was not constituted to obviate the actual payment of dividends. The English case of *Re L.B. Holliday & Co*,[1] which seems to tighten the test and to get out of the grip of s.74(2)(f), requires that the claimant must show that the unpaid dividends were (a) the subject of some agreement express or implied between the claimant and the company or (b) the company must, with the passage of time, be taken necessarily to be in the same position as if the dividends had in fact been paid and then paid back to the company as a loan; in other words recognition necessarily of a loan situation.[2]

Forfeiture of shares

4–117   If shares have been forfeited within a year before the winding up, or if the shares have been transferred within the year and forfeited, the shareholder is still liable as a past member.[3] Where shares have been forfeited more than one year before the winding up, the former owner is not liable as a contributory even where the articles provide that their member remains "liable to pay to the company all calls owing on such shares at the time of such forfeiture, though he may be sued for the calls even after the expiry of one year from the forfeiture".[4]

A and B classes of contributories

4–118   The practice in preparing the list is to have an A list of contributories who are present members and primarily liable, and a B list of contributories who are the past members who have ceased to be members

---

[1] [1986] B.C.L.C. 227.

[2] See also *Re Rural & Veterinary Requisites Ltd* (1978) 3 A.C.L.R. 597; *Re Harry Simpson & Co Pty Ltd* (1963) 81 W.N. (Pt 1) (NSW) 207; and *Re Associated Electronics Services Pty Ltd* [1965] Qd R. 36.

[3] *Re Blakely Ordnance Co, Creyke's Case* (1869) 5 Ch. App. 63; *Re Accidental & Marine Insurance Corporation, Bridger's Case and Neill's Case* (1869) 5 Ch. App. 266.

[4] *Re Blakeley Ordnance Co, Needham's Case* (1867) L.R. 4 Eq. 135; *Ladies' Dress Association Ltd v Pulbrook* [1900] 2 Q.B. 376.

within a year preceding the winding up. The list must contain a statement of the name and address of, and the number of shares and extent of interest to be attributed to, each contributory, the amount called up, and the amount paid up in respect of such shares or interest, and distinguish between the several classes of contributories.[5] It is competent to settle the A and B lists separately.[6]

Representative and unrepresentative contributories

When settling the list of contributories, the court or the liquidator **4–119** must distinguish between persons who are contributories in their own right and persons who are contributories as being representatives of or liable for the debts of others.[7]

(a) Trustees in bankruptcy

When a contributory becomes bankrupt either before or after he has **4–120** been placed on the list, his trustee in bankruptcy represents him for all purposes of the winding up and is a contributory.[8] There may be proved against the bankruptcy estate the estimated value of his liability to future calls as well as calls already made.[9] The discharge of the bankrupt frees him entirely from liability to calls made after its date.[10]

(b) Executors

If a contributory dies either before or after he has been placed on the **4–121** list of contributories, his personal representatives, and the heirs and legatees of heritage of his heritable estate in Scotland, are liable to contribute to the assets of the company in discharge of his liability.[11] Where executors themselves apply for shares, they are personally liable as contributories, but where the executors are holders of a deceased member's shares they are liable only to the amount of the estate and not personally liable unless they have acted in some way which shows that they are to be treated as members.[12] They have two options with different legal effects. They may have the shares transferred into their own names and become members of the company or, if they do not wish to have the shares transferred into their own names, they have a reasonable time to sell the shares and to produce a purchaser who will take the transfer of them.[13] The question will be whether the placing of their names on the register was authorised by the executors, but personal liability will not be inferred from the mere form of entries in the company's ledger and dividends received by him.[14]

---

[5] Rules of the Court of Session, r.211(1)(a).
[6] *Liquidator of Caledonian Heritable Security Co Ltd* (1882) 9 R. 1130.
[7] Insolvency Act 1986, s.148(3).
[8] *ibid.*, s.82.
[9] *ibid.*, s.82(4).
[10] *Cresswell Ranch and Cattle Co v Balfour Melville* (1901) 29 S.L.R. 841.
[11] Insolvency Act 1986, s.81(1).
[12] *Buchan v City of Glasgow Bank* (1879) 6 R. (HL) 44.
[13] *ibid.*
[14] *ibid., per* Lord Selborne at 49.

(c) Trustees

4–122   Notice of trust may be entered on the register but, unlike executors who are generally not personally liable as contributories, trustees are personally liable, with a right of indemnity against the trust estate. The law was laid down by Lord Chancellor Cairns in one of four cases taken by trustees to the House of Lords arising out of the collapse of the City of Glasgow Bank.[15] Lord Cairns stated:

> "On the whole, my Lords, I am of the opinion that the decision of the Court of Session now under appeal is correct, and I must move your Lordships to dismiss the appeal. It is difficult to use words which will adequately express the sympathy I feel for those who have been overwhelmed in the disaster of the City of Glasgow Bank; and that sympathy is peculiarly due to those who, without any possibility of benefit to themselves, and probably without any trust estate behind them sufficient to indemnify them, have become subject to loss or ruin by entering, for the advantage of others, into a partnership attended with risks of which they probably were forgetful or which they did not fully realise."[16]

The trustee whose name is on the register, and who resigns office but does not intimate the resignation to the company, remains liable as a contributory.[17] Assumed trustees are liable where new certificates have been issued and their names are on the register though their names had not been entered in the "stock ledger".[18] The trustee's name may not be removed from the register if, before the date of the winding up, the company had become hopelessly insolvent.[19]

6. Rectification of Register

4–123   The liquidator may apply to the court to have the register rectified as may any contributory or aggrieved person.[20] This right is important mainly in the case of unlimited companies or where there are partly-paid shares, as in recent privatisations. Transfers after the commencement of a winding up are void, except on the sanction of the court, in a compulsory winding up.[21] In a voluntary winding up a transfer may be made with the sanction of the liquidator.[22] The power of rectification may be retrospective to a date before the liquidation so as to allow the transferee the right of a dissentient.[23]

---

[15] See Chap.1.

[16] *Muir v City of Glasgow Bank* (1879) 6 R. (HL) 21 at 27, reaffirming the Lord Justice-Clerk, who observed: "It is now well settled that in this or any like company no one can become a partner with a limited liability, or with any other liabilities than such as are borne in common by all the partners".

[17] *Kerr v City of Glasgow Bank* (1879) 6 R. (HL) 52.

[18] *Bell v City of Glasgow Bank* (1879) 6 R. (HL) 55.

[19] *Mitchell v City of Glasgow Bank* (1879) 6 R. (HL) 60.

[20] Companies Act 1985, s.359; Insolvency Act 1986, ss.148(1) and 112(1).

[21] Insolvency Act 1986, s.127.

[22] *ibid.*, s.88.

[23] *Re Sussex Brick Co* [1904] 1 Ch. 598.

Until the register is rectified the liquidator is bound to enter on the A list the name of every person who is on the register of members.[24] There are several grounds on which persons may ask the liquidator to apply to the court for rectification of the register or, if the liquidator is unwilling, apply themselves.

(a) Unnecessary delay

If shares have been sold and a transfer has been presented for **4–124** registration but, owing to the delay of the company, the transfer has not been registered, the register will be rectified in favour of the transferor.[25] The test is whether the name of any person is, without sufficient cause, entered in or omitted from a company's register of members, or whether default has been made or unnecessary delay taken place in entering on the register the fact of any person having ceased to be a member.[26] The shareholder is not entitled on the eve of liquidation to insist on registration; the directors ought to refuse registration if the facts are such that the rights of creditors have intervened although a winding up has not commenced.[27] The transfer ought to be confirmed by the directors at the first meeting at which, in the ordinary course of business, it can be confirmed, and thereupon registered. If not so confirmed, there is "unnecessary delay".[28] Although transferors know that the company is on the eve of winding up voluntarily, this will not prevent their validly transferring their shares.[29]

(b) Default of company

What amounts to default on the part of the company is a matter of **4–125** circumstances. For example, if before the winding up the transfer duly executed has been left for registration, and the directors have neglected to approve or disapprove of it, and if there is no reason why they should have disapproved, the court will rectify the register.[30] If the reason for the non-registration is the default of the company, the court will not rectify on the application of the liquidator, whatever may be the right of the transferor to rectification. The liquidator represents only the company to whose default the error is owing. The contributories have no interest except through the company, and the creditors have no right in equity against the person who has never been held out to them.[31] Conversely, however, if a shareholder has sold his shares, he is not relieved from being a contributory if, owing either to his own neglect or that of his transferee, or if, in fact, owing to any cause except the neglect of the company, his transferee's name has not been substituted for his at

---

[24] *Reese River Silver Mining Co v Smith* (1869) L.R. 4 (HL) 64.
[25] *Dodds v Cosmopolitan Insurance Corporation*, 1915 S.C. 992.
[26] Companies Act 1985, s.359(1).
[27] *Nelson Mitchell v City of Glasgow Bank* (1879) 6 R. (HL) 66.
[28] *Re Joint Stock Discount Co, Nation's Case* (1866) L.R. 3 Eq. 77.
[29] *McLintock v Campbell*, 1916 S.C. 966; *Re Taurine Co* (1883) 25 Ch. D. 118.
[30] *Hill's Case* (1867) 4 Ch. App. 769, n.
[31] *Sichell's Case* (1867) 3 Ch. App. 119.

the date of the winding up. Only if the omission to substitute the name of the transferee is owing entirely to the neglect and default of the company will the register be rectified.[32] The default by the company will not, however, be sufficient in itself to have a name removed from the register. The court's power is discretionary and regard must be had to the "justice of the case".[33] Accordingly, where there is a dispute between two individuals as to who should be registered as a member of the company, then a default of the company takes second place to the merits of their competing claims.[34] Where a formal requirement in relation to a transfer has not been met, such as if the articles require that the transfer be executed by both transferor and transferee, the court will not interfere if that formal requirement has not been met and as a result the transfer has not been reflected in the register.[35] If, however, the transfer is void by, for example, being *ultra vires* of the company, the court may reduce (quash) the transfer and rectify the register to put the transferor back on the register even if there is a delay of several years.[36]

(c) Misrepresentation and fraud

4–126   A transfer which has been executed before insolvency may not be reduced on the grounds of fraudulent misrepresentation inducing purchase of the shares and the register rectified if the entry on the register is prior to insolvency.[37] If, however, it can be shown that the alleged member has never agreed to become a shareholder and accordingly any contract was void, it is immaterial that the name is on the register at the commencement of insolvency.[38] If, before the insolvency of the company, the shareholder has stopped all connection with the company and has commenced proceedings to have his name removed from the register, and to rescind the contract, he will be entitled to relief, although between the date of bringing his action and the judgment of the court upon it, an order has been obtained to wind up the company.[39] He will not be able to claim damages but only be entitled to rank as a creditor for money paid to the company.[40] The fact that a shareholder may only rank for his money subscribed on shares allotted and registered may not in normal circumstances be of much help. However, where there are likely calls on insolvency, it is critical that the member is quick off the mark in bringing his action for rescission of the contract on the ground of fraud or misrepresentation. The case of *Tennent v City of Glasgow Bank*[41] puts the critical date back to the date of the stoppage of the bank and a notice of a meeting to propose a resolution to wind up. It is unclear whether after the commencement of a receivership or an

---

[32] *Marshall v Glamorgan Iron and Coal Co* (1868) L.R. 7 Eq. 129 at 137, *per* Giffard V.C.
[33] *Sichell's Case*, above, at 122.
[34] *Howe v City of Glasgow Bank* (1879) 6 R. 1194.
[35] *Marino's Case* (1867) 2 Ch. App. 596.
[36] *General Property Investment Co and Liquidator v Matheson's Trs* (1888) 16 R. 282.
[37] *Tennent v City of Glasgow Bank* (1879) 6 R. (HL) 69.
[38] *Gorrissen's Case* (1873) 8 Ch. App. 507.
[39] *Smith's Case* (1867) L.R. 2 Ch. 604.
[40] *Houldsworth v City of Glasgow Bank* (1880) 7 R. (HL) 53.
[41] (1879) 6 R. (HL) 69.

administration order it would be too late to bring an action of rescission. It is suggested that a receivership does not have this effect but that an administration order, where it is clear that the company is going to go into liquidation, would have that effect.

7. MAKING CALLS

In a creditors' voluntary winding up the liquidator makes calls.[42] In a **4–127** winding up by the court, the call is made by the court.[43] This is done by the liquidator applying to the court by way of a note, stating the proposed amount of call and the reasons for making it.

The call may be made at any time either before or after the court or the liquidator has ascertained the sufficiency of the company's assets, and calls may be made on all or any of the contributories who are on the list of contributories to the extent of their liability. The liability extends to the satisfying of the company's debts and liabilities, the expenses of winding up, and the liability for the adjustment of the rights of the contributories among themselves.[44] Terms varying liability cannot be implied into a company's articles of association based on extrinsic evidence linked to surrounding circumstances, and a member therefore cannot be forced by such an implication to contribute sums to a company over and above the amounts he has subscribed for.[45]

The liability of a contributory is a debt due as from "the time when his liability commenced", but payable only when a call is made. Prescription can accordingly operate to extinguish liability five years after the date of the call.[46] Also, if a call has been made by the directors and it has prescribed, the liquidator or court cannot make the call for the same money. The court or liquidator may recover interest on calls at the rate of five per cent.[47] If, however, the liquidator is repeating calls made before by the directors, he may demand payment of a higher rate of interest if it is provided for in the articles of association of the company.[48] The call, if and when the liquidator determines to make it, will be made by an instrument in writing under his hand, and notice of the making of the call is sent to the contributories. He may call a meeting first before making the calls, to consider the matter and invite the members to attend. In the case of a compulsory winding up, the call is effectively a decree by the court. The procedure is first to make calls on those on the A list, and if these calls are not sufficient to satisfy the debts, to make a call on those on the B list.

Calls should be made *pari passu*, there being an implied condition of equality among shareholders in a company.[49]

---

[42] Insolvency Act 1986, s.165(4)(b).
[43] *ibid.*, s.150(1).
[44] *ibid.*, ss.150(1) and 165(4)(b).
[45] *Bratton Seymour Service Company Ltd v Oxborough, The Times*, March 2, 1992.
[46] Prescription and Limitation (Scotland) Act 1973, s.6, Sch.1.
[47] Insolvency Act 1986, ss.161, 165(4)(b).
[48] *Liquidators of Benhar Coal Co Ltd* (1882) 9 R. 763.
[49] *British and American Trustee and Finance Corporation Ltd v Couper* [1894] A.C. 399.

Where calls are not answered it is open to the liquidator under s.161 of the Insolvency Act 1986 in the case of a compulsory winding up, or in terms of s.112(2) of the Insolvency Act 1986 in the case of a voluntary winding up, to produce a list certified by him of the names of the contributories liable in payment of any calls and the court may forthwith pronounce a decree against these contributories for payment of the sums certified, and the liquidator may enforce these calls by summary diligence. Where a company has been wound up, all books and papers of the company and of the liquidator are, as between the contributories, *prima facie* evidence of the truth of all matters purporting to be recorded.[50]

8. ADJUSTMENT OF RIGHTS

4–128 Where the assets turn out to be sufficient to pay off creditors and pay the costs of the winding up, before any payment by way of a distribution may be made to members, the surplus funds must be first applied to adjusting the rights of the contributories among themselves. This is mandatory in a compulsory and a voluntary winding up. In the case of a compulsory winding up it is effected by the court,[51] and in a voluntary winding up it is done by the liquidator.[52] Accordingly, unless the articles provide otherwise,[53] where shares are unequally paid up an adjustment must be made between the contributories, or if the surplus assets are not sufficient to make the adjustment, a further call must be made to allow this if there is still uncalled share capital.[54]

9. TAKING CONTROL OF ASSETS

Custody and control of assets

The liquidator, as soon as he is able after his appointment, must take possession of all the assets of the company and any property, books, papers or records in the possession or control of the company or to which the company appears to be entitled.[55] In the case of a creditors' voluntary winding up, there is also statutory power under which a liquidator proposed at a members' meeting may exercise the power to take custody and control of the property of the company prior to his appointment by the creditors' meeting.[56] Only companies registered under the Companies Acts may be wound up voluntarily,[57] but some unregistered companies may register and then wind up voluntarily.[58]

---

[50] Insolvency Act 1986, s.191.

[51] *ibid.*, s.154.

[52] *ibid.*, s.165(5).

[53] *Ex p. Maude* (1870) L.R. 6 Ch. App. 51.

[54] See *Re Phoenix Oil and Transport Co Ltd* [1958] Ch. 560 for the meaning of "adjustment".

[55] Insolvency (Scotland) Rules 1986, r.4.22, inserted by para.18 of the Schedule to the Insolvency (Scotland) Amendment Rules 1987.

[56] Insolvency Act 1986, s.166(3).

[57] *ibid.*, s.221(4).

[58] *Southall v British Mutual Life Assurance Society* (1871) LR 6 Ch 614.

10. Keeping Records

Sederunt book

The liquidator must maintain a "sederunt" book during his term of **4–129** office for the purpose of providing an accurate record of the liquidation process, and in particular he must make up and maintain an inventory and valuation of the assets which he must retain in the sederunt book.[59] By "maintain" it is perhaps suggested that the valuations must be kept up to date but such expense is not usually justified and it is not the practice. Rule 7.33(1) of the Insolvency (Scotland) Rules 1986 makes it mandatory for each insolvency practitioner to maintain a sederunt book in which must be recorded everything that is required to be recorded by any provision of the Insolvency Act 1986 or the Insolvency (Scotland) Rules 1986. There is no prescribed form for the "sederunt" book. The expression can mean a loose leaf lever-arch file on a retrieval system if it can be reproduced in legible form. All minutes of meetings, resolutions, notices, interlocutors, accounts, schemes of division, compromises, schemes of arrangement and voluntary arrangements must be kept in it. The sederunt book must be made available for inspection at all reasonable hours by any interested person.

Access to records

Certain documentation may be withheld from interested parties in **4–130** terms of r.7.27 of the Insolvency (Scotland) Rules 1986 as amended by Art.50 of the Schedule to the Insolvency (Scotland) Amendment Rules 1987. If the liquidator considers that it should be treated as confidential, or that it is of such a nature that its disclosure would be calculated to be injurious to the interests of the company's creditors or its members or the contributories in its winding up, he is entitled to decline to allow the record to be inspected by a person who would otherwise be an interested party. Members of the liquidation committee may be refused access, but on refusal any person who is interested may seek an order from the court allowing them inspection of the record.[60]

11. Annual and Final Meetings

(a) First meeting

The interim liquidator must summon a first meeting of creditors and **4–131** contributories primarily to appoint a liquidator in terms of s.138 of the Insolvency Act 1986. Similarly in a creditors' voluntary winding up, the company summons a first meeting of creditors in terms of s.98 of the Insolvency Act 1986 primarily to nominate a liquidator.

---

[59] Insolvency (Scotland) Rules 1986, r.4.22(1)(b), inserted by para.18 of the Schedule to the Insolvency (Scotland) Amendment Rules 1987.
[60] *ibid.*, r.7.27(3).

(b) Annual meetings

4–132 After the first meetings mentioned above, the liquidator, in both a voluntary winding up and a compulsory winding up must summon a meeting of the creditors in each year during which the liquidation is in force, and has the discretion to summon a meeting of the creditors or the contributories at any time for the purpose of ascertaining their wishes in all matters relating to the liquidation.[61] In a creditors' voluntary winding up he must summon a general meeting of the company and a meeting of creditors at the end of the first year from the commencement of the winding up, and of each succeeding year or at the first convenient date within three months from the end of the year or such longer period as the Secretary of State may allow.[62] The liquidator must lay before each of the meetings an account of his acts and dealings and of the conduct of the winding up during the preceding year.[63] These provisions in relation to annual meetings are not new in relation to creditors' voluntary windings up.[64] The duty of the liquidator, in a compulsory winding up, to call an annual meeting of creditors (but not a general meeting of the company as in a creditors' voluntary winding up) is new and does not apply to compulsory windings up commenced prior to December 29, 1986.

Final meeting

4–133 In both a creditors' voluntary winding up and a compulsory winding up, the liquidator shall summon a final meeting of the creditors.[65] In a compulsory winding up the liquidator summons the meeting "if it appears to him that the winding up is for practical purposes complete".[66] In a creditors' voluntary winding up, the liquidator summons meetings of the company and of the creditors as soon as the company's affairs are fully wound up and he has made up an account of the winding up, showing how it has been conducted and how the company's property has been disposed of.[67] In a final meeting of creditors in a compulsory winding up the creditors receive the liquidator's report of the winding up, and determine whether the liquidator should have his release. In a creditors' voluntary winding up the creditors receive an 'account' as well as a report.

The law has not, for practical purposes, changed in relation to a creditors' voluntary winding up, but in relation to windings up commenced after December 29, 1986 it has changed in relation to compulsory windings up. Formerly there was no duty to summon a final meeting of creditors in a compulsory winding-up. Previously the company was dissolved by the liquidator making an application to the

---

[61] Insolvency (Scotland) Rules 1986, r.4.23.
[62] Insolvency Act 1986, s.105(1).
[63] *ibid.*, s.105(2).
[64] Companies Act 1985, s.595.
[65] Insolvency Act 1986, ss.106, 146.
[66] *ibid.*, s.146(1).
[67] *ibid.*, s.106(1).

court.[68] This is no longer the case. There is no need to have a final meeting or annual meeting where an early dissolution is sought by the liquidator under ss.202 or 112 of the Insolvency Act 1986.

12. Dissolution of the Company and Striking Off Register

(a) Dissolution of the company

In a creditors' voluntary winding up, within one week from the date **4–134** of the final meeting at which the liquidator's final account was presented to creditors, he must send a copy of the account to the Registrar of Companies and make a return to him.[69] The Registrar, on receiving the account and return, must forthwith register them, and on the expiration of three months from the registration of the return the company is deemed to be dissolved.[70] However, the court may, on the application of the liquidator or any other person who appears to the court to be interested, make an order deferring the date at which the dissolution of the company is to take effect.[71]

The procedure in a compulsory winding up is similar. The liquidator has to send a notice to the court and to the Registrar of Companies (Form 4.17 (Scot)) that the meeting has been held and of the decisions (if any) of the meeting.[72] The registrar must register the notice forthwith on receipt and at the end of three months, beginning with the day of the registration of the notice, the company is dissolved.[73] Again, as in a voluntary winding up, the court may, on application of any person who appears to have any interest, defer the dissolution of the company for such period as the court thinks fit.[74]

(b) Early dissolution of company

In a compulsory winding up and in a creditors' voluntary winding **4–135** up, if after the first statutory meeting it appears to the liquidator that the realisable assets of the company are insufficient to cover the expenses of the winding up, he may apply to the court for an order that the company be dissolved.[75] Where the liquidator makes the application, if the court is satisfied that the realisable assets of the company are insufficient to cover the expenses of the winding up and it appears to the court appropriate to do so, the court shall make an order that the company be dissolved.[76] The liquidator must then forward to the

---

[68] Companies Act 1985, s.568(1).
[69] Insolvency Act 1986, s.106(3).
[70] *ibid.*, s.201(2).
[71] *ibid.*, s.201(3).
[72] *ibid.*, s.172(8).
[73] *ibid.*, s.205(2).
[74] *ibid.*, s.205(5).
[75] *ibid.*, ss.112(1) and 204(2); for discussion of the jurisdiction under s.112.
[76] *ibid.*, s.204(3).

registrar within 14 days of the date of the order a copy of the order. The registrar must register it forthwith and at the end of a period of three months beginning from the day of the registration of the order, the company is dissolved.[77] As in the usual dissolution, the court may defer the dissolution on the application of any person who appears to the court to have an interest.[78]

(c) Effect of dissolution of company

4–136   When a company is dissolved, all property and rights vested in or held in trust for the company immediately before its dissolution are deemed to be *bona vacantia* (unowned goods) and belong to the Crown.[79] That does not include property held by the company on trust.[80] When a company is dissolved, the court has no longer any jurisdiction to reach it, for there is no company,[81] because there are no officers or other agents who can be served with notices or writs on behalf of the company.

(d) Power to declare dissolution void

4–137   Where a company has been dissolved, the liquidator or any other person appearing to the court to be interested, may apply to the court for an order declaring the dissolution void.[82] Before the coming into force of the amending provisions of the Companies Act 1989[83] it had been necessary in terms of the statute that the application be made within two years of the date of dissolution, although the Scottish courts had granted an order under that section 10 years after dissolution in exercise of its *nobile officium*.[84] In an English case, *Bradley v Eagle Star Insurance Co Ltd*,[85] a former employee of a company which had been dissolved raised proceedings against insurers under the Third Parties (Rights against Insurers) Act 1930 in which it was claimed that the plaintiff had suffered a disability by reason of her employment by the company. Under that Act, if a winding-up order is made in respect of a company and the company is insured against liabilities to third parties, any rights of the company against the insurer, whether arising before or after that event, are transferred to the third party.[86] Because in the *Bradley* Case the company had been dissolved before the existence and amount of the company's liability had been established, it was held by the House of Lords that the employee's claim could not succeed because no right of the company against the insurers capable of being transferred to the employee had arisen at the time of dissolution. Because the

---

[77] Insolvency Act 1986, s.204(4).
[78] *ibid.*, s.204(5).
[79] Companies Act 1985, s.654(1).
[80] *ibid.*, s.654(1).
[81] *Re Westbourne Grove Drapery Co* (1879) 39 L.T. 30.
[82] Companies Act 1985, s.651; *Liqr of McCall & Stephen*, 1920 S.L.T. 26.
[83] Companies Act 1989, s.141.
[84] *Coffins Brothers & Co Ltd*, 1916 S.C. 620.
[85] [1989] A.C. 957; [1989] 1 All E.R. 961 (HL).
[86] Third Parties (Rights against Insurers) Act 1930, s.1(1).

dissolution of the company had occurred more than two years previously, the company could not be restored to the register for the purpose of the employee's claim against the company being established, and therefore the plaintiff was left without a remedy. Because of this decision, s.651 of the Companies Act 1985 was amended to provide that an application for the purpose of bringing proceedings against the company for damages in respect of personal injuries or under the Fatal Accidents Act 1976 or the Damages (Scotland) Act 1976 may be made at any time, provided that it appears to the court that those proceedings will not be time-barred.[87] In terms of s.651(5) of the Companies Act 1985: "'Personal injuries' includes any disease and any impairment of a person's physical or mental condition.'

It has been held in England that the court may take into account any power that the court in those proceedings has to extend the prescriptive period which would otherwise apply.[88] On the making of an order the court may direct that the period between the dissolution of the company and the making of the order is not to count for the purposes of statutory prescription or limitation.[89] The time limits under s.651, apart from the above exception are: (a) The company must not have been dissolved more than two years from the date of the application, and (b) an application under the exception is not competent over twenty years from the date of the dissolution.[90]

In any event the order of the court may be made after the expiry of the two-year period, provided the application is made within the two years.[91]

If property has gone to the Crown as *bona vacantia*, it must account to the company for the proceeds after the dissolution has been declared void.[92] The effect of an order declaring a dissolution void is that all consequences flowing from such dissolution are themselves voided.[93] If facts come to light which would require the dissolution being declared void, an application to the court should be made as soon as possible after these facts come to light.[94]

(e) Striking off Register

Companies which are not carrying on business or have minimal assets **4–138** are often disposed of without a winding up, under the provisions of s.652 of the Companies Act 1985. Under that provision, where the Registrar has reasonable cause to believe that a company is not carrying on business or in operation, he may send to the company a letter of

---

[87] Companies Act 1985, s.651(5) (added by the Companies Act 1989, s.141(3)).
[88] *Re Workvale Ltd* [1992] 1 W.L.R. 416.
[89] Companies Act 1985, s.651(6) as amended.
[90] Companies Act 1985, s.651(4) as added and Companies Act 1989, s.141(4).
[91] *Dowling Petr,* 1960 S.L.T. (Notes) 76.
[92] Companies Act 1985, s.655(2).
[93] *ibid.,* s.651(2); *Re C W Dickson* [1947] Ch. 251; *Champdany Jute Co Ltd,* 1924 S.C. 209.
[94] *Re Thompson and Riches Ltd* [1981] 1 W.L.R. 682.

inquiry. If he does not within a month receive an answer, he is, within 14 days, to send a second letter by registered post and if he does not receive a reply to this, in terms that the company is carrying on business, or receives a reply stating that the company is not carrying on business or in operation, he may publish in the *Gazette* and send a notice by post to the company in terms that, at the expiration of three months, the name of the company will be struck off the register and the company dissolved. The notice may be addressed to the company at its registered office or, if no office has been registered, to the care of some officer of the company, or if there is no officer of the company whose name and address are known to the Registrar, to each of the persons who subscribe to the memorandum at the addresses mentioned on it. At the expiry of the period mentioned in the notice, the name is struck off and the company dissolved. However, the liability of every director, managing officer and member is continuous, and may be enforced as if the company had not been dissolved. Section 13 and Sch.5 to the Deregulation and Contracting Out Act 1994 introduced ss.652A to F into the Companies Act 1985. These sections set up a process in terms of which private companies—but not public companies—file an application to the Registrar of Companies in a prescribed form and containing prescribed information. These new sections merely formalise the previous practice of directors of companies writing to the Registrar and asking that their companies be struck off under s.652. The Registrar, however, is not allowed to strike off a company under s.652A unless three months have elapsed after the publication of a notice in the Edinburgh Gazette stating that he may exercise his powers under s.652A in relation to the company, and inviting anyone to show cause why he should not do so.[95] If the Registrar decides to strike off a company then a notice is to be published in the Edinburgh Gazette,[96] the effect of which is to dissolve the company.[97] If a company has been struck off, a court may order its subsequent winding up.[98] There are a number of procedural matters which must be followed, set out in the sections dealing with having a company struck off in this manner.

Where a company is being wound up, if the Registrar has reasonable cause to believe that no liquidator is acting, or that the affairs of the company are fully wound up, and the proper returns have not been made by the liquidator for six months, and the Registrar has published in the *Gazette* and sent a notice to the company, or to the liquidator at his last known place of business, the company's name may be struck off the Register with the same result.

The main difference between the company being dissolved in this manner and through a winding-up is that the liabilities mentioned above continue. Further, any company, member, or creditor aggrieved by the proceeding may, within 20 years from the publication of the

---

[95] Companies Act 1985, s.652A(3).
[96] *ibid.*, s.652A(4).
[97] *ibid.*, s.652A(5).
[98] *Re Anglo-American Exploration & Development Co* [1898] 1 Ch. 100; *Re Waterford Improved Dwellings Co Ltd* [1934] I.R. 631.

notice in the *Gazette*, apply to the court in which the company is liable to be wound up, and the court, if satisfied that the company was carrying on business or in operation when struck off, or that it is just to do so, may order its restoration to the Register and, on an office copy of the order being delivered to the Registrar, it is deemed to have continued in existence as if its name had never been struck off.[99]

Applications under s.653 of the Companies Act 1985 for restoration to the Register are not confined to parties who are creditors of the dissolved company but to all persons who have an interest and who are in some way legally prejudiced as a result of the dissolution. The main object of the provision allowing the declaration of a dissolution void is to enable assets which subsequently come to light to be distributed properly[1] and that a person who has a claim, whether against the company or against the third party such as an insurer or guarantor, will have a remedy in a situation where he can only enforce the claim if the company is restored to the Register.[2] The Secretary of State also may seek to restore a company to the Register under s.653(2) where he wishes to commence disqualification proceedings against the company's directors.[3]

In the case of *Conti v UeberseeBank A.G.*[4] the Scottish Court of Session (Inner House) distinguished the English authorities which had held to the effect that a person who was instrumental in bringing about the striking off of a company could not be a person aggrieved for the purposes of s.653(1) of the Companies Act 1985, because the person must be aggrieved at the time of the striking off and would not seek a striking off if he were not aggrieved. The argument was accepted in the Inner House that a person who was instrumental in the application for striking off could not be aggrieved at that time. However, he could be aggrieved, for the purposes of s.653(1), not by the original action of striking off itself, but by the occurrence of some new event post-dissolution and involving the company. Lord Prosser stated:

"The considerations which established that a member or creditor who had taken no part in the striking off could rely upon subsequent or supervening circumstances, in showing that he was aggrieved by the company having been struck off, applied equally to a person who had deliberately or intentionally been involved in having the company struck off, but had not, in so doing, intended to deprive the company (or members or creditors) of benefits

---

[99] Companies Act 1985, s.653(3).

[1] See *Re Blue Note Enterprises Ltd* [2001] 2 B.C.L.C. 427, in which the High Court considered the circumstances when it would be appropriate to restore a company to the Register, and in that case held that to refuse to restore a company to the Register where it had been struck off for failing to file an annual return would be an excessive penalty, and that the court in exceptional circumstances could apply conditions to any restoration to the Register.

[2] *City of Westminster Assurance Co Ltd v Registrar of Companies* [1997] B.C.C. 960 (C.A.); *Re Blenheim Leisure (Restaurants) Ltd* [2000] B.C.C. 554 (C.A.).

[3] *Re Townreach Ltd (No. 002081 of 1994)* [1994] 3 W.L.R. 983.

[4] 2000 S.C. 240; 2000 S.L.T. 1015; [2000] B.C.C. 172.

which, as things turned out, would have accrued but for the company having thus been struck off''.

CHAPTER 5

ADMINISTRATIONS

History and background to administration in the United Kingdom

The regime of administration was first introduced into the Scottish law **5–01** of corporate insolvency by ss.27 to 44 of the Insolvency Act 1985, which were consolidated as ss.8 to 27 inclusive of the Insolvency Act 1986. The introduction of an administration order procedure was one of the proposals made in Chap.9 of the *Cork Report*.[1] The proposal suggested the introduction of a procedure by which a failing company could be financially reconstructed with a view either to procuring the rehabilitation and survival of the company as a going concern or, failing that, to secure a better realisation of the company's assets than would result from the immediate winding up of a failed company. The administration order procedure derived from the Cork Report, applied exclusively to companies. Since the introduction of the new form of legal entity known as a "limited liability partnership" by the Limited Liability Partnerships Act 2000,[2] the administration provisions of the Insolvency Act 1986 (as well as the winding up and receivership provisions) have applied to limited liability partnerships.[3]

The administration order procedure, as advocated in the Cork Report, was comparable to procedures under certain foreign systems of insolvency law.[4] However in many ways, it really took as a model what had sometimes taken place under an imaginative use of floating charge receivership in England and Wales. It had proved possible in some cases for the receiver and manager of a company's entire undertaking, to produce a corporate rescue which left the company in a better economic

---

[1] Cmmd. 8558 (1982).

[2] S.1 was commenced on April 6, 2001 by the Limited Liability Partnerships Act 2000 (Commencement) Order 2000 (SI 2000/3316).

[3] The relevant instruments effecting this, made under s.14 of the Limited Liability Partnerships Act 2000, are the Limited Liability Partnerships Regulations 2001 (SI 2001/1090) and the Limited Liability Partnerships (Scotland) Regulations 2001 (SI 2001/128), which came into force on April 6, 2001. The Scottish Regulations are effective in relation to insolvency in devolved areas under the Scotland Act 1998.

[4] See Chap.11 of the US Bankruptcy Reform Act 1978 (11 U.S.C). There are of course numerous differences in detail between 11 U.S.C. and the administration procedure derived from the *Cork Report*, such as that under Chap.11 the board of directors remains in control of the company. For comparisons see Westbrook (1990) I.L.&P.86–90. A comprehensive account of the subject of administration and reorganisation including international comparisons, is to be found in *Corporate Rescue*, by David Brown. See also Fletcher, Higham & Trower, *The Law & Practice of Corporate Administrations*; Grier & Floyd, *Corporate Recovery: Administrations & Voluntary Arrangements*.

condition than that in which it had been found, but at the same time had safeguarded the interests of the secured creditor and holder of the instrument under which the receiver and manager was appointed.[5] What the *Cork Report* proposed was a rehabilitative process for a company that would be generally available, rather than relying on a floating charge and initiatives coming from a receiver. In furtherance of this policy, the general powers conferred upon an administrator following the Cork Report were identical to those conferred on an administrative receiver in terms of Chap.1 of Pt III of the Insolvency Act 1986. There have been several well publicised administrations, such as those of *Olympia & York/Canary Wharf* and *Maxwell Communications Corporation*. Generally, however, the administration procedure has not been widely adopted. For example in England and Wales between 1987 and 1997 there were on average only 172 administrations, although on average 3751 administrative receiverships. Since then the number of administrative receiverships has gone down and the number of administrations have gone up. For example, in England and Wales in 2001 there were just under 2000 administrative receiverships and just under 700 administrations. It is perhaps too early to read anything into these latest figures since they may merely reflect the economic cycle. The figures in relation to Scotland which are available for the years 1996 to 2001 inclusive show on average 91 administrative receiverships per year and four administrations.[6] The low level of take-up of administrations in England and Wales and in Scotland, is further emphasised by the fact that administration has often been employed as a convenient antichamber to liquidation in situations where immediate break-up and liquidation of a company was for some reason not attractive. There may be procedural reasons for the low level of utilisation of administration. It is a complex process, involving judicial intervention with an exacting standard set by the courts in deciding whether any of the authorised purposes of an administration are likely to be achieved. There is also the existence of the administrator's power to remove directors, and of course the possibility that a floating charge holder may exercise his powers and place the company in administrative receivership. Finally, there is the sheer cost of the procedure.[7]

In judging whether the administration procedure as derived from *Cork* has achieved its purpose, the low level of uptake cannot in itself be

---

[5] In terms of ss.29(2) and 251 of the Insolvency Act 1986, a receiver and manager is now known in England and Wales as an "administrative receiver". In Scotland an "administrative receiver" is still known as a "receiver" and is a person appointed under a floating charge which comprises the whole (or substantially the whole) of the company's property in terms of s.251 of the Insolvency Act 1986.

[6] There were 10 administrations in the millennium year. Excluding the millennium year there would, on average, have been only three administrations per year. The statistics for the years 1996 to 2001 in relation to England and Wales and Scotland may be found on the Website of the Insolvency Service at: *www.//insolvency.gov.uk/information/stats/statistics.htm*. The figures for voluntary arrangements in Scotland show on average one voluntary arrangement per year during those six years.

[7] In Scotland, there is a general perception that an administration is sufficiently unusual a procedure that it needs the supervision of the Court of Session, sheriffs being unlikely to have any expertise dealing with them. This adds significantly to the expense of the procedure and makes local control more difficult.

seen as a stigma of failure. It may be that, set in the context of the defining objective of corporate insolvency, liquidation was the type of restructuring that was required in most cases. Secondly, administrative receiverships may have allowed the business to be salvaged, although the company went under. Indeed the rescue culture in the US with its "debtor-in-possession", in the form of a retention by existing management of their full powers as contained in Chap.11 of the US Bankruptcy Code, has been much debated and come in for much adverse criticism in the US.[8] Several countries in recent years have introduced variations on the administration order procedure including Canada, Australia, and the Irish Republic.[9] Drawing on experience in other jurisdictions, and in particular the working of the Australian model,[10] the Government in July 2001 published proposals in a White Paper, *Insolvency—A Second Chance*.[11] The proposals were subsequently incorporated into the Enterprise Act 2002, which effects what is a wholesale reform of the administration and administrative receivership procedure in the UK. Much of the thinking behind the proposals in the Enterprise Act 2002 is based on the assumption that, if only the procedures of administration were simplified and more finely tuned, many more companies would be rescued as going concerns. The evidence adduced to support this assumption was largely anecdotal, and shows little regard to the difficulty of transposing a company rescue model from one jurisdiction to another with a different history and culture.

Reforms introduced by the Enterprise Act 2002

Section 248 of the Enterprise Act 2002 replaces Pt II of the Insolvency Act 1986 with a new Sch.B1—as set out in Sch.16 to the Insolvency Act 2002. Schedule B1 now contains in one document almost all of a code governing companies and administration.[12] **5–02**

The focus of new corporate insolvency code contained in the Enterprise Act 2002 is to restrict the use of administrative receivership. The aim is to make the procedure more a collective procedure in favour of all the creditors rather than administrative receivership which gives the floating charge holder effective control of any reorganisation. A second aim is to streamline and speed up the administration process.

Restriction on the appointment of an administrative receiver

The key section of the Enterprise Act 2002 in relation to the restriction on the appointment of an administrative receiver is s.250. A new Ch.IV of Pt III of the Insolvency Act 1986 is inserted by s.250. In terms of new **5–03**

---

[8] See Bradley & Rosenzweig (1992) 101 Yale L.J. 1043; Lopucki (1992) 91 Mich. L. Rev. 79 and (1993) Wisc.L.Rev. 729; and Warren (1992) 102 Yale L.J. 437.

[9] For accounts of procedures in other jurisdictions see Tay (1993) 2 I.I.R. 43; Ogilvie [1994] J.B.L. 304; Harmer (1993) 2 I.I.R. 74; Fruchtman (1994) 3 I.R.R. 33; and G. McCormack (1990) 1 I.L.L.& P.94. Comparative observations are given in Fletcher (1994) 2 *Insolvency Law Journal* 110–125.

[10] See the voluntary administration procedure contained in Pt 5.3A of the Australian Corporations Act 1989, as inserted in 1993. A key difference between the Australian model and that eventually adopted by the UK Government in the Enterprise Act 2002 is that, in Australia, the second objective of maximising the return to creditors is only open if it is not possible for the company or its business to continue in existence.

[11] Cmnd. 5234, July 2001.

[12] Certain types of companies are exempt from the code or have their own special administration regimes (see paras 5–07 to 5–10).

s.72A(2) of the Insolvency Act 1986, now contained in Chap.IV of Pt III of the Insolvency Act 1986; "[i]n Scotland, the holder of a qualifying floating charge in respect of a company's property may not appoint or apply to the court for the appointment of a receiver who on appointment would be an administrative receiver of property of the company". Previously a holder of a qualifying floating charge could effectively frustrate the administration procedure by the appointment of an administrative receiver.[13]

Transitional provisions and "prescribed part"

5–04   The new restriction on the appointment of an administrative receiver is, however, subject to an important qualification. It only applies to floating charges created on or after September 15, 2003.[14] This means that for years ahead—perhaps decades—receivership shall continue in Scotland alongside the new administration procedure. If, of course, the new administration procedure proved a success, it might encourage holders of qualifying floating charges created before the appointed day to create new charges, and thus be subject to the new administration procedure. There is, however, one significant disincentive to this manoeuvre. Floating charges created after September 15, 2003 do not catch the "prescribed part",[15] which is a specified part of the assets (if they are sufficient) of a company which are now set aside for ordinary creditors but which previously would have gone to the holder of the floating charge. A sort of understood *quid pro quo* for the "prescribed part" was the abolition of Crown preferences. What holders of floating charges created on or after September 15, 2003 were to lose in the "prescribed part" they would recoup from the assets which previously would go to the Crown as preferred debts. The holders of floating charges created before September 15, 2003,[16] however, get the *quid* without giving the *quo*. They are in the paradoxical position of now participating in the assets which previously would have gone to the Crown as Crown preferences, but without having to forego the "prescribed part". The banks have been handed a large short term windfall.[17]

Streamlining of procedure

5–05   The second most important change in relation to administration is that administrators may now be appointed by an out-of-court route by holders of floating charges, companies or their own directors.[18] A court route, however, is still retained.

---

[13] See generally *Re Croftbell Ltd* [1990] B.C.C. 781. An "administrative receiver" in terms of s.251 of the Insolvency Act 1986 in relation to Scotland means a receiver appointed under s.51 of that Act in a case where the whole (or substantially the whole) of the company's property is attached by the floating charge.

[14] S.72A(4) of the Insolvency Act 1986 as inserted by s.250 of the Enterprise Act 2002.

[15] SI 2003/2097 (see para.19–25).

[16] The appointed date for the purposes of s.72A(4)(a) of the Insolvency Act 1986 was September 15, 2003 (Insolvency Act 1986, S.72A (Appointed Date) Order 2003 (SI 2003/2095)).

[17] It is difficult to estimate the size of this windfall, but it is many hundreds of millions of pounds. See Jill Treanor, in the *Guardian*, June 23, 2003, where it is stated that insolvency practitioners estimate that for several years the banks will get a windfall of £400m a year as a result of changes to the rules for winding up companies with pre-existing loans.

[18] Previously only a court could appoint an administrator (s.8 of the Insolvency Act 1986, as originally enacted).

Duty of administrator to all creditors

An administrative receiver primarily owes duties to his or her **5–06** appointer—usually the main creditor—and any guarantor of that debt, but not to the company's creditors as a whole and also an administrative receiver has no duty to seek to put together a company rescue in the same way that an administrator has.[19] In terms of the new legislation an administrator is an officer of the court, whether or not he is appointed by the court,[20] and in exercising his functions the administrator of a company acts as its agent.[21] Finally, and most importantly from a legal point of view, there is a general duty on an administrator "to perform his functions in the interests of the company's creditors as a whole"[22] and to realise property in order to make a distribution to one or more secured or preferential creditors, only if he does not unnecessarily harm the interests of the creditors of the company as a whole.[23]

It is difficult to know whether the legal fine tuning in relation to the status and duties of an administrator will change the attitudes and culture of insolvency practitioners (who still have a monopoly of this type of work[24]). They may continue instinctively and for business reasons to see their interests very much bound up with the interests of their main clients—their sponsoring banks. The banks with qualifying floating charges[25] will effectively have the right to intervene and appoint their own man as administrator instead of the one proposed by the company or its directors.[26]

Companies not subject to the new administration procedure

Special administration regimes

Certain types of organisation, prior to the coming into force of the **5–07** Enterprise Act 2002, had their own statutory administration regimes usually because there was a public interest in the activity of the

---

[19] For duties owed by an administrative receiver, see *Medford v Blake* [1999] 2 B.C.L.C. 221.

[20] See para.5 of new Sch.B1 to the Insolvency Act 1986.

[21] Paragraph 69 of new Sch.B1 to the Insolvency Act 1986.

[22] See para.3(2) of new Sch.B1 to the Insolvency Act 1986.

[23] See para.3(4)(b) of new Sch.B1 to the Insolvency Act 1986.

[24] See para.6 of new Sch.B1 to the Insolvency Act 1986.

[25] A "qualifying floating charge" is defined in paragraph 14(2) of new Sch. B1 to the Insolvency Act 1986 as an instrument which:

"(a) states that paragraph 14 applies to the floating charge,

(b) purports to empower the holder of the floating charge to appoint an administrator of a company,

(c) purports to empower the holder of the floating charge to make an appointment which would be the appointment of an administrative receiver within the meaning given by s.29(2), or

(d) purports to empower the holder of a floating charge in Scotland to appoint a receiver who on appointment would be an administrative receiver."

Alternatively, in terms of sub-paragraph (3), a person is a holder of a "qualifying floating charge" if he holds one or more debentures secured over the whole or substantially the whole of the company's property.

[26] Paragraphs 14 and 26 of new Sch.B1 to the Insolvency Act 1986 give the holder of a qualifying charge the opportunity to appoint his own administrator while the notice period is running of a notice by the company or its directors of intention to appoint an administrator.

organisation continuing intact. The special administration regimes in relation to these organisations are preserved by s.249 of the Enterprise Act 2002, and they are not subject to the administration regime introduced by that Act. The organisations concerned are:

(a) a company holding an appointment under Chap.I of Pt II of the Water Industry Act 1991;

(b) a protected railway company within the meaning of s.59 of the Railways Act 1993 including that section as it has effect by virtue of s.19 of the Channel Tunnel Rail Link Act 1996;

(c) a licensed company within the meaning of s.26 of the Transport Act 2000;

(d) a public private partnership company within the meaning of s.210 of the Greater London Authority Act 1999;

(e) a building society within the meaning of section 119 of the Building Societies Act 1986.

Incidentally the bodies referred to in (a) to (c) above are still entitled to appoint an administrative receiver.[27] Also a public-private partnership company within the meaning of s.210 the Greater London Authority Act 1999 may appoint an administrative receiver in terms of s.72C of the Insolvency Act 1986.[28] (That is because all present project companies in category (d) meet the criteria of s.72C.) The final category (e)—building societies—cannot grant a floating charge.

Special administration regimes/Insurance companies and banks

5–08   The provisions in relation to administration contained in new Sch.B1 to the Insolvency Act 1986 also does not apply to insurance companies, which—apart from Lloyd's—have their own administration procedure in terms of the Financial Services and Markets Act 2000 (Administration Orders Relating to Insurers) Order 2002 (S.I. 2002/1242), as amended by the Financial Services and Markets Act 2000 (Administration Orders Relating to Insurers) (Amendment) Order 2003 (S.I. 2003/2134).[29]

---

[27] See s.72GA of the Insolvency Act 1986, as inserted by the Insolvency Act 1986 (Amendment) (Administrative Receivership and Urban Regeneration Etc.) Order 2003 (SI 2003/1832). That Order was made under s.72H of the Insolvency Act 1986, which was inserted by s.250 of the Enterprise Act 2002.

[28] S.72C of the Insolvency Act 1986 was inserted by s.250 of the Enterprise Act 2002.

[29] Paragraph 9(2) of new Sch.B1 to the Insolvency Act 1986. Since April 20, 2003, a UK court may not make an administration order in respect of an EEA insurer (an insurer authorised in an EEA state other than the UK to carry out direct insurance within the meaning of the first life and first non-life directives (Nos 79/276/EEC and 73/239/EEC)) under the terms of reg.4(1) of the Insurers (Reorganisation and Winding Up) Regulations 2003 (SI 2003/ 1102), which implement EC Directive 2001 /17/EC. In general terms the effect of the directive and the implementing regulations is that an insurer which is authorised in the European Economic Area may only be the subject of relevant insolvency proceedings in its home Member State, and requires mutual recognition across the EEA of this home Member State proceedings. That mutual recognition is facilitated, for example, by provisions requiring States to ensure that insolvency officials such as liquidators or administrators may exercise the powers conferred under the home Member State law in all other Member States. Like the EC Insolvency Regulation (Council Regulation (EC) No. 1346/2000), from the scope of which insurance undertakings and credit institutions are excluded with their own directives, there are exceptions such as set-off, retention of title, security over real property, etc.

Administration as regards insurers came into force on May 31, 2002.[30] This restriction, however, does not apply to companies which are exempt from the general prohibition in relation to effecting or carrying out contracts of insurance in terms of s.19 of the Financial Services and Markets Act 2000.[31] The restriction does not apply also to an authorised deposit taker effecting or carrying out contracts of insurance in the course of a banking business.[32] An "authorised deposit taker" means a person with permission under Pt IV of the Financial Services and Markets Act 2000 to accept deposits.

Administration orders used not to be available to banks and to authorised institutions under the Banking Act 1987. Administrators may now be appointed in the case of banks which are authorised institutions or former authorised institutions under the Banking Act 1987, which have their own specially tailored regime.[33] Still not covered by any administration regime is a person who has a liability in respect of a deposit which is accepted in accordance with the Banking Act 1979 or 1987, but is not an authorised deposit taker under Pt IV of the Financial Services and Markets Act 2000.[34] However, power is taken in the Enterprise Act 2000 to apply to non-authorised deposit takers a regime similar to that for authorised deposit takers.[35]

Companies subject to new regime but preserving right to appoint administrative receiver

A halfway house to the full administration regime under the new **5–09** procedures are six types of organisation which are subject to the new administration regime, but nevertheless are entitled to appoint an administrative receiver if they choose. The types of organisation are set out in ss.72B to 72G of the Insolvency Act 1986.[36] The organisations are: market arrangement companies,[37] public private partnerships,[38] util-

---

[30] It is thought that the first case of an administration order on an insurance company was that on July 19, 2002 in respect of Folksam International Insurance Company (UK) Limited, an English registered company. Details of that administration are to be found in a website dedicated to the administration by PriceWaterhouseCoopers. (It details also, *inter alia*, how US courts extended the protection available to the administrator in respect of US assets under s.304 of the United States Bankruptcy Code.)

[31] Paragraph 9(3) of new Sch.B1 to the Insolvency Act 1986.

[32] *ibid.*

[33] The Banks (Administration Proceedings) Order 1989 (SI 1989/1276, as amended by SI 1998/1129, art.2, Sch.1, para.9) which applies Pt II of the Insolvency Act 1986 to companies which are authorised institutions or former authorised institutions under the Banking Act 1987.

[34] Paragraph 9(1) of new Sch.B1 to the Insolvency Act 1986.

[35] S.422 of the Insolvency Act 1986, as amended by para.35 of Sch.17 to the Enterprise Act 2000.

[36] These sections were inserted by s.250(1) of the Enterprise Act 2002.

[37] These are arrangements of a kind described in para.1 of new Sch.2A to the Insolvency Act 1986, as inserted by s.72H(2) of the Insolvency Act 1986 (inserted by s.250(1) of the Enterprise Act 2002). The definition in para.1 was amended as soon as it came into force by art.2 of the Insolvency Act 1986 (Amendment) (Administrative Receivership and Capital Market Arrangements) Order 2003 (SI 2003/1468).

[38] The relevant companies are "project companies" as described in para.7 of Sch.2A to the Insolvency Act 1986.

ities,[39] a financed project company,[40] companies subject to special charges,[41] and Registered Social Landlords.[42]

Companies which are fully subject to the new administration regime

5–10   Apart from the special cases outlined in the previous paragraphs, the full new administration procedure applies to all other companies which may be wound up including limited liability partnerships.[43] "Company" also includes unregistered companies.[44] Companies with a paid up share capital of under £120,000 may be wound up concurrently by the Court of Session and the Sheriff Court.[45] And since Art.3 of the EC Regulation on Insolvency Proceedings[46] came into force on May 31, 2002, an administration order may also be made where a company has its "centre of main interests" in Scotland irrespective of where it is registered.[47]

Circumstances in which an administrator may be appointed

5–11   The reforms of administration effected by the Enterprise Act 2002 are best understood as a development of the previous administration procedure. The circumstances in which an administration order could be

---

[39] A project company is an exception when it is a utility project designed wholly or mainly for the purpose of a "regulated business" of a kind listed in para.10 of new Sch.2A to Insolvency Act 1986.

[40] This is a project company within the meaning given in para.7 of Sch.2A of the Insolvency Act 1986, financed under an agreement carrying a debt of at least £50m for the purposes of carrying out the project (s.72E of the Insolvency Act 1986, as inserted by s.250(1) of the Enterprise Act 2002).

[41] The special charges concerned are:
   (a) a market charge within the meaning of s.173 of the Companies Act 1989;
   (b) a system-charge within the meaning of the Financial Markets and Insolvency Regulations 1996 (SI 1996/1469); and
   (c) a collateral security charge within the meaning of the Financial Markets and Insolvency (Settlement Finality) Regulations 1999 (SI 1999/2979).
These definitions are contained in s.72F of the Insolvency Act 1986, as inserted by s.250 of the Enterprise Act 2002.

[42] "Registered Social Landlord" is a company which is registered as a social landlord under Pt III of the Housing (Scotland) Act 2001 (asp 10).

[43] See the Limited Liability Partnerships Act 2000 and the modifications to the Insolvency Act 1986 set out in the provisions of reg.5 and Sch.3 to the Limited Liability Partnerships Regulations 2001 (SI 2001/1090).

[44] See s.220 of the Insolvency Act 1986.

[45] See s.120 of the Insolvency Act 1986. The sheriff may not put into administration companies limited by guarantee or unlimited companies: see *Pearce, Petr*, 1991 S.C.L.R. 861. There is no good reason why the sheriff court should not be given jurisdiction in the case of a company limited by guarantee, subject to the amount of the guarantee. However, this anomaly has not been rectified in the Enterprise Act 2002.

[46] Council Regulation 1346/2000.

[47] Effect is given to Art.3 of the EC Regulation by an amendment of s.8 of the Insolvency Act 1986. In the Insolvency Act 1986 (Amendment) (No.2) Regulations 2002 (SI 2002/1240), para.5 (effective May 31, 2002), Art.2 and Annexes A—C of the EC Regulation apply to administration proceedings. In Scotland the EC Regulation on Insolvency Proceedings on the Scottish law of administration has been implemented by the Insolvency (Scotland) Regulations 2003 (No.2109 (s.8)). See also for the interpretation of the EC Regulation's effect *Re BRAC Rent-A-Car Inc., The Times*, February 24, 2003; [2003] E.W.H.C. 128; [2003] 1 W.L.R. 1421 and *Re The Salvage Association, The Times*, May 21, 2003; [2003] E.W.H.C. 128; [2003] 3 All E.R. 246, *per* Blackburne J. He held that in terms of Art.3 of the EC Regulation, the court had jurisdiction to make an order in respect of a company and a "legal person". Hence an association incorporated by Royal Charter would be covered.

made were previously contained in s.8(1) of the Insolvency Act 1986. That section laid down two main conditions which had to be satisfied in order that a court might exercise the power to make an administration order in relation to a company. The first condition, imposed by s.8(1)(a), was that the court had to be satisfied that the company was, or was likely to become, unable to pay its debts. The second condition, imposed by former s.8(1)(b) of the Insolvency Act 1986 was that the court had to consider that the making of an administration order would be likely to achieve one or more of the administration purposes mentioned in s.8(3).

Court and new out of court route into administration/new administration purposes

The reforms contained in the Enterprise Act 2002 preserve the court **5–12** route into administration with more or less the same procedure as before. The two tests in former s.8(1) of the Insolvency Act 1986 are maintained, except that in the second test in s.8(1)(b) "likely to achieve" is watered down to "reasonably likely to achieve". The major changes are that (a) there is now a new out of court route into administration, which is described below; and (b) there is a new set or structure of administration purposes (which are described at para.5–16).

Having an out-of-court route into administration[48] necessarily has complicating knock-on procedural consequences. The scheme, as now contained in new Sch.B1 to the Insolvency Act 1986, envisages that the test of the company being, or likely to become, unable to pay its debts shall remain, subject to one qualification mentioned below. In an out-of-court route, this judgment must obviously be made by someone other than the court. In terms of the reforms, this judgment, in the case of a company, or its directors or the holder of a floating charge appointing an administrator, must be made by the company, or its directors or the holder of the floating charge—*i.e.* not by the administrator. However in the case of a holder of a floating charge, the test is different to that applying to the other categories of appointors. The test is whether the charge is enforceable at the date of the appointment,[49] which is not the same as the insolvency test in s.123 of the Insolvency Act 1986.[50] A second difference between the procedure where a holder of a floating charge appoints an administrator—as opposed to the company or its directors—is that the lodging of the statutory declaration and other documentation with the court is at the time of the appointment, whereas

---

[48] Although it is called an out-of-court route, documentation must still be filed or, in Scotland, lodged with a court, and the administrator is an officer of the court. It is doubted by the authors that these two nexuses with the court are sufficient to bring out of court administrations within "insolvency proceedings" for the purposes of the EC Insolvency Regulation (Council Regulation (EC) 1346/2000), and thus have their acts recognised in all the Member States (see also para.22–60 in relation to voluntary windings up and para.7–02 in relation to voluntary arrangements).

[49] See para.18(2)(b) of new Sch.B1 to the Insolvency Act 1986.

[50] This difference is described as a "qualification" because a floating charge would normally include an insolvency test, such as set out in s.123 of the Insolvency Act 1986, but it can also include other covenants, which if breached, would trigger the crystallisation of the floating charge.

with a company, or its directors, the lodging must be prior to the appointment—at the stage when there is notice being given of the intention to appoint an administrator.[51]

Administrator takes on court's role in judging the merits of proposals

5–13   A second important necessary difference in the way out-of-court routes work is that the judge's decision on the viability of an administration proposal is now transferred to the administrator himself. Accordingly when a holder of a floating charge appoints an administrator under para.14 of new Sch.B1 to the Insolvency Act 1986 or the company or its directors appoint an administrator under para.22 of that Schedule, a notice of appointment must be filed or in Scotland lodged with the court.[52] The notice of appointment must identify the administrator and must be accompanied by a statement by the administrator:

(a) that he consents to the appointment;
(b) that in his opinion the purpose of administration is reasonably likely to be achieved; and
(c) giving such other information and opinions as may be prescribed under rules made under s.411 of the Insolvency Act 1986.[53]

The provisions concerning the notice of appointment are identical for the holder of a floating charge and a company or its directors.[54] The effect of these provisions is to transfer the decision making in relation to whether an administration proposal is viable to the administrator himself. No further procedure is required, once the relevant notices of appointment have been lodged with the court, with the administration and the appointment of the administrator taking effect at the date of the lodging of the notice of appointment and the accompanying documentation with the court.[55]

Company "unable to pay its debts"

5–14   The first test to qualify for administration in former s.8(1)(a) of the Insolvency Act 1986 was that the court had to be satisfied that the company was, or was likely to become, unable to pay its debts (within

---

[51] In relation to Scotland the rules governing the appointment of administrators are contained in the Insolvency (Scotland) Rules 1986, as amended by the Insolvency (Scotland) Amendment Rules 2003 (SI 2003/2111)(S9)). That last instrument basically inserts a new Pt II into the Insolvency (Scotland) Rules 1986. That Part sets out the relevant rules in relation to the appointment of an administrator and also prescribes forms that must be used.

[52] Paragraph 18 of new Sch.B1 to the Insolvency Act 1986 in respect of a floating charge holder, and para.29 of that Schedule in respect of a company or its directors appointing an administrator.

[53] The relevant rules in relation to the documentation are contained in the Insolvency (Scotland) Amendment Rules 2003 (SI 2003/2111(S.9)), which amend the Insolvency (Scotland) Rules 1986 to substitute a new Pt 2 of those Rules covering the appointment of administrators, with also the relevant forms specified.

[54] Paragraph 18(3) of new Sch.B1 to the Insolvency Act 1986 in respect of a holder of a floating charge, and para.29(3) of that Schedule in respect of a company or its directors.

[55] Paragraph 19 of new Sch.B1 to the Insolvency Act 1986 in respect of an administrator appointed by a floating charge holder and para.31 of that Schedule in respect of the appointment of an administrator by a company or its directors.

the meaning of the provision contained in s.123 of the Insolvency Act 1986).[56] A particular problem arose early as to the threshold of probability necessary to satisfy the test if a company was not presently unable to pay its debts. The threshold of that test and the further tests of likelihood of achieving administration purposes contained in former s.8(1)(b) were discussed by Hoffmann J. in the case of *Re Harris Simons Construction Ltd*[57] and in the case of *Re Imperial Motors (UK) Ltd*,[58] in which he dealt with the degree of likelihood required by s.8(1)(b). In the latter case he held that on the facts of that case the company was not unable to pay its debts within the meaning of s.123 of the Insolvency Act 1986 by its being insolvent in the sense that its liabilities exceeded its assets. It was, however, insolvent within the meaning of s.123(1)(e) of the Insolvency Act 1986 as it could not pay its debts as they fell due. Nevertheless, in determining whether or not to make an administration order he held that he had to balance the interests of the petitioning creditor company in achieving a more advantageous realisation of the company's assets on the one hand, and on the other hand the interests of the company, its shareholders and management in not having the business of the company taken out of their hands. Because the interests of the petitioning creditor appeared to be adequately secured, and therefore the risk to them in not making the order was not great, it was not appropriate to make an order. It is difficult to know whether the appointer of an administrator, under the new procedure, should exercise that type of discretion before appointing an administrator, or whether merely to show that the company is unable to pay its debts is sufficient. It is thought on balance that the Hoffmann test should be applied, and that a slight risk to a secured creditor is not sufficient to warrant an administration. The issue of the threshold of likelihood was considered in depth in the recent case of *Highberry Limited v Colt Telecom Group plc (No.2)*[59] in which it was held that the court had to be satisfied that insolvency was more likely than not. The different wording in s.8(1)(a) and 8(1)(b) indicated different thresholds of persuasion, and it could not have been intended that companies be exposed to petitions for administration unless it was shown that rescue was probably needed.

Reasonable likelihood of attainment of an authorised purpose

Section 8(1)(b) of the Insolvency Act 1986 imposed a condition that the court must consider that the making of an administration order would be likely to achieve one or more of the purposes mentioned in subs.(3).[60] **5–15**

[56] For a full discussion of the meaning of this term see paras 4–106 to 4–111 in Chap.4.
[57] [1989] 5 B.C.L.C. 11 at 13.
[58] [1990] B.C.L.C. 29.
[59] *Sub nom. Colt Telecom Group plc, Re (No.2)* [2002] E.W.H.C. 2815; [2003] B.P.I.R. 324, Ch.D. (Companies Court), *per* Jacob J.
[60] S.8(3) of the Insolvency Act 1986 listed the following four purposes:
"(i) the survival of the company, and a whole or any part of its undertaking, as a going concern;
(ii) the approval of a voluntary arrangement under Part I of the Insolvency Act;
(iii) the sanctioning under section 425 of the Companies Act 1985 of a compromise or arrangement between the company and any such persons as are mentioned in that section; and
(iv) a more advantageous realisation of the company's assets than would be realised on a winding up."

The test now is that the administration order is "reasonably likely" to achieve the purpose of administration.[61] It is thought that the qualification of the likelihood by reasonableness is not significant, given the courts' attitude to commercial judgements of administrators.[62] Unsurprisingly the word "likely" in s.8 of the Insolvency Act 1986 has proved contentious and controversial. Its construction has been the main area of focus of any court contemplating administration proceedings. In the early case of *Re Consumer & Industrial Press*,[63] Peter Gibson J. adopted a restrictive interpretation in holding that an administration order would only be granted if it was more probable than not that it would achieve its aim. He stated:

> "As I read s8 the court must be satisfied on the evidence put before it that at least one of the purposes in s8(3) is likely to be achieved if it is to make an administration order. That does not mean that it is merely possible that such purpose will be achieved; the evidence must go further than that to enable the court to hold that the purpose in question will more probably than not be achieved."

By contrast, in *Re Harris Simons Construction Ltd*,[64] Hoffman J. held that it sufficed that there was a real prospect that one or more of the stated purposes would be achieved, even if not as high on the probability scale as a figure in excess of 50 per cent. The same approach was adopted by Vinelott J. in *Re Primlaks (UK) Ltd*.[65] That approach would seem to be the proper test and is now the accepted position.[66]

Purposes of administration

5–16   Paragraph 3 of new Sch.B1 of the Insolvency Act 1986 replaces the four statutory purposes under former s.8(3) of the Insolvency Act 1986. In terms of para.3(1) to new Sch.B1 to the Insolvency Act 1986, the administrator of a company must perform his functions with the objective of:

> "(a) rescuing the company as a going concern, or
> (b) achieving a better result for the company's creditors as a whole than would be likely if the company were wound up (without first being in administration), or
> (c) realising property in order to make a distribution to one or more secured or preferential creditors."[67]

---

[61] Paragraph 11(b) (in relation to court appointed administrators) and paras 18(3)(b) and 29(3)(b) (in relation to administrators appointed by a floating charge holder or by a company or its directors) of new Sch.B1 to the Insolvency Act 1986.

[62] See *Re: T & D Industries* plc *(in administration)* [2000] 1 B.C.L.C. 471; [2000] 1 All E.R. 333.

[63] [1988] B.C.L.C. 177.

[64] [1989] 5 B.C.C.11.

[65] [1989] 5 B.C.C.510.

[66] See *Re Rowbotham Baxter Ltd* [1990] B.C.L.C. 397, *per* Harman J.; and *Re SCL Building Services Ltd* [1990] B.C.L.C. 1998; and *Re Land and Property Trust Co plc* [1991] B.C.C. 446.

[67] No longer are there specific references to the approval of voluntary arrangements or sanctioning of schemes under s.425 of the Companies Act 1985, but this is only to give these two methods of achieving restructuring less emphasis and not in any way to preclude them.

Although a certain scepticism may be in order[68] as to whether the change of the purposes of administration will in practice lead to an increased success rate in salvaging financially viable companies which have hit problems, there is no doubt that the legal language used in the reforms introduced by the Enterprise Act 2002 is very different to that in s.8(3) of the Insolvency Act 1986. The change of language was bitterly contested in Parliament.[69] The wording of para.3(1) of new Sch.B1 to the Insolvency Act 1986 can only be understood with the aid of the Ministerial statements made to Parliament. First, the expression "rescuing the company" was stated by Ministers to mean much more than saving the company as a rump or shell. It was stated by the Minister for E-Commerce and Competitiveness, Douglas Alexander, to mean "to rescue it as a going concern, with the whole or much of its business intact.[70] (This formulation of Douglas Alexander is different to the interpretation given in the Explanatory Notes at para.647 where the expression is taken to mean "the company and as much of its business as possible".)

The statement by Douglas Alexander that a company must be rescued as a going concern, with the whole or much of its business intact sets a higher objective for administration than that set in s.8(3) of the Insolvency Act 1986, where the test is the survival of the company, and the whole or any part of its undertaking, as a going concern. "Much" must mean a substantial part of the formulation. Concern was expressed during the passage of the Enterprise Act through Parliament that it failed to address the importance of the preservation of employment by not making a purpose of administration the survival of a business, as opposed to the survival of the company as a going concern. The original Cork Committee had been concerned to salvage viable parts of businesses as going concerns to preserve employment and prevent the dissipation of economic assets and collections of skills. Its original formula was "rehabilitating the company or preserving all or part of its business as a going concern". The new formula does not have a primary objective of the hiving-off from the company of the whole or part of its undertaking as a going concern, if the company itself does not survive as a going concern. Those promoting a proposal along the second lines would have to fall back on the second purpose in para.3(1), namely "achieving a better result for the company's creditors as a whole than would be likely if the company were wound up (without first being in administration). Indeed, Douglas Alexander stated in Parliament that he recognised that there would be some cases in which the break up and sale of some or all of a company's individual businesses as a going concern would result in a better return for the creditors.

However, in making the statement Douglas Alexander was underplaying, or rather fudging, his rejection of the *Cork* option[71] of having

---

[68] See para.5–01.

[69] All the *Hansard* references and dates of debates are to be found in para.801 of the Explanatory Notes which are published on the HMSO website.

[70] House of Commons, Standing Committee B, 14th sitting on May 9, 2002 at col.549.

[71] And also very much a primary objective of the Australian model, on which the DTI was saying the new UK model was based.

the survival of a business (as opposed to the survival of the company) as an objective of administration. His implication was that, if businesses were viable, their sale should obtain a better return for creditors than a break up. This, of course, is not necessarily the case. Businesses, for example, might have to have an injection of capital to make them acceptable to the transferee, with the financing at the expense of creditors.

The new formulation of objectives, which was subject to much debate within government, now underlines just how much the British system of administration is tilted in favour of creditors' rights. This is further underlined by the fact that an administrator, in terms of para.3(3)(b) of new Sch.B1 to the Insolvency Act 1986, has the alternative option of organising the company's affairs through administration in order to get the best deal for creditors as a whole without any attempt to rescue the company as a going concern. To qualify for this option two conditions must be met: (a) administration must be likely to achieve a better deal for creditors as a whole than rescuing the company as a going concern[72]; and (b) administration must implicitly be likely to achieve a better result for creditors as a whole than going straight into winding up.[73]

A final objective of administration in terms of para.3(1)(c) of new Sch.B1 to the Insolvency Act 1986 is to realise property in order to make a distribution to one or more secured or preferential creditors. This objective is not an alternative objective to rescuing the company as a going concern or achieving a better result for the company's creditors as a whole than going straight into winding up. Rather it may only be set as an objective if the first two objectives are not reasonably practicable. There is a further condition that it must not unnecessarily harm the interests of the creditors of the company as a whole.[74]

Restrictions on appointment of an administrator

(1) Winding up

5–17   An administrator may not be appointed if the company is in liquidation by virtue of a resolution for voluntary winding up, or a winding up order.[75] This restriction is subject to a new procedure set out in paras 37 and 38 of new Sch.B1 to the Insolvency Act 1986. It is now open to the holder of a qualifying floating charge, who but for a liquidation order could appoint an administrator under the new legislation to apply to the court for an administration order which discharges the winding up order and institutes an administration.[76] Similarly a liquidator of any company which has gone into liquidation may apply to the court for an administration order.[77]

---

[72] Insolvency Act 1986, para.3(3)(b) of new Sch.B1.
[73] *ibid.*, para.3(1)(b) of new Sch.B1.
[74] *ibid.*, para.3(4)(b) of new Sch.B1.
[75] *ibid.*, para.8(1) of new Sch.B1.
[76] *ibid.*, para.37 of new Sch.B1.
[77] *ibid.*, para.38 of new Sch.B1.

(2) Administrative receivership

An administrator may not be appointed if a holder of a floating **5–18** charge has appointed an administrative receiver, unless the person by or on behalf of whom the receiver was appointed consents to the making of the administration order.[78] An administration order may also not be made if the court thinks that the security by virtue of which the receiver was appointed would be avoided under s.245 (avoidance of floating charge) if an administration order were made,[79] or the court thinks that the security by virtue of which the receiver was appointed would be challengeable under ss.242 (gratuitous alienations) or 243 (unfair preferences) or under any rule of law in Scotland.[80] On a strict wording of para.39(1) of new Sch.B1 to the Insolvency Act 1986 the court is only deciding a hypothetical issue as to whether floating charges may be challengeable under ss.242, 243 and 245 of the Insolvency Act 1986. Nevertheless, it is thought that the court would determine the question of the validity of the floating charge before making an administration order.

Although administrative receivership is destined to be reserved for special cases of companies, transitional provisions mean that old floating charges created before September 15, 2003 remain effective. This gives the holders of those floating charges the potentially valuable option of blocking an administration. The option is virtually uncircumscribed because the court will not look behind a floating charge or disregard it simply because it may have been demanded by a bank solely to give it the option of forestalling the possibility of an administration order. A floating charge, by its very nature, is capable of covering *acquirenda*, and it is therefore immaterial that, at the date that the floating charge was granted, there were little or no assets to be secured by the charge. A charge created merely for its function of being able to block the appointment of an administrator has become known as a "lightweight floating charge".[81]

Administration procedure

Prior to the reforms in the Enterprise Act 2002, administrators could **5–19** only be appointed by a court order in terms of s.8 of the Insolvency Act 1986. Now that paras 14 to 34 of new Sch.B1 to the Insolvency Act 1986 allow for the holder of the floating charges and companies or their directors to appoint administrators without a court hearing, two procedures are obviously needed, *i.e.* a court route procedure and an out of-court route procedure.

Court route procedure

Paragraph 12 of new Sch.B1 to the Insolvency Act 1986 lists the **5–20** persons who are entitled to present a petition for an administration order. These are the company itself or the directors; or a creditor or

---

[78] Insolvency Act 1986, para.39(1)(a) of new Sch.B1.
[79] *ibid.*, para.39(1)(c) of new Sch.B1.
[80] Paragraph 39(1)(c) and (d) of new Sch.B1. The "any rule of law" provision is to cover challenges at common law.
[81] See Oditah: "Lightweight Floating Charges", Journal of Business Law [1991] 49: and *Re Croftbell Ltd* [1990] B.C.C. 781.

creditors (which includes any contingent or prospective creditor or creditors); or all or any of those parties acting together or separately.

A company has sufficient title and interest to present a petition to be wound up under s.124 of the Insolvency Act 1986. The company has an interest, quite apart from the members as contributories who would have no interest in a company that is wholly insolvent, in having its affairs properly conducted and adequately wound up, and in satisfying its duties to pay its debts, or at least, to have them met *pari passu* out of its assets when it is wholly insolvent. By the same token, because of the close similarities between a winding up under s.124 and a petition for an administration order under para.12 to new Sch.B1 to the Insolvency Act 1986, a company has sufficient interest to present a petition for an administration order.[82]

In relation to the directors, the Act requires the directors to act collectively in presenting a petition for an administration order. The use in para.12(1)(b) of new Sch.B1 to the Insolvency Act 1986 of the expression "the directors" and the lack of any alternative reference to "director" in the singular form, means that an individual director, or indeed a group of directors forming a minority on the board may not present a petition for an administration order.[83] Where the board of directors acts collectively, there is no requirement within the Insolvency Act 1986 that the directors must obtain the prior endorsement of a general meeting of the members before they validly present a petition. The members themselves, of course, can resolve that the company shall apply for an administration order in terms of para.12(1)(a). In exceptional cases, it has been held that the Chief Executive Officer of a parent company had presumptive authority to act in the name of the company, but this was only because such a presumption existed at law in the place of registration of the company.[84] Where the administration order is sought by secured creditors, their interests are weighted lighter than those of unsecured creditors, since the unsecured creditors have been held to have more to lose.[85] It is thought that this principle is now reflected in the emphasis in para.3 of new Sch.B1 to the Insolvency Act 1986 on the interests of the creditors "as a whole". In addition to the persons listed above, the Financial Services Authority may make an application for an administration order in relation to certain persons in terms of section 359 of the Financial Services and Markets Act 2000.[86]

Once an administration application has been made, the applicant must notify the persons prescribed by r.2.3(1) of the Insolvency (Scotland)

---

[82] *Re Land and Property Trust Co plc* [1991] B.C.L.C. 845.

[83] *Re Instrumentation Electrical Services Ltd* [1988] 4 B.C.C. 301, as interpreted in *Re Equiticorp International plc* [1989] 5 B.C.C. 599. See also the definition in para.105 of new Sch.B1 to the Insolvency Act 1986.

[84] *Re MTI Trading Systems Ltd* [1997] B.C.C. 703.

[85] *Re Consumer & Industrial Press Ltd* [1988] 4 B.C.C. 68; *Re Imperial Motors (UK) Ltd* [1989] 5 B.C.C. 214.

[86] S.359 was substituted by para.55 of Sch.17 to the Enterprise Act 2002; see that section also for special test of "unable to pay its debts".

Rules 1986.[87] The contents of the petition are also prescribed. The application for administration cannot be withdrawn without the permission of the court.[88] On hearing an administration application, the court may make the administration order sought, dismiss the application, adjourn the hearing conditionally or unconditionally, or make such other order which the court thinks appropriate.[89]

Effect of dismissal of administration petition

If the court decides not to make an administration order, the normal **5–21** practice will be to dismiss the petition, leaving winding up as the likeliest alternative route for the company to follow. Where an administration order petition has been presented reasonably and on appropriate professional advice, it has been held that the costs incurred in the administration order application down to the hearing at which it was dismissed, could be treated as allowable costs in the subsequent winding up.[90] The underlying rationale is that it would otherwise be difficult for directors, solicitors or accountants to act in good faith in preparing and presenting an administration order to recover the costs thereby incurred. This would work against the legislative intention which is that the administration course should be adopted wherever practical as the best method of averting a winding up. Harman J. held in the case of *Re Land and Property Trust Co (No 3),*[91] that that course had not been followed. He stated:

"I entirely follow that directors who are doing their best to save their companies and who make an ill-advised, as it turns out, presentation of an administration petition, should not normally be penalised by an order to pay costs personally. I do accept that it has to be shown that there are exceptional reasons in the conduct of the matter why the directors personally should be called upon to answer for what are undoubtedly their personal resolutions . . . But the facts of these petitions do not give any hint that that careful process was here adopted. The main petition, seeking an administration order in respect of the parent company of the group was first presented. There then followed in pell-mell haste these 29 petitions in respect of the subsidiary companies. The petitions existed for only a few days including a weekend, and were abandoned by leading counsel for the companies without any attempt to urge the court to grant the petitions. I can only infer that experienced leading counsel on reading the evidence available in opposition considered, and if he did he was in my judgment correct, that the petitions were all absolutely doomed to failure. The gap of 21 days between the board's resolution and the date of presentation does not seem to have been taken up, at least there is

---

[87] As amended by SI 2003/2111; para.12(2) of new Sch.B1 to the Insolvency Act 1986.
[88] Paragraph 12(3) of new Sch.B1 to the Insolvency Act 1986.
[89] Paragraph 13(1) of new Sch.B1 to the Insolvency Act 1986.
[90] *Re Gosscott (Groundworks) Limited* [1988] B.C.L.C. 363; see in contrast *Re W.F. Fearman Ltd (No. 2)* (1988) 4 B.C.C. 141.
[91] [1991] B.C.L.C. 856; this view of Harman J. has superseded his previous judgment in *Re W.F. Fearman Ltd (No. 2)*, which is thought to be wrong.

no evidence that it was, by consultation with and consideration of the advice of the proposed administrators.

Thus the costs of the petitions were incurred not in reliance on the reports under r 2.2, although the costs were no doubt largely incurred after the signing of the report, but in pursuance of the directors' resolutions all passed in so short a space of time at noon on 7 January. It was those resolutions which authorised solicitors to incur costs on behalf of the companies. In my judgment I am entitled on the evidence and on the conduct of all these petitions before me to conclude that the directors never properly considered the matter on a basis of whether there was any real risk of flooding the market or any real benefit to be attained by the making of administration orders, and simply embarked on a course of action which had no rational prospect of succeeding in a perhaps desperate attempt to free the companies from the intense pressure by the various creditors."

First it is clear from this extract from Harman J.'s judgment that directors of companies could be exposed to the costs of unsuccessful administration order applications, if they are irresponsibly brought. Secondly, it is thought that the directors could be personally exposed, if third parties suffer unnecessary losses as a result of the bringing of an administration order application in these circumstances. Thirdly, it is thought that solicitors acting for directors contemplating the bringing of an administration order petition are under a duty of care to advise the directors of these risks.

Interim orders of the court in Scotland

5–22   As regards the power to make an interim order, the courts initially interpreted the predecessor s.9(4) of the Insolvency Act 1986 as enabling them to appoint an interim administrator prior to a final decision on the petition.[92] In that case its competence was not disputed, but the competence was later disputed in the case of *Avenel Hotel Ltd*, March 1987 (unreported), but again such an order was held to be competent. In England and Wales, the court took the view that, although it was competent to appoint a person to take control of the company and manage its affairs, it was not competent to appoint an interim administrator as such.[93] This is now rejected in the light of the cases of *Secretary of State for Trade & Industry v Palmer*,[94] and *Care Scotland plc*,

---

[92] *Air Ecosse Ltd* (1987), unreported in relation to the initial decision to make an interim order. In England an administration order can be made even prior to the presentation of the petition, where supporting evidence convinces a court that an administration order would, in due course, be made (*Cavco Floors Limited* [1990] B.C.L.C. 940; and *Re Chancery plc* [1991] B.C.L.C. 712, where Harman J. granted an administration order, when there had not been proper service and held the hearing in camera). For a detailed comparison of the issue of interim orders in England and Wales, and Scotland, see Donna McKenzie Skene and Yvonne Enoch, "Petitions for Administration Orders where there is a Need for Interim Measures: a Comparative Study of the Approach of the Courts in Scotland and in England and Wales", *Journal of Business Law*, March 2000.

[93] *Re a Company (No.00175 of 1987)* [1987] B.C.L.C. 467.

[94] 1995 S.L.T. 188.

petrs.[95] In that case although it was held that the appointment of an administrator *ad interim* as such was not competent, the court did appoint the proposed administrator to manage the company *ad interim.*[96] In addition to those powers there is now power under the reforms in the Enterprise Act 2002[97] to treat the application as a winding up petition and make any order which the court could make under s.125 of the Insolvency Act 1986. This gives statutory backing to the approach adopted by the court in refusing to make an administration order on the ground that a compulsory liquidation was the appropriate option in the circumstances in the case of *Re Arrows Ltd (No.3).*[98] In that case the court had the option of making a winding up order because there was a parallel petition for winding up on behalf of creditors.

Service of petition

Rule 2.3(1) of the Insolvency (Scotland) Rules 1986, as amended by the **5–23** Insolvency (Scotland) Rules 2003,[99] sets out the persons on whom a petitioner for an administration order must serve the petition. As well as any holder of a qualifying floating charge, the other persons are—

(a) an administrative receiver, if appointed;
(b) a member State liquidator, if one has been appointed in the main proceedings in relation to the company;
(c) if a petition for the winding up of the company has been presented but no order for winding up has yet been made, the petitioner under that petition;
(d) a provisional liquidator, if appointed;
(e) a person proposed in the petition to be the administrator;
(f) the registrar of companies;
(g) the Keeper of the Register of Inhibitions and Adjudications for recording in that register;
(h) the company, if the application is made by anyone other than the company; and
(i) the supervisor of a voluntary arrangement under Part I of the Insolvency Act 1986, if such has been appointed. The court can also order that the petition is served on other persons.

Contents of petition

Where an application is made by way of petition for an administration **5–24** order there a Statement of the Proposed Administrator must be lodged with a petition.[1] The Statement must be made by each of the persons proposed to be administrator of the company and must be in the form

---

[95] June 6, 1996, Outer House, unreported.
[96] For a full discussion of this issue see Donna McKenzie Skene and Yvonne Enoch, *Journal of Business Law*, March 2000, *supra.*
[97] Paragraph 13(1)(e) of new Sch.B1 to the Insolvency Act 1986.
[98] [1992] B.C.C. 131. The power in former s.9(4) of the Insolvency Act 1986 is very wide but it does not expressly allow a winding up order.
[99] SI 2003/2111 (S.9).
[1] Rule 2.2(1) of the Insolvency (Scotland) Rules 1986 as amended by the Insolvency (Scotland) Amendment Rules 2003.

required by r.7.30 of and Sch.5 to the Insolvency (Scotland) Rules 1986, as amended by SI 2003/2111. The Statement of the proposed administrator must state that he consents to accept appointment as administrator of the company, and must give details of any prior professional relationship that he has had with the company. It must also state that in his opinion it is reasonably likely that the purpose of administration will be achieved.

Indemnity for administrator appointed out of court

5–25   The statutory declarations to be made by the appointer out of court of an administrator, will no doubt force such appointors to carefully consider the validity of their right to appoint. In Scotland in terms of s.63(2) of the Insolvency Act 1986, where the appointment of a person as a receiver by the holder of a floating charge is discovered to be invalid (whether by virtue of the invalidity of the instrument or otherwise), the court may order the holder of the floating charge to indemnify the person appointed against any liability which arises solely by reason of the invalidity of the appointment.[2] A similar provision now applies to those who appoint administrators out of court, *i.e.* the holder of a floating charge, the company or its directors.[3]

Appointment of an administrator when a company is in liquidation

Prior to the Enterprise Act 2002, it was not competent to apply for an administration order when a company had gone into liquidation.[4] Under the reforms where a company has gone into compulsory liquidation it is now competent for the holder of a qualifying floating charge to make an administration application.[5] A liquidator in both a voluntary and compulsory winding up may make such an application.[6] If the court makes an administration order the court shall discharge any winding up order.[7] The court shall also specify which of the powers under new Sch.B1 are to be exercisable by the administrator and it may modify that Schedule.[8] In addition, where a court in Scotland makes an administration order in relation to a company which is in liquidation, the administration order shall contain consequential provisions, including—

(a) in the case of a liquidator in a voluntary winding up, his removal from office;
(b) provisions concerning the release of the liquidator, including his entitlement to recover expenses and to be paid his remuneration;

---

[2] In England the relevant section is s.34 of the Insolvency Act 1986.
[3] Paragraph 21 in respect of the holder of a qualifying floating charge, and para.34 in respect of a company or its directors, of new Sch.B1 to the Insolvency Act 1986.
[4] Former s.8(4) of the Insolvency Act 1986.
[5] Paragraph 37(1) and (2) of new Sch.B1 to the Insolvency Act 1986.
[6] Paragraph 38(1) of new Sch.B1 to the Insolvency Act 1986.
[7] Paragraphs 37(3)(a) and 38(2)(a) of new Sch.B1 to the Insolvency Act 1986.
[8] Paragraph 37(3)(d) and (e) and para.38(2)(d) and (e) of new Sch.B1 to the Insolvency Act 1986.

(c) provision for payment of the costs of the petitioning creditor in the winding up;

(d) provisions regarding any indemnity given to the liquidator;

(e) provisions regarding the handling or realisation of any of the company's assets under the control of the liquidator; and

(f) such other provisions as the court shall think fit.[9]

At present a court may sist or stay a compulsory winding up under s.147(1) of the Insolvency Act 1986.[10] This power,[11] if expressed in unlimited terms, has the effect of bringing the winding up process to an end with the company thereupon resuming the conduct of its business and affairs as if no winding up had existed.[12] The circumstances in which it is envisaged that a liquidator or holder of a qualifying floating charge might seek an administration order, would be where they were convinced that the company could be salvaged as a going concern or a much better result achieved for creditors than would result from an immediate break-up of the company. For this provision to be effective an administration application really needs to be as soon as possible after a winding up order has been made, or the company has gone into a creditors' voluntary liquidation. Otherwise changes to the commercial position of the company become irreversible. Perhaps it was a step too far for the Enterprise Act 2002 to impose a duty on liquidators, as soon as possible after taking office, to consider whether it might be better for the company and/or its creditors if an administration order were made, with a corresponding duty on courts hearing winding up petitions, to consider whether an administration order might be more appropriate.

Effect of administration

Dismissal of winding up petition

On the making of an administration order, or if the company is in **5–26** administration following an appointment of an administrator by the holder of a qualifying floating charge, any petition for the winding up of the company shall be dismissed.[13] That provision does not apply to a winding up petition presented under s.124A (public interest) or s.367 of the Financial Services and Markets Act 2000 (petition by the Financial Services Authority), and where an administrator becomes aware that a petition was presented under either of these provisions before his appointment he is obliged to apply to the court for directions.[14]

---

[9] These provisions are prescribed under paras 37(3)(b) and 38(2)(b) of new Sch.B1 to the Insolvency Act 1986 and are contained in r.2.3(1) of the Insolvency (Scotland) Rules 1986 (SI 1986/1915), as amended by the Insolvency (Scotland) Amendment Rules 2003 (SI 2003/2111 (s.9)).

[10] In the case of a voluntary winding up the proper approach is an application to the court under s.112 of the Insolvency Act 1986.

[11] Discussed in para.4–114.

[12] See *Austral Brick Co PTY Ltd v Falgat Constructions PTY Ltd* (1990) 2 A.C.S.R. at 766.

[13] Paragraph 40(1) to new Sch.B1 to the Insolvency Act 1986.

[14] Paragraph 40(2) and (3) of new Sch.B1 to the Insolvency Act 1986.

Dismissal of administrative or other receiver

5–27   When an administration order takes effect in respect of a company, any administrative receiver of a company must vacate office.[15] Also where a company is in administration, any receiver of part of the company's property must vacate office if the administrator requires him to.[16] Where an administrative receiver or receiver vacates office on respectively an administration order taking effect or a company being in administration, his remuneration is charged on and paid out of any property of the company which was in his custody or under his control immediately before he vacated office.[17]

Effect of administration on management of the company and the directors

5–28   Once the administrator is appointed, he has the general powers outlined later in this chapter. In addition, he has the power to appoint and remove directors,[18] and the power to call meetings of members and creditors.[19] This last power means that, although no resolution may be passed while an administration order is in force for the winding up of the company, the administrator may convene meetings for the purpose of commencing winding up, and time them so that when he has obtained a discharge he is ready to be appointed liquidator (as provided for in s.140(1) of the Insolvency Act 1986). Legal proceedings may be brought against the company only with the leave of the court or the administrator.[20] This would allow, for example, action under ss.459 to 461 of the Companies Act 1985 (protection of minority interests) although no order could be made for winding up. A petition in respect of unfair harm to interests by the administrator would not require leave.[21]

In terms of para.64 of new Sch.B1 to the Insolvency Act 1986 all powers of the company or its officers which could be exercised in such a way as to interfere with the exercise by the administrator of his powers cease to be exercisable except with the consent of the administrator, which may be given either generally or in relation to particular cases. The language suggests that the test for the continuance of any power in the directors is not whether a particular exercise of a particular power *would* interfere, but whether any exercise *could* interfere. This suggests that no powers will survive in the directors. It is difficult, however, to believe that the Insolvency Act 1986 intended to stop the directors

---

[15] Paragraph 41(1) of new Sch.B1 to the Insolvency Act 1986. This restriction applies only to an administration order taking effect because, in terms of para.17(b) of new Sch.B1 to the Insolvency Act 1986, an administrator may not be appointed by a holder of a floating charge under para.14(1) of that Schedule if an administrative receiver of the company is in office. Similarly, in terms of para.25(c) of new Sch.B1 to the Insolvency Act 1986, a company or its directors may not appoint an administrator under para.22 of that Schedule if an administrative receiver of the company is in office.

[16] Insolvency Act 1986, para.41(2) of new Sch.B1.

[17] *ibid.*, para.41(3)(a) of new Sch.B1.

[18] *ibid.*, para.61 of new Sch.B1.

[19] *ibid.*, para.62 of new Sch.B1.

[20] *ibid.*, para.43(6) of new Sch.B1.

[21] *ibid.*, para.74 of new Sch.B1.

applying to the court in the name of the company for the discharge of the administrator or of the administration order, or from appealing against the making of the administration order only because the administrator is given statutory powers to bring or defend proceedings in the name of the company. The granting of the directors' parallel powers to bring proceedings in the name of the company could not interfere with his own powers. Provided that the action is in relation to the appointment of an administrator, the administrator is entitled to defend any action or appeal, and none of his duties are interfered with. It is not an interference in his power to challenge his appointment, whereas to challenge an act of his would be.[22] There might be a problem, however, of how the directors would fund their legal action. They would probably not be able to use company money unless successful.

Moratorium on insolvency proceedings and other legal process

The provisions, formerly in s.11 of the Insolvency Act 1986, providing **5–29** the company with a moratorium on insolvency proceedings and other legal process have been largely re-enacted in paras 42 to 44 of new Sch.B1 to the Insolvency Act 1986. It is this moratorium or protection from creditors which is the defining feature of administration, as opposed to receivership or winding up. The main changes are dictated by the new out of court administration appointment procedure. As before, no resolution may be passed for the winding up of a company or order made for the winding up of a company where there is an administration order.[23] This provision also applies where there is an out of court appointment of an administrator.[24] These provisions create absolute prohibitions. The only exceptions being petitions to wind up the company under s.124A (public interest) of the Insolvency Act 1986, or s.367 of the Financial Services and Markets Act 2000 (a petition by the Financial Services Authority).[25] Prior to the making of an administration order or the out of court appointment of an administrator, the presentation of a winding up petition is not precluded.[26] Once a petition for an administration order has been presented, the court will accede to an application to restrain advertisement of the winding up petition until the administration petition has been heard, since the administration process has priority over all other processes. The reason is that it is contrary to the whole essence of the administration petition procedure that anything be done while the petition is pending to continue legal proceedings or do anything which might be seen in public to damage the company, such as the advertisement of a winding up petition. The reason that a winding up petition is allowed to be presented at any stage prior to the making of the administration order, is because of all the many important consequences that follow from the date of presentation of a winding up petition.[27] These considerations will apply in two cases in relation to out

---

[22] See discussion of residuary powers of directors (para.4–06).
[23] Paragraph 42 of new Sch.B1 to the Insolvency Act 1986.
[24] Paragraph 42 of new Sch.B1 to the Insolvency Act 1986.
[25] Paragraph 42(4) of new Sch.B1 to the Insolvency Act 1986.
[26] In relation to a petition for an administration order, this was formerly spelt out in s.10(2)(a) of the Insolvency Act 1986.
[27] *Re Manlon Trading Ltd* [1988] 4 B.C.C. 455; *Re a Company* (No. 001992 of 1988) [1989] B.C.L.C. 9; and *Re a Company* (No. 001448 of 1989) [1989] B.C.L.C. 715.

of court appointments where there is a notice period prior to the actual appointment.[28] Where a company enters administration following an appointment by the holder of a qualifying floating charge under para.14 of new Sch.B1 to the Insolvency Act 1986, a pending petition for the winding up of the company is suspended only.[29]

Moratorium on other legal process

5–30   When an administration order is made or a company enters admin-istration the company is given protection from its creditors.[30] Creditor action against the company is precluded without the consent of the administrator or the permission of the court.[31] This protection from creditors commences on an interim basis prior to the administration in the case of the court route where an administration application has been made, and any lifting of the moratorium would require permission of the court.[32] Similarly, in the case of the out of court route, protection commences in respect of an appointment of an administrator by a holder of a qualifying floating charge, from the lodging with the court of a notice of appointment.[33] Where a company or its directors are appointing an administrator, the protection begins when a copy of notice of intention to appoint an administrator is lodged with the court under para.27(1) of new Sch.B1 to the Insolvency Act 1986.[34] The protection, however, ceases if the period of notice required by para.26(1) of new Sch.B1 to the Insolvency Act 1986 has expired without an administrator having been appointed.[35] During the period of interim protection from creditors, in out of court administration appointments, any legal process requires the consent of the court.[36]

During the administration, while the protection from creditors is effective, and during any interim protection or moratorium period—

---

[28] See para.15(1)(a) and 26(1) of new Sch.B1 to the Insolvency Act 1986.

[29] Paragraph 40(1)(b) of new Sch.B1 to the Insolvency Act 1986.

[30] Paragraph 43 of new Sch.B1 to the Insolvency Act 1986.

[31] Paragraph 43 of new Sch.B1 to the Insolvency Act 1986.

[32] Paragraph 44(1) and (5) of new Sch.B1 to the Insolvency Act 1986.

[33] Paragraph 44(2) of new Sch.B1 to the Insolvency Act 1986. There would appear to be confused drafting in relation to the interim moratorium in respect of an appointment of an administrator under para.14 of new Sch.B1 to the Insolvency Act 1986. Paragraph 44(2) of that Schedule refers to the filing of "a copy of notice of intention to appoint an adimnstrator". However, that procedure is not laid down in relation to an appointment under para.14 of that Schedule. It applies to an appointment under para.22 of the Schedule. This is clear from para.19 of that Schedule, which states that the appointment of an administrator under para.14 takes effect when the requirements of para.18 are satisfied. In other words the appointment of an administrator commences immediately a notice of appointment is lodged with the court. A holder of a floating charge appoints an administrator with the appointment to take effect as at the date of the lodging of the notice with the court.

[34] Paragraph 44(4) of new Sch.B1 to the Insolvency Act 1986.

[35] Paragraph 44(4)(b) of new Sch.B1 to the Insolvency Act 1986. The authors take this period to mean the notice period given under para.26(1) of that Schedule which may be more than five business days' written notice.

[36] Paragraph 44(5) of new Sch.B1 to the Insolvency Act 1986.

(a) no step may be taken to enforce security over the company's property[37];

(b) no step may be taken to repossess goods in the company's possession under a hire purchase agreement[38];

(c) a landlord may not exercise a right of forfeiture by peaceable re-entry in relation to premises let to the company;

(d) in Scotland, a landlord may not exercise a right of irritancy in relation to premises let to the company;

(e) no legal process (including legal proceedings, execution, distress and diligence) may be instituted or continued against the company or property of the company;

(f) where the court gives permission for one of the transactions referred to above, it may impose a condition on or a requirement in connection with the transaction[39];

(g) the landlord may not exercise a right of irritancy in relation to premises let to the company.[40]

Meaning of no legal process in paragraph 43(6) of new Schedule B1

It was decided during the first year of the operation of the Insolvency **5–31** Act 1986 in Scotland in the case of *Air Ecosse*[41] that the expression "no other proceedings" in the relevant predecessor, ss.10(1)(c) and 11(3)(d) was confined to proceedings such as proceedings by a creditor to recover a debt, but would not extend to administrative procedures such as applications by a Chief Constable for suspension of a public house licence or other administrative constraints which might otherwise affect a company, such as the exercise of its functions by a civil aviation authority in determining whether a company was fit to operate aircraft and had the requisite financial resources to carry on business to a requisite statutory standard. In dealing with previous s.11(3)(d), that case held that that paragraph must be construed *ejusdem generis* with (confined to the categories outlined in) s.11(3)(a) to (c). Similarly, it had

---

[37] In terms of s.248(b)(ii) of the Insolvency Act 1986 a "security" means, in relation to Scotland, any security (whether heritable or moveable), any floating charge and any right of lien or preference and any right of retention (other than a right of compensation or set-off). Excluded are the special charges referred to in s.72F of the Insolvency Act 1986, as inserted by s.248(1) of the Enterprise Act 2002. Unless a consent is obtained to lifting a protection, a person having a lien over goods is not entitled to retain them: see *Re Sabre International Products Ltd* [1991] B.C.L.C. 470, *per* Harman J.

[38] In terms of para.111(1) of new Sch.B1 to the Insolvency Act 1986 a "hire-purchase agreement" includes a conditional sale agreement, a chattel leasing agreement. These terms are defined in s.251 of the Insolvency Act 1986.

[39] Paragraph 43 of new Sch.B1 to the Insolvency Act 1986.

[40] This is a new provision in relation to Scotland. The English provision previously contained in s.10(1)(aa) of the Insolvency Act 1986, as inserted by s.9 of the Insolvency Act 2000 and its corresponding provision in s.11(3)(ba), effective from April 2, 2001 (SI 2001/766), was designed to reverse the decisions in a series of cases including *Re Lomax Leisure* [1999] 1 B.C.L.C. 126 and *Razzaq v Pala* [1998] B.C.C. 66. The original view, delivered in the case of *Exchange Travel Agency Ltd v Triton Property Trust* [1991] B.C.C. 341, was reinstated by statute. See also in relation to Scotland, *Scottish Exhibition Centre Ltd v Mirestop Ltd (No. 2)* 1996 S.L.T. 8.

[41] 1987 S.L.T. 751; (1987) 3 B.C.C. 492 (Court of Session, Inner House).

been held that an application for leave to register a charge out of time does not amount to proceedings which require consent of the administrator or leave of the court.[42] In England the case of *Air Ecosse Ltd* was distinguished in the case of *Carr v British International Helicopters Ltd*,[43] in which the Employment Appeal Tribunal held that a complaint to an employment tribunal, alleged unfair selection for redundancy by the administrators in dismissing the company's employees, fell under the description of "other proceedings" within the meaning of former s.11(3)(d) of the Insolvency Act 1986. The courts in England and Wales have also not followed the restrictive reading of the expression "other proceedings" applied by the Court of Session in Air Ecosse Ltd, and it must surely be open to doubt as an authority on this point.[44] Although it is thought that the expression "no legal process" should be interpreted widely, there are limits and, for example, it has been held that the service of contractual notice purporting to make time of the essence, or for the purpose of terminating a contract by reason of repudiatory breach by the company, did not amount to the type of proceedings to which former s.11(3)(d) applied.[45] In contrast a statutory right to detain an aircraft under s.88 of the Civil Aviation Act 1982 in security of landing fees and dues, has been held to constitute a passive right, even if there was not actual security until the aircraft was detained, and would require the leave of the court before it could be lawfully exercised.[46]

Lifting of the protection of moratorium

5–32 Whether a court or an administrator should give leave to lift any protection of the company against enforcement proceedings by creditors is now subject to a growing body of case law. The problem in relation to the rights of security holders and those wanting to enforce liens or take other proceedings is how to balance their interests against the interests of the company and the other creditors. Certain guidelines were issued by Sir Nicholas Browne-Wilkinson V.-C. in the case of *Bristol Airport plc* in 1990.[47] These guidelines were referred to with approval and much expanded in the English Appeal Court in the case of *Atlantic Computer Systems plc (No. 1)*.[48]

In that case the company in administration carried on the business of leasing computer equipment to end users, for which purpose it needed to borrow funds to finance the purchase of the equipment which it then

---

[42] *Re Barrow Borough Transport Ltd* [1990] Ch. 227, 5 B.C.C. 646.

[43] [1993] B.C.C. 855. See also *Re Paramount Airways Ltd* (No.3) [1993] B.C.C. 664.

[44] See, for example, *Biosource Technologies Inc. v Axis Genetics plc* [2000] B.C.L.C. 286, where, in his judgement, Ferris J. reviewed the authorities and held that a party who was a competitor, rather than a creditor of a company in administration, was prohibited from bringing proceedings complaining of infringement of intellectual property rights unless there was consent of the court or administrator.

[45] *Re Olympia and York Canary Wharf Ltd, American Express v Adamson* [1993] B.C.C. 154.

[46] *Bristol Airport plc v Powdrill*, sub nom. *Paramount Airways Ltd (No.1)* Re [1990] Ch. 744; [1990] 2 W.L.R. 1362; [1990] 2 All E.R. 493; [1990] B.C. C. 130; [1990] B.C.L.C. 585.

[47] *ibid.*

[48] *Re Atlantic Computer Systems plc (Nos 1 and 2)* [1992] Ch. 505; [1992] 2 W.L.R. 367; [1992] 1 All E.R. 476; [1990] B.C.C. 859; and [1991] B.C.L.C. 606.

leased out. Two funders were the Norwich Union Group and the Allied Irish Group. There were two methods by which the funders provided finance. The first was for the funder to supply the equipment to the company under a hire-purchase agreement and the second was for the funder to lease the equipment to the company, in each case the company subletting the equipment to the end users. An administration order was made in relation to the company for the purpose of achieving a more advantageous realisation of the company's assets. After administrators had been appointed, rental payments from the end users were paid to the administrators. During their appointment the administrators did not pay any monies which were due to the funders. The administrators declined to consent to the funders exercising their rights to terminate the head leases.

Two of the funders applied to the court to decide whether the equipment leased to end users constituted "goods in the company's possession under any hire-purchase agreement". If they were such, the next question was whether the court would grant leave under s.11(3)(c) of the Insolvency Act 1986, entitling the funders to enforce their security. In the court of First Instance Ferris J. held that the equipment was not in the possession of the company for the purposes of section 11(3)(c) of the Insolvency Act 1986.[49] If, however, leave to bring an action had been needed, the case for granting it would be very strong and to the extent that property of the funders was being used in the company's business while the administration order was in force, the funders would be entitled as "expenses of the administration" to receive the payments provided for in their agreements with the company.

The Court of Appeal discussed the differences between a liquidation and an administration. Briefly an administration was intended to be an interim and temporary regime. Whether or not those with proprietary rights against the company should be allowed to enforce those rights against the company depended on all the circumstances of the case, and it would be inappropriate to adopt the inflexible rule for winding up that if land or goods in the company's possession under an existing lease or hire-purchase agreement were used for the purposes of the administration, the continuing rent or hire charges should automatically be treated as expenses of the administration. This was backed up by the terms of s.19(5) of the Insolvency Act 1986, in terms of which there is no automatic priority on third parties whose contracts with the company are adopted by the administrator, except in the case of contracts of employment. Secondly the equipment being leased, as far as between the company and the funders, remained in the possession of the company. Therefore the funders needed the consent of the court, or the administrators, to remove the equipment. At the end of a long and complicated judgment, the court laid down certain guidelines for future reference which state in detail the principles which courts must follow when making decisions in this complicated area of administration law. They have become known as the "the Atlantic Computer Guidelines".

---

[49] *Re Atlantic Computer Systems plc (Nos 1 and 2)* [1990] B.C.L.C. 729.

The Atlantic Computer guidelines

5–33 Nicholls L.J. ended the opinion of the Appeal Court as follows:

"There is one final matter to which we now turn. In the course of argument we were invited to give guidance on the principles to be applied on applications for the grant of leave under s 11. It is an invitation to which we are reluctant to accede, for several reasons: first, Parliament has left at large the discretion given to the court, and it is not for us to cut down that discretion or, as it was put in argument, to confine it within a straitjacket. However much we emphasise that any observations are only guidelines, there is a danger that they may be treated as something more. Secondly, s 11(3)(c) and (d) applies to a very wide range of steps and proceedings, and the circumstances in which leave is sought will vary almost infinitely. Thirdly, it is the judges who sit in the Companies Court who have practical experience of the difficulties arising in the working out of this new jurisdiction, not the members of this court.

However, we have already drawn attention to the important role of the administrator in this field. He should respond speedily and responsibly to applications for consent under s 11. Parliament envisaged that in the first place s 11 matters should be dealt with by him. It is to be hoped, in the interests of all concerned, that applications to the court will become the exception rather than the rule. But we recognise that for this to be so, authorised insolvency practitioners and their legal advisors need more guidance than is available at present on what, in general, is the approach of the court on leave applications. We feel bound, therefore, to make some general observations regarding cases where leave is sought to exercise existing proprietary rights, including security rights, against a company in administration:

(1) It is in every case for the person who seeks leave to make out a case for him to be given leave.

(2) The prohibition in s 11(3)(c) and (d) is intended to assist the company, under the management of the administrator, to achieve the purpose for which the administration order was made. If granting leave to a lessor of land or the hirer of goods (a 'lessor') to exercise his proprietary rights and repossess his lands or goods is unlikely to impede the achievement of that purpose, leave should normally be given.

(3) In other cases when a lessor seeks possession the court has to carry out a balancing exercise, balancing the legitimate interests of the lessor and the legitimate interests of the other creditors of the company (see Peter Gibson J in *Royal Trust Bank v Buckler* [1989] BCLC 130 at 135).

The metaphor employed here, for want of a better, is that of scales and weights. Lord Wilberforce adverted to the limitations of this metaphor in *Science Research Council v Nassé, BL Cars Limited (formerly Leyland Cars) v Vyas* [1979] 3 All ER 673 at 681 [1980] AC 1028 at 1067. It must be kept in mind that the exercise under s 11 is not a mechanical one; each case calls for an exercise in judicial judgment, in which the court seeks to give effect to the purpose of the statutory provisions, having regard to the parties' interests and all the circumstances of the case. As already noted, the purpose of the prohibition is to enable or assist the company to achieve the object for which the administration order was made. The purpose of the power to give leave is to enable the court to relax the prohibition where it would be inequitable for the prohibition to apply.

(4) In carrying out the balancing exercise great importance, or weight, is normally given to the proprietary interests of the lessor. Sir Nicholas Browne-Wilkinson V-C observed in *Bristol Airport plc v Powdrill* [1990] BCLC 585 at 602, [1990] 2 All ER 493 at 507 that, so far as possible, the administration procedure should not be used to prejudice those who were secured creditors when the administration order was made in lieu of a winding-up order. The same is true regarding the proprietary interest of a lessor. The underlying principle here is that an administration for the benefit of unsecured creditors should not be conducted at the expense of those who have proprietary rights which they are seeking to exercise, save to the extent that this may be unavoidable and even then this will usually be acceptable only to a strictly limited extent.

(5) Thus it will normally be a sufficient ground for the grant of leave if significant loss would be caused to the lessor by a refusal. For this purpose loss comprises any kind of financial loss, direct or indirect, including loss by reason of delay, and may extend to loss which is not financial. But if substantially greater loss would be caused to others by the grant of leave, or loss which is out of all proportion to the benefit which leave would confer on the lessor, that may outweigh the loss of the lessor caused by the refusal.

Our formulation was criticised in the course of the argument, and we certainly do not claim for it the status of a rule in those terms. At present we say only that it appears to us the nearest we can get to a formulation of what Parliament had in mind.

(6) In assessing these respective losses the court will have regard to matters such as: the financial position of the company, its ability to pay the rental arrears and the continuing rentals, the administrator's proposals, the period for which the administration order has already been in force and is expected to remain hi force, the effect on the administration if leave were given, the effect on the applicant if leave were refused, the end result sought to be achieved by the administration, the prospects of that result being achieved, and the history of the administration so far.

(7) In considering these matters it will often be necessary to assess how probable the suggested consequences are. Thus if loss to the applicant is virtually certain if leave is refused, and loss to the others a remote possibility if leave is granted, that will be a powerful factor in favour of granting leave.

(8) This is not an exhaustive list. For example, the conduct of the parties may also be a material consideration in a particular case, as it was in *Bristol Airport v Powdrill*. There leave was refused

on the ground that the applicants had accepted benefits under the administration, and had only sought to enforce their security at a later stage: indeed, they had only acquired their security as a result of the operations of the administrators. It behoves a lessor to make his position clear to the administrator at the outset of the administration and, if it should become necessary, to apply to the court promptly.

(9) The above considerations may be relevant not only to the decision whether leave should be granted or refused, but also to a decision to impose terms if leave is granted.

(10) The above considerations will also apply to a decision on whether to impose terms as a condition for refusing leave. Section 11(3)(c) and (d) makes no provision for terms being imposed if leave is refused, but the court has power to achieve that result. It may do so directly, by giving directions to the administrator: for instance, under s 17, or hi response to an application by the administrator under s 14(3), or in exercise of its control over an administrator as an officer of the court. Or it may do so indirectly, by ordering that the applicant shall have leave unless the administrator is prepared to take this or that step in the conduct of the administration.

Cases where leave is refused but terms are imposed can be expected to arise frequently. For example, the permanent loss to a lessor flowing from his inability to recover his property will normally be small if the administrator is required to pay the current rent. In most cases this should be possible, since if the administration order has been rightly made the business should generally be sufficiently viable to hold down current outgoings. Such a term may therefore be a normal term to impose.

(11) The above observations are directed at a case such as the present where a lessor of land or the owner of goods is seeking to repossess his land or goods because of non-payment of rentals. A broadly similar approach will be applicable on many applications to enforce a security: for instance, an application by a mortgagee for possession of land. On such applications an important consideration will often be whether the applicant is fully secured. If he is, delay in enforcement is likely to be less prejudicial than in cases where his security is insufficient.

(12) In some cases there will be a dispute over the existence, validity or nature of the security which the applicant is seeking leave to enforce. It is not for the court on the leave application to seek to adjudicate upon that issue, unless (as in the present case, on the fixed or floating charge point) the issue raises a short point of law which it is convenient to determine without further ado. Otherwise the court needs to be satisfied only that the applicant has a seriously arguable case.''

The guidelines in *Atlantic Computer Systems plc* have been approved and applied in Scotland.[50] The authors do not consider that the reformulation

---

[50] *Scottish Exhibition Centre Ltd v Mirestop Ltd*, 1993 S.L.T. 1034.

of the objectives of administration mean that the Atlantic Systems guidelines will have to be reworked. Apart from the "prescribed part"[51] there is nothing in the reformulation of the objectives which undermines the rights of holders of securities.

This is underlined by the fact that an administrator's statement of proposals under para.49 of new Sch.B1 to the Insolvency Act 1986 may not include any action which affects the right of a secure creditor of the company to enforce his security, or would result in a preferential debt of the company being paid otherwise than in priority to its non-preferential debts, or would result in one preferential creditor of the company being paid a smaller proportion of his debt than an other.[52]

Legal status of administrator

It is thought that the administrator acts in several capacities. He is (1) **5–34** an officer of the company; (2) an agent of the company; (3) a public officeholder; and (4) an officer of the court.

(1) Officer of the company

The administrator, like a liquidator (but unlike a receiver), is an officer **5–35** of the company because, like the liquidator, he is the governing body of the company managing its affairs as well as its business and property.[53] As an officer of the company, he is liable to misfeasance proceedings.[54] As an "officer of the company" an administrator is entitled to protection under s.727 of the Companies Act 1985. In the case of *Re Home Treat Ltd*, Harman J. stated[55]:

> "The answer may be that the court can afford protection to the administrators pursuant to s 727 of the 1985 Act. That allows, in proceedings for negligence, default, breach of duty or breach of trust—and this, I think, would be an allegation of default—against an officer of the company or person employed by the company, the court, if it appears that that officer may be Liable in respect of the wrong but has acted honestly and reasonably and ought fairly to be excused, to relieve him. Those phrases are, of course, reminiscent of the phrases in s 61 of the Trustee Act 1925.
> The question is whether under that power to relieve officers of the company, an administrator can be relieved. I have been shown a decision of Parker J as he then was, later Lord Parker of Waddington, who was a very great authority in all these matters. In *Re X Co Limited* [1907] 2 Ch 92 Parker J held that a liquidator might be

---

[51] See paras 5–04 to 19–25.
[52] Paragraph 73(1) of new Sch.B1 to the Insolvency Act 1986.
[53] Paragraph 68(1) of new Sch.B1 to the Insolvency Act 1986.
[54] Paragraph 75 of new Sch.B1 to the Insolvency Act 1986. An important change introduced by para.75—apart from clearer drafting—is that the examination of the conduct of the administrator may be at any time and is not now restricted to being in the course of a winding up.
[55] [1991] B.C.L.C. 705.

given relief on the footing that he is an officer of the company to do a certain act concerned with the memorandum under the Stamp Act 1891. The notes to s 448 of the Companies Act 1948 in *Buckley on the Companies Act* [14 edn 1981]p 892, that section being the direct predecessor of s 727 of the 1985 Act, say 'firstly, *semble* a liquidator is an officer within the meaning of this section', and they refer to *Re X Co Limited,* and they go on to say that s 448 extends to a transaction *ultra vires* of the company . . .

It seems to me quite clear that the word 'officer', which merely means somebody who holds an office, and an office in relation to the company, can apply to an administrator. That is so although he is also an officer of the court, there being in that context no conflict of duties between his duty as officer of the company and his duty as an officer of the court. In both capacities his duties are to manage the business and property of the company for the better effecting of the purpose for which the court made the order, in the interests of the creditors and it may be eventually of the contributories of the company.

I therefore come, at the end of this somewhat lengthy recitation, to the conclusion that the application under s 727 of the 1985 Act is justified and the administrators ought to be given a direction as set out in the intended application which has been put before me, validating their conduct of the affairs of the company."

(2) Agent of the company

5–36   The administrator acts as agent of the company.[56] He is not personally liable on any contract including a contract of employment entered into or adopted by him in the carrying out of his duties as administrator, except if the contract provides otherwise, the liabilities rather being charged on and payable out of the property of the company over which he has custody or control.[57] However, people must be put on notice that the company is subject to an administration order. Every invoice, order for goods and business letter, on or in which the company's name appears issued by or on behalf of the administrator or the company, must contain the administrator's name and a statement that the affairs, business and property of the company are being managed by the administrator.[58] The administrator may expose himself to personal liability for breach of this provision if in ignorance of the administration order persons supply goods to the company not knowing that it is insolvent or likely to become insolvent. Suppliers, including utilities, may insist on personal guarantees from the administrator before the provision of services or goods,[59] but he is entitled to secure the provision of continued supply by utilities without providing arrears accrued prior to the date of the administration order.[60]

---

[56] Paragraph 69 of new Sch.B1 to the Insolvency Act 1986.
[57] Paragraph 99(4) and (5) of new Sch.B1 to the Insolvency Act 1986.
[58] See discussion of residuary powers of directors at para.5–28.
[59] S.233 of the Insolvency Act 1986.
[60] S.233 of the Insolvency Act 1986.

(3) Officeholder

The administrator is an officeholder. He is vested with special powers **5–37** and privileges under ss.230 to 246 of the Insolvency Act 1986. He has powers to inquire into the company's dealings.[61] He has power to challenge prior transactions of the company (ss.242, 243, 244 and 245 of the Insolvency Act 1986) and is given special exemption from liability for loss or damage occasioned by his seizure or disposal of property which does not belong to the company.[62] His acts as administrator are also validated even if there has been a defect in his appointment or qualifications.[63]

(4) Officer of court

The administrator like the liquidator appointed on a compulsory **5–38** liquidation is an officer of the court.[64] This status involves special privileges and responsibilities. He is protected by the law of contempt against any interference with the performance of his duties and has a right of access to the court for directions. Finally, the administrator owes to the company fiduciary duties to exercise good faith and a duty to exercise the professional skill and care of an insolvency practitioner. He is not allowed to have any conflict of interest between his duty as administrator and any private interest. If the administrator is a solicitor or accountant, he may however be free to employ his own firm to assist in the performance of his duties as administrator.[65]

Duties and powers of administrators

The overriding duty of an administrator can be characterised as that **5–39** of exercising responsible care for the company whose property and affairs has been entrusted to him.[66] In this pursuit the administrator of a company may do anything necessary or expedient for the management of the affairs, business and property of the company.[67] All other powers conferred on an administrator to do a specified thing are without prejudice to the generality of that general power.[68] So, for example, it has been held that an administrator has the power to replace trustees of a company pension fund and to change the trust deed, in that there is a close connection between the management of the pension scheme and the management of the company's affairs.[69] In addition to that general power, the administrator of a company has the powers specified in Sch.1 to the Insolvency Act 1986.[70] These provisions have not been changed by the Enterprise Act 2002.

---

[61] S.236 of the Insolvency Act 1986.
[62] S.234(3) and (4) of the Insolvency Act 1986.
[63] S.232 of the Insolvency Act 1986.
[64] Paragraph 5 of new Sch.B1 to the Insolvency Act 1986. A liquidator in a voluntary liquidation is not an officer of the court: *Re Bateson (John) & Co* [1985] B.C.L.C. 259.
[65] See *Bridal Centre* (1985) 9 A.C.L.R. 481.
[66] *Re Charnley Davies Ltd* (No. 2) [1990] B.C.L.C. 760; [1990] B.C.C. 605.
[67] Paragraph 59(1) of new Sch.B1 to the Insolvency Act 1986.
[68] Paragraph 59(2) of new Sch.B1 to the Insolvency Act 1986.
[69] *Denny v Yeldon* [1995] 1 B.C.L.C. 560.
[70] Para.60 of new Sch.B1 to the Insolvency Act 1986.

The powers listed in Sch.1 to the Insolvency Act 1986 are the same powers as an English administrative receiver has,[71] including the power to present or defend a winding up petition (a power unlikely to be used in practice). The administrator also has powers under ss.133, 134, 236 and 237 of the Insolvency Act 1986 to apply to the court for an order of a public and private examination of directors etc. of the company and production of documents.[72]

The administrator has no greater powers than the company itself has in its memorandum, with the result that the administrator has no power to do acts which are *ultra vires* of the company. Although section 4 of the Companies Act 1985 allows the company to change its objects, it allows the change only in certain limited ways, and these do not include a power to change its objects to carry on some business other than its then authorised business. A company may be able to change its objects within the course of an administration subject to that proviso.[73] A person who deals with the administrator of a company in good faith and for value need not enquire whether the administrator is acting within his powers.[74]

Restrictions on administrator exercising powers

5–40   The main restriction on the administrator's powers is that he must manage the company's affairs, business and property in accordance with any proposals approved at an initial creditors' meeting to which an administrator's proposals are presented, including any revision of those proposals which is made by him and which he does not consider substantial, and in accordance with any revision of those proposals approved by a meeting called to consider revised proposals.[75] A second restriction is that the administrator must comply with directions of the court in connection with any aspect of his management of the company's affairs, business or property.[76] Because it is thought that most administrations arising from floating charges created after September 15, 2003 will be out of court administrations, the scope for court directions generally has been circumscribed with power of direction only if the direction is consistent with proposals approved by creditors' meetings, or there is some procedural vacuum or irregularity.[77] There is a third important restriction, which governs how the administrator may deal with property which is subject to a charge or security, which is described below.

Administrative duties of administrator

(1) Taking custody of property

5–41   The administrator of a company is under a duty to take custody or control of all the property to which he thinks the company is entitled.[78] He may also apply to the court for orders for the restoration to the

---

[71] S.42(1) of the Insolvency Act 1986.
[72] See paras 4–70 to 4–75.
[73] *Re Home Treat Ltd* [1991] B.C.L.C. 705.
[74] Insolvency Act 1986, para.59(3) to new Sch.B1.
[75] *ibid.*, para.68(1) of new Sch.B1.
[76] *ibid.*, para.68(2) of new Sch.B1.
[77] *ibid.*, para.68(3) of new Sch.B1.
[78] *ibid.*, para.67 to new Sch.B1 (formerly a similar formulation was contained in repealed s.17(1) of the Insolvency Act 1986).

company of assets disposed of for no consideration or inadequate consideration,[79] or assets disposed of which create a preference in favour of a creditor to the prejudice of the general body of creditors.[80]

(2) Notification of appointment

As soon as is reasonably practicable after his appointment, the **5–42** administrator must send a notice of his appointment to the company.[81] He must also advertise his appointment once in the *Edinburgh Gazette* and once in a newspaper circulating in the area where the company has its principal place of business or in such newspaper as he thinks appropriate for ensuring that the order comes to the notice of the company's creditors.[82] At the same time he must give notice of his appointment to:

(a) a receiver, if appointed;
(b) a petitioner in a petition for the winding up of the company, if there is a petition pending;
(c) any provisional liquidator of the company, if one has been appointed;
(d) any supervisor of a voluntary arrangement under Part I of the Insolvency Act 1986; and
(e) the Keeper of the Register of Inhibitions and Adjudications for recording in that Register.[83]

The administrator must also send a notice of his appointment to the Registrar of Companies before the end of the period of seven days beginning with the date of the administration order or, in the case of administrators appointed by a holder of a qualifying floating charge or a company or its directors, the date on which the administrator has received his statutory notice of appointment from his appointor in terms of respectively paras 20 and 32 of new Sch.B1 to the Insolvency Act 1986.[84] Finally, an administrator must as soon as is reasonably practicable obtain a list of the company's creditors and send a notice of his appointment to each creditor of whose claim and address he is aware.[85] The various notices referred to in this paragraph must be in the forms prescribed by the Insolvency (Scotland) Rules 1986, as amended by the Insolvency (Scotland) Amendment Rules 2003 (SI 2003/2111 (S. 9)).[86]

(3) Notification on stationery

While a company is in administration, every invoice, order for goods **5–43** or services, and business letter issued by or on behalf of the company or the administrator must state the name of the administrator and that the

---

[79] S.242(1)(b) of the Insolvency Act 1986 ("gratuitous alienations").
[80] S.243(4)(b) of the Insolvency Act 1986 ("unfair preferences").
[81] Paragraph 46(2) of new Sch.B1 to the Insolvency Act 1986.
[82] Rule 2.19(1) of the Insolvency (Scotland) Rules 1986, as amended by the Insolvency (Scotland) Amendment Rules 2003 (SI 2003/2111 (S. 9)).
[83] Rule 2.19(2) of the Insolvency (Scotland) Rules 1986, as amended by the Insolvency (Scotland) Amendment Rules 2003, *supra*.
[84] Paragraph 46(4) and (6) of new Sch.B1 to the Insolvency Act 1986.
[85] Paragraph 46(3) of new Sch.B1 to the Insolvency Act 1986. The sending of the notice to each creditor may be waived by the court in terms of para.46(7)(a) of that Schedule.
[86] The form for notification of appointment of an administrator for a newspaper or in the *Edinburgh Gazette* is Form 2.10B (Scot) and that for a notice of an administrator's appointment pursuant to para.46 of Sch.B1 to the Insolvency Act 1986 and r.2.19 of the Insolvency (Scotland) Rules 1986, is Form 2.11B (Scot).

affairs, business and property of the company are being managed by him. It is an offence for the administrator, any officer of the company, and the company itself to contravene these provisions except with reasonable excuse.[87] The wording of the provisions is not exhaustive of the type of dealings which a company may have with third parties. There is no reference to oral communications, or to electronic communications such as e-mails. Similarly, catalogues and brochures, and company cheques may also be outside the scope of the publicity requirement. It is suggested that the high standards of good faith and probity in dealings expected of officers of the court mean that all reasonable efforts must be made by administrator to alert persons dealing with him as to the status of the company, and in this he should go beyond the strict interpretation of the provisions.

Administrator's powers to deal with company's property

Charged or secured property

5–44   Paragraphs 70 and 71 of new Sch.B1 to the Insolvency Act 1986 gives the administrator power to dispose of, or exercise his powers in relation to, charged property. Charged property is divided into two categories: (1) property subject to a floating charge; and (2) property subject to any other security.

Property subject to a floating charge

5–45   The administrator of a company may dispose of or take action relating to property which is subject to a floating charge as if it were not subject to the charge.[88] Where property is disposed of in reliance of this power, the holder of the floating charge has the same priority in respect of the proceeds of the disposal as he had in respect of the property disposed of.[89] Hence, cash received from a sale, or goods bought with any proceeds of a sale, remain secured by the floating charge. Although a floating charge which has crystallised in Scotland acts as an assignation insecurity of company debts in favour of the holder of the floating charge, these provisions are quite clear that such assets are to be treated as if they were not subject to a security (*i.e.* had not been assigned) and hence are able to be collected in for the running of the business.

Effectively, because an administrator may "exercise his powers in relation to the property", this means that the company's cash or other assets may thus be used to buy goods and services, and the business may be conducted as if the floating charge had not crystallised. Although the holder of the floating charge has his priority maintained, his fear, of course, will be that his position may be worsened if the effect of the administration order leads to a deterioration in the financial position of the business. This can easily happen if funds that are secured are used to buy the stock, which ends up being sold at fire sale prices. If,

---

[87] Insolvency Act 1986, para.45 of new Sch.B1.
[88] *ibid.*, para.70(1) of new Sch.B1.
[89] *ibid.*, para.70(2) of new Sch.B1.

however, a creditor or member of a company feels that the administrator is acting or has acted so as unfairly to harm his interests (whether alone or in common with some or all other members or creditors), or he thinks that the administrator is proposing to act in a way which would unfairly harm his interests, he may apply to the court for relief.[90] Similarly, a creditor or member of a company in administration may apply to the court claiming that the administrator is not performing his functions as quickly or as efficiently as is reasonably practicable.[91] In those situations the court has discretion to make a range of orders, including directing the administrator to act in a particular way or requiring a creditors' meeting to be held for a specified purpose.[92] The court may even provide for the appointment of the administrator to cease to have effect.[93] These discretionary powers of the court may not be exercised in a way which would impede or prevent the implementation of a voluntary arrangement approved under Pt I of the Insolvency Act 1986 or a compromise or arrangement sanctioned under s.425 of the Companies Act 1985, or proposals which have been approved at creditors' meetings more than 28 days before an application for relief has been made.[94] Where property in Scotland is disposed of under these provisions, the administrator must grant to the disponee an appropriate document of transfer or conveyance of the property, with that document or recording, intimation or registration of that document (where recording, intimation or registration of the document is a legal requirement for completion of title to the property), having the effect of disencumbering the property of or, as the case may be, freeing the property from, the security.[95]

Property subject to securities other than a floating charge

The court may by order enable the administrator of a company to dispose of property which is subject to a security (other than a floating charge) as if it were not subject to the security.[96] Such an order may only be made on the application of the administrator and be granted where there court thinks that the disposal of the property would be likely to promote the purpose of the administration in respect of the company.[97] There is a similar discretion on the court in relation to goods in the possession of the company under a higher purchase agreement, chattel-leasing agreement or conditional sale agreement.[98] Where these powers are exercised the order must be subject to the condition that the net proceeds of any disposal of the goods are first applied towards discharging the sums secured by the securities.[99] If the sums realised are less than could be realised in an open market, any deficiency has to be

5–46

---

[90] Insolvency Act 1986, para.74(1) and (3) of new Sch.B1.
[91] *ibid.*, para.74(2) of new Sch.B1.
[92] *ibid.*, para.74(4)(a), (b) and (c) of new Sch.B1.
[93] *ibid.*, para.74(4)(d) of new Sch.B1.
[94] *ibid.*, para.74(6) of new Sch.B1.
[95] *ibid.*, para.113 of new Sch.B1.
[96] *ibid.*, para.71(1) of new Sch.B1.
[97] *ibid.*, para.71(2) of new Sch.B1.
[98] *ibid.*, para.72(1) and (2) of new Sch.B1.
[99] *ibid.*, para.71(3) and 72(3) of new Sch.B1.

made up to the holder of the type of security.[1] It can be assumed that, unless the company is in a position to make up this deficiency, the court would not lift the security. As with goods disposed of which were subject to a floating charge, the disponee must be given an appropriate document of transfer.[2]

Getting in the company's property

5-47   When a company is in administration, the court may require any person who has in his possession or control any property, books, papers or records to which the company appears to be entitled, to pay, deliver, convey, surrender or transfer the property, books, papers or records to the administrator.[3] If the administrator seizes or disposes of any property which is not the property of the company but had reasonable grounds for believing that he was entitled to seize or dispose of that property, he is not liable to any person in respect of any loss or damage resulting from the seizure or disposal except in so far as that loss or damage is caused by the administrator's own negligence.[4] These powers of getting in property are backed up by statutory duties imposed on persons associated with the company to give the administrator co-operation and such information concerning the company and its promotion, formation, business, dealings, affairs of property as the administrator may at any time after the company goes into administration reasonably require, and those persons have a duty to attend on the administrators at such times as the administrator may reasonably require.[5] There are further back-up powers of enquiry into a company's dealings in s.236 of the Insolvency Act 1986. In terms of subs.(3) of that section the court may require any one of a number of persons associated with the company and listed to submit an affidavit to the court containing an account of his dealings with the company or to produce any books, papers or other records in his possession or under his control relating to the company. In the case of *Re British & Commonwealth Holdings plc (No.2)*[6] the House of Lords unanimously confirmed the principles that are to apply in relation to a court's power to order discovery of information under s.236 on the application of an office holder in insolvency proceedings.

Administrator selling the whole undertaking of the company prior to approval of proposals

5-48   It has been held in relation to former s.17(2) of the Insolvency Act 1986 that the provisions contained in that subsection are sufficient to allow an administrator to sell the entire undertaking of a company.

---

[1] Paragraph 71(3)(b) and 72(3)(b) of new Sch.B1 to the Insolvency Act 1986.

[2] Paragraph 133 of new Sch.B1 to the Insolvency Act 1986.

[3] S.234(1) and (2) of the Insolvency Act 1986.

[4] S.234(3) and (4)(a) of the Insolvency Act 1986.

[5] S.235(1) and (2) of the Insolvency Act 1986; see *Re Cloverbay Ltd* [1989] B.C.L.C. 724; and *Re Cloverbay Ltd* (No.2) [1990] B.C.C. 299, where the court disallowed further attempts to obtain even more information on the ground that they were oppressive to the party concerned.

[6] [1992] Ch. 342 (CA); [1993] 3 A.C. 426 (H.L.). The court enjoys an unfettered and general discretion in the exercise of this extraordinary power, and must balance the requirement of the office holder against possible oppression to the person from whom information is sought. On the other hand, there is no rule of limitation to the effect that the office holder is confined to reconstituting that knowledge which the company once had and was entitled to possess.

There are conflicting decisions as to whether the administrator prior to the approval of his proposals, is obliged to seek the specific permission of the court, or whether it is merely something which he should consider, when exercising a professional judgement in the light of all known circumstances, and also taking into account that this would be a sensible precaution against a later challenge to his actions.[7] It is thought by the authors that the emphasis of the new objectives of administration on the survival of the company as a going concern should tip the argument against an administrator being allowed to sell the whole undertaking of a company prior to his proposals being considered by a meeting of creditors, or without express direction of the court. Secondly, the terms of para.68 of new Sch.B1 to the Insolvency Act 1986 gives the administrator of a company the overriding duty to manage its affairs, business and property in accordance with proposals or revised proposals approved by creditors' meetings. The predecessor s.17(2) treats the duties of an administrator differently, whether proposals have been approved or have not yet been approved. This distinction is no longer adhered to. Thirdly, there are sufficient powers in the Act and in the Regulations to allow an expedited creditors' meeting to be called to consider proposals. It is also thought by the authors that the emphasis of the new objectives of administration on the survival of the company as a going concern should tip the argument against an administrator being allowed to sell the whole undertaking of a company prior to his proposals being considered by a meeting of creditors, or without express direction of the court.

Limitation periods

The Insolvency Act 1986 makes no provision about the effect of an **5–49** administration order on the running of time for the purposes of limitation of actions, and it has been held that the moratorium on proceedings during administration does not amount to a permanent transformation of creditors' rights in the same way as occurs in a compulsory winding up, where the court have ruled that limitation periods are arrested.

Statement of affairs

An important part of an administrator's duties on taking office is to **5–50** find out as soon as possible the present state of affairs of the company. He is under a statutory duty to require one or more of the following persons to provide a statement of the affairs of the company:

(a) a person who is or has been an officer of the company,
(b) a person who took part in the formation of the company during the period of one year ending with the date on which the company enters administration,

---

[7] *Re Consumer & Industrial Press Ltd (No. 2)* [1988] 4 B.C.C. 72; *Re Smallman Construction Ltd* [1998] 4 B.C.C. 784; *Re NS Distribution Ltd* [1990] B.C.L.C. 169; *Re Charnley Davies Ltd* [1990] B.C.C. 605; *Re Montin Ltd* [1999] 1 B.C.L.C. 663; *Re Osmosis Group Ltd* [1999] 2 B.C.L.C. 329; *Re P.D. Fuels Ltd* [1999] B.C.C. 450; and *Re T & D Industries plc* [2000] 1 ALL E.R. 333.

(c) a person employed by the company during that period;

(d) a person who is or has been during that period an officer or employee of a company which is or has been during that year an officer of the company.[8]

In Scotland the Statement of Affairs must be a statutory declaration made in accordance with the Statutory Declarations Act 1835,[9] and give particulars of the company's property, debts and liabilities, and the names and addresses of the company's creditors, including securities held by each creditor and the date on which each security was granted.[10] A notice requiring a Statement of Affairs must be in the prescribed form.[11] A person required to submit a Statement of Affairs must do so before the end of the period of 11 days beginning with the day on which he receives notice of the requirement.[12] There is a prescribed form for the Statement of Affairs,[13] where the administrator thinks that it would prejudice the conduct of the administration for the whole or part of the Statement of the company's affairs to be disclosed, he may apply to the court for an order of limited disclosure in respect of the Statement, or any specified part of it.[14] A person who provides to the administrator a Statement of the company's affairs, or Statement of Concurrence shall be allowed, and paid by the administrator out of his receipts, any expenses incurred by that person in so doing which the administrator considers reasonable.[15]

Administrator's proposals

5–51   Paragraph 48 of new Sch.B1 to the Insolvency Act 1986 provides that as soon as is reasonably practicable or, in any event, within eight weeks of the administration commencing, the administrator is required to make a Statement setting out proposals for achieving the statutory objective of administration, although this period can be extended with the permission of the court or with the consent of creditors in terms of paras 107 and 108 of that Schedule. The administrator must send a copy of the proposals to the Register of Companies, the company's creditors

---

[8] Insolvency Act 1986, para.47(1) and (3) of new Sch.B1.

[9] *ibid.*, para.47(4) of new Sch.B1.

[10] *ibid.*, para.47(2)(c), (d), (e) and (f) of new Sch.B1.

[11] *ibid.*, para.47(1)(b) of new Sch.B1; Rule 2.20(2) of the Insolvency (Scotland) Rules 1986, as amended by SI 2003/2111, with the required form being Form 2.12B (Scot).

[12] Paragraph 48(1) of new Sch.B1 to the Insolvency Act 1986. The period of 11 days may be extended by the administrator in terms of para.48(2)(b) of that Schedule.

[13] See r.2.21 of the Insolvency (Scotland) Rules 1986 as amended by SI 2003/2111. The form is Form S2.13B (Scot.). Where one or more persons specified in a company is being asked to submit a Statement of Affairs the administrator may instead require a Statement of Concurrence in terms of r.2.21(2) of the Insolvency (Scotland) Rules 1986 as amended, and the requisite form is Form 2.14B (Scot.). A Statement of Concurrence must be returned within five business days of receipt from the administrator of the Statement of Affairs being concurred with in terms of r.2.21(4) of the Insolvency (Scotland) Rules 1986. The administrator shall, as soon as is reasonably practicable, file a copy of the Statement of Affairs and any Statement of Concurrence with the Registrar of Companies (r.2.21(6) of the Insolvency (Scotland) Rules 1986) and that must be with Form 2.15B (Scot.).

[14] Rule 2.22(1) of the Insolvency (Scotland) Rules 1986 as amended by SI 2003/2111.

[15] Rule 2.24 of the Insolvency (Scotland) Rules 1986 as amended by SI 2003/2111.

and every member of the company, although the last obligation may be fulfilled by publishing a notice[16]. The notice shall give an undertaking to provide a copy of the Statement of Proposals free of charge to any member of the company who applies in writing to a specified address,[17] be published once in the Edinburgh Gazette and once in the newspaper in which the administrator's appointment was advertised.[18] It must state the full name of the company, full name and address of the administrator, and give details of the administrator's appointment and specify an address to which any member of the company may apply in writing for a copy of the Statement of Proposals to be provided free of charge.[19] The period within which the administrator must send out the proposals (now set at eight weeks) is reduced from the three months which it was under former s.23(1) of the Insolvency Act 1986.

Each copy of the administrator's proposals sent to the creditors must be accompanied by an invitation to an initial creditors' meeting, which must be held as soon as reasonably practicable or, and in any event, within 10 weeks of the administration commencing, and on 14 days' notice.[20] The time periods may be extended with the permission of the court or the consent of creditors.[21] If the administrator does not consider that it is reasonably practicable to rescue the company and/or achieve a better result for the creditors than on a winding up (without first being in administration), his or her Statement must explain why.[22] Only if these first two objectives cannot be met may the third objective be set of realising property in order to make a distribution to one or more secured or preferential creditors, provided of course that that objective does not unnecessarily harm the interests of the creditors of the company as whole.[23] A meeting of creditors need not be summoned to consider the administrator's proposals where the Statement of Proposals states that the administrator thinks:

(a) that the company has sufficient property to enable each creditor of the company to be paid in full;

(b) that the company has insufficient property to enable a distribution to be made to unsecured creditors other than by virtue of section 176A(2)(a) of the Insolvency Act 1986 (the prescribed part set aside for unsecured creditors); or

(c) that neither of the objectives contained in paragraphs 3(1)(a) and (b) of new Schedule B1 to the Insolvency Act 1986 can be achieved.[24]

Where a Statement of Proposals is set in those terms and no meeting is requisitioned, the administrators' proposals shall be deemed to have

---

[16] Insolvency Act 1986, para.49(4) and (6) of new Sch.B1.

[17] *ibid.*, para.49(6) of new Sch.B1.

[18] Rule 2.25(6) of the Insolvency (Scotland) Rules 1986 as amended by SI 2003/2111.

[19] *ibid.*

[20] Paragraph 51(1) and (2) of the new Sch.B1 to the Insolvency Act 1986; r.2.27(1) of the Insolvency (Scotland) Rules 1986, as amended by SI 2003/2111.

[21] Insolvency Act 1986, paras 107 and 108 of new Sch.B1.

[22] *ibid.*, para.49(2)(b) of new Sch.B1.

[23] *ibid.*, para.3(4) of new Sch.B1.

[24] *ibid.*, para.52(1) of new Sch.B1.

been approved by the creditors on the expiry of 12 days from the date upon which the administrator sent out his Statement of Proposals.[25] However, an administrator must summon an initial creditors' meeting if it is requested by creditors of the company whose debts amount to at least 10 per cent of the total debts of the company.[26] Further meetings of creditors may also be demanded of an administrator by creditors on the same basis, or be directed by the court in terms of para.56(1) of new Sch.B1 to the Insolvency Act 1986.

Approval and revision of administrator's proposals

5–52   The initial creditors' meeting to which an administrator's proposals are presented may approve the proposals, or approve them but with modification provided that the administrator consents to the modification.[27] After the conclusion of an initial creditors' meeting, the administrator must, as soon as is reasonably practicable, report any decision taken to the court, the Registrar of Companies, every creditor who received notice of the meeting, and any creditors who did not receive notice of a meeting and of whose claim the administrator has become subsequently aware.[28] The administrator has the option of doing anything that has to be done at a creditors' meeting by correspondence between the administrator and the creditors.[29]

The administrator must summon a second creditors' meeting if he wishes to make a substantial revision to his proposals,[30] although in cases of genuine urgency, where the spirit and substance of the terms first approved is observed, the court may grant authority to the administrator under para.63 of new Sch.B1 to the Insolvency Act 1986 to implement modifications without further creditors' approval.[31] A creditors' meeting may establish a creditor's committee which may require the administrator to attend on the committee at any reasonable time, of which he is given at least seven days' notice, and to provide the committee with information about the exercise of his functions.[32] Through its regular supply of information, the creditors' committee should be able to monitor how far the administration order is fulfilling its intended purposes, and thus put a creditor into a position to invoke the intervention of the court under para.74 of new Sch.B1 to the Insolvency Act 1986 and challenge the administrator's conduct of the company, on the ground that the administrator has acted, is acting, or is proposing to act, in a way that unfairly harms the interests of the

---

[25] Rules 2.25(3) and 2.31 of the Insolvency (Scotland) Rules 1986, as amended by SI 2003/2111. The 12 days specified in these provisions is the period within which an administrator must send out a request for an initial creditors' meeting from the date upon which he sends out his Statement of Proposals.

[26] Insolvency Act 1986, para.52(2) of new Sch.B1.

[27] *ibid.*, para.53(1) of new Sch.B1.

[28] *ibid.*, para.53(2) of new Sch.B1 and r.2.35 of the Insolvency (Scotland) Rules 1986 as amended by SI 2003/2111.

[29] Paragraph 58(1) of new Sch.B1 to the Insolvency Act 1986, with procedures set out in r.2.28 of the Insolvency (Scotland) Rules 1986, as amended by SI 2003/2111.

[30] Paragraph 54 of the new Sch.B1 to the Insolvency Act 1986.

[31] *Re Smallman Construction Ltd* (1988) 4 B.C.C. 784.

[32] Paragraph 57 of new Sch.B1 to the Insolvency Act 1986.

creator.[33] The courts will normally only interfere with an administrator's commercial decisions if they are wrong in law or unfair to creditors or contractors, but such an intervention may provide an occasion for the court to state the fundamental principles on which an administration should be conducted.[34]

Failure to obtain approval of administrator's proposals

If an initial creditors' meeting or a creditors' meeting summoned to **5–53** approve a revision to proposals, fails to approve the proposals, a report of the outcome of the meeting is sent to the court under para.53(2)(a) of new Sch.B1 to the insolvency Act 1986, and the court then had a wide range of options including providing that the appointment of an administrator shall cease to have effect from a specified time, adjourning the hearing conditionally or unconditionally, making an interim order, making an order on a petition for winding up suspended by the appointment of an administrator by a holder of a floating charge, and making any other order that it thinks appropriate.[35]

Content of Statement of Proposals

The Statement of Proposals by the administrator must contain full **5–54** details of the administration, the names of the directors and secretary of the company and details of any shareholdings which they have in the company.[36] It must also include an account of the circumstances giving rise to the appointment of the administrator, and if a statement of the company's affairs has been submitted, a copy or summary of it, with the administrator's comments, if any.[37] If a full Statement of Affairs is not provided, the administrator must give the names and addresses of the creditors, and details of the debt owed to, and security held by, each of them.[38] If no Statement of Affairs has been submitted, there must be included details of the financial position of the company at the latest practicable date (which must, unless the court otherwise orders, be a date not earlier than that on which the company entered administration), the names and addresses of the creditors, and details of the debts owed to, and security held by, each of them, and an explanation as to why there is no Statement of Affairs.[39] The proposals must also include details of how it is envisaged that the purpose of administration will be achieved and how it is proposed that the administration shall end, setting out any proposal for a voluntary arrangement under Part I of the Insolvency Act 1986 and any proposal for a compromise or arrangement to be sanctioned under section 425 of the Companies Act 1985 (compromise with creditors or members).[40] Where a creditors' voluntary liquida-

---

[33] See *O'Neill v Phillips* [1999] 1W.L.R. 1092, in which the House of Lords, *per* Lord Hoffmann, analysed "unfair prejudice" in s.459(1) of the companies act 1985.

[34] *Re C.E. King Ltd* [2000] 2 B.C.L.C. 297.

[35] Paragraph 55 of new Sch.B1 to the Insolvency Act 1986.

[36] Rule 2.25(1)(a) to (d) of the Insolvency (Scotland) Rules 1986, as amended by SI 2003/2111.

[37] Rule 2.25(1)(e) and (f) of the Insolvency (Scotland) Rules 1986, as amended by SI 2003/2111.

[38] Rule 2.25(1)(h) of the Insolvency (Scotland) Rules 1986, as amended by SI 2003/2111.

[39] Rule 2.25(i) of the Insolvency (Scotland) Rules 1986, as amended by SI 2003/2111.

[40] Rule 2.25(1)(l) of the Insolvency (Scotland) Rules 1986, as amended by SI 2003/2111; para.49(3) of new Sch.B1 to the Insolvency Act 1986.

tion is proposed, details must be provided of the proposed liquidator and a statement that the creditors may nominate another person to act as liquidator.[41] There must be included in the statement a history of how the administration has been managed and financed and how, if the administrator's proposals are approved, the administration will continue to be managed and financed.[42] There must be included the basis upon which it is proposed that the administrator's remuneration should be fixed.[43] The proposals must also state whether the EC Regulation on Insolvency Proceedings applies, and if so, whether the proceedings are main proceedings or territorial proceedings.[44]

Pari passu rule and rights of security holders preserved in administrator's proposals

5–55   The administrator's Statement of Proposals may not include any action which would result in one preferential creditor of the company being paid a smaller proportion of his debt than another, or would result in a preferential debt of the company being paid otherwise than in priority to non-preferential debts, or would affect the right of a secured creditor of the company to enforce his security.[45]

Distribution of moneys

5–56   An administrator has no power to make a partial distribution of assets to creditors where the assets of the company are less than its liabilities except through the mechanism of a voluntary arrangement or a compromise under s.425 of the Companies Act 1985.[46] There is a statutory exception now, in that the administrator may make a distribution to secured and preferential creditors provided preferential creditors are paid in accordance with the ranking rules in s.175 of the Insolvency Act 1986.[47] There was some authority that administrators could make payments to pre-administration creditors in order to ensure the future of the company as a going concern.[48] The administrator is now given express power to make payment otherwise than to secured or preferential creditors if he thinks it is likely to assist achievement of the purpose of administration in addition to his general power under para.13 of Sch.1 to the Insolvency Act 1986 to make any payment which is necessary or incidental to the performance of his functions.[49]

---

[41] Rule 2.25(1)(m) of the Insolvency (Scotland) Rules 1986, as amended by SI 2003/2111.
[42] Rule 2.25(1)(p) of the Insolvency (Scotland) Rules 1986, as amended by SI 2003/2111.
[43] Rule 2.25(1)(j) of the Insolvency (Scotland) Rules 1986, as amended by SI 2003/2111.
[44] Rule 2.25(1)(q) of the Insolvency (Scotland) Rules 1986, as amended by SI 2003/2111.
[45] Paragraph 73(1) of new Sch.B1 to the Insolvency Act 1986.
[46] *Re St Ives Windings Ltd* [1987] 3 B.C.C. 634; *Re British and Commonwealth Holdings plc* (No.3) [1992] 1 W.L.R. 672.
[47] Paragraph 65 of new Sch.B1 to the Insolvency Act 1986.
[48] See Fletcher, Higham and Trower, *The Law and Practice of Co-operative Administrations*, at pp.190–191 and cases there referred to.
[49] Paragraph 66 of new Sch.B1 to the Insolvency Act 1986.

Ending of administration

(a) Automatic end of administration

The administrator must perform his functions as quickly and effi- **5–57** ciently as is reasonably practicable,[50] but, in any event, the administration will end automatically after one year from the date on which it takes effect.[51] However, this term may be extended for an additional period of up to six months with the consent of each secured creditor of the company and, if the company has unsecured debts, creditors whose debts amount to more than 50 per cent of the company's unsecured debts, disregarding debts of any creditor who does not respond to an invitation to give or withhold consent.[52]

(b) Court ending administration on application of administrator

The administrator may apply to the court to end his administration, **5–58** and he must make such an application if he thinks that the purpose of administration cannot be achieved, or that the company should not have entered administration, or a creditors' meeting requires him to make such an application.[53] Similarly, an administrator must also make an application to end his administration if the administrator thinks that the purpose of administration has been sufficiently achieved in relation to the company.[54] In those circumstances the court may provide that the appointment of an administrator shall cease to have effect from a specified time, and may make a range of other orders.[55]

(c) Out of court termination of administration where objective achieved

Where an administrator is appointed by a holder of a floating charge **5–59** or by a company or its directors, and the administrator thinks that the purpose of administration has been sufficiently achieved in relation to the company, he may file a notice with the court, and with the Registrar of Companies, and the administrator's appointment shall cease to have effect when the notice has been lodged with the court and with the Registrar of Companies.[56] In addition the administrator must send a copy to every creditor of the company of whose claim and address he is aware of the notice within five business days of lodging the notice with the court, although this last obligation may be satisfied by publication in the Edinburgh Gazette and another newspaper.[57]

---

[50] Insolvency Act 1986, para.4 of new Sch.B1.

[51] *ibid.,* para.76(1) and (2) of new Sch.B1.

[52] *ibid.,* para.78(1) of new Sch.B1. If the administrator has made a statement that the company has insufficient property to enable a distribution to be made to unsecured creditors other than the prescribed part of the company's assets set aside for unsecured creditors, the requisite consents are the consents of each secured creditor of the company, and preferential creditors whose debts amount to more than 50% of the preferential debts of the company, disregarding debts of any creditor who does not receive an invitation to give or withhold consent (para.78(2) of that Schedule).

[53] Insolvency Act 1986, para.79(1) and (2) of new Sch.B1.

[54] *ibid.,* para.79(3) of new Sch.B1.

[55] *ibid.,* para.79(4) of new Sch.B1.

[56] *ibid.,* para.80(2) and (3) of new Sch.B1.

[57] Rule 2.45(2) and (3) of the Insolvency (Scotland) Rules 1986, as amended by SI 2003/2111.

(d) Court ending administration on application of a creditor

5–60   A creditor of a company may apply to the court for the appointment of an administrator of a company to cease to have effect on the grounds of there being an improper motive on the part of the applicant for an administration order, or on the part of the person who appointed the administrator out of court.[58]

(e) Exit into a winding up

5–61   The court shall order that the appointment of an administrator shall cease to have effect, if a winding up order of the company in administration is made on a petition presented under s.124A (public interest) of the Insolvency Act 1986, or under s.367 of the Financial Services and Markets Act 2000 (petition by financial services authority).[59] Administration may also end by an exit into a voluntary winding up if the administrator thinks that the preferential and secured creditors will receive payment in respect of their debts, and that there will be money left over for a distribution to unsecured creditors.[60] If the administrator thinks these conditions will be met, he may send a notice to that effect to the Registrar of Companies to be registered, with a copy of the notice filed with the court as soon as reasonably practicable after that, and a copy also sent to each creditor of whose claim and address he is aware of.[61] On the registration by the Registrar the appointment of an administrator in respect of the company ceases to have effect and the company is then wound up as if a resolution for voluntary winding up under s.84 of the Insolvency Act 1986 were passed on the day on which the notice was registered, with the liquidator being a person nominated by the creditors[62] or, if no person is nominated by the creditors, the administrator.[63]

(f) Exit into dissolution

5–62   Paragraph 84 of new Sch.B1 to the Insolvency Act 1986 provides that the administrator may take steps to dissolve the company where he finds that the company has no further assets to make a distribution to creditors; in which case he may send a notice to the Registrar of Companies and send a copy to the court and to each of the creditors. The company is then considered dissolved after three months from the registration of the notice by the Registrar of Companies.

Replacement[64] of an administrator

(a) Resignation of administrator

5–63   An administrator may resign only on the grounds of ill-health or because he intends ceasing to be in practice as an insolvency practitioner, or there is some conflict of interests or change in personal

---

[58] Insolvency Act 1986, para.81(1) and (2) of new Sch.B1.

[59] *ibid.*, para.82(1) to (3) of new Sch.B1.

[60] *ibid.*, para.83(1) and (2) of new Sch.B1.

[61] *ibid.*, paras 83(3) to (5) of new Sch.B1.

[62] Rule 2.47(3) of the Insolvency (Scotland) Rules 1986, as amended by SI 2003/2111, sets out the procedure for nomination.

[63] Paragraph 83(6) and (7) of new Sch.B1 to the Insolvency Act 1986.

[64] "Replacement" is where an administrator dies, resigns, is removed from office by the court or vacates office through ceasing to be qualified as an administrator; para.90 of new Sch.B1 to the Insolvency Act 1986.

circumstances, which precludes or makes impracticable the further discharge by him of the duties of administrator or on court sanctioned grounds.[65]

(b) Application to replace administrator

Where the administrator was appointed by an administration order, the court may replace the administrator on an application made by a creditors' committee of the company.[66] An application may also be made by the company, the directors of the company, one or more creditors of the company, or where more than one person was appointed to act jointly or concurrently as the administrator, any of those persons who remains in office, but only if there is no creditors' committee or the court is satisfied that the creditors' committee or a remaining administrator is not taking reasonable steps to make a replacement, or the court is satisfied that for another reason it is right for the application to be made.[67] In the case of out of court appointments of administrators, the replacement of the administrator may be made by the appointer of the administrator.[68]

(c) Substitution of administrator: competing floating charge holder

Where an administrator of a company is appointed out of court by the holder of a qualifying floating charge, the holder of a qualifying floating charge which has priority of ranking in accordance with s.464(4)(b) of the Companies Act 1985, may apply to the court for the administrator to be replaced by an administrator nominated by the holder of the prior floating charge.[69] **5–64**

(d) Substitution of administrator appointed by company or directors: creditors' meeting

Where an administrator of a company is appointed by a company or its directors, and there is no holder of a qualifying floating charge in respect of the company's property, the administrator may be replaced by a creditors' meeting, but only if the new administrator's written consent to act is presented to the meeting before the replacement is made.[70] **5–65**

Discharge from liability of administrator

Where a person ceases to be the administrator of a company (whether because he vacates office by reason of resignation, death or otherwise, because he is removed from office or because his appointment ceases to **5–66**

---

[65] Rule 2.49 of the Insolvency (Scotland) Rules 1986, as amended by SI 2003/2111. Rules 2.50 and 2.51 of these Rules set out detailed procedures to be followed in the case of resignations, and r.2.52 sets out the procedure to be followed where an administrator has died or has ceased to be qualified to act as an insolvency practitioner.

[66] Paragraph 91(1)(a) of new Sch.B1 to the Insolvency Act 1986.

[67] Paragraph 91 of new Sch.B1 to the Insolvency Act 1986.

[68] Paragraphs 92 and 93 of new Sch.B1 to the Insolvency Act 1986. Paragraphs 94 and 95 of that Schedule make further provisions in relation to the replacement of an administrator.

[69] Insolvency Act 1986, para.96 of new Sch.B1.

[70] *ibid.*, para.97 of new Sch.B1.

have effect) he is discharged from liability in respect of any action of his as administrator.[71] The discharge takes effect:

(a) in the case of an administrator who dies, on the lodging with the court of notice of his death;

(b) in the case of an administrator appointed by a holder of a floating charge or a company or its directors, at a time appointed by resolution of the creditors' committee or, if there is no committee, by resolution of the creditors; or

(c) in any case, at a time specified by the court.[72]

Although an administrator is discharged, he remains liable to misfeasance action under para.75 of new Sch.B1 to the Insolvency Act 1986.[73]

Remuneration of the administrator

5–67   The administrator's remuneration is to be determined from time to time by the creditors' committee or, if there is no creditors' committee by the court, and is paid out of the assets of the company as an expense of the administration. The relevant rules are those applicable to liquidators and trustees in bankruptcy.[74]

---

[71] Insolvency Act 1986, para.98(1) of new Sch.B1.
[72] *ibid.*, para.98(2) of new Sch.B1.
[73] *ibid.*, para.98(4) of new Sch.B1.
[74] Rule 2.39 of the Insolvency (Scotland) Rules 1986, as amended by SI 2003/2111 applying, with modifications, rr.4.32–4.35, and s.53 of the Bankruptcy (Scotland) Act 1985.

CHAPTER 6

RECEIVERSHIP

Introduction

Although the Enterprise Act 2002 effectively abolished administrative **6–01** receivership in Scotland,[1] the transitional provisions in that Act mean that administrative receivership in its old form is going to be around for many years. The authors have decided, therefore, to give this insolvency regime as full a treatment in this chapter as in the second edition of the book but, as in that edition, not to go into those areas of practical detail which are very well covered in *The Law and Practice of Receivership in Scotland* by Greene and Fletcher, a third edition of which is soon to be published.

Format of chapter

This chapter is divided into three parts as follows: part I covers the **6–02** general nature of floating charges, the legal effects of the crystallisation of floating charges, and receivership; part II covers the appointment of receivers, joint receivers, the resignation of receivers, the removal of receivers, and the remuneration of receivers; and part III covers the duties and powers of receivers.

PART I

NATURE OF FLOATING CHARGE AND EFFECT OF CRYSTALLISATION OF FLOATING CHARGE AND RECEIVERSHIP

Administrative receivers and receivers/new importance of distinction

Floating charges are legal instruments which give the holder of the **6–03** floating charge a security or charge over the assets of a company to the extent described in the charge. In terms of s.51(1) of the Insolvency Act 1986 the holder of a floating charge over all or any part of the property (including uncalled capital) may appoint a receiver under certain defined circumstances. Where the floating charge covers the whole (or substantially the whole) of the company's property, the receiver so appointed is known as an "administrative receiver".[2] Where the floating

---

[1] See para.5–03.
[2] Enterprise Act 2002, s.251.

charge does not cover the whole (or substantially the whole) of the company's property, then the receiver is known merely as a "receiver".[3] A receiver in Scotland may only be appointed by the holder of a "floating" charge.[4] The test then is not what property could at the time of the floating charge being created, be caught, but rather that when the floating charge crystallises, "substantially the whole of the company's property" has been attached. Accordingly if the holder of the floating charge, before it has crystallised, restricts the scope of the assets covered by the floating charge, what started out as potentially an administrative receivership could on crystallisation lose that status.[5]

Since September 15, 2003, when the insolvency provisions of the Enterprise Act 2002 came into force,[6] this distinction between the two types of floating charge has added importance in that from then there are restrictions on the appointment of an administrative receiver. A new Chap.IV of Pt III of the Insolvency Act 1986 is inserted by s.250 of that Act, and in terms of new s.72A(2) in that Chap.IV: "In Scotland, the holder of a qualifying floating charge in respect of a company's property may not appoint or apply to the court for the appointment of a receiver who on appointment would be an administrative receiver of property of the company". The new restriction on the appointment of an administrative receiver is, however, subject to an important qualification. It only applies to floating charges created on or after September 15, 2003.[7] There are some exceptions to the restriction on the appointment of an administrative receiver on the back of post-September 15, 2003 floating charges,[8] but they are very limited. Secondly, it will still be competent to appoint a receiver if it is over property below the threshold required for an administrative receivership. However, receivership as it has been generally known in Scotland—an all assets receivership—is effectively abolished. However, the fact that pre-September 15, 2003 floating charges are not restricted—and there are considerable benefits to the holder in not having the right restricted[9]—means that the familiar receivership will be used for years. This chapter must be read in this context. It must also be understood that the restriction on the right to appoint an administrative receiver does not affect the law of floating charges and the nature of the security. All the changes mean, is that the enforcement of the floating charge will be in the hands of an administrator and not an administrative receiver, with the holder of the floating charge still effectively appointing the officeholder.

Companies able to create floating charges

6–04   The floating charge may be created by any incorporated company which the Court of Session has jurisdiction to wind up.[10] Effect will accordingly be given to floating charges by companies which have been

---

[3] Insolvency Act 1986, s.251.

[4] *ibid.*, s.51(1).

[5] *Scottish and Newcastle Breweries plc v Ascot Inns Ltd (in receivership)* [1993] B.C.C. 634; 1994 S.L.T. 1140.

[6] The Enterprise Act 2002 (Commencement No. 4 and Transitional Provisions and Savings) Order 2003 (SI 2003/2093).

[7] s.72A(4) of the Insolvency Act 1986 as inserted by s.250 of the Enterprise Act 2002.

[8] See para.5–09.

[9] See para.5–04.

[10] Companies Act 1985, s.462(2).

incorporated by a private Act of Parliament or by a Royal Charter, or under predecessor legislation to the Companies Act. Also charges granted by companies incorporated in other parts of Great Britain and by foreign companies are given effect to. The recognition in Scotland of a floating charge by a foreign company is not dependent on either the company itself or the charge in question being registrable in Scotland under ss.424 or 691 of the Companies Act. It is necessary only that the company is "incorporated", *i.e.* that it has a separate status as a legal person in its local legal system and that the charge is seen to be of the nature of a "floating charge".

Fixed and floating charges

Important legal consequences arise from the difference between **6–05** "fixed" and "floating" charges, and it is thought that an understanding of charges or securities generally would be helpful to aid appreciation of the legal rights of the holder of the floating charge on the crystallisation of the floating charge by the appointment of a receiver or winding up. Briefly, a fixed security is a security over land and any other type of property of the company which will be effective on the winding up of the company.[11] The statutory definition follows the old legal maxim that bankruptcy is the test of all legal rights. A fixed security therefore gives the holder of the fixed security the effective and almost unqualified right in competition with any other creditors to have the secured assets realised for the benefit of the holder of the security. In contrast, where there is a floating charge, although the security has legally the same effect in relation to the assets secured "as if it were" a fixed security,[12] this is subject to a major qualification. Before the security holder is entitled to the proceeds of the sale of an asset secured by a floating charge, the rights of any person who holds a fixed security over the property must be satisfied. Secondly, before the holder of the floating charge is entitled to the proceeds of any sale of assets secured by a floating charge, preferential creditors must be paid.[13] Preferential debts are a category of debts as defined by s.386 of and Sch.6 to the Insolvency Act 1986. They used to form quite an extensive category of debts but, since the abolition of Crown preferences by s.251 of the Enterprise Act 2002,[14] the category is much reduced. The "prescribed part"[15] to be made available to unsecured creditors operates like a preference— although not scheduled as such—and may amount to the value of the lost Crown preferences. These preferences etc may leave no proceeds for the holder of the floating charge.

A second major difference between a fixed charge and a floating charge is that a fixed charge is specific to a particular asset, whereas a floating charge is not specific. *In Re Yorkshire Woolcombers Association*,[16] Vaughan-Williams L.J. explained the nature of a fixed security:

---

[11] Insolvency Act 1986, s.70(1).
[12] Companies Act 1985, s.463(2).
[13] Insolvency Act 1986, s.59(1).
[14] See para.19–18.
[15] See para.19–25.
[16] [1903] 2 Ch. 284 at 294.

"I do not think that for a 'specific security' you need have a security of a subject-matter which is then in existence. I mean by 'then' at the time of the execution of the security; but what you do require to make a specific security is that the security whenever it has come into existence, and has been identified or appropriated as a security, shall never thereafter at the wish of the mortgagor cease to be a security. If at the wish of the mortgagor he can dispose of it and prevent it being any longer a security, although something else may be substituted more or less for it, that is not a 'specific' security."

In contrast, a floating charge is not immediately effective or enforceable. Rather it "floats" over the company's assets, entitling the company to deal with the property in the ordinary course of business. When the floating charge becomes effective, it is said to "crystallise", which occurs on the winding up of the company or on the appointment of a receiver.[17] It then attaches the property of the company as if it were a fixed security. What assets are then secured depends on the terms of the floating charge.[18] Where the floating charge stipulates that the assets of the company, present and future, are covered by the charge, the charge attaches assets re-acquired after the receiver's appointment, and indeed any property which comes into the company's hands.[19]

In the *Yorkshire Woolcombers* case,[20] Romer L.J. set out three characteristics of a floating charge: (1) a charge on a class of assets of a company present and future; (2) that class is one which in the ordinary course of business of the company would be changing from time to time; and (3) it is contemplated that until some future step is taken by the chargee the company may carry on in its ordinary course of business in respect of the charged assets.

There is a further qualification to the rights of the holder of a floating charge. When an administration order takes effect in respect of a company, any administrative receiver of a company must vacate office.[21] Also, where a company is in administration, any receiver of part of the company's property must vacate office if the administrator requires him to.[22] Where an administrative receiver or receiver vacates office on respectively an administration order taking effect or a company being in administration, his remuneration is charged on and paid out of any property of the company which was in his custody or under his control immediately before he vacated office.[23]

---

[17] Companies Act 1985, s.463(1); Insolvency Act 1986, s.53(7).

[18] Companies Act 1985, s.462(1).

[19] *Ross v Taylor*, 1985 S.L.T. 387.

[20] [1903] 2 Ch. 284 at 295.

[21] Paragraph 41(1) of new Sch.B1 to the Insolvency Act 1986. This restriction applies only to an administration order taking effect, because in terms of para.17(b) of new Sch.B1 to the Insolvency Act 1986 an administrator may not be appointed by a holder of a floating charge under para.14(1) of that Schedule if an administrative receiver of the company is in office. Similarly, in terms of para.25(c) of new Sch.B1 to the Insolvency Act 1986 a company or its directors may not appoint an administrator under para.22 of that Schedule if an administrative receiver of the company is in office.

[22] Paragraph 41(2) of new Sch.B1 to the Insolvency Act 1986.

[23] Paragraph 41(3)(a) of new Sch.B1 to the Insolvency Act 1986.

During the period in which the administration order is in force, the administrator is allowed to dispose of or deal in the property attached as if the floating charge had not crystallised.[24] This is not the position with fixed securities, where a court order would be required.[25] Nevertheless, the floating charge is still crystallised and secures the assets or replacement assets.[26] The wording of the statute does not limit the appointment of a receiver to floating charges created after the introduction of receivers to Scotland by the Companies (Floating Charges and Receivers) (Scotland Act) 1972. It would also appear possible to limit the circumstances in which a receiver could be appointed.[27] There would seem no reason in principle why the holder of a floating charge could not have all his rights to appoint a receiver limited by contract, so that the floating charge would crystallise only in the event of a winding up.

Types of fixed security

In general, all assets of a company may be made subject to a fixed **6–06** security in Scotland. In the case of certain assets, however, any security is void unless it is registered by the company. The following fixed securities must be registered:

(1) a charge on land or any interest in land;
(2) a security over the uncalled share capital of a company;
(3) a security over incorporeal (non-physical) moveable property of any of the following categories:

    (a) the book debts of a company;
    (b) calls made but not paid;
    (c) goodwill;
    (d) a patent or a licence under a patent;
    (e) a trademark;
    (f) a copyright or a licence under a copyright; and

(4) a security over a ship or aircraft or any share in a ship.[28]

In relation to rights (of which the most valuable in relation to a company are usually receivables or book debts), the mechanism for creating a fixed security is the assignation of the right to the security holder and, in the case of receivables, intimation to the debtor. This is important in relation to insolvency because the courts have interpreted the crystallisation of the floating charge having effect as if the charge were a fixed charge[29] literally to mean that the holder of the floating charge was to be in the same position as he would have been had he set up the mechanics of a normal fixed charge.[30] The fact that the crystallisation of a floating

---

[24] Insolvency Act 1986, para.70(1) of new Sch.B1.
[25] *ibid.*, para.71 of new Sch.B1.
[26] *ibid.*, para.70(2) of new Sch.B1.
[27] See the Insolvency Act 1986, s.52(1), which speaks of a receiver being able to be appointed "in so far as not otherwise provided for by the instrument on the occurrence of any of the following events".
[28] Companies Act 1985, s.410(4); see also Companies Act 1989, s.93.
[29] *ibid.*, s.463(1); Insolvency Act 1986, s.53(7).
[30] *Forth v Clyde Construction Ltd v Trinity Timber & Plywood Ltd*, 1984 S.L.T. 94.

charge effectively assigns receivables to the holder of the floating charge, is important in relation to set off.[31]

Registration of floating charges/obligations securable

6–07   As in the case of the fixed charges referred to above, a floating charge must be registered in Scotland if it is to have the effect of securing assets[32]. The floating charge may be to secure a debt (*i.e.* in an instrument known as a "debenture"). However, it may also be used to secure other obligations including a guarantee.[33] The attachment of a floating charge on the appointment of a receiver, or in the case of winding up, gives security not only for the principal of the debt or obligation in question but also for both pre- and post-receivership interest until payment of the sum due under the charge.[34]

Crystallisation of floating charges/assets charged

6–08   When a floating charge crystallises and attaches on the company going into liquidation, the property which is attached is "the property then comprised in the company's property and undertaking or, as the case may be, in part of that property and undertaking".[35] The wording of ss.53(7) and 54(6) of the Insolvency Act 1986 is slightly different. In terms of these sections the property attached is "the property then subject to the charge". It is not clear that the different wording has any legal import.

Acquirenda

6–09   Where a floating charge is expressed to relate to the whole assets of the company, present and future, *acquirenda*[36] would appear to be charged on the crystallisation of the floating charge.

In the case of *Ross v Taylor*[37] the Inner House considered the effect of a floating charge which was expressed to relate to the whole assets of a company, present and future, while the instrument was in force. According to Lord President Emslie, the true question was not "what was the property comprised in the company's property and undertaking on the date of the receiver's appointment?" Rather, the question was what property was subject to the charge. Upon a proper construction of the instrument the charge was over the whole of the property of the company existing and from time to time emerging, and it followed that, under the provisions of that floating charge, goods which were reac-

---

[31] See Chap.17.
[32] Companies Act 1985, s.410(4)(e).
[33] *ibid.*, s.462(1).
[34] Companies Act 1985, s.463(4); *National Commercial Bank of Scotland Ltd v Liquidators of Telford Grier Mackay & Co*, 1969 S.C. 181.
[35] Companies Act 1985, s.463(1).
[36] *Acquirenda* is a Scots legal dog Latin term meaning assets acquired subsequently.
[37] 1985 S.L.T. 387.

quired after the receiver's appointment fell under the attachment of the charge. Any property which came into the company's hands after the appointment of the receiver would be attached and available, if need be, for realisation by the receiver. A second question put to the court in *Ross v Taylor*[38] was, if goods did not form part of a company's assets at the date of the appointment of a receiver, on the liquidation of the company would the floating charge re-crystallise to the effect that any *acquirenda* since the date of the receiver's appointment would fall within the assets covered by the floating charge for distribution purposes in a liquidation? The court answered the question in the affirmative, on the grounds that the floating charge, on the commencement of a winding up, attached to the property then comprised in the company's property and undertaking, and had effect as if it were a fixed security over the property. The reason for the court arriving at a "double crystallisation" solution was their strict reading of the wording of s.1(2) of the Companies (Floating Charges and Receivers) (Scotland) Act 1972, which provided that a floating charge "shall, on the commencement of the winding-up . . . attach to the property then comprised in the company's property and undertaking etc." On consolidation the terminology was altered, and s.463(1) of the Companies Act provided that: "On the commencement of the winding-up of a company, a floating charge created by the company attaches to the property then comprised in the company's property and undertaking, etc."

This wording has been further altered by s.140(1) of the Companies Act 1989 which substitutes for "on the commencement of the winding-up of a company" the words "where a company goes into liquidation within the meaning of section 247(2) of the Insolvency Act 1986". Sections 53(7) and 54(6) of the Insolvency Act 1986 provide that on the appointment of a receiver the charge "attaches to the property then subject to the charge".

It is not possible to say whether in future a court, on the new wording, would stick to the concept of "double attachment". What is clear however is that future assets of the company are attached.

Assets of the company

Heritable property

Crystallisation of a floating charge attaches heritable property pro- **6–10** vided the company has beneficial ownership of the property.[39]

Moveable property

Moveable property owned by a company is caught by the crystillisa- **6–11** tion of a floating charge, subject to any securities such as a landlord's hypothec.[40]

---

[38] 1985 S.L.T. 387.

[39] See *Sharp v Thomson*, 1997 S.L.T. 636; [1998] B.C.C. (H.L.) 115.

[40] *Grampian Regional Council v Drill Stem (Inspection Services) Ltd (in receivership)*, 1994 S.C.L.R. 36 (*Cumbernauld Development Corporation v Mustone*, 1983 S.L.T. (Sh. Ct.) 55 not followed).

Consigned funds

6–12   It is not clear always what are assets of the company for the purposes of being covered by a Scottish charge. Where funds have been consigned to court to await the result of pending litigation it has been held in Scotland that the funds are not "property" of a company and hence are not attached by a floating charge.[41]

Trust assets

6–13   Where property is held by the company subject to a valid trust in favour of a third party, that property is not attached by the floating charge on the appointment of a receiver.[42]

Unfair preferences and gratuitous alienations

6–14   It has been held in England in *Re Yagerphone Ltd*[43] that money recovered from a creditor on the grounds that it had been paid out as a fraudulent preference was not subject to a floating charge over the company's assets as the money at the time that the charge crystallised did not constitute property of the company nor a "contingent interest". Following on that reasoning the court also was of the opinion that the right to recover money from a creditor who had been fraudulently preferred was conferred for the purpose of benefiting the general body of creditors and therefore should form part of the general assets of the company for distribution to the general creditors. The Inner House in *Ross v Taylor*[44] said that the English cases of *Re Yagerphone Ltd*[45] and *N W Robbie & Co v Witney Warehouse Co Ltd*,[46] did not afford any reliable assistance, but turned upon their own facts and the particular terms of the relevant debentures. It is thought that the reasoning in *Re Yagerphone Ltd* is open to challenge in Scotland. It may be argued, and is thought by the authors, that the right to recover assets paid out as a preference or as a gratuitous alienation is an asset of the company. Both these actions are available at common law to a creditor as well under statute to a creditor, administrator and liquidator. It is thought that these categories of action under statute are machineries to vindicate rights of the company. They are also designed to allow the creditors to benefit collectively.[47] The reduction of voidable transactions in Scotland is not entirely without retrospective effect, and reduction may have the effect of bringing the relevant asset within the "assets of the company".[48]

Extortionate credit transactions

6–15   Slightly more problematical—if only because it is a relatively new procedure with little case law—is the position of sums recovered under the "extortionate credit transactions" provisions of s.244 of the Insol-

---

[41] *Hawking v Hafton House Ltd*, 1990 S.L.T. 496.
[42] *Toy Valley Joinery Ltd v Cf Financial Services Ltd*, 1987 S.L.T. 207. (See Chap.9.)
[43] [1935] Ch. 392.
[44] 1985 S.L.T. 387.
[45] [1935] Ch. 392.
[46] [1963] 3 All E.R. 613.
[47] D.P. Sellar, 1983 S.L.T. 253; see also for an excellent discussion *Oxford Journal of Legal Studies*, Vol. 10, No 2.
[48] In the case of *N.A. Kratzmann Pty Ltd (No 2) v Tucker* (1970–71) 123 C.L.R. 295, 301–2, the Australian courts were prepared to recognise an exception to the *Yagerphone* rule where specific property which had been the subject of a fraudulent preference is recovered and it was covered by the terms of the charge.

vency Act 1986. Section 244(2) provides that: "[t]he court may, on the application of the office holder, make an order with respect to the transaction if the transaction is or was extortionate and was entered into in the period of three years ending with the day in which the administration order was made or (as the case may be) the company went into liquidation."

Section 244(4) provides for the remedy of reduction. This type of order may therefore be obtained by a receiver when the company is in liquidation or by an administrator when the company is in administration. It is thought that sums recovered under the extortionate credit transaction provisions of s.244 would be treated in the same way as sums recovered under the gratuitous alienations and unfair preferences provisions of ss.242 and 243. It is difficult to see why any action brought under s.244 could not also in essence be brought under statute and at common law as a gratuitous alienation.

Misfeasance proceedings

It is thought that sums recovered under s.212 of the Insolvency Act **6–16** 1986 would be caught by an appropriately drafted floating charge, because the misfeasance provisions create no new liabilities but merely establish a summary procedure for compelling directors to account for any breach of duty. The right being vindicated is a right which inheres in the company at the time the directors breach their duty.[49]

Fraudulent trading and wrongful trading

The position of sums recovered under the fraudulent trading pro- **6–17** visions of s.213 of the Insolvency Act 1986 and the "wrongful trading" provisions of s.214 of that Act is thought to be in different to the position of sums recovered under the provisions of the unfair preferences, gratuitous alienations and misfeasance proceedings, which are not thought to be caught by a crystallising floating charge. However, this is not beyond doubt and produces a serious anomaly.[50]

Remedies in England and Scotland

In relation to ss.238 and 242 of the Insolvency Act 1986, which deal **6–18** with "transactions at an undervalue" in England and Wales and "gratuitous alienations" in Scotland, and ss.239 and 243, which deal with "preferences" in England and Wales and "unfair preferences" in Scotland, there is a further problem in relation to the types of remedy available. Briefly, in terms of ss.238(3) and 239(3) of the Insolvency Act 1986 the court in England and Wales will make an order restoring the position to what it would have been had there not been a challengeable transaction. This means that if heritage was bought at an undervalue, the recipient of the alienation is ordered to make up the difference. In Scotland in contrast, in such a situation the transaction has to be

---

[49] See para.3–05 for a fuller discussion.
[50] For a fuller discussion see para.8–19.

reduced, the heritage reverts to the company and the recipient only ranks for the non-gratuitous element; and accordingly invariably gets nothing.[51] This discrepancy may be rectified by the workings of the Human Rights Act 1998 bringing the Scottish position into line with the English position.[52]

Until such an event, it is thought that, in cross border situations, the English/Welsh and Scottish jurisdictions will enforce each other's rulings. It is thought that the inconsistency of treatment is not sufficient to make one jurisdiction's approach against public policy in private international law in the other's jurisdiction and hence a reason for refusing enforcement under s.426 of the Insolvency Act 1986.[53]

Date of commencement of receivership

6–19   Receivership commences and the floating charge crystallises on the appointment of a receiver.[54] Receivership is deemed to commence on the day on which, and at the time at which, the instrument of the receiver's appointment is delivered to the receiver, as evidenced by a written docquet.[55] It must be accepted by the receiver by the end of the first business day following that on which the instrument of appointment is received.[56]

Effect of receivership on carrying on of the business

6–20   Unlike a winding up, which can be carried on only for the purpose of the beneficial winding up of the company, there is no restriction on the right of the company to carry on business on the appointment of a receiver. Indeed he is given the explicit power "to carry on the business of the company or any part of it" covered by the charge.[57]

---

[51] Insolvency Act 1986, ss.242(4), 243(5) and *Shorts (Alexander) Trustee v Chung*, 1991 S.C.L.R. 269.

[52] See para.3–05.

[53] S.72(1) of the Insolvency Act 1986 provides that: "a receiver appointed under the law of either part of Great Britain in respect of the whole or any part of any property or undertaking of a company and in consequence of the company having created a charge which, as created, was a floating charge may exercise his powers in the other part of Great Britain so far as their exercise is not inconsistent with the law applicable there" (see *Norfolk House plc (in receivership) v Repsol Petroleum*, 1992 S.L.T. 235, for working of provision effectively of English charge covering Scottish heritable property, despite floating charge converted to a fixed charge in England); and s.426(5) of the Insolvency Act 1986 provides that: "for the purposes of sub-section (4) a request made to a court in any part of the United Kingdom by a court in any other part of the United Kingdom or in a relevant country or territory is authority for the court to which the request is made to apply, in relation to any matters specified in the request, the insolvency law which is applicable by either court in relation to comparable matters falling within its jurisdiction"; and "In exercising its discretion under this subsection, a court shall have regard in particular to the rules of private international law."

[54] Insolvency Act 1986, s.53(7).

[55] *ibid.*, s.53(6)(b); *Secretary of State for Trade and Industry v Houston*, 1994 S.L.T. 775.

[56] *ibid.*, s.53(6)(a).

[57] *ibid.*, s.42(1) and Sch.2, para.14.

Effect of receivership on directors' powers

The directors of a company remain in office on receivership. Indeed **6–21** the Insolvency Act 1986 refers to the current directors of a company being required to make a statement of affairs to the receiver.[58] When a receiver is appointed over property, the power of the directors to deal with the property over which the receiver has been appointed is superseded but not extinguished.[59] The extent of the directors' remaining power depends on the scope of the floating charge. If the floating charge covers all the assets and undertaking of the company, present and future, the powers of the directors will be very limited. Where, however, the floating charge only covers a part of the company, the directors may run the rest of the company.

When looking to what powers the directors have, a good test of the extent of the directors' powers is to inquire whether the powers which the board are said to have lost are ones which can be said to have been assumed by the receiver.[60] The general rule is that the appointment of a receiver: "entirely supersedes the company in the conduct of its business, deprives it of all power to enter into contracts in relation to that business, or to sell, pledge or otherwise dispose of the property put into the possession, or under the control of the receiver and manager. Its powers in these respects are entirely in abeyance".[61] The board has, during the currency of the receivership, no powers over assets in the possession or control of the receiver.[62] This, however, does not preclude the directors from raising actions in connection with the charged property.[63] In the case of *Newhart Developments Ltd v Co-operative Commercial Bank Ltd*,[64] directors were held to have residual powers to bring proceedings against a debenture holder who had appointed the receiver. In that case, however, the Court of Appeal had been impressed by two matters. First, it was impressed by the fact that the company had been indemnified by outside sources against all liability, not only for its own costs, but also for costs which the company might be ordered to pay to the other party. Therefore the bringing of proceedings by the directors in the company's name could not, in any circumstances, prejudice the property over which the receiver had a charge. The court was also impressed by the fact that the receiver was in an invidious position in deciding whether or not to take proceedings by reason of the fact that he was being invited to sue those who had appointed him. Doubt was thrown on that decision by Sir Nicholas Browne-Wilkinson V-C, in *Tudor Grange Holdings Ltd v Citibank NA*,[65] where he stated:

---

[58] Insolvency Act 1986, s.66(3)(a).

[59] *Imperial Hotel (Aberdeen) Ltd v Vaux Breweries Ltd*, 1978 S.L.T. 113; *Independent Pension Trustee Ltd v LAW Construction Co Ltd*, 1997 S.L.T.1105.

[60] *Re Union Accident Insurance Co Ltd* [1972] 1 All E.R. 1105 at 1113; although that case concerned directors' residuary powers on liquidation, the test, it is suggested, is also a good test on receivership.

[61] *Moss Steamship Co v Whinney* [1912] AC 254 at 263, *per* Lord Atkinson.

[62] *Gomba Holdings UK Ltd v Homan*; *Gomba Holdings UK Ltd v Johnson Matthey Bankers Ltd* [1986] B.C.L.C. 331 at 336.

[63] *Shanks v Central Regional Council*, 1987 S.L.T. 410, *per* Lord Weir, disapproving of a judgment of Lord Grieve in *Imperial Hotel (Aberdeen) Ltd v Vaux Breweries Ltd*, 1978 S.C. 86.

[64] [1978] 2 All E.R. 896; [1978] Q.B. 814.

[65] [1991] B.C.L.C 1009 at 1019.

"I have substantial doubts whether the *Newhart* case was correctly decided . . . The decision seems to ignore the difficulty which arises if two different sets of people, the directors and the receivers, who may have widely differing views and interests, both have power to bring proceedings on the same cause of action. . .. Further, the Court of Appeal in the *Newhart* case does not seem to have had its attention drawn to the fact that the embarrassment of the receiver in deciding whether or not to sue can be met by an application to the court for directions as to what course should be taken, an application now envisaged in s 35 of the Insolvency Act 1986."

Because, during receivership, the conduct of the business of the company is taken out of the hands of the directors, the directors' residual powers do not create any duty upon their part to the creditors such as to advise them that their interests could be jeopardised unless they petitioned for the winding-up of the company.[66]

A company in receivership may sue a receiver who acts improperly and in breach of his duties to the company. In *Watts v Midland Bank plc*[67] Gibson J. stated:

"It is common ground between the parties, and I suggest, common sense, that there must be some redress obtainable by a company in receivership against a receiver who acts improperly and in breach of his duties to the company to the detriment of the company. It is also common ground that the liquidator of a company in receivership can sue the receiver. Why should a company in receivership have to go into liquidation before the receiver could be sued by the company? There is no doubt that a mortgagor can sue a mortgagee improperly exercising a power of sale. Why should not a mortgagor company in receivership sue the receiver appointed by the mortgagee to realise the security so as to repay the mortgagee if the receiver acts improperly and to the detriment of the company? Of course the court will not allow any interference by the company in receivership with the proper exercise by a receiver of a power of sale, but I can see no reason in principle why the court should not allow the company to sue the receiver in respect of an improper exercise of his powers."

A decision of a receiver could be challenged by a company on the grounds of bad faith or that it was a decision which no reasonable receiver could have made[68] and a company may at the earlier stage seek

---

[66] *Re Joshua Shaw & Sons Ltd* [1989] B.C.L.C. 362; that case concerned a company which had been in receivership for nine years. The directors had submitted that the company was absolutely solvent. The receivers said that it was unlikely that there would be any money for unsecured creditors. However, after nine years of receivership, there was a surplus of £350,000 available for ordinary creditors. This the court ordered to be paid to the contributories through a voluntary winding-up on the basis that the creditors were time barred. Hoffmann J. said that there may be a gap in the law in that the appointment of a receiver does not stop time running for the purposes of limitation.

[67] [1986] B.C.L.C. 15 at 21.

[68] *Gomba Holdings UK Ltd v Homan; Gomba Holdings UK Ltd v Johnson Matthews Bankers Ltd* [1986] B.C.L.C. 331 at 337.

suspension and interdict against the appointment of a receiver by a floating charge holder.[69] The court may order the company under s.736(2) of the Companies Act 1985 to find caution for expenses if it is the pursuer, and generally has power to order the company to find caution where the company is the defender.[70]

EFFECT OF RECEIVERSHIP ON CONTRACTS OTHER THAN EMPLOYMENT CONTRACTS

Contracts other than contracts of employment

A receiver is deemed to be the agent of a company in relation to such **6–22** property of the company as is attached by the floating charge by virtue of which he was appointed.[71] Any contract entered into by or on behalf of the company prior to the appointment of a receiver continues in force (subject to its terms) notwithstanding that appointment, but the receiver does not, by virtue only of his appointment, incur any personal liability on any such contract.[72] The position in relation to new contracts entered into by him in the performance of his functions is different. He incurs personal liability on those contracts, except in so far as the contract otherwise provides.[73] This stipulation means that receivers invariably seek to exclude personal liability, but sometimes may be obliged to accept personal responsibility for payments due in respect of goods or services. If the supplier refuses to supply unless a new contract is entered into on the same basis as an old contract, the receiver does not "adopt" the original contract but enters into a new contract on the same terms with a new arrangement for payment.[74] A receiver who is personally liable by virtue of s.57(2) of the Insolvency Act 1986 is entitled to be indemnified out of the property of the company in respect of which he was appointed which the administrator considers reasonable.[75] The statutory provisions apply to both "administrative" receivers and ordinary receivers.[76]

Section 233 of the Insolvency Act 1986 provides that an administrative receiver can secure continuing provision of gas, electricity, water and telecommunications from public suppliers, but the supplier may make it a condition of the giving of the supply that the administrative receiver personally guarantees the payment of any charges in respect of the supply, but shall not make it a condition of the giving of the supply, or do anything which has the effect of making it a condition of the giving of the supply, that any outstanding charges in respect of the supply given to the company before the effective date are paid.[77]

---

[69] *Taynor Ltd v Whitbread & Co plc* [1988] S.L.T. 433.
[70] *Balfour Beatty Ltd v Brinmoor Ltd* 1997 S.L.T. 888; *Atlas Hydraulic Loaders Ltd v Seabond Ltd* 1998 S.L.T. 6; and *Pioneer Seafood Ltd v Braer Corp.* 1999 S.L.C.L.R. 1126.
[71] Insolvency Act 1986, s.57(1).
[72] *ibid.,* s.57(4).
[73] *ibid.,* s.57(2).
[74] *Lindop v Stuart Noble & Sons Ltd* [1998] S.C.L.R. 648; aff'd 1999 S.C.L.R. (I.H.) 889.
[75] Rule 2.24 of the Insolvency (Scotland) Rules 1986, as amended by SI 2003/2111.
[76] *ibid.,* s.57(1).
[77] S.233(2) of the Insolvency Act 1986.

Rates

6–23   A receiver acts as agent for the company in relation to the property which is subject to the floating charge under which he was appointed, and when he carries on the business of the company from the heritable property owned by the company it is the company which remains in rateable occupation during the receivership with the receiver having no personal liability.[78]

Contracts of employment

6–24   Contracts of employment are dealt with in Chap.11.

PART II

APPONTMENT, REMOVAL AND RESIGNATION OF RECEIVERS

Qualifications of receivers

Appointment of receivers

6–25   Only an individual is qualified to act as an "administrative receiver",[79] and he must be qualified to act as an insolvency practitioner by virtue of being authorised by a recognised professional body, or by holding an authorisation from those bodies themselves or from the Secretary of State.[80] Sections 51(3) to (5) prohibit the appointment of undischarged bankrupts, firms or bodies corporate as receivers. Section 390(4) of the Insolvency Act 1986 also precludes a person from acting as an insolvency practitioner (and hence an administrative receiver) if the person is subject to a disqualification order under the Company Directors Disqualification Act 1986, or if a disqualification undertaking has been accepted by the Secretary of State. Similarly, patients under the various Mental Health Acts are precluded, as well as a person who has had a guardian appointed to him under the Adults with Incapacity (Scotland) Act 2000.[81]

Power of holder of floating charge and court to appoint a receiver

6–26   The receiver may be appointed by the holder of a floating charge over any part of the property of a company,[82] or alternatively a receiver may be appointed by the court on the application of the holder of the floating

---

[78] *Murdoch Lang McKillop v Tayside R.C.*, 1994 S.C.L.R. (Notes) 746; *Ratford & Hayward v Northavon R.D.C.* [1987] Q.B. 357; for discussion see I.F. Fletcher (1988) 1 *Insolvency Intelligence*; Lightman & Moss, paras 20–004 to 20–019; and for position in respect of winding ups see: *Re Beckford Foods Ltd* [2001] E.W.C.A.Civ. 1934. The fact that the company is in occupation for rating purposes does not mean that the receiver cannot, for other statutory purposes, be held to be in occupation of premises (see *Lord Advocate, Petr*, 1990 S.C.L.R. (Notes) 794; *McKillop, Receiver of Rowan Leisure Ltd, Petr*, 1995 S.L.T. 216).
[79] Insolvency Act 1986, ss.388 and 390(1).
[80] *ibid.*, ss.390, 391 and 392.
[81] *ibid.*, s.390(4) as amended by the Adults with Incapacity (Scotland) Act 2000.
[82] Insolvency Act 1986, s.51(1).

charge.[83] The authors know of no case where the court has appointed a receiver. There is no power in Scotland as in England[84] for creditors to apply to the court to appoint a receiver in a winding up.

Circumstances justifying appointment by the holder of a floating charge

Section 52 of the Insolvency Act 1986 outlines the circumstances when **6–27** a receiver may be appointed. They are:

(1) On the occurrence of circumstances specified in the instrument creating the floating charge as entitling the holder of the floating charge to appoint a receiver, a receiver may be appointed by the holder of the floating charge.[85]
(2) On the occurrence of events laid down by statute, the holder of a floating charge, unless it provides otherwise, may appoint a receiver. The events laid down by statute are:

    (a) the expiry of a period of 21 days after the making of a demand for payment of the whole or any part of the principal sum secured by the charge, without payment having been made;
    (b) the expiry of a period of two months during the whole of which interest due and payable under the charge has been in arrears;
    (c) the making of an order or the passing of a resolution to wind up the company; and
    (d) the appointment of a receiver by virtue of any other floating charge created by the company.[86]

Provided no other receiver has been appointed, the court may appoint a receiver in the same circumstances, provided it is satisfied that the position of the holder of the charge is likely to be prejudiced if no appointment of a receiver is made.[87] A debenture holder in exercising a contractual power to appoint a receiver is under no duty to be altruistic to the borrowing company when deciding whether to exercise that power. The only requirement is one of good faith.[88]

Payment on demand

There is a frequent provision in a floating charge that a receiver may **6–28** be appointed on default by the company to pay on demand what is due. This causes difficulties, because on the one hand justice to the company suggests that the company should be given a reasonable time to pay,

---

[83] Insolvency Act 1986, s.51(2).
[84] *ibid.*, s.32.
[85] *ibid.*, s.52(1).
[86] *ibid.*, s.52(1).
[87] *ibid.*, s.52(2).
[88] *Shamji v Johnson Matthey Bankers* [1991] B.C.L.C. 36.

whereas on the other hand the lender may legitimately wish to take immediate action to avoid jeopardy to the assets of the company which are secured. "Once a decision [has] been made by the Bank to call up its money, there must be a risk that delay of any length would enable assets secured by the debenture to disappear or to be seized by other creditors".[89] Greene and Fletcher suggest that an "on demand" facility would allow a period of 24 hours from the making of the demand for repayment.[90] However, in England it has been held that an "on demand debenture" allowed the borrower merely sufficient time during banking hours to collect the money from its bank or some other "convenient place" to make payment, and the company was not entitled to raise the money either from its bank or elsewhere,[91] which was a case concerning the money markets. It is suggested that what the contracting parties have in contemplation is the key aspect. A loan to a crofter in Benbecula may envisage more time on an "on demand" notice than one to a commodity dealer.

In the case of *Toynar Ltd v Whitbread & Co Ltd*[92] interim suspension of the appointment of receivers was applied for by the company and interim interdict against their continuing to act in that capacity on the ground that the alleged arrears in interest relied on in appointing the receivers was not in fact owed. Although there was an argument that the arrears were not owed, the Inner House upheld the Lord Ordinary's rejection of the application on the ground that the Lord Ordinary had correctly applied the "balance of convenience" test in finding that the holders of the floating charge would be subject to greater prejudice than the petitioners if the interim relief were granted.

Mode of appointment by holder of charge

6–29   The appointment of a receiver by the holder of a floating charge must be made by means of a validly executed instrument in writing, a copy of which must be delivered by or on behalf of the person making the appointment to the Registrar of Companies and the Accountant in Bankruptcy for registration within seven days of its execution and must be accompanied by a notice.[93]

An instrument of appointment of a receiver by a company which is dated on or after July 31, 1990 requires no greater formality than being

---

[89] *ANZ Banking Group (NZ) Ltd v Gibson* [1981] 2 N.Z.L.R. 513 at 519, *per* Holland J.

[90] *Greene and Fletcher*, para.1.31.

[91] *Titford Property Co Ltd v Cannon Street Acceptances Ltd*, May 22, 1975, Goff J., unreported, referred to in *Williams & Glyns Bank Ltd v Barnes* [1981] Com. L.R. 205 at 210. See also *Bank of Baroda v Penessar* [1987] Ch. 335, where it was held that, because a debenture was a commercial matter, a short but adequate period limited to the implementation of the mechanics of payment was to be preferred to the test of a "reasonable time depending on the circumstances of the case"; and *Sheppard & Cooper Ltd v TSB Bank Plc (No.2)* [1996] B.C.C. 965, where a similar approach was taken. The precise form of demand envisaged by the charge must be adhered to: *Elwick Bay Shipping Co Ltd v Royal Bank of Scotland Ltd*, 1982 S.L.T. 62.

[92] 1988 S.L.T. 433.

[93] Insolvency Act 1986, s.53(1). Since the relevant provisions of the Scotland Act 1998 came into force, documentation must be sent to the Accountant in Bankruptcy as well as the Registrar of Companies by virtue of s.125 and para.23 of Sch.8 to that Act.

executed by a single director, the secretary or a duly authorised person, in accordance with s.36B(2) of the Companies Act 1985.[94] There is no requirement that it should be a probative document.

Although an unregistered floating charge is void, unless already presented for registration within 21 days of its creation,[95] it is not thought that mere failure to file the notice with the Registrar would invalidate the appointment of a receiver. Although there is a statutory duty to register the appointment, there is no provision deeming an unregistered appointment void.

Joint receivers, etc.

Joint receivers may be appointed.[96] The appointment of any joint **6–30** receiver has no effect unless the appointment is accepted by all of them.[97] Their appointment as joint receivers is deemed to be made on the day on, and at the time at which, the instrument of appointment is received by the last of them.[98] At the date of the commencement of the joint receivership each joint receiver may docquet receipt of the instrument of appointment.[99] They must both indorse on the instrument of appointment the receipt of the instrument of appointment.[1] It is the joint receiver who last endorses his docquet of acceptance who is required to send a copy of the instrument of appointment to the holder of the floating charge.[2] If there are two or more floating charges, each holder of the floating charge may appoint a receiver, but if one charge has priority to the other, the receiver appointed under that charge shall have the powers given to a receiver to the exclusion of any other receiver.[3] If two or more floating charges rank equally, the receivers appointed under them are deemed to be appointed as "joint receivers".[4] Two equally-ranking floating charges would not entail "joint receivers" unless the assets covered are the same assets. The one floating charge would not have priority to the other floating charge in such a case. If a receiver, under a floating charge that has priority of ranking, is appointed subsequently to another, the powers of the previous receiver are suspended.[5] However, the suspension of the powers of a receiver does not have the effect of requiring him to release any part of the property (including any letters or documents) of the company from his control

---

[94] Inserted by s.130(3) of the Companies Act 1989; substituted by s.14(1) of and para.51 of Sch.4 to the Requirements of Writing (Scotland) Act 1995.

[95] Companies Act 1985, s.410(2); see *N.V. Slavenburg's Bank v Intercontinental National Resources Ltd* [1980] 1 All E.R. 955; the court has power in terms of s.420 of that Act to allow late registration on cause shown (see *Prior v Murray Ventures*, 1989 S.C.L.C. 640 (O.H.)).

[96] Insolvency Act 1986, s.56(3).

[97] Receivers (Scotland) Regulations 1986, reg.5(a).

[98] *ibid.*, reg.5(b).

[99] Insolvency Act 1986, s.53(6).

[1] Insolvency (Scotland) Rules 1986, r.3.1.

[2] *ibid.*, r 3.1(4).

[3] Insolvency Act 1986, s.56(1).

[4] *ibid.*, s.56(2).

[5] *ibid.*, s.56(4).

until he receives from the receiver superseding him a valid indemnity (subject to the limit of the value of such part of the property of the company as is subject to the charge by virtue of which he was appointed) in respect of any expenses, charges and liabilities he may have incurred in the performance of his functions as receiver.[6] The suspension of the powers of a receiver, however, does not cause the floating charge by virtue of which he was appointed to cease to attach to the property to which it attached.[7] Because joint receivers must act together, unless there is provision made in the instrument of appointment,[8] in the event of disagreement, the only option is for the holder of the floating charge or a receiver to seek directions from the court using the provisions of s.63 of the Insolvency Act 1986.

Publication of receivership

6–31   On the appointment of a receiver he must forthwith send to the company and publish notice of his appointment.[9] He must also within 28 days after his appointment, unless the court directs otherwise, send notice of his appointment to all the company's creditors so far as he is aware of their addresses.[10]

Removal of receiver

6–32   A receiver may be removed by the court under s.62(3) of the Insolvency Act 1986. It is suggested that conflict of interest or misconduct would be grounds for removal of a receiver. It is only open to the holder of the floating charge to apply to the court under the statute to remove a receiver. There is, however, another remedy open to a creditor in terms of s.62(2) of the Insolvency Act 1986, which states: "A receiver shall vacate office if he ceases to be qualified to act as an insolvency practitioner in relation to the company". Although only "administrative receivers" need to be insolvency practitioners,[11] it is thought that the effect of the section is that any receiver (whether he needed to be a "qualified insolvency practitioner" or not) must vacate office if he ceases to be a qualified insolvency practitioner. Accordingly, if a creditor thinks that a receiver is abusing his position, representations could be made by him to the Secretary of State or to the recognised professional body, laying the evidence before them and requesting them to withdraw their authorisation for the accused receiver to act as an insolvency practitioner.[12]

Resignation of receiver

6–33   A receiver may resign his office.[13] Where a receiver resigns or vacates office on completion of the receivership or in consequence of his ceasing to be qualified as an insolvency practitioner, he must give the Registrar

---

[6] Insolvency Act 1986, s.56(5).
[7] *ibid.*, s.56(6).
[8] *ibid.*, s.56(3).
[9] *ibid.*, s.65(1)(a).
[10] *ibid.*, s.65(1)(b).
[11] *ibid.*, s.388(1)(a).
[12] *ibid.*, s.393(4).
[13] *ibid.*, s.62(1).

of Companies and the Accountant in Bankruptcy notice to that effect and the Registrar enters the notice in the Register of Charges.[14] He must also give notice of his vacating office to:

(1) the holder of the floating charge by virtue of which he was appointed;
(2) the members of the creditors' committee, if any;
(3) the company or, if it is in liquidation, the liquidator; and
(4) the holder of any other floating charge and any receiver appointed by him.[15]

In the case of a resignation, there must be at least seven days' notice of the resignation[16] and in all other cases the notice must be within 14 days of the vacation of the office.[17]

Remuneration

The remuneration of a receiver is to be determined by agreement **6–34** between the receiver and the holder of the floating charge by virtue of which he was appointed.[18] If the receiver's remuneration cannot be determined in accordance with an agreement or, where it is determined but disputed by the receiver, the holder of any floating charge or fixed security over all or any part of the property of the company, the company itself, or the liquidator of the company, it may be determined by the Auditor of the Court of Session by an application of the receiver or any of these other persons disputing it.[19] The payment to the receiver of his remuneration has priority to the payment of the floating charge-holder.[20]

If there is no agreement between the receiver and the holder of the floating charge, in terms of which the holder of the floating charge undertakes to pay the remuneration of the receiver, the receiver has to look to the assets of the company for the payment of his remuneration, and in this regard he is similar to the liquidator of a company, in so far as, except by express agreement, the creditors who have appointed a liquidator have no liability to pay his remuneration.[21] Unless there is an agreement between the charge-holder and the receiver, the fact that the charge-holder appoints the receiver does not entail that there is an implied obligation on the charge-holder to pay for the services of the receiver.[22]

Refloating

On the expiry of one month following upon the removal of a receiver **6–35** or his ceasing to act as a receiver, if no other receiver has been appointed, the floating charge under which he was appointed ceases to

---

[14] Insolvency Act 1986, s.62(5); Form 3 (Scot).
[15] Insolvency (Scotland) Rules 1986, r.3.11; Receivers (Scotland) Regulations 1986, reg.6.
[16] Receivers (Scotland) Regulations 1986, reg.6.
[17] Insolvency (Scotland) Rules 1986, r.3.11.
[18] Insolvency Act 1986, s.58(1).
[19] *ibid.*, s.58(2).
[20] *ibid.*, s.60(1)(d).
[21] *Hill Samuel & Co Ltd v Laing*, 1989 S.L.T. 760.
[22] *ibid.* at 761.

attach the property subject to it, and again subsists as a floating charge.[23] It will, of course, crystallise again on a winding up,[24] and there seems no reason why a receiver should not be appointed at a subsequent date if there is a subsequent default.

PART III

DUTIES AND POWERS OF A RECEIVER

A. DUTIES OF RECEIVER

6–36 The receiver has certain duties laid on him by statute and certain general duties of care. The general duties of care arise from the statutory duties.

Statutory duties

(1) Payment of floating charge-holder after satisfaction of prior claims

6–37   A receiver has one main statutory duty to perform. He must pay moneys received by him to the holder of the floating charge, by virtue of which he was appointed in or towards satisfaction of the debt secured by the floating charge. He must first, however, pay the following persons:

(a) the holder of any fixed security which is over property subject to the floating charge and which ranks prior to, or *pari passu* with, the floating charge;

(b) all persons who have effectually executed diligence on any part of the property which is subject to the charge by virtue of which the receiver is appointed;

(c) creditors in respect of all liabilities, charges and expenses incurred by or on behalf of the receiver;

(d) the receiver in respect of his liabilities, expenses and remuneration, and any indemnity to which he is entitled out of the property of the company; and

(e) the preferential creditors entitled to payment.[25]

(2) Reporting to creditors and creditors' committee

6–38   A receiver has a statutory duty (within three months or such longer period as the court may allow) after his appointment to send to the Registrar of Companies and the Accountant in Bankruptcy, to the holder of the floating charge by virtue of which he was appointed and to any trustees for secured creditors of the company and (so far as he is aware of their addresses) to all such creditors a report.[26] The report must detail:

---

[23] Insolvency Act 1986, s.62(6).
[24] Companies Act 1985, s.463(1).
[25] Insolvency Act 1986, s.60(1).
[26] *ibid.*, s.67(1).

(a) the events leading up to his appointment, so far as he is aware of them;

(b) the disposal or proposed disposal by him of any property of the company and the carrying on or proposed carrying on by him of any business of the company;

(c) the amounts of principal and interest payable to the holder of the floating charge by virtue of which he was appointed and the amounts payable to preferential creditors; and

(d) the amount (if any) likely to be available for the payment of other creditors.[27]

In addition, he must also, within three months, send a copy of the report (so far as he is aware of their addresses) to all *unsecured* creditors of the company, or publish a notice stating an address to which unsecured creditors of the company should write for copies of the report to be sent to them, which is to be free of charge.[28] He must also summon a meeting of the company's unsecured creditors on not less than 14 days' notice and lay a report before the meeting.[29] Where a meeting of creditors is summoned, the meeting may establish a "creditors' committee".[30]

(3) Keeping records

The receiver must keep a sederunt book as an insolvency practitioner.[31] **6–39**

(4) Notification on notepaper, etc.

All invoices, orders for goods, business letters issued by the company or the receiver or the liquidator must contain a statement that a receiver has been appointed.[32] **6–40**

(5) Statement of affairs

In terms of s.66(1) of the Insolvency Act 1986, where a receiver is appointed "he *shall* forthwith require" a statement of affairs from certain designated persons (for details see Chap.18). **6–41**

This statutory duty extends to all receivers in Scotland but only to administrative receivers in England.[33] This discrepancy is strange and apparently gives the Scottish receiver jurisdiction over the affairs of the company not covered by the floating charge. The rule[34] says: "where the receiver decides to require from any person a statement of affairs . . . he shall send a notice" on a Form 3.1 (Scot.). Given the statutory duty, the discretionary decision implied by the rule must only be as to who shall be required to make a statement.

---

[27] Insolvency Act 1986, s.67(1).
[28] *ibid.,* s.67(2).
[29] *ibid.,* s.67(2).
[30] *ibid.,* s.68(1).
[31] Insolvency (Scotland) Rules 1986, r.7.33(1).
[32] Insolvency Act 1986, s.64(1).
[33] *ibid.,* s.47(1).
[34] Insolvency (Scotland) Rules 1986, r.3.2(1).

Standard of care

6–42   A receiver must exercise his powers without negligence and exercise care in disposing of assets to make sure that they achieve the value which they might reasonably be expected to realise.[35] He must exercise any power of sale bona fide and with regard to the interests of the company and obtain a fair price.[36] He has a general duty of care as regards the rights of members of a company pension scheme over which he exercises control.[37]

Duty to company and guarantor

6–43   The Scottish courts have suggested that the approach to the duties of a receiver and holder of a floating charge should be as close as possible in Scotland and England.[38] The position in English law is now settled. Both the holder of the floating charge and the receiver owe duties of care to the company and any guarantor of the sums secured by the floating charge. In *Standard Chartered Bank Ltd v Walker*,[39] Lord Denning MR said:

> "We have had much discussion on the law. So far as mortgages are concerned the law is set out in *Cuckmere Brick Co Ltd v Mutual Finance Ltd.*[40] If a mortgagee enters into possession and realises a mortgaged property, it is his duty to use reasonable care to obtain the best possible price which the circumstances of the case permit. He owes this duty not only to himself (to clear off as much of the debt as he can) but also to the mortgagor so as to reduce the balance owing as much as possible, and also to the guarantor so that he is made liable for as little as possible on the guarantee. This duty is only a particular application of the general duty of care to your neighbour which was stated by Lord Atkin in *Donoghue v Stevenson*[41] and applied in many cases since: see *Home Office v Dorset Yacht Co Ltd*[42] and *Anns v Merton London Borough*.[43] The mortgagor and the guarantor are clearly in very close 'proximity' to those who conduct the sale. The duty of care is owing to them, if not to the general body of creditors of the mortgagor. There are several dicta to the effect that the mortgagee can choose his own time for the sale, but I do not think this means that he can sell at the worst possible time. It is at least arguable that, in choosing the time, he must exercise a reasonable degree of care.
>
> So far as the receiver is concerned, the law is well stated by Rigby LJ in *Gosling v Gaskell*,[44] a dissenting judgment which was approved

---

[35] *Forth & Clyde Construction Co Ltd v Trinity Timber & Plywood Co Ltd*, 1984 S.L.T. 94 at 97, *per* Lord President Emslie; for England see *Medforth v Blake* [1999] B.C.C. 771.
[36] *Rimmer v Thomas & Sons Ltd*, 1967 S.L.T. 7.
[37] *Larsen's Executrix v Henderson*, 1990 S.L.T. 498.
[38] See comments of Lord Weir in *Shanks v Central Regional Council*, 1987 S.L.T. 410 at 414, and of Lord Grieve in *Imperial Hotel (Aberdeen) Ltd v Vaux Breweries Ltd*, 1978 S.C. 86.
[39] [1982] 3 All E.R. 938 at 942.
[40] [1971] Ch. 949.
[41] [1932] A.C. 562.
[42] [1970] A.C. 1004.
[43] [1978] A.C. 728.
[44] [1896] 1 Q.B. 669.

by the House of Lords.[45] The receiver is the agent of the company, not of the debenture holder, the bank. He owes a duty to use reasonable care to obtain the best possible price which the circumstances of the case permit. He owes this duty not only to the company (of which he is the agent) to clear off as much of its indebtedness to the bank as possible, but he also owes a duty to the guarantor, because the guarantor is liable only to the same extent as the company. The more the overdraft is reduced, the better for the guarantor. It may be that the receiver can choose the time of sale within a considerable margin, but he should, I think, exercise a reasonable degree of care about it. The debenture holder, the bank, is not responsible for what the receiver does except in so far as it gives him directions or interferes with his conduct of the realisation. If it does so, then it too is under a duty to use reasonable care towards the company and the guarantor.

If it should appear that the mortgagee or the receiver have not used reasonable care to realise the assets to the best advantage, then the mortgagor, the company, and the guarantor are entitled in equity to an allowance. They should be given credit for the amount which the sale should have realised if reasonable care had been used. Their indebtedness is to be reduced accordingly."

Standard Chartered Bank Ltd v Walker has subsequently been referred to, seemingly with approval, by Lord Ross in *Lord Advocate v Maritime Fruit Carriers Ltd*,[46] and the principles which Lord Denning stated have since been reinforced by the Privy Council in 1983 in the case of *Tse Kwong Lam v Wong Chit Sen*[47] and followed in *American Express International Banking Corpn v Hurley*.[48] Unfortunately in the only Scottish case on the subject, *Imperial Hotel (Aberdeen) Ltd v Vaux Breweries Ltd*[49] Lord Grieve followed a much earlier English case, *Re Johnson & Co (Builders) Ltd*,[50] which had been already superseded and discredited by the case of *Cuckmere Brick v Mutual Finance Ltd*.[51] Accordingly, it is suggested (especially since Lord Grieve was trying to follow English authority) that his decision that "there is no duty on the mortgagee to see that there is as much as possible left over for those interested in the 'equity' of the company" was wrongly decided.

Duty to creditors

(1) Preferential creditors

The receiver is under a statutory duty to pay preferential creditors **6–44** before paying the holder of a floating charge.[52] It is a positive duty, not simply a negative one not to pay the holder of the instrument containing

---

[45] See [1897] A.C. 575.
[46] 1983 S.L.T. 357.
[47] [1983] 1 W.L.R. 1349.
[48] [1986] B.C.L.C. 52.
[49] 1978 S.C. 86 at 91.
[50] [1955] Ch. 634.
[51] [1971] Ch. 949.
[52] Insolvency Act 1986, s.59(1).

the floating charge without paying the preferential creditors.[53] If the receiver carries on the business in such a way as to dissipate assets which would otherwise be available to pay preferential creditors or accounts to the company or the holder of the instrument containing the floating charge before paying the preferential creditors, he will be liable for breach of statutory duty.[54] The statutory duty to pay preferential creditors is imposed by s.59(1) of the Insolvency Act 1986. That section applies only where the company is not being wound up. However, s.60 of the Insolvency Act 1986 lays down that the receiver shall pay monies received by him to the floating charge-holder after satisfaction of the category of creditors including preferential creditors. He then must pay over any surplus to "the company or its liquidator as the case may be".[55] This envisages a situation where the receiver makes these distributions, although the company is in liquidation. This is in keeping with the Scottish law that a receiver's powers supersede those of a liquidator,[56] and that a receiver may be appointed after the commencement of a liquidation.[57] The result is that there is a duty to the preferred creditors by the receiver if he is appointed before or after the company is in liquidation. It is important because, if the receiver pays over the money for the liquidator to distribute, he could render himself liable to the preferential creditors. This is because the order of priority in distribution by the liquidator is different to the order of priority imposed by statute on the receiver.[58] The liquidator has the expenses of the liquidation as a prior claim to preferential debts. Accordingly, the expenses of the liquidation could eat into or use up moneys available to pay preferential creditors. One effect of this is that preferential creditors will have a financial incentive often to persuade the holder of a floating charge to appoint a receiver. If the sums were significant, they might underwrite the receiver's costs. A problem arises, however, where a liquidation has commenced and a receiver is appointed. Liquidation expenses will have been incurred, and it would appear, following *Manley, Petr,*[59] that the liquidator could be at risk for them. Nevertheless, the question of entitlement to such expenses has not been the subject of a judicial decision. Common sense suggests that, in Scotland, the liquidator should be entitled to his expenses until he hands over to the receiver.

In the English case of *Re First Express Ltd*[60] a company went into liquidation. Shortly afterwards, the bank appointed an administrative receiver under its debenture. The liquidator accounted to the bank— under its fixed charge—for money collected from the company's book debts, but retained a small amount against the liquidation costs. Hoffmann J. accepted that there were liquidation costs as to the payment of which the liquidator was entitled to priority and, therefore,

---

[53] *Westminster Corp. v Haste* [1950] Ch. 442.
[54] See *IRC v Goldblatt* [1972] Ch. 498; and *Westminster Corp. v Haste, above.*
[55] Insolvency Act 1986, s.60(2)(c).
[56] *Manley, Petr,* 1985 S.L.T. 42.
[57] *Libertas-Kommerz GmbH v Johnson,* 1977 S.C. 191.
[58] Insolvency (Scotland) Rules 1986, r.4.66.
[59] 1985 S.L.T. 42.
[60] See *Greene and Fletcher,* para.3.51.

might retain some of the money collected. The authors cannot see any special provision in the English insolvency rules why that ruling should be applicable only to England.

Administrative receivers often seek an indemnity from a liquidator when they pass funds to the liquidator. Because an administrative receiver is under a statutory duty to pay surplus funds not required for the discharge of his obligations to the company over which he is appointed, which is in liquidation, he is not entitled to an indemnity in respect of the performance of this obligation. If, however, a liquidator for some reason seeks to receive monies earlier than the time when the administrative receiver would normally be in a position to pay over, it is thought that in those situations an indemnity should be demanded.

(2) *Duty to ordinary creditors?*

It has been suggested that the receiver owes a duty to manage the **6-45** business of the company with due diligence.[61] Does this mean there is a duty of care to ordinary creditors? Although the proximity between the receiver and creditors is perhaps closer since the Insolvency Act 1986 set up a "creditors' committee" on receivership, and although the English law of equity is pushing boundaries in this area of the law, it is thought incorrect in Scots law to suggest that the receiver owes a duty of care to creditors merely as creditors. Unless there is a breach of a statutory duty in relation to distribution, creditors' interests are represented and their rights enforced through the company. In *Standard Chartered Bank Ltd v Walker*[62] Lord Denning MR said: "the mortgagor and the guarantor are clearly in very close 'proximity' to those who conduct the sale. The duty of care is owing to them, if not to the general body of creditors of the mortgagor."

Nevertheless, a receiver may owe a direct duty of care to creditors whose relationship with the company extends beyond that of mere creditors. The rationale of the rule suggested in the last paragraph is that the creditors' claim is in respect of a debt owed by the company, and such a claim should therefore be made through the company. In certain cases, however, the claim in issue does not relate to a debt owed by the company, and the fact that the claimant is a creditor of the company is merely incidental to the claim. For example, a receiver will clearly owe a duty of care to persons who have deposited property with the company; in such cases the duty arises out of their ownership of the property deposited. If the property cannot be retained by the company, the receiver must notify the owners of that fact and must give them a reasonable opportunity to remove their property; until it is removed the receiver must continue to look after it. Likewise, a receiver owes a duty of care not to prejudice the rights as against third parties of persons dealing with the company. A good example of this is the pension and life assurance entitlement of employees of the company; the receiver

---

[61] *Medforth v Blake* [2000] Ch. 949; [1999] 3 All E.R. 97; see also *Downsview Nominees Ltd v First City Corp. Ltd* [1993] A.C. 295; and for analysis *Sealey* [2000] C.L.J. 31.
[62] [1982] 3 All E.R. 938 at 942.

clearly owes a duty to preserve that entitlement, by continuing to pay the pensions to the institution providing the pension and life assurance until such time as the employees have had a reasonable opportunity to make alternative arrangements on their own account. This means that employees must be given notice that the receiver is to stop paying the premiums in time for them to take action to preserve their rights. In the case of *Larsen's Executrix v Henderson*,[63] the executrix of a deceased employee of a company had sought damages from the receiver appointed to the company for loss allegedly sustained through the termination by the receiver of life insurance provisions effected through the company which it would have been open to the deceased to have continued, despite his fatal illness. The court held that there existed a duty of care on the part of the receiver of a company to employees with rights under a pension scheme not to terminate the pension scheme without first giving an indication that such an event might occur, but that in this particular case the receiver had given adequate notice.

If the receiver has been negligent, the ordinary creditors' rights may be enforced through the company or its liquidator. Alternatively, in the case of an administrative receivership only, the court may, on application of the liquidator, or of any creditor or contributory examine into the misfeasance of an administrative receiver under s.212(1)(b) of the Insolvency Act 1986. This remedy open to a creditor (not just the liquidator) enables the court to order the administrative receiver concerned: (a) to repay, restore or account for moneys; or (b) to contribute a sum to the company's assets by way of compensation in respect of the misfeasance or breach of fiduciary or other duty as the court thinks just.[64] Again here, the emphasis is on the former administrative receiver paying the *company* compensation.

B. POWERS OF RECEIVER

Agency of receiver

6–46 In Scotland a receiver is deemed to be the agent of a company in relation to such of the property of the company as is attached by the floating charge by virtue of which he was appointed.[65] This is in contrast to England, where only an administrative receiver is deemed to be the company's agent. In England the administrative receiver is only the agent unless and until the company goes into liquidation.[66] There is no corresponding provision in Scotland that the agency of a receiver terminates on liquidation.

Statutory powers of Scottish receiver

6–47 All Scottish receivers (not just administrative receivers) have whatever powers are specified in the instrument creating the floating charge in relation to property covered by the floating charge.[67] In addition the

---

[63] 1990 S.L.T. 498.
[64] Insolvency Act 1986, s.212(3).
[65] *ibid.*, s.57(1).
[66] *ibid.*, s.44(1)(a).
[67] *ibid.*, s.55(1).

receiver has a further set of powers specified by statute, provided they are not inconsistent with any provision of the instrument creating the floating charge, in relation to the property covered by the floating charge,[68] but subject to the rights of any person who has effectually executed diligence on all or any part of the property of the company prior to the appointment of the receiver, and subject to the rights of any person who holds over all or any part of the property of the company a fixed security or floating charge which has priority over, or ranks *pari passu* with, the floating charge by virtue of which the receiver was appointed.[69] The statutory powers given by the Insolvency Act 1986 included in addition to minor amendments five new powers which are those listed at the end of the list and starred. These powers are available to receiverships commenced after December 29, 1986 unless written into the instrument creating the floating charge.[70] The powers are as follows:

(1) To take possession of property

A receiver has the power to take possession of, collect and get in the **6–48** property from the company or a liquidator or any other person, and for that purpose to take such proceedings as may seem to him expedient.[71] This is the power which enables the receiver to fulfil his main function, which is to realise on behalf of his appointer the assets subject to the floating charge in order to satisfy the claim of the holder of the floating charge. Where a liquidator has been appointed on the winding up of a company, whether this is before or after the receiver's appointment, the liquidator must hand over property covered by the charge to the receiver and his powers are superseded.[72] The provision also allows him to collect debts due to the company by taking proceedings in the name of the company.[73]

(2) Power to sell property

The receiver has the power to sell, hire out or otherwise dispose of the **6–49** property by public roup or private bargain and with or without advertisement.[74]

(3) Power to borrow

The receiver has power to raise or borrow money and grant security **6–50** for it over the property.[75]

(4) Power to appoint solicitor or accountant

The receiver has the power to appoint a solicitor or accountant or **6–51** other professionally qualified person to assist him in the performance of his functions.[76]

---

[68] Insolvency Act 1986, s.55(2).
[69] *ibid.*, s.55(3).
[70] *ibid.*, Sch.11, para.3.
[71] *ibid.*, s.55(2) and Sch 2, para 1.
[72] *Manley, Petr*, 1985 S.L.T. 42.
[73] *McPhail v Lothian R.C.*, 1981 S.L.T. 173; *Forth & Clyde Construction Ltd v Trinity Timber & Plywood Co Ltd*, 1984 S.L.T. 94.
[74] Insolvency Act 1986, s.55(2) and Sch.2, para.2.
[75] *ibid.*, s.55(2) and Sch.2, para.3.
[76] *ibid.*, s.55(2) and Sch.2, para.4.

(5) Power to bring or defend legal actions

6–52   The receiver has the power to bring or defend any action or any other legal proceedings in the name and on behalf of the company.[77] The action must have the company—just the receiver as the pursuer—with an indication that the company is in receivership.[78] Where a receiver brings an action in the name of the company, he acts as agent but does not incur any personal liability, other than in relation to contracts he may enter into by, for example, instructing solicitors or counsel, when he has a right of relief against the property of the company subject to the floating charge[79]. Where a receiver litigates, he is entitled to have his liabilities, expenses and any indemnity to which he is entitled paid out of the property of the company covered by the floating charge before payment of the proceeds of the realisations of secured assets covered by a floating charge to the holder of a floating charge.[80] Where he litigates, he merely incurs a liability on behalf of the company, and is not personally liable for that liability. In contrast, where a liquidator litigates, he is personally held to warrant the sufficiency of the funds in his hands and is personally liable for expenses.[81] Accordingly, when a company litigates, it will not normally be required to find caution in terms of s.726(2) of the Companies Act 1985 if there is no suggestion that the liquidator, if he is bringing the action, would be unable to honour the obligation.[82] In contrast, because a receiver will not be personally liable, the company will normally be ordered to find caution to pay the defender's expenses, if it litigates in receivership and there is reason to believe that the company will be unable to pay the defender's expenses.[83]

(6) Power to refer to arbitration

6–53   The receiver has power on behalf of the company to refer to arbitration all questions affecting the company.[84]

(7) Insurance

6–54   The receiver has power to effect and maintain insurances in respect of the business and property of the company.[85] A receiver will have to be very careful with company insurance policies. In relation to insurance

---

[77] Insolvency Act 1986, s.55(2) and Sch.2, para.5; The administrative receiver may oppose a winding up petition (*Foxhill & Gyle (Nurseries) Ltd*, 1978 S.L.T. (29) and may petition for the recall of diligence (see *Iona Hotels Ltd v Craig*, 1991 S.L.T. 11).

[78] See *Myles J. Callaghan Ltd (in receivership) Ltd v City of Glasgow District Council*, 1988 S.L.T. 227 (O.H.); 1987 S.C.L.R. 627; and *Graham Ritchie and John Readman (as joint receivers of Madame Foods Ltd) v EFT Industrial Ltd*, 1997 S.C.L.R. 955 (in that case the action was dismissed because action not brought in the name of the company).

[79] Insolvency Act 1986, s.57(3).

[80] *ibid.*, ss.60(1)(e) and 57(3).

[81] *Sinclair v Thurso Pavement Syndicate* (1903) 11 S.L.T. 364.

[82] *Stewart v Steel*, 1987 S.L.T. (Sh. Ct.) 60.

[83] Companies Act 1985, s.726(2); see *Balfour Beatty Ltd v Brinmoor Ltd*, 1997 S.L.T. 888; *Atlas Hydraulic Loaders Ltd v Seabon Ltd*, 1998 S.L.T. 6; and *Pioneer Seafood Ltd v Braer Corp.*, 1999 S.C.L.R. 1126.

[84] Insolvency Act 1986, s.55(2) and Sch.2, para.6.

[85] *ibid.*, s.55(2) and Sch.2, para.7.

policies entered into prior to the receivership, he will not be personally liable for the premiums. However, if he renews a contract he will be personally liable.[86] Most company policies will cover public liability for which he may not have a concern in their being insured. He should check his exposure before entering into unnecessary policies.

Section 1 of the Third Parties (Rights against Insurers) Act 1930 provides that, where under any contract of insurance a company is insured against liabilities to third parties which it may incur, then in the event of a receiver being appointed, if any such liability is incurred by the insured, the rights of the insured against the insurer under the contract in respect of the liability shall, notwithstanding anything in any Act or rule of law to the contrary, be transferred to and vest in the third party to whom the liability was so incurred. This means that the crystallisation of the floating charge does not attach the insured's rights against the insurance company in such a way that the third party was left merely ranking for a claim.

(8) Power to use company's seal

The receiver has the power to use the company's seal.[87]   **6–55**

(9) Execution of deeds

The receiver has the power to do all acts and to execute in the name **6–56** and on behalf of the company any deed, receipt or other document.[88]

(10) Negotiable instruments

The receiver has power to draw, accept, make and endorse any bill of **6–57** exchange or promissory note in the name of, and on behalf of, the company.[89]

(11) Agents and employees

The receiver has power to appoint agents, to do any business which **6–58** he is unable to do himself, or which can more conveniently be done by an agent, and power to employ and dismiss employees.[90] The receiver has much greater scope to appoint an agent than a liquidator. He may appoint an agent to do any business "which can more conveniently be done by an agent". A liquidator does not have this latitude.[91]

(12) Work on property

The receiver has the power to do all such things (including the **6–59** carrying out of work) as may be necessary for the realisation of the property.[92]

---

[86] Insolvency Act 1986, s.57(2).
[87] *ibid.*, s.55(2) and Sch.2, para.8.
[88] *ibid.*, s.55(2) and Sch.2, para.9.
[89] *ibid.*, s.55(2) and Sch.2, para.10.
[90] *ibid.*, s.55(2) and Sch.2, para.11.
[91] *ibid.*, ss 165, 167 and Sch.4, para.12.
[92] *ibid.*, s.55(2) and Sch.2, para.12.

(13) Incidental payments

6–60   The receiver has power to make any payment which is necessary or incidental to the performance of his functions.[93]

(14) Power to carry on the business of the company

6–61   The receiver has the power to carry on the business of the company or any part of it.[94]

(15) Winding-up petitions

6–62   The receiver has power to present or defend a petition for the winding up of the company.[95] The receiver may wish to petition to wind up the company if there is a surplus on assets after payment of the floating charge-holder but that surplus is insufficient to pay all the ordinary creditors on a winding-up, or if the holder of a floating charge is owed money by the company which is not secured by the floating charge. He would have the same grounds, as agent of the company, in opposing a petition for the winding up of the company as the company itself would have. Where a creditor seeks a winding-up order on the ground that a company is unable to pay its debts, the petition for winding up will not be dismissed unless there are compelling reasons for it.[96]

(16) Ranking in debtors' estates

6–63   The receiver has power on behalf of the company to rank and claim in the bankruptcy, insolvency, sequestration or liquidation of debtors of the company, to receive dividends and to accede to trust deeds for creditors of the debtors.[97]

(17) Leases and tenancies

6–64   The receiver has power on behalf of the company to grant or accept a surrender of a lease or tenancy of any of the property, and to take a lease or tenancy of any property required or convenient for the business of the company.[98]

(18) Uncalled capital

6–65   The receiver has power to call up any uncalled capital of the company.[99]

(19) Establishment of subsidiaries

6–66   The receiver has a statutory power to establish subsidiaries of the company.[1]

---

[93] Insolvency Act 1986, s.55(2) and Sch.2, para.13.
[94] *ibid.*, s.55(2) and Sch.2, para.14.
[95] *ibid.*, s.55(2) and Sch.2, para.21.
[96] *Foxhall and Gyle (Nurseries) Ltd, Petrs*, 1978 S.L.T. (Notes) 29.
[97] Insolvency Act 1986, s.55(2) and Sch.2, para.20.
[98] *ibid.*, s.55(2) and Sch.2, para.15.
[99] *ibid.*, s.55(2) and Sch.2, para.17.
[1] *ibid.*, s.55(2) and Sch.2, para. 18.

(20) Power to transfer business to subsidiaries

The receiver, as in establishing subsidiaries, has the power to transfer **6–67**
to subsidiaries of the company the business of the company or any part
of it and any of the property of the company.[2] That power and the above
power are necessary to enable a receiver to hive down businesses of the
company into newly established subsidiaries in order to sell them.

(21) Compromises and arrangements

The receiver has power to make any arrangements or compromise on **6–68**
behalf of the company. It is thought that compromises and arrangements on behalf of the company would be contracts and, accordingly,
the receiver would be personally liable on the compromises and
arrangements under s.57(2) unless the contract provided otherwise.

(22) Power to change company's registered office

The receiver has power to change the situation of the company's **6–69**
registered office.[3] A company may change the situation of its registered
office only in the part of the United Kingdom in which it is registered.

(23) Disposal of interest in property

Where a receiver sells or disposes of, or wishes to sell or dispose of **6–70**
property of the company which is subject to the floating charge by
virtue of which he was appointed, and which is subject to the security or
interest of a prior *pari passu* or postponed ranking creditor, or is
property affected by effectual diligence, and the receiver cannot obtain
the consent of the creditor or the person entitled to the effectual
diligence, the receiver may apply to the court for authority to sell or
dispose of the property.[4] The court may authorise the sale or disposal of
the property or interest in question free of the security, interest, burden,
encumbrance or diligence, and on any terms or conditions it thinks fit.[5]

However, where there is a fixed security over the property or interest
in question which ranks prior to the floating charge, and has not been
met or provided for in full, the court will not authorise the sale or
disposal of the property or interest in question unless it is satisfied that
the sale or disposal would be likely to provide a more advantageous
realisation of the company's assets than would otherwise be the case.[6]
There is a further condition to an authorisation to sell. In terms of s.61(4)
of the Insolvency Act 1986, the authorisation must have as a condition
that the net proceeds of the disposal are applied towards discharging
the sums secured by the fixed security, and if the net proceeds are less
than what is determined by the court to be the net amount which would
be realised on a sale of the property or interest on the open market by a
willing seller, that deficit has to be made good.[7] There is a similar

---

[2] Insolvency Act 1986, s.55(2) and Sch.2, para.22.
[3] *ibid.*, s.55(2) and Sch.2, para.22.
[4] *ibid.*, s.61(1).
[5] *ibid.*, s.61(2).
[6] *ibid.*, s.61(3).
[7] *ibid.*, s.61(4).

provision in relation to administrators under para.71(3) of new Sch.B1 to the Insolvency Act 1986.

(24) Incidental powers

6–71　　The receiver has the power to do all other things incidental to the exercise of the powers contained in the instrument creating the floating charge and his statutory powers.[8]

(25) Exercise of powers in England

6–72　　The Scottish receiver may exercise his powers in England in so far as their exercise is not inconsistent with English law.[9]

---

[8] Insolvency Act 1986, s.55(2) and Sch.2, para.23.
[9] *ibid.*, s.72(1).

CHAPTER 7

VOLUNTARY ARRANGEMENTS

History and background to company voluntary arrangements ("CVAS")

Although it is often assumed that CVAs were introduced by the **7–01** Insolvency Act 1986, precursors of arrangements under s.425 of the Companies Act 1985 can be traced back to the Joint Stock Companies Arrangement Act 1870. The main procedure today, however, is the CVA introduced in Pt I of the Insolvency Act 1986, with significant amendments being made to the procedure by the Insolvency Act 2000, with, in particular, the introduction of a moratorium on creditor action where a voluntary arrangement is proposed under Pt I of the Insolvency Act 1986 by the directors of a company. The relevant provisions in relation to that moratorium are contained in Sch.A1 to the Insolvency Act 1986, inserted by s.1 of and para.4 of Sch.1 to the Insolvency Act 1986. In this chapter any reference to "Sch.1A" shall be a reference to that Schedule. CVAs under Pt I of the Insolvency Act 1986 are described in Pt I of this chapter.

Arrangements under s.425 of the Companies Act 1985 are still valid. This is a procedure by which a company comes to a compromise or arrangement with its creditors, or any class of any, or with its members or any class of them, which is legally binding on all the creditors and/or members. It is available in all windings up, administrations, receiverships and to a company at any time. To be legally binding, there must be approval by a majority in number of the creditors or the members voting and with that majority representing three quarters of those voting, whereas in a CVA only the second condition needs to be met. There is a second drawback, in that the sanction by the court of a 425 arrangement is necessary.[1] Another disadvantage of the 425 arrangement is that there is no moratorium on creditor action until it becomes effective.[2] The s.425 arrangement procedure has one advantage over a CVA, in that, when a s.425 scheme is sanctioned by the court, the court may also sanction arrangements external to the company under s.427 of the Companies Act 1985 which effect reconstructions or amalgamations

---

[1] S.425(2) of the Companies Act 1985.
[2] The Insolvency Service of the DTI published a consultation document called *A Review of Company Rescue and Business Reconstruction Mechanisms*. The report by the review group, published in May 2000, recommended at para.43 that full consideration be given to introducing a moratorium procedure to be available in support of s.425 arrangements. However this proposal was not taken up in the Enterprise Act 2002.

involving other companies. This type of reconstruction involving out-side parties is not open in conjunction with voluntary arrangements under Pt I of the Insolvency Act 1986. However, that one advantage has not proved sufficient to outweigh the other disadvantages of s.425 schemes, and they are now uncommon. For completeness, however they are described in Pt II of this chapter. Similarly, for completeness described in Pt III of this chapter, are compromises by a company at common law, by liquidators under their powers granted by ss.165 and 167 of the Insolvency Act 1986, by administrators under their powers in terms of para.60 of new Sch.B1 to the Insolvency Act 1986, and by receivers under their powers conferred by s.55(2) of, and Sch.2 to the Insolvency Act 1986, which are also described below in para.6–68.

The CVA, as recommended by the Cork Committee,[3] and introduced in Pt I of the Insolvency Act 1986, did not prove popular, especially in Scotland, where the uptake of this procedure has been minimal.[4] The comparable figures in Northern Ireland show a nil return. The low incidence of uptake of a CVA was widely regarded as indicative of a failure to develop a "rescue culture". It was also suggested that insolvency practitioners were advising directors to place their com-panies into liquidation rather than voluntary arrangements because insolvency practitioners themselves were much more familiar with the liquidation process, as opposed to the voluntary arrangement process. It was also probably the case that many companies had deteriorated too far to enable them to be put into a CVA, because directors had delayed in taking professional advice. It was often very difficult to show creditors or other interested parties that sufficient funding could be obtained to allow the company to continue trading in a voluntary arrangement.

In addition to these reasons a widespread consensus emerged that a most important reason for the low uptake of CVAs was the lack of a statutory moratorium against creditor action during the period when efforts were in progress to conclude a voluntary arrangement. This was in contrast to the Individual Voluntary Arrangement under Part VIII of the Insolvency Act 1986, where a moratorium was an integral aspect of the process.[5] In a consultative document issued in April 1995, with the title *Revised Proposals for a New Company Voluntary Arrangement Procedure*, the Insolvency Service proposed an additional type of CVA which would exist alongside that available under Pt I of the Insolvency Act 1986. There would be a few preliminary formalities, and a 28–day moratorium on creditor action would be obtainable by the company by the filing of notice in court of a proposal for a CVA, supported by a statement by the directors that they had supplied correct information to a prospective nominee, whose consent to act would also have to be

---

[3] Cmnd. 8558 (1982).

[4] According to the figures published on the DTI website there were only five CVAs in the whole six-year period to the end of 1999.

[5] For comments on the operation of the CVA and the Individual Voluntary Arrange-ment, see S. Hill (1990) I.L. & P.47; J. Gibson (1992) 5 *Insolvency Intelligence* 60; and J.B. Bannister (1994) 10 *Insolvency Lawyer* 5–8.

lodged at the time of filing. Only viable business would be accorded access to this mode of rescue, and meetings of creditors and share-holders would be convened within 28 days to vote upon the proposal. If the proposals were not accepted, there would be a smooth transition into winding up, on the basis that the company would be deemed unable to pay its debts within the meaning of s.123 of the Insolvency Act 1986.

The Insolvency Act 2000

The proposals put forward in the consultative document in 1995 were enacted by the Insolvency Act 2000, with the main provisions being brought into force from January 1, 2003.[6] Briefly ss.1 and 2 of that Act, together with Schs 1 and 2, insert a new s.1A, and a new Sch.A1 into the Insolvency Act 1986 and amend some of the CVA procedure under Pt I of that Act. A facility for obtaining a moratorium in advance of a CVA is now an option, but is restricted to companies which meet defined qualifying conditions, the chief of which is that a company satisfies two or more of the requirements for being a small company as set out in s.247(3) of the Companies Act 1985. The original form of CVA available under Part I of the Insolvency Act 1986 continues to be available to companies which do not meet the qualifying conditions, and which therefore do not obtain the benefit of the moratorium against creditor action.

Council Regulation on Insolvency Proceedings

The CVA procedure is a type of proceedings which is subject to the European Council Regulation on Insolvency Proceedings 2000.[7] From May 31, 2002, all types of insolvency proceedings, which include CVAs, are within the scope of the Regulation if the company subject to the CVA has its centre of main interests in the European Community. It then becomes subject to uniform rules governing jurisdiction, applicable law, recognition and enforcement. Foreign companies which do not have their centre of main interests in the UK, or in one of the other EC Member States are not affected by the EC Regulation. Article 37 of the European Council Regulation on Insolvency Proceedings provides for the conversion of a voluntary arrangement into a winding up, which is reflected in rr.1.46 to 1.48 of the Insolvency (Scotland) Rules 1986.[8] Under these provisions a liquidator appointed in the European Union but outside the UK may apply to the court for the conversion of a CVA into a winding up.

7–02

---

[6] SI 2002/2711.

[7] Council Regulation 1346/2000. That Regulation has been implemented by Pt II of the Insolvency (Scotland) Regulations 2003 (SI 2003/2109), which amends the Insolvency (Scotland) Rules 1986 (SI 1086/1915, amended by SI 1987/192 and SI 2002/2709). See para.5–12, where doubt is cast on whether, as implemented in the UK, an out of court administration is outwith the scope of the Brussels Convention. The same considerations apply to CVAs.

[8] As inserted by art.25 of SI 2003/2109.

PART I

CVAS UNDER PART I OF THE INSOLVENCY ACT 1986

CVAs without a moratorium and CVAs with a moratorium

7–03   With the bringing into force of the voluntary arrangement provisions of the Insolvency Act 2000 on January 1, 2003, there are now two modes of company voluntary arrangements under the Insolvency Act 1986. The first mode is a company voluntary arrangement under Pt I of the Insolvency Act 1986 without a moratorium against creditor action; and a voluntary arrangement with a moratorium under s.1A of the Insolvency Act 1986,[9] and under the procedures set out in Sch.A1 to the Insolvency Act 1986.[10] It is proposed in this chapter to describe first the original mode of arrangement, without initial moratorium, and then to describe a CVA with a moratorium. It is thought highly likely that most free-standing voluntary arrangements, *i.e.* those not linked to an administration or liquidation, will use the moratorium route.

CVA under Part I of the Insolvency Act 1986 without a moratorium

Nature of a voluntary arrangement

7–04   A CVA is a deal or arrangement between a company and its creditors, in which there is a composition of the company's debts with the creditors or some wider arrangement with the creditors. If the arrangement follows the procedure prescribed by statute, the composition or arrangement becomes by statute binding on all the creditors. A composition involves the creditors' writing off a proportion of their debts. The leading case to date on the interpretation of "composition" and "arrangement" is the case of *Inland Revenue Commissioners v Adam & Partners Ltd*, in which it was held that an agreement in terms of which creditors received no return whatsoever could not be classed as a composition, but could be described as an arrangement.[11] Although there is statutory intervention, the underlying nature of a voluntary arrangement is contractual, with the creditors of the company being presented with a proposal in relation to their debts.[12]

Proposal for a voluntary arrangement

7–05   Section 1 of the Insolvency Act 1986 authorises the directors of a company (other than one in administration or winding up) to make a proposal to the company and its creditors for a composition in satisfac-

---

[9] S.1A was inserted into the Insolvency Act 1986 by para.2 of Sch.1 to the Insolvency Act 2000.

[10] Schedule A1 to the Insolvency Act 1986 was inserted by para.4 of Sch.1 to the Insolvency Act 2000.

[11] [2001] 1 B.C.L.C. 222.

[12] The contractual nature of a voluntary arrangement is discussed by Michael Rutstein in *Insolvency Intelligence* (February 2000), and this approach has been confirmed in *Re Kudos Glass Ltd* [2001] 1 B.C.L.C. 390.

tion of its debts or a scheme or arrangement of its affairs. Unlike the company rescue route through administration, there is no requirement that it be established first that the company is insolvent, or unable to pay its debts at the time of the proposal. If the company is in administration or in winding up, a proposal for a CVA may only be made by the administrator or the liquidator.[13] It is not uncommon for a company in administration to enter a CVA, and indeed this was one of the purposes of administration prior to the reforms introduced by the Enterprise Act 2002. It is relatively rare for a liquidator to propose a CVA, and it is not clear whether the appropriate route is for there to be a sist or discharge of the winding up order. In the case of *Re Dollar Land (Feltham) Ltd*[14] there was rescission (discharge) but it was meant to operate as a breathing space to consider a CVA and not as a dismissal of the winding up petition.

Functions of the nominee

The nominee must, within 28 days (or such longer period as the court **7–06** may allow) after he is given notice of the proposal for a voluntary arrangement, submit a report to the court stating:

(a) whether in his opinion, the proposed voluntary arrangement has a reasonable prospect of being approved and implemented,
(b) whether in his opinion, meetings of the company and of its creditors should be summoned to consider the proposal, and
(c) if in his opinion such meetings should be summoned, the date on which, and time and place at which, he proposed the meetings should be held.[15]

For the purposes of enabling the nominee to prepare his report, the person (usually the director) intending to make the proposal must submit to the nominee a document setting out the terms of the proposed voluntary arrangement and a statement of the company's affairs.[16] The nominee must be more than a mouthpiece of the directors of the company and needs to apply his own independent judgement to what goes into his report, with the prospect of creditors approving the proposal resting on their faith in his skill and independent judgement. The nominee has powers to call on the directors for further information.[17] Valuable guidance on the nominee's duties in preparing a report is to be found in Statement No.3 of Insolvency Practice issues by the Association of Business Recovery Professionals to be found on the website of that organisation.[18]

---

[13] S.1(3) of the Insolvency Act 1986.
[14] [1995] B.C.C. 74; [1995] 2 B.C.L.C. 270 (Ch. D.); for discussion of this issue and further citations, see paras 8.79–8.90 of G. Weisgard, *Company Voluntary Arrangements* (2003, Jordans).
[15] S.2(2) of the Insolvency Act 1986 as amended by s.2 of and paragraphs 1 and 3(a) of Schedule 2 to the Insolvency Act 2000.
[16] S.2(3) of the Insolvency Act 1986. Rule 1.5 of the Insolvency (Scotland) Rules 1986 sets out the prescribed particulars which must be in the Statement of Affairs.
[17] Rule 1.6 of the Insolvency (Scotland) Rules 1986.
[18] For duties and standards of care of a nominee, see *Re A Debtor (No. 222 of 1990)* [1993] B.C.L.C. 233; *Re Greystoke* [1996] B.C.L.C. 429; *Hook v Jewson Ltd* [1997] 1 B.C.L.C. 664; and *Re Cooper v Fearnley a Debtor (No. 103 of 1994)* [1997] B.P.I.R. 20.

Meetings of the company and of its creditors to approve proposal

7–07   The key event in relation to a voluntary arrangement is the meetings of the members and creditors of the company to consider and approve with or without modifications the proposal. If in his report, the nominee states that in his opinion meetings of the company and its creditors should be summoned to consider the directors' proposal, the date on which the meetings are to be held must be not less than 14, nor more than 28 days from the date on which the nominee lodged his report in the court under s.2 of the Insolvency Act 1986.[19] The notice summoning the meeting must specify to the court in which the nominee's report has been lodged and with each notice he must also send a copy of the directors' proposal, a copy of the Statement of Affairs or, if he thinks fit, a summary of it (the summary to include a list of creditors and the amount of their debts), and the nominee's comments on the proposal.[20] Meetings of members and of creditors summoned under s.3 of the Insolvency Act 1986 must be conducted under the provisions of Chap.1 of Pt VII (meetings) of the Insolvency (Scotland) Rules 1986 as amended by Chap.5 of Pt I of those Rules.[21] Rule 1.14 of the Insolvency (Scotland) Rules 1986[22] provides that, in fixing the date, time and place for the creditors' meeting and the company's meeting, the person summoning the meetings must have regard primarily to the convenience of the creditors. The meetings may be held on the same day or on different days. If held on the same day, the meetings must be held in the same place, but in either case the creditors' meeting must be fixed for a time in advance of the company meeting, and where the meetings are not held on the same day, they must be held within seven days of each other. At any meeting of creditors, the approval or modification of any proposal requires a majority of at least three-quarters in value of the creditors' present or represented in voting, in person or by proxy, in favour of the resolution.[23] Votes of creditors are calculated according to the amount of a creditor's debt up to the date of the meeting.[24] Although the CVA procedure is primarily an out of court procedure, it is conducted under the auspices of the court,[25] with all the key documents lodged with the court.

---

[19] Insolvency (Scotland) Rules 1986, r.1.9.

[20] *ibid.*, r.1.9(2).

[21] *ibid.*, r.1.13 of the Insolvency (Scotland) Rules 1986. The provisions in Chap.5 of Pt I of the Insolvency (Scotland) Rules 1986 have been significantly amended by paras 5 to 9 inclusive of the Schedule to the Insolvency (Scotland) Amendment Rules 2002 (SI 2002/2779).

[22] As amended by para.5 of the Schedule to the Insolvency (Scotland) Amendment Rules 2002.

[23] Insolvency (Scotland) Rules 1986, r.7.12(2).

[24] *ibid.*, r.7.9(3), read with r.4.15(5), and r.7.9(4)(c).

[25] The Court of Appeal has indicated in relation to individual voluntary arrangements that the self-contained statutory code relating to voluntary arrangements means that the supervisor of the arrangement is an officer of the court, and subject to its control in the course of performing his functions and duties (*King v Anthony* [1998] 2 B.C.L.C. 517 (CA)). It is suggested that the ruling would be exactly the same in relation to voluntary arrangements under Pt I of the Insolvency Act 1986.

Right of challenge to a CVA

There is also a right of challenge by an interested member or creditor, **7–08** or liquidator, administrator or nominee in terms of s.6 of the Insolvency Act 1986. If the above-mentioned parties choose to challenge the arrangements, the grounds of challenge are (a) that the voluntary arrangement "unfairly prejudices the interests of a creditor, member or contributory of a company", or (b) that there has been a material irregularity at the meetings summoned under s.3 of the Insolvency Act 1986.[26] The expression "unfairly prejudices" has not been defined in relation to this section. It has been considered in relation to s.459(1) of the Companies Act 1985,[27] which uses almost identical wording in relation to the interests of a member of a company being prejudiced, and it is suggested that the terms have the same meaning in both sections.[28] The key to understanding seems to be that there must not only be prejudice. It must be to the creditor's or member's interest as a creditor or member.[29] The arrangement must cause "unfair" prejudice.[30]

If the court is satisfied in relation to a challenge on the ground of irregularity or unfair prejudice, it may suspend or revoke the decision approving the proposal of the meetings and at its discretion order new meetings to consider revised proposals or make any other order.[31] Except challenged in the above manner, meetings are deemed regularly conducted.[32] If the court refuses the approval but allows further meetings and then is satisfied that no revised proposals are being submitted, it must revoke or suspend the decision approving the voluntary arrangement.[33] The right of challenge is exercisable only within the period of 28 days beginning with the first day on which reports of the outcome of the meeting required to be sent to the court by the chairman of the meeting under s.4(6) of the Insolvency Act 1986 are sent to the court.[34] There is no jurisdiction on the court to the extend time limits of 28 days imposed by s.6(3) of the Insolvency Act 1986 for making an application to challenge a CVA which has been approved at the meetings.[35]

---

[26] In *Individual Voluntary Arrangements*, by S. Lawson, there is a list of examples of possible irregularities suggested (at para.A13).

[27] "Unfair prejudice" was also used in s.27(1)(a) of the Insolvency Act 1986 as the ground on which an aggrieved interested party might legally challenge an administrator's management of a company's affairs. The test now in para.74 of new Sch.B1 to the Insolvency Act 1986 is "unfairly harm the interests", which is thought to be more or less the same as the previous test.

[28] It is unlikely that the legislature would have originally (prior to the Enterprise Act 2002 reforms) tied these two types of voluntary arrangement together as justifying purposes of an administration order, if it had in contemplation that the court would use different principles for accepting one and rejecting another.

[29] *Re a Company (No 004475 of 1982)* [1983] Ch. 178.

[30] The concept of "unfair prejudice" was considered in detail in the House of Lords in relation to s.459(1) in the case of *O'Neill v Phillips* [1999] 1 W.L.R. 1092, in which Lord Hoffman went through the authorities.

[31] Insolvency Act 1986, s.6(4).

[32] *ibid.*, s.6(7).

[33] *ibid.*, s.6(5).

[34] S.6(3) of the Insolvency Act 1986, as amended by paras 1, 7(1) and (4) of Sch.2 to the Insolvency Act 2000.

[35] *Re Bournemouth & Boscomb Athletic Football Club Co Ltd* [1998] B.B.I.R. 183.

Effect of voluntary arrangements under Part I of the Insolvency Act 1986

7–09　　An approved voluntary arrangement under Pt I of the Insolvency Act 1986 takes legal effect as if made at the creditors' meeting and binds every person who, in accordance with the rules, had notice of and was entitled to vote at that meeting (whether or not he was present or represented at the meeting), as if he were a party to the voluntary arrangement.[36] These arrangements do not operate as an agreement between the parties affected but have a statutory force. One set of legal obligations is substituted for another by statute (known legally as "statutory novation"). Consequently the discharge under a scheme of one of several debtors who are jointly and severally liable does not discharge the others[37] unless there is an express provision in the scheme to that effect.[38] It is also not legal for a company, which has become bound by a scheme approved, to vary the scheme by agreement with the other parties affected.[39] If the parties wish to do that they have to petition for another scheme.

Implementation of voluntary arrangements under section 1 of the Insolvency Act 1986

7–10　　Section 1(2) of the Insolvency Act 1986 stipulates that the "nominee" shall act as trustee or otherwise supervise the implementation of a voluntary arrangement. He is to be known as the supervisor.[40] The Insolvency (Scotland) Rules 1986 give details on the procedure in relation to the supervisor's duties, such as his duty to keep accounts and records and annually to send an abstract to the court, the Registrar of Companies, creditors, members and auditors, etc.[41] The directors stay in control of the company except where powers have been delegated to the supervisor in terms of the voluntary arrangement. Section 7(3) of the Insolvency Act 1986 gives any of the company's creditors, or any other person who is dissatisfied by any act, omission or decision of the supervisor, the power to apply to the court for a court order in relation to the supervisor's dealings. It is thought that the court would not interfere with the supervisor's conduct of the arrangement unless he acted contrary to the voluntary arrangement or purported to exercise powers beyond those implied to him as supervisor, or acted unreasonably. The court does not have power to vary a voluntary arrangement once approved, and it is therefore essential that the proposal is thought out ahead and contains all the powers that a supervisor might need[42]; such as a power to call meetings of creditors to approve variations or to have the discretion to make minor changes himself. Failing such

---

[36] Insolvency Act 1986, s.5(2).
[37] *Re Garner's Motors* [1937] Ch. 594.
[38] *Shaw v Royce Ltd* [1911] Ch. 138.
[39] *Srimati Premil Den v People's Bank of Northern India* [1938] 4 All E.R. 337.
[40] Insolvency Act 1986, s.7(2).
[41] Insolvency (Scotland) Rules 1986, First Pt, Chap.6, as amended by paras 10 to 15 of the Schedule to the Insolvency (Scotland) Amendment Rules 2002 (SI 2002/2709).
[42] See the Court of Appeal case of *Re Alpa Lighting Ltd* [1997] B.P.I.R. 341; compare *Re FMS Financial Management Services Ltd* (1989) 5 B.C.C. 191.

provisions, any variation would have to have the unanimous consent of all interested parties (*i.e.* not just the requisite majority).[43]

Termination of voluntary arrangement without moratorium under Part I of the Insolvency Act 1986

Not more than 28 days after the final completion or termination of the **7–11** voluntary arrangement, the supervisor must send, to creditors and members of the company who are bound by it, a notice that the voluntary arrangement has been fully implemented or (as the case may be) has terminated.[44] With the notice there must be sent to each creditor and member a copy of a report by the supervisor summarising all receipts and payments made by him in pursuance of the arrangement, and explaining in relation to implementation of the arrangement any departure from the proposals as they originally took effect, or (in the case of termination of the arrangement) explaining the reasons why the arrangement has terminated.[45] The supervisor must also, within the 28 days, send to the Registrar of Companies and to the court a copy of the notice to creditors and members, together with a copy of the report referred to above, and he must not vacate office until these copies have been sent.[46]

Trust funds and failure of voluntary arrangement

A voluntary arrangement may fail to attain its objective of rescuing **7–12** the company for a number of reasons. It may then be followed by winding up. If, in terms of the voluntary arrangement, funds have been placed in trust for creditors, the supervisor may retain and administer those funds in accordance with those terms.[47] There was no default rule that, where the CVA failed to state clearly what was to happen on liquidation to a trust created by a CVA, the liquidation caused the CVA itself to fail or terminate and the trust over the assets for the purpose of the CVA also terminated.[48]

CVA under Part I of the Insolvency Act 1986 with a moratorium

In terms of para.3(2) of Sch.A1 to the Insolvency Act 1986,[49] the **7–13** proposed moratorium procedure applies only to "small" companies as defined by s.247(3) of the Companies Act 1985 as amended. These are companies which fulfil two or more of the following requirements:

(a) an annual turnover of £2.8m or less;

---

[43] *Raja v Rubin* [1999] 1 B.C.L.C. 621.
[44] Insolvency (Scotland) Rules 1986, r.1.23(1).
[45] *ibid.*, r.1.23(2).
[46] *ibid.*, r.1.23(3).
[47] *Re Halson Packaging Ltd* [1997] B.C.C. 993; [1997] B.P.I.R. 194; *Re Brelec Insulations Ltd* [2000] 2 B.C.L.C. 576; and *Re Kudos Glass Ltd* [2001] 1 B.C.L.C. 390.
[48] *Re N.T. Gallagher & Son Ltd. Shierson v Tomlinson* [2002] B.C.C. 867.
[49] As inserted by para.4 of Sch.1 to the Insolvency Act 1986.

(b) a "balance sheet total" of £1.4m or less[50]; and
(c) a workforce of 50 employees or fewer.

The effective abolition of administrative receivers by the Enterprise Act 2002 perhaps makes it unfortunate that only small companies are able to gain a moratorium against creditor actions, as there may well be occasions when larger companies would benefit from a CVA without having to go through administration. However, the Secretary of State does have powers to make regulations to modify the eligibility qualifications of a company in relation to a moratorium.[51]

A company cannot seek a moratorium if it is:

(a) an insurance company within the meaning of the Insurance Companies Act 1982;
(b) an authorised institution or former authorised institution within the meaning of the Banking Act 1987;
(c) a party to a market contract, a money market contract or a related contract or any of its properties is subject to a market charge, a money market charge or a system-charge; or
(d) it is a participant (within the meaning of the settlement finality regulations) or any of its property is subject to a collateral security charge (within the meaning of those regulations).

Three further categories were added by the Insolvency Act 1986 (Amendment) (No.3) Regulations 2002.[52] A company is also not eligible to obtain a moratorium if:

(a) it is party to a capital market arrangement, according to the criteria set out in para.4A of Sch.A1 and one or more of the criteria set out in para.4D;
(b) a project company of a public-private partnership project which includes step-in rights (paras 4(h) and 4(j)); or
(c) it is a company which has incurred a liability under an agreement of £10m or more.[53]

Further factors precluding a moratorium

7–14   A further set of factors which preclude a moratorium are listed in para.4(1) of Sch.A1 to the Insolvency Act 1986, as inserted by para.4 of Sch.1 to the Insolvency Act 2000. The factors are:

(a) an administration order is in force in relation to the company;

---

[50] "Balance sheet total" means the total of called up share capital not paid, fixed assets (intangible, tangible and investments), current assets, stock, work in progress, debtors, investments and cash and bank balances (and prepayments and accrued income). Assets are to be included whether or not secured. Book values are to be used, not forced sale realisable values.

[51] Paragraph 5 of Sch.A1 to the Insolvency Act 1986.

[52] SI 2002/1990.

[53] These are the same exclusions which apply to administrations and liquidations.

(b) the company is being wound up;

(c) there is an administrative receiver of the company;

(d) a voluntary arrangement has effect in relation to the company;

(e) there is a provisional liquidator of the company;

(f) a moratorium has been in force for the company at any time during the period of 12 months ending with the date of lodging and—

    (i) no voluntary arrangement had effect at the time at which the moratorium came to an end, or

    (ii) a voluntary arrangement which had effect at any time in that period has come to an end prematurely[54]; or

(g) a voluntary arrangement in relation to the company which had effect in pursuance of a proposal under s.1(3) has come to an end prematurely and, during the period of 12 months ending with the date of lodging, an order under s.5(3)(a) has been made.

Initiative in relation to a moratorium

The initiative in obtaining a moratorium, lies with the directors. When **7–15** the directors of a company wish to apply for a moratorium, they must supply a nominee (a person nominated to supervise the arrangement) with a copy of:

(a) the proposed arrangements;

(b) a statement of affairs;

(c) other information prescribed in the Insolvency (Scotland) Rules 1986; and

(d) any other information required by the nominee to enable him to form an opinion as to whether the proposal is viable. This further information must include an explanation as to how the arrangement is to be financed.[55]

The nominee must then issue a statement indicating whether or not, in his opinion, the proposal is viable and whether meetings of creditors and members should be convened.[56] He must also indicate whether or not, in his opinion, the proposed arrangement has a reasonable prospect of being approved and implemented and whether the company is likely to have sufficient funds.[57] These requirements seem somewhat onerous and are likely to add to the cost and time involved in setting up a CVA. It may even mean that nominees err on the side of caution to avoid any potential liability, and thus promising proposals are ditched. New r.1.25

---

[54] A CVA ends prematurely if, when it ceases to have effect, it has not been fully implemented in respect of all persons bound by it (s.7B of the Insolvency Act 1986), as inserted by para.10 of Sch.2 to the Insolvency Act 2000.

[55] Insolvency Act 1986, para.6(1) of Sch.A1, as inserted by para.4 of Sch. 1 to the Insolvency Act 2000.

[56] *ibid.*, para.6(2) of Schedule A1, as inserted by para.4 of Sch.1 to the Insolvency Act 2000.

[57] *ibid.*, para.6(2) of Schedule A1.

of the Insolvency (Scotland) Rules 1986 provides that the directors can amend the proposal prior to the nominee issuing his statement. This will allow the directors to change the proposal if the nominee is not satisfied with the proposal as initially given to him.[58] Once the nominee has prepared his statement, the directors should lodge the following documents in court:

(a) the proposed arrangement;
(b) the statement of affairs;
(c) a statement that the company is eligible for a moratorium;
(d) a statement that the nominee has consented to act; and
(e) the nominee's statement as to viability and funding.[59]

New r.1.29 of the Insolvency (Scotland) Rules 1986 provides that the documents are to be delivered with four copies of a Schedule listing them within three working days of the submission by the nominee of his paragraph 6(2) statement. Upon lodging, the court endorses the four copies of the Schedule of Documents, returning three copies. The directors then pass two copies to the nominee and the third to the company.[60]

Duration and effect of the moratorium

7–16   The moratorium comes into effect when the requisite documents are lodged with the court, and terminates at the end of the day on which the meetings of the company and its creditors are first held, unless an extension is granted under para.32 of Sch.A1 to the Insolvency Act 1986. The time limit for the holding of the first two meetings is 28 days from the beginning of the moratorium, and if either of those meetings has not taken place before the end of that period, the moratorium comes to an end at the end of the day on which the meetings were to be held, unless it is extended under para.32 of Sch.A1 to the Insolvency Act 1986.[61] Unless it has previously come to an end, the moratorium terminates at the end of the day in which a decision to approve a voluntary arrangement under para.31 of Sch.A1 to the Insolvency Act 1986 takes effect.[62] When a moratorium comes into force, the directors must forthwith notify the nominee, who in turn must advertise the fact, and notify the Registrar of Companies, the Keeper of the Register of Inhibitions and Adjudications, the company and any petitioning creditor of the company of whose claim he is aware of at the coming into force of the moratorium.[63] A similar procedure is required when the moratorium comes to an end.[64]

---

[58] The proposal of course is likely to have been prepared by the nominee with the directors. New r.1.28 of the Insolvency (Scotland) Rules 1986 also provides that the nominee must submit his para.6(2) statement to the directors within 28 days of his receiving the proposal, with the statement and the nominee's comments on the forms prescribed by that Rule.
[59] Insolvency Act 1986, para. 7 of Sch.A1, as inserted by para.4 of Sch.1 to the Insolvency Act 2000.
[60] New r.1.30(1) of the Insolvency (Scotland) Rules 1986.
[61] Insolvency Act 1986, para.8 of Sch.A1.
[62] *ibid.*, para.8 of Sch.A1 1986.
[63] New r.1.30 of the Insolvency (Scotland) Rules 1986.
[64] New r.1.32 of the Insolvency (Scotland) Rules 1986.

During the moratorium the company is protected from creditor action as provided for in para.12(1) of Schedule A1 to the Insolvency Act 1986, which is in almost identical terms to the moratorium when a company is in administration, with similar rights of creditors and others to ask the court to lift the moratorium in a particular regard, and to challenge the nominee's conduct.[65] A provision in an instrument creating a floating charge is rendered void if it provides for the obtaining of a moratorium, or anything done with a view to obtaining one, to be an event causing the charge to crystallise or causing restrictions which would not otherwise apply to be imposed on the disposal of property by the company or a ground for the appointment of a receiver.[66] A further important provision in the legislation is that, while a moratorium is in force, there is a prohibition imposed on the company on obtaining credit to the extent of £250 or more from a person who has not been informed that a moratoria is in force.[67]

PART II

Schemes under section 425 of the Companies Act 1985

The wording used in s.425 of the Companies Act 1985 and in s.1 of the **7–17** Insolvency Act 1986 is different. In terms of s.1 of the Insolvency Act 1986, a "voluntary arrangement" is a "composition in satisfaction of a company's debts or a scheme of arrangement of its affairs". Section 425 of the Companies Act 1985 talks of a "compromise or arrangement between a company and its creditors, or any class of them, or between the company and its members, or any class of them". An examination of these two expressions suggests that the wording should be read as legally synonymous in Scotland.

Compromise

In certain English cases, the expression "compromise" has been **7–18** discussed.[68] These cases suggest that in England for there to be a compromise there must be some dispute, *e.g.* as to the power to enforce rights, or as to what those rights are. In Scotland, "compromise" in most circumstances means the settlement of a claim where there is a dispute.[69] However, in liquidation the word seems to be stretched to mean a "composition", which is an agreement by which a creditor accepts a portion of the debts owed to him by the debtor in full discharge of the debtor's obligations.[70] A deal, where the debt has been admitted by the liquidator, and the creditors have agreed to accept a sum of money, has

---

[65] Insolvency Act 1986, paras 12 to 23 of new Sch.A1.

[66] *ibid.*, para.43(1) of Sch.A1.

[67] *ibid.*, para.17 of Sch.A1.

[68] *Sneath v Valley Gold Ltd* [1893] 1 Ch. 477 at 491n; *Mercantile Investment and General Trust Co v International Co of Mexico* [1893] 1 Ch. 484n; *Mercantile Investment and General Trust Co v River Plate Trust, Loan and Agency Co* [1894] 1 Ch. 578.

[69] Stair, I, xvii, 2.

[70] Bell, *Comm.*, ii, 398.

been described as a "compromise".[71] This type of arrangement is exactly the same as a "composition" under Pt I of the Insolvency Act 1986.[72]

Arrangement of affairs

7–19   The expression "arrangement of its affairs" used in s.425 of the Companies Act 1985 is to be interpreted "broadly", in Scotland, to cover a wide variety of different types of arrangement.[73] It covers, *inter alia*, consolidations of shares,[74] arrangements with creditors,[75] alterations of class rights in memoranda of association,[76] and schemes by which the holder of the majority of shares acquires the minority on favourable terms.[77] It would not cover arrangements *ultra vires* the company[78] nor where there is another statutory procedure.[79]

Main difference between compromises and arrangements under section 425 of the Companies Act 1985 and voluntary arrangements under Part I of the Insolvency Act 1986

7–20   The main difference between compromises and arrangements under s.425 of the Companies Act 1985 and voluntary arrangements under Pt I of the Insolvency Act 1986 is in their implementation. Under Pt I of the Insolvency Act, in terms of s.4, unless the person concerned agrees, a secured creditor may not be affected by any proposal, and the holder of a preferential debt must be given priority and paid *pari passu* with the other preferential debtors. This restriction gives the secured creditor or preferential creditor an absolute veto. Under s.425, by contrast, provided that the requisite majorities are obtained in the different classes under a s.425 scheme, a dissenting minority can be bound by an arrangement (subject to the sanction of the court).[80] In determining what is a "class", it must be confined to those persons whose rights are not so dissimilar as to make it impossible for them to consult together with a view to their common interest, and if there is a different state of facts existing among different creditors which may differently affect their minds and their judgments, they must be divided into different classes.[81] Accordingly, it is not just a question of "secured" and "unsecured", etc. The underlying interests must be looked at to ensure equity. The Court of Appeal has laid down guidance in determining what constitutes a class for the purposes of voting on a scheme of arrangement, and on the procedure

---

[71] *Liquidator of RD Simpson Ltd* (1908) 15 S.L.T. 649; and *RD Simpson Ltd and Liqudator v Hudson Beare* (1908) 15 S.L.T. 875.

[72] See judgment of the Court of Appeal in *Commissioners of Inland Revenue v Adam & Partners Ltd* [2001] 1 B.C.L.C. 222

[73] *Singer Manufacturing Co v Robinow*, 1971 S.C. 11 at 14, *per* Lord President Clyde.

[74] Companies Act 1985, s.425(6).

[75] *Shandon Hydropathic Co Ltd, Petrs*, 1911 S.C. 1153.

[76] *Edinburgh Railway Access and Property Co v Scottish Metropolitan Assurance Co*, 1932 S.C. 2.

[77] *Singer Manufacturing Co v Robinow*, *supra*.

[78] See *Re Cooper, Cooper v Johnson* [1902] W.N. 199; *Re Stephen Walters & Sons* [1926] W.N. 236; *Re Oceanic Steam Navigation Co* [1939] Ch. 41.

[79] *Re Guardian Assurance Co* [1917] 1 Ch.431.

[80] *La Lainière de Roubaix v Glen Glove Co*, 1925 S.C. 91.

[81] *Sovereign Life Assurance Co v Dodd* [1892] 2 Q.B. 573, approved in *La Lainière*, above.

in general to be followed in order to secure the necessary approvals for a scheme of arrangements.[82] A further difference is the absence of any species of moratorium from creditor action in a s.425 arrangement.[83]

Procedure for approval of scheme of arrangement under section 425 of the Companies Act 1985

The procedure in a s.425 arrangement is for the liquidator, or **7–21** administrator, or any member or creditor, or the company (*i.e.* through the directors) to petition the court.[84] It is thought that the receiver may petition the court. Only the company is given a statutory right under s.425 of the Companies Act 1985, as only the directors have a statutory right under s.1 of the Insolvency Act 1986 to put forward proposals. The holder of a floating charge, however, could petition as a creditor. Where the petition is for sanction of an arrangement between a company and its members, the practice is to omit from the petition any reference to the meeting of the members of the company, and to ask only for an order for separate meetings of special classes of shareholders.[85] Where the arrangement is between the company and its creditors, an order for separate meetings of different classes of creditors is sought.[86] Where the creditors are not involved it is unnecessary to call a creditors' meeting.[87] The first order of the court will be an order for intimation and for summoning the necessary meetings in the manner the court prescribes.[88] The court may then appoint a reporter.

The meetings will ordinarily be summoned not only by individual notices to the shareholders and others concerned, but also by advertisement in newspapers.[89] If the notice is sent to the creditors or members, there must also be sent a statement explaining the effect of the compromise or arrangement, and notice given by the advertisements must also contain this statement. These requirements are essential[90] and, if they are not met, the meetings have to be reconvened.[91] When the compromise or arrangement under s.425 is duly passed at the meetings[92] it is submitted to the court, answers are allowed, and a remit is made to the reporter if ordered in the first order. The reporter acts very much

---

[82] *Re Hawk Insurance Co Ltd* [2001] 2 B.C.L.C. 480.

[83] A Report by the Review Group following the DTI consultation document *A Review of Company Rescue and Business Reconstruction Mechanisms* (May 2000) recommended (at para.43) that full consideration be given to introducing a moratorium procedure to support s.425 arrangements.

[84] Companies Act 1985, s.425(1).

[85] *Cayzer, Irvine & Co, Petrs*, 1963 S.C. 25.

[86] *Tritonia*, 1948 S.N. 11.

[87] *Clydesdale Bank, Petrs*, 1950 S.C. 30.

[88] Companies Act 1985, s.425.

[89] *Merchiston Castle School*, 1946 S.C. 23.

[90] Companies Act 1985, s.426.

[91] *Rankin and Blackmore*, 1950 S.C. 218, applied in *Scott & Co*, 1950 S.C. 507; *Coltness Iron Co*, 1951 S.C. 476; *City Property Investment Trust Corp.*, 1951 S.C. 507, followed in *Scottish Eastern Investment Trust*, 1966 S.L.T. 285; *Second Scottish Investment Trust*, 1962 S.L.T. 392.

[92] There must be approval by a majority in number representing three-quarters in value of the creditors or class of creditors or members voting (s.425(2) of Companies Act 1985).

like the "insolvency practitioner" in relation to a voluntary arrangement under Pt I of the Insolvency Act 1986.

Criteria applicable when court sanctioning scheme under section 425 of the Companies Act 1985

7–22   The criteria by which the Scottish courts decide whether to sanction a scheme under s.425 were set down by Lord President Dunedin in the case of *Shandon Hydropathic Co Ltd*[93] as follows:

> "What the Court has to do is to see first of all that the statutory provisions have been complied with; and secondly, that the majority has been acting *bona fide*. The Court also has to see that the minority is not being overridden by a majority, having interests of its own clashing with those of the minority whom they seek to coerce. Further than that, the Court has to look at the scheme and see whether it is one as to which persons, acting honestly and viewing the scheme laid before them in the interests of those whom they represent, take a view which can be reasonably taken by business men. The Court must look at the scheme and see whether the Act has been complied with, whether the majority are acting *bona fide* and whether they are coercing the minority in order to promote interests adverse to those of the class whom they purport to represent; and then see whether the scheme is a reasonable one, or whether there was any reasonable objection to it, or such an objection to it as that any man might say that he could not approve of it."

(Lord Dunedin also held that, in considering and coming to the conclusion that a scheme was a reasonable one, the court was entitled to take into consideration the fact that the requisite majority of creditors who approved the scheme were businessmen in Glasgow.)

Effect of sanctioning of scheme under section 425 of the Companies Act 1985

7–23   Where an order is made sanctioning a scheme under s.425 of the Companies Act 1985 it becomes binding (subject to registration under subs.(3) of that section), and in the same way as a scheme approved under Pt I of the Insolvency Act 1986, the arrangements have a statutory force and amount to a statutory novation.

PART III

Compromises, arrangements and compositions at common law

7–24   Compromises, arrangements and compositions at common law (*i.e.* non-statutory agreements, unlike agreements under Pt I of the Insol-

---

[93] 1911 S.C. 1153 at 1155, quoting Lindley L.J. in *Re Alabama, New Orleans, Texas and Pacific Junction Ry Co* [1891] 1 Ch. 213 at 238.

vency Act 1986, which are made legally binding by statute) may be made by a company which is insolvent (although it would have to be careful that there was no fraudulent preference), or by a company under an administration order or by a company in liquidation with the sanction of the court or by a company in receivership.[94] All the statutes do is to give the company in liquidation, etc. the same power of compromise both with creditors and debtors as an individual would have.[95] These types of common law arrangements are likely to be less common now in view of the voluntary arrangements which can be effected under Pt I of the Insolvency Act 1986. However they are still an option, and may be used where requisite majorities are difficult to get or would be inconvenient to get. The power, however, should not be used to effect the sort of compromise or arrangement contemplated in Pt I of the Insolvency Act 1986 or under s.425 of the Companies Act 1985,[96] *e.g.* distributing assets of the company otherwise than strictly in accordance with the rights of creditors in the liquidation.

Composition contracts or compromise contracts are purely contractual and hence only binding on the contracting parties. Where the sanction of the court is required, there is no legally binding agreement until the sanction is obtained,[97] and the court will not give a general power to compromise.[98] If the court has given its sanction without having a material fact disclosed the court will grant reduction of the decree sanctioning the compromise.[99] The terms of the contract vary as well as the number of acceding parties. It may be made a condition of the contract that there must be agreement of all the creditors.[1] A trust deed is sometimes granted to secure payment of the composition.[2] A composition agreement does not imply that a debtor has been given a discharge, although that can be agreed.[3] Non-acceding creditors are not bound by a non-statutory agreement, although they may by their actings be barred from claiming that they are not bound.[4] Whether a composition agreement gives a discharge depends on the terms of the agreement and subsequent actings.[5] Accession to a composition agreement may be proved by any form of writing—a signature is sufficient.[6]

If the debtor under a composition agreement defaults, the other party to the contract can sue for the whole amount of his debt.[7] In this way, a non-statutory composition or compromise agreement differs radically

---

[94] Insolvency Act 1986, ss.14, 55(2), 165 and 167.

[95] *Re Albert Life Assurance Co* (1871) L.R. 6 Ch. 381.

[96] *Re Trix Ltd* [1970] 3 All E.R. 397.

[97] *Reid & Laidlaw v Reid* (1905) 7 F. 457.

[98] *Pattisons Ltd, Liqr of* (1899) 6 S.L.T. 372; *Bennett & Co, Liquidator of* (1906) 13 S.L.T. 718.

[99] *Henderson & Co v Stewart* (1894) 22 R. 154.

[1] *Brown v M'Intyre* (1830) 8 S. 847.

[2] *Miller v Downie* (1876) 3 R. 548.

[3] *Ogilvie & Son v Taylor* (1887) 14 R. 399.

[4] *Weighton v Cuthbert & Sons* (1906) 14 S.L.T. 251.

[5] *Campbell & Co v Scott's Trs* (1913) 1 S.L.T. 149; *Craig v Somerville* (1894) 2 S.L.T. 139 and 243.

[6] *Henry v Strachan & Spence* (1897) 24 R. 1045.

[7] *Alexander and Austine v Yuille* (1873) 1 R. 185; *Woods Parker and Co v Ainslie* (1860) 22 D. 723.

from a statutory compromise agreement where the fact of statutory novation means that default does not allow one to sue for the previous debt. Where there is a composition in satisfaction of debts, it is important in relation to securities whether the composition is with the company in winding up or not. If there is no liquidation, the creditors are entitled to a composition on the full amount of their debts without deduction of any security they have.[8] Where there is a winding-up, securities must be deducted before a ranking is admitted.[9] Where a creditor grants a discharge to the debtor under a composition contract, the guarantor of any debt is thereby freed, unless the consent, express or implied, of the guarantor to remaining bound has been obtained, or unless the guarantor has failed to pay the debt and claim against the debtor when called upon by the creditor to do so, or unless the contract expressly reserves the right to go against the guarantor.[10] The corollary of course is that where no discharge is granted or implied the guarantor remains bound.

---

[8] *McBride v Stevenson* (1884) 11 R. 702.

[9] Bankruptcy (Scotland) Act 1985, Sch.1, para.5, as applied by Insolvency (Scotland) Rules 1986, r.4.16(1).

[10] Bell, *Comm.*, i, 376; Goudy on *Bankruptcy*, p.494; *Smith v Ogilvie* (1821) 1 S. 159 (NE 152); aff'd (1825) 1 W. and S. 315; *Flemming v Wilson* (1823) 2 S. 336 (NE 296); *Morton's Trs v Robertson's J.F.* (1892) 20 R. 72.

EFFECT OF INSOLVENCY

CHAPTER 8

DIRECTORS' LIABILITIES ON INSOLVENCY

Introduction

Limited liability was introduced by statute over a century ago to **8–01**
encourage the taking of risks with capital—what the economist John
Maynard Keynes called "the animal spirits of capitalism".[1] It has always
however been recognised that there are attendant risks of creditors and
companies being defrauded or abused. The opposition last century to
"limited liability" was largely on that ground.[2]

The Cork Committee concluded in the 1970s that the then law was
totally inadequate in dealing with problems of fraud, both by liquidators
and by delinquent directors. The Cork Committee was, of course,
addressing fraud in the strict legal sense and not looking at the
corporate governance issue of how to stop those who control corporate
treasuries from looting them—albeit legally—through unbridled pay
awards to themselves. In relation to criminal fraud, the Committee
stated:

"We believe that this is an urgent problem which demands immediate attention, before the law falls into even greater disrespect and
contempt. An entirely fresh approach is now required. The nature
of the problem is vividly illustrated by the following extracts from
written evidence submitted by a Divisional Consumer Protection
Officer of the South Yorkshire County Council:
'The doctrine of limited liability may have its good points, but it
also leads to some indifference and lack of concern when company
officials know that if the company goes down, they will not have a
financial liability . . . There are many fraudulent practices concerned
with the formation and liquidation of companies. Companies are
formed, debts run up, the assets milked and the company put into
liquidation. Immediately a new company is formed and the process
is repeated ad infinitum. Associated with the basic fraud is the
practice of new companies buying the remaining stock of the old
company (from the liquidator) at give away prices, taking on the
premises complete with fittings which are unpaid for, again at
nominal prices.'"

The Cork Committee had two main proposals for change in the
law to meet the problems in relation to directors:

---

[1] J.M. Keynes, *General Theory of Employment, Interest and Money* (New York, Harcourt,
Brace, 1935), pp.160–161.
[2] See para.1–06.

(1) the introduction of a new concept of "wrongful trading", so that those concerned in the management of a company's affairs would be made liable for the financial consequences of their wrongful or reckless conduct ("wrongful trading"); and

(2) the disqualification of delinquent directors, and their being made personally liable for the debts of their companies in certain defined circumstances ("disqualification procedure").

As regards the problem of delinquent liquidators, the problem was to be solved by handing over a monopoly of insolvency to professional "insolvency practitioners" (mostly accountants)—a new profession subject only to self regulation.[3]

(1) Wrongful trading

8–02   The concept of "wrongful trading" was contained in s.214 of the Insolvency Act 1986. The provision applied only to a company in a creditors' winding-up or a winding-up by the court. Briefly, what the law did was to significantly widen directors' exposure to action by a liquidator in relation to how they conducted the affairs of the company when they ran it. Any action under the section has to be brought by the liquidator. No action might be brought by a creditor or contributory under this section. A full discussion of "wrongful trading" to be found at paras 8–10 to 8–19.

(2) Disqualification procedure

8–03   Sections 8 and 10 of the Company Directors Disqualification Act 1986 gave two new grounds for making a disqualification order on a director, which were additional to the previously existing grounds which were contained in ss.295 to 302 of, and Sch.12 to, the Companies Act 1985, now largely consolidated into the Company Directors Disqualification Act 1986. (The legal framework for making and registering disqualification orders, which was also contained in the Companies Act 1985, was continued in the Company Directors Disqualification Act 1986.) The two additional grounds for making a disqualification order advocated in the Cork Report are:

(a) being held responsible as a director for a company's "wrongful" or "fraudulent" trading[4]; and

(b) "unfitness" found following an investigation of a company's affairs on the order of the Secretary of State for Trade and Industry.[5]

The procedure introduced by the Company Directors Disqualification Act 1986 was not a success. It took a long time, involving, as it did, a

---

[3] The Association for Accountancy & Business Affairs, of which the Labour M.P. Austin Mitchell, is a leading light, publishes on its web site very disturbing evidence of how the self regulation of this very restricted profession acts against the public interest, with fees set at exorbitant levels. World-wide winding up costs in BCCI have already passed $1,200,000,000.

[4] Company Directors Disqualification Act 1986, s.10.

[5] *ibid.*, s.8.

court hearing on every occasion. It could also be very expensive for all those involved. Only 10 per cent of disqualification proceedings were contested and went to a full hearing, whereas 60 per cent were unopposed and in the remaining 30 per cent of cases directors consented to the making of the order. This suggested a procedure, not involving the court, was required where directors were willing to accept that they should be disqualified. This idea, promoted by the Vice-Chancellor, Sir Richard Scott, led to an important change to the disqualification procedure effected by the Insolvency Act 2000. That Act changed the Insolvency Act 1986, to the effect that where there is agreement between the Secretary of State and the director, disqualification can be achieved without involvement of the courts. It is also provided that a breach of the terms of an undertaking has the same criminal consequences as a breach of a disqualification order only where agreement cannot be reached, must the case go to court.

This latest change in the law in relation to disqualification proceedings, has been successful in its aim of saving court time. In the first 17 months of the procedure being available, 1,621 undertakings were accepted and 756 disqualification orders made. That compared with 2,070 orders in the preceding 17 months. The disqualification process has accordingly speeded up offering earlier protection for both business and the public, with the courts no longer clogged up with undisputed applications.

Format of chapter

It is proposed in Pt I of this chapter to look first at the common law **8–04** remedies against directors before dealing with statutory remedies. Part II of the chapter deals with disqualification proceedings against directors.

PART I

DIRECTORS DUTIES AND LIABILITIES

Common law and statutory remedies against delinquent directors

The wrongful trading reforms had a significant continuity and overlap **8–05** with the previous pre-Cork law. For example, directors' liability for negligence generally and their liability for breach of duty were not changed by the reforms except in relation to action brought under statute by a liquidator. (There was thus no change in the type of action a company in receivership, or the administrator of a company could bring against directors.) Secondly, an action (formerly under s.631 (now repealed) of the Companies Act 1985) ("misfeasance") was still able to be brought by the liquidator or a creditor or contributory under s.212 of the Insolvency Act 1986. Action for fraudulent trading under s.213 of the Insolvency Act 1986 re-enacted s.630 of the Companies Act 1985 except that action may only be brought by the liquidator and not by a creditor or contributory. The type of action open to a liquidator under the "wrongful trading" provision of s.214 of the Insolvency Act 1986 was in contrast a radical addition to the previously existing law. It is, however, best understood by looking at the general law in relation to the duties of directors and seeing how wrongful trading goes beyond them, and also how action based on it by a liquidator is a parallel remedy to action based on the "fraudulent trading" provision of s.213 of the Insolvency Act 1986.

Accordingly, it is proposed to deal with:

(a) negligence breach of duty of directors;
(b) misfeasance action under s.212 of the Insolvency Act 1986;
(c) fraudulent trading action under s.213 of the Insolvency Act 1986; and
(d) wrongful trading under s.214 of the Insolvency Act 1986.

(a) Negligence and breach of duty

8–06   The duties of a director to a company, until the reforming legislation, were those set out by Romer J. in *Re City Equitable Fire Insurance Co*[6] where he stated:

"In order, therefore, to ascertain the duties that a person appointed to the board of an established company undertakes to perform, it is necessary to consider not only the nature of the company's business, but also the manner in which the work of the company is in fact distributed between the directors and the other officials of the company, provided always that this distribution is a reasonable one in the circumstances, and is not inconsistent with any express provisions of the articles of association. In discharging the duties of his position thus ascertained a director must, of course, act honestly, but he must also exercise some degree of both skill and diligence. To the question of what is the particular degree of skill and diligence required of him, the authorities do not, I think, give any very clear answer. It has been laid down that so long as a director acts honestly, he cannot be made responsible in damages unless guilty of gross or culpable negligence in a business sense. But as pointed out by Neville J in *Re Brazilian Rubber Plantations and Estates Limited*,[7] one cannot say whether a man has been guilty of negligence, gross or otherwise, unless one can determine what is the extent of the duty which he is alleged to have neglected. For myself, I confess to feeling some difficulty in understanding the difference

---

[6] [1925] Ch. 407 at 427; see also *Re D'Jan of London Ltd* [1994] 1B.C.L.C. 561, in which Hoffmann J. took the view that the common law standard of care could now be equated with the standard of care owed by a director under s.214 of the Insolvency Act 1986; and *Norman v Theodore Goddard (a firm)* [1992] B.C.L.C. 1028, in which Hoffmann J. cited *Re Equitable* and stated that that standard was that now stated in s.214(4) of the Insolvency Act 1986 and that directors might trust others until there was a reason to distrust them.
[7] [1911] 1 Ch. 425.

between negligence and gross negligence, except in so far as the expressions are used for the purpose of drawing a distinction between the duty that is owed in one case and the duty that is owed in another . . .

There are, in addition, one or two other general propositions that seem to be warranted by the reported cases: (1) A director need not exhibit in the performance of his duties a greater degree of skill than may reasonably be expected from a person of his knowledge and experience. A director of a life insurance company, for instance, does not guarantee that he has the skill of an actuary or of a physician. In the words of Lindley MR: "If directors act within their powers, if they act with such care as is reasonably to be expected from them, having regard to their knowledge and experience, and if they act honestly for the benefit of the company they represent, they discharge both their equitable as well as their legal duty to the company".[8] It is perhaps only another way of stating the same proposition to say that directors are not liable for mere errors of judgment; (2) A director is not bound to give continuous attention to the affairs of his company. His duties are of an intermittent nature to be performed at periodical board meetings; and at meetings of any committee of the board upon which he happens to be placed. He is not, however, bound to attend at all such meetings, though he ought to attend whenever in the circumstances, he is reasonably able to do so. (3) In respect of all duties that, having regard to the exigencies of the business, and the articles of association, may properly be left to some other official, a director is, in the absence of grounds for suspicion, justified in trusting that official to perform such duties honestly."

The level of diligence and skill therefore required of directors is the reasonable care which an ordinary man might be expected to take, in the circumstances, on his own behalf, but not without the need to exhibit a greater degree of skill than could reasonably be expected from a person of his knowledge and experience. The duties of a director whether executive or non-executive were considered to be the same, and a non-executive director could not plead that he did not have any duties to perform.[9] However, the responsibility of a person who nominates directors to the board of directors of a particular company which subsequently becomes insolvent relates only to the question of negligence in the making of the initial appointment. The person nominating is not responsible for the acts and defaults of those nominees whilst acting as company directors. Such responsibility lies at the door of the company for which they are acting as directors.[10]

Romer J. did not set an absolute standard for a director's duty of diligence. He quoted with approbation Lord Macnaghten's judgment in *Dovey v Cory*[11]: "I do not think it desirable for any tribunal to do that

---

[8] *Lagunas Nitrate Co v Lagunas Syndicate* [1899] 2 Ch. 392 at 435.
[9] *Dorchester Finance Co Ltd v Stebbing* [1989] B.C.L.C. 498.
[10] *Kuwait Asia Bank EC v National Mutual Life Nominees Ltd* [1990] 3 W.L.R. 297.
[11] [1901] A.C. 479.

which Parliament has abstained from doing—that is to formulate precise rules for the guidance or embarrassment of businessmen in the conduct of business affairs." The problem with Romer J.'s definition and that running through other attempts at definitions is that a director is not thought to be like a professional man with professional skills. He can be anybody off the street, and the thinking is that one cannot legally require of him anything more than one could expect from the man off the street. Hence "errors of judgment" are acceptable. If there is to be a basis of fault it has to go beyond errors of judgment, and be something like "gross negligence". Gross negligence, or something similar, is the traditional test in Scotland.[12] The law in this area really is not formed with a modern economy in mind, requiring as it does only a level of skill to be expected of the particular individual—not of a person filling a particular job, however responsible the job. Not surprisingly, in view of the exceptionally low level of skill legally required of them, there are few reported cases in England or Scotland of directors being sued for negligence, although quite a number on breach of trust, or breach of contract. In addition to the duty of diligence as described in the *City Equitable* case, directors are also trustees for the company, in that they must act in good faith for the benefit of the general body of members.[13]

If directors are negligent or in breach of these duties as detailed above, they may be sued by the company.[14] The action will be open to an insolvent company, an insolvent company in receivership and an insolvent company under an administration order. If the company is in liquidation, the action should be brought under s.212 of the Insolvency Act 1986.

In exceptional circumstances directors may be sued directly by third parties, where for example the directors effectively "are the company" by being owners and directors.[15] The company may have a right of action against a negligent director in addition to a claim for any breach of an employment contract it might have with him.

Section 310 of the Companies Act 1985 makes void any article of association of a company or contract with the company or other provision providing indemnity to the director for negligence. There are, however, policies of negligence insurance available to directors, but it is unsettled whether the company may pay the premiums.

---

[12] *Lees v Tod* (1882) 9 R. 807 at 833, *per* Lord Deas; *Thompson v J Barke & Co (Caterers) Ltd*, 1975 S.L.T. 67. The concept of "gross negligence" is almost unknown elsewhere in the law of Scotland and is not known in the law of professional negligence (*Hunter v Hanley*, 1955 S.C. 200). It is still applicable to trustees, who, like directors, can be anyone "off the street". If there were a professional standard required, people might be reluctant to accept the responsibility.

[13] *Re City Equitable Fire Insurance Co* [1925] Ch. 407; *Harris v Harris (A) Ltd*, 1936 S.C. 183; *Selangor United Rubber Estates v Cradock* [1968] 2 All E.R. 1073.

[14] *Western Bank v Baird's Trs* (1872) 11 M. 96; *Industrial Development Consultants Ltd v Cooley* [1972] 2 All E.R. 162.

[15] *Brenes & Co v Downie*, 1914 S.C. 97 at 104.

(b) Action under section 212 of the Insolvency Act 1986 ("misfeasance action")

The liquidator has a right to apply to the court asking the court to **8–07** examine into the conduct of a director if it appears that the director has misapplied or retained or become liable or accountable for any money or property of the company, or been guilty of misfeasance or breach of any fiduciary duty or any other duty in relation to the company, and the court may then compel a delinquent director to repay or restore any money which he has misapplied or retained or become liable or accountable for to the company or to contribute to the company's assets an appropriate sum by way of compensation.[16] The section also permits the court to enforce the company's right at the initiative of a creditor or a contributory. The contributory need not have a financial interest in the outcome.[17]

An action under this section or its statutory predecessors going back to the Companies Act 1862 has been traditionally known in England, but not in Scotland as a "misfeasance action", initiated by a "misfeasance summons". Misfeasance, however, is only one of the grounds of action, and the slightly exotic word "misfeasance" is used as shorthand for a basketful of grounds including misfeasance. In fact a "misfeasance action" does not create any additional grounds of action to those listed above. It is a procedural matter only. The statute merely provides a summary method of enforcing the liabilities that might have been enforced by the company itself or by its liquidator by means of an ordinary action.[18] The fullest recent Scottish analysis of the meaning of the section, with citation of authorities, was that by Lord Penrose in the case of *Ross v Davy*,[19] in which he stated that a "breach of fiduciary duty" may, at one end of the spectrum, include simple carelessness, and at the other extend to acts which on any view are criminal in the narrowest sense of that expression. Embezzlement liable to action under the criminal law would fall within the provision, as would negligent investment. Action may also be taken under this section against other persons connected with the formation, promotion or running of the company in addition to directors, and also against liquidators, administrative receivers and administrators.[20]

A Scottish example of the section at work was the case of *Farquhar v McCalls*.[21] In that case the court had ordered an examination into the conduct of two directors of a company proceeding on an application by a creditor in the liquidation of *Ardtalla Yachts Ltd* which sought to compel them to contribute sums to the company's assets by way of

---

[16] Insolvency Act 1986, s.212.

[17] S.212(5) of the Insolvency Act 1986.

[18] *Blin v Johnstone*, 1988 S.L.T. 335 at 338; *Cohen v Selby* [2001] 1 B.C.L.C 135

[19] 1996 S.C.L.R. 369; see also *Westlowe Storage &Distribution, Re* [2000] 2 B.C.L.C. 590 for scope of s.212.

[20] This came into effect only after April 28, 1986.

[21] April 10, 1991, Oban Sheriff Court, unreported. See also *Blin v Johnstone*, 1988 S.L.T. 335 and *Gray v Davidson*, 1991 S.C.L.R. 38, Sh. Ct; see also *Ross v Davy*, 1996 S.C.L.R. 369 for Lord Penrose's dicta on procedure in the Court of Session.

compensation in respect of misfeasance or breach of fiduciary or other duty. The court had held that, in the liquidation, the court had first to be satisfied that there was a *prima facie* case against the directors before an examination was ordered. At the *prima facie* stage, *ex parte* statements and affidavits were sufficient to substantiate the Note in the liquidation. In that case the court held that the sale by a company of its business and assets without consideration for a goodwill element amounted to a breach of fiduciary duties. There had also been a breach of fiduciary duty by putting into liquidation a viable company which could have traded out of a short-term liability.

For there to be an action under s.212 of the Insolvency Act 1986, it is necessary that loss is shown to have been borne by the company. It is not sufficient that there has been misappropriation of funds if the funds have been paid back.[22] If a company is solvent and likely to remain so, it is open to its members to ratify what would otherwise have been a breach of duty by directors provided that the conduct to be ratified was not itself unlawful or a fraud in the company or its creditors.[23] In that case the liquidator would have no cause of action to pursue in the company's name.[24] If, however, a transaction is likely to cause loss to creditors because the company is insolvent a purported approval or ratification by the members of a breach of duty by the directors causing loss to the company will be ineffective.[25]

Most of the cases in England brought under this section, or its statutory predecessors, have involved breach of trust or breach of other duties or improper or *ultra vires* actions, *e.g.* payment of dividends out of capital[26]; the making of secret profits by a promoter.[27] In Scotland procuring the payment of private claims to directors after a winding-up petition was caught.[28] The substantive law in Scotland appears from the interchangeability of authorities cited in court to be the same as in England.[29]

(c) Fraudulent trading under section 213 of the Insolvency Act 1986

8–08   Section 213 of the Insolvency Act 1986 continued the pre-Cork law in relation to fraudulent trading. It re-enacted s.630 of the Companies Act 1985 (formerly s.332 of the Companies Act 1948) with the exception that

---

[22] *Derek Randall Enterprises Ltd (in liquidation) v Randall* [1991] B.C.L.C. 379; [1990] B.C.C. 749.

[23] *Atwool v Merryweather* (1867) L.R. 5 Eq. 464n; *Attorney-General's Reference (No 2)* [1984] 1 Q.B. 624.

[24] *Salomon v A. Salomon & Co Ltd* [1897] A.C. 22; *Multinational Gas & Petrochemical Co v Multinational Gas & Petrochemical Services Ltd* [1983] Ch. 258; *Rolled Steel Products (Holdings) Ltd v British Steel Corp.* [1982] Ch. 478; upheld in this point [1986] Ch. 246; and *Brady v Brady* [1988] 2 All E.R. 617.

[25] *Walker v Wimborne* (1976) 50 A.L.J.R. 446; *Re Horsley & Weight Ltd* [1982] Ch. 442; *Nicholson v Permakraft (NZ) Ltd* [1985] 1 N.Z.L.R. 242; and *Kinsela v Russell Kinsela Pty Ltd* (1986) 10 A.C.L.R. 395.

[26] See *Flitcroft's Case* (1882) 21 Ch. D 519.

[27] *Gluckstein v Barnes* [1900] A.C. 240.

[28] *Liqr of Bankers and General Insurance Co Ltd v Lithauer*, 1924 S.L.T. 775.

[29] *Liqrs of City of Glasgow Bank v Mackinnon* (1882) 9 R. 535.

an action might no longer be brought by a contributory or a creditor.[30] In terms of the section, if in the course of the winding up of a company it appears that any business of the company has been carried on with the intent to defraud creditors of the company or creditors of any other person, or for any fraudulent purposes, the court may, on the application of the liquidator of the company, declare that any persons who were knowingly parties to the carrying on of the business in such manner are to be liable to make such contributions (if any) to the company's assets as the court thinks proper. The restriction that only the liquidator may bring the action makes the section in line with the provisions relating to "wrongful trading" which also may only be brought by the liquidator.

This section, and its statutory predecessors, apply not only to directors, but to "any persons who are knowingly parties to the carrying on of the business". Accordingly, not only officers of the company are liable, but any person who is party to the carrying on of the business. The class would include, for example, a creditor who accepts money which he knows has been procured by carrying on the business with intent to defraud creditors for the very purpose of making the payment,[31] although it is not clear whether the creditor needs to have given some prior encouragement to the fraud or whether he could have acquiesced in it after the event. In setting up the liability under the section, the case law suggests the following:

(1) What is required is to show a criminal intent, which is accordingly a subjective and not an objective test. It is accordingly necessary to show "actual dishonesty involving, according to current notions of fair trading amongst commercial men, real moral blame".[32] There can either be intent to defraud or reckless indifference, whether or not the creditors were defrauded.[33]

(2) The onus of proving that the person charged has been guilty of dishonesty is upon the person who alleges it.[34]

(3) One transaction alone may be sufficient to set up liability, *e.g.* the acceptance of a deposit or the purchase price for goods in advance, knowing that the goods cannot be supplied and the deposit or price will not be repaid.[35] The mere giving or receipt of preference over other creditors will not necessarily constitute fraudulent trading.[36]

(4) In order to be party to the trading in question, the company itself must have been party to the fraud[37] and the individual

---

[30] Insolvency Act 1985, Sch.6, para.6.

[31] *Re Gerald Cooper Chemicals Ltd* [1978] Ch. 262.

[32] *Re Patrick and Lyon* [1933] Ch. 786; *R v Cox; R v Hodges* [1983] B.C.L.C. 169; *R v Lockwood* [1986] Crim. L.R. 244.

[33] *Hardie v Hanson* (1960) 105 C.L.R. 451, High Court of Australia; *Rossleigh v Carlaw,* 1986 S.L.T. 204.

[34] *Re Patrick and Lyon* [1933] Ch. 796 at 790.

[35] *Re Gerald Cooper,* above; *R v Lockwood,* above.

[36] *Re Sarflax* [1979] Ch. 592; *R v Grantham* [1984] Q.B. 675; *Rossleigh v Carlaw,* 1986 S.L.T. 204.

[37] *Re Augustus Barnett* [1986] B.C.L.C. 170.

took some active part. It is not enough that he failed to prevent it or failed to advise against it.[38] Carrying out orders from superiors is not enough to set up fraudulent trading without an element of participation,[39] but actively assisting in the carrying on of the fraudulent business may be enough to set up fraudulent trading, without an involvement in its management.[40]

(5) There is constructive intent to defraud established if credit is obtained at a time when the person knows that there is no good reason for thinking that funds will become available to pay the debt when it becomes due or shortly thereafter. It is unnecessary to establish knowledge that funds will never become available.[41]

(6) Persons may also be criminally liable under s.458 of the Companies Act 1985 (whether or not the company is in liquidation), but a s.213 action is civil in its nature and accordingly allegations have to be proved on the balance of probabilities.[42] "Shadow directors" are also liable, as they are also for "wrongful trading". This expression is defined in both s.22(5) of the Company Directors Disqualification Act 1986 and s.741(2) of the Companies Act 1985 to mean a person in accordance with whose directions or instructions the directors of a company are accustomed to act (excluding a person who gives advice in a professional capacity). It obviously covers the case where a board is really taking directions from some outside controller. It could cover a holding company,[43] or even a bank if the company invariably takes its instructions from its bank.

The case of *R v Grantham* mentioned in (5) above somewhat lowered the hitherto very tight definition of "fraudulent" in this context, by holding that the dishonest intent (which has to be proved for a prosecution case to succeed) does not have to extend to an intention to deprive a creditor of his property permanently, and that dishonesty may be inferred if credit is taken or lengthened in circumstances where there is no reasonable prospect of the debts being paid as they fall due, or shortly thereafter. That important case, although a criminal case, indicates that the courts were already moving in the direction of "wrongful trading".

A section 213 action is compensatory and not punitive

8–09   Where an action is brought under s.213 of the Insolvency Act 1986 for fraudulent trading, the court is entitled to make a compensatory order for the amount of loss incurred by the company as a result of the

---

[38] *Re Maidstone Builders* [1971] 1 W.L.R. 1085.
[39] *R. v Miles* [1992] Crim. L.R. 657.
[40] *Morris v Banque Arabe & Internationale d'Investissement S.A. (No.2)* [2001] 1.B.C.L.C. 263.
[41] *R v Grantham*, above.
[42] *Aktieselskabet Dansk Skibsfinansiering v Brothers* [2001] 2 B.C.L.C. 324.
[43] This is the nearest that the law has got to detraction from the limited liability of a company to open up the concept of "group liability" as proposed in the EEC Ninth Directive on Company Law. The Cork Committee thought the matter of "group liability" too complex for them, but one requiring urgent attention.

fraudulent trading. In the English case of *Re a Company (No. 001418 of 1988)*,[44] Judge Bromley Q.C. laid down principles in terms of which relief would be granted under s.213 and how liability should be measured. Going through previous authorities, he concluded that there should not only be a compensatory element in damages to reflect how far the assets of a company had been depleted causing loss to creditors, but also that there could be a punitive element. Recently the Court of Appeal in the important case of *Morphites v Bernasconi*,[45] went through all the main authorities again and considered the scope of liability for fraudulent trading under s.213 of the Insolvency Act 1986. It overruled the decision of the lower court on the test under the section and on the question of whether a punitive element was competent.[46] The Court of Appeal also provided valuable guidance for liquidators considering the use of a s.213 action and for directors defending such claims.

According to the Court of Appeal, the principle on which the contribution power had to be exercised was that the contribution to the assets in which the company's creditors would share in the liquidation should reflect (and compensate for) the loss which had been caused to those creditors by the carrying on of the business in the manner which gives rise to the exercise of the power. The precondition for the exercise of the court's powers under s.213 of the Insolvency Act 1986 is that it should appear to the court "that any business of the company had been carried on with intent to defraud creditors of the company". Parliament did not provide that the powers under those sections might be exercisable whenever it appeared to the court "that any creditor of the company had been defrauded in the course of carrying on the business of the company". The Court of Appeal also held that punishment of those who had been party to the carrying on of the business in a manner of which the court disapproved—beyond what was inherent in requiring them to make contributions to the assets of a company with limited liability which they could not otherwise be required to make—was foreign to the compensatory principle. Further, the power to punish a person knowingly party to fraudulent trading—formerly contained in s.332(3) of the 1948 Act—had been re-enacted (and preserved in s.458 of the Companies Act 1985). It could not have been Parliament's intention that the court would use the power to order contribution under s.213 of the 1986 Act in order to punish the wrongdoer. The contribution gained by a s.213 action is on behalf of the creditors collectively, not just the victims.[47] There may be cases where a director's liability under ss.212 (misfeasance), 213 (fraudulent trading), 214 (wrongful trading) or 243 (unfair preferences) might run concurrently. It is thought that, in Scotland, a court would have to bear in mind the overlapping nature of these remedies, so that no element of compensation was duplicated.[48]

---

[44] [1991] B.C.L.C. 197.

[45] [2003] E.W.C.A. Civ. 289; [2003] B.C.C. 540; [2003] 2 B.C.L.C. 53; [2003] Ch. 552.

[46] [2001] 2 B.C.L.C. 1.

[47] See also *Re Esal (Commodities) Ltd.* [1997] 1 B.C.L.C. 705 (C.A.).

[48] In England there are conflicting decisions on whether liability under the various sections can be imposed cumulatively or whether "net" compensation is the proper approach: see *Re DKG Contractors Ltd* [1990] B.C.C. 903; *Re Purpoint Ltd* [1991] B.C.C. 121; *R v Holmes* [1991] B.C.C. 394.

(d) Wrongful trading

8–10   Section 214 of the Insolvency Act 1986 created the legal concept of "wrongful trading". It applies only to directors and shadow directors, and former directors or shadow directors.[49] Persons who act as *de facto* directors without having been validly appointed are also subject to s.214 of the Insolvency Act 1986.[50] Fraudulent trading on the other hand applies to a larger class of persons.[51] A similar concept to wrongful trading was already established in several European countries, and this provision was introduced in large measure as a result of the anticipated need to conform with the draft EEC Bankruptcy Convention.

The Cork Committee had put forward its own draft definition of "wrongful trading",[52] the essential part of which read: "at any time when the company is insolvent or unable to pay its debts as they fall due it incurs further debts or other liabilities to other persons without a reasonable prospect of meeting them in full".

The above definition, which is echoed in the case of *R v Grantham*, above, was not adopted by Parliament, and is wider in its scope than that of s.214.

For the section to apply the following two conditions must be met:
  (a) the company must have gone into insolvent liquidation (*i.e.* liquidation at a time when its assets are insufficient for the payment of its debts and other liabilities and the expenses of winding up[53]); and
  (b) at some time before the commencement of the winding-up of the company, the person to be held liable was a director or a shadow director, and either knew or ought to have concluded that there was no reasonable prospect that the company would avoid going into insolvent liquidation.[54]

Where these conditions are met the court may, on the application of the liquidator, declare that the director in question is liable to make a contribution to the company's assets as the court thinks proper.

There is a defence to the liability in s.214(3), in terms of which the declaration that the director shall make a contribution shall not apply where the court is satisfied that, after the date of the actual or constructive knowledge, there was no reasonable prospect that the company would avoid going into insolvent liquidation, the director took *every* step with a view to minimising the potential loss to the company's creditors that he ought to have taken (assuming him to have known that

---

[49] Insolvency Act 1986, s.214(1), (2) and (7).
[50] *Re Hydrodan (Corby) Ltd* [1994] B.C.C. 161, where the distinction between a "shadow director" and a "*de facto* director" and a "*de jure*" director is drawn.
[51] See paras 8–08 to 8–09.
[52] Cork Report, Cmnd. 8558, para.1806.
[53] Insolvency Act 1986, s.214(6).
[54] *ibid.*, s.214(2)(b) and (c).

there was no reasonable prospect that the company would avoid going into insolvent liquidation). The onus of proof of "having taken all the necessary steps" is accordingly placed on the director.

For the purpose of determining the fact which a director of a company ought to have known or ascertained, and the conclusions which he ought to have reached and the steps which he ought to have taken, the test is:

What would a reasonably diligent person have done, having both:

(a) the general knowledge, skill and experience that may reasonably be expected of a person carrying out the same functions as are carried out by that director in relation to the company; and
(b) the general knowledge, skill and experience that that director has?[55]

Differences between "wrongful trading" and "fraudulent trading"

There would appear to be the following key distinctions between **8–11** wrongful trading and fraudulent trading apart from the fact that only directors and shadow directors may be liable for wrongful trading:

(a) in the case of fraudulent trading the onus of proof is on the person alleging fraud whereas in the case of wrongful trading once the conditions establishing liability are set up, the onus is on the director to prove that he was sufficiently diligent to avoid loss to creditors;
(b) in the case of fraudulent trading a positive act is required to establish liability whereas in the case of wrongful trading acts of omission may be sufficient;
(c) for the purpose of establishing fraudulent trading there would need to be actual knowledge that the company was unable to pay its debts, whereas with wrongful trading it is sufficient that the director ought to have known this; and
(d) going by the case of *R v Grantham*, fraudulent trading involves usually failure to have proper regard to the interests of future creditors (*i.e.* those extending credit to the company) whereas wrongful trading involves a failure to have regard to the interests of creditors as a class.

"Wrongful trading" and negligence

The concept of "wrongful trading" extends the usual ambit of a **8–12** director's liability for negligence. Previously the emphasis had been on the need for honesty and conscientiousness rather than a particular degree of professional skill, diligence or competence.[56] There are two tests:

---

[55] Insolvency Act 1986, s.214(4).
[56] See para.8–06.

(1) What would a reasonably diligent person having the general knowledge, skill and experience reasonably to be expected of any person carrying out the same functions (a) have concluded about the prospects of the company avoiding insolvent liquidation; and (b) have done to minimise loss?

This is an objective test and looks to the job that the director is doing rather than to the particular skills of the director himself. Accordingly if a cost accountant is over-promoted to the job of finance director, he will not be able to argue that given his training and background he could not be reasonably expected to have the skills necessary to run a finance department. Section 214(5) of the Insolvency Act 1986 makes a further refinement. The director is first assumed to have the general knowledge, skill and experience that may reasonably be expected of a person carrying out "the same functions" as are carried out by that director.[57] He is also, however, assumed to have these attributes in relation to functions entrusted to him by the company but which he does not carry out.[58] Hence if the finance director is responsible for the "treasury" function in a company, it will not be open to him to say he did not understand anything about foreign exchange fluctuations and left it all to his treasurer.

The objective test, having been thus established, is then applied both in determining whether the director ought to have known that there was no reasonable prospect that the company would avoid going into insolvent liquidation, and in determining what steps a reasonably diligent person would have taken.[59] In relation to deciding whether there is any reasonable prospect of the company avoiding going into insolvent liquidation, the courts have not yet had to lay down guidelines as to what each director is supposed to know. Previously he was not thought obliged to attend all board meetings,[60] but this may now have to be revised in the light of this potentially higher duty.

(2) What was "the general knowledge, skill and experience" that the director had?

This is a subjective test and is in line with the pre-Cork law on negligence. It should be noted, however, that because the subjective test is in addition to the objective test, the director will be judged by the subjective test, if his skill, knowledge and experience is higher than that which could be reasonably expected from a person carrying out the same functions.

Aspects of wrongful trading

8–13   In relation to determining whether there is no reasonable prospect that the company would avoid going into "insolvent liquidation", a company goes into "insolvent liquidation" at a time when its assets are

---

[57] Insolvency Act 1986, s.214(4)(a); see *DKG Contractors Ltd.* [1990] B.C.L.C. 903.
[58] *ibid.*, s.214(5).
[59] *ibid.*, s.214(4).
[60] See para.8–06.

insufficient for the payment of its debts and other liabilities and the expenses of the winding up.[61] ("Insolvent liquidation" on the ingenious definition would not, however, cover a creditors' or compulsory winding up, where it turns out at the end of the day that there is a surplus of assets because of course in that event (*e.g.* Rolls-Royce Ltd) the creditors recover their debts, or where creditors had time-barred debts.[62]) The inclusion of the "expenses of the winding up" in the definition probably means that the director has to look not only to the state of the balance sheet when the company is trading to see if the company is solvent, but also to whether, if it was forced into a winding up, there would be a surplus after taking into account the distress element in the realising of assets and the winding-up expenses. The test is probably therefore on a prospective "balance sheet" rather than a "liquidity" basis. This matter is still not resolved by the courts, and it may be that the courts decide that "going into insolvent liquidation" means that assets are to be valued on a "going concern" basis and not on a "break-up" basis.[63] The authors think that on a "break-up" basis is correct. The image the directors are meant to have in stark relief *is* a "break-up" and the question is whether creditors would lose—if so, urgent action is required. It is also not clear how contingent liabilities are to be valued.[64] Although the implications of s.214 appear stringent, it is directed only at pronounced cases; namely, where there is "no reasonable prospect" that the company would avoid going into insolvent liquidation. That does not mean that it was "likely" that the company would go into insolvent liquidation. It only covers a situation where it would be unreasonable to say that there was any prospect of the company avoiding insolvent liquidation. Optimistic trading, or company doctors going in with a reasonable hope that they might turn round a company, would seem not to be covered. It is thus much more directed at a situation where directors pay out to themselves large fees, or run up credit, when the company is obviously going into liquidation, or recklessly overtrade. There is, however, a practical problem with venture capital firms when only two in 10 survive, and they are known from the outset as likely to go under. It may be objected that directors of venture capital firms are therefore unnecessarily inhibited, with the consequent discouragement of this type of important "seed-corn" investment. The objection is unsound because directors of venture capital firms are not any more at risk than other directors, provided they insist that the firms are kept sufficiently capitalised, so that it is the "venture capital" that is put at risk, not creditors' money.

The duty of directors is to cut the potential loss to the company's creditors. This goes against recent decisions of the courts denying the possibility that directors owe duties of any kind to creditors.[65] The

---

[61] Insolvency Act 1986, s.214(6).

[62] See *Re Joshua Shaw and Sons Ltd* [1989] B.C.L.C. 362.

[63] See *Re a* Company [1986] B.C.L.C. 261, where Nourse J. decided that, in relation to "inability to pay debts", one should look to whether money would be available at the time the debts became due (*i.e.* liquidity basis).

[64] For the different approaches to valuation including contingent liabilities, see para.4–107.

[65] *Multinational Gas and Petrochemical Co v Multinational Gas and Petrochemical Services Ltd* [1983] Ch. 258; see *Winkworth v Edward Baron Development Co Ltd* [1986] 1 W.L.R. 1512 at 1516, *per* Lord Templeman.

measure of liability of the directors is also not the usual liability measured by loss to the creditors. It is "such contribution" (if any) to the company's assets as the court thinks proper.[66] The Act is silent as to the criteria the courts should apply in deciding the measure of contribution (if any) which directors should make. The formula gives the court wide discretion. It is drafted in an open fashion and does not, for example, say whether the financial means of the director are to be taken into account. The same formula is now used in relation to a contribution to be made by a director in the case of fraudulent trading.[67] Despite the open endedness of the section, it is thought that, given the relevant formulation in respect of contribution is the same in ss.214 as in 213, the approach in *Morphites v Bernasconi*,[68] should be followed.

Case of *Re Produce Marketing Consortium Ltd (No.2)*

8-14   Since the introduction of "wrongful trading" by s.214 of the Insolvency Act 1986, the courts have had to deal with remarkably few cases. The reason for this may be that the section is having a deterrent effect both on directors and banks, who are potentially liable as "shadow directors". The leading and first case was *Re Produce Marketing Consortium Ltd (No.2)*,[69] which was heard in the Chancery Division of the High Court by Knox J. over nine days in February and March 1989. Too much reliance perhaps should not be placed in one case, but Knox J. took the opportunity to elaborate on certain of the propositions mentioned above which are extractable from the wording of s.214 itself. He laid down guidelines in the following areas:

(a) Standard by which director's conduct to be judged

8-15   Knox J. stated[70] that the test to be applied in judging a director was by the standards of what can reasonably be expected of a person fulfilling his functions, and showing reasonable diligence in doing so. In this connection the requirement to have regard to the functions to be carried out by the director in question, in relation to the company in question, involved having regard to the particular company and its business. Accordingly the general knowledge, skill and experience postulated will be less extensive in a small company in a modest way of business, with simple accounting procedures and equipment, than it would be in a large company with sophisticated procedures. He then laid down what should be the minimum standards. He stated:

> "Nevertheless, certain minimum standards are to be assumed to be attained.
> Notably there is an obligation laid on companies to cause accounting records to be kept which are such as to disclose with reasonable accuracy at any time the financial position of the

---

[66] Insolvency Act 1986, s.214(1).
[67] *ibid.*, s.213(2).
[68] [2003] E.W.C.A. Civ. 289; [2003] B.C.C. 540; [2003] 2 B.C.L.C. 53; [2003] Ch. 552.
[69] [1989] B.C.L.C. 520.
[70] *ibid.*, at 550.

company at that time: see the Companies Act 1985, s 221(1) and (2)(a). In addition directors are required to prepare a profit and loss account for each financial year and a balance sheet as at the end of it: Companies Act 1985, s 227(1) and (3). Directors are also required, in respect of each financial year, to lay before the company in general meeting copies of the accounts of the company for that year and to deliver to the registrar of companies a copy of those accounts, in the case of a private company, within 10 months after the end of the relevant accounting reference period (see the Companies Act 1985, ss 241(1) and (3) and 242(1) and (2)).

As I have already mentioned, the liquidator gave evidence that the accounting records of PMC were adequate for the purposes of its business. The preparation of accounts was woefully late, more especially in relation to those dealing with the year ending 30 September 1985 which should have been laid and delivered by the end of July 1986.

The knowledge to be imputed in testing whether or not directors knew or ought to have concluded that there was no reasonable prospect of the company avoiding insolvent liquidation is not limited to the documentary material actually available at the given time. This appears from s 214(4) which includes a reference to facts which a director of a company ought not only to know but those which he ought to ascertain, a word which does not appear in sub-s (2)(b). In my judgment this indicates that there is to be included by way of factual information not only what was actually there but what, given reasonable diligence and appropriate level of general knowledge, skill and experience, was ascertainable. This leads me to the conclusion in this case that I should assume, for the purposes of applying the test in s 214(2), that the financial results for the year ending 30 September 1985 were known at the end of July 1986 at least to the extent of the size of the deficiency of assets over liabilities."

(b) Amount the court would order to be contributed

Knox J. held that the amount to be contributed was primarily **8–16** compensatory and not penal. He stated:

"On the nature of that discretion there were conflicting submissions made to me. Counsel for the first respondent submitted that the court's discretion is entirely at large, and he pointed to no less than three sets of words indicating the existence of a wide discretion: the court *may* declare that the person is to be liable to make *such* contribution *(if any)* to the company's assets as the court thinks *proper*. He also submitted that the provision is both compensatory and penal in character. He referred me to *Re William C Leitch Bros Ltd* [1932] 2 Ch 71 at 79, [1932] All ER Rep 892 at 896 where Maugham J said of s 275 of the Companies Act 1929:
   'I am inclined to the view that s 275 is in the nature of a punitive provision, and that where the Court makes such a declaration in relation to 'all or any of the debts or other liabilities of the company', it is in the discretion of the Court to make an order without limiting the order to the amount of the debts of those

creditors proved to have been defrauded by the acts of the director in question, though no doubt the order would in general be so limited.'

However, counsel for the first respondent also submitted that the amount which the court concluded had been lost as a result of the wrongful trading should provide a ceiling for the figure which the court declared should be contributed to the company's assets, which is of course the exact opposite of what Maugham J said in that regard. He also relied on the provisions of s 214(3) which prevent the exercise of the discretion under sub-s (1) in any case where, to put it briefly, the director has done everything possible to minimise loss to creditors, and he suggested that it would be inequitable for a director who has just failed to escape scot-free under the provision because he had only done nearly but not quite everything to that end to be treated on a par with a director who had done nothing to minimise loss to creditors.

Counsel for the liquidator . . . submitted that s 214 of the 1986 Act gave a purely civil remedy, unlike the predecessors of s 213 of that Act, such as s 275 of the Companies Act 1929 and s 332 of the Companies Act 1948 which combined the civil and criminal. More significantly for my purpose she submitted that s 214 was compensatory rather than penal. What is ordered to be contributed goes to increase the company's assets for the benefit of the general body of creditors. On that basis she submitted that the proper measure was the reduction in the net assets which could be identified as caused by the wrongful activities of the persons ordered to contribute. This jurisdiction, it was submitted, is an enhanced version of the right which any company would have to sue its directors for breach of duty, enhanced in the sense that the standard of knowledge, skill and experience required is made more objective.

On this analysis, once the circumstances required for the exercise of discretion under s 214(1) are shown to exist, she submitted that the situation was analogous to that obtaining where a tort such as negligence was shown to have been committed in that *quantum* was a matter of causation and not culpability. The discretion given to the court was to enable allowance to be made for questions of causation and also to avoid unjust results such as unwarranted windfalls for creditors. Thus in *West Mercia Safetywear Ltd (in liq) v Dodd* [1988] BCLC 250 at 253, Dillon LJ said of s 333 of the Companies Act 1948:

'The section in question, however, s 333 of the Companies Act 1948, provides that the court may order the delinquent director to repay or restore the money, with interest at such rate as the court thinks fit, or to contribute such sum to the assets of the company by way of compensation in respect of the misapplication as the court thinks fit. The court has a discretion over the matter of relief, and it is permissible for the delinquent director to submit that the wind should be tempered because, for instance, full repayment would produce a windfall to third parties, or, alternatively, because it would involve money going round in a circle or passing through the hands of someone else whose position is equally tainted.'

In my judgment the jurisdiction under s 214 is primarily compensatory rather than penal. *Prima facie* the appropriate amount that a director is declared to be liable to contribute is the amount by which the company's assets can be discerned to have been depleted by the director's conduct which caused the discretion under subs (1) to arise. But Parliament has indeed chosen very wide words of discretion and it would be undesirable to seek to spell out limits on that discretion, more especially since this is, so far as counsel were aware, the first case to come to judgment under this section. The fact that there was no fraudulent intent is not of itself a reason for fixing the amount at a nominal or low figure, for that would amount to frustrating what I discern as Parliament's intention in adding s 214 to s 213 in the 1986 Act, but I am not persuaded that it is right to ignore that fact totally."

(c) Interest

Knox J held that he was entitled to allow interest to be ordered to be **8–17** contributed on the director's contribution from the commencement of the winding-up.

Penal element in Scotland

As will be noted from what was said in para.8–16 in relation to **8–18** fraudulent trading, and above in relation to wrongful trading, the English courts have in the past[71] allowed there to be a penal element in the financial order made against directors for fraudulent trading, and, in the case of *Re Produce Marketing Consortium (No 2)*,[72] had not ruled out a penal element for wrongful trading. It is not clear which approach the Scottish courts would take. In the case of s.212(3) of the Insolvency Act 1986 in relation to misfeasance the court may only order compensation. In relation to fraudulent trading in terms of s.213 of the Insolvency Act 1986: "[t]he court on the application of the liquidator may declare that any persons who are knowingly parties to the carrying on of the business . . . are to be liable to make such contributions (if any) to the company's assets as the court thinks proper."

The payment provision is the same for wrongful trading under s.214(1) of the Insolvency Act 1986. Both these provisions are different from the previous s.630 of the Companies Act 1985 which provided that:

"The court, on the application of the official receiver, or the liquidator or any creditor or contributory of the company, may, if it thinks proper to do so, declare that any persons who are knowingly parties to the carrying on of the business in the manner above-mentioned are to be personally responsible, without any limitation of liability, for all or any of the debts or other liabilities of the company as the court may direct."

---

[71] *Morphites v Bernasconi* [2003] E.W.C.A. Civ. 289; [2003] B.C.C. 540; [2003] 2 B.C.L.C. 53; [2003] Ch. 552. changed the position. This case brought the law into line with thought the authors have previously suggested should be the position.

[72] [1989] B.C.L.C. 520.

The above provision sets an upper limit of liability as the debts of the company. A second difference is that the director is to be made liable for the debts; not to make a contribution to the assets of the company. It is not clear in s.630(2) whether the director would be guaranteeing the debts of the company and have a right of subrogation against the company or would have no right of subrogation. A further approach is given in ss.216 and 217 of the Insolvency Act 1986, which provide that a person is personally responsible for all the relevant debts of a company if at any time he is involved in the management of the company and it is trading under a restricted name. Section 217(2) states that where a person is personally responsible, he is jointly and severally liable in respect of those debts with the company and any other person who, whether under that section or otherwise, was so liable. Accordingly, under that provision the director would be guaranteeing the debts only and would have a right of relief against any assets of the company. Accordingly he would effectively be underwriting the deficit of the company. A further complication is that s.215(5) provides that ss.213 and 214 are to have effect notwithstanding that the person concerned may be criminally liable in respect of matters on the ground of which the declaration under these sections is to be made. Accordingly a criminal fine is not ruled out. What Judge Bromley Q.C. seemed to say in *Re a Company (No 001418 of 1988)*[73] was that there was now no upper limit on the sum which the court could order a director to pay. The starting point was compensation, of which the ceiling was the loss of the company as a result of the fraudulent trading, but there was no limit in theory to the punitive element.

It is thought that that approach of Judge Bromley Q.C. was misconceived. It is thought that the upper limit of liability of the director should be his being liable without relief for all the debts of the company from the date of the fraudulent trading whether induced by the fraudulent trading or not. It is thought that it is not the role of the civil court to impose a liability of a punitive nature in addition to that maximum limit. It is also thought that, given that the wrongful trading provision is in the same terms and that there is an express provision that there may also be a criminal liability, that a punitive approach would be incorrect for wrongful trading. What is thought to be the correct approach is for the court to take a view as to what the upper limit should be, and then to order a contribution based on the degree of culpability and the extent, where knowable, that debts of the company have been induced by the fraudulent trading.

Proceeds of actions under sections 213 and 214 of the Insolvency Act 1986

8–19   Actions under ss.213 and 214 of the Insolvency Act vest solely in the liquidator, unlike an action under s.212, which may be brought by the liquidator, or any creditor or contributory. The right is a statutory one, which the liquidator alone has a standing to pursue. Accordingly it is

---

[73] [1991] B.C.L.C. 197.

certainly the law in England that proceeds of a s.214 action (and probably a s.213 action following the same logic) are not classed as "property of the company" as supplied by s.436 of the Insolvency Act 1986.[74] Because in England proceeds of these actions are not classed as "property of the company", it means that these proceeds are not caught by a crystallised floating charge. It is difficult to see how the definition of "property" could have been wider drawn, unless there had been express reference to proceeds of s.213 and s.214 actions. If the English approach is followed this creates a serious anomaly. The type of director action which may be caught by a s.212 action is so wide, ranging from carelessness to embezzlement, that for practical purposes the grounds of action overlap with s.213 and s.214 actions. This means that if a liquidator chooses the s.212 route, proceeds of any actions are caught by the crystallisation of the floating charge, whereas if he opts for a s.213 or a s.214 action, they are not caught by the crystallisation of the floating charge. It may need statutory intervention to cut this particular knot.

Relief in terms of section 727 of the Companies Act 1985

Section 727 of the Companies Act 1985 is a protective section for **8–20** directors and other officers of a company. It provides that in any proceedings against, *inter alia*, a director for negligence, default, breach of duty or breach of trust, if a director who is or may be liable has, in the opinion of the court, acted honestly and reasonably, and if, having regard to all the circumstances of the case, including those connected with his appointment, he ought fairly to be excused, the court may wholly or partly relieve him from his liability, with the court having a discretion in the matter, and being able to impose terms. It is not enough to prove that a director acted reasonably and honestly. It is necessary, in addition, to prove that he ought fairly to be excused.[75] It has been held that the section applies only to actions brought by or on behalf of the company against its directors for breach of duty, and not to acts related to third parties.[76] Section 727 of the Companies Act 1985 may be raised as a defence to an action brought under s.212 of the Insolvency Act 1986.[77] In the English case of *Re Produce Marketing Consortium Ltd*[78] it was held that a s.727 defence was not available against an action for

---

[74] In that section "property" is defined to include "money, goods, things in action, land and every description of property wherever situated and also obligations and every description of interest, whether present or future or vested or contingent, arising out of, or incidental to, property". See *Re Oasis Merchandising Services Ltd, Ward v Aitken* [1997] 1 B.C.L.C. 689 (C.A.); affirming [1995] B.C.C. 911; *Grovewood Holdings plc v James Capel & Co Ltd* [1995] B.C.C. 760.

[75] *National Trustee Co of Australasia v General Finance, etc Co* [1905] A.C. 373; *Re Smith, Smith v Thompson* (1902) 71 L.J. Ch. 411; *Re Turner Barker v Ivimey* [1897] 1 Ch. 536; *Re Second Dulwich 745 Starr-Bowkett Building Society* (1899) 68 L.J. Ch. 196; *Re Grindey, Clews v Grindey* [1898] 2 Ch. 593; *Perrins v Bellamy* [1899] 1 Ch. 797; *Re Lord de Clifford* [1900] 2 Ch. 707.

[76] *Customs & Excise Commrs v Hedon Alpha Ltd* [1981] Q.B. 818, CA.

[77] See *Re Claridges' Patent Asphalte* [1921] 1 Ch. 543, where directors acted upon an opinion of counsel that the act was *intra vires*; and *Farquhar v McCall*, April 10, 1991, Oban Sheriff Court, unreported.

[78] [1989] 3 All E.R. 1; see also *Re Brian D. Pierson (Contractors) Ltd* [1999] B.C.C. 26; [2001] 1 B.C.L.C. 275.

wrongful trading under s.214 of the Insolvency Act 1986. In a subsequent English case of *Re DKG Contractors Ltd*,[79] the court was prepared to entertain a s.727 defence to an action under s.214 of the Insolvency Act 1986, but held on the facts that the respondents had not acted reasonably, and therefore ought not to be excused. It is thought that the provisions of s.727 should not excuse liability under s.214 of the Insolvency Act 1986. It is thought that s.214(2) and (3) provide the only statutory excuse; *i.e.* in terms of s.214(2) that the person did not know or ought not to have concluded that there was no reasonable prospect that the company would avoid going into insolvent liquidation or, in terms of s.214(3), that the person took every step with a view to minimising the potential loss to the company's creditors. It is difficult to see how Parliament could countenance a second excuse, having set up a specific excuse tailored for the circumstances of that particular type of action. In relation to an action under s.213 of the Insolvency Act 1986, it is thought that s.727 of the Companies Act 1985 would not *a fortiori* be available.

Time limits on bringing a section 214 action

8–21   There is no statutory limit for bringing proceedings under s.214. In England it has been held that an action under s.214 must be made within six years of the company going into insolvent liquidation.[80] In Scotland a claim under s.214 would prescribe after five years from the date on which, acting with reasonable diligence, the liquidator could have discovered the basis of the action.[81]

Part II

Director Disqualification Procedure

Disqualification of directors

8–22   The Company Directors Disqualification Act 1986 built on the previous law relating to director disqualification consolidated in ss.295 to 302 of, and Sch.12 to, the Companies Act 1985, which set out the legal framework for making and registering disqualification orders, and set out the grounds on which a disqualification order should be made under the law then in force. The previous provisions relating to the disqualification of directors by reference to association with insolvent companies were repealed and tighter provisions introduced. There are *six* grounds for disqualifying a person as a director. In terms of ss.2, 3, 4 and 5 of the Company Directors Disqualification Act 1986 a person may be disqualified for one of four criminal or apparently criminal activities. Fifthly, he may also be disqualified where the court has declared a director liable to make a contribution for fraudulent trading under s.213

---

[79] [1990] B.C.C. 903.
[80] *Re Farmizer Properties Ltd* [1995] B.C.C. 926; affirmed, *sub nom. Moore v Gadd* [1997] B.C.C. 655.
[81] Prescription and Limitation (Scotland) Act 1973, s.11.

of the Insolvency Act 1986, or wrongful trading under s.214 of the Insolvency Act 1986.[82] The sixth ground and most usual is when the court is satisfied that he is "unfit" to take part in the management of a company.

A disqualification order after a declaration of liability for "fraudulent trading" or "wrongful trading" under ss.213 and 214 can be made by the court itself or on the application of any person,[83] but in relation to "unfitness" it must be brought by the Secretary of State for Trade and Industry, if he thinks it is expedient in the public interest.

There are two distinct procedures leading to an application by the Secretary of State for the disqualification on the grounds of "unfitness":

(a) a report by a liquidator, administrator, or administrative receiver under s.6 leading to an application; and
(b) an inspector's report after a Department of Trade and Industry investigation leading to an application.

Procedure for disqualification for unfitness under section 6

Since the Insolvency Act 2000 came into effect there are now two **8–23** distinct routes into director disqualification. The first is the traditional court route to disqualification. The second is by way of undertakings given by the delinquent director to the Secretary of State. It is proposed to deal with the court route first. The considerations informing that part of the Chapter apply equally to the out of court route.

(a) Court route to disqualification

The procedure prior to a court hearing an application for a dis- **8–24** qualification order under s.6 is two-stage:

First stage—report by officeholders

First the office-holders of a company (*i.e.* liquidators, administrative **8–25** receivers and administrators) have a statutory duty in terms of s.7(3) of the Company Directors Disqualification Act 1986 to report to the Secretary of State any person who is, or has been, a director of a company which has at any time become insolvent (whether while he was a director or subsequently) where it appears to the officeholders that the person's conduct as a director of that company (and conduct in relation to any other company may be taken into account) makes him unfit to be concerned in the management of a company. In this context director will include a "shadow director", as defined by s.22(5) of the Company Directors Disqualification Act 1986 and s.741(2) of the Companies Act 1985, which is construed widely to include management

---

[82] Company Directors Disqualification Act 1986, s.10.
[83] *ibid.*, s.10(1).

consultants actively engaged in the running of a company.[84] Where it is alleged that the person concerned is a shadow director there should be a fairly arguable case that the individual exercised a degree of control over the company's affairs as to indicate that he was acting as more than just a professional adviser.[85] Conduct has to relate to matters connected with the insolvency of the company.[86] Reports must be made on prescribed forms.[87] In terms of s.6(2) of the Company Directors Disqualification Act the company is said "to have become insolvent" only if an administrative receiver is appointed, or an administration is entered into, or the company goes into liquidation and its assets cannot meet its liabilities including winding-up expenses.

Second stage—application by Secretary of State

8–26   The second stage is that, if it appears to the Secretary of State that it is expedient in the public interest that a disqualification order should be made, he may make an application to the court for an order. He may not, except with the leave of the court, apply after the end of the period of two years beginning with the day on which the company of which the person accused is or has been a director became insolvent.[88]

It is thought that the courts have power to disqualify a director in respect of a foreign company that is being wound up in Scotland and that, in proceedings against the director of a Scottish company, his conduct in relation to foreign companies of which he was also a director may be taken into consideration.[89]

The court may waive some of the normal constraints attendant upon a disqualification order and allow the person subject to the order to remain as a director of a particular company that has not featured in the disqualification proceedings on giving suitable undertakings as to his future behaviour and the future administration of that named company.[90] In the case of *Re Chartmore Ltd*[91] Harman J. accepted an undertaking that board meetings in future would be held monthly and would be attended by a representative of the company's auditors. This would be for a trial period of one year with liberty for there to be an application for an extension of that period.

Provided applications are lodged with the court within the two-year period, it does not matter if the warrant for service is granted or service is effected after the expiry of the two-year period.[92] For the purposes of

---

[84] *Re Tasbian Ltd (No.3)* [1991] B.C.C. 435.

[85] *Official Receiver v Nixon*, Financial Times, March 6, 1992; [1993] B.C.L.C. 297.

[86] Company Directors Disqualification Act 1986, s.6(2).

[87] See the Insolvency Companies (Reports on Conduct of Directors) (Scotland) Rules 1996 (SI 1996/1910), as amended by the Insolvent Companies (Reports on Conduct of Directors) (Scotland) (Amendment) Rules 2001 (SI 2001/768).

[88] Companies Directors Disqualification Act 1986, s.7(1) and (2).

[89] *Re Eurostem Maritime Ltd* [1987] P.C.C. 190.

[90] *Cargo Agency Ltd* [1992] B.C.L.C. 686; *Secretary of State for Trade and Industry v Palfreman* 1995 S.C.L.R. 172 (O.H.).

[91] [1990] B.C.L.C. 673.

[92] *Secretary of State for Trade and Industry v Josolyne*, 1990 S.C.L.R. 32; 1990 S.L.T. (Sh. Ct.) 48: followed in *Secretary of State for Trade and Industry v Normand*, 1994 S.C.L.R. 930 (O.H.).

the time limit the company "becomes insolvent" at the first occurrence of insolvent liquidation, administration, or administrative receivership. The occurrence of one of these regimes after the other, such as liquidation following administrative receivership, does not start running again for the purposes of the time limit.[93] As regards the exercise by the court of its discretion to allow an extension of the two-year period, the Court of Appeal has indicated that the court will grant leave to commence disqualification proceedings out of time, provided there is an arguable case for disqualification, an adequate explanation for the delay in commencing proceedings, and there is no prejudice to the director who is the subject of those proceedings.[94] The exercise of this discretion must now be read against the context of the Human Rights Act 1998 in the case of *EDC v UK (Application No. 24433/94)* [1998] B.C.C. 370, the Commission upheld a complaint that disqualification proceedings which lasted nearly four and a half years constituted an infringement of the "reasonable time" provision in Art.6(1) of the European Convention on Human Rights. Statements obtained compulsorily under s.235 of the Insolvency Act 1986 may be used in disqualification proceedings without infringing Art.6(1) of the Convention, because these proceedings are regulatory rather than criminal.[95]

Procedure for disqualification for unfitness under section 8

In addition to and parallel to information being received from office **8–27** holders of companies, the Secretary of State has power under the Companies Act 1985[96] to appoint inspectors to investigate the affairs of a company in a number of situations (*e.g.* on the application of the company itself or a section of its members)[97] if the court so orders,[98] or of his own accord (if it appears to him that there are circumstances suggesting fraud or irregularity),[99] and has powers to require production to him of books or papers relating to a company and to ask for an explanation of them to be given. If it appears to the Secretary of State from a report made to him, or from information or documents obtained by him under certain of these parallel powers, that it is expedient in the public interest that a disqualification order should be made against that person,[1] he may apply under s.8 for a court order against a director or former director of any company.

---

[93] *Official Receiver v Nixon, The Times*, February 16, 1990, CA; [1991] B.C.L.C. 54; affirming *Re Tasbian Ltd* [1989] B.C.L.C. 720.

[94] *Secretary of State for Trade and Industry v Langridge* [1991] B.C.L.C. 543; [1991] B.C.C. 148 C.A.; followed in *Secretary of State v Martin* [1998] B.C.C. 184; The majority decision in *Langridge* was followed in Scotland in *Secretary of State for Trade and Industry v Lovat*, 1995 S.C.L.R. 180 (Sh. Ct), which was affirmed by the Inner House of the Court of Session, 1996 S.C.L.R. 195.

[95] *DC, HS and AD v UK (Application No. 39031/97)*, September 14, 1999, unreported. That case was heard by the European Court of Human Rights and the same approach was taken by the Courts of Appeal in *R. v Secretary of State for Trade and Industry, ex p. McCormick* [1998] B.C.C. 379.

[96] Companies Act 1985, ss.431–441.

[97] *ibid.*, s.431.

[98] *ibid.*, s.432(1).

[99] *ibid.*, s.432(2).

[1] Company Directors Disqualification Act 1986, s.8.

Applications for disqualification under s.8 of the Company Directors Disqualification Act 1986 appear to be comparatively rare in comparison to applications under s.6 of that Act. In the case of *Re Samuel Sherman plc*,[2] Paul Barker Q.C., sitting as a High Court judge, said that that case was the first to be presented under s.8 of the Company Directors Disqualification Act, in which the test "whether it was expedient in the public interest", following a report by inspectors fell into two distinct disqualification categories. The director persistently failed to comply with a range of statutory duties, which were of an administrative kind, and did not denote dishonesty. He also speculated wildly (and beyond the company's constitutional capacity) with the surplus cash received by the company from the sale of its assets; thereby turning a surplus of £300,000 into one of £26,000. The disqualification in that case was for five years. The fact that the respondent had not been dishonest, that he had not concealed any information, that he had himself lost a valuable investment and that he had co-operated with the DTI, could not, in the opinion of the court, save him from disqualification. On the issue of the length of the disqualification period, the judge adopted the division of the 15-year maximum period which Dillon L.J. had adopted in *Re Sevenoaks Stationers (Retail) Ltd*.[3] The respondent should have gone into the middle bracket. Little or no disqualification "would give a signal that directors of public companies could readily avoid disqualification despite breaches of statutory provisions designed to inform and protect the investing public". In fact the court placed him at the top of the most lenient category.

Activities constituting unfitness under sections 6 and 8 of the Company Directors Disqualification Act 1986

8–28   In the case of applications brought under s.6 of the Company Directors Disqualification Act 1986 by the Secretary of State, following on the report of an office-holder of a company, the court is under a statutory duty to disqualify the unfit director, if it is satisfied that his conduct makes him unfit to be concerned in the management of a company.[4] In the case of an application brought by the Secretary of State following on reports by inspectors, the disqualification is not mandatory. The court has a discretion whether to disqualify or not.[5]

Where the disqualification is mandatory, this means only that the court must disqualify him from acting *without leave of the court*, so that the court imposing the disqualification is entitled at the same time to grant leave, either generally or subject to restrictions, *e.g.* to specified companies or for a specified time. The director's conduct in relation to other companies, whether or not they themselves have become insolvent, may be taken into account, but there must be some misconduct in relation to the insolvent company before s.6 applies.[6]

---

[2] [1991] B.C.C. 699.

[3] [1991] Ch. 164 at 174; [1990] B.C.C. 765 at 771; [1991] B.C.L.C. 325 at 328 (see para.8–28).

[4] Company Directors Disqualification Act 1986, s.6(1).

[5] *Re Bath Glass Ltd* (1988) 4 B.C.C. 130; [1988] B.C.L.C. 329.

[6] Company Directors Disqualification Act 1986, s.8(2).

In determining whether a person is unfit under the s.6 and s.8 procedures the court must have regard to the matters mentioned in Sch.1, as amended, to the Company Directors Disqualification Act 1986.[7] These matters may be summarised as follows:

(1) any misfeasance or breach of a fiduciary duty or other duty owed by the director to the company;
(2) any misapplication of assets or conduct making him accountable to the company;
(3) his part in any improper transfer;
(4) his part in any failure by the company to keep proper records and registers and to file annual returns, etc.;
(5) the director's part in any failure to prepare annual accounts and directors' and auditor's reports;
(6) the extent of the director's responsibility for the causes of the company becoming insolvent;
(7) the extent of the director's responsibility for any failure by the company to supply any goods or services which have been paid for (in whole or in part);
(8) the extent of the director's responsibility for the company entering into any transaction which is at an "undervalue" or which is voidable as a preference;
(9) the extent of the director's responsibility for any failure to summon a creditors' meeting in a creditor's voluntary winding up; and
(10) the director's failure to comply with certain procedural obligations imposed on directors in insolvency (*e.g.* the preparation of a statement of affairs).

All these criteria are to be looked to in the case of a company having become insolvent.[8] (When the company has not become insolvent the court only has to have regard to (1) to (5).) The list is not exhaustive since the court is to have regard to these matters "in particular" and the list may be amended by order of the Secretary of State by statutory instrument, subject to annulment in pursuance of a resolution of either House of Parliament.[9]

A disqualification order under s.6, *i.e.* following a report by an officeholder, has a minimum period of two years and a maximum period of 15 years.[10] A disqualification following an inspector's report has only a maximum penalty of a 15-year disqualification.[11]

In cases which have been brought to court, a general picture is now clear of the type of situations in which a court will hold that a person is unfit to be a director. The level of blameworthiness that has to be established for there to be a finding that a person is unfit to be

---

[7] Company Directors Disqualification Act 1986, s.9(1).
[8] *ibid.*, s.9(1).
[9] *ibid.*, s.9(4) and (5).
[10] *ibid.*, s.6(4).
[11] *ibid.*, s.8(4).

concerned in the management of a company has been stated in different ways by different judges. In *Re Bath Glass Ltd*,[12] Peter Gibson J. stated the test as follows:

> "To reach a finding of unfitness the court must be satisfied that the director has been guilty of a serious failure or serious failures, whether deliberately or through incompetence, to perform those duties of directors which are attendant on the privilege of trading through companies with limited liability."

Hoffmann J. suggested a somewhat higher degree of culpability. He said:

> "There must, I think, be something about the case some conduct which if not really dishonest is at any rate in breach of standards of commercial morality, or some really gross incompetence which persuades the court that it would be a danger to the public if he were to be allowed to continue to be involved in the management of companies, before a disqualification order is made."[13]

Following the reasoning in that case Hoffmann J. held that the fact that the unpaid debts include taxes does not in itself prove that there had been a sufficient breach of commercial morality to merit disqualification, and in *Re CU Fittings Ltd*[14] he held that the benefiting of ordinary creditors to a greater extent than the Crown was not necessarily a type of mismanagement which merited disqualification. A different view was taken by Vinelott J. in *Re Stanford Services Ltd*,[15] who made the point that the Crown is an involuntary creditor and that a director owes not merely a duty to keep a full and up to date record of tax deducted and collected but a duty to account for it and not use such tax to finance his business.[16] In the case of *Re Lo-line Electric Motors Ltd*,[17] Browne-Wilkinson V.-C. considered the non-payment of Crown debts as more culpable than non payment of other debts and the implication was that that rendered a person unfit to be a director. He stated:

> "The debts owed by the companies included substantial Crown debts, ie sums for which the company was liable to the Inland Revenue or Customs and Excise in respect of PAYE, national insurance and value added tax. There is a slight difference of judicial approach to Crown debts. In *Re Dawson Print Group Ltd* [1987] BCLC 601 Hoffmann J, on the facts of that case, did not draw

---

[12] (1988) 4 B.C.C. 130.

[13] *Re Dawson Print Group Ltd* (1987) B.C.C. 322 at 324, cited with approval by Browne-Wilkinson V.-C. in *Re McNulty's Interchange Ltd* (1988) 4 B.C.C. 533; see also *Re Douglas Construction Services Ltd* (1988) 4 B.C.C. 553.

[14] [1989] B.C.L.C. 556.

[15] (1987) 3 B.C.C. 326.

[16] In *Re McNulty's Interchange Ltd* [1989] B.C.L.C. 709, 4 B.C.C. 533, Browne-Wilkinson V.-C. did not regard it as improper that payment of Crown debts had been withheld where agreements had been reached with the Customs and Excise and the Inland Revenue for payment by instalments.

[17] [1988] B.C.L.C. 698 at 704–705.

any distinction between a failure to pay Crown debts and the failure to pay other trading debts. However, in *Re Wedgecroft Ltd* (7 March 1986, unreported) Harman J treated crown debts as *'quasi-trust'* monies and the failure to pay them as being more morally culpable than failure to pay ordinary commercial debts. In *Re Stanford Services Ltd* [1987] BCLC 607 Vinelott J treated the failure to pay Crown debts as more serious than the failure to pay commercial debts. He described the Crown as an involuntary creditor and said (at 617): 'the directors of a company ought to conduct its affairs in such a way that it can meet these liabilities when they fall due, not only because they are not monies earned by its trading activities, which the company is entitled to treat as part of its cash flow (entitled that is in that the persons with whom it deals expect the company to do so) but more importantly, because the directors ought not to use monies which the company is currently liable to pay over to the Crown to finance its current trading activities. If they do so, and if, in consequence, PAYE, national insurance contributions and VAT become overdue, and, in a winding-up, irrecoverable, the court may draw the inference that the directors were continuing to trade at a time when they ought to have known that the company was unable to meet its current and accruing liabilities, and were unjustifiably putting at risk monies which ought to have been paid over to the Crown as part of the public revenues to finance trading activities which might or might not produce a profit. It is, I think, misleading (or at least unhelpful) to ask whether a failure to pay debts of this character would be generally regarded as a breach of commercial morality. A director who allows such a situation to arise is either in breach of his duty to keep himself properly informed, with reasonable accuracy, as to the company's financial position . . . or is acting improperly in continuing to trade at the expense and jeopardy of monies which he ought not to use to finance the company's current trade.'

I agree with those remarks and add this. Although the Crown debts are not strictly trust monies, the failure to pay them over does not only prejudice the Crown, as creditor, but in the case of PAYE and national insurance may also have a prejudicial effect on the company's employees. The use of monies obtained by compulsory deductions from wages for the financing of the company's business is to use monies which morally, if not legally, belong either to the employees or to the Crown without the consent of either. I consider the use of the monies which should have been paid to the Crown to finance contribution of a insolvent company's business more culpable than the failure to pay commercial debts."

This approach has now been overturned in England by the Court of Appeal in the case of *Re Sevenoaks Stationers (Retail) Ltd*.[18] Giving the opinion of the court, Dillon L.J. held that the non payment of Crown debts did not in itself indicate a higher degree of culpability than the non-payment of other debts. The test was to see what the significance of the non-payment of Crown debts was. He stated:

---

[18] [1991] B.C.L.C. 325.

"I would see validity in this if it were correct, as the Vice-Chancellor apparently thought [in *Re Lo-Line Electric Motors Ltd*[19]], that failure to pay over to the Crown monies deducted from the wages of employees might have a prejudicial effect on the employees. On the hearing of this appeal, however, both sides have made enquiries, including enquiries from the Inland Revenue, to see what prejudice there may be to the employees, and no trace of any prejudice has been found. On the contrary, the Revenue rightly accept that the burden of a failure by the employer as the Crown's appointed collector, to pay over to the Crown monies deducted from wages for PAYE or national insurance contributions must fall on the Crown and not on the employees. Therefore the employees are credited with what has been deducted from their wages even though what has been deducted has not been paid over to the Crown.

Moreover though the Crown had powers under the Social Security Act 1975 and previous such Acts to sue the directors personally for non remittance of national insurance contributions deducted from wages of their company's employees, those powers were abolished by the Insolvency Act 1985, following an earlier public announcement by the Secretary of State for Trade that it had been decided as a matter of policy that no proceedings should be brought against directors for the recovery of such contribution.

As for VAT, no one suggests that a customer who pays VAT to a company as part of the price to him of goods sold or services rendered to him by the company has to pay VAT again to the Customs and Excise or is in any other way prejudiced by the failure of the company to account to the Customs and Excise for the VAT which the company has received. Moreover, for instance, a retailer (and the instance could apply equally to a manufacturer) sells goods to a customer and receives VAT in respect of the price, whether the price is quoted ex-VAT or inclusive of VAT, I find it very difficult to regard it as automatically more heinous on the part of the retailer not to account to the Customs and Excise for the VAT paid than it would be not to pay the supplier, who may be in a small way of business, in due time for the goods sold to the retailer's customer.

The Official Receiver cannot, in my judgment, automatically treat non payment of any Crown debt as evidence of unfitness of the directors. It is necessary to look more closely in each case to see what the significance, if any, of the non payment of the Crown debt is."

In that case the Court of Appeal noted that there had been a deliberate decision to pay only those creditors who pressed for payment. The result was that companies had traded when they were insolvent and known to be in difficulties at the expense of those creditors who, like the Crown, had happened not to be pressing for payment. It held that such conduct on the part of a director could well be relied on as a ground for

---

[19] [1988] B.C.L.C. 698.

saying that the director was unfit to be concerned in the management of a company. What, however, was relevant in the Crown's position was not that the debt was a debt which arose from a compulsory deduction from the employees' wages or a compulsory payment of VAT, but that the Crown was now pressing for payment, and the director was taking unfair advantage of that forbearance on the part of the Crown, and, instead of providing adequate working capital was trading at the Crown's expense while the companies were in jeopardy. The court held it would be equally unfair to trade in that way and in such circumstances at the expense of creditors other than the Crown. It is thought by the authors that the opinion of Dillon L.J. in *Re Sevenoaks Stationers*[20] is the correct approach. In the case of *Re Sevenoaks Stationers (Retail) Ltd*,[21] which was the first decision of the Court of Appeal on a disqualification under s.6 of the Company Directors Disqualification Act 1986, the court pronounced certain guidelines as to the applicable period of disqualification which should be imposed. In what might have been thought an obvious observation, the Court of Appeal affirmed that the potential 15–year disqualification period should be divided into three brackets; namely (1) the top bracket of disqualification for a period over 10 years, which should be reserved for particularly serious cases. These may include cases where a director who has already had one period of disqualification imposed on him, is disqualified for a second period; (2) the minimum of two to five years' disqualification, which should be applied where, though disqualification is mandatory, the case is relatively, not very, serious; and (3) the middle bracket of disqualification for six to 10 years, which should apply for serious cases which do not merit the top bracket.[22] The guidelines in *Sevenoaks* are followed in Scotland.[23]

Other grounds for disqualification

Apart from the special provisions of s.10 of the Company Directors **8–29** Disqualification Act 1986 which allow the court to make a disqualification order of its own motion or on the application of any person, where there has been wrongful or fraudulent trading, there are *four* other grounds on which the court may disqualify a person from being a director, which are listed in sections 2, 3, 4 and 5, of the Company Directors Disqualification Act 1986. They are: (1) conviction of an indictable offence, in connection with the promotion, formation, management or liquidation of a company, or with the receivership or management of a company's property; (2) persistent breaches of the companies legislation; (3) summary conviction under the companies

---

[20] [1991] B.C.L.C. 325.

[21] Above; see also *Re Keypak Homecare Ltd* [1990] B.C.L.C. 440; *Re T & D Services (Timber Preservation and Damp Proofing Contractors) Ltd* [1990] B.C.C. 592; and *Re Travel Mondial (UK) Ltd* [1991] B.C.L.C. 120.

[22] Examples of the use of the three "brackets" are to be found in *Re Peppermint Park Ltd* [1998] B.C.C. 23; *Re Saver Ltd* [1999] B.C.C. 221. Guidance on the policy thinking behind the legislation on disqualification and its purpose was given by the Court of Appeal in *Secretary of State v Griffiths* [1998] B.C.C. 836 and in *Secretary of State v McTighe* [1997] B.C.C. 224.

[23] See *Secretary of State for Trade and Industry v Palfreman* 1995 S.C.L.R. 172.

legislation; and (4) fraud, fraudulent trading or breach of duty revealed in winding up. In those cases an application for a disqualification order may be made by the Secretary of State, or by the liquidator, or by any past or present member or creditor of any of the companies concerned. The grounds are essentially unchanged from the former reasons applicable prior to April 28, 1986, and the only ground of disqualification relevant in insolvency is the fourth ground; namely a disqualification order based on fraudulent trading. There is overlapping because a disqualification order may also be made on that ground under s.10 of the Company Directors Disqualification Act 1986. However, for s.10 to apply an order must first have been made declaring the person liable to contribute to the company's assets under s.213 of the Insolvency Act 1986.

(b) Out of court route/disqualification undertakings

8–30　　The sheer weight of cases coming before the courts under the Company Directors Disqualification Act 1986, and the prospect that delay in the determination of pending disqualification proceedings could amount to a violation of the director's rights under Art.6(1) of the European Convention on Human Rights, led to a development of alternative consensual arrangements aimed at reducing the time consumed by the hearing itself. The director and the DTI through the Insolvency Service reached agreement on the terms of a formal statement of facts constituting a case of unfitness, and indicating the length of an appropriate disqualification period. The court would then be invited to incorporate those terms into an order based on a finding of unfitness, and thus a full hearing would be avoided. This procedure was first allowed in *Re Carecraft Construction Co Ltd*,[24] and soon became established as the norm in uncontested cases.

Section 6 of the Insolvency Act 2000 further expedited the system by amending the Company Directors Disqualification Act 1986 to allow disqualification without a court hearing. A new s.1A was inserted into the Company Directors Disqualification Act 1986 to allow the Secretary of State to accept a disqualification undertaking through a procedure which bypasses the need for a court hearing, but has the same consequences as though a disqualification order had been made by the court. The terms of the undertaking must embody the same terms of prohibition from acting as a director or in any of the other ways specified in s.1 (as amended), and the period to be specified in the undertaking must fall within the prescribed range of between two years (as a minimum) and 15 years (as a maximum). The Secretary of State, represented normally by the Insolvency Service, has a discretion whether or not to adopt this out of court determination of a case. A new s.7(2A), also inserted into the Company Directors Disqualification Act 1986, provides that the Secretary of State may accept the undertaking if it appears to him that it is expedient in the public interest that he should do so instead of applying, or proceeding with an application, for a

---

[24] [1993] B.C.C. 336.

disqualification order. If agreement with a director cannot be reached, the Secretary of State may revert to the court based procedure. This new procedure came into effect from April 2, 2001.[25]

Main weakness of reforms

The weakness of the statutory reporting system and the liabilities **8–31** which directors may incur is that it depends on the appointment of liquidators, administrators and administrative receivers to make the necessary investigations and report. If the company does not have sufficient funds to pay an office-holder, there will be no automatic vetting, only spot-checking by the Department of Trade and Industry. Paradoxically, under the system the more ruthless directors are at stripping their companies bare, leaving nothing for creditors, the less likely they are to be caught.

Criminal liabilities of directors outlined above

In addition to the civil liabilities outlined in this chapter and their **8–32** openness to public examination proceedings, directors are also subject to a criminal code. For example, contravention of a disqualification order risks conviction of up to two years in prison, or a fine, or both.[26] There is also a quasi-criminal penalty in s.15 of the Company Directors Disqualification Act 1986, in that a person breaching a disqualification order becomes personally liable for all the debts of a company incurred while acting in breach of the order whether or not his actings had anything to do with their being run up. Further offences and their penalties in relation to insolvency may be found in Sch.11 to the Insolvency Act 1986.

Use of prohibited name

Section 216 of the Insolvency Act 1986 prohibits, except with the leave **8–33** of the court, former directors of companies which have gone into insolvent liquidation from being directors of, or concerned in, another company with the same or similar name for five years from the liquidation. They are liable to imprisonment for breach, and under s.217 liable for the debts of the subsequent company. Acting in the management of a company known by a prohibited name contrary to s.216 of the Insolvency Act 1986 is an offence of strict liability, requiring no proof of *mens rea*.[27]

In the case of *Re Bonus Breaks Ltd*,[28] a director (whose previous company had become insolvent) was given leave by the court to act as a director of a new company with a similar name to the unsuccessful

---

[25] SI 2001/766.
[26] Company Directors Disqualification Act 1986, s.13.
[27] *R v Doring* [2002] B.C.C. 838; following the approach in *R v Brockley* [1994] B.C.C. 131.
[28] [1991] B.C.C. 546.

predecessor. Assurances, however, were required from the director that the capital base of the new company would be maintained and that there would be no purchase or redemption of the company's shares for the next two years unless the transaction was approved by an independent director. Persons have been convicted under this section for using the name "Ardtalla Yacht Services Limited" without permission of the court, where the liquidated company had been called "Ardtalla Yachts Limited".[29]

---

[29] *Farquhar v McCall,* April 10, 1991, Oban Sheriff Court unreported.

CHAPTER 9

EFFECT OF CORPORATE INSOLVENCY ON DILIGENCE

Introduction

Since the last edition of this book in 1993, far reaching changes have **9–01** been made in the Scottish law of diligence by the Debt Arrangement and Attachment (Scotland) Act 2002, which rebranded "poindings" as "attachments", and replaced warrant sales with a new procedure. Neither of these measures really impacts on the area of corporate insolvency law. In that field the greatest impact has come from Strasbourg, through the European Court of Human Rights and the Human Rights Act 1998, and the series of cases flowing from them; especially *Karl Construction Ltd v Palisade Properties plc*[1] and *Advocate General for Scotland for and on behalf of the Commissioners of Inland Revenue v Maureen Taylor*,[2] which abolished an automatic right to inhibitions and arrestments on the dependence of a court action, which had often been used in a wholly unscrupulous manner to bludgeon small companies, sometimes to ruin. Although these cases are to be welcomed, it is to be regretted that neither the legislature nor the judiciary had earlier stopped this mischief, which might have carried on for many more years but for the chance intervention of the Human Rights Act 1998.

As regards the effect of corporate insolvency on diligence, these developments have had no impact, and it is thought that the promised Diligence and Bankruptcy (Scotland) Bill (which was published in draft in June 2004) has no read across to the corporate insolvency and diligence field.

Definition of diligence

Diligence is a collective name traditionally given in Scotland to an **9–02** assortment of legal procedures. It is perhaps better defined as any judicial process whereby a creditor freezes ("litigiosity") or seizes ("nexus") assets of a debtor. Litigiosity merely stops the debtor from disposing of the assets. Nexus gives the creditor a real right ("judicial security"). There are *four* main types of diligence which creditors may use against a company. These are: (1) arrestment; (2) inhibition; (3) attachment; and (4) adjudication.

In addition to these four main types of diligence there are three other types, namely, real adjudication, mails and duties and real poinding

---

[1] 2002 S.L.T. at 312.
[2] 2003 S.L.T. 1340.

("poinding of the ground"). The last three types of diligence are uncommon in modern practice and are unlikely to be scrapped. They are accordingly dealt with only briefly at para.9–13. The general nature of the four main types of diligence is as follows:

(1) Arrestment

9–03   Arrestment is the diligence appropriate to attach financial obligations owed to the debtor by a third party; and corporeal moveables (*i.e.* physical assets) belonging to the debtor which are in the hands of the third party. In relation to the arrestment, the arresting creditor is known as the "arrester", the third party as the "arrestee" and the debtor as "the common debtor".[3] Arrestment to enforce payment of a decree is known as arrestment in execution. Arrestment to keep frozen some asset of the defender so that the asset may be realised to satisfy the decree which the pursuer hopes he is going to obtain is known as "arrestment on the dependence", which right is of course now circumscribed[4]. The effect of an arrestment is to prevent the arrestee from paying over the sum attached to the common debtor. If he does so, he is liable to the arrester for the loss caused thereby. The arrestment freezes the assets, *i.e.* introduces "litigiosity". It gives the arrester no title to the assets which have been arrested. The arresting creditor completes his diligence (realises the assets subject to the arrestment) by bringing an action of "furthcoming" against the arrestee and the common debtor in order to obtain "a decree effectually transferring from the common debtor to the arresting creditor the obligation which was originally prestable to the former by the arrestee".[5] In this way the arrester obtains payment of the debt owed by the arrestee to the common debtor.

In addition to arrestment so defined, which is intended as diligence, foreigners may be made subject to the jurisdiction of the Scottish courts by the arrestment of their assets in the hands of third parties in Scotland. This is known as arrestment to found jurisdiction (*ad fundandam juridictionem*).

(2) Inhibition

9–04   The classical definition of an "inhibition", was that it was "a writ passing under the signet, prohibiting the debtor from alienating any part of his estate, and from contracting debt by means of which it may be carried off, to the prejudice of the creditor inhibitor; and interdicting third parties from taking conveyancing of the heritage".[6] The effect of an inhibition is as classically formulated, but it affects only the heritable estate of the debtor. It is not a complete diligence and its effect is merely prohibitory and preventive. It may be in execution of a decree, or on the dependence of an action. This latter right is, of course, now circumscribed.[7]

---

[3] Wilson on *Debt* (2nd ed., 1992), Chap.16.
[4] *Karl Construction Ltd v Palisade Properties plc,* 2002 S.L.T. at 312.
[5] *Lucas's Trs v Campbell and Scott* (1894) 21 R. 1096 at 1103, *per* Lord Kinnear.
[6] Bell, *Prin.,* 2306.
[7] *The Advocate General for Scotland for and on behalf of the Commissioners of Inland Revenue v Maureen Taylor,* 2003 S.L.T. 1340.

Where a debtor has granted a heritable security and another creditor has inhibited, on the sale of the security subjects the heritable creditor is entitled to be paid in full from the proceeds, and the inhibiting creditor is entitled to the balance in preference to creditors whose debts were contracted after the date of the inhibition, but not in preference to other creditors whose debts were contracted before the date of the inhibition.[8] Although, in principle, an inhibition is a protective diligence only, and does not divest the debtor of any of his property, on the debtor's liquidation the inhibitor is entitled to receive the same dividend from the heritable property as he would have received if no debts affecting it had been created after the date of the inhibition. This is achieved by a complicated process, which in effect results in the inhibitor being compensated for any shortfall in his dividend at the expense of posterior creditors.[9]

(3) Attachment

Attachment (which, prior to the coming into force of the Debt **9–05** Arrangement and Attachment Act 2002, was known as a "poinding") is the form of diligence appropriate to attach corporeal moveables belonging to the debtor himself which are in the custody or control of the debtor himself. It can also be used where corporeal moveables belonging to the debtor are in the possession of the creditor.[10] "The essence of attachment is that the goods attached may be taken to the market cross and sold".[11] The effect of attachment is to lay a nexus on the goods and create a security over them in favour of the creditor.[12]

(4) Adjudication

Adjudication is the appropriate diligence to attach heritable property **9–06** of the debtor. The subjects of the diligence are land and heritable rights. The procedure is by an action which can be raised only in the Court of Session.

The effects of insolvency on diligence

In the absence of a provision to the contrary, an advantage at the **9–07** expense of the general body of creditors might be secured by a creditor enforcing his debt by diligence against funds or assets belonging to the

---

[8] For a full discussion, see Maher & Cusine, *The Law and Practice of Diligence*, Chaps 4 and 9; Wilson on *Debt* (2nd ed.), Chaps 19 and 23, and cases referred to in these works.

[9] Bell, *Comm.*, ii, 413; see also *Baird & Brown v Stirrat's Tr.* (1872) 10 M. 414 at 419, where Lord President Inglis said that: "[t]he rule contemplates an inhibiting creditor, creditors whose debts were contracted prior to the inhibition, and creditors whose debts were contracted subsequent to the inhibition. All those creditors adjudge within a year and a day of one another, so that it does not matter which is the leading adjudication. In respect of their adjudications they all rank *pari passu*. But the inhibiting creditor has a preference over those whose debts were contracted subsequent to the inhibition. The prior creditors are to be neither hurt nor benefited by the inhibition. In these circumstances the clear and equitable rule of ranking was established, that the inhibitor's preference must be secured to him entirely at the expense of the subsequent creditors, while creditors whose debts were contracted prior to the inhibition draw just what they would have done had the whole creditors been ranked *pari passu*." See *Graham Stewart*, p.567, for the proposition that liquidation acts like sequestration.

[10] *Lochead v Graham* (1883) 11 R. 201.

[11] *Trowsdale's Tr v Forcett Ry Co* (1870) 9 M. 88 at 95, *per* Lord Neaves.

[12] *Stephenson v Dobbins* (1852) 14 D. 510.

debtor. Any inequalities which might otherwise arise from the use of diligence are eliminated in *three* ways:

  (a) by the equalisation of some forms of diligence (arrestments, attachments and adjudications) outside liquidation;
  (b) by the equalisation or reduction of these forms of diligence in the event of liquidation; and
  (c) by the suspension of diligence during liquidation.

In addition, where there is an administration, diligence may not be commenced or proceeded with in terms of para.43 of new Sch.B1 to the Insolvency Act 1986, except with the leave of the court or the administrator.[13] This is also the case where there is a voluntary arrangement in contemplation with a moratorium against creditor action.[14] The voluntary arrangement itself, if approved under Part I of the Insolvency Act 1986, could have as an arrangement condition that one or more creditors be obliged to lift diligence.)

(1) EQUALISATION OF DILIGENCE OUTSIDE LIQUIDATION

9–08 Scots law is unusual among legal systems in creating rules for the *pari passu* ranking of creditors on the proceeds of diligence outside liquidation. These rules were designed to discourage a race of diligence among creditors, which might precipitate or aggravate the debtor's insolvency and lead to greater inequalities among the unsecured creditors. Independently of liquidation, provision is made for the *pari passu* ranking of creditors on the proceeds of adjudications for debt, arrestments and attachments.

In the case of the two most common forms of diligence, *i.e.* arrestments and attachments, equalisation depends on "apparent insolvency". "All arrestments and attachments which have been executed within 60 days prior to the constitution of the apparent insolvency of the debtor, or within four months thereafter, shall be ranked *pari passu* as if they had all been executed on the same date".[15] The rule about equalisation of diligences outwith liquidation applies equally to sequestration (a full discussion is to be found in *Clark v Hinde, Milne & Co*[16]). Moreover, any creditor producing in that period a decree for payment or liquid grounds of debt is entitled to rank as if he had executed an arrestment or a attachment.[17] The same law applies to the arrestment of ships, but not to the arrestment of earnings and maintenance arrestment.[18] There is

---

[13] The moratorium can be preceded by an interim moratorium in terms of para.44 of new Sch.B1 to that Act.

[14] See Chap.7.

[15] Bankruptcy (Scotland) Act 1985, Sch.7, para.24(1); see also Gretton, "Multiple Notour Bankruptcy" 28 J.L.S.S. 18.

[16] (1884) 12 R. 347 at 353, *per* Lord Shand.

[17] Bankruptcy (Scotland) Act 1985, Sch.7, para.24(3).

[18] *Harvey v MacAdie* (1888) 4 Sh.Ct Rep. 254; *Munro v Smith*, 1968 S.L.T. (Sh.Ct) 26; Bankruptcy (Scotland) Act 1985, Sch.7, para.24(8).

a similar provision in principle although different in detail in relation to the equalisation of adjudications for debt under the Diligence Act 1661 (c.34), and the Adjudication Act 1672 (c.45). The equalisation of adjudications is unrelated to apparent insolvency, and operates only in favour of creditors actually adjudging before or within a year and a day after an effectual adjudication, not in favour of creditors who merely hold decrees or liquid grounds of debt.

"Apparent insolvency" is constituted if the company gives written notice to its creditors that it has ceased to pay its debts in the ordinary course of business; or if it grants a trust deed.[19] It is thought by the authors that an administration must be equivalent to a written notice to the company's creditors that it has ceased to pay its debts in the ordinary course of business.[20] "Trust deed" does not seem to apply to voluntary arrangements under Pt I of the Insolvency Act 1986.[21]

(2) Equalisation or Reduction of Prior Diligence on Liquidation

The justification for reducing or equalising diligences effected within a **9–09** short period prior to liquidation is simply stated in the Bills of Exchange (Scotland) Act 1772,[22] which, with reference to the diligences of arrestment and attachment, proceeded on the narrative that:

"The personal estates of such debtors as become insolvent are generally carried off by the diligences of arrestment and poinding, executed by a few creditors, who, from the nearness of their residence to, and connection with such debtors, get the earliest notice of their insolvency, to the great prejudice of creditors more remote and unconnected, and to the disappointment of that equality which ought to take place in the distribution of estates of insolvent debtors among their creditors."

(1) Equalisation of arrestments and attachments

The equalisation of arrestments and attachments arises independently **9–10** of winding up. However, the commencement of a winding-up during the period of equalisation nevertheless has important consequences for the equalisation process. In terms of s.37(1) of the Bankruptcy (Scotland) Act 1985[23]:

"The commencement of winding up[24] . . . shall have the effect in relation to diligence done (whether before or after the commence-

---

[19] Bankruptcy (Scotland) Act 1985, s.7(1)(b) and (c)(i).

[20] An exception would be if the holder of a floating charge appoints an administrator relying on a breach of the debenture other than insolvency.

[21] *ibid.*, ss.5(2)(c) and 73(1).

[22] 12 Geo. 3, c.72.

[23] As applied to windings up in Scotland by Insolvency Act 1986, s.185.

[24] Commencement of winding up for the purposes of s.37 as applied to equalisation of diligence in windings up means, where the company is being wound up by the court, the day on which the winding up order is made.

ment of winding up) in respect of any part of the company's estate of—

(a) a decree of adjudication of the heritable estate of the company for payment of its debts which has been duly recorded in the register of inhibitions and adjudications on that date; and

(b) an arrestment in execution and decree of furthcoming, and arrestment in execution and warrant sale, and a completed attachment,

in favour of the creditors according to their respective entitlements."

Section 37(4) of the Bankruptcy (Scotland) Act 1985[25] provides that:

"No arrestment or attachment of the estate of the company . . . executed

(a) within the period of 60 days before the commencement of winding up and whether or not subsisting at that date; or

(b) on or after the commencement of winding up,

shall be effectual to create a preference for the arrester; and the estate so arrested or attached, or the proceeds of sale thereof, shall be handed over to the liquidator."

Equalisation of arrestments and attachments arises independently of liquidation, but a winding up commenced during the period of equalisation has consequences for the equalisation process. If the winding up is the first constitution of "apparent insolvency", then arrestments and attachments are cut down within 60 days of the liquidation because any arrestment or attachment executed within the period of 60 days preceding the winding up is ineffectual to secure a preference. A similar result is achieved where there has been an antecedent constitution of "apparent insolvency" within the period of four months preceding the commencement of winding up, because the winding up has in terms of s.37(1) of the Bankruptcy (Scotland) Act 1985 the effect of a completed diligence in favour of creditors according to their respective entitlements. This effectively ranks their entitlements *pari passu* with any arrestment or attachment executed on or after the sixtieth day before the earlier constitution of "apparent insolvency".[26]

Section 185(3) of the Insolvency Act 1986 provides that, where a company is being wound up by the court (and that would include a voluntary winding up converted into a compulsory one), the date of the commencement is to be the date of the order. If the first constitution of "apparent insolvency" on a converted winding up is the winding-up resolution and the order is more than four months and 60 days thereafter the order will not be effective to equalise with diligence effected prior to the resolution.

---

[25] As applied to liquidations by Insolvency Act 1986, s.185(1).

[26] For an illustration of this effect, see *Stewart v Jarvie*, 1938 S.C. 309.

(2) Equalisation of inhibitions

Inhibitions, although different from arrestments and attachments in **9–11**
that they do not attach to a specific asset, do give the inhibiting creditor
a preference over those whose debts were contracted subsequent to the
inhibition. In order to establish this equalisation, the law was changed in
1986 by s.37(2) of the Bankruptcy (Scotland) Act 1985, as applied by
s.185(1) of the Insolvency Act 1986, which enacts:

> "No inhibition on the estate of the company which takes effect
> within the period of 60 days before the commencement of winding
> up shall be effectual to create a preference for the inhibitor and any
> relevant right of challenge shall, at the commencement of winding
> up, vest in the liquidator, as shall any right of the inhibitor to
> receive payment for the discharge of the inhibition:—
>
> Provided that this subsection shall neither entitle the liquidator to
> receive any payment made to the inhibitor before the commence-
> ment of winding up nor affect the validity of anything done before
> that date in consideration for such payment."

(3) Effect of administration on equalisation of diligences

In administration procedure both an interim moratorium and a **9–12**
moratorium preclude diligence being commenced or continued.[27] There
is provision for the administrator to sell, with the permission of the
court, property which is subject to a security other than a floating
charge.[28] This the authors interpret to mean that the security remains in
place and no further legal steps may be taken by way of diligence
whether by commencement or continuation. The authors do not interpret this to mean that a diligence is lifted. (There is no provision for
diligences to be reactivated at the end of an administration order.) There
would appear, however, to be perhaps an undesirable mischief created
as a result. Because diligences are only struck at within 60 days of
commencement of winding up, an administration order has the effect of
depriving ordinary creditors of one means of striking at diligences
within the 60 days by seeking a winding up. Because, however, it is
thought that an administration constitutes "apparent insolvency", diligences will effectively be reduced if made within 60 days before the
apparent insolvency provided the commencement of the winding up is
within four months after the "administration order".[29] If an administration lasts more than four months, those creditors who have not arrested,
or produced a decree or liquid grounds of debt, will be disadvantaged.

---

[27] Insolvency Act 1986, paras 43 and 44 of new Sch.B1.
[28] *ibid.*, para.71(2) of new Sch.B1 to the Insolvency Act 1986.
[29] The proposition that "administration" constitutes "apparent insolvency" was disputed by Professor Wilson—see Wilson on *Debt* (2nd ed.), p.282. This is thought incorrect,
with one exception. An administration only takes effect if the company is or is likely to be
unable to pay its debts; all the company's correspondence must state this, and it must be
advertised publicly to creditors in terms of r.2.19(1) of the Insolvency (Scotland) Rules
1986, as amended by SI 2003/2111. The exception is where the administrator is appointed
by a holder of a floating charge, relying on a breach of the debenture other than
insolvency in terms of para.45 of new Sch.B1 to the Insolvency Act 1986.

If the justifying purpose of an administration is "a better result for the creditors as a whole than would be likely on a winding up" (without first being in administration), it is suggested that "better result" could be read to mean not just that more money is realised for creditors, but that the balance of interests in the winding up is not upset. In particular, a public policy consideration in the four-month rule should not lightly be discarded. Accordingly, it is suggested that the creditor who has legitimate fears about the running of the four months could bring a challenge. He would have to argue that he had title and interest to object, which is not expressly written into the Insolvency Act 1986.

(3) Suspension of Diligence on Winding Up

9–13 Arrestments and attachments are ineffectual within 60 days of the commencement of liquidation or after the commencement of liquidation.[30] Adjudications are also ineffectual after the commencement of winding up.[31] Another type of action—"poinding of the ground"—is a diligence open to a creditor holding a *debitum fundi,* such as a superior or a heritable creditor. It enables the creditor to attach moveables on the heritable property affected by the diligence. The underlying principle is that the creditor is merely giving effect to a pre-existing right arising by virtue of his *debitum fundi* and accordingly no competition of diligence can arise between creditors poinding the ground, since they have priority according to the dates of their respective infeftments. This type of action is now restricted by statute. In terms of s.37(6) of the Bankruptcy (Scotland) Act 1985,

> "No poinding of the ground in respect of the estate of the company . . . executed within the period of 60 days before the commencement of winding up or on or after that date shall be effectual in a question with the liquidator, except for the interest on the debt of a secured creditor, being interest for the current half yearly term and arrears of interest for one year immediately before the commencement of that term".

In contrast an action of maills and duties is available to a secured creditor whose security includes an assignation of rents during a winding up. The creditor becomes vested in the landlord's rights and accordingly may recover rents. A standard security contains no assignation of rents but, under the Conveyancing and Feudal Reform (Scotland) Act 1970, the creditor has, on default by the debtor, a right to enter into possession of the security subjects and receive or recover the rent. It may seem anomalous that, whereas an action of maills and duties is unaffected by a liquidation, a poinding of the ground is affected.

---

[30] Bankruptcy (Scotland) Act 1985, s.37(4) as applied to liquidations by Insolvency Act 1986, s.185(1). Section 37 was amended by s.61 of, and para.15(4) of Sch.3 to, the Debt Arrangement and Attachment (Scotland) Act 2002 to have poindings renamed attachments.

[31] S.37(8) of the Bankruptcy (Scotland) Act 1985, as applied to liquidations by s.185(1) of the Insolvency Act 1986.

However, an action of maills and duties, which puts a heritable creditor in the position of the landlord in relation to the tenants, has a natural connection with the company's heritable property, whereas the remedy of poinding of the ground is directed not at the company's heritable property but at moveables on the property. Adjudications within a year and a day of the first adjudication are equalised.[32] In terms of s.37(1) of the Bankruptcy (Scotland) Act 1985: "winding up has the effect of—(a) a decree of adjudication of the heritable estate of the company for payment of its debts which has been duly recorded in the Register of Inhibitions and Adjudications on that date; . . . in favour of the creditors according to their respective entitlements." This means that although adjudication is competent during liquidation, any adjudication within a year before or a year after liquidation is effectively cut down. This does not apply to "real adjudications" by which a creditor who already holds real security over heritable property enforces it.

Effectually executed diligence in receivership and winding up

(a) Effectually executed diligence in receivership

All persons who have effectually executed diligence on any part of the **9–14** property of a company which is subject to the charge by which a receiver is appointed have priority to the holder of the floating charge.[33] The expression "effectually executed diligence" has been the subject of some discussion.[34]

Arrestments

An arrestment followed by a decree of furthcoming is an effectually **9–15** executed diligence.[35] The commencement of winding up has the effect of being a completed diligence, and gives guidance to interpretation. Section 37(1) of the Bankruptcy (Scotland) Act 1985 states that commencement of winding up will have the effect "of (b) an arrestment in execution and decree of furthcoming, an arrestment in execution and warrant of sale, and a completed attachment."

The statute envisages that an arrestment is not completed without a decree of furthcoming, or in the case of a ship, a warrant of sale. This is totally in line with the decision of the First Division in *Lord Advocate v Royal Bank of Scotland*,[36] in which Lord President Emslie stated:

---

[32] Diligence Act 1661; Adjudications Act 1672.

[33] Insolvency Act 1986, s.60(1)(b).

[34] See cases cited in next footnote and *Armour and Mycroft, Petrs*, 1983 S.L.T. 453; *Sim*, 1984 S.L.T. (News) 25; *Grampian R.C. v Drill Stem (Inspection Services) Ltd (In Receivership)* (Sh.Ct) 1994 S.C.L.R. 36, in which case it was, it is suggested, correctly decided that a landlord's hypothec gave the landlord a real right in security, which prevailed over a subsequent crystallised floating charge; *Gretton*, 1983 S.L.T. (News) 145; JADH, 1983 S.L.T. (News) 177; Wilson on *Debt*, p.202.

[35] *Lord Advocate v Royal Bank of Scotland Ltd*, 1977 S.C. 155; see also *Gordon Anderson Plant Ltd*, 1977 S.L.T. 7; *Cumbernauld Development Corp. v Mustone Ltd*, 1983 S.L.T. (Sh.Ct.) 55; and *Forth and Clyde Construction v Trinity Timber and Plywood Co*, 1984 S.L.T. 94.

[36] 1977 S.C. 155 at 169.

"The accurate description of an arrestment, however, is that it is merely an 'inchoate' diligence,[37] a 'step' of diligence or an 'inchoate or begun' diligence.[38] It has never been held otherwise and is succinctly described in *Lucas's Trustees v Campbell & Scott*[39] by Lord Kinnear—a master in this field of law—in these terms: 'An arrestment and furthcoming is an adjudication preceded by an attachment and the essential part of the diligence is the adjudication'.[40] It is accordingly part but not the essential part of a diligence consisting of arrestment and furthcoming."

The conclusion, however, that the arrestment is totally defeated (*i.e.* the arrester gains no possible advantage in the competition) by a subsequent effectually executed diligence seems an unfounded further deduction. In the case of *Iona Hotels Ltd (In Receivership) Petitioners*[41] the First Division of the Court of Session addressed the case where a floating charge had been granted over the assets of a company after an arrestment had been laid on a debt. In the case *of Lord Advocate v Royal Bank of Scotland*[42] the arrestment had been after the creation of the floating charge. In the *Iona Hotels Ltd* case, applying the analogy of a fixed security the court held that property which is the subject of an assignation in security remains the property of the company subject to the rights of the assignee. Litigiosity which results from the arrestment restricts the power of a common debtor to affect his own property by his subsequent voluntary act, but it does not render that act worthless for all purposes. The rights of the assignee of a subsequent assignation in security are subject to the rights of the arrester whose advantage cannot be defeated by that security. But the extent of that advantage will depend on the outcome of the process in which the arrestment is used. If the action fails the arrestment falls and there is no longer any restriction on the rights of the assignee, and the fixed security will be effective in regard to any balance which may remain after any successful claim by the arrester has been satisfied. The same approach was appropriate in the case of a posterior floating charge. This was not in conflict with any of the provisions of the statute. The property to which the floating charge attaches is subject to the rights of an arrester whose arrestment was prior to the date of registration of the floating charge. The extent of those rights may be such as to render the floating charge worthless on crystallisation in regard to the property held by the arrestee, but they may not. The receiver must await the outcome of the process until the debt arrested for has been satisfied. What remains at that stage will be for him to collect because it is, as it all along had been, property of the company to which the floating charge had attached.

The court in the *Iona Hotels* case recognised that it would be anomalous if a debtor company which granted a bond and floating

---

[37] Stair, III, i, 42.
[38] Ersk., III, vi, 11 and 15.
[39] (1894) 21 R. 1096.
[40] At 1103.
[41] 1991 S.L.T. 11.
[42] 1977 S.C. 155.

charge in favour of its creditor should be in a better position in regard to prior arrestments than a debtor which granted an assignation in security. It was not possible to distinguish between these two forms of security for the purpose of the competing security situation. This tackled the problem of circularity where a bare arrestment ranks before a subsequent intimation of an assignation in security but on the *Lord Advocate v Royal Bank of Scotland*[43] case behind a floating charge, but an assignation in security being a fixed security ranked ahead of a floating charge. The court, however, did not seem to examine whether the crystallisation of a floating charge was the critical fact, or the registration itself of the floating charge. Lord Hope stated:

"Against this background one must ask oneself why it should be that a debtor who grants a bond and floating charge in favour of his creditor should be in any better position in regard to prior arrestments than a debtor who grants an assignation in security. In principle I do not find it possible to distinguish between these two forms of security for present purposes. Both can be seen to be voluntary acts of the debtor at the date of granting of the relevant deed. The assignation in security is completed by intimation, which can be taken to be the equivalent of registration in the case of a floating charge: see s 410 of the Companies Act 1985. The assignation is of course a fixed security over the moveables to which it relates, whereas the floating charge does not acquire this character until the receiver is appointed. But on the appointment of a receiver the holder of a floating charge enjoys all the protection in relation to any item of attached property that the holder of a fixed security over that item would enjoy under the general law: *Forth & Clyde Construction Co Ltd v Trinity Timber & Plywood Co Ltd* 1984 SLT at p 96 per Lord President Emslie. The analogy is clearly seen in the case of a book debt. In regard to that kind of moveable property the only form of fixed security which is available under the general law is an assignation in security which has been duly intimated. Section 53(7) of the Insolvency Act 1986 provides that the attachment which takes place when the receiver is appointed under a floating charge has effect as if the charge were a fixed security over the property to which it has attached, so its effect in regard to book debts is the same as if they had been the subject of duly intimated assignation in security. No doubt there is this difference, that in contrast to the holder of a fixed security the rights of the holder of the floating charge are incomplete until the receiver has been appointed, because it is only then that the attachment can take place. But I think that this point merely serves to emphasise that the holder of a duly registered floating charge should not be in a better position in regard to prior arrestments than the assignee in security of the common debtor whose assignation has been intimated to the arrestee. In both cases the voluntary act of the common debtor has been completed, in the one case by registration which makes public the creation of the floating charge and in the other by intimation to

---

[43] 1977 S.C. 155.

complete the security. It seems to me to be clear in principle that the arrestment should prevail in both cases, since the litigiosity extends to any voluntary deed of the common debtor which is posterior to the arrestment."

It is very difficult to see why Lord Hope considered that the arrestment has to be prior to the date of registration of the floating charge. The correct date, it is thought, should be the date of crystallisation of the floating charge when the assignation takes place. If the crystallisation takes place prior to the arrestment, the debt which is being purportedly arrested no longer may be competently arrested. However, until crystallisation, the floating charge floats. There may by registration of the floating charge be intimation of a future assignation; but until such an actual assignation by crystallisation the company may still assign its debts, and they are accordingly arrestable.

The *Lord Advocate v Royal Bank of Scotland*[44] case and *The Iona Hotels Ltd* case[45] leave the law in this area in an unsettled state, although it looks as if the *Iona Hotels* judgment of Lord Hope may just not be followed by the judges even without it being amended by statute or overturned by a superior court. Lord Hardie effectively refused to follow it in *Commissioners of Custom and Excise v John D. Reid Joinery Ltd*,[46] arguing that a floating charge holder whose charge, even if created prior to an arrestment, takes the property on crystyllisation subject to any rights of an arrester.[47]

If arrestments not followed by a furthcoming, are completely trumped by the crystallisation of a floating charge, this has the benefit to the receiver that if a receiver is appointed after the arrestment he will not be compelled to liquidate the company within 60 days of the arrestment being executed in order to have the arrestment cut down under the provisions for equalisation of diligence in terms of s.37 of the Bankruptcy (Scotland) Act 1985, as applied to liquidations by s.185(1)(a) of the Insolvency Act 1986. On the other hand, following the *Iona Hotels Ltd* case,[48] liquidations may unnecessarily be prematurely instituted.

Attachments

9–16   The Bankruptcy (Scotland) Act 1985 only talks about a "completed attachment". It has been an open question for a century whether a attachment is held to be "effectually executed" at (a) the date of execution of the attachment (when the officer "adjudges" the goods to belong to the attachment creditor); or (b) only when the report of the sale is lodged, or there is delivery of the goods to the creditor.[49] It is not

---

[44] *ibid.*

[45] 1991 S.L.T. 11.

[46] 2001 S.L.T. (O.H.) 588.

[47] He followed the approach in the sheriff court case of *Commercial Aluminium Windows Ltd v Cumbernauld Development Corp.*, 1987 S.L.T. (Sh. Ct.) 91.

[48] 1991 S.L.T. 11.

[49] Support for the latter view is found in *Tullis v Whyte*, June 18, 1817, F.C.; *Samson v McCubbin* (1822) 1 S. 407; *S. Yuile Ltd v Gibson*, 1952 S.L.T. (Sh.Ct.) 22. The former view appears to receive recognition in *New Glenduffhill Coal Co Ltd v Muir and Co* (1882) 10 R. 372; *Galbraith v Campbell's Trs* (1885) 22 S.L.R. 602; *Bendy Bros Ltd v McAlister* (1910) 26 Sh.Ct Rep. 152.

clear as a result of the *Iona Hotels Ltd* case (above) whether an attachment also has to be executed prior to the registration of a floating charge to give the attacher a claim to the property to which the holder of the floating charge would have to be subject, or whether there might also need to be a completed attachment.

Inhibitions

An inhibition is neither a "completed diligence" nor an "effectually **9–17** executed diligence", and where a creditor refuses to lift it the receiver may apply to the court to have it lifted under s.61 of the Insolvency Act 1986.[50] A liquidator may sell heritable property, and this is not challengeable on the ground of any prior inhibition (reserving any effect of such inhibition on ranking) in a winding up by the court.[51] The liquidator in a voluntary winding up does not have this statutory power and would have to apply to the court for it under s.112 of the Insolvency Act 1986.

In the case of *Armour v Mycroft*[52] an inhibition had been registered against a company after it had granted a floating charge but before receivers were appointed. Following the appointment of joint receivers it was agreed between the joint receivers and the inhibitors that the inhibitors would grant a partial discharge of their inhibition, releasing heritable property which the receivers had sold to a third party, provided that the proceeds of sale would be consigned into court pending a determination by the court as to the relative entitlements of the floating charge holders and the inhibitors. Though the inhibitors initially argued that the inhibition represented an effectually executed diligence on the company's property, they eventually conceded that point and argued instead that an order should be made by the court that the inhibitor's debt should be met out of the proceeds of sale, either before payment to the floating charge holders, or after payment but before payment to the company. The court held that the inhibitors should be paid after the debt of the floating charge holders had been met but before any payment was made to the company. That decision failed to recognise that at common law an inhibition itself would confer no priority on the inhibitors in respect of the proceeds of sale. Unfortunately in a subsequent case, *Taymech Ltd v Rush & Tompkins Ltd*,[53] when a similar situation was dealt with by Lord Coulsfield it was not suggested by the counsel for the pursuers that a receivership might not prevail against the inhibitions and there was no indication that it was even possible that such an argument might be considered at a later stage in the proceedings. Also there was no suggestion that the inhibitions might be of any value to the pursuers in any competition with other creditors apart from those by whom the receiver had been appointed.

---

[50] Formerly s.477 of the Companies Act 1985. See Wilson on *Debt* (2nd ed.), p.117. As to whether an inhibition is an effectually executed diligence, see *Armour and Mycroft, Pets*, 1983 S.L.T. 453.

[51] Bankruptcy (Scotland) Act 1985, s.31(2) as conferred on liquidators by Insolvency Act 1986, s.169(2).

[52] 1983 S.L.T. 453.

[53] 1990 S.C.L.R. 789; 1990 S.L.T. 681.

Accordingly Lord Coulsfield recalled the inhibitions, but included a condition in the interlocutor to the effect of preserving any priority that the pursuers might have against the company.

Adjudications

9–18   The same problems arising out of *Lord Advocate v The Royal Bank of Scotland*[54] and the *Iona Hotels Ltd* case[55] arise in the case of adjudications. The first question would be whether a notice of litigiosity registered in connection with an adjudication could compete with a floating charge. The second problem would usually arise, in that the notice of litigiosity is invariably registered after the creation of the floating charge and so would only affect future advances secured by the floating charge. A third problem is caused by the terms of s.60(1) of the Insolvency Act 1986, which requires a receiver to rank a voluntary heritable security prior to an effectually executed diligence, which the authors read to include an effectually executed adjudication, irrespective of the times of infeftment and, even though under the general law of ranking, the adjudication would have priority over the security. By this provision, floating charges distort the ranking of heritable securities and adjudications in a competition between them, although the competition has nothing to do with the floating charges. This would seem to require statutory amendment. A further problem is that, under the ordinary common law, a duly registered inhibition gives the inhibitor a preference over a subsequently registered adjudication for debt when the debt enforced by the adjudication was "contracted" after the registration of the inhibition. If an inhibition can never be ranked before a floating charge, but an adjudication can be so ranked, it follows that in a ranking by a receiver the adjudication will have priority over the inhibition in violation of the ordinary common law.[56]

(b) Effectually executed diligence in winding up

9–19   Although arrestments or attachments executed within 60 days before the commencement of winding up are ineffectual to create a preference for the arrester or attacher,[57] this has been interpreted by the court in the case of arrestments only to apply to arrestments that were actually subsisting at the date of commencement of winding up, and therefore had no application where the arrestment had been superseded by payment and was no longer subsisting at that date.[58] Accordingly, an arrestment followed by a furthcoming (*i.e.* an effectually executed diligence) would seem not to be reducible by a winding up. It is thought that the law would be the same in relation to attachments followed by a sale (*i.e.* an unequivocally completed attachment).

In terms of s.37(4) of the Bankruptcy (Scotland) Act 1985, as applied to liquidations by s.185(1) of the Insolvency Act 1986:

---

[54] 1977 S.C. 155.

[55] 1991 S.L.T. 11.

[56] See Scot. Law Com. Discussion Paper No.78, "Adjudications for Debt and Related Matters" (November 1988, p.173).

[57] Bankruptcy (Scotland) Act 1985, s.37(4) as applied to liquidations by Insolvency Act 1986, s.185(1).

[58] *Johnston v Cluny Estates Trs*, 1957 S.L.T. 293.

"No arrestment or poinding of the estate of the debtor (including any estate vesting in the permanent trustee under section 32(6) of that Act) executed—

(a) within the period of 60 days before the date of sequestration and whether or not subsisting at that date; or
(b) on or after the date of sequestration,

shall be effectual to create a preference for the arrester or attacher; and the estate so arrested or attached, or the proceeds of sale thereof, shall be handed over to the permanent trustee".

It had been held, before the passing of the Bankruptcy (Scotland) Act 1985, in the case of *Johnston v Cluny Estates Trs*,[59] that the provisions concerning the effect of sequestration on diligence contained in s.327(1)(a) of the Companies Act 1948 did not apply to funds arrested within 60 days of a sequestration if, during that time, the arrestment had been withdrawn or superseded by payment. The Scottish Law Commission in their *Report on Bankruptcy and Related Aspects of Insolvency and Liquidation*[60] proposed a provision as follows:

"No arrestment or poinding of the estate of the debtor (including any estate vesting in the permanent trustee under section 31(5) of this Act [the Bill of the Scottish Law Commission]) executed within the period of 60 days before the date of sequestration or after that date, and no inhibition taking effect within that period, shall be effectual to create a preference for the arrester, poinderer or inhibitor; and the benefit of any such arrestment or attachment executed within that period or after that date, or inhibition taking effect within that period, shall vest in the permanent trustee."

The last statement in that clause of the Bill would have entailed that any benefit gained by an arrester or attacher would have gone into the estate of the bankrupt. If "the benefit of any such arrestment or attachment" were read to mean the sale proceeds of any article attached or arrested in the hands of the attacher or arrester, or any money paid over to an arrester, in the hands of an arrester, the perceived mischief of the case of *Johnston v Cluny Estates Trs*[61] would have been met. The mischief is that, although subsisting arrestments or attachments are cut down, depriving the arresters or attachers of any benefit, the arresters or attachers would be benefited if the goods were sold and the proceeds handed over to them on the authority of the bankrupt, or the bankrupt had paid the arrester the sum claimed or instructed one of his debtors to pay the arrester. The clause proposed by the Scottish Law Commission would have produced an anomaly, in that, unless payments could otherwise be struck down as "unfair preferences", any benefit induced by an arrestment or attachment within the 60 day period would vest in the company; and this would put the arrester or attacher in a worse position

---

[59] 1957 S.L.T. 293.
[60] Scot. Law Com. No. 68.
[61] 1957 S.L.T. 293.

than if the payments had been forthcoming without that type of legal pressure. Section 37(4) of the Bankruptcy (Scotland) Act takes the proposal of the Scottish Law Commission further. Because "the estate so arrested or attached, or the proceeds of sale thereof, shall be handed over to the permanent trustee" this would seem to attach a *vitium reale* to the proceeds of sale. But non-connected third parties seem to be required to hand over the proceeds of sale to the permanent trustee (the liquidator). It is thought that, in terms of s.37(4) of the Bankruptcy (Scotland) Act 1985, even if read alone, an effectually executed diligence, whether an arrestment followed by a furthcoming or attachment followed by a sale would be reducible in a winding up, provided the diligence was within the 60 days. The reason would be that the furthcoming legally flowed from the arrestment and was dependent on the arrestment and the sale flowed legally from and was dependent on the attachment. This result is, in any event, entailed by the terms of s.37(1)(a) of that Act. Section 37(4), however (unlike the proposed provision suggested by the Scottish Law Commission), poses a separate problem as regards interpretation for cases where an arrestment has been only followed by payment by the debtor or by an instruction by the debtor to one of his debtors to pay the arrester. In addition to the anomalous consequences flowing from the provisions in relation to arrestments and attachments in s.37(4) of the Bankruptcy (Scotland) Act 1985 as described above, there is an express provision that the proceeds of a sale must be handed over to the permanent trustee. This the authors read to cover both a judicial sale dependent on an attachment and a situation where the owner of the attached goods, namely the debtor, authorises the attacher to sell the goods and take the proceeds. However, where there is an arrestment of a debt (as opposed to the arrestment of corporeal moveables in the hands of a third party), there is a real problem as to the interpretation of s.37(4) of the Bankruptcy (Scotland) Act 1985. On a very broad reading, the expression "the estate so arrested . . . shall be handed over to the permanent trustee" could mean money paid to an arrester by the debtor of a company on the instruction of the company or by the company itself to persuade the arrester to lift the arrestment. It is thought, however, by the authors that, where debts are arrested, one could not properly describe money paid to the arrester by a debtor of the company or by the company to lift the arrestments as "the estate so arrested". Neither could money paid over ever be classed as "proceeds of sale". If that interpretation is right, the problem raised in the case of *Johnston v Cluny Estates Trs*[62] is not met.

There is accordingly an incentive to creditors of any company to arrest the debts of a company whose creditworthiness is suspect, on the basis that debts paid even within the 60–day period, the payment of which has been induced by the arrestment, would not be clawed back under s.37(4) of the Bankruptcy (Scotland) Act 1985 as applied to liquidations. The provisions of s.37(4) of the Bankruptcy (Scotland) Act 1985 are ambiguous and create anomalies. They probably do not achieve their intended purpose in relation to meeting the problem in the case of

---

[62] 1957 S.L.T. 293.

Johnston v Cluny Estates Trs[63] and are likely to create confusion in this area of corporate insolvency.

Diligence outwith statutory periods

Diligence outwith the statutory 60 days from winding up creates a **9–20** preference even if not completed.[64]

---

[63] 1957 S.L.T. 293.
[64] *Commercial Aluminium Windows Ltd v Cumbernauld Development Corp.*, 1987 S.L.T. (Sh.Ct.) 91.

CHAPTER 10

CHALLENGEABLE TRANSACTIONS

Background

The present law on challengeable transactions has not significantly **10–01** changed since the Insolvency Act 1986 and its accompanying reforms. (The Enterprise Act 2002 made only minor adjustments.[1]) The Insolvency Act 1986 (which consolidated provisions in the Companies Act 1985 introduced on April 1, 1986 by the Bankruptcy (Scotland) Act 1985) first of all replaced the provisions in the Bankruptcy Act 1621[2] and the Bankruptcy Act 1696,[3] which made challengeable "gratuitous alienations" and "fraudulent preferences" on bankruptcy. Secondly, s.617 of the Companies Act 1985,[4] which allowed challenges to floating charges created within 12 months of the commencement of a winding-up, was replaced by s.245 of the Insolvency Act 1986, which strengthened the former rules and abolished the previous provision contained in s.617(3) of the Companies Act 1985, under which, in Scotland, a floating charge was only reducible under the Companies Acts. (This followed the recommendation of the Scottish Law Commission contained in its report on bankruptcy and related aspects of insolvency and liquidation.[5]) Thirdly, there was a major new enactment introduced by s.244 of the Insolvency Act 1986 under which "extortionate credit transactions" may be reduced on an application to the court by an administrator or a liquidator, with the onus being on the provider of the credit to prove that the transaction was not extortionate. Fourthly, with the introduction of administration procedure in 1986, some of the rights of challenge, previously vesting in creditors and liquidator, were extended to administrators.

There are now accordingly *four* major categories of transactions which may be challenged in a liquidation:

(a) gratuitous alienations;

---

[1] A liquidator now requires the sanction of the court or the creditors' committee to bring an action under ss.242 or 243 of the Insolvency Act 1986 (para.3A of Sch.4 to the Insolvency Act 1986, as inserted by s.253 of the Enterprise Act 2002). This provision is also applicable to the corresponding English provisions: see, for Scotland, *Dyer v Mislop*, 1994 S.C.L.R. 171 and *Dyer v Craiglaw Developments Ltd*, 1999 S.L.T. 1228; and in England *Re Floor Fourteen Ltd* [2001] 2 B.C.L.C. 392.

[2] (c.18).

[3] (c.5).

[4] Derived from the Companies Act 1948, s.322, the Companies (Floating Charges and Receivers) (Scotland) Act 1972, s.8.

[5] Scot. Law Comm. No. 68.

(b) unfair preferences;
(c) floating charges; and
(d) extortionate credit transactions.

GRATUITOUS ALIENATIONS

Common law

10–02 The Scottish common law has long recognised that there is always a risk that a debtor, appreciating that his affairs are becoming embarrassed and that he may be insolvent, may seek to put his assets out of the reach of his creditors by transferring them to other persons, particularly to friends and relations. Accordingly, the common law allows challenge of a gift by an insolvent donor on the ground that such a gift amounts to a fraud upon his creditors. Indeed the common law allows a successful challenge of a voluntary alienation by a debtor, irrespective of proof of intention to defraud, where it can be shown that:

(1) the debtor was insolvent at the time of the challenge and was either insolvent at the time of the alienation or was made insolvent by it; and
(2) the alienation was made without onerous consideration; and
(3) the alienation was to the prejudice of the challenging creditor.

The common law challenge may be made by any creditor, whether his debt was contracted before or after the alienation.[6] Insolvency in the context of the common law challenge means the debtor's absolute insolvency, in the sense that his overall liabilities are greater than his assets. Such insolvency is difficult for a creditor to establish in any event, but it is especially difficult in relation to a point of time in the past. The common law, therefore, was strengthened by the Bankruptcy Act 1621. Both the common law rules relating to gratuitous alienations as well as the 1621 Act apply to companies (including limited liability companies) as well as to individuals. This was unequivocally stated by the First Division of the Court of Session in the case of *Bank of Scotland v Pacific Shelf (Sixty-Two) Ltd*,[7] affirming the case of *Abram Steamship Co Ltd v Abram*.[8] Lord Brand, delivering the opinion of the court, stated:

> "We have no doubt that the petitioners have the rights of creditors at common law. The common law conferred upon creditors the right to challenge certain actions by their debtors. There is no reason in principle why, after 1856, this right should not, in the absence of statutory provision to the contrary, have been available against debtors who happen to be limited companies. We are in complete agreement with the opinion of the Lord Ordinary that this

---

[6] Goudy, H., *Bankrutpcy*, p.33 and cases cited there. See in particular *Wink v Speirs* (1867) 6 M. 77 at 79, *per* Lord Justice Clerk Patton.
[7] 1988 S.C.L.R. 487; 1988 S.L.T. 690.
[8] 1925 S.L.T. 243.

right has survived successive statutory enactments regulating the affairs of limited companies. As my Lord in the chair pointed out it would not have been difficult in the course of the debate, to restrict the common law rights of creditors in clear language, if that had been the intention of the legislature. In our opinion those rights could only be abrogated by clear statutory provision of necessary implication. We were not referred to any such statutory provision and the implications point in the opposite direction."

In terms of s.242(7) of the Insolvency Act 1986 a liquidator and an administrator are expressly stated to have the same common law rights as a creditor to challenge an alienation of a company made for no consideration or no adequate consideration. The granting of a floating charge may be challenged as a gratuitous alienation at common law as well as under s.245 of the Insolvency Act 1986[9].

The law contained in the 1621 Act (although it is repealed) still applies to all transactions entered into before April 1, 1986. Such transactions may only be set aside as gratuitous alienations to the extent that they could have been set aside under the 1621 Act.[10] For some time, therefore, that Act will remain of some significance.

Bankruptcy Act 1621 ("the Act")

The Act provided that when a debtor makes an alienation to "any **10–03** conjunct or confident person without true just and necessary causes and without a just price truly paid, the same being done after the contracting of lawful debts from true creditors", the latter may challenge the gift.

> "'Conjunct and confident persons' are described in the preamble to the Act as 'wives, children, kinsmen, allies and other confident and interposed persons'. Case law has interpreted the expression 'conjunct persons' to include those who are closely related to the debtor, such as a spouse, parent, children, brothers, sisters, uncles and sons-in-law. It has also been held to include those in a confidential relationship with the debtor, such as business partners, clerks, servants, etc. There is no rule to the same effect in the common law, but Bell suggests that 'where the connection between the parties has been very close and intimate, the Court has raised a presumption to the effect of throwing the *onus probandi* of solvency on the holder of the deed".[11]

The Act has been interpreted in such a way that, if it can be established that the debtor was insolvent at the date of the challenge, it is presumed (a) that he was also insolvent at the date of the alienation; and (b) that the alienation was made without onerous consideration. It is not wholly

---

[9] See para.39(1)(d) of new Sch.B1 to the Insolvency Act 1986.
[10] Insolvency Act 1986, Sch.11, para. 9(1).
[11] Bell, *Comm.*, ii, 184, citing *Crs of Marshall v His children* (1709) Mor. 48 Note; *Inglis v Boswell* (1676) Mor. 11567; *McChristian v Monteith* (1709) Mor. 4931.

clear whether, if the debtor was insolvent at the date of the alienation, the gift will be set aside where it can be shown that its effect was to render the debtor insolvent.[12] If, however, it is established that the debtor was or became solvent after the date of the alienation, the right of challenge disappears.

The Act provided that the person making the challenge may be "any true creditor". This has been construed to mean only creditors whose debts were contracted before the alienation. Challenge under the Act is therefore in this respect more restricted than under the common law. The liquidator may make the challenge whether representing prior creditors or not.

The words "true, just and necessary causes", although in terms conjunctive, have always been construed disjunctively.[13] Accordingly a challenge under the Act can be defeated where it can be shown that the alienation was made for a "true" or "just" cause even if strict necessity is absent. The cause must be "existing and operating at the date of the deed".[14] It is not a condition of any challenge under the common law or under the Act that the alienation was entirely gratuitous. It suffices that there was a materially inadequate consideration in money or in money's worth. Where there is a material inadequacy, the transaction is held to be gratuitous to the extent of the inadequacy and may be reduced.[15] Although the Act declares the alienations, dispositions, etc. to which it refers "to have been from the beginning and to be in all times coming null and of no avail force nor effect", it nevertheless extends protection to "any of His Majesty's good subjects (no way partakers of the said frauds) having purchased one of the said bankrupt's lands or goods by true bargains". Accordingly a third party, receiving the subject matter of the alienation for value and in good faith, is protected. The donee, however, is liable to make good to the bankrupt's creditors the price he receives.

Challenges at common law and under statute to prior transactions of a company are excluded in terms of s.165 of the Companies Act 1989 in relation to a market contract to which a recognised investment exchange or recognised clearing house is a party or which is entered into under its default rules, or in relation to a disposition of property pursuant to such a market contract. Where margin is provided under a market contract which is thus excluded, the protection extends to the provision of the margin, to any contract effected by the exchange or clearing house for the purpose of realising the property provided as margin, and to a disposition of property in accordance with the rules of the exchange or clearing house as to the application of such property.

---

[12] Contrast *McLay v McQueen* (1899) 1 F. 804 with *Abram Steamship Co v Abram*, 1925 S.L.T. 243, OH.

[13] Bell, *Comm.*, ii, 176, citing *Grant v Grant of Tullifour* (1748) Mor. 949 at 952.

[14] *Horne v Hay* (1847) 9 D. 651 at 665, *per* Lord Justice-Clerk Hope.

[15] *Glencairn v Brisbane* (1677) Mor. 1011; *Miller's Tr. v Shield* (1862) 24 D. 821; *Gorrie's Tr. v Gorrie* (1890) 17 R. 1051; *Tennant v Miller* (1897) 4 S.L.T. 318; *Abram Steamship Co v Abram*, 1925 S.L.T. 243, OH.

Effect of challenge

The effect of a successful challenge is that the subject of the alienation **10–04** becomes an asset of the debtor's estate and may be attached by the diligence of any creditor.[16] The challenging creditor is not entitled to delivery of the asset.

Alienations

The Act applies to "all alienations, dispositions, assignations, and **10–05** translations, whatsoever made by the debtor of any of his lands, teinds, reversions, actions, debts, or goods whatsoever". The subjects of the alienation must be able to be attached by the diligence of the creditors.[17] The following would be included: the granting of a bill[18] or a promissory note,[19] the assignation of a life interest or insurance policy, a lease,[20] the discharge of a claim,[21] a decree allowed to pass in absence,[22] the abandonment of an action.[23] It applies to the delivery of goods.[24] The conveyance may be direct or indirect.[25] Accordingly, a conveyance from the seller to the conjunct or confident person, the price being paid by the insolvent, is an alienation.[26] Cash payments are not alienations under the Act,[27] whereas under the common law they are.[28]

Gratuitous alienations under the Insolvency Act 1986

In terms of s.242(1) of the Insolvency Act 1986 certain alienations are **10–06** challengeable in the case of a winding up by either the liquidator, or any creditor who is a creditor by virtue of a debt incurred on or before the date of the commencement of the winding up. Where an administration is entered into, an alienation is challengeable by the administrator but not by the creditors.[29] Alienations prior to April 1, 1986 and thereafter may be challenged under the Insolvency Act 1986.[30] Section 242 of the Insolvency Act 1986 concerns itself with companies, and is accordingly much clearer than challenges under the old Bankruptcy Act 1621, the enactment of which preceded the institution of sequestration, let alone windings up or administrations. The question of who was a confident or conjunct person in relation to a company was never totally clear and

---

[16] *Cook v Sinclair and Co* (1896) 23 R. 925.
[17] Bell, *Comm.*, ii, 178–179.
[18] *ibid.*, ii, 177.
[19] *Thomas v Thomson* (1865) 3 M. 1160.
[20] *Gorrie's Tr. v Gorrie* (1890) 17 R. 1051.
[21] *Laing v Cheyne* (1832) 10 S. 200.
[22] McKenzie, *Works*, II, p 8.
[23] *Wilson v Drummond's Reps* (1853) 16 D. 275.
[24] *NB Ry Co v White* (1882) 20 S.L.R. 129.
[25] Bell, *Comm.*, ii, 174.
[26] *Ross v Hutton* (1830) 8 S. 916; *Bolden v Ferguson* (1863) 1 M. 552.
[27] *Gilmour Shaw and Co's Tr v Learmonth*, 1972 S.C. 136.
[28] *Dobie v Mitchell* (1854) 17 D. 97; *Main v Fleming's Trs* (1881) 8 R. 880.
[29] Insolvency Act 1986, s.242(1)(b), as amended by para.28(2) of Sch.17 to the Enterprise Act 2002.
[30] *ibid.*, s 242(2)(a).

had to be inferred by analogy from that of a personal debtor. This is clarified by statute. The expression "associate" as defined by the Bankruptcy (Scotland) Act 1985, s.74, as amended by reg.11 of the Bankruptcy (Scotland) Regulations 1985, replaces the old expression "conjunct and confident" person.

Ground of challenge and onus of proof

10–07   A challenge may be brought under s.242(1) of the Insolvency Act 1986 by a pre-liquidation creditor, liquidator with the sanction of the court or liquidation committee,[32] or administrator, on the grounds that an alienation has favoured some person. The court must grant a decree of reduction or for such restoration of property to the company's assets or other such redress as may seem appropriate.[33]

If reduction is competent in the situation, it has been held by the Second Division of the Inner House in the case of *Alexander Short's Tr. v Tai Lee Chung*[34] that reduction must be granted.[35] Also the purpose of s.34 of the Bankruptcy (Scotland) Act 1985 and s.242 of the Insolvency Act 1986 is to restore property improperly alienated, and the court did not have discretion to decide matters on general equitable principles.[36] This means that, if heritable property has been alienated for less than the full value, the heritable property is returned to the company and the person to whom the property was gratuitously alienated ranks as a "postponed creditor" for the consideration which was given. That would normally mean that the postponed creditor got nothing. This remedy is different to the English remedy under s.238(3), in terms of which the court makes an order restoring the position to what it would have been if the company had not entered into the transaction. This discrepancy between the English and the Scottish approach to these transactions at undervalue, or gratuitous alienations, may lead to problems when these orders are being enforced in the different jurisdictions under s.426 of the Insolvency Act 1986. It is thought that the Second Division took the then legally correct although restrictive view in the case of *Alexander Short's Tr. v Tai Lee Chung*, in their interpretation of s.34 of the Bankruptcy (Scotland) Act 1985 which is the counterpart to s.242 of the Insolvency Act 1986 for sequestration purposes. The court stated:

---

[32] A liquidator now requires the sanction of the court or the creditors' committee to bring an action under ss.242 or 243 of the Insolvency Act 1986 (para.3A of Sch.4 to the Insolvency Act 1986, as inserted by s.253 of the Enterprise Act 2002). This provision is also applicable to the corresponding English provisions: see, for Scotland, *Dyer v Mislop*, 1994 S.C.L.R. 171 and *Dyer v Craiglaw Developments Ltd*, 1999 S.L.T. 1228; and in England *Re Floor Fourteen Ltd* [2001] 2 B.C.L.C. 392.

[33] Insolvency Act 1986, s.242(4).

[34] 1991 S.C.L.R. 629.

[35] See, however, comments on human rights implication of this principle described in Chap.3.

[36] *Alexander Short's Tr. v Tai Lee Chung*, 1991 S.C.L.R. 629 and *Cay's Tr. v Cay*, 1997 G.W.D. 4–162; aff'd 1998 S.C.L.R. 456; 1999 S.L.T. 321; *Baillie Marshall Ltd (in liquidation) v Avian Communications Ltd*, 2002 S.L.T. 189; *Nottay's Tr. v Nottay*, 2001 S.L.T. 769.

"The starting point in a case of this nature for interpretation of section 34(4) is that the original alienation has been avoided and the transaction has been vitiated. This is not a good starting-point for an argument which is based solely on equity. It is in our opinion clear from a reading of section 34(4) that the general purpose is to provide that as far as possible any property which has been improperly alienated should be restored to the debtor's estate. In the case of a disposition of heritable property this can easily be done by reduction of that disposition. We consider that the reference to 'other redress as may be appropriate' is not intended to give the court a general discretion to decide a case on equitable principles but is designed to enable the court to make an appropriate order in a case where reduction or restoration of the property is not a remedy which is available. As reduction is available in this case, we consider that it is the proper remedy and for this reason we would refuse the reclaiming motion."

The Scottish law in this area under statute seems intended disproportionately to penalise the recipient of a gratuitous alienation.[37] The interpretation of the judges is obviously what Parliament intended at the passing of the Insolvency Act 1986. If restoration of the status quo was what was sought, it is difficult to see why the legislature would have prescribed in terms of s.51(3)(c) of the Bankruptcy (Scotland) Act 1985 and r.4.66(2)(a) of the Insolvency (Scotland) Rules 1986 that a creditor's right to any alienation which has been reduced or restored to the company's assets under s.242 of the Insolvency Act 1986 or to the proceeds of sale of such an alienation, is to be classed as a "postponed debt".

Reduction is, however, not always available. The House of Lords took the view that, if the decree related to land to which the Land Registration (Scotland) Act 1979 applied, it could not be registered. Whereas, in relation to the Register of Sasines, the problem did not arise because that Act did not apply to that Register. While the Keeper had power to rectify the title sheet and thereby give effect to the decree, this was only available in limited circumstances in terms of s.9 of the Land Registration (Scotland) Act 1979, which might not include the circumstances in the case in which a decree had been obtained. If rectification was not available the Keeper would be obliged to indemnify any person who suffered loss as a result of the inaccuracy in the title sheet.[38] Because of this, the liquidator should not seek reduction of a conveyance of registered land but an order for the reconveyance of the property to the company, on the basis that reduction is not open.[39]

As with the construction of ss.123(2) and 214(6), a question arises under s.242(4)(a) whether the test to be applied in relation to the

---

[37] See further arguments in Chap.3.
[38] *Short's Tr. v Keeper of the Registers of Scotland*, 1994 S.C.L.R. 135; 1994 S.L.T. 65; aff'd (H.L.) 1996 S.C.L.R. 571; 1996 S.L.T. 166.
[39] See *Short's Tr. v Chung (No. 2)*, 1997 S.C.L.R. 1181; 1998 S.L.T. 200; aff'd 1999 S.L.T. 751; 1999 S.C. 471, where it was suggested that a conclusion for such an order ought to be included in the action of reduction, so as to avoid a possible argument that a later application was incompetent as *res judicata*.

valuation of a company's assets to test whether it is solvent is a test based on valuation as a "going concern" or, on a "break up" basis.[40] It is thought by the authors that the "going concern" test will be applied. Even though there is a legal presumption of insolvency, to be rebutted by the person granting the alienation, any benefit of the doubt is given to the donor trying to establish his solvency. Bell states[41]:

> "It has been held sufficient if the debtor had at the time of the deed a *visible* estate, although *ex eventu*, he should prove insolvent. The subsequent depression of the funds, or the fall of markets for land or goods, will therefore afford a good answer on the question of insolvency, where, on a fair reckoning of the estate as at the date of the deed, the debtor was solvent. This retrospective reckoning is to be favourably viewed where the challenge is at a distant time".

In England, by contrast, the test is whether the company is "unable to pay its debts" within the terms of s.123 of the Insolvency Act 1986, and hence is both a "balance sheet" test and a "liquidity or cash flow" test.

It is thought that in Scotland a person may seek a declarator that there has been a gratuitous alienation, and not have it preceded by an action of reduction.[42] It is thought that the court may look behind a series of transactions to see whether collectively they may be struck at as a gratuitous alienation and come within the terms of s.242 of the Insolvency Act 1986.[43] It is thought by the authors that, although that proposition has been decided where transactions were being challenged at common law, the same would apply to a series of transactions being challenged under s.242 of the Insolvency Act 1986.[44] The court, however, shall not grant such a decree if the person seeking to uphold the alienation establishes:

(a) that immediately, or at any other time, after the alienation, the company's assets were greater than its liabilities, or
(b) that the alienation was made for adequate consideration, or
(c) that the alienation—

    (i) was a birthday, Christmas or other conventional gift; or
    (ii) was a gift made, for a charitable purpose to a person who is not an associate of the company,

which, having regard to all the circumstances, it was reasonable for the company to make.[45]

As in the 1621 Act, the rights of any person who acquires in good faith and for value from or through the transferee in the alienation are not prejudiced.[46]

---

[40] See para.4–111.
[41] Bell, *Comm.*, ii, 186.
[42] *Mycroft v Boyle* 1987 S.C.L.R. 621.
[43] *ibid.*
[44] *ibid.*
[45] Insolvency Act 1986, s.242(4).
[46] *ibid.*, s.242(4).

Types of alienation struck at

All types of alienation are struck at if they are for no consideration or **10–08** no adequate consideration including payments in cash, even if there was a prior obligation.[47] "Adequate consideration" implies the application of an objective standpoint and while not necessarily equivalent to the best price that could be obtained, it should be what could reasonably be expected in the circumstances as between parties acting in good faith and at arm's length. "Adequacy" must be tested at the time of the transaction, but the matters of which the valuer might take account include events which affected the value but took place between the transactions and the valuation, particularly the extent to which they were foreseeable at the transaction date.[48] Collateral arrangements may be relevant.[49]

As regards guarantees, the definition of consideration is again that it is something which has to have a patrimonial worth at the time it is given and, where a guarantee is given, the adequacy of the consideration can only be assumed if the transaction as a whole appears commercial, provided it is assessed strictly and full consideration in money or money's worth has moved from the creditor.[50] In all cases it was for the creditor in the guarantee to aver and prove that consideration was provided, and that the consideration was adequate.[51] The payment of a sum in exchange for an assignation of debts is not a preference if the value of the debts adequately reflects the sum paid.[52] A gratuitous discharge by the company of a security would be for "adequate consideration" if it had not made any advances to the debtor.[53] The granting of a security (which in itself does not diminish the assets of a company) is not a "gratuitous alienation" although it may be an "unfair preference".[54] However, a guarantee granted at a time when the principal obligant was insolvent is a gratuitous alienation.[55] A bond granted to the Inland Revenue in respect of another party's liabilities was held to have been for "adequate consideration" on the basis that, in return, the Revenue granted a certificate under s.70 of the Finance (No. 2) Act 1975, which allowed the company to carry on in business.[56]

Because an alienation in implementation of a prior obligation is deemed in terms of s.242(6) of the Insolvency Act 1986 to be one for which there was no consideration or no adequate consideration to the extent that the prior obligation was undertaken for no consideration or

---

[47] Insolvency Act 1986, s.242(6).
[48] *Nova Glaze Replacement Windows Ltd v Clark Thomson & Co.*, 2001 S.C. (OH) 815.
[49] *Phillips v Brewin Dolphin Bell Lawrie Ltd* [2001] 1 B.C.L.C. 145 (H.L.); [2001] 1 W.L.R. 143 (H.L.); [2001] B.C.C. 864 (H.L.); *Nottay's Tr. v Nottay*, 2001 S.L.T. 769.
[50] *Jackson v Royal Bank of Scotland Plc*, 2002 S.L.T. (O.H.) 1123, *per* Lord Drummond Young.
[51] *ibid.*
[52] *Cay's Trs v Cay*, 1998 S.C.L.R. 456.
[53] *Rankin v Meek*, 1995 S.L.T. 526.
[54] *Mistral Finance (In Liquidation), Re* [2001] B.C.C. 27 (decided on the equivalent English law in s.238 of the Insolvency Act 1986).
[55] *Jackson v Royal Bank of Scotland Plc*, 2002 S.L.T. 1123.
[56] *John E. Rae (Electrical Services) Linlithgow Ltd v Lord Advocate*, 1994 S.L.T. 788.

no adequate consideration, this means that rights to claim on the company's property such as under guarantees, etc. are ineffectual because they are liable to be frustrated to the extent that the guarantee is quashed by the gratuitous alienation provision. It does seem strange that the company is still entitled to make a birthday, Christmas or other conventional gift, which would appear to be more appropriate in the case of personal debtors. However, this is qualified by what would be reasonable having regard to all the circumstances. It may also be struck at as *ultra vires* of the company.

Time limits

10–09   There are no time limits at common law or under the Bankruptcy Act 1621. Section 242(3) of the Insolvency Act 1986 sets time limits. In terms of that section, an alienation may be struck at if it becomes effectual, where an "associate" of the company is favoured, within five years of the commencement of the winding up of the company, or within five years of an administration being entered into. In all other cases the alienation must become effectual in favouring the "non-associate" of the company within two years before the commencement of the winding up or the administration being entered into.[57] Section 242(3) accordingly brings alienations to "non-associates" within the scope of statutory challenge, whereas before the coming into force of the Insolvency Act 1986 such alienations could only be challenged under the common law. The time limits apply to challenges applying the former law.[58]

Definition of "associate"

10–10   "Associate" is defined in terms of s.435 of the Insolvency Act 1986. It includes:

(1) Other companies

   A company is an associate of another company if one person has control of both, or where a person has control of one company and persons who are associates of that person, or the person and persons who are his associates, have control of the other. Alternatively, companies are associated if a group of two or more persons has control of each company, and the groups either consist of the same persons, or could be regarded as consisting of the same persons, by treating (in one or more cases) a member of either group as replaced by a person of whom he is an associate.[59]

   Individuals are associated if the "associate" is the individual's husband or wife or is a relative, or the husband or wife of a relative of the individual or if the individual's husband or wife, and a relative of an individual includes the individual's brother, sister, uncle, aunt, nephew,

---

[57] Insolvency Act 1986, s.242(3).
[58] *ibid.*, s.242(2).
[59] *ibid.*, s.435(6).

niece, lineal ancestor or lineal descendant, treating any relationship of the half blood as a relationship of the whole blood and the step-child or adopted child of any person as his child and an illegitimate child as the legitimate child of his mother and reputed father. Husband or wife includes a former husband or wife and a reputed husband or wife.[60]

(2) Employers

A person is an associate of any person whom he employs or by whom **10–11** he is employed, and any director or other officer of a company is to be treated as employed by that company.[61]

(3) Controllers

A company is an associate of another person if that person has control **10–12** of it or if that person and his associates have control. In deciding whether a person shall be taken to have control of a company, a person is deemed to have control of the company if (a) the directors of the company or of another company which has control of it (or any of them) are accustomed to act in accordance with his directions or instructions; or (b) he is entitled to exercise, or control the exercise of, one-third or more of the voting power at any general meeting of the company or of another company which has control of it; and where two or more persons together satisfy either of these conditions, they are taken to have control of the company.[62]

UNFAIR PREFERENCES

Common law

An "unfair preference" (formerly described as a "fraudulent prefer- **10–13** ence") may be challenged at common law. Essentially a creditor may challenge voluntary transactions by which, after the insolvency of a debtor, another creditor receives a preference, or in the words of Bell, a debtor "after his funds have become inadequate to the payment of all his debts, intentionally, and in contemplation of his failing, confers on favourite creditors a preference over the rest".[63] The challenge can be at the instance of any creditor[64] or the liquidator or administrator.[65] The courts have readily permitted the awareness of the debtor of his insolvency to be inferred from circumstances. Knowledge of the debtor's insolvency or collusion on the part of the preferred creditor need not be established.[66] Conversely, the creditor's knowledge of the debtor's absolute insolvency does not transform the payment of the debt into an

---

[60] Insolvency Act 1986, s.435(2) and (8).
[61] *ibid.*, s.435(4).
[62] *ibid.*, s.435(6).
[63] Bell, *Comm.*, ii, 226.
[64] *Goudy*, p.42.
[65] Insolvency Act 1986, s.243(6).
[66] *McCowan v Wright* (1853) 15 D. 494; see also *Whatmough's Tr. v British Linen Bank*, 1932 S.C. 525 and 1934 S.C. (H.L.) 51.

unfair preference where the payment would not otherwise be so regarded.[67]

Bankruptcy Act 1696

10–14   Although the Bankruptcy Act 1696 has been repealed, preferences which have been effected before April 1, 1986 may only be set aside, as in the case of gratuitous alienations, to the extent that they could have been set aside under the law in force immediately before that day.[68] Legal time limits applying to the Bankruptcy Act 1696 mean that it will not be applied any longer, but an understanding of the Act elucidates the new law.

The Bankruptcy Act 1696 provided:

> "All and whatsoever voluntary dispositions, assignations, or other deeds which shall be found to be made or granted directly or indirectly, by the aforesaid debtor or bankrupt either at or after his becoming bankrupt or in the space of 60 days before in favour of his creditors, either for their satisfaction or further security, in preference to other creditors, to be void and null."

The reference to "becoming bankrupt" is a reference to the old concept of notour bankruptcy, replaced now by apparent insolvency.[69] The period of 60 days was increased to six months in terms of s.115(3) of the Companies Act 1947. Accordingly, any fraudulent preference within six months of notour bankruptcy could be reduced. A company could be rendered notour bankrupt to the effect of permitting the reduction of preferences struck at by the 1696 Act.[70]

Under the common law and the 1696 statute, challenge was excluded in the case of (a) *nova debita* (transactions where the bankrupt and another party have undertaken reciprocal obligations); (b) cash payments of debts actually due; and (c) transactions in the course of ordinary trade or business.[71] Such transactions and payments are completely protected unless they form part of a collusive arrangement to create a preference. The rational basis of these exceptions was stated by Lord President Inglis in *Anderson's Trustee v Flemming*.[72]

> "It would be a very unfortunate thing for the trade of this country if such exception did not exist; because if the Act of 1696 were allowed to extend to all the ordinary transactions of traders, not

---

[67] *Nordic Travel Ltd v Scotprint Ltd*, 1980 S.L.T. 189 at 198, *per* Lord President Emslie.
[68] Insolvency Act 1986, Sch.11, para.9(1).
[69] See para.9–08.
[70] *Clark v Hinde, Milne & Co* (1884) 12 R. 347.
[71] See *Nordic Travel, supra*; *Horsburgh v Ramsay & Co* (1885) 12 R. 117; *Walkraft Paint Co Ltd*, 1964 S.L.T. 103 and 104; *Whatmough's Tr., supra* which qualify the classic statements of the law in important ways.
[72] (1871) 9 M. 718 at 722.

contemplating bankruptcy, and not aware of their being insolvent, it would disturb their business relations to a most calamitous extent. A man may go on trading in the honest belief of his own solvency, and that even up to the date of bankruptcy, and his ordinary transactions will not be held to fall under the operation of this statute. The law is fixed, both in expediency and equity, that they shall not be so."

Unfair preferences under section 243 of the Insolvency Act 1986

Unlike s.242, which makes major changes to the Bankruptcy Act 1621, **10–15** s.243 follows in large part the Bankruptcy Act 1696. The same provisions apply in relation to *nova debita*[73] with the added clarification that the performance of the reciprocal obligations need not take place at the same time. Similarly, transactions in the ordinary course of business or trade are exempt.[74] Cash payments for debts which have become payable are also exempt.[75]

In the case of *Nicoll v Steelpress (Supplies) Ltd*[76] the court held that in relation to *nova debita* reciprocity meant full consideration for any new transaction. It stated:

"Having considered the foregoing contentions of the parties we are not persuaded by the argument for the defenders that the passage cited from Bell and Goudy proceeds on the basis of broad equivalence between the contributions of debtor and creditor in transactions to be excepted from the general rule against unfair preferences. It appears to us that paragraph 3 of Goudy, read short from page 90 to the top of page 91, gives its overall sense quite clearly as follows:

'A *novum debitum* strictly signifies an obligation undertaken by the bankrupt in respect of some present consideration received. . . the implement of such obligations within the days of bankruptcy is protected from the operation of the statute on the ground that the bankrupt does not thereby give a preference by way of satisfaction or further security but simply gives the specific subject which he bargained to give, and in respect of which an equivalent has accrued to his estate. . . Moreover. . . the parties do not *quoad hoc* stand in any prior relation of debtor and creditor. The consideration given to the bankrupt must be a real one and fair value.'

We consider that the passage from Bell is to be read in a similar sense. The principle behind both passages, as we see it, is that the consideration given to the debtor in the transaction cannot be less than full value to qualify for the exception. Strict equivalence is essential in that the debtor's estate must not be diminished as a result of the transaction . . .

---

[73] Insolvency Act 1986, s.243(2)(c).
[74] *ibid.*, s.243(2)(a).
[75] *ibid.*, s.243(2)(b).
[76] 1993 S.L.T. 533; 1992 S.C.L.R. 332.

Further, we doubt whether reduction of prior indebtedness could ever qualify as a valid consideration in a *novum debitum*. That appears to be the effect of the second-last sentence of the passage from Goudy quoted above. Such consideration clearly arises from indebtedness previously incurred which is precisely the area struck at by the law of preferential repayment of creditors. In reality, it is an old debt disguised as a new consideration."

Arrestments

10–16   The Scottish Law Commission highlighted a complication where the debtor has taken action within the period of challenge to fulfil an obligation which he has already assumed and gave the example of a case where, following an arrestment placed by a creditor, the debtor arranges to pay the debt by means of a mandate granted to the arrestee. Although in one sense such a payment is a voluntary payment, since the debtor could have allowed the arrestment to proceed to a furthcoming, there could be an alternative view that he was merely anticipating the inevitable. It was not clear from the authorities whether such a payment would be protected either as a cash payment or as being made involuntarily.[77] Following the Law Commission's recommendations, there was constituted a statutory exemption to challenge as an unfair preference where the transaction consists of:

"the granting of a mandate by a company authorising an arrestee to pay over the arrested funds or part thereof to the arrester where—

(i) there has been a decree for payment or a warrant for summary diligence, and

(ii) the decree or warrant has been preceded by an arrestment on the dependence of the action or followed by an arrestment in execution".[78]

Protection of third parties

10–17   Again following the recommendation of the Scottish Law Commission, as in the case of gratuitous alienations, the rights of innocent third parties are now expressly protected where the third party has acquired a right or interest in good faith and for value from or through the creditor in whose favour a preference has been created, although the preferred creditor will of course have to account.[79]

Persons entitled to challenge unfair preferences

10–18   Unfair preferences may be challenged by any creditor who is a creditor by virtue of a debt incurred on or before the date of commencement of winding up, or by the liquidator.[80] In the case of an administra-

---

[77] Scot. Law Com. No. 68 at 12.39.
[78] Insolvency Act 1986, s.243(2)(d).
[79] *ibid.*, s.243(5); (gratuitous alienations, s.242(5)).
[80] *ibid.*, s.243(4)(a).

tion, the administrator only may make the challenge.[81] This follows the scheme in relation to the persons who may challenge a gratuitous alienation under s.242 of the Insolvency Act 1986.

Remedies

The remedies are the same as under s.242(4) in relation to gratuitous **10–19** alienations.[82]

Challengeable period

The period covered by a challenge is now restricted to six months **10–20** prior to the commencement of winding up or administration order. The provisions previously existing by which a company could be made notour bankrupt for this purpose have been replaced by s.243(1) of the Insolvency Act.

Types of transactions struck at

The type of transactions which a company may enter into which **10–21** create a preference in favour of a creditor to the prejudice of the general body of creditors is only limited by human deviousness. The following types of transaction have been held to be unfair preferences:

    (a) the return of moveables bought but not paid for under an arrangement made in view of the buyer's insolvency[83];
    (b) the discharge of a right[84];
    (c) the abandonment of a competent defence[85];
    (d) the allowance of a decree by default[86];
    (e) the granting of a delivery order for moveables[87]; and
    (f) the payment of a long standing debt on the eve of a liquidation.[88]

FLOATING CHARGES

Common law

For the avoidance of doubt, s.613(3) of the Companies Act 1985 (first **10–22** introduced by s.8 of the Companies (Floating Charges and Receivers)

---

[81] Insolvency Act 1986, s.243(4)(b).
[82] See *Baillie Marshall Ltd. (in liquidation) v Avian Communications Ltd*, 2002 S.L.T. (O.H.) 189.
[83] *Watson & Sons Ltd v Veritys Ltd* (1908) 24 Sh. Ct Rep. 148.
[84] *Keith v Maxwell* (1795) Mor. 1163.
[85] *Wilson v Drummond's Reps* (1853) 16 D. 275.
[86] *Lauries' Tr. v Beveridge* (1867) 6 M. 85.
[87] *Wright v Mitchell* (1871) 9 M. 516; *Price & Pierce Ltd v Bank of Scotland*, 1910 S.C. 1095; 1912 S.C. (HL) 19; for a fuller list and for further analysis of cash payments, transactions in the ordinary course of business and *nova debita*, see Wilson on *Debt*, pp.239–240.
[88] See *Secretary of State for Trade and Industry v Burn*, 1998 S.L.T. 1009.

(Scotland) Act 1972) provided that, where a company was being wound up in Scotland, a floating charge over all or any part of its property was not to be held an alienation or preference avoidable by statute (other than by that provision) or at common law on the ground of insolvency or notour bankruptcy. That provision has now been repealed. The previous doubt now resurfaces, and it is now an open question whether floating charges may be struck at under common law or under the provisions as to gratuitous alienations and unfair preferences under the Insolvency Act 1986. It is suggested that floating charges may now be reduced as gratuitous alienations or unfair preferences in terms of ss.242 and 243 of the Insolvency Act 1986 and at common law. Challenges under ss.242 and 243 are different in result to a challenge under s.245 of the Act. The different results as described later show why these should be seen as parallel challenges. The scheme of the Insolvency Act 1986 allows overlapping challenges in terms of different sections of that Act.

Avoidance of certain floating charges under section 245 of the Insolvency Act 1986

10–23   In relation to floating charges created after December 29, 1986 they may be reduced in terms of s.245. In relation to those created before December 29, 1986 they are only reducible to the extent that they would have been reducible under the law previously in force.[89] Unlike the provisions in relation to gratuitous alienations and unfair preferences, which were introduced on April 1, 1986 by the Bankruptcy (Scotland) Act 1985 amending the Companies Act 1985, this provision only came into force on December 29, 1986. Accordingly, the previous law applies to all floating charges created prior to December 29, 1986.

Floating charges created before December 29, 1986

10–24   Section 617 of the Companies Act 1985 provided that, where a floating charge had been created within 12 months of the commencement of a winding up, then unless it was proved that the company was solvent immediately after the creation of the charge it was to be invalid except to the amount of any cash paid to the company at the time of or subsequent to the creation of, and in consideration for, the charge, together with interest.

Provisions under section 245 of the Insolvency Act 1986

10–25   Section 245 of the Insolvency Act 1986 changed the law in several important aspects:

(1) Categories of floating charge holders

10–26   Section 245 divides floating charge holders into two categories: (a) connected persons; and (b) any other persons.

---

[89] Insolvency Act 1986, Sch.11, para.9.

A "connected person" is a person who is a director or shadow director of the company (i.e. a person in accordance with whose directions or instructions the directors are accustomed to act), or an associate of such person, or an associate of the company, "associate" being as defined by s.435 of the Insolvency Act 1986.[90]

(2) Time limits

In the case of floating charges created in favour of unconnected **10–27** persons, they are challengeable if created within 12 months of the commencement of winding up, where a company goes into liquidation, and within 12 months of the presentation of a petition for an administration order where there is an administration order.[91] In the case of persons connected with the company, the time limit is a period of two years ending with the presentation of the petition for an administration order, or the commencement of winding up.

(3) Defence to challenge

In the case of persons not connected with the company, the floating **10–28** charge may be challenged only if, at the time of the creating of the floating charge, the company was unable to pay its debts in terms of s.123 of the Insolvency Act 1986,[92] or became unable to pay its debts within the meaning of that section in consequence of the transaction under which the charge is created.[93] Accordingly, if it can be shown that at its creation, the company was solvent and not likely to become insolvent, the charge is not struck down.

The defence that the company was able to pay its debts, however, is not open, even to an unconnected person if the floating charge has been granted between the presentation of a petition for an administration order and the granting of the administration order or, in the case of an appointment by the company or its directors under para.22 of new Sch.22 to the Insolvency Act 1986, between the lodging of the notice of intention to appoint an administrator and the appointment.[94]

(4) Challenge to a floating charge

A successful challenge to a floating charge has the effect of invalidat- **10–29** ing the security created by the floating charge except to the extent of the aggregate of—

    (a) the value of so much of the consideration for the creation of the charge as consists of money paid, or goods or services supplied,

---

[90] Insolvency Act 1986, s.249.
[91] *ibid.*, s.245(3) and (5).
[92] See paras 4–106 to 4–111.
[93] Insolvency Act 1986, s.245(4).
[94] S.245(3) and (5) of the Insolvency Act 1086, as amended by para.31 of Sch.17 of the Enterprise Act 2002. Paragraph 31 is confused because the reference to the time between the notice of intention to appoint an administrator and the appointment in the case of an appointment under para.14 of Sch.B1 is not apt, since there is no notice to appoint in the case of such an appointment.

to the company at the same time as, or after, the creation of the charge;

(b) the value of so much of that consideration as consists of the discharge or reduction, at the same time as, or after, the creation of the charge, of any debt of the company; and

(c) the amount of such interest (if any) as is payable on the foregoing amount in pursuance of any agreement under which the money was paid for the goods or services supplied.[95]

In other words, the floating charge is invalidated except to the extent of new money granted in return for the floating charge or company debt reduced as a result of the granting of the floating charge, or interest on either of these. The floating charge is not allowed merely to secure debt already in place without new considerations being given.

As an extra safeguard, in the case of goods or services supplied, if an unrealistic price is set on them, the value of any goods or services supplied by way of a consideration for a floating charge is now by statute the amount in money which, at the time of their supply, could reasonably have been expected to be obtained for supplying them in the ordinary course of business and on the same terms (apart from the consideration) as those on which they were supplied to the company.[96] In deciding whether cash payments qualify for the exception, it is necessary to look at the substance to see whether the payments were truly made for the benefit of the company or were indirectly to give a preference to an existing creditor.[97]

The expression "at the same time as, or after the creation of the charge" in ss.245(2)(a) and (b) defines what is "new" and "old" consideration with respect to the consideration. The formalities of setting up a floating charge may mean external delays, in the case of *Power v Sharp Investments Ltd*,[98] the Court of Appeal stipulated that the simultaneous nature of the transactions had to be interpreted strictly, although with a degree of practical latitude as stated by Sir Christopher Slade:

"In a case where no presently existing charge has been created by any agreement or company resolution preceding the execution of the formal debenture . . . no moneys paid before the execution of the debenture will qualify for the exemption under [section 245(2)(a)], unless the interval between payment and execution is so short that it can be regarded as minimal and execution can be regarded as contemporaneous."

(5) Effect of challenge to a floating charge

10–30   A floating charge is only avoided (without reduction) in the course of an administration or a winding up under s.245 of the Insolvency Act 1986. The floating charge holder is then not entitled to rely on his

---

[95] Insolvency Act 1986, s.245(2).
[96] *ibid.*, s.245(6).
[97] *Libertas-Kommerz GmbH*, 1978 S.L.T. 222.
[98] [1993] B.C.C. 609.

security in an administration or a winding up to the extent that the security is invalidated in terms of s.245 of the Insolvency Act 1986 as described above. If, however, prior to the winding up or the administration, a receiver has been appointed under a floating charge and money ingathered for payment to the debenture holder, neither is the appointment of the receiver invalid nor the payment of sums towards the debenture holder reduced, if subsequently it is held that the floating charge is invalid. There also seems to be no reason why, in the course of a winding up, a receiver may not be appointed over assets secured by that part of the floating charge which is not invalidated. The effects described above differ radically from the effects of gratuitous alienations and unfair preferences which are struck at. In *Mace Builders (Glasgow) Ltd v Lunn*,[99] Scott J. compared the differing effects of a challenge under s.320 of the Companies Act 1948[1] with that of a floating charge avoided under s.322 of the Companies Act 1948.[2] He stated:

> "I have no difficulty in accepting counsel for the plaintiffs submission as to the effect of section 320 on a mortgage. The purpose of section 320 is to enable to be avoided transactions which constitute fraudulent preferences. If a mortgage is granted by way of a fraudulent preference, it is not only the charge which is tainted but the whole contents of the mortgagee's powers and remedies and the mortgagor's covenants for payment of principal and interest are as much a part of the fraudulent preference as the charge itself. The purpose of the fraudulent preference is to enable the creditor to obtain repayment with priority over the other creditors. It must follow that the avoidance of the transaction which constitutes the fraudulent preference will include the avoidance of the act whereby the creditor's debt is repaid. It is to be noted that section 320 in terms incorporates the law of bankruptcy. Fraudulent preference in bankruptcy is dealt with by section 44 of the Bankruptcy Act 1914. Subsection (1) of that section provides for the avoidance of transactions of fraudulent preference. Subsection (2) provides that: 'this section shall not affect the rights of any person taking title in good faith and for valuable consideration through or under a creditor of the bankrupt'.
>
> Accordingly, on the avoidance of a transaction under section 320, the position of purchasers who have dealt with the preferred creditor before the commencement of the bankruptcy is protected. Section 322 does not have any similar saving for the rights of the purchasers. If the effect of section 322 is, as counsel for the defendant contends, simply to avoid the charge in the winding-up, there is no need for any such saving. The validity of the pre-winding up transactions of the debenture holder or of a receiver appointed by the debenture holder are not affected by section 322.
>
> [The] subsection[3] reads: 'where a company is being wound up, a floating charge . . . shall be invalid.'' This is language which focuses

---

[99] [1986] Ch. 459; aff'd [1987] Ch. 191, CA.
[1] Companies Act 1985, s.615, now revised in Insolvency Act 1986, s.243.
[2] Subsequently Companies Act 1985, s.617, now revised extensively in Insolvency Act 1986, s.245.
[3] Companies Act 1948, s.322(1).

attention on the course of the winding up and which avoids the charge in and for the purpose of the winding up.

Counsel for the plaintiffs analogy with section 320 is not, in my view, an apt one. Section 320 incorporates the law of bankruptcy, and declares that transactions of fraudulent preference shall 'be invalid accordingly'. Section 322 has no analogous content. Further, the legislative intention under section 320 is to avoid transactions of fraudulent preference. It is inherent in that intention that transactions which pre-date the commencement of the winding up or bankruptcy will have to be set aside. But I can discern in section 322 no legislative intention beyond an intention that in the circumstances specified in the section, the debenture holder should not be permitted in the winding up to have the benefit of the security. That intention does not, in order to be satisfied, require more than that the charge cannot be relied on in the winding up."

The differing effects support the contention that different grounds of challenge are open against floating charges, the most root and branch being that it is an unfair preference or gratuitous alienation. It could also be challenged as an extortionate credit transaction under s.244 of the Insolvency Act 1986 as described in the following sections.

English cases of *Re M.C. Bacon Ltd and Re M C Bacon (No 2) Ltd*

10–31   Decisions of Millett J. in *Re M.C. Bacon Ltd*[4] and *Re M.C. Bacon Ltd (No 2)*[5] have been treated by certain authorities as of significance in relation to the granting of securities by insolvent companies to their banks. The facts of the case were briefly as follows: M.C. Bacon Limited ("the company") went into creditors' voluntary liquidation on August 24, 1987 with an estimated deficiency as regards unsecured creditors of £329,435. At the date of liquidation the company's overdraft at the National Westminster Bank ("the Bank") stood at £235,530. The overdraft was secured by a fixed and floating charge dated May 20, 1987. On September 4, 1987 the bank demanded payment and on the same date it appointed an administrative receiver. Mr Ian Clark ("the liquidator") was appointed liquidator of the company at a meeting of creditors on September 7, 1987, thereby replacing a liquidator who had been appointed on August 24, 1987. On September 28, 1987 he issued an application seeking (1) to have the bank's security set aside, (a) under s.239 of the Insolvency Act 1986 as a voidable preference or (b) under s.238 of the Insolvency Act 1986 as a transaction at an undervalue; and (2) a declaration under s.214 of the Insolvency Act 1986 that the bank was liable to make a substantial contribution to the company's assets on the ground that, for the last few months of the company's life, it had been a shadow director of the company and had thereby rendered itself responsible for what was alleged to have been wrongful trading by the company. An application by the bank to strike out the proceedings

---

[4] 1990 B.C.C. 78; [1990] B.C.L.C. 324; the approach was also followed in *Re Ledingham-Smith* [1993] B.C.L.C. 635.

[5] [1990] 3 W.L.R. 646; [1990] B.C.L.C. 607; [1991] Ch. 127.

failed before Knox J., and the trial began before Millet J. on October 23, 1989. It lasted for 17 days. On the twelfth day of the trial and, after nearly six days of oral evidence, the liquidator abandoned the wrongful trading claim. The bank led no evidence. On November 30, 1989, Millet J. dismissed the proceedings on the basis that the transaction did not amount to a preference under s.239 of the Insolvency Act 1986, and that the creation of the security over the company's assets did not come within s.238(4)(b) of the Insolvency Act 1986 since it did not diminish or deplete the value of the assets. He also ordered the liquidator to pay the costs personally. Subsequently the liquidator unsuccessfully sought an order that the liquidator should be reimbursed so far as possible for the bank's costs which he had been ordered to pay, and for his own costs out of the assets subject only to the bank's floating charge, as "expenses incurred in the winding up" within the meaning of s.115 of the Insolvency Act 1986 and "expenses of the winding up" within s.175(2)(a) of that Act. In the course of his judgments after these hearings, Millet J. held:

(1) Because in terms of s.239(5) an order striking at a preference in England and Wales, may not be made unless the company which gave the preference was influenced in deciding to give it by a desire to create a preference, it was incumbent upon the party seeking to have a prior transaction set aside as a voidable preference to establish that the debtor company "positively wished" to improve the creditor's position in the event of its own insolvent liquidation. Section 239(5) did not require that this motive should have been a dominant factor influencing the decision to enter into the transaction, nor even that it should have had any special force in "tipping the scales" nor have been a *"sine qua non"*. All that was required by the subsection was that the requisite desire should have "influenced" the decision; which is hardly an exacting requirement, if all that has to be shown is that this was one of the factors which operated on the minds of those who made the decision.

(2) The relevant time at which the requisite desire had to be shown to have been operative was the time when the decision was taken to grant the preference, rather than the actual date of the transaction.

(3) Because in terms of s.238(4)(b) for there to be a transaction at undervalue in England and Wales, the company has to enter into a transaction with a person for a consideration the value of which . . . is significantly less than the value . . . of the consideration provided by the company, the creation of a security over a company's assets was not caught by that subsection since it did not diminish or deplete the value of the assets.

(4) Any sums recovered from a creditor who has been wrongly preferred enures for the benefit of the general body of creditors, not for the benefit of the company or the holder of a floating charge. It does not become part of the company's assets but is received by the liquidator impressed with a trust in favour of those creditors among whom he has to distribute the assets of the company. *Re Yagerphone Ltd*[6] was still the

---

[6] [1935] Ch. 392.

law in England and Wales, notwithstanding s.239(3) of the Insolvency Act 1986, which empowers the court on finding a voidable preference proved to make such order as it thinks fit for "restoring the position to what it would have been if the company had not given that preference", and s.241(1)(c) which empowers the court to "release or discharge . . . any security given by the company". Those powers were not intended to be exercised so as to enable a debenture holder to obtain the benefit of the proceedings brought by the liquidator.

It has been suggested by certain authorities that the decisions of Millet have important implications. For example, Professor Ian F. Fletcher, in discussing the first judgment,[7] states:

> "This decision will be welcomed by companies and by banks and by other institutional lenders alike, for it ensures that, provided the company is motivated only by proper commercial considerations, it is possible for a company in economic difficulties to seek financial assistance, and to effect a security in exchange for the injection of fresh funds into the company, without the risk that the lender's security will be subsequently rendered voidable in the event of the company's insolvency. This surely accords with common sense, and with commercial expediency, and is also consistent with the traditional concept of what should amount to an impeachable preference, namely a debtor's conscious attempt in contemplation of the onset of insolvency to place certain creditors—typically friends, relatives or associates—in an advantageous position vis-à-vis the general body of creditors. Such conduct is readily distinguishable from the orthodox commercial practice of a prudent lender taking a standard form of registrable security in the context of providing the funds for the company's continued effort to trade through a period of crisis."

It is thought by the authors that the Scottish courts should take a very guarded approach to the findings in *Re M.C. Bacon Ltd*[8] for a number of reasons. First the authors can see no reason why a floating charge granted in the circumstances of that case would not be caught by the provisions of s.245 of the Insolvency Act 1986. Though new money was granted, the floating charge was mainly to secure old money and hence would have been invalid to that extent in terms of s.245(2) of the Insolvency Act 1986. The company certainly was insolvent within 12 months of the date of the creation of the floating charge, and hence would be caught by s.245(3)(b) of the Insolvency Act 1986. It may even have been caught by s.245(3)(a) of that Act if the bank had been found to be a "shadow director" and hence a "connected" person in terms of

---

[7] The *Journal of Business Law* (1991) at p.74; see *Barclays Bank plc v Homan*, Independent, September 1, 1992 (aff'd C.A. [1992] B.C.C. 757), where Hoffmann J. accepted that a "subjective intention" to prefer was necessary if s.239 of the Insolvency Act 1986 were invoked in an English administration, but refused an injunction preventing ancillary US examiner applying to US court for recovery under para.541 of US Bankruptcy Code in terms of which no intention was necessary.

[8] 1990 B.C.C. 78; [1990] B.C.L.C. 324.

s.249 of that Act. This ground of challenge does not seem to have been pled in that case. Secondly, it is thought that, in Scotland, the granting of a security would be caught by the gratuitous alienation provision of s.242(4)(b) when read with s.242(6) of the Insolvency Act 1986. Even where a company is solvent, secured debt is more valuable than unsecured debt. For there to be adequate consideration, with a solvent company there would have to be a premium to reflect the upgrading in the value of a debt in translating it from an unsecured to a secured debt. The less creditworthy a company becomes, the greater is the premium in value of its secured debt over its unsecured debt. If a company in any circumstances grants a floating charge over its whole business and undertaking, it is giving up the right to grant other persons a first charge; which is an economic asset of a company. Thirdly, in Scotland there is no equivalent provision of s.239(5) of the Insolvency Act 1986. "Desire" is not necessary in terms of the Scottish s.243 of the Insolvency Act 1986 to create a preference. A transaction is struck at, which creates a preference, unless it falls within the exceptions.

It is difficult to see how the transaction mentioned in *Re M.C. Bacon Ltd*,[9] could come within the Scottish excepting provisions. It is not a payment in cash for a debt which has become payable in terms of s.243(2)(b) of the Insolvency Act 1986. It is not a transaction whereby the parties undertake reciprocal obligations in terms of s.243(2)(c) because there was not strict equivalence in value of the obligations as required in Scotland.[10] It is finally difficult to see how the transaction could be classed as "a transaction in the ordinary course of trade or business" and be covered by s.243(2)(a) of the Insolvency Act 1986. Although the type of transaction mentioned in *Re M.C. Bacon Ltd* may happen often in the business world, it is not "in the ordinary course" of trade or business. It is an extraordinary transaction if but for it, the ordinary course of business or trade ceases.[11] In relation to Millet J.'s finding that property made over to a company following an order under s.239 of the Insolvency Act 1986 does not form part of the assets of the company and accordingly would not be attached by a floating charge, see para.8–19.

EXTORTIONATE CREDIT TRANSACTIONS

In terms of s.244 of the Insolvency Act 1986, an administrator or a **10–32** liquidator may seek a court order in relation to transactions under which credit has been extended to a company within the period of three years ending with the day on which the administration order was made or the commencement of the liquidation.

Definition of "extortionate"

In terms of s.244(3) of the Insolvency Act 1986 "a transaction is **10–33** extortionate if, having regard to the risk accepted by the person providing the credit—(a) the terms of it are or were such as to require

---

[9] [1990] B.C.C. 78; [1990] B.C.L.C. 324.
[10] See *Peter Nicoll v Steelpress (Supplies) Ltd*, 1992 S.C.L.R. 332.
[11] See *Bob Gray (Access) Ltd*, 1987 S.C.L.R. 720 and cases cited there.

grossly exorbitant payments to be made (whether unconditionally or in certain contingencies) in respect of the provision of the credit, or (b) it otherwise grossly contravened ordinary principles of fair dealing."

The definition is largely modelled on the provisions in ss.137 to 139 of the Consumer Credit Act 1974, which allowed the re-opening of extortionate creditor bargains in cases falling within the ambit of that Act.

The test of "grossly exorbitant" in relation to the payments will be a question of fact and circumstance. There is a presumption in terms of s.244(3) that a transaction is extortionate, unless the contrary is proved. The power which the liquidator or administrator has to strike at a credit transaction under s.244 is in addition to his right to strike at the transaction as a gratuitous alienation under s.242 of the Insolvency Act 1986.

Remedies under section 244 of the Insolvency Act 1986

10–34 An order under s.244 may contain one or more of the following provisions:

(a) a provision setting aside the whole or part of any obligation created by the transaction;

(b) a provision otherwise varying the terms of the transaction or varying the terms on which any security for the purposes of the transaction is held;

(c) a provision requiring any person who is or was a party to the transaction to pay to the office holder any sums paid to that person, by virtue of the transaction, by the company;

(d) a provision requiring any person to surrender to the office holder any property held by him as security for the purposes of the transaction;

(e) a provision directing accounts to be taken between any persons.

CHAPTER 11

EMPLOYMENT LAW AND PENSIONS

Format of Chapter

In this chapter, Part I deals with the effect of liquidations, administra- **11–01** tions and receiverships on contracts of employment; Part II deals with the particular problems associated with the Transfer of Undertakings (Protection of Employment) Regulations 1981[1] ("TUPE") in the context of corporate insolvency; and Part III deals with Pensions and Corporate Insolvency.

PART I

Effect of Liquidations, Administrations and Receiverships on Contracts of Employment

Liquidations

The legal effect of a winding up order, or winding up, was not **11–02** judicially considered in depth in any reported case until 1978, when the First Division (the Scottish Appeal Court) in the case of *Smith v Lord Advocate*[2] looked at the effects of liquidation.[3] The case, however, was concerned with whether there was a change of employer on the appointment of a liquidator. Having decided that there was not, the court went on to hold that there was continuous employment as far as redundancy payments were concerned from the date of the company's employment of the employees initially until eventual dismissal by the liquidator on the grounds of redundancy. The court did not have to decide the legal effect of a winding up order on contracts of employment. However, Counsel for the Lord Advocate (the future Lord Chancellor Lord McKay of Clashfern) argued that a winding up order acted as "constructive notice" of termination but did not itself terminate the contract. This legal expression was also used by Lord Stormonth

---

[1] SI 1981/1794 as amended primarily by SI 1987/442.
[2] 1978 S.C. 259.
[3] The liquidation in question was the liquidation of Upper Clyde Shipbuilders Ltd. The liquidation was important politically in leading to the Heath Administration's change of policy in the face of rising unemployment. It was also legally important in that the government showed that it did not regard itself as constitutionally bound to underwrite the debts of a limited company in public ownership in the same way that it constitutionally underwrote the debts of nationalised industries, although not necessarily of certain statutory bodies in public ownership, *e.g.* Mersey Docks Board.

Darling in the case of *Day v Tait*[4] in holding that, where an employer acts in a particular way (such as in that case going into insolvent liquidation), he can be held to have committed a breach of contract sufficiently serious in employment law to amount to constructive notice of termination, entitling the employee no longer to be bound by the contract and to claim damages. It is suggested by the authors, following *Day v Tait* (above), that a winding up order amounts to repudiatory breach entitling the employee to affirm the contract or to treat it as discharged. If he elects to treat the contract as discharged he must do so within a reasonable period.[5] Otherwise the contract of employment continues.

In England the position is slightly different. The effect of the making of a winding up order by the court on the contract of employment in England is that, from the date of its publication,[6] the order has the effect of automatically dismissing all the employees of the company with immediate effect.[7]

In relation to voluntary windings up, the law depends on the circumstances of the winding up. In England, the mere fact of a voluntary winding up has been held not to operate as dismissal,[8] but a voluntary winding up coupled with the sale of the company's business has been held to operate as a dismissal.[9] For the purpose of determining in a voluntary liquidation whether there has been dismissal the following facts have been held to be relevant in England: whether the company is solvent or insolvent[10]; whether the company has previously intimated to the relevant employee that his employment is likely to terminate on liquidation[11]; whether the liquidation involves the immediate cessation of the company's business and whether the employee's continuation in office is inconsistent with the role of the liquidator, *e.g.* the case of the managing director.[12] The Scottish cases of *Day v Tait* (above) and *Smith v Lord Advocate* (above) suggest that the insolvency of the company is the key aspect; which is consistent with the underlying reasoning running through the English cases; namely "can the employee rely on having a job and being paid his wages?" In relation to all types of winding up, there are constraints on the liquidator carrying on the business. The liquidator in a voluntary winding up has only a limited power to continue to carry on the business of the company so far as it is necessary for the beneficial winding up of the company.[13] The effect of

---

[4] (1900) 8 S.L.T. 40.

[5] *Crown Estate Commissioners v Liquidators of Highland Engineering Ltd*, 1975 S.L.T. 58.

[6] See *Re General Rolling Co; Chapman's* case (1866) L.R. 1 Eq. 346.

[7] See *Re General Rolling Co; Re Oriental Bank Corp.; MacDowall's* case (1886) 32 Ch. D. 366; and *Commercial Finance Co Ltd v Ramsingh-Mahabir* [1994] 1 W.L.R. 1297.

[8] *Midland Counties District Bank Ltd v Attwood* [1905] 1 Ch. D. 357; *Fox v Bryant*, 1979 I.C.R. 64

[9] *Reigate v Union Manufacturing Co* [1918] 1 K.B. 592.

[10] *Gerard v Worth of Paris* [1936] 2 All E.R. 1905; *Fowler v Commercial Timber* [1930] 2 K.B. 1; *Reigate Union Manufacturing Co* [1918] 1 K.B. 592.

[11] *Reigate v Union Manufacturing Co*, above.

[12] *Fowler v Commercial Timber Co* [1930] 2 K.B. 1 at 16.

[13] Insolvency Act 1986, s.87.

the passing of a resolution for the voluntary winding up of a company is that the company is likely to cease to carry on business after a short time, which will terminate the employment of all the employees. In the case of a compulsory winding up the carrying on of the company's business again is allowed so far as may be necessary for its beneficial winding up, but only with the sanction of the court or the creditors' committee.[14]

Continuity of employment

If the business of the company in liquidation is carried on and the **11–03** continued employment is accepted by the employee, the employee's contract of employment with the company continues.[15] This Scottish formulation is different to the English formulation in terms of which the company through the liquidator and the employee are held to have agreed that there has been no termination of employment.[16] However, even in a TUPE situation (see below) it is difficult to see when the different approaches could matter.

Administrators and receivers

The appointment of an administrator or a receiver has been held not **11–04** in itself to act as constructive notice of dismissal or terminate the contract of employment.[17] In the case of an administration, the reason for this approach was that the primary purpose of the appointment of the administrator was to preserve the continuation of the business of the company. However, in the case of *Re Atlantic Computers Systems plc*[18] the Court of Appeal suggested that the position of an administrator was closer in some respects to that of a liquidator than to that of the receiver. The key difference between the two regimes was that, in the case of a winding up a company, the company had reached the end of its life, whereas an administration was intended to be only an interim and temporary regime. It is thought by the authors that in all cases of administration (whether by application to the court under paragraph 12, or by an out of court appointment under paras 14[19] or 22, of new Sch.14 to the Insolvency Act 1986) the company has to be certified as unable to pay its debts or likely to be unable to pay its debts.[20] Only if the administration purpose likely to be achieved is the first purpose of rescuing the company as a going concern (with a likelihood of employment being preserved) is the presumption of likely or actual insolvency displaced. It is thought that unless the presumption is displaced, the

---

[14] Insolvency Act 1986, s.167(1)(a) and Sch.4, para.5; see for limits on the powers of liquidators to carry on business: *Re Wreck Recovery and Salvage Co* (1880) 25 Ch. D353; and *Re Great Eastern Electric Co Ltd* [1941] Ch. 241.

[15] *McEwan v Upper Clyde Shipbuilders Ltd* (1972) 13 K.I.R. 141 and *Smith v Lord Advocate* (1978) S.C. 259.

[16] See *Re English Joint Stock Bank, ex Harding* (1867) 3 Eq. 341; *Re Oriental Bank Corp.; McDowall's case* (1886) 32 Ch. D. 366; *Reid v The Explosives Co Ltd* (1887) 19 Q.B.D. 265.

[17] *Powdrill v Watson* [1995] 2 A.C. 394 at 448F.

[18] [1992] Ch. 505; [1992] 1 All E.R. 476.

[19] Except where in terms of para.18(2)(b) of new Sch.14 to the Insolvency Act 1986, the floating charge is enforceable only by a reason other than the insolvency of the company.

[20] Paras 11(2), 18(2)(b) and 27(2)(a) of new Sch.14 to the Insolvency Act 1986.

company entering administration works as constructive notice of dismissal as in the case of an insolvent liquidation. However, it is accepted that the position has not been clearly settled in Scotland, and that making the type of analysis required for this approach is not helped by the way the purposes of administration are run together in the Enterprise Act 2002, making the necessary distinctions difficult to arrive at.

In the case of an administration and a receivership, the company remains the employer.[21] There is also continuity of employment with a company where a receiver arranges for it to continue to trade.[22]

Adoption of contracts by administrators and receivers

11–05　　Prior to amending legislation in the Insolvency Act 1994, the courts in a series of cases identified an anomaly in former ss.19 and 44 (equivalent of s.44 in Scotland is s.57) of the Insolvency Act 1986, in terms of which contracts of employment, "adopted" by receivers and administrators, were respectively subject to a personal guarantee of receivers, or, in the case of administrators, given a first charge over the assets of the company. These cases were subject to a combined appeal to the House of Lords with judgments given in March 1995,[23] by which time Parliament had already enacted the Insolvency Act 1994 to deal with the perceived mischief. The amending legislation corrected the perceived anomaly in relation to contracts of employment adopted in administrations and receiverships/administrative receiverships after March 15, 1994. In theory contracts adopted prior to that may still be subject in certain rare circumstances to the unamended insolvency law. However, given the distance in time and the limitations on bringing actions, it is not proposed to deal with the effect of the unamended provisions or the legal history.[24]

In Scotland the provision as regards receivers is now set out in s.57 of the Insolvency Act 1986, as amended by s.3 of the Insolvency Act 1994. The comparable position in relation to administrators is now contained in para.99(4) to (6) of new Sch.14 to the Insolvency Act 1986. The position of administrators and receivers/administrative receivers is still slightly different. Receivers incur personal liability in terms of the statute (except of course—as is usual—to the extent that they provide otherwise in the contract), although they may be indemnified out of the assets of the company if these are adequate. In contrast where the adoption provision gives employees in an administration priority, this becomes a first charge over the assets of the company, i.e. it ranks before a floating charge. The amending legislation clarified that for contracts adopted on or after March 15, 1994, special priority was only given for a "qualifying liability".[25] The term "qualifying liability" was defined so that it was limited to a liability under the contract of employment:

---

[21] *Powdrill v Watson* [1995] 2 A.C. 394 at 448F.

[22] *Re Mack Trucks (Britain) Ltd* [1987] 1 A11 E.R. 977 at 982.

[23] *Paramount Airways, Leyland Daf and Ferranti, sub nom. Powdrill v Watson* [1995] 2 A.C. 394.

[24] For an analysis see Palmer's *Company Law* (Sweet & Maxwell), Vol.3, paras 14.049.1–9 and 14.225.1–9; and D. Pollard, Corporate *Insolvency: Employment and Pension Rights*, (Butterworths, 2000), paras 9.63–9.130.

[25] Ss.19(6) and 57(2) of the Insolvency Act 1986.

(a) to pay a sum by way of wages or salary or contribution to an occupational pension scheme[26];

(b) incurred while the administrator or receiver (in England administrator/receiver) is in office[27]; and

(c) which is in respect of services rendered wholly or partly after the adoption of the contract of employment.[28]

These provisions have been re-enacted in similar terms in para.99(4) to (6) of new Sch.14 to the Insolvency Act 1986, with the main difference being that the expression "qualifying liability" has been dropped. Holiday pay including pay in lieu of holiday is covered by para.99 (6)(a) and (c) of new Sch.14 to, and s.57(2C)(b) of, the Insolvency Act 1986.

What is covered by "wages or salary"[29] and contributions to an occupational pension scheme[30] is important. The key fact is that under the current law priority is limited to ongoing claims for cash payment. Excluded therefore are statutory claims (*e.g.* for unfair dismissal) and contractual non-cash claims (*e.g.* for benefit in kind) which are not liabilities under a contract of employment. Claims for back wages and termination claims are also excluded in so far as they will not be with reference to anything done or which occurs after the adoption of the contract of employment. Pension contributions will be covered if contractual including a money purchase occupational scheme.[31] The term "occupational pension scheme" is not defined, but it would appear probable that the definition in s.1 of the Pensions Scheme Act 1993 would be applied. On that basis any liability to a personal pension scheme would not be covered (except to the extent that it would fall within the definition of an occupational pension scheme).[32] The personal liability of the insolvency practitioner is to the employee; so, for example, trustees of a pension scheme may not enforce the liability directly unless the insolvency practitioner has taken some other step to adopt liabilities to the scheme.

Order of priority in receiverships/No special priority if contracts of employment simply continued

The changes introduced by the Insolvency Act 1994 did not change **11–06** the order of priorities in a receivership set out in s.60 (of which there is no comparable provision in England and Wales) of the Insolvency Act 1986. Section 60(1)(c) gave creditors a special priority over a receiver in respect of the receiver's liabilities, expenses and remuneration, and any indemnity to which he is entitled out of the property of the company "in respect of all liabilities, charges and expenses incurred by or on behalf of

---

[26] Insolvency Act 1996, ss.19(7)(a) and 57(2A)(a).

[27] *ibid.*, s.19(6) and 57(2A)(b).

[28] *ibid.*, s.19(7)(b) and 57(2A)(c).

[29] *ibid.*, para.99(5) and (6) of new Sch.14.

[30] *ibid.*, para.99(6)(e) of new Sch.14.

[31] See *Paramount Airways* [1993] B.C.C. 662 at 675C–D, *per* Evans-Lamb J. at first instance.

[32] For a discussion of candidate pension claims for inclusion see D. Pollard, *Corporate Insolvency: Employment and Pension Rights* (Butterworths, 2000).

the receiver". In the case of *Roger Lindop v Stuart Noble & Sons Ltd*,[33] the Inner House (the Scottish Court of Appeal) held that a receiver adopting a contract of employment in Scotland did not give the employee this special priority over the receiver's claims. To come within the terms of s.60(1)(c) the liabilities would have to be confined to new contractual obligations incurred by the receiver in the performance of his functions. It could apply not only to a new contract but also, depending on the particular circumstances, to the amendment of or innovation upon an existing contract, so long as, on a proper construction, a new contractual obligation was thereby incurred. Simply to continue an existing contract of employment in force and thereby to adopt it, as had happened in that case, did not involve the incurring of a new contractual obligation.

PART II

TUPE IN THE CONTEXT OF CORPORATE INSOLVENCY

11–07 The Transfer of Undertakings (Protection of Employment) Regulations 1981[34] ("TUPE") were designed to implement the Acquired Rights Directive[35] but, in fact, from the insolvency practitioner's point of view differ in several key respects from the Directives. The "Acquired Rights Directive" was "on the approximation of the laws of the Member States relating to the safeguarding of employees' rights in the event of transfers of undertakings, business or parts of business". The Directive did not make any exception where the transferring business had become insolvent or had entered into insolvency proceedings. However, in *Abels v Administrative Board of the Bedrijfsvereniging voor de Metaalindustrie en de Electrotechnische Industrie*[36] the European Court of Justice ruled that the Acquired Rights Directive did not apply to transfers "where the transferor had been adjudged insolvent and the undertaking or business in question formed part of the assets of the insolvent transferor". In that case Mr Abels worked for a Dutch company which ran into difficulties. On September 2, 1981 a judicial order was made protecting the company from its creditors and it was finally put into liquidation on June 9, 1982. The liquidator sold the undertaking to another company which took over the business and most of the workforce. The Dutch court asked the ECJ to rule whether the Acquired Rights Directive applied to such an insolvency, or if it would have applied to a sale during the currency of the judicial protection from creditors. Having answered the first question that the Directive did not apply to such an insolvency, the court

---

[33] 1999 S.C.L.R. at 889.

[34] SI 1981/1794 as amended by the Transfer of Undertakings (Protection of Employment) (Amendment) Regulations 1987 (SI 1987/442), the Trade Union Reform and Employment Rights Act 1993, the Collective Redundancies and Transfer of Undertakings (Protection of Employment) (Amendment) Regulations 1995 (SI 1995/2587) and the Collective Redundancies and Transfer of Undertakings (Protection of Employment) (Amendment) Regulations 1999 (SI 1999/1925).

[35] Initially enacted as Council Directive EEC/77/187 and now Council Directive 2001/23/EC.

[36] [1985] E.C.R. 469; [1987] 2 C.M.L.R. 406; followed in *D'Urso v Ercole Marelli Elettromeccanica Generale (C-363/89)* [1992] I.R.L.R. 136, ECJ; [1993] 3 C.M.L.R. 513.

replied that it would have applied to a transfer during the currency of judicial protection from creditors.

There are good economic reasons why the Acquired Rights Directive did not apply to transfers from an insolvent entity. The main reason is that it is easier to find a purchaser or "rescuer" of a going concern if the purchaser can take on the workforce without assuming responsibility for all their accumulated rights while employed by the previous employer. The level, or even the uncertainty, of these liabilities could deter potential buyers of the business and hence lead to the break-up of an otherwise viable concern.[37]

A second reason why it might not be thought sensible to apply the Acquired Rights Directive to insolvency situations is that it privileges one group of creditors over another and has the *de facto* effect of upsetting the *pari passu* principle. This is because the purchaser of a business taking over the employees would take over their accumulated contractual entitlements and, provided the acquirer is financially sound, secure the entitlements of the transferring employees. Because the acquiring purchaser will insist on paying less for the business than he otherwise would have without the accumulated liabilities, not only do the transferring employees gain a privileged position in relation to the other creditors, but the assets of the insolvent firm are lessened and thus less is available to pay the other creditors. A third drawback of the approach is that only those workers who transfer have their entitlements secured. Thus, one group of workers may be privileged over another group of workers. Therefore, applying the Directive to insolvencies potentially leads to discrimination against creditors who are not employees and discrimination between groups of employees.

Although the Acquired Rights Directive was designed to exclude transfers out of insolvency, applying the terms of the Directive to such situations is permitted by virtue of Art.7 of the Directive, which states that the Directive does not affect the right of Member States to introduce laws which are more favourable to employees. The ECJ so held in the case of *Botzen v Rotterdamsche Droogdok Mattschappij BV*.[38] The UK Government introduced in TUPE provisions that in some regards may go beyond the EC worker protection legislation.

The fact that TUPE was not intended to exclude transfers from insolvent companies is indicated by reg.4, which covers hive-downs by receivers, administrators and liquidators in creditors' voluntary winding ups. The fact that members' voluntary winding ups are not referred to is because there is no question of their exclusion in so far as there is no insolvency. Compulsory winding ups are not referred to, and this must be taken as intended, presumably on the basis that, under English law, there would be an automatic dismissal of all employees. This is

---

[37] The Council's and the EC's views on this matter appear to be unchanged. See, *e.g.* Directive 98/50 EC, Arts (7) and (8).

[38] [1986] 2 C.M.L.R. 50.

anomalous because this is not the law in Scotland, and in England there is always the possibility of the liquidator and the dismissed employee agreeing to the continuation of the employment. However, as the TUPE Regulations operate so as to transfer employees employed in an undertaking (or part of one) immediately before the transfer,[39] any employees who have agreed a continuation with the company throught the liquidator in such a situation would nevertheless be protected under the TUPE Regulations.

Hive-downs/Transfers

11–08   The general principles of TUPE applicable to transfers from solvent entities apply to transfers from insolvent entities which are covered by TUPE. An exception to the normal rules is provided for in reg.4 in relation to hive-downs. These are transfers from receivers, administrators and liquidators in creditors' voluntary winding ups. The regulation therefore encompasses transfers from receiverships which do not necessarily involve a determination that a company is insolvent, which are likely to be covered by the Acquired Rights Directive.[40] Regulation 4 also encompasses transfers from administrations concerned with the survival and sale of the business as a going concern, which are also likely to be within the scope of the Acquired Rights Directive.[41] Transfers from administrations concerned with a more advantageous realisation of the company's assets without the sale of the business as a going concern will be outwith the scope of the Acquired Rights Directive, as will transfers from creditors' voluntary winding ups, which are also outwith the scope of the Directive.[42]

Hiving-down (which is less common now following the change in the tax position in relation to tax losses effected by the Finance Act 1986) is the practice by which the insolvency practitioner transfers the undertaking in which the employees are employed to a new company, with the intention of selling the new company free of the problems of the insolvent entity. Under normal TUPE rules, the employees would transfer at the same time as the undertaking is hived-down, which would mean that if there were then to be no sale of the hived-down undertaking, the employees would have lost their special rights in the initial insolvency. A further reason for the special provision was probably to give the insolvency practitioner time to select employees for dismissal before the ultimate on sale of the hived-down entity to the third party, so that only selected employees transferred under the rule. However, in the case of *Litster v Forth Dry Dock & Engineering Co Ltd* (in receivership),[43] the House of Lords held that TUPE must be construed

---

[39] See TUPE, reg.5(3).
[40] See *Mythen v Employment Appeals Tribunal* [1990] 1 I.R. 98 (a decision of the Irish High Court).
[41] See *Spano v Fiat Geotech SpP* [1995] E.C.R. 1–4321; *Jules Dethier Equipement SA v Jules Dassy* [1998] I.R.L.R. 266.
[42] The analysis of the scope of TUPE as regards the various insolvency regimes given in this paragraph is supported by *dicta* in the EAT decision in *Perth and Kinross Council v Donaldson* [2004] I.R.L.R. 121.
[43] [1990] 1 A.C. 546.

"purposely" to afford the employees the protection intended by the Directive. In that case this required finding that employees would have been employed immediately before the transfer within the terms of the Regulations had they not been dismissed unfairly for a reason connected to the transfer which followed shortly afterwards. Therefore those employees who had been dismissed were also to be taken to have transferred to the purchasing company. It was accepted that it was open to the transferee to argue that the employees had not been dismissed unfairly but for an economic, technical or organisational reason within reg.8. However, in that case this had not been demonstrated. Again using the "purpose" test, the court held in *Re Maxwell Fleet & Facilities Management Ltd (in administration) (No.2)*[44] that, where a company in administrative receivership had passed on its business through a series of transactions via a subsidiary company to a third company, the series of transactions should be interpreted as in substance a single trans-action, amounting to a protected transfer under reg.4 sufficient to pass on liability for the employees to the transferee company.

TUPE and pensions

Regulation 5 of TUPE broadly provides for all the rights, powers, **11–09** duties and liabilities of the transferor employer to be automatically assumed by the transferee. Regulation 7, however, currently provides an exclusion for rights under or relating to occupational pension schemes. The exclusion has the effect of reducing the range of protection of the employee. The employee is left with his preserved rights under the company's scheme but with no entitlement to pension rights as regards future service or as regards any shortfall resulting from his having been treated as an early leaver in the transferor's scheme in relation to past service.

Although Art.3(3) of the Acquired Rights Directive provides an exclusion for pension schemes in respect of an employee's right to old age, invalidity or survivors' benefits under supplementary company or inter-company pension schemes outside the statutory social security schemes in Member States, s.33 of the Trade Union Reform and Employment Rights Act 1993 amended reg.7 of TUPE for transfers after August 30, 1993. The amendment clarified that any provisions in an occupational pension scheme that did not relate to benefits for old age, invalidity or survivors were to be treated as part of the scheme. This could cover, for example, redundancy or early retirement benefits, provided that the benefit does not itself consist of a pension.[45]

---

[44] [2000] 2 All E.R. 860; [2000] I.R.L.R. 368.

[45] See *Frankling v BPS Public Sector Ltd* [1999] I.C.R. 347; and *Beckmann v Dynamco, Whicheloe, MacFarlane* [2002] I.R.L.R. 578; [2002] All E.R. (EC) 865. In the *Beckmann* case, Beckmann had been employed by the NHS and her employment was transferred to DWM under TUPE. When DWM dismissed her for redundancy it refused to pay her the early retirement pension, lump sum and other benefits to which she would have been entitled under the NHS scheme on the grounds that those benefits were excluded from TUPE. The ECJ held that: "early retirement benefits and benefits intended to enhance the conditions of such retirement, paid in the event of dismissal to employees who have reached a certain age, such as the benefits in the main proceedings, are not old-age, invalidity or survivors' benefits within the meaning of Article 3(3) of Council Directive 77/187/EEC". This approach was also followed in *Martin v South Bank University (Case C-4/01)* [2004] I.C.M.L.R. 15; [2004] I.R.L.R. 74. Clauses 203 and 204 of the Pensions Bill 2004 going through Parliament at the date of writing this book will effectively abolish the exclusion, if passed as presently drafted.

Directive 2002/74 EC

11–10 Some of the rights of employees referred to earlier in this chapter are embodied and/or expressed in Pt XIII of the Employment Rights Act 1996. The rights set out in that Part stem from Directive 80/987 EC on protection of employees in the event of the insolvency of their employer. Directive 2002/74 EC amends the 1980 Directive. Member States are to implement the amending Directive's provisions by October 8, 2005. In brief, the aim of the 2002 Directive is to "ensure equitable protection for . . . employees concerned", where their employer is insolvent, and one means of doing that is to redefine "insolvency" to include within the concept insolvency proceedings other than liquidation. Member States are directed to clarify the arrangements under which employees pay claims will be met in the event of their employer's insolvency.[46]

PART III

PENSIONS AND CORPORATE INSOLVENCY

Contractual obligations and trusts

11–11 Where a company with a pension scheme becomes insolvent, the rights and liabilities of the employing company in relation to the scheme will depend on whether or not a trust exists. If the pension scheme is a simple contractual obligation of the company to pay a pension at a later date, or a promise to contribute to a personal pension scheme, an employee of the insolvent company will have no greater remedies than those of any other unsecured creditors.

This general rate is subject to the proviso that certain contributions owed by the employing company to occupational pension schemes and state scheme premiums are made preferential debts being category four under Sch.6 to the Insolvency Act 1986 (amounts owed by the company which fall within Sch.4 of the Pensions Schemes Acts 1993).[47] Schedule 4 to the Pension Schemes Act 1993 covers (a) any sum owed on account of an employee's contributions to an occupational pension scheme (not a personal pension scheme) that has been deducted by the employer from earnings paid to the employee during the four months preceding the relevant date or otherwise due in respect of earnings paid or payable in that period but not yet paid into the scheme[48]; (b) any sum owed on account of an employer's contributions to a contracted-out scheme (*i.e.*

---

[46] See also Directive 03/41/EC on the activities and supervision of institutions for occupational retirement provisions, which covers provision of security for pensions, but is of more general application than just insolvency.

[47] Sch.4 to the Pension Schemes Act 1993 was amended by the Pensions Act 1995, ss.137(6) and (7) and Sch.5, para.85.

[48] Sch.4 to the Pension Schemes Act 1993; "relevant date" is the date at which preferential claims are assessed in terms of s.387 of the Insolvency Act 1986, which is usually the date of the appointment of a receiver, the date of the making of an administration order or the date of the relevant winding up order or resolution.

an occupational pension scheme which is contracted out of SERPS, the state earnings related pension scheme),[49] but only in respect of the 12–month period preceding the relevant date and only where they are attributable to the provision of guaranteed minimum pensions[50] or protected rights[51] under the scheme; and (c) "state scheme premiums" within the meaning of ss.55 to 68 of the Pension Schemes Act 1993 payable by the company in relation to service in the 12 months prior to the date of fixing the amount of the premium.

If the pension scheme involves a trust—and all inland revenue approved private sector funded schemes involve trusts[52]—the assets of the trust will not be assets of the insolvent company at the disposal of the insolvency practitioner.[53] A "trust scheme" is defined in terms of s.124 of the Pensions Act 1995 as an occupational pension scheme established under a trust. It is distinguished in the legislation from a "public service pension scheme", which is defined in terms of s.1 of the Pension Schemes Act 1993 as "an occupational pension scheme established by or under an enactment or the Royal Prerogative or a Royal Charter, being a scheme, all the particulars of which are set out in, or a legislative instrument made under, an enactment, Royal warrant or charter", where there is no trust.[54]

Powers and discretions of the insolvent company in relation to pension scheme trust

The powers and discretions of the trustees and the employer company 11–12 depend on the construction of the particular pension scheme and specialist pensions law advice should be sought. In some pension schemes, discretion over how to manage and deal with the assets of the pension scheme is vested in the trustees, in some schemes it is vested in the trustees acting jointly with, or with the consent of, the employer and in some it is vested in the employer alone. Where the employer company has a discretion, it is important to establish whether the discretion is fiduciary. If it is, the company in a fiduciary capacity owes

---

[49] Pension Schemes Act 1993, s.7(3).

[50] See s.8(2) of the Pension Schemes Act 1993. If the contributions attributable solely to the provision of guaranteed minimum pensions cannot be identified, the preferential amount is deemed in terms of para.2(3) of Sch.4 to the Pension Schemes Act 1993 to be a particular percentage of "total reckonable earnings" as defined in para.2(4) of Sch.4 to the Pension Schemes Act 1993.

[51] See s.10 of the Pension Schemes Act 1993.

[52] An unfunded scheme can be approved by the Inland Revenue providing its benefits are within Inland Revenue limits. That will then provide taxation benefits in respect of contributions to and benefits out of it. Going one stage further, however, is exempt approved scheme status, which also gives exemption to investment income and capital gains. For that to be claimed schemes must be set up in trust or in some other method approved by the Inland Revenue. The other method will be somehow to set aside the assets for the member. The usual example given is *Hancock v General Revertionary and Investment Co Limited* [1919] 1 K.B 25. See also *Christie's Tr. v Leith, Hull and Hamburg Steam Packet Company*, 1915 S.C 848.

[53] *Re Kayford Ltd* [1975] 1 All E.R. 604; *Heritable Reversionary Company Ltd v Millar* [1892] A.C. 598.

[54] *Donald Bain, Petrs*, 2002 S.L.T. (I.H.) 1112.

a duty to the trust beneficiaries as to how and when to exercise the discretion. If the discretion is not fiduciary, the company may exercise the discretion in its own interest.

Most powers and discretions of the company in relation to a pension trust are not fiduciary, such as a power to agree with trustees to increases of benefits or to amendments of the pension scheme.[55] There is no reason why the instrument setting up the trust should not set out which powers and discretions are fiduciary.[56] Even where a power or discretion held by the insolvent company is not fiduciary, there may still be an implied duty that it must be exercised in good faith and not arbitrarily or capriciously.[57] It would appear that the duty of good faith may be enforced by the trustees as well as by employees or ex-employees.[58] The sorts of powers and discretions which may be fiduciary, would include (a) powers vested in the company in its capacity as a trustee of the pension scheme[59]; (b) unilateral powers of amendment in a pension scheme without the need for the consent of the trustees, although in *British Coal Corp. v British Coal Staff Superannuation Scheme Trs*,[60] Vinelott J. held that such a unilateral amendment power was not a fiduciary power in a case where there were restrictions on its scope; and (c) power to appoint or remove a trustee.[61]

Administrators, receivers and liquidators

In relation to non-fiduciary powers and discretions, these can come within the scope of the powers of liquidators, administrators and receivers.[62] The reasoning for this was succinctly stated by Street C.J. in the Supreme Court of New South Wales in a case concerning the powers of a receiver and manager. He said:

> "The administration of a superannuation plan is but one aspect of the overall industrial relationship between the company and its staff. The control of the relationship in all its aspects whether by way of wages, working conditions or superannuation, lies at the heart of managing the staff of a company, and hence is an integral part of the management of the business of the company".[63]

---

[55] See *Imperial Group Pension Trust Ltd v Imperial Tobacco Ltd* [1991] 2 All E.R. 597; *Mettoy Pension Trustees Ltd v Evans* [1991] 2 All E.R. 513; and *Re Courage Group's Pension Schemes* [1987] 1 All E.R. 528.

[56] For a discussion of fidiciary powers, see D. Pollard, *Corporate Insolvency: Employment and Pension Rights* (2nd ed., Butterworths, 2000), at paras 12.5 to 12.33.

[57] *Mihlenstedt v Barclays Bank International Ltd* [1989] I.R.L.R. 522; and *Stannard v Fisons* [1992] I.R.L.R. 27.

[58] *Imperial Group Pensions Trust Ltd v Imperial Tobacco Ltd* [1991] 2 All ER 597.

[59] *Icarus (Hertford) Ltd v Driscoll* [1989] P.L.R. 1.

[60] [1995] 1 All E.R. 912.

[61] See *IRC v Schroder* [1983] STC 480; and *Mettoy Pension Trustees Ltd v Evans* [1991] 2 All ER 513; see in contrast *Simpson Curtis Pension Trustees Ltd v Readson Ltd* [1994] O.P.L.R. 231.

[62] *Re Edgar* (1971–73) A.C.L.C. 27,492; *Simpson Curtis Pension Trustees Ltd v Readson Ltd* [1994] O.P.L.R. 231; *Denny v Yeldon* [1995] 1 B.C.L.C. 560; in Scotland, *per* Lord Hamilton, *Independent Pension Trustee Ltd v LAW Construction Co Ltd* [1996] O.P.L.R. 259.

[63] *Re Edgar*, above.

In relation to insolvency practitioners exercising the fiduciary powers of the company, there has been an enormous amount of conflicting case law.[64] The position in relation to the exercise of fiduciary powers has been largely resolved by provisions now contained in ss.22 to 26 of the Pensions Act 1995, originally introduced by Sch.4 to the Social Security Act 1990,[65] which provide that where an insolvency practitioner begins to act in relation to an employer participating in an occupational pension scheme, the practitioner has a duty to ensure that at least one of the trustees of the scheme is an independent person.[66] Any discretionary power vested in the employer, which is of a fiduciary nature, is to be exercised by the independent trustee. Any member of the scheme may apply to the appropriate court for an order requiring the practitioner to carry out this duty if he fails or refuses to do so.

Pension scheme surpluses

Where it has been actuarially established that the pension scheme has a **11–13** surplus, depending on the terms of the trust, discretion to allocate the surplus may be within the sole discretion of the trustees, or the trustees with the consent of the company, or exclusively within the control of the company. How the surpluses are allocated is highly charged politically. On the one hand it may be argued that the trust is for the benefit of the employees, but on the other hand any surplus after an actuarial valuation, would represent over-funding by the employer.

The position is as follows. Where increase in benefits is at the discretion of the employer, or the employer's consent is necessary, then the insolvency practitioner is entitled to have any surplus transferred into the assets of the company, although this may be subject to a duty of good faith.[67] Where the discretion is within the control of the trustees, it might be supposed that the trustees should give more weight to the interests of the members, as opposed to the employer. In the case of *Thrells Ltd (1974) Pension Scheme v Lomas*,[68] the company was the sole trustee and the liquidator arranged for its powers to be surrendered to the court; an option not really available in Scotland.[69] Sir Donald

---

[64] See, *e.g. Icarus (Hertford) Ltd v Driscoll* [1990] P.L.R. 1; *Mettoy Pension Trustees Ltd v Evans* [1991] 2 All E.R. 513; *Re William Makin & Sons Ltd* [1993] B.C.C. 453; *Imperial Group Pension Trust Ltd v Imperial Tobacco Ltd* [1991] 2 All E.R. 597; *Re Eastern Capital Futures Ltd (1989)* 5 B.C.C. 224; *Re Telesure Ltd* [1997] B.C.C. 580; and *Tom Wise Ltd v Fillimore* [1999] B.C.C. 129.

[65] The provisions introduced by Sch.4 to the Social Security Act 1990 as ss.57C and 57D of the Social Security Pensions Act 1975 were modified by the Occupational Pension Schemes (Independent Trustee) Regulations 1990 (SI 1990/2075).

[66] For the procedures to ensure that there is an independent trustee, see s.47 of the Child Support, Pensions and Social Security Act 2000, which inserts ss.26A—26C into the Pensions Act 1995, and the Occupational Pension Schemes Independent Trustee) Regulations 1997 (SI 1997/252, as amended by SI 1997/3038). For the exercise of trust functions, see Chap.12.

[67] *Imperial Group Pension Trust Ltd v Imperial Tobacco Ltd* [1991] 2 All E.R. 597.

[68] [1992] O.P.L.R. 21; [1993] B.C.C. 441.

[69] See petition of *Peter Harding*, 2000 S.L.T. (I.H.) 843 and authorities cited in the sole judgment of the Lord President. The full judgment is on the Scottish Courts website, to which readers are referred.

Nicholls V.-C. set out what he considered should be material considerations which a reasonable trustee could take into account in deciding whether to increase benefits, or pay all or part of any surplus to an employer. The material circumstances listed would include:

(a) the scope of the power;
(b) the purpose of the power;
(c) the source of the surplus;
(d) the size of the surplus and the provisions of s.11(3) of the Social Security Act 1990, which provided that payment could not be made out of the resources of a pension scheme to an employer unless the scheme provided for pensions when they became payable to be given a limited price increase[70];
(e) the financial position of the employer; and
(f) the needs of the members of the scheme.

In that case the court decided that it would exercise the discretion to increase benefits, with the result that the surplus, after securing LPI increases on pensions in payment, should be used to provide LPI increases on deferred pensions, with the remaining balance only then being paid to the company to benefit its creditors. These material considerations, however, should not be seen as loose guidelines. In the case of *Peter Harding*[71] in the sole judgment, Lord President Rodger approved of the observations of Sir Richard Scott V.-C. in *Edge v Pensions Ombudsman*[72] in dealing with particular provisions in that case:

> "They had a discretionary power to make amendments to the rules in order to provide additional benefits to members, whether pensioners or still in service. It was within their discretion to provide benefits to members in service to the exclusion of members no longer in service. They certainly had a duty to exercise their discretionary power honestly and for the purposes for which the power was given and not so as to accomplish any ulterior purposes. But they were the judges of whether or not their exercise of the power was fair as between the benefited beneficiaries and other beneficiaries. Their exercise of the discretionary power cannot be satisfied simply because a judge, whether the Pensions Ombudsman or any other species of judge, thinks it was not fair."

Lord President Rodger also agreed with the Vice-Chancellor's judgment in emphasising that, in exercising a power, the trustees did not need to act impartially among different classes of members. Equally, the Vice-Chancellor was satisfied that the trustees were entitled to take into account the possible effect of any course of action on the position of the employers.[73]

---

[70] S.11(3) was later consolidated as s.108(1) of the Pension Schemes Act 1993.
[71] 2000 S.L.T. (I.H.) 843.
[72] [1998] Ch. 512.
[73] See also the New Zealand case which went to the Privy Council: *Wrightson Ltd v Fletcher Challenge Nominees Ltd, sub nom. Fletcher Challenge Nominees Ltd v Wrightson Ltd* [2001] U.K.P.C. 23; [2001] Pens. L.R. 207, Lord Millett, P.C.

The whole area of surpluses is more closely regulated than previously. First, the tax approval regime of the Income and Corporation Taxes Act 1988, Pt XIV, Chap.II, requires any surplus on winding up to be destined back to the employer. This is not always clearly reflected, particularly in older schemes, and even where it is, questions can arise as to apportionment of surplus among several employers, past and/or present (see, for example, *Davis v Richards & Wallington Industries Limited* [1991] 2 All E.R. 563). Secondly, there are tight controls in s.37 of the Pensions Act 1995 on payments to employers out of a scheme. Sections 76 and 77 of the Pensions Act 1995 also lay down conditions for payment of surplus to an employer when a scheme is being wound up, and where no other power exists, trustees are given power to decide how to dispose of surplus. Any payment back to an employer is subject to a tax charge under Income and Corporation Taxes Act 1998, Sch.22.

Winding up or restructuring of occupational pension scheme on the insolvency of the employer

In most occupational pension schemes there is usually an express **11–14** provision covering the effect on the scheme of the insolvency of the employer company or the company's failure to pay contributions or meet other obligations under the scheme. If the company is merely a participating employer in a centralised scheme and not the sponsor or establisher of the scheme, the insolvency would usually only necessitate the end of the participation of the company, with perhaps a partial winding up of the scheme in respect of that company's participation. If, however, the insolvent company is the principal company, the winding up provisions in the scheme may provide that a liquidation of the principal company will automatically mean the winding up of the scheme. A receivership or administration would not commonly automatically trigger the winding up of the scheme. The Inland Revenue requires the deed and rules of an approved scheme to specify whether the scheme is to be wound up (or simply paid up) if the employer's contributions cease.[74]

A scheme which provides for the participation of more than one employer is also required by the Inland Revenue to provide for that part of the scheme relating to a participating employer that goes out of business or leaves the scheme for other reasons to be wound up.[75] The date upon which the scheme enters winding up will depend upon the terms of the trust deed. There are specific provisions in the Occupational Pension Schemes (Winding up) Regulations 1996,[76] which deal with the date upon which winding up is treated as having commenced where this is not set out in the scheme itself. In relation to winding ups started after April 6, 1997, s.73 of the Pensions Act 1995[77] sets out an overriding

---

[74] Tolley's *Pensions Law H4.2.*
[75] *ibid.*
[76] SI 1996/3126.
[77] As modified by the Occupational Pension Schemes (Winding Up) Regulations 1996 (SI 1996/3126).

order of priority on winding up.[78] The order of priority is set out in s.73(3), with first priority given to any liability for pensions or other benefits which, in the opinion of the trustees, are derived from the payment by any member of the scheme of voluntary contributions. The second priority is where the entitlement to payment of a pension or other benefit has arisen and is secured by an insurance policy (entered into before April 6, 1997) which may not be surrendered (or whose surrendered amount is less than the liability secured); excluding increases to pensions.[79] The third in priority is where a person's entitlement to payment of pension or other benefit has arisen. In such a case the priority is accorded to the liability for that pension or benefit and for any pension or other benefit which will be payable to dependents of that person on his death (but excluding increases to pensions).[80] The fourth in priority are any liabilities for pensions or other benefits which have accrued to or in respect of members of the scheme (but excluding increases to pensions), or in respect of members with less than two years pensionable service, the return of contributions.[81] The fifth in priority are increases in the above mentioned pensions.

The order of priorities set out in s.73 of the Pension Schemes Act applies to occupational pension schemes subject to the minimum funding requirement under s.56 of that Act. Section 56 of the Pension Schemes ·Act does not apply to money purchase schemes,[82] nor to schemes prescribed under s.56(2)(b) of that Act. Excluded are public sector schemes and schemes not approved under ss.590 or 591 of the Income and Corporation Taxes Act 1988.[83]

Section 75 of the Pensions Act 1995/Debt on the employer

11–15   Section 75(1) of the Pensions Act 1995 provides that, in the case of an occupational pension scheme, if the value of the assets is less than its liabilities, an amount equal to the difference is to be treated as a debt due from the employer to the trustees or managers of the scheme. Where the employer has gone into liquidation, then this debt is taken (for the purposes of the insolvency legislation) to arise immediately before the liquidation occurred.[84] A s.75 debt is not a preferential debt in the insolvency.[85]

A particularly charged issue is how the deficiency is calculated. The main Regulations dealing with this are the Occupational Pension

---

[78] The order of priority described is supplanted by a transitional order of priorities set out .in the Occupational Pension Schemes (Deficiency on Winding up, etc.) Regulations 1996 (SI 1996/3128, as amended by SI 1997/786, SI 1999/3198, SI 2000/2691, SI 2002/380 and SI 2004/403). This transitional order of priority is to apply to any winding up commencing before April 6, 2007.

[79] Pension Schemes Act 1975, s.73(3)(aa), as inserted by reg.3(3) of SI 1996/3126.

[80] *ibid.,* s.73(3)(b).

[81] *ibid.,* s.73(3)(c).

[82] *ibid.,* s.56(2)(a).

[83] Occupational Pension Schemes (Minimum Funding Requirement and Actuarial Valuations) Regulations 1996 (SI 1996/1536), reg.28.

[84] Pension Schemes Act 1995, s.75(2).

[85] *ibid.,* s.75(8).

Schemes (Deficiency on Winding up etc.) Regulations 1996.[86] In effect these provided that the deficit was to be assessed on the basis that the liabilities were to be on the minimum funding requirement standard (MFR). This is a statutory solvency standard introduced by the Government in 1997, and liabilities assessed on that basis are significantly less than the actual cost of buying out members' benefits by purchase of annuities on the insurance market

Effective from March 15, 2004 are the Occupational Pension Schemes (Winding Up and Deficiency on Winding up etc.) (Amendment) Regulations 2004.[87] These Regulations change the method of assessing liabilities so that solvent employers will have to pay the total buyout cost of annuities for all members of the pension scheme. The main Regulations were amended following a number of high-profile pension scheme wind ups where members were not provided with their full pension entitlement because there was not enough money in the pension scheme to buy out members' pensions in full. The MFR standard meant that employers could avoid having to provide the additional money to meet the full extent of the deficit. The amended Regulations, however, only apply to wind ups of schemes which have commenced on or after June 11, 2003 and only apply where the employer is not insolvent. The definition of solvent in the Regulations is "not in liquidation", including a members' voluntary winding up.[88]

---

[86] SI 1996/3128, as amended by SI 1997/786, SI 1999/3198, SI 2000/2691, SI 2002/380 and SI 2004/403.

[87] SI 2004/403.

[88] This definition may encourage company restructurings to avoid the new and more expensive basis of valuation.

PART 4

SECURITIES AND SPECIAL CREDITOR RIGHTS

CHAPTER 12

TRUSTS

Trust prevails on insolvency

The right of a beneficiary of a trust against the trustee is anomalous in **12–01** nature, in that it has features of both a real right and a personal right.[1] On the liquidation or sequestration of the trustee it is the features akin to a real right that are important. In the leading case, *Heritable Reversionary Co Ltd v Millar*,[2] it was held that the right of a beneficiary under a trust prevailed on the trustee's sequestration against his trustee in sequestration and his personal creditors. Ostensibly the decision turns upon the meaning of the word "property" in s.102 of the Bankruptcy Act 1856 (now represented by s.31 of the Bankruptcy (Scotland) Act 1985), which provided that the "property" of a bankrupt should vest in his trustee. Lord Watson said:

"That which, in legal as well as conventional language, is described as a man's property is estate, whether heritable or moveable, in which he has a beneficial interest which the law allows him to dispose of. It does not include estate in which he has no beneficial interest, and which he cannot dispose of without committing a fraud."[3]

This reasoning is equally applicable on both a creditors' voluntary winding-up of a company and a winding-up by the court. In the former case, s.107 of the Insolvency Act 1986 provides that "the company's property in a voluntary winding up shall on the winding up be applied in satisfaction of the company's liabilities *pari passu*". In the latter case, s.143(2) of the Insolvency Act 1986 provides that the functions of the liquidation are "to secure that the assets of the company are got in, realised and distributed to the company's creditors", while the word "assets" is used instead of "property" Lord Watson's reasoning clearly

---

[1] This topic is dealt with more fully in Chaps 1 and 10 of Wilson and Duncan on *Trusts, Trustees and Executor* (2nd ed., 1995). The former chapter, in particular, provides an extremely valuable historical discussion of the rights of the parties to a trust. See also "Trusts", "Rights of the Beneficiaries against Trustees" and "Trust Property" in *Stair Memorial Encylopaedia*, Vol.24, paras 49–52.

[2] (1891) 18 R. 1166; reversed on appeal (1892) 19 R. (HL) 43. See also *Forbes' Trs v Macleod* (1898) 25 R. 1012; *Hinkelbein v Craig* (1905) 13 S.L.T. 84; *Turnbull v Liquidator of Scottish County Investment Co Ltd*, 1939 S.C. 5

[3] (1892) 19 R. (H.L.) 43 at 49–50.

applies.[4] Before the decision in *Heritable Reversionary Co Ltd v Millar*, it had been held that the right of a beneficiary under a trust prevailed against the diligence of the trustee's personal creditors.[5] It had also been held that the right prevailed against the alienation of trust property in breach of trust as long as the person acquiring it either has given less than full value for the property or has acquired it with actual or constructive knowledge of the trust.[6] If the trustees transact as such, there will obviously be knowledge of the trust.[7] Nevertheless, the beneficiary's right does not prevail against a person who acquires trust property in good faith, without knowledge of the trust, and who gives full value.[8] It is in this respect that the rights of a beneficiary are in the last resort personal rather than real. This does not, however, affect the beneficiary's rights on winding up.

The rationale for the rule regarding an ordinary acquirer in good faith and for full value is that any other rule would impose an unacceptable degree of uncertainty on purchasers of property, who could never be certain whether the property acquired was subject to a latent trust.[9] An alternative formulation is that of Lord Watson in *Heritable Reversionary Co Ltd v Millar*:

"It must be kept in view that the validity of a right acquired in such circumstances by a *bona fide* onerous disponee for value does not rest upon the recognition of any power in the trustee which he can lawfully exercise, because breach of trust duty and wilful fraud can never be in themselves lawful, but upon the well-known principle

---

[4] In *Turnbull v Liquidator of Scottish County Investments Co Ltd*, above, and *Gibson v Hunter Home Designs Ltd*, 1976 S.C. 23, it was assumed without argument that the same reasoning applied on a winding up by the court. For the purposes of the insolvency legislation, "property" is defined in s.436 of the Insolvency Act 1986 as including "money, goods, things in action [incorporeal moveables, *i.e.* debts, shares and the like], land and every description of property wherever situated and also obligations and every description of interest whether present or future or vested or contingent, arising out of, or incidental to, property". Although this definition is very wide, it does not appear to add to the notion of property at common law, and the statement of principle by Lord Watson in *Heritable Reversionary Co Ltd v Millar* (1892) 19 R. (HL) 43 at 49–50 is still relevant. Any other view would cause difficulty in the application of various sections of the Insolvency Act 1986; notably ss.107 (distribution of company's property in voluntary winding up) and 127 (avoidance of dispositions of company's property after commencement of winding up) and Sch.1, paras 1,2,3,12 and 16 (powers of administrator) and Sch.4, para.6 (power of liquidator to sell company's property).

[5] At para.12–04.

[6] *Redfearn v Somervail* (1813) 1 Dow 50; 1 Pat. App. 707; *Taylor v Forbes* (1830) 4 W. and S. 444; *Macgowan v Robb* (1864) 2 M. 943.

[7] See Halliday, *Conveyancing Law and Practice*, Vol.1, ss.1–24.

[8] Referred to as a *bona fide* onerous disponee; *Heritable Reversionary Co Ltd v Millar* (1892) 19 R. (HL) 43 at 47, *per* Lord Watson. "Good faith" means simply that the acquirer should not have actual or constructive knowledge of the trust. See *Redfearn v Somervail*, above; *Burns v Lawrie's Trs* (1840) 2 D. 1348; *Thomson v Clydesdale Bank* (1893) 20 R. (HL) 29. It is essential that the person acquiring the property should have a real right, duly completed by the legal procedures appropriate to the type of property in question, in order that his right may prevail against the trust.

[9] *Redfearn v Somervail* (1813) 1 Dow 50 at 72, *per* Lord Eldon and in the Court of Session at 3 *Scots Revised Reports* (H.L.) at 16, *per* Lord Hermand. Where the purchaser of the trust property does not give full value, it is obvious that no equity arises in his favour.

that a true owner who chooses to conceal his right from the public and to clothe his trustee with all the *indicia* of ownership is thereby barred from challenging rights acquired by innocent third parties for onerous considerations under contracts with his fraudulent trustee."[10]

These reasons do not, however, apply to the generality of creditors who are the persons in whose interests a winding up takes place. The general creditors are not persons who have purchased property subject to the trust, and then have not, as a general rule, acquired rights on the faith of the trustees' apparent ownership. Lord Watson further stated:

"It is also necessary to keep in view that the rule of personal bar which must protect transactions with the trustee from challenge by the [beneficiary] only applies to transactions which affect and create an interest in the trust-estate. Personal creditors of the trustee who neither stipulate for nor obtain any conveyance to that estate do not, in the sense of law, transact on the faith of its being a property of the trustee. As Lord McLaren observed[11] . . . 'Creditors in general do not give credit to a bankrupt in reliance upon any supposed presumptions that property standing in his name is his private property. Unless they are going to advance money on heritable security they know nothing of his title-deeds and trust only to his personal credit.' Accordingly, the contraction of debts by the trustee whilst the trust is latent creates no *nexus* [attachment] over the trust-estate in favour of personal creditors. If they proceeded to attach the trust-estate on the footing of its belonging to their debtor, the beneficiary could defeat their diligence by appearing to vindicate his right. An adjudging creditor gives no new consideration for the interest in the estate which he secures by the process of adjudication, and, in my opinion, he can be in no better position in a question with the *cestui que* trust [beneficiary] than if he had obtained a conveyance without value from the trustee."[12]

The rule laid down in *Heritable Reversionary Co Ltd v Millar*,[13] that the rights of a beneficiary under a trust prevail on the insolvency of the trustee against his personal creditors, applies whether or not the trust is latent, that is, whether or not the trust appears on the face of the deed or other document which constitutes the trustee's title to the property in question. In *Heritable Reversionary Co*, the trustee's title to the heritable properties in question was absolute and unqualified and accordingly the trust was latent.[14] The beneficiary's rights were still preferred to the claim of the trustee's sequestrated estate. A case where the trust appeared on the face of the trustee's title would plainly be *a fortiori*.

Administration; voluntary arrangements

Under s.14 of the Insolvency Act 1986 an administrator is entitled: "to do all such things as may be necessary for the management of the affairs, business and property of the company". The specific powers **12–02**

---

[10] (1892) 19 R. (H.L.) 43 at 47. See also Lord Craig at 3 *Scots Revised Reports* (HL) at 16.
[11] (1891) 18 R. 1166 at 1175.
[12] (1892) 19 R. (HL) 43 at 47.
[13] (1892) 19 R. (HL) 43.
[14] *ibid.* at 46, *per* Lord Watson.

conferred by Sch.1 similarly refer to the "property" of the company as that word is used in particular in relation to taking possession of, collecting and getting the company's property (para.1), selling the company's property (para.2), granting security over the company's property (para.3) and realising the company's property (para.12). The administrator's general duties, specified in s.17, involve taking into his custody or under his control "all the property to which the company is or appears to be entitled", and managing "the affairs, business and property of the company". In these repeated references to the "property" of the company, that expression must be given the sense referred to in *Heritable Reversionary Co Ltd v Millar*.[15] Consequently, an administrator is in exactly the same position in relation to a trust as a liquidator.

This result will not usually be affected by new Sch.B1 to the paras 42 to 44 of the Insolvency Act 1986.[16] These provisions prohibit the enforcement without consent of the administrator or leave of the court of any security over the property of a company in respect of which a petition for an administration order has been presented or an administration order has been made. The only cases where these provisions will have an effect on a trust are where the trust is used as a pure form of security.[17] In most cases where a trust is used in a commercial agreement it involves part implement of a contract of sale of debts, or possibly other assets, and thus does not involve a "security" in the sense of the companies legislation.[18] Para.43 of the new Sch.B1 to the Insolvency Act 1986 prohibits other proceedings, execution (diligence) or other legal process against a company in administration or its property without the consent of the administrator or leave of the court. It has been held that the expressions "other proceedings" and "other legal process" must be construed *ejusdem generis* with the other provisions of s.11(3), the predecessor of para.43,[19] and it seems that this provision will not prevent the enforcement of a trust directly against trust property, as long as court proceedings or diligence against the company itself are not involved. If an administration order is made in respect of the trustee, the beneficiary will often be able to enforce the trust by using a power of attorney or a power to appoint a fresh trustee.[20] Alternatively, an application can be made for the appointment of a judicial factor, but in that case para.43 will apply as the company must, as trustee, be called as a respondent.[21]

Part 1 of the Insolvency Act 1986 does not specify that a voluntary arrangement made thereunder must only deal with the "property" or

---

[15] See *supra*. The definition of property in s.436 of the Insolvency Act 1986 is again relevant: see n.4, *supra*.

[16] See generally, Chap.5.

[17] See Chap.13 on the nature of a security.

[18] *Re George Inglefield Ltd* [1933] Ch. 1, discussed further at para.13–05; see also *Armour v Thyssen Edelstahlwerke A.G.*, 1990 S.L.T. 991.

[19] *Air Ecosse Ltd v Civil Aviation Authority*, 1987 S.L.T. 752; see generally, paras 5–29—5–33.

[20] See para.12–24.

[21] *ibid.*

"assets" of the company. Nevertheless, s.1(1) refers to a proposal to the company and to its creditors "for a composition in satisfaction of its debts or a scheme of arrangement of its affairs". It is thought that these words only authorise a composition or scheme which affects the property of the company, in the sense defined by Lord Watson, and the creditors of the company, who are thought not to include the beneficiaries under a trust. It is also thought that trust property is not "property of the company [which is] subject to a security" in terms of s.15 of the 1986 Act unless the trust is in reality a security in the sense discussed in Chap.13.

Floating charges and receivers

The effect of the grant of a floating charge or the appointment of a **12–03** receiver on property held in trust by a company has not been judicially considered.[22] The result of these two events is determined by the nature of a floating charge. The crucial feature of such a charge is that it does not attach to any property of the company until either winding up[23] or the appointment of a receiver of the property subject to the charge.[24] Until then it lies dormant, and does not prevent the company from dealing with the property subject to the charge. If the company alienates property before crystallisation of the charge, that property simply drops out of the charge. Not only outright alienation is permitted. Lesser rights, such as leases and rights in security, may be created over the property subject to the charge prior to crystallisation.[25] In exactly the same way, property subject to the charge can be subjected to a trust, and there seems to be no reason that the trust should not prevail. The floating charge holder expects, because of the nature of his security, that items of the company's property will be alienated, and a trust is simply a means of achieving that. Even if a latent trust has been created before the creation of the floating charge, it is thought that that trust should still prevail. The floating charge does not of itself create real rights over specific items of property, and it assumes that in future property may be alienated by the company. Thus the holder cannot be said to transact on the faith of a specific item of trust property's being or remaining the property of the company.[26] Consequently the floating charge holder is, in relation to trust property, in the same position as the general creditors, rather than the acquirer for value of a specific item of property.

---

[22] In *Tay Valley Joinery Ltd v C.F. Financial Services Ltd*, 1987 S.L.T. 207 it was argued that a latent trust had been created which did not prevail against the receiver, on the authority of *Burns v Lawrie's Trs* (1840) 2 D. 1348, as he was an assignee for full value in good faith and neither he nor the floating charge holder had knowledge of the trust. This argument was rejected on the ground that the special case did not disclose adequate facts for any such argument.
[23] Companies Act 1985, s.463.
[24] Insolvency Act 1986, ss.53(7), 54(6).
[25] This is subject to an exception if the creation of security rights is prohibited by the instrument creating the charge in terms of s.464 of the Companies Act 1985; this is a very frequent stipulation.
[26] Compare Lord Watson in *Heritable Reversionary Co Ltd v Millar* (1892) 19 R. (H.L.) 43 at 47.

When a receiver is appointed, the floating charge attaches to "the property subject to the charge". On the commencement of the winding up of a company that has granted a floating charge, the charge attaches to "the property then comprised in the company's property and undertaking".[27] In the expressions quoted, it seems clear that the word "property" must have the same meaning as that explained by Lord Watson in *Heritable Reversionary Co Ltd v Millar*,[28] with the result that property that has been rendered subject to a trust is excluded from the attachment of the floating charge. In virtually all cases involving receivership or winding up, the company will be insolvent, and the meaning accorded by Lord Watson is appropriate in any insolvency regime. Moreover, if the floating charge attached to trust property, the result would be a circular series of priorities. The trust prevails over the creditors of the company, including preferential creditors and creditors who have done diligence. Those categories of creditor, however, prevail over the floating chargeholder.[29] It is thought that this result cannot be correct, and that in the legislation governing floating charges, "property" is used in the sense explained by Lord Watson. In addition, the floating chargeholder knows when he takes the charge that property may drop out of it as a result of alienation. The creation of a trust is merely one form of alienation. Thus there is no reason to regard his equity, and that of the receiver who represents him, as in any way preferable to that of the beneficiary of the trust, who has merely taken property which everyone concerned contemplated could be alienated. Moreover, the floating chargeholder cannot be said to have transacted on the faith of any item of property remaining the property of the trustee.

After the receiver has been appointed, the security created through attachment of the floating charge will obviously prevail over any trust that the company may subsequently try to create. The principle *assignatus utitur jure auctoris* applies.[30]

Diligence

12–04 The rules on the use of diligence in relation to a trust are consistent with those on insolvency. Private creditors of the trustee may not do any form of diligence against the trust estate.[31] The general rule is that arresters, inhibitors and adjudgers take the estate of the common debtor

---

[27] Insolvency Act 1986, ss.53(7), 54(6); see Chap.5; Companies Act 1985, s.463(1).

[28] (1892) 19 R. (H.L.) 43 at 49–50; see para.12–01.

[29] See para.12–01 (trust and creditors) and para.12–04 (trust and diligence); Companies Act 1985, s.463(3) as amended and Insolvency Act 1986, ss.60(1)(e) and 175 (preferential creditors); Companies Act 1985, s.463(1)(a) and Insolvency Act 1986, s.60(1)(b) (creditors who have done diligence).

[30] The transferee of a right can acquire no higher right than the person who transfers the right to him has. See *Scottish Widows' Fund v Buist* (1876) 3 R. 1078.

[31] For arresters, see *Mackenzie v Watson* (1678) Mor. 10188; *Brugh v Forbes* (1715) Mor. 10213; Bell *Commentaries*, i.33; G. Stewart on *Diligence*, pp.67–68. For adjudgers, see *Livingston and Shaw v Lord Forrester and Creditors of Grange* (1644) Mor. 10200; *Preston v Earl of Dundonald's Creditors* (1805) Mor. "Personal and Real", App. No.2; G. Stewart on *Diligence*, p.620. Inhibition is clearly *a fortiori* of adjudication.

tantum et tale as it stands vested in him, and if the common debtor holds property as a trustee the diligence of his personal creditors will not affect that property.[32] Creditors of the trustee *qua* trustee may, however, do diligence against the trust estate; the primary remedy of a creditor of a trust is to obtain payment out of the trust estate.[33] Creditors of the beneficiary of a trust may do diligence against his beneficial interest in the trust estate. Normally arrestment will be appropriate but, if the beneficiary's interest is heritable, inhibition must be used.[34] Creditors of one of a number of beneficiaries cannot, however, attach the trust estate beyond the amount specifically destined to their debtor.[35]

Constitution of trust

If an alleged trust is to receive effect on the insolvency of the trustee, **12–05** it is essential that it should have been properly constituted. The detailed requirements for the constitution of a trust are beyond the scope of this work.[36] Nevertheless, certain matters that may assume significance in the context of insolvency should be mentioned. The traditional form of trust is constituted by (a) the declaration of certain trust purposes by the truster; (b) the acceptance of those purposes by the trustee; and (c) the transfer of property by either the truster or a third party to the trustee to be held for the purposes of the trust.[37] The transfer of property to the trustees must be effected in such a way as to confer real rights on them; otherwise the property will not be subjected to the trust and, on the insolvency of the trustee, it will be the donor or seller of the property who can claim it, not the beneficiary. The procedure necessary to confer real rights will, of course, vary according to the type of property concerned. Generally speaking, recording in the General Register of Sasines (or registration in the Land Register) is required for heritage, assignation followed by intimation to the debtor for incorporeal moveables and delivery for corporeal moveables, except in the anomalous case of sale of goods, where mere intention to transfer will suffice.[38]

It is also important to bear in mind that, if a person is to declare himself the sole trustee of his own property or any property which he may acquire, a written document complying with s.2 of the Requirements of Writing (Scotland) Act 1995 is normally required.[39] Section 2

---

[32] *Erskine*, 3.6.16; *Mackenzie v Watson, supra.*

[33] *Stewart v Forbes* (1888) 15 R. 383. If such a creditor cannot obtain payment from the trust estate, he has a personal right of action against the trustee, unless it has been agreed, expressly or by implication, that only the trust estate is to be liable. For a fuller discussion of a trustee's personal liabilities, see Wilson and Duncan on *Trusts, Trustees and Executor* (2nd ed., 1995), Chaps 28 and 29; *Stair Memorial Encyclopaedia*, Vol.24, para.225.

[34] G. Stewart on *Diligence*, pp.61–62.

[35] *ibid.*, pp.61–62.

[36] See Wilson and Duncan, pp.23–40.

[37] *Camille and Henry Dreyfus Foundation Inc v Inland Revenue*, 1955 S.L.T. 335 at 337, *per* Lord Normand.

[38] Sale of Goods Act 1979, ss.17, 18. The detailed rules regarding the transfer of real rights to trustees are discussed in Wilson and Duncan, pp.33–39.

[39] Requirements of Writing (Scotland) Act 1995, s.1(2)(a)(iii). The same rule applies to the variation of such a trust: s.1(6). See Wilson and Duncan, pp.37–40, for a discussion of the law.

provides that no document required by s.1(2) shall be valid in respect of the formalities of execution unless it is subscribed by the granter of it or, if there is more than one granter, by each granter. Apart from such subscription, however, nothing more is required for the document to be valid. If, however, a trust of the sort mentioned in s.1(2)(a)(iii) is not constituted in a written document complying with s.2, but a beneficiary under the trust has acted or refrained from acting in reliance on the trust with the knowledge and acquiescence of the truster, the truster is not entitled to withdraw from the trust, and the trust is not to be regarded as invalid on the ground that it is not properly constituted, provided that the beneficiary's position has been affected to a material extent by his acting or refraining from acting in reliance on the trust or would be adversely affected to a material extent by such withdrawal from the trust.[40]

Certain particular types of trust require special mention because of their importance in a commercial context. These are bare trusts, constructive trusts arising out of a fiduciary relationship, trusts implied where a fiduciary acquires property with funds derived from the person for whom he acts, and trusts where the truster declares himself a trustee.

Bare trusts

12–06   In a commercial context the most usual example of the traditional trust will be a nominee holding, or bare trust, under which the trustee simply holds property for the behoof of a beneficiary, who may or may not be the truster. In such a case, the trust property will in the last resort be under the control of the beneficiary, who can call for it to be transferred into his own name at any time,[41] even if the trustee is insolvent. The declaration of trust in such cases will generally be simple in nature. It is generally essential, however, that the requirements of s.1(2)(a)(iii) of the Requirements of Writing (Scotland) Act 1995 should be satisfied.

Constructive trusts[42]

12–07   Constructive trusts are implied by law in two main sets of circumstances. The first is where a non-trustee acquires property from a trustee in breach of trust and either in the knowledge that it has been transferred to him in breach of trust or without giving full value for the property so transferred.[43] In such cases the transferee from the trust holds the property so transferred on a constructive trust for the beneficiaries of the original trust. The second case where a constructive trust arises is where a fiduciary acquires a benefit in consequence of his fiduciary position or from any breach of his fiduciary duties.[44] The latter

---

[40] Requirements of Writing (Scotland) Act 1995, s.1(3) and (4).
[41] *Millet's Trs v Miller* (1890) 18 R. 301.
[42] See Wilson and Duncan, pp.98–103
[43] See n.6 to this chapter.
[44] The law relating to fiduciaries and constructive trusts arising therefrom is discussed in the Stair *Memorial Encyclopaedia*, vol.24, paras 170–188 on "Trusts, Fiduciary Duties of Trustees and Others". The law relating to fiduciaries and their duties has developed from the law on trustees' duties of good faith; the trustee is the archetypal fiduciary.

type of constructive trust is of importance in a commercial context. Fiduciaries include, in addition to trustees, company directors,[45] certain partners,[46] agents[47] and persons to whom confidential information is imparted.[48] Every fiduciary is under a duty not to place himself in a position where his personal interest and his duty to look after the affairs of the person to whom the fiduciary duty is owed may possibly conflict.[49] If a fiduciary acts in breach of that duty, any profit or advantage or benefit that he receives as a result of the breach is held by him as a constructive trustee for the beneficiary of the fiduciary duty. That means that the rights of the beneficiary will prevail even on the fiduciary's insolvency. The breach of fiduciary duty is automatic; no inquiry is generally allowed as to the fairness of the transaction. An example of a transaction involving a breach of fiduciary duty which gives rise to a constructive trust is the purchase of trust estate by a trustee acting in his private capacity.[50] In such a case both the property purchased by the trustee and any proceeds following the resale of such property, including any profits accruing to the trustee, will be held on constructive trust for the purposes for which the trustee held the property so purchased.[51] Likewise, when a trustee or other fiduciary defeats the legitimate expectations of those to whom he stands in a fiduciary relationship, he will be a constructive trustee of the benefit so acquired. Examples include a trustee's obtaining a renewal of a lease to a trust in his own name,[52] and a company director's diverting to himself contracts which the company might reasonably have expected to obtain.[53] The taking of unauthorised remuneration by a fiduciary such as an agent[54] and the use of confidential information acquired in a fiduciary capacity for the fiduciary's own purposes[55] will similarly give rise to a constructive trust.

---

[45] *Aberdeen Ry Co v Blaikie Bros* (1854) 16 D. 470,1 Macq. 461; *Regal (Hastings) Ltd v Gulliver* [1967] 2 A.C. 134n. See also Chap.8.

[46] Partnership Act 1890, ss.26, 30; *McNiven v Peffers* (1868) 7 M. 181; *Roxburgh Dinardo's J.F. v Dinardo*, 1992 G.W.D. 6–322.

[47] See *Lothian v Jenolite Ltd*, 1969 S.C. 111; *Boardman v Phipps* [1967] 2 A.C. 46.

[48] *Boardman, supra; Seager v Copydex Ltd* [1967] 1 W.L.R. 923; [1969] W.L.R. 809.

[49] *Aberdeen Ry Co v Blaikie Bros, supra.*

[50] See *Magistrates of Aberdeen v University of Aberdeen* (1876) 3 R. 1087; aff'd. (1877) 4 R. (HL) 48; *Johnston v MacFarlane*, 1987 S.L.T. 593; *Elias v Black* (1856) 18 D. 1225; *Wright v Morgan* [1926] A.C. 788, PC. In England it has been held that the purchase of property held for fiduciary purposes by an agent is not an automatic breach of fiduciary duty, but that an inquiry into the fairness of the transaction should be allowed: *Spencer v Topham* (1856) 22 Beav. 573. This does not appear to accord with the Scottish authorities: *cf. Elias v Black, supra; Aberdeen Ry Co v Blaikie Bros, supra.*

[51] *cf. Inglis v Inglis*, 1983 S.C. 8; 1983 S.L.T. 437. The sale to the trustee will also be reducible at the instance of a beneficiary.

[52] *Keech v Sandford* (1726) Sel. Cas. Ch. 61; *McNiven v Peffers, supra.*

[53] *Cook v Deeks* [1916] 1 A.C. 554, PC; *Regal (Hastings) Ltd v Gulliver* [1967] 2 AC 143. Considerable case law exists on this point; reference should be made to the standard works on company law.

[54] See *Brown v IRC*, 1964 S.C. (H.L.) 180; *Stair Memorial Encyclopaedia*, Vol.24, para.183.

[55] *Boardman v Phipps* [1967] 2 A.C. 46; see *also Stair Memorial Encyclopaedia*, Vol. 24, paras 184–185. In certain English cases involving the receipt of secret commissions by agents and directors, it has been held that the sum received by the agent or director was not held on constructive trust for the principal or company; *Metropolitan Bank v Heiron* (1880) 5 Ex D. 319, CA; *Lister & Co v Stubbs* (1890) 45 Ch. D. 1, CA; *Powell and Thomas v Evan James & Co* [1905] 1 K.B. 11, CA. It is thought that those cases do not represent the law of Scotland, and that a constructive trust would be held to arise, as in any other case of breach of fiduciary duty; see *Stair Memorial Encyclopaedia*, Vol.24, para.188.

A trust will not be implied in the absence of a pre-existing fiduciary relationship. In particular a trust will not be inferred from a mere personal obligation.[56]

Implied trusts—fiduciary relationships

12–08   The existence of a fiduciary relationship is also significant in that, where a fiduciary acquires property with funds derived from the person for whom he acts as fiduciary, it will readily be implied that he holds such property on trust for that person. Thus an agent who acquires property with funds provided by his principal[57] will frequently hold that property on trust for the principal.[58] The same point applies in relation to company directors, whose relationship to the company is essentially that of principal and agent[59]. Even if funds are provided by a third party, such as a bank, if the loan is arranged in connection with the principal's business, it is likely that property acquired with such funds will be held on trust for the principal[60]. The question of whether parties are in fact in the relationship of principal and agent must be determined objectively, according to the commercial realities of the situation; the fact that a party is described as an agent for another, or as an independent principal, is not conclusive[61]. In some cases, however, even though the relationship of principal and agent exists, funds acquired by the agent but destined for the principal may not be subject to a trust. That is especially so if the underlying commercial reality of the transactions in question does not accord with that of a trust. In such cases the relationship between the principal and the agent will be that of debtor and creditor. The result, of course, is that, in the event of the insolvency of the agent, the principal will not be protected by the existence of a trust. An example of a case where the relationship between principal and agent was held not to involve a trust is *Style Financial Services Limited v Bank of Scotland*,[62] which is discussed below.

It is thought that the requirements of s.1(2)(a)(iii) of the Requirements of Writing (Scotland) Act 1995 do not apply to implied trusts of this nature. That paragraph, taken together with s.2 of the Act, requires writing for the constitution of "any trust whereby a person declares himself to be sole trustee of his own property or any property which he may acquire". Where parties stand in a relationship such as principal

---

[56] See *Bank of Scotland v Liqrs of Hutchison Main & Co Ltd*, 1914 S.C. (HL) 1 at 8, *per* Lord Kinnear and at 17, *per* Lord Shaw of Dunfermline; *Gibson v Hunter Home Designs Ltd*, 1976 S.C. 23 at 27–28, *per* Lord President Emslie, and at 31, *per* Lord Cameron; *National Bank of Scotland Glasgow Nominees Ltd v Adamson*, 1932 S.L.T. 492. See para.12–11, *infra*.

[57] The original situation in *Heritable Reversionary Co v Millar, supra*: see (1892) 19 R. (H.L.) 43 at 46.

[58] Wilson and Duncan, pp.12–13. But see *Style Financial Services Limited v Bank of Scotland (No 2)*, 1998 S.L.T. 851, discussed below

[59] See *Aberdeen Ry Co v Blaikie Bros, supra*.

[60] See *Bank of Scotland v Liquidators of Hutchison, Main & Co Ltd*, 1914 S.C. (H.L.) 1 at 15, *per* Lord Shaw of Dunfermline.

[61] *Michelin Tyre Co Ltd v Macfarlane (Glasgow) Ltd (in Liquidation)* (1917) 2 S.L.T. 205, where criteria for distinguishing agency are discussed by Lord Dunedin at 212.

[62] Above; discussed below at para.12–14.

and agent, however, and the agent acquires property with the principal's funds, it cannot be said that the agent declares himself to be a trustee. The relationship of trustee and beneficiary is a legal conclusion implied from the actings of both parties rather than the result of a declaration by the agent that he is to be a trustee. In any event, the mischief struck at by s.1(2)(a)(iii) is clearly the possibility that a person facing insolvency, or declared insolvent, asserts that he holds substantial parts of his assets on trust for third parties when in fact no such trust has been declared. Where, however, trustee and beneficiary stand in the relationship of principal and agent, or company and director, or partnership and partner, the trust is based on an antecedent relationship which will nearly always be capable of proof by evidence extrinsic to the trust. In these circumstances, the mischief that underlies s.1(2)(a)(iii) will not normally exist. Even though the trust cannot be proved by documentary evidence, the relationship that gives rise to it will be capable of such proof, or at least of proof that goes well beyond the existence of trust itself.

Declaration of self as trustee

In the traditional form of Scottish trust, property was transferred to **12–09** the trustees by the truster, or on occasion by a third party after the trust had been constituted by the truster. It is now clear, however, in view of the decision in *Allan's Trustees v Lord Advocate*,[63] that it is competent for a truster to declare himself trustee of his own property, as long as the trust is intimated to the beneficiary, or to someone acting on his behalf. In that case Lord Reid stated:

> "I think that we can now accept the position, as a reasonable development of the law, that a person can make himself a trustee of his own property, provided that he also does something equivalent to delivery or transfer of the trust fund. I reject the argument . . . that mere proved intention to make a trust coupled with the execution of a declaration of trust can suffice. If that were so it would be easy to execute such a declaration, keep it in reserve, use it in case of bankruptcy to defeat the claims of creditors, but, if all went well and the trustee desired to regain control of the fund, simply suppress the declaration of trust".[64]

It was held in *Allan's Trustees* that intimation to the beneficiaries was equivalent to delivery of the trust fund, and brought the trust into

---

[63] 1971 S.C. (H.L.) 45.

[64] *Allan's Trs*, 1971 S.C. (H.L.) 45 at 54, *per* Lord Reid. The practice appears to have originated in the commercial field, where a partner or employee took title to property in his own name but in trust for his employer or the partnership of which he was a member. *Heritable Reversionary Co Ltd v Millar*, *supra* can be regarded as an example of the former type of case, although the disposition to the employee trustee was clearly made in anticipation of the declaration of trust; *Hinkelbein v Craig* (1905) 13 S.L.T. 84 is an example of the latter type of case. Other early authorities are collected in Lord Reid's speech in *Allan's Trs* at 53–54. Of these, the dissenting judgment of Lord Kyllachy in *Cameron's Tr. v Cameron*, 1907 S.C. 407 deserves notice.

operation, and further[65] that intimation to one beneficiary out of several was sufficient, because it was the equivalent of delivery of the trust property, to bring the whole trust into operation.[66]

Allan's Trustees has been followed in a number of cases.[67] As the more recent of these cases illustrate, the possibility of a truster's declaring himself trustee of his own property is of considerable commercial importance, principally because it provides a simple and informal method of obtaining security for the performance of contractual obligations. It is probably fair to say that the implications of this device are only starting to be worked out, and consequently it is thought appropriate to deal with this area of the law in some detail.

The requirements for declaring oneself a trustee were summarised by the Lord President in *Clark Taylor & Co Ltd v Quality Site Development (Edinburgh) Ltd*[68] in the following terms:

> "In order to complete the successful constitution of a trust recognised as such by our law, where the truster and trustee are the same person, there must be in existence an asset, be it corporeal or incorporeal or even a right to future *acquirenda* [property coming into the estate in future], there must be a dedication of the asset or right to defined trust purposes; there must be a beneficiary or beneficiaries with defined rights in the trust estate, and there must also be delivery of the trust deed or subject of the trust or a sufficient and satisfactory equivalent to delivery, so as to achieve irrevocable divestiture of the truster and investiture of the trustee in the trust estate".

The two features which cause the greatest difficulty in practice are the declaration of trust (the "dedication of the asset or right to defined trust purposes") and the equivalent of delivery.

DECLARATION OF TRUST

Formal requirements of declaration of trust

12–10   In the first place it should be noted that any trust whereby a person declares himself to be sole trustee of his own property or any property which he may acquire must normally be constituted by a written document subscribed by the granter. That is the result of s.1(2)(a)(iii) of the Requirements of Writing (Scotland) Act 1995, taken together with s.2 of the Act. Section 1(2) is subject to subss.(3) and (4) of the same section, which deal with the situation where a beneficiary under the trust has

---

[65] Lord Guest dissenting.

[66] See Lord Reid in *Allan's Trs, supra*, at 55–56.

[67] *Clark's Trs v Lord Advocate*, 1972 S.C. 177; *Ken's Trs v Lord Advocate*, 1974 S.C. 115; *Export Credit Guarantee Department v Turner*, 1979 S.C. 286; *Clark Taylor & Co Ltd v Quality Site Development (Edinburgh) Ltd*, 1981 S.C. 111; and *Tay Valley Joinery Ltd v C.F. Financial Services Ltd*, 1987 S.L.T. 207.

[68] 1981 S.C. 111 at 118; the facts of the case are discussed below at para.12–12.

acted or refrained from acting in reliance on the trust with the knowledge and acquiescence of the trust her. In such cases the truster is not entitled to withdraw from the trust and the trust is not to be regarded as invalid, provided that the beneficiary has either been affected to a material extent as a result of acting or refrained from acting as aforesaid, or if a withdrawal from the trust would have an adverse effect on the beneficiary to a material extent. Normally, however, a person who wishes to declare himself a trustee of his own property should declare the trust purposes in writing, and subscribe that writing.

Trust and contract

A declaration of trust must be sharply distinguished from a contract **12–11** creating merely personal rights. The distinction is made clearly in the leading case, *Bank of Scotland v Liquidators of Hutchison Main & Co Ltd*.[69] In that case it was agreed between the bank and the company in liquidation that the bank would surrender a security held by it over certain of the company's assets, and that the company would obtain a debenture from one of its debtors and assign it to the bank in lieu of the surrendered security. At the date of the company's liquidation, the agreement had been implemented except for the assignation of the debenture in favour of the bank. It was argued for the bank that the debenture was held by the company in trust for the bank; *Heritable Reversionary Co Ltd v Millar* was relied upon in support. That claim was rejected by the House of Lords. Lord Kinnear, distinguishing the trust in *Heritable Reversionary Co Ltd v Millar*, said:

> "The trust so established was declared in express terms, and directly affected the constitution of the real right. It is a very different thing to say that a personal obligation to give the benefit of a specific fund to a particular creditor creates a trust which attaches to the fund and excludes it from the estate for distribution.[70]"

Lord Kinnear went on to refer to Lord Westbury's dictum in *Fleeming v Howden*[71] that "an obligation to do an act with respect to property creates a trust" and expressed the view that it must be confined to obligations which affect the real right, and should not be extended to personal obligations[72].

---

[69] 1914 S.C. (H.L.) 1.
[70] *Bank of Scotland v Liquidators of Hutchison Main & Co Ltd*, 1914 S.C. (H.L.) 7, above.
[71] (1868) 6 M. (H.L.) 113 at 121.
[72] Lord Shaw of Dunfermline at 17 stated that the dictum did not represent the law of Scotland; it involved "an invasion into the well-settled principle that a contractual obligation with regard to property, which has not effectually and actually brought about either a security upon it or a conveyance of it, is not *per se* the foundation of a trust or of a declarator of trust". While that statement emphasises that a mere contractual obligation will not give rise to a trust, it must not be taken as detracting from the principle, established definitively in *Allan's Trs v Lord Advocate, supra*, that a trust may be created by a truster's declaring himself trustee and carrying out an equivalent of delivery. In any event, it is hard to see how a contractual obligation can of itself bring about a security or, outside the anomalous case of sale of goods, a conveyance of property. Further criticism of

Clark Taylor

12–12   In *Clark Taylor & Co Ltd v Quality Site Development (Edinburgh) Ltd*[73] an attempt was made to set up a trust in favour of a supplier of goods over the proceeds of resale of those goods. The contract of sale between the supplier and the purchaser of a quantity of bricks contained the following clause (condition 11(b)):

> "In the event of the buyer reselling or otherwise disposing of the goods or any part thereof before the property therein has passed to him by virtue of clause 11(a) hereof, then the buyer will, until payment in full to the seller of the price of goods, hold in trust for the seller all his rights under such contract of resale or any other contract in pursuance of which the goods or any part thereof are disposed of or any contract by which property comprising the said goods or any part thereof is or is to be disposed of and any money or other consideration received by him thereunder."

The bricks were used by the purchaser in carrying out building works and the purchaser received payments under the building contracts, which were paid into its current bank account. Payments received under the building contracts were in all cases greater than the price of the bricks used in the contracts. The purchaser of the bricks went into liquidation while the price of the bricks was still outstanding to the supplier, and it was argued by the supplier that a trust had been constituted over the sums received under the building contracts. This argument was rejected as follows:

> "Condition 11(b) cannot be read as containing any declaration of trust by the Company [the purchaser]. It is, rather, a condition which imposes upon the Company a contractual obligation to hold certain alleged "trust" subjects in "trust", in accordance with its precise terms. It cannot, therefore, by itself, in the context of the Contract as a whole, demonstrate that a trust was ever created in terms of the obligation. But there are more formidable objections than this to the submission of the first parties [the supplier]. Even if we assume, contrary to the opinion we have expressed, that condition 11(b) could fairly be read as containing a purported acceptance by the [Company] of an alleged trust over their own property, corporeal and incorporeal, the question is whether there can be identified any true trust in accordance with the law of Scotland. The alleged trust is to hold "for the seller" all the rights and all the moneys to come under all contracts not yet entered into

---

Lord Westbury is found in the speech of Lord Watson in *Heritable Reversionary Co Ltd v Millar* (1892) 19 R. (H.L.) 43 at 49. It should be noted that English law is in this respect radically different from Scots Law, and English authorities cannot be relied upon. In particular, English law will frequently imply an equitable assignment, giving rise to rights analogous to those under a trust, in circumstances where purely personal contractual obligations would arise in Scots law. See also *Gibson v Hunter House Designs Ltd*, 1976 S.C. 23 at 27–28, *per* Lord President Emslie and at 31, *per* Lord Cameron; *National Bank of Scotland Glasgow Nominees Ltd v Adamson*, 1932 S.C. 492.

[73] 1981 S.C. 111.

in which any of the bricks sold are used, until the price of the bricks has been paid in full. It is at once obvious that the value of the alleged "trust" subjects might be (and as it proved in the event to be) infinitely greater than the price to which the first parties were entitled under the Contract with the [Company]. Yet according to the submission for the [first parties] all had ceased to be part of the [Company's] own estate and could not be released from the fetters of the trust unless and until such time as the [Company's] debt was paid, in full, presumably out of funds which were not burdened by any trust. What is really significant here is, of course, that in the so-called trust no beneficial interest whatever in the subjects thereof is or was conferred upon the alleged beneficiaries, the first parties. All they were entitled to receive was the price of the bricks. It is not provided that they should be entitled to have recourse to any part of the "trust" fund for this purpose. Properly construed, what condition 11(b) purports to do is to secure the freezing of the defined subjects, regardless of their value, under an alleged trust which gives no beneficial interest therein to the supposed "beneficiary" until they receive the price of the bricks which they sold to the [Company]. In our opinion the essential ingredients of a trust are entirely lacking and condition 11(b) can be seen for what it really is—as no more than an attempt, under the guise of an alleged trust, to keep valuable assets of the [Company] out of the hands of its other creditors, at least until the [suppliers] have themselves received payment in full of the price of the bricks sold to the [Company]. Before leaving this submission we ought to say two things. The first is that, even if the [purchaser] had on receipt of the various interim payments gone through the exercise of executing and intimating declarations of "trust" in the exact terms of condition 11(b) in relation to these payments, the essential ingredients of a trust would still be absent and the position of the first parties could not have been strengthened thereby. The second is that if a condition such as condition 11(b), designed only to freeze assets of a debtor and to keep them out of other creditors' hands until a particular creditor's debt is paid in full, were to be regarded as constituting a proper trust in accordance with the law of Scotland, and were to be adopted widely by sellers of goods, the damage which would be done to the objectives of the law of bankruptcy and of liquidation would be incalculable. Other interesting complications can easily be figured, and a person creating more than one such 'trust' in favour of his creditors could readily find himself in trouble under the criminal law."[74]

Tay Valley

In *Tay Valley Joinery Ltd v C F Financial Services Ltd*[75] the validity of a **12–13** trust in an invoice discounting agreement, a type of debt factoring agreement, was considered.[76] The agreement involved the sale of the

---

[74] 1981 S.C. 111 at 115–116, *per* Lord President Emslie.

[75] 1987 S.L.T. 207.

[76] In an invoice discounting agreement intimation to the trading company's debtors is avoided, whereas in the more traditional type of factoring agreement such intimation is effected.

present and future book debts of a trading company (which were referred to in the agreement as "receivables") to a factoring company. In a factoring or invoice discounting agreement, the factoring company makes payment to the trader for book debts shortly after they arise. The point of such an agreement is to assist the trading company's cash flow. This leaves the factoring company exposed, because unless it takes a formal assignation and intimates it to the trading company's debtors it has no real right to the debts. Thus if the trading company becomes insolvent, it is the receiver or liquidator, not the factoring company, who will be entitled to recover them. To avoid this, it is usual to create a trust over the outstanding book debts in favour of the factoring company, and this can most easily be achieved by the trading company's declaring itself a trustee.[77]

The factoring agreement in *Tay Valley* was governed by English law. It provided that the purchase of receivables should be complete and that the right to receivables should vest in the factoring company upon such receivables coming into existence. It further provided that the trading company would (1) record the sale of receivables to the factoring company in its books; (2) notify the factoring company on special forms of receivables arising from time to time; (3) note on customers' accounts that they were held on trust for the factoring company (although this was not observed in practice); (4) as trustee for the factoring company keep remittances received in payment of any receivables separate from other moneys and pay those into a separate account; and (5) send the factoring company each month an aged analysis of receivables. It was agreed in the special case that, under English law, the invoice discounting agreement effected an equitable assignment to the factoring company of those book debts the proper law of which was English law, in consequence of which the trading company held those book debts for the factoring company under a constructive trust.[78]

The court held that the invoice discounting agreement was effective as a declaration of trust in Scotland. Lord Robertson[79] held that the terms of the agreement, in the light of the practice followed by the parties, were sufficient for a trust to be inferred. Lord Dunpark, who discussed this question most fully,[80] held that the agreement must be construed in accordance with English law, under which it constituted a declaration of trust. This construction was supported by the two references to a trust in the agreement[81] which, while they did not amount by themselves to a declaration of trust, clearly assumed that a trust had been created. Lord McDonald[82] held that a trust could be established from (a) the require-

---

[77] Halliday, *Conveyancing Law and Practice*, Vol.I, para.8.63.

[78] The result would have been different if Scots law had been the proper law of the invoice discounting agreement; in that event, without an actual declaration of trust over specific assets, only personal rights would have been created, and there would have been no trust.

[79] 1987 S.L.T. 20, at 212L—213G.

[80] *ibid.* at 214H—215L.

[81] See cls (3) and (4) above.

[82] 1987 S.L.T. 20, at 219B—D.

ments that the trading company note on customers' accounts that they were held on trust for the finance company and (b) the fact that a note was made on copies of the trading company's consolidated monthly statements that the debts contained therein had been assigned to the factoring company.

Requirements of effective declaration of trust—underlying commercial reality

As will be clear from the cases discussed so far, it is difficult to lay **12–14** down any definitive rules for determining what amounts to an effective declaration of trust as against an agreement creating merely personal rights. The wording used by the alleged truster is clearly important. In an agreement whose construction is governed by Scots law, there must be a clear declaration that specific subjects are held on trust, or will when they come into existence be held on trust, for another person.[83] Such a declaration is not enough by itself, however. It is also essential to determine whether the alleged deed of trust is a genuine declaration of trust. For this purpose it is essential to consider the practical working of the supposed trust; a declaration of trust is not a mere form of words, but represents an underlying commercial or economic reality. If the wording used, purportedly creating a trust, does not conform to the underlying reality of a trust, it will be treated as a nullity. This can be clearly seen in the passage quoted above from *Clark Taylor & Co Ltd v Quality Site Development (Edinburgh) Ltd*[84] where it was held that the alleged trust was merely a device to keep valuable assets of the company out of the hands of its creditors. In that case the contractual entitlement of the supplier was to receive the price of the bricks sold, but the alleged trust, which was designed to create a security for the fulfilment of the purchaser's obligations under the contract for the sale of the bricks, extended to the whole of the rights enjoyed by the purchaser under the building contracts in which the bricks were used. The underlying commercial reality of the contract was the sale of the bricks, but the supplier attempted to create a trust security for the price over much more valuable rights under another, distinct contract. In these circumstances it was clear that the purported trust and the security created thereby had no connection with the commercial reality of the contract under which it bore to arise. The declaration of trust was accordingly treated as not being genuine. *Tay Valley* also involved the

---

[83] As a matter of practical drafting, the expression "in trust for" should always be used, but expressions such as "for behoof of" may, if the context supports the construction, be held equivalent. The use of agreements governed by other legal systems should be avoided. These are drafted against a different legal background. In particular, English agreements are drafted in the light of rules relating to equitable assignments which have no equivalent in Scots law. This means that agreement must be reached as to the construction of the agreement in the foreign legal system, or evidence must be led of foreign law. In any event, it is not clear that Scots law should, as a matter of policy, allow a foreign deed to affect real or trust rights in property which throughout the transaction remains in Scotland where that deed can be understood only by reference to foreign law. If a deed is to affect Scottish property which does not move out of Scotland it should at least be comprehensible to a Scots lawyer.

[84] 1981 S.C. 111 at 115–116.

use of a trust to create a form of security for the performance of contractual obligations; under the invoice discounting agreement the factoring company was ultimately entitled to payment of the receivables, and the trust was designed to secure that obligation. In this case, however, the amount over which the trust subsisted was precisely the factoring company's entitlement, and the trust could be regarded as involving the part implement of the contract for sale of the receivables.[85] Thus the trust corresponded to the underlying commercial reality and there was no question of its being anything other than genuine.

The consequences of according validity to a trust-security which does not represent the underlying commercial reality can be seen from *Clark Taylor & Co Ltd v Quality Site Development (Edinburgh) Ltd*.[86] If the trust in that case had been held valid, the supplier of the bricks would have effectively frozen a major source, perhaps the only source, of the purchaser's income. This would have an obvious impact on the purchaser's cash resources. In many cases it would disable him from paying his other debts. Moreover, if one supplier is allowed to impose such a trust-security, others will obviously attempt to do so over the same funds. In *Clark Taylor*, for example, suppliers of sand, gravel and the like might have tried to impose trusts identical to the brick supplier's. The subjects of these purported trusts would necessarily be the same as the subjects of the brick supplier's trust; namely, the rights under the building contract of the purchaser in the supply contracts. If the brick supplier's trust is valid, however, the purchaser's rights under the building contract have passed out of its estate and have become part of the brick supplier's estate, and thus the purchaser would be disabled from creating any subsequent trusts. In these circumstances the court concluded in *Clark Taylor*[87] that "a person creating more than one such 'trust' in favour of his creditors could readily find himself in trouble under the criminal law".[88]

The concept of the underlying commercial reality was applied to an alleged trust in the context of the relationship of principal and agent in *Style Financial Services Ltd v Bank of Scotland (No 2)*.[89] In that case, a company running a department store, Goldberg, were customers of the defenders. The pursuers were a finance company which provided credit to customers of Goldberg, through the medium of an in house credit card known as the "Style card". When a customer repaid the pursuers,

---

[85] See para.12–22, *infra*. The fact that the trust involved part implement of a contract of sale meant that it did not constitute a charge or security for the purposes of the statutory provisions governing the registration of charges: *Re George Inglefield Ltd* [1933] Ch. 1.

[86] 1981 S.C. 111 at 116.

[87] 1981 S.C. 111 at 116.

[88] In a number of English and Australian cases, the concept of the underlying commercial reality has been used to determine whether or not a trust subsists: *Foley v Hill* 2 HL Cas 28 (bank who mixes money deposited with his own is debtor, not trustee); *South Australian Insurance Co v Randell* (1869) L.R. 3 P.C. 101 (mixing of corn by miller incompatible with ownership of farmers); *Re Nevill* (1871) L.R. 6 Ch. App. 397 (parties' actings inconsistent with fiduciary relationship); *Re Bond Worth Ltd* [1980] Ch. 228 (terms of contract of sale incompatible with trust).

[89] 1998 S.L.T. 851; see above at para.12–08 and below at para.12–29.

he could do so either directly or by making payment to Goldberg, and in the latter event he could do so by a cheque drawn in favour of either Goldberg or the pursuers. When Goldberg received such payments (which were known as "Style collections") it lodged them in a bank account held in its own name, and from time to time transferred the sums at credit to the pursuers. The pursuers had granted a mandate authorising the defenders to credit Goldberg's account with cheques drawn in favour of the pursuers. Goldberg's account was overdrawn at all material times. A receiver was appointed over the property and undertaking of Goldberg, at a time when a substantial sum was owed by Goldberg to the pursuers. The pursuers brought an action against the defenders for payment of the sums owed by Goldberg. They contended that the relationship between Goldberg and the pursuers with regard to the Style collections was that of agent and principal. Consequently Goldberg's obligation to the pursuers in respect of those monies was fiduciary rather than one of debtor and creditor. Thus Goldberg's failure to pay the sums sued for constituted a breach of trust on their part and there was accordingly a misapplication of trust funds in violation of the fiduciary obligation. The defenders were aware of a breach of trust, and that put them in bad faith in a question with the pursuers. The defenders argued that the relationship between Goldberg and the pursuers was at all times that of debtor and creditor, no trust being created over the monies paid into Goldberg's account with the defenders.

Lord Gill held that the Style collections were not the subject of a trust. Moreover, even if they had been, the defenders had given onerous consideration for the payments made into Goldberg's account and had been in good faith in using those payments in reduction of Goldberg's overdraft. The defenders were accordingly not liable to pay the pursuers at the sums owed to the pursuers by Goldberg.

Lord Gill's analysis of the law begins with a discussion of the incidents of the banker-customer relationship.[90] He concluded that the existence of the mandate granted by the pursuers in favour of the defenders was of critical importance; it amounted to a clear authorisation by the pursuers to the defenders to credit to Goldberg's account any cheque or postal order drawn in favour of the pursuers that Goldberg should lodge as a payment to their own account. He went on to hold[91] that the agreements entered into between the pursuers and Goldberg had the effect of making Goldberg the pursuers' agents for the purpose of collecting payments made in Goldberg stores by Style cardholders in settlement of their accounts. Where one party appointed another as its agent to collect funds due to him, it did not necessarily follow that the funds so collected were impressed with a trust. Such a trust might be created by express agreement or by necessary implication, but the agent's authority might be such that he was at liberty to deal with the funds free of any trust and to settle with his principal on a debtor-

---

[90] This is discussed in a later part of this chapter at para.12–29.
[91] 1998 S.L.T. 865L—866B.

creditor basis. This was such a case. The agreements entered into
between the pursuers and Goldberg nowhere used the word "trust".
While they used the expressions "on behalf of" or "on Style's behalf",
those words did not, in the context of the agreement as a whole, signify
anything more than a debtor-creditor relationship. Lord Gill was prepared to reach the foregoing conclusion on the basis of the agreements
between the pursuers and Goldberg considered by themselves. When
the agreements were considered together with the mandate granted by
the pursuers in favour of the defenders, however, it was clear that
Goldberg were authorised to mix payments made by Style card holders
with their other receipts, and to pay all such monies into their account.
On that basis, it was impossible to segregate the Style collections from
the other monies, and the defenders could not know how much, if
anything, of any individual pay-in represented Style, collections. Consequently, if such monies had been subject to a trust, the defenders could
never have known how much of the sums credited to Goldberg's
account could be drawn on by Goldberg, and that would render the
mandate unworkable. These considerations were conclusive against the
existence of a trust.[92]

Declaration of trust must affect specific property

12–15   A declaration of trust must take effect in relation to specific property,
and it must be ensured that the wording of the declaration is appropriate to cover any particular property that is claimed to be subject to the
trust. This is illustrated by *Export Credits Guarantee Department v
Turner*,[93] where the Export Credits Guarantee Department entered into a
number of agreements with a company whereby they guaranteed
advances to the company made by its bank against invoices for goods
exported by the company. Under one of the agreements known as the
recourse agreement, it was declared that: "all sums received by the
[company] or any person on its behalf in respect of any transaction
which is the subject of a Guaranteed Advance shall . . . be received and
held in trust by the [company] for the [Department] until the [company]
has made repayment to the Bank or has paid to the [Department] the
amount of any demand made". The company became insolvent and
went into liquidation. At that time certain debts which were the subject
of guaranteed advances made by the bank to the company were
outstanding, and those debts were subsequently paid to the liquidator.
The Department claimed that those debts had been subject to the trust
constituted by the recourse agreement and were thus held for its behoof.
This claim was rejected by the Second Division. The main ground of
decision was that debts could not be included in the subjects of trust,
since the declaration of trust referred only to "sums received" and not
to "debts".[94] In *Tay Valley*, on the other hand, the trust was constituted

---

[92] 1998 S.L.T. 851.
[93] 1979 S.C. 286.
[94] *Export Credits Guarantee Department v Turner*, above at 294. The reference to "sums
recovered" seems to be an error. The Lord Justice-Clerk went on to say that "'debts' could

over "receivables", which were defined in the factoring agreement as meaning:

> "all the book debts, invoice debts, accounts, notes, bills, acceptances and/or other forms of obligations owed by or owing to the [trading company] which are in existence at the date of commencement of this Agreement or which come into existence during the currency of this Agreement in respect of contracts entered into by the [trading company] for the sale of goods or the provision of services in the ordinary course of business."

It is essential that the trust subjects should be defined as fully as possible but not so widely that the trust goes beyond the underlying commercial purpose of the contract.

EQUIVALENTS OF DELIVERY

Intimation to beneficiaries

In *Allan's Trustees v Lord Advocate*[95] it was held that intimation to the **12–16** beneficiaries was equivalent to delivery of the trust fund and brought the trust into operation, and further[96] that intimation to one beneficiary out of several was sufficient, because it was the equivalent of delivery of the trust property, to bring the whole trust into operation.[97] It has subsequently been held that intimation to an agent for the beneficiaries will suffice as an equivalent of delivery, even if the agent is also acting for the truster.[98] Intimation to the beneficiary or his agent is thus a sufficient overt act to give rise to the "irrevocable divestiture of the truster and investiture of the trustee in the trust estate",[99] and at the same time to create the rights enjoyed by the beneficiary of a trust.

Trust property must exist before intimation

When intimation is effected, however, it is essential that there should **12–17** be in existence specific property which is to be rendered subject to the trust. In *Kerr's Trustees v Lord Advocate*[1] a truster purported to declare

---

not become part of the trust subjects unless the company has divested themselves of them and they could only do so by assignation [intimated] to the debtors." This is clearly incorrect: see *Tay Valley*, at 212G—I, *per* Lord Robertson, at 215G—K, *per* Lord Dunpark and at 219G—J, *per* Lord McDonald. Assignation followed by intimation would transfer the full real rights in a debt from cedent to assignee. A declaration of trust followed by intimation to the beneficiary, as in *Allan's Trs v Lord Advocate* does not transfer full real rights to the beneficiary, but only the quasi-real rights of a beneficiary under a trust (see above, at paras 12–01 and 12–09). The function of intimation in the two cases is thus quite different. See also Lord Dunpark at 1979 S.C. 286 at 290.

[95] 1971 S.C. (H.L.) 45.
[96] Lord Guest dissenting.
[97] Lord Reid at 55–56.
[98] *Clark's Trs v Lord Advocate*, 1972 S.C. 177. The agent must have a right or duty to act on behalf of the beneficiaries: *Kerr's Trs v Lord Advocate*, 1974 S.C. 115 at 127, *per* Lord Kissen and at 132, *per* Lord Fraser.
[99] *Clark Taylor & Co Ltd v Quality Site Development (Edinburgh) Ltd*, 1981 S.C. 111 at 118.
[1] 1974 S.C. 115.

herself trustee of certain policies of assurance by intimating the trust to agents for the beneficiaries, but she did so before the policies had been taken out. It was held that a trust had not been validly created. Lord Fraser, after referring to the speech of Lord Reid in *Allan's Trustees*,[2] expressed the rationale of the decision as follows[3]:

> "What we are looking for . . . is something equivalent to delivery or transfer of a trust fund, and I cannot see how there can be such an equivalent until after the trust fund has come into existence.[4]"

In *Kerr's Trustees* it was further held that intimation, to be effective, must follow the declaration of trust. Lord Fraser stated[5]:

> "It appears to me that anything said by an intended settlor to an intended beneficiary before the settlor has executed a declaration of trust cannot be more than an expression of intention and the intention could be changed at any time before the declaration is executed. The only exception would be where there is some contractual obligation by the settlor towards the beneficiary".

It thus appears that, if a prospective truster agrees with a prospective beneficiary that he will set up a trust, then intimates to the prospective beneficiary that certain assets will be subject to the trust, and finally executes a declaration of trust, that will suffice. Lord Fraser went on to discuss the practical difficulties that would arise if intimation could precede the declaration of trust in cases where there is no antecedent contract: in particular, if the terms of the intimation differed from those of the declaration, or if the declaration only followed the intimation after a long interval, considerable doubts would arise as to the validity of the alleged trust. *Kerr's Trustees*[6] further makes it clear that the information given by way of intimation must be sufficient to specify the property held in trust.[7]

Intimation distinguished from acceptance of contractual obligation

12–18   In *Clark Taylor & Co Ltd v Quality Site Development (Edinburgh) Ltd*[8] it was argued on behalf of the supplier that the terms of the contract were sufficient to impose on the purchaser an obligation to create a trust of

---

[2] 1971 S.C. (H.L.) 45 at 54.

[3] 1974 S.C. 115 at 129; see also Lord Kissen at 126.

[4] In *Allan's Trs* the policy of assurance did not in fact come into existence until after the intimation (see 1971 S.C. (H.L.) 45 at 47–48) but this point was not argued.

[5] 1974 S.C. 115 at 130.

[6] Lord Kissen at 127; Lord Fraser at 131.

[7] In *Tay Valley Joinery Ltd v C.F. Financial Services Ltd, supra* Lord Dunpark indicated at 215H—I that some trust property (debts in that case) must exist when the declaration of trust is executed, because there must be at that time some property to which the beneficial right may be transferred to a beneficiary by delivery or its equivalent. It is thought that this dictum was made *per incuriam*, and that "executed" should read "intimated". That would bring the *dictum* into line with *Kerr's Trs, supra*. In any event, it is difficult to see why a prospective trustee cannot execute a declaration of trust purposes, then obtain trust property, and finally intimate to the beneficiaries that that property is held for those purposes. In such a case the trust would come into existence on intimation.

[8] 1981 S.C. 111. See above at para.12–12.

moneys received under the building contracts for behoof of the supplier, and that that contractual obligation was a continuing intimation that as soon as any such moneys reached the hands of the purchaser they would be held in trust in implement of that obligation. This continuing intimation was said to be a sufficient equivalent of delivery. The argument was rejected[9] on the ground that the alleged equivalent of delivery was not intimation of action taken in relation to existing assets or rights for behoof of the beneficiary; it was merely the acceptance of an obligation to hold in trust certain moneys that might be received in future. A contractual obligation to constitute a trust does not by its own vigour have the effect of constituting a trust in favour of one of the contracting parties. There must be "some overt extraneous and ostensible act which involves acceptance of the trust and marks definitely the character of the trustee's possession".[10] The court nevertheless stated[11] that intimation to the beneficiary or his agent was not the only equivalent to delivery of the subjects. Delivery of the trust deed will suffice, although that is essentially a form of intimation, but it appears that in appropriate cases other equivalents will be admitted.

Intimation in relation to debts and *acquirenda*

The court also indicated in *Clark Taylor*[12] that the property subjected to a trust could be a right to *acquirenda*; that is, a right to items of property which the truster may acquire in future. It is clear that rights of this nature may be the subject of an ordinary assignation either absolutely or in security,[13] and accordingly there seems no reason that they should not be the subject of a trust. Nevertheless, while an assignation of *acquirenda* will be effective as between cedent and assignee, intimation to the debtor is still required to create real rights which will prevail against third parties. For intimation to take place, the identity of the debtor must be known. That means that a distinction must be drawn between cases where a debt exists, even though it is not payable until a future date, or is contingent (the classic case of the *spes successionis*[14]), or is uncertain in amount, and cases where no debt yet exists. In the latter case no debtor exists to whom intimation can be made, and accordingly no real rights in the debt can be transferred to an assignee. Consequently an assignation of, for example, all debts which may in future become due to the cedent from his trade customers will only create personal rights between

12–19

---

[9] *ibid.* at 118–119.
[10] Following Lord Kyllachy in *Cameron's Trs v Cameron*, 1907 S.C. 407 at 415. See also *Gibson v Hunter Home Designs Ltd*, 1976 S.C. 23.
[11] 1981 S.C. 111 at 118.
[12] *ibid.* at 117–118.
[13] *Browne's Tr. v Anderson* (1901) 4 F. 305; Gloag and Irvine, *Rights in Security*, pp.441–443. See McBryde, *Contract*, 12–35 to 12–37.
[14] The authorities are discussed in the passages cited in the preceding footnote. The expression *spes successionis* is normally used to describe a contingent right to succeed to the estate of a deceased person, but, at least in the last century, it was also used to describe the right of the heir (at law and *in mobilibus*) of a person who was still alive and the right of the spouse and children of such a person to legal rights; the reason for treating the latter two types of right as a *spes* is that they would prevail unless defeated by a testamentary writing. A *spes successionis* cannot be arrested.

cedent and assignee. Real rights in relation to any particular debt will pass to the assignee only after intimation has been made to the customer who owes the debt, and for that purpose it is essential to know who the customer is. It is thought that the creation of trust rights is limited in a similar way. If a truster declares himself trustee for, say, a factoring company of future debts from trade customers, that may give rise to a personal right in the factoring company (if the wording of the declaration is appropriate), but no real rights will pass until a debt has actually become due from a specific customer, and the truster intimates to the factoring company that the debt is held for the purposes of the trust. This appears to be in accordance with the approach of the Inner House in *Kerr's Trustees v Lord Advocate*,[15] where it was held that a trust cannot be created over property that does not yet exist. A trust can, however, be created over a future or contingent debt. In such cases the debt exists, even though it may never be payable, or may not be payable until a future date. Nor is it essential that the debt or other incorporeal moveable that is made subject to the trust should be capable of precise quantification or valuation. Thus a claim to damages against a particular person can be the subject of both an assignation and a trust.

In *Tay Valley Joinery Ltd v C.F. Financial Services Ltd*[16] the trading company was required by the invoice discounting agreement to notify book debts to the factoring company on special forms. Each form included a schedule which listed the receivables that had arisen since the last form had been prepared. Such forms were prepared and sent every few days, and on receipt the factoring company gave credit to the trading company for the receivables specified in the schedule. The sending of each form was held to amount to sufficient intimation that a trust had been created over the debts specified in the schedule to the form.[17] It is thought that a factoring agreement must incorporate an arrangement of this nature if its trust provisions are to be valid, in view of the considerations discussed in the last paragraph.

In *Export Credits Guarantee Department v Turner*[18] it was argued that intimation was effected when the recourse agreement, which contained the alleged trust, was delivered to the department, or alternatively when trust property came into existence following such delivery. Both of these contentions were rejected[19] on the ground that intimation cannot be effected until there is a trust fund. If, however, a procedure similar to that in *Tay Valley* had been followed, there can be little doubt that the trust in favour of the Department would have been effective, on the assumption that the recourse agreement had been properly worded.

Use of trusts in commercial agreements

12–20   The validity of a trust in a commercial agreement is likely to depend on two main factors; whether the trust truly represents the underlying commercial reality of the agreement, and whether an appropriate

---

[15] 1974 S.C. 115. See para.12–17.
[16] 1987 S.L.T. 207; discussed above at para.12–13.
[17] Lord Robertson at 213F—G; Lord Dunpark at 216A—217A; Lord McDonald at 219E—K.
[18] 1979 S.C. 286; discussed above at para.12–15.
[19] See 1979 S.C. 286 at 294–295.

equivalent of delivery has been effected in relation to any particular asset. The most common case where a trust will represent the underlying commercial reality is likely to be where the trust is used to provide interim security for the performance of a contractual obligation, as in *Tay Valley*. It is essential, however, that the rights of the beneficiary under the trust should not extend to any greater assets than do his contractual rights. Such a trust can be regarded as a form of part-implement of the contract, and appears unobjectionable from a policy standpoint.

It is also possible to use a trust to create a simple and informal type of security, in a manner similar to an *ex facie* absolute assignation. The owner of an asset, such as shares in a company, executes a declaration of trust in favour of the person who is to take the security, the trust being expressed in absolute terms, so that the truster becomes a bare trustee. At the same time a back letter similar to the type used for an *ex facie* absolute assignation[20] is executed. This should state that the beneficial interest of the beneficiary under the trust is truly enjoyed in security and should specify the terms of the security. Formal intimation of the trust should then be made to the beneficiary.[21] In the case of incorporeal property, the same result[22] can be reached by an *ex facie* absolute assignation. Nevertheless, there appears to be a considerable demand in commercial circles for a more informal type of security which does not involve intimation to the debtor. This can be seen in the practice followed by banks of taking a so-called "pledge" of shares; the certificates for which are deposited with the bank along with an executed transfer, which in theory can be registered if insolvency threatens.[23]

The use of a trust to create a security in the manner suggested is in accordance with the underlying commercial reality of the transaction as long as the back letter is framed appropriately. This should provide expressly that the lender beneficiary is entitled to call upon the trustee to denude in his favour (a right which would be implied anyway). It should further provide that, if the trustee is called upon to denude, the lender beneficiary will at once sell the trust subjects, will use the proceeds to satisfy his debt, and will account for the balance to the trustee. An arrangement of this nature goes no further by way of security than the trust that was upheld in *Tay Valley*, and there seems no reason to deny its validity. Where a trust of this sort may fail to represent the underlying commercial reality, however, is where the subjects selected are of a fluctuating nature, such as stock-in-trade. In such cases the trust is likely in any event to amount to an attempt to

---

[20] Styles of back letter are found in Halliday, *Conveyancing Law and Practice*, Vol.I, Chap.7; those paras 7–77 and 7–83 are especially useful, although they will need minor modification for a trust-security.

[21] It may be possible to incorporate the intimation into the back letter.

[22] Without the risk of the *bona fide* onerous assignee, whose rights prevail over a latent trust.

[23] This device obviously creates no form of security in Scots law until the transfer is registered, or unless the shares are bearer securities. See Halliday, paras 7–76 *et seq.*

create a floating charge by means other than those specified in s.462 of the Companies Act 1985. It is thought that a trust may be used to create a security over heritable property, notwithstanding the terms of s.9(3) of the Conveyancing and Feudal Reform (Scotland) Act 1970, which provides that a grant of any right in an interest in land for the purpose of securing any debt by way of a heritable security shall be capable of being effected only if it is embodied in a standard security. A trust does not involve a heritable security, as defined in s.9(8). Care should in all cases be taken to ensure that a trust-security granted by a company does not require registration under s.410 of the Companies Act 1985.[24] It must also be ensured that the creation of further securities is not prohibited or restricted by any prior security; such prohibitions or restrictions, imposed under s.464 of the Companies Act 1985, are common in floating charges.[25]

Attempts are made from time to time to create securities over Scottish property by means of an English equitable charge, which is a type of security analogous to a trust.[26] Apart from floating charges,[27] these are ineffective, since it is clearly established that the creation of security rights over property situated in Scotland is governed by Scots law.[28] An English declaration of trust followed by intimation sufficient to satisfy the requirements of Scots law will be effective in Scotland, as *Tay Valley* makes clear. It is nevertheless unsafe to rely on English forms of deed in this area of law. In English law, equitable interests (which are similar to the interests of a beneficiary under a trust) are implied in a wide variety of transactions, and English deeds tend to be based on the assumption that such inferences will be drawn. It would plainly be quite unsatisfactory if the beneficial tide to Scottish property depended upon inferences drawn from a foreign deed in accordance with the rules of a foreign legal system. For this reason it is thought that English equitable interests other than express trusts followed by intimation to the beneficiary should not be recognised as affecting Scottish property.

Securitisation agreements

12–21   Trusts may also be used in connection with the securitisation of debts, a form of financing that has become fairly common in recent years in England and is starting to spread to Scotland. The details of a securitisation agreement are beyond the scope of the present work, but it is proposed to indicate how trusts are used in such agreements to avoid the risk of insolvency.

---

[24] In *Tay Valley* the trust over the book debts did not require registration because it involved part-implement of a contract rather than a security; see *Re George Inglefield Ltd* [1933] Ch. 1, and Chap.13.

[25] In the case of a factoring or invoice discounting agreement the trust will normally involve part-implement of the contract for sale of the debts, and in such a case the consent of any prior floating charge holder will not be required; see Chap.13.

[26] In part this seems to reflect the desire of the commercial community for a simple and informal type of security of general application.

[27] English floating charges are recognised in Scotland by virtue of the Companies Act 1985, s.462(1).

[28] *Mitchell v Burnet and Mouat* (1746) Mor. 4468; *Inglis v Robertson and Baxter* (1898) 25 R. (H.L.) 70.

Typically, a securitisation will involve selling the benefit of a large number of relatively small debts, usually arising out of hire-purchase contracts or loans secured over heritable property, to noteholders, and using the proceeds of sale to finance further lending. The original creditor in the debts which are sold is usually a hire-purchase or other consumer finance company. It sells the debts for their market value to a trustee company,[29] specially set up for the securitisation and, as instalments of the debts are paid to it, it passes these on to the trustee company. The trustee company in turn sells and communicates the benefit of the debts to the company which issues the notes to the public. It does this in two ways. First, at the start of the transaction the trustee company grants an assignation in favour of the note-issuing company of all debts and payments due to it from the finance company; that assignation must obviously be intimated to the finance company, in order to complete a real right in the assignee. Alternatively, the trustee company may declare a trust over the debts and payments due to it from the finance company in favour of the note-issuing company. Either of these methods provides protection against the possible insolvency of the trustee company. Secondly, as instalments of the hire-purchase or other debts are paid by the finance company to the trustee company, the trustee company passes these on to the note-issuing company. The note-issuing company uses such payments to meet interest and capital repayments due on the notes.

For such an arrangement to be financially viable it is essential that the notes issued to the public should receive a high credit rating, and for that to be obtained it is important that the debts should be protected against the insolvency of the intermediaries. The assignation granted by the trustee company, or the trust declared by that company, is designed to achieve that result. The more substantial risk of insolvency, however, is that of the original finance company. Consequently it is usual for the finance company to declare a trust over the debts due to it from its customers. Conventional terminology uses the expression "receivables" to cover both these debts and the payments made in respect of the debts.[30] When the finance company offers to sell a quantity of receivables to the trustee company, and the offer is accepted, one of the terms of the resulting contract is that the finance company declares a bare trust over those receivables (which must be specified in detail) in favour of the trustee company. That trust is then intimated to the trustee company as beneficiary, the intimation once again referring to the specific receivables that are to be subject to the trust.[31] Thereafter the debts owed

---

[29] In order to avoid stamp duty the sale will usually be completed offshore.

[30] Debts and payments are distinct items of property, and it is important that the expression "receivables" should be defined in such a way as to cover both.

[31] In conventional practice, it is usual to have the trust declared and intimated offshore, where the completion meeting takes place. Normally the trust is intimated verbally, and the trustee company provides a written acknowledgment, in order to avoid any risk of stamp duty. It is thought that verbal intimation of a trust will be adequate, on the basis of the speeches in *Allan Trs v Lord Advocate*, 1971 S.C. (H.L.) 45 and the opinions of the Second Division in *Kerr's Trs v Lord Advocate*, 1974 S.C. 115, but that a written acknowledgment is desirable to provide evidence that intimation has been made: see *Donaldson v Ord* (1855) 17 D. 1053 at 1061–1070, *per* LJC Hope. In spite of the usual practice, it is thought by the authors that no stamp duty is payable on either an intimation or an acknowledgment of intimation in any event, and that the only duty is the fixed duty of 50p on the declaration of trust (if that is made in or brought to the UK).

to the finance company are owed to the trustee company. When a payment is made to the finance company in respect of one of those debts, it is received by the finance company as a trustee, and held for the purposes of the trust in favour of the trustee company.[32]

The declaration of trust made by the trustee company in favour of the note-issuing company should relate not only to payments received from the finance company but also to the whole beneficial interest of the trustee company in the trust declared by the finance company. In this way the total entitlement of the trustee company is held on trust for the note-issuing company, and the risk of the trustee company's insolvency is avoided. The trust declared by the trustee company must be intimated to the note-issuing company.[33] If the trust declared by the finance company is a single trust, over all the receivables sold by that company, it is probably sufficient that the trustee company makes a single intimation to the note-issuing company that the beneficial interest under the finance company's trust is held on trust for the note-issuing company. Nevertheless, it is safer if a fresh intimation is made by the trustee company to the note-issuing company following each sale of receivables by the finance company to the trustee company. The intimation should refer to the trustee company's entire beneficial interest in the specific debts that have been sold.[34] When a payment is made by the finance company to the trustee company there is no need for any further intimation, as the payment amounts to actual delivery of property (cash) to the trustee (the trustee company). Intimation is only necessary as an equivalent of delivery where there is no actual delivery.

Nature of beneficiary's interest in securitisation trusts

12–22　　　The trusts created for the purposes of a securitisation transaction involve a part-implement of the sale of receivables, and as such do not constitute a charge or security for the purposes of registration in the register of charges of either the finance company or the trustee company.[35] It is thought that this characterisation, as part-implement of a sale rather than a security, applies generally,[36] with the result that any negative pledge that has been granted by either the finance company or the trustee company will not strike at the securitisation trusts.[37] Like-

---

[32] In practice such payments received from the finance company's debtors will be paid into a trust account for behoof of the trustee company set up for the purposes of the securitisation. That procedure is not necessary, however, to impress the trust on the payments received by the finance company.

[33] This is so even if the trust declared by the trustee company is subject to English law (because both Scottish and English debts are involved in the securitisation), as it is essential that the trust is properly impressed on the beneficial interest in the trust declared by the finance company over Scottish receivables (which will usually be a Scottish trust).

[34] As with the declaration of trust by the finance company, it is normal to use a verbal intimation followed by a written acknowledgment. See n.31 to this para.

[35] Under the Companies Act 1985, ss.410–424, to be replaced by the Companies Act 1989, ss.92–107; see *Re George Inglefield Ltd* [1933] Ch. 1, discussed at para.13–05, below.

[36] See *Armour v Thyssen Edelstahlwerke A.C.*, 1990 S.L.T. 891, discussed at paras 13–03 and 13–04.

[37] See para.13–06.

wise, if either company is placed in administration, the trusts will not be regarded as a security for the purposes of ss.10(1)(b) and 11(3)(b) of the Insolvency Act 1986.[38] It is immaterial that the finance company grants a trust over heritably secured debts, as a trust over heritable property does not contravene s.9(3) of the Conveyancing and Feudal Reform (Scotland) Act 1970.[39]

The ability to use trusts to protect the noteholders in a securitisation against the insolvency of the finance company or the trustee company is nevertheless limited in one significant respect. If the contract between the finance company and its debtor ceases to oblige the debtor to make payments, as where goods are repossessed under a hire-purchase contract or where a standard security is called up, the trust created by the finance company will not apply to the proceeds of sale of the goods or security subjects. The contract for the resale of the goods or land in question will inevitably be created after the declaration of trust and relative intimation, and thus sums payable under the contract of resale cannot be the subject of that trust. A fresh trust can be created over such sums, but if the finance company is insolvent it will have no incentive to do so; the liquidator, administrator or receiver is likely to repudiate any personal liability to create such a trust and thus restrict the trustee company to a claim against the insolvency for breach of contract. The only means of avoiding this difficulty is by creating a floating charge over the finance company's rights in the subjects that it may have a right to repossess, and in any entitlement it may have in the proceeds of sale of those subjects. Thus in the case of a finance company which lets vehicles on hire purchase, a floating charge would be taken over that company's interest in the vehicles and its interest in any contract for the sale of those vehicles following repossession. Any such floating charge would require registration; it cannot be regarded as part-implement of a contract for sale of the debts.

Enforcement of trust rights

The general rights of the beneficiary in a trust to enforce it against the **12–23** trustee were described in *Inland Revenue v Clark's Trs*[40] in the following terms:

> "When counsel was asked to state what rights of action a benefici- ary has by our law to protect his interest in the trust estate, he was obliged to admit that these rights of action were a right to interdict the trustee from committing any breach of trust, and a right of personal action, for example a declarator or an action of accounting against the trustees, to compel them to administer the trust accord- ing to its terms. There is also a personal action for damages against the trustees for breach of trust, and it is open for the beneficiary, by suitable procedure in this court, to bring about a change of

---

[38] See para.13–06.
[39] See para.13–20.
[40] 1939 S.C. 11.

administration of the trust either by a transfer of the administration to new trustees or by transfer of the administration to a judicial factor. But there is no action by which a beneficiary as such can in any way vindicate for himself any of the trust property . . . It is no exception from, but rather a confirmation of, this proposition, that a beneficiary may compel trustees to give the use of their names or to grant an assignation of their claim against a third party".[41]

Where the trustee is insolvent, a personal action for damages will obviously be of no assistance. An action for accounting may be of help if trust property can be traced in the hands of the trustee or elsewhere.[42] If the liquidator, administrator or receiver of an insolvent trustee attempts to interfere with trust property in such a way as to defeat the beneficiary's rights, an interdict against breach of trust will be appropriate. That is a competent course against an administrator, notwithstanding paras 42 and 43 of the new Sch.B1 to the Insolvency Act 1986, as only the administrator, and not the company, need be called as a defender. Likewise, interdict may be obtained against a liquidator without consent, notwithstanding s.130(2) of the same Act. Thus, if the liquidator of a finance company that had entered into a securitisation agreement attempted to renegotiate hire-purchase contracts that had been made subject to a trust, the beneficiary in that trust could obtain interdict against such actings.[43]

Change in administration of trust

12–24   In appropriate cases, as Lord President Normand indicates in *Clark's Trs*,[44] a beneficiary can change the administration of a trust. On the insolvency of a trustee, its liquidator, administrator or receiver is unlikely to be interested in continuing the administration of the trust, as the benefit will enure to the beneficiary, not the insolvency. Thus a change in administration is likely to be the beneficiary's most effective remedy. If no specific provision is made in the trust documents, the most appropriate course of action is the appointment of a judicial factor.[45] This is achieved by the presentation of a petition to the court.[46]

---

[41] Lord President Normand at 22; see also Lord Moncrieff at 26.

[42] See para.12–26.

[43] Such interference, to be actionable, need not be with the actual rights of the beneficiary. It is sufficient that a liquidator or administrator of the trustee acts in such a way as to defeat or diminish the reasonable expectations of the beneficiary. On reasonable expectations, see *Inglis v Inglis*, 1983 S.C. 8; *McNiven v Peffers* (1868) 7 M. 181; *Keech v Sandford* (1726) Sel. Cas. Ch. 61; *Cook v Deeks* [1916] 1 A.C. 554; and *Boardman v Phipps* [1967] 2 A.C. 46.

[44] 1939 S.C. 11.

[45] On judicial factors, see generally Walker *Judicial Factors* (1974); and *Stair Memorial Encyclopaedia*, Vol.24, paras 237 *et seq.*

[46] When an administrator has been appointed, it will be necessary to obtain his consent or the leave of the court, as para.4.3 of the new Sch. B1 to the Insolvency Act will apply. Likewise, with a liquidator, s.130(2) requires leave of the court; the company, as trustee, must be called as a respondent in the petition for appointment of a judicial factor. It is thought that there will be no difficulty in obtaining the leave of the court in such cases, even if the administrator will not give consent: see *Re Atlantic Computer Systems plc* [1992] 2 W.L.R. 367; especially at 374–375, 381 and 395C—F. See further Chap.5.

The petition should normally ask for the appointment of an *interim* judicial factor to deal with the position prior to the making of a final appointment. With most forms of commercial agreement involving trusts, notably factoring and securitisation agreements, there will be a constant inflow of funds into the trust, and immediate action will be needed to deal with these. In addition, in securitisation agreements, in particular, it is critical that the flow of funds from debtors through the finance and trustee companies to the note-issuing company should be maintained in order that the latter company can make payments of interest and capital to the noteholders. The note-issuing company will have no other source of income. The petition should also seek powers that will be necessary to enable the judicial factor to administer the trust properly. With a factoring or securitisation agreement, those powers must include power to enforce all of the trustee's rights and powers in respect of the debtors, to collect and if necessary sue for all receivables due from debtors, and to pay all sums collected to the beneficiary of the trust, after deduction of expenses. The factor should also be empowered to appoint agents to assist him in the performance of his duties.

It will usually be more satisfactory to include in the trust documents a specific power, exercisable by the beneficiary, to change the administration of the trust. One possibility is a simple power to appoint a new trustee in the event of the insolvency of the original trustee. It is more common, however, to make use of a power of attorney granted by the trustee, exercisable on the trustee's insolvency.[47] Such a power must be contained expressly in the trust documents. It should entitle the attorney (as mandatory for the trustee) to administer the trust in place of the original trustee. The attorney should be expressly authorised to exercise the whole rights and powers of the original trustee, including any discretions exercisable by it. Power to collect and sue for debts or other trust property should also be conferred, and a power to appoint agents will probably be of assistance.

Another useful provision in the trust documents is a power, exercisable by the beneficiary, to call on the trustee to make over the whole rights that are subject to the trust. That is an example of the general principle that a beneficiary who is absolutely entitled to trust property (the beneficiary of a bare trust) and *sui juris* can call on the trustee to denude in his favour.[48] It should further be provided that the right of the beneficiary to call for a transfer of the trust funds is exercisable notwithstanding the insolvency of the trustee, and that in that event an assignation or other transfer of the trust property in favour of the beneficiary may be exercised by an attorney or other mandatory on behalf of the trustee.[49] Such a power merely involves the beneficiary's fundamental right to compel the trustee to denude, and it provides a convenient method of superseding the trustee's administration in the event of its insolvency. Following an assignation or other transfer

---

[47] On powers of attorney in insolvency, see Chap.15.
[48] *Miller's Trs v Miller* (1890) 18 R. 301; *Yuill's Trs v Thomson* (1902) 4 F. 815; *Stair Memorial Encyclopaedia*, Vol.24, para.72; Wilson and Duncan, pp.167 *et seq.*
[49] On the validity of such provisions, see Chap.15.

executed by the attorney, the beneficiary must take all necessary steps to complete its real rights. Thus, if an assignation of debts is involved, the beneficiary must intimate the assignation to each of the debtors.

Administration of trust by liquidator, administrator or receiver

12–25   In certain cases the liquidator, administrator or receiver or a company that acts as a trustee may continue the administration of the trust, even though it does not benefit the insolvency. In such a case the person administering the trust is subject to the rights and duties of a trustee, and may be liable for breach of trust if he fails to administer the trust properly. In England it has been held that, in such cases, the liquidator or other insolvency practitioner is entitled to payment of his expenses and reasonable remuneration out of the trust funds.[50] It is thought that the result in Scotland would be the same. So far as expenses and outlays are concerned, the liquidator would be in the position of a *negotiorum gestor*.[51] The right to reasonable remuneration was founded on the equitable nature of trust rights, and that is a feature of Scottish trusts.[52]

Tracing of trust property

12–26   While the rights of a beneficiary against trust property on the trustee's insolvency are clearly established,[53] practical difficulties often arise in determining what is trust property. There is obviously no problem if trust property is in the name of the trustee and if its state has not been altered. The trustee may, however, have used trust property to acquire other property, which may or may not be in his own name, or he may have mixed the trust property with his own, for example, by paying both his own funds and trust funds into a common bank account in his name. He may have granted real rights over the trust property in favour of a third party. Such cases are governed by two general principles. The first is that the rights of the beneficiary will continue to affect trust property in the hands of the trustee, or any person who acquires such property from the trustee, as long as it remains identifiable as trust property. The application of this principle is generally referred to as the tracing of the trust property. This first principle, however, is subject to the second, which is that the rights of the beneficiary will be defeated if trust property has found its way to a transferee who gives full value and takes in good faith without notice of the trust.[54] It is thought that the test for the identifiability of trust property should be a practical one—as long as it is possible to discover a fund or an item of property in the hands of the trustee or an acquirer from the trustee which contains trust property or was bought using trust property, or represents the proceeds of trust property, that item will be identifiable as trust property.[55] Provided that

---

[50] *Re Berkeley Applegate (Investment Consultants) Ltd* [1989] B.C.L.C. 28.

[51] See Gloag on *Contract*, pp.334–335.

[52] The word "equitable" is here used in the Scottish sense, and not in the technical sense that it has acquired in English law.

[53] See paras 12–01 *et seq.*

[54] *Redfearn v Somervail* (1813) 1 Dow 50; 1 Pat. App. 707. See above at para.12–01.

[55] No test has been laid down judicially, but a practical approach has clearly been followed in the cases discussed below. See Bell, *Comm.*, I, 216.

this test is satisfied, it does not matter what the nature of the transaction was. Nor does it matter how many transactions may have affected the trust property.[56]

Inmixing of trust funds with trustee's own money

It frequently occurs in practice that an insolvent trustee has inmixed **12–27** trust funds with his own money, usually in a bank account operated by him. The general rule in such cases is that: "the court will, if it can, disentangle the account and separate the trust funds from the private monies, and award the former specifically to the beneficiaries."[57] If the trustee makes payments out of the account for his own purposes, the presumption is that these are made from his private money, and that what is left, or as much of that as is necessary, remains subject to the trust.[58] In such cases the rule in *Clayton*[59] does not apply to trust funds that have been inmixed with a trustee's own funds. It is also established that the onus of proving which part of a mixed fund is the trustee's lies on him. "If a man mixes trust funds with his own, the whole will be treated as the trust property, except so far as he may be able to distinguish what is his own."[60] The result is different, however, when the trustee's bank account is overdrawn and trust money paid into it. In such cases, if the bank has no notice of the trust and applies the payments to reduce the trustee's overdraft, the trust money paid into the account will become the property of the bank and the beneficiaries' rights will be defeated.[61] In cases where the bank uses trust money to reduce the trustee's overdraft in ignorance of the trust, it is in the position of a transferee of trust money in good faith and for value, and thus its rights prevail against those of the trust beneficiaries. If, by contrast, the trustee's account is at credit, the bank does not give value when funds are paid into the account, and thus its rights do not prevail

---

[56] See *Newton's Exrx v Meiklejohn's J.F.*, 1959 S.L.T. 71, where the pledging of shares by a stockbroker under a general letter of hypothecation was held not to be sufficient to destroy the identity of those shares as trust property.

[57] *Smith v Liquidator of James Birrell Ltd*, 1968 S.L.T. 174 at 175, *per* Lord Fraser; see also *Macadam v Martin's Tr.* (1872) 11 M. 33; *Jopp v Johnston's Tr.* (1904) 6 F. 1028. The leading English cases on this problem are *Re Hallett's Estate* (1879) 13 Ch. D. 696 and *Sinclair v Brougham* [1914] A.C. 398. English law differs markedly from Scots law in this area, however. In England distinct rights to trace property are recognised at law and in equity, and many of the cases turn on somewhat narrow distinctions that have not become part of Scots law.

[58] *Jopp v Johnston's Tr.*, *supra*, where *Re Hallett's Estate*, *supra*, was followed.

[59] 1 Mer. 572, discussed in Gloag on *Contract* at pp.713–715 and McBryde on *Contract* at paras 22–26 and 22–27.

[60] *Frith v Cartland* (1865) 2 H. and M. 417 at 420–421, *per* Wood V.-C., cited with approval by Jessel M.R. in *Re Hallett's Estate*, *supra*, at 719; and by Lord Justice-Clerk Macdonald in *Jopp v Johnston's Tr*, *supra*, at 1035.

[61] *Thomson v Clydesdale Bank Ltd* (1891) 18 R. 751; (1893) 20 R. (H.L.) 59; *Hofford v Gowans* (1909) 1 S.L.T. 153; *Bank of Scotland v MacLeod Paxton Woolard & Co*, 1998 S.L.T. 258; *Style Financial Services Ltd v Bank of Scotland*, 1996 S.L.T. 421; *Style Financial Services Ltd v Bank of Scotland (No 2)*, 1998 S.L.T. 851, at 863–864 and 867–868. It is necessary that the bank should actually apply the money to reduce the overdraft if the beneficiaries' rights are to be defeated. This explains why the opposite result was reached in *Smith v Liquodator of James Birrell Ltd*, *supra*, where the bank did not consolidate the trustee's two accounts, one of which was overdrawn.

against the trust. Consequently, in such cases the beneficiaries are entitled to trace the trust money into the trustee's bank account. If, however, the bank subsequently allows the account holder to draw cheques on the account in reliance on the sums at credit of the account, or itself issues banker's drafts in reliance on the account's being in credit, it thereby gives value and is accordingly not liable for the sums so transferred from the account.[62] The bank will only escape liability in such cases is it has no knowledge of the trust. If it is aware that the monies in question are indeed trust monies it will lack good faith, and consequently its rights will not prevail over the rights of the beneficiaries of the trust.[63] If a bank, or any other recipients of trust funds, either fails to provide onerous consideration or is aware that funds have been applied in breach of trust, it will be liable to the trust on the basis of the principle analogous to recompense that no one can profit from another person's fraud or breach of trust.[64] That general principle is only defeated by the combination of good faith and onerous consideration.

Case law

12–28   The leading case in this area is *Thomson v Clydesdale Bank*.[65] A stockbroker paid a sum of money into his overdrawn bank account by endorsing a cheque received by him from another stockbroker to whom he had sold certain shares. The shares had been sold on the instructions of trustees, who had further instructed him to place the price on deposit with certain banks. The ordinary course of business on the stock exchange was that the selling broker received the buying broker's cheque and make payment to his own customer by his own cheque or, where he had instructions to reinvest, by delivery of the new investments. The sum paid by the broker into his account was applied by the bank in reduction of the overdraft, but did not extinguish it. The broker did not reinvest the funds as instructed by the trustees, and a few days later he absconded without having made any further significant operations on his bank account. The bank's officials gave evidence that they believed the money to have come into the broker's hands in the course of his business as a broker, and there was no evidence that the bank knew that the broker had improperly paid the money into his own account. It was held that the bank was under no obligation to repay the money in question to the trustees. The relevant principles of law were stated by Lord Watson in the following terms[66]:

> "When a broker, or other agent entrusted with the possession and apparent ownership of money, pays it away in the ordinary course of his business, for onerous consideration, I regard it as settled law

---

[62] *Bank of Scotland v MacLeod Paxton Woolard & Co, supra.*
[63] *Taylor v Forbes* (1830) 4 W. & S. 444; *Bank of Scotland v MacLeod Paxton Woolard & Co, supra; Style Financial Services Ltd v Bank of Scotland, supra.*
[64] 155a *Gibbs v British Linen Company* (1875) 4 R. 630; *Clydesdale Bank v Paul* (1877) 4 R. 626; *Thomson v Clydesdale Bank, supra; Bank of Scotland v MacLeod Paxton Woolard & Co, supra; Style Financial Services Ltd v Bank of Scotland (No 2), supra.*
[65] Above.
[66] At 20 R. (H.L.) 61. See also L.C. Herschell at 60 and Lord Shand at 62–63, and the Lord Ordinary (Kyllachy) at 18 R. 754.

that a transaction which is fraudulent as between the agent and his employer will bind the latter, unless he can shew that the recipient of the money did not transact in good faith with his agent . . .

The payment to the bank was onerous in so far as concerned the respondents, because, whenever made, it operated in law as a discharge by them pro tanto of the broker's liability for the debit balance on his account; and several drafts were made by him and honoured before his dishonesty became known

The broker knew that he was insolvent, and that he was using his customers' money to pay his own debt to the bank without any reasonable expectation of his being able to replace it. That was an undoubted fraud upon the appellants; but, in my opinion, the broker's fraud is of no relevancy in this case, unless it is coupled with bad faith on the part of the respondents. The onus of proving that they acted in *mala fide* rests with the appellants. It is not enough for them to prove that the respondents acted negligently; in order to succeed, they must established that the respondents knew, not only that the money represented by the cheque did not belong to the broker, but that he had no authority from the true owner to pay it into his bank account".

Thomson has been followed in two recent cases, *Bank of Scotland v MacLeod Paxton Woolard & Co*[67] and *Style Financial Services Limited v Bank of Scotland*.[68] In the first of these, funds that had been obtained by fraud were paid into two accounts with the Bank of Scotland in Glasgow. Those accounts were in the name of a firm of accountants, and the sums paid in were much larger than any previous transactions carried out by that firm. The bank made certain inquiries to comply with regulations designed to combat money laundering, but they were unable to discover the true nature of the fraud. Consequently they complied with instructions to pay banker's drafts to third parties, reimbursing themselves from the funds in the two accounts.[69] Eventually the nature of the fraud became apparent, and at that point the bank stopped transactions on the two accounts and subsequently raised an action of multiplepoinding in order to determine entitlement to the funds remaining in the accounts. The bank had stopped certain of the banker's drafts before payment. In one case the payee had raised an action against the bank and had ultimately obtained decree for the sum in the draft. The bank claimed to be entitled to take credit for that sum out of the funds remaining in one of the accounts. The parties who had been defrauded claimed that they were entitled to the whole sums standing at credit of the accounts, and that the bank were not entitled to take any credit for sums paid under banker's drafts. They argued that the bank had failed to make sufficient inquiries and was thus reckless or wilfully blind as to the true position.

---

[67] Above.

[68] Above.

[69] A banker's draft involves an obligation on the bank itself that is not in any way dependent upon the availability of funds in its customer's account. Consequently, the normal practice followed by banks, which was followed by the Bank of Scotland in the case under discussion, is that the bank reimburses itself with funds from its customer's account before issuing a draft on the customer's instructions.

Lord Coulsfield held that the bank had at all times acted in good faith and had given onerous consideration, in the form of issuing a banker's draft on the faith of the funds that had been paid into the two accounts in the name of the firm of accountants. The bank had accordingly brought themselves within the principle that a party who receives funds in good faith and gives onerous consideration is not affected by any breach of trust that may have affected the funds in the past. Lord Coulsfield summarised the result of the decision in *Thomson* as follows[70]:

> "That decision, therefore, establishes . . . that in order to establish liability against the recipient of a payment who has given valuable consideration, it is not enough to show the mere receipt of the payment nor even the negligent receipt of the payment. The person seeking recovery, as true owner, must show that the recipient was not in bona fide. It is true that, in [*Thomson*], Lord Shand refers to facts 'which put the bankers on inquiry', but, in context, that seems to me to be a reference to the particular facts of the case, in which there was no evidence of anything of the kind, not a qualification on the principle which he had earlier expressed both in *Thomson* and in *Gibbs*. The same can, I think, be said of the Lord Chancellor's reference to the recipient having 'reason to believe' and of Lord Kyllachy's reference to constructive knowledge. The question upon which the present dispute terms, therefore, is what the pursuers have to prove in order to show that the bank were not in bona fide".

12–29 On that matter Lord Coulsfield stated that there was no Scottish authority directly in point, but that the matter had been considered in a tract of English and Privy Council authority, which he then analysed at length.[71] He concluded, on the basis of these cases, that it must now be taken to be clear that the dishonesty is an essential element in the establishing of liability against a third party in cases such as this. As to the precise meaning of dishonesty for this purpose, Lord Coulsfield held that the correct standard appeared from the speeches in *Thomson v Clydesdale Bank*.[72] He concluded[73]:

> "What these passages seem to me to show is that evidence of acts or omissions which might be described as showing wilful blindness, will fall or reckless failure to ask questions, commercially unacceptable conduct or any other form of doubtful behaviour, is evidence which can properly be considered, along with any other evidence in the case, in deciding whether an inference should be drawn that the person in question was acting dishonestly, but that the question is not whether there was blindness or recklessness per se but whether there was dishonesty or improbity".

---

[70] At 1998 S.L.T. 274B—D.
[71] Notably the decision of the Privy Council in *Royal Brunei Airlines v Tan* [1995] 2 A.C. 378. Lord Coulsfield expressly rejected the five-point analysis of dishonesty suggested by Peter Gibson J. in *Baden v Societe Generale pour Favoriser le Developement du Commerce et de l'Industrie en France SA* [1993] 1 W.L.R. 509.
[72] Above.
[73] At 1998 S.L.T. 276G—H.

On the facts of the case before him, Lord Coulsfield held that no dishonesty or improbity had been established. There was no evidence from which it could be inferred that any officer of the bank knew or actually suspected that a fraud had been committed for that the funds remitted to the two accounts in question were the proceeds of fraud. Nor could it be said that any bank officer shut his eyes to the fact that a fraud was taking place; there was nothing in the way of reckless or wilful blindness, or any other doubtful or unacceptable behaviour on the part of those officers. Steps had in fact been taken to find out what was happening, and it was significant that, even when it began to appear that some sort of fraud had been or was being committed, there was great uncertainty as to what exactly that fraud was. It followed that the bank were entitled to take credit for the sum relating to the banker's draft that they had been compelled to pay. The bank were further held entitled to retain sums held in suspense accounts against other banker's drafts that had been issued, even though no attempt to enforce those drafts had yet been made. Those sums could be held until the drafts prescribed.

The facts and general conclusions of *Style Financial Services Limited v Bank of Scotland (No 2)*[74] are set out above.[75] Lord Gill's analysis of the law begins with a discussion of the incidents of the banker-customer relationship. He states[76]:

"In general, the relationship of banker and customer is simply that of debtor and creditor . . . In receiving funds from his customer and crediting them to the customer's account, the banker is in general under no obligation to inquire as to the source of those funds . . . The mere fact that the banker knows that the funds have been received by the customer on behalf of a third party will not put the banker in bad faith in such circumstances, provided that the funds are credited in the ordinary course of the customer's business. There may however be circumstances in which the banker has notice, actual or constructive, that the payment is being supplied by the customer and is therefore liable to the third party.

In the absence of express authorisation the banker has no right to credit to the account of a customer cheques made payable to a third party; but such express authorisation may be given in the form of an appropriate mandate to the banker from the third party. Where the banker credits such cheques to the customer's account in pursuance of the mandate, that transaction, in my opinion, will be a transaction in ordinary course. Moreover, if money is paid in in virtue of such a mandate, the credit resulting from such a pay-in is available to the account holder to be drawn on by him for any purpose . . . If that consequence is to be excluded, the third party must qualify his mandate appropriately".

The critical feature of the present case was the existence of the mandate. **12–30** Lord Gill considered that it constituted "a clear and unambiguous

---

[74] Above.
[75] At para.12–14.
[76] At 1998 S.L.T. 863C—F.

authorisation by the pursuers to the defenders to credit to Goldberg's account any cheque or postal order payable to the pursuers that Goldberg should lodge as a payment to their own account". The mandate did not limit Goldberg's right to deal with the money, or earmark the Style collections in any way. Goldberg's receipts would in any event include payments for their own sales as well as Style collections, and the defenders would be unaware of the extent to which monies received by them were referable to Style collections and would have no duty to inquire as to that matter. In these respects the position of the defenders was a fortiori of that of the bank in *Thomson v Clydesdale Bank*.[77]

Lord Gill held[78] that the agreements entered into between the pursuers and Goldberg gave rise to the relationship of principal and agent between the pursuers and Goldberg, in relation to the collection of payments made in Goldberg stores by Style cardholders. That did not, however, give rise to a trust relationship between Goldberg and the pursuers. The conclusion followed from both the wording of the agreements themselves and the commercial context in which they operated. Even if the Style collections had been subject to a trust, however, Lord Gill would have held that Goldberg could not have been in breach of it by paying the monies into their account, because the mandate expressly authorised them to do so. The only breach of trust that could have occurred would have been that involved in Goldberg's failing to pay the sums due by them to the pursuers after the agreed interval.

There had in fact been such delays and, if Goldberg had been guilty of a breach of trust, the question would have arisen as to whether the defenders were liable to the pursuers for such breach. Lord Gill held that the defenders would not have been so liable. He stated the relevant principles as follows[79]:

> "On the assumption that Goldberg were in breach of trust in failing to remit the sums sued for to the pursuers, the defenders would have been liable to the pursuers for those sums only on the principle that no one is entitled knowingly to profit from another's breach of trust and . . . The defenders would not have incurred such a liability if they gave value for the monies received and were in good faith".

Lord Gill held that the defenders had acquired the relevant monies for onerous consideration and were in good faith in doing so. Onerous consideration arose because the monies were paid into Goldberg's overdrawn account; thus they were applied in payment of a debt lawfully due by Goldberg to the defenders. On the authority of *Thomson v Clydesdale Bank Limited*,[80] such a payment is received by the bank for

---

[77] Above.
[78] At 1988 S.L.T. 865K. See para.12–14, above.
[79] *ibid.* at 1998 S.L.T. 867C–D.
[80] Above.

an onerous consideration. Moreover, in reliance on Goldberg's continued payment of the Style collections into their account, including those collections to which the mandate applied, the defenders continued and extended Goldberg's overdraft. But for the mandate, the defenders would have set the overdraft limit at a lower level, and would have appointed receivers over Goldberg's property much sooner. This to involve giving value for the receipt of the relevant monies.

So far as bad faith was concerned, the pursuers relied solely on knowledge that funds were paid in breach of trust; consequently it was unnecessary to consider other circumstances, of the sort discussed in *Bank of Scotland v MacLeod Paxton Woolard & Co*,[81] that might amount to bad faith. Lord Gill held that, for bad faith to exist, the defenders' knowledge must extent to two crucial matters: first, that the monies deposited did not belong to Goldberg, and secondly, that Goldberg had no authority to pay the monies into their overdrawn account. He held that the pursuers' case failed on both of these grounds. On the first, the defenders had not seen any of the contracts entered into between the pursuers and Goldberg, and were never put on notice as to the terms of those contracts. Nor were they ever told that the relevant monies were subject to a trust. On the second, the defenders had the mandate from the pursuers in their favour, and that authorised them to credit cheques and postal orders made payable to the pursuers to Goldberg's account.[82] That meant that the defenders could not have been said knowingly to be in receipt of unauthorised payments of trust funds, if the funds had been subject to a trust.

Inmixing of trust funds with funds of third party

Trust money may be inmixed with the funds of persons other than the **12–31** trustee. In the only reported Scottish case on this area of the law, *Magistrates of Edinburgh v McLaren*,[83] the funds of two trusts were inmixed and administered together. It was held that the combined fund should be divided rateably between the trusts, according to the amounts derived from each. In making the division, income and capital were divided separately in such a way as to reflect the different periods during which the property of each trust had been part of the common fund. This result appears just, and is certainly preferable to the application of the rule in *Clayton*, which may have very arbitrary consequences. When trust money is inmixed with the funds of a third party who acts in good faith, without knowledge of the trust, but does not give full value, it is thought that the result should be the same as with the inmixing of the funds of two trusts. In such cases, if the third party removes more than his share from the mixed fund, the beneficiaries of

---

[81] Above.

[82] At 1998 S.L.T. 867E—868J. The New Zealand case, *Westpac Banking Corporation v Savin* [95] 2 N.Z.L.R. 41, was distinguished, as were *Stephens Travel Service International Pty Ltd v Qantas Airways Ltd* (1988) 13 N.S.W.L.R. 331; and *Extruded Welding Wire (Sales) Ltd v McLachlan & Brown*, 1986 S.L.T. 314.

[83] (1881) 8 R. (H.L.) 1, above at 40.

the trust are entitled to recover the excess from him, since he has not given value for the money removed.[84]

Property derived from trust property

12–32   A trustee may use trust property held by him, either by itself or together with his own property, to acquire other property. In all such cases the property so acquired will be subject to the trust, and the beneficiaries will be entitled to claim it in the event of the trustee's insolvency.[85] It is essential, however, that the property should remain identifiable as trust property, in the manner discussed above.[86] If a third party who either knows of the trust or does not give full value acquires property using trust funds, the result is the same; the rights of such persons do not prevail against the trust.

If a trustee or third party acquires property using both his own funds and trust funds, it is thought that any increase in the value of the property so acquired should be shared rateably by the acquirer and the trust so long as the acquirer is acting honestly. If, on the other hand, the trustee commits a wilful breach of trust, or the third party knows that he is dealing with trust property, it is thought that any increase in value should accrue to the trust. In such cases there is a deliberate breach of trust, or deliberate acquiescence in a breach of trust, and it seems inequitable that the party guilty of such breach or acquiescence should profit in any way from his actions. Furthermore, if a third party takes title to trust property or deals with it in knowledge of the trust, he will take that property, or anything representing it, as a constructive trustee. The beneficiaries will thus be entitled to enforce the trust against him, and to claim any profits arising from the use of the trust property in exactly the same way as against the original trustee.[87]

Enforcement of creditors' rights against trustee[88]

12–33   A trustee who enters into a contractual obligation with a third party to the trust is generally personally liable on such an obligation.[89] It is possible for a trustee to contract in such a way that the trust estate only

---

[84] In so far as the English decision in *Re Diplock* [1948] Ch. 465 goes beyond this proposition, it does not appear to be in accordance with Scots law.

[85] *Jopp v Johnston's Tr.* (1904) 6 F. 1028, where money was withdrawn from a bank account that included both trust funds and the trustee's own funds and was placed on deposit receipt in the trustee's name.

[86] See para.12–26.

[87] In England those who intermeddle with trust property are distinguished from those who act as agents for the trust within the scope of their authority as such agents; the latter are generally not held liable as constructive trustees: *Barnes v Addy* (1874) L.R. 9 Ch. App. 244; *Mara v Browne* [1896] 1 Ch. 199; *Williams-Ashman v Price and Williams* [1942] Ch. 219; *Carl Zeiss Stiftung v Herbert Smith & Co (No 2)* [1969] 2 Ch. 276. If such a rule represents die law of Scotland, it is thought that it should not apply where an agent deals with or takes control of property in the knowledge that a breach of trust is being committed; in such cases the agent is actively and knowingly taking part in a breach of trust.

[88] See generally *Stair Memorial Encyclopaedia*, Vol. 24, para.225; Wilson and Duncan, pp.451 *et seq.*

[89] *Cullen v Baillie* (1856) 8 D. 511.

is bound, but that requires the agreement, express or clearly implied, of the other contracting party.[90] Even if the trustee is unable to meet his obligations from his own resources, a creditor who has contracted with the trustee in his capacity of trustee may claim payment from the funds of the trust.[91] That is so whether or not the creditor was aware of the existence of the trust. What matters is whether the trustee in fact contracted on behalf of the trust. It follows that, in the event of the trustee's insolvency, the creditors who contracted with the trustee acting in that capacity may take steps to secure the administration of the trust so that they may be paid out of the trust assets. To this end, it will not usually be appropriate to appoint a liquidator to the trustee, as that will not segregate the trust funds from the trustee's own property.[92] Instead, it will generally be preferable to have a judicial factor appointed on the trust estate. The factor's duty is then to ingather the trust property and to pay the creditors of the trust and thereafter the beneficiaries.

Creditors of the trust are invariably entitled to payment out of trust funds in preference to beneficiaries of the trust, unless the creditor's claim involved a breach of trust by the trustee and (1) the creditor was aware of that breach of trust, or (2) the creditor did not give full value for his debt.[93] The beneficiary's right is only to the balance of the trust funds after all debts properly constituted by the trustee have been paid. Consequently, if it appears likely that a trustee will make the whole of the trust property over to the beneficiaries without first paying all creditors of the trust, those creditors may obtain an interdict against the transfer to the beneficiaries. A trustee has a right to reimbursement out of the trust estate in respect of debts that he has properly contracted on behalf of the trust.[94] Moreover, in security of his right to reimbursement a trustee has a lien over trust property,[95] and may in some circumstances have a right of general retention.[96] It follows that a trustee should not make over trust funds to a beneficiary unless he has made full provision for the debts of the trust. If he fails to make provision for the debts of the trust, his personal liability on such debts remains. If his own estate is not sufficient to meet those debts, the transfer to the beneficiary will constitute a gratuitous alienation,[97] on the basis that there is no obligation to transfer funds to the beneficiary until the debts of the trust have been paid.

---

[90] *Cullen v Ballie* (1856) 8 D. 511; *Lumsden v Buchanan* (1865) 3 M. (H.L.) 89 at 95, *per* Lord Cranworth.

[91] *Cunnigham v Montgomerie* (1879) 6 R. 1333.

[92] If the creditor has a prospect of recovering funds from the trustee's own estate, the appointment of a liquidator will be appropriate, but corporate trustees generally have no significant assets apart from the trust funds under their charge.

[93] See para.12–01, above.

[94] See generally Wilson and Duncan, pp.472 *et seq.*; *Stair Memorial Encyclopaedia*, Vol.24, paras 232 *et seq.*

[95] Gloag & Irvine, *Rights in Security*, pp.403–405.

[96] Gloag & Irvine, pp.330–340.

[97] See Chap.17.

CHAPTER 13

THE NATURE OF A SECURITY

Introduction

In common with other systems based on Roman law, Scots law has **13–01** taken a restrictive approach to the creation of real securities. Three general categories of real security[1] existed at common law. Over land and heritable rights generally, the *ex facie* absolute disposition, normally accompanied by a back letter indicating the terms of the security, was the usual form, although two other forms, the bond and disposition in security and bond of cash credit, were both available.[2] Over corporeal moveable property (goods), the only form of security was the pledge.[3] Over incorporeal moveable property (debts, shares, policies of assurance and contractual rights generally), the only form of security was an assignation in security; the terms of the security might be set out on the face of the assignation or in a separate back letter.[4] In each case, security rights could be created only by delivery of possession or its equivalent. In the case of heritable securities, this was achieved by recording in the Register of Sasines. In the case of pledge, delivery of the goods, or of a document of title representing the goods, to the security holder was essential. The only exception occurred if the security holder already had possession, in which case retention served as the equivalent of delivery. In the case of assignation in security, intimation to the debtor formed the equivalent of delivery.

The common law has been modified by statute in two important respects. First, the old forms of heritable security were replaced in 1970 by the standard security.[5] Recording in the Register of Sasines (or, since 1979,[6] registration in the Land Register) is still necessary, however, to

---

[1] In a real security rights are created in favour of the security holder over items of property. That should be contrasted with personal security, or caution, which takes the form of a guarantee. A real security is enforceable over the property notwithstanding the insolvency of its owner (subject, in the case of petitions, for the appointment of an administrator and administration orders, to Insolvency Act 1986, ss.10(1)(b) or 11(3)(c)). A guarantee, by contrast, merely gives a personal right of action against the guarantor (unless it is backed by a real security), and on his insolvency the creditor can only rank for a dividend.

[2] See Halliday, *Conveyancing Law and Practice*, Vol.3, Chaps 32–34; Gloag and Irvine, *Rights in Security*, Chaps 2–6.

[3] Gloag and Irvine, Chap.7; C. Miller, *Corporeal Moveables in Scots Law*, paras 11.04–11.14.

[4] Gloag and Irvine, Chaps 13–16.

[5] Conveyancing and Feudal Reform (Scotland) Act 1970, ss.9–31; see *Halliday*, Chaps 36–40, 42.

[6] Land Registration (Scotland) Act 1979.

create real security rights which will prevail on the insolvency of the owner of the property. Secondly, the floating charge was introduced in 1961.[7] It is ineffective without registration in the company's register of charges.[8]

Apart from the foregoing general categories of security, rights of retention and lien are recognised, founded on ownership or possession or on the principle of mutuality of contractual obligations.[9] Finally, there exist a number of highly specific securities in the nature of a hypothec (a security without delivery of possession or its equivalent); namely the landlord's and superior's hypothecs and a variety of securities over ships and aircraft.[10] These form exceptions of a limited nature to the rule that delivery or its equivalent is necessary to constitute a security.

The importance of identifying whether a right purportedly created by parties is of the nature of a real security is that, if it does not fit into one of the recognised categories of security, it will be ineffective on the insolvency of the granter. In particular, apart from the limited number of hypothecs and the floating charge, if delivery or retention of possession of the security subjects or an equivalent of delivery does not occur, any right of the nature of a security will be ineffective. Further, any attempt to achieve the result of a real security by means of a mere personal contract will not be recognised.

Nature of a security—right accessory to creditor's primary right to sue for debt

13–02   Perhaps the most satisfactory description of a security in Scottish legal literature is that of Gloag and Irvine[11]:

> "[A]ny right which a creditor may hold for ensuring the payment or satisfaction of his debt, distinct from, and in addition to, his right of action and execution against the debtor under the latter's personal obligation. A creditor, in other words, who holds a right in security, has at his disposal some means of realising payments or exacting performance of the obligation due to him, distinct from, and in addition to, the means which are at the disposal of the debtor's general creditors, who have relied solely on the debtor's personal credit. Whatever the special form of the right in security may be, its effect is in all cases to put the party entitled to it in a position of advantage, and to render his power of realising payment of his debt more sure . . . Further, a right of this kind is always necessarily accessory in its nature, being constituted for the merely

---

[7] Companies (Floating Charges) (Scotland) Act 1961. The law is now contained in ss.462–466 of the Companies Act 1985. See Chap.5.

[8] See para.6–07.

[9] See Gloag and Irvine, Chaps 10 and 11; Gloag on *Contract*, pp.623–644.

[10] See Gloag and Irvine, pp.406–437 (landlord's and superior's hypothecs), 291–302, 437–439 (securities over ships).

[11] Gloag and Irvine, *Rights in Security*, pp.1–2.

subsidiary purpose of enabling the person entitled to it to make sure of receiving a certain sum which is due to him, if not otherwise, then at all events by means of the right in question".

The critical feature of this description is the accessory nature of a security right; it is a right additional to the primary right to sue for payment of the debt.

Qualifications

Gloag and Irvine's description of a right in security must now be **13–03** regarded as qualified by the decision of the House of Lords in *Armour v Thyssen Edelstahlwerke A.G.*[12] Lord Keith[13] drew attention to the following passage in Gloag and Irvine's introduction to their chapter on securities over moveables:

> "It is proposed in this and the succeeding chapters to consider by what method a party in possession of [corporeal moveable] property may convey or transfer it in security; that is, by what methods he may, while retaining the ownership in, or at least the ultimate right to, the subject, confer on a particular creditor a right over it, which will enable that creditor to vindicate that subordinate right in a question with the general creditors of his author, with particular creditors attaching the subject by diligence, or with a third party to whom it may have been transferred."[14]

He continued:

> "Can it be said that Carron [the purchasers of goods under an 'all sums' retention of tide clause] somehow attempted to create a security over the goods in favour of the appellants [the sellers of the goods]? In order that it might do so it would require to have both the ownership and the possession, actual or constructive, of the goods. The essence of a right in security is that the debtor retains at least what Gloag and Irvine call the ultimate right to the goods. Can it be said that Carron obtained anything which gave it the capacity to retain an ultimate right to the goods? That could be so only if the contract of sale gave it the property in the goods, but the contract of sale said that the property in the goods was not to pass until all debts due to the appellants had been paid. We are now very far removed from the situation where a party in possession of corporeal moveables is seeking to create a subordinate right in favour of a condition while retaining the ultimate right to himself . . . Carron had no interest of any kind whatever in any particular goods. Carron was never in a position to confer upon the appellants any subordinate right over the [goods], nor did it ever seek to do so".[15]

---

[12] 1990 S.L.T. 891; the decision in that case is discussed at paras 13–04 and 13–05, below.
[13] *ibid.* at 894F—H.
[14] Chap.7; the passage occurs at p.187.
[15] 1990 S.L.T. 891 at 894I—L.

In a later passage in his speech, Lord Keith stated:

> "In all cases where a right in security is conferred the debtor retains an ultimate right over the subject matter in question. The creditor, having realised out of that subject matter a sufficient sum to meet the debt, is obliged to account to the debtor for any surplus".[16]

Ultimate right over subject matter

13–04   The main criterion in Lord Keith's analysis of the nature of a security is that the person granting the security should have an "ultimate right" over the subject matter of the security. It is not wholly clear from the speech itself what the exact nature of such an "ultimate right" should be. It is nevertheless thought that the right in question must be either a real right to the security subjects or an absolute personal right—that is, a personal right which is not qualified by any contingency.

In *Armour v Thyssen Edelstahlwerke A.G.*[17] the purchasers had agreed to buy a quantity of steel, but the contract provided that property in the steel would not pass until all debts due by the purchasers to the sellers had been paid. The purchasers' right to property in the steel was accordingly contingent upon their payment of all debts to the sellers, and it was held that the purchasers were unable to create a security. On the other hand, the passage from Gloag and Irvine, *Rights in Security*[18] quoted by Lord Keith clearly differentiates between ownership, or a full real right, and the "ultimate right" to the security subjects, which must therefore be something less than a full real right.[19] Likewise rights of retention founded on *ex facie* absolute ownership of property[20] involve the creation of a security right in favour of the actual owner of the property by a person, usually a purchaser or the beneficiary of a trust, who has a merely personal right, or at least a right less than a full real right, to the property. The problem with the view that an absolute personal right to property is necessary in order to create a security over it is that it is competent to assign a contingent debt, for example a term assurance policy, in security. Likewise a *spes successionis* can be assigned absolutely or in security.[21] While a *spes successionis* can be regarded as a form of property right, the right of the holder of a life assurance policy as against the issuing company is a right arising under a personal contract, just as Carron's right to the goods in *Armour* was a right, albeit contingent, under a personal contract. The contingency in *Armour* was

---

[16] 1990 S.L.T. 891 at 895c.

[17] 1990 S.L.T. 891.

[18] Gloag and Irvine, p.187; see para.13–02, above. It does not appear from the passage referred to that Gloag and Irvine intended that the "ultimate right" to the security subjects should be the criterion of what amounts to a security. The concept does not even appear in the general discussion of the nature of a security in Chap.1 of their work.

[19] Lord Keith does, however, suggest at 894l that, in order to create a security, a person must have both ownership and possession of goods. That seems inconsistent with the other examples discussed in this paragraph.

[20] Gloag and Irvine, pp.330–340.

[21] *Browne's Tr. v Anderson* (1901) 4 F. 305.

under the control of Carron, in that by making payment of all sums due to Thyssen they could obtain ownership, but continued payment of premiums is likewise a condition for the validity and enforceability of a life policy. It is in any event difficult to see as a matter of principle why a contingent right should not form the subject of a security, either by assignation or by retention.

Earlier Scottish cases

In earlier Scottish cases under what is now s.62(4) of the Sale of Goods **13–05** Act 1979[22] the approach taken by the court was to consider the substance of the transaction to determine whether it was intended to operate by way of security. The general approach was summarised by Lord Moncrieff in *Robertson v Hall's Tr.*

"The form of the contract is not conclusive. The reality of the transaction must be inquired into; and if, contrary to the form of the contract, and even the declaration of the parties, it appears from the whole circumstances that a true sale was not intended, it will be held that the property has not passed and that no effectual security has been acquired".[23]

It is thought that such a substantive approach should be applied in all cases where the question of whether a transaction is truly a security is in issue. Nevertheless, under s.62(4) a formal approach is clearly impossible, as the subsection applies only to transactions in the form of a contract of sale, and the reference in the subsection to the way the transaction is intended to operate invites a substantive approach.

In *Gavin's Tr. v Fraser*[24] a contractor sold his plant to the timber merchant for whom he was working, at its fair value, and it was agreed that the contractor might buy back the plant within a year for the same price with interest at six per cent. The contractor gave no personal obligation to repay the price, but merely had an option to repurchase. It was held that the agreement was in fact a contract of sale, and was not intended to operate by way of security. The critical point was that there was no personal obligation to be secured by any intended security arrangement.[25] In other words, an obligation in security must be accessory to a principal obligation. If an obligation stands alone, it cannot be a security.

The approach of the House of Lords in *Armour v Thyssen Edelstahlwerke A.G.*[26] suggests that, in future, a more formal and less substantive

---

[22] Formerly s.61(4) of the Sale of Goods Act 1893. The statutory context (see head (6) in para.13–07) has coloured these decisions to a considerable extent.
[23] (1896) 24 R. 120 at 134. See also *Hepburn v Law*, 1914 S.C. 918 at 921; *Newbigging v Morton*, 1930 S.C. 273; and *Scottish Transit Trust v Scottish Land Cultivators*, 1955 S.C. 254.
[24] 1920 S.C. 674.
[25] See Lord President Clyde at 634; Lord Mackenzie at 688–689.
[26] 1990 S.L.T. 891.

approach is likely to be taken to the question of whether a particular right is truly a right in security. In this connection the classic English description of a security is likely to be of assistance. In *Re George Inglefield Ltd*[27] Romer L.J. differentiated a transaction of sale and a transaction of mortgage or charge (in Scottish terminology a security) in the following terms:

"In a transaction of sale the vendor is not entitled to get back the subject-matter of the sale by returning to the purchaser the money that has passed between them. In the case of a mortgage or charge, the mortgagor is entitled, until he has been foreclosed, to get back the subject-matter of the mortgage or charge by returning to the mortgagee the money that has passed between them. The second essential difference is that if the mortgagee realises the subject-matter of the mortgage for a sum more than sufficient to repay him, with interest and the costs, the money that has passed between him and the mortgagor he has to account to the mortgagor for the surplus. If the purchaser sells the subject-matter of the purchase, and realises a profit, of course he has not got to account to the vendor for the profit. Thirdly, if the mortgagee realises the mortgage property for a sum that is insufficient to repay him the money that he has paid to the mortgagor, together with interest and costs, then the mortgagee is entitled to recover from the mortgagor the balance of the money, either because there is a covenant by the mortgagor to repay the money advanced by the mortgagee or because of the existence of the simple contract debt which is created by the mere fact of the advance having been made. If the purchaser were to resell the purchased property at a price which was insufficient to recoup him the money that he paid to the vendor, of course he would not be entitled to recover the balance from the vendor".[28]

The critical features of a security, according to this description, are first that the granter of a security is entitled to recover the subject matter by paying his debt to the security holder, and secondly that, if the security subjects are realised by the security holder, he is entitled to recover his full debt, but only that sum, regardless of the amount realised by the sale of the security subjects. Those features look to the practical operation of a right to discover whether it is a security, rather than to any underlying concept of what a security is. Nevertheless, while it cannot be regarded as a comprehensive description of a security right, Romer L.J.'s opinion provides workable criteria for distinguishing a security, and is likely to be helpful in practice.

As the decision in *Re George Inglefield Ltd*[29] makes clear, if a right involves part implement of a contract of sale it will not constitute a security. In that case a furnishing company which carried on a consider-

---

[27] [1933] Ch. 1.
[28] *ibid.* at 27–28.
[29] At n.4, above.

able hire-purchase business had gone into creditors' voluntary liquidation. To finance its lending, the furnishing company had entered into agreements with a discount company, in terms of which the discount company purchased goods not on hire-purchase together with the benefit of the relative hire-purchase agreements. The furnishing company executed assignments of all such goods and hire-purchase agreements in favour of the discount company, but these were not intimated to the hirers of the goods.[30] It was claimed by the liquidator that the assignments were mortgages or charges of book debts which were void against the creditors of the furnishing company for want of registration. The Court of Appeal held that the agreements were for an out-and-out sale of the goods and the benefit of the hire-purchase contracts, and that the assignments, even though unintimated, were only the part-implement of that sale. The furnishing company had no right to the return of the property assigned, and was entitled to a definite sum (albeit calculated in accordance with a formula) which did not vary according to how much the discount company realised from the contracts assigned or from the resale of the goods which formed the subject matter of those contracts.

Significance of characterisation as security

Characterisation of a right as a security rather than some other form **13–06** of transaction such as a sale is important in a number of respects. These are enumerated below. For the most part the substantive law which governs the enumerated areas falls outwith the scope of the present work. References are given to the principal writings on each subject, to which reference should be made for the detailed law.

(1) A security right must fit into one of the categories of security recognised in Scots law. Otherwise it will be wholly invalid.[31]

(2) Certain categories of security must be registered under ss.410 to 424 of the Companies Act 1985; otherwise they will be void against a liquidator and creditors of the company. If, however, a right does not amount to a security, it will not require registration. Sections 410 to 424 of the 1985 Act are due to be replaced by new provisions enacted by ss.97 to 107 of the Companies Act 1989. These will form ss.395 to 420 of the 1985 Act as amended, and will constitute a uniform scheme of registration for all companies registered under the Companies Acts throughout Great Britain.[32] In practice the most important

---

[30] In Scotland assignation of goods is not competent, but the basic principle in the case still applies.

[31] See paras 13–01 and 13–02. The classic work on rights in security is Gloag and Irvine, *Rights in Security*. For more up to date treatments of particular subjects, see the other works cited in the footnotes to para.13–01, and also: Wilson, *Debt* (2nd ed., 1991), Chaps 7–9; Gloag and Henderson, *Introduction to the Law of Scotland* (9th ed., 1987), Chap.20; Carey Miller, *Corporeal Moveables in Scots Law*, Chap.11; Gordon, *Scottish Land Law*, Chap. 20; McBryde, *Contract*, paras 14–33 to 14–48 (retention and lien), and 22–44 to 22–88 (compensation and balancing of accounts on insolvency); Gloag on *Contract*, pp.623–644 (retention, lien, compensation, balancing of accounts on insolvency).

[32] See Palmer's *Company Law*, Chaps 49 and 46, so far as relevant to Scotland.

categories of security are charges on land wherever situated (standard securities in Scotland), securities over book debts,[33] securities over patents, trademarks and copyrights and associated licences, securities over ships and aircraft and floating charges. Under the new provisions in the 1989 Act there will be added a charge on goods or any interest in goods other than a charge under which the chargee is entitled to possession either of the goods or of a document of title to them.[34] It is thought that that provision will not affect practice in Scotland, where only securities over ships and aircraft will be registrable. The only general form of security over corporeal moveables recognised by Scots law, other than securities arising by operation of law, is pledge. It is established by *Armour v Thyssen Edelstahlwerke AG*[35] that a right of retention of title is not a security.

Section 395(2) of the 1985 Act, as amended by the 1989 Act, makes it clear that security interests arising by operation of law are not registrable. That is thought to cover rights of retention and lien, and the landlord's and superior's and maritime hypothecs.

(3) In terms of s.9(3) of the Conveyancing and Feudal Reform (Scotland) Act 1970, a grant of any right over an interest in land for the purpose of securing any debt by way of heritable security may be effected only by means of a standard security. If a right is not granted for security purposes, the restriction does not apply,[36] as in a securitisation agreement. "Heritable security" is defined in s.9(8)(a) as any security capable of being constituted over an interest in land by disposition or assignation of that interest in security and of being recorded in the Register of Sasines. Thus, rights under a trust over land or heritably secured debts will not be affected by s.9(3).

13–07   (4) It is common for floating charges to contain a prohibition on the grant without the consent of the security holder of further securities other than those arising by operation of law. Such provisions, commonly known as negative pledges, are authorised in floating charges by s.464(1) of the Companies Act 1985. If a right is not a security, it is not struck at by a negative pledge. It should be noted that, under s.464(2), a fixed security arising by operation of law has priority over a floating charge, notwithstanding a negative pledge—that applies to rights of retention and lien and the landlord's and superior's and maritime

---

[33] For definition of a book debt, see Palmer's *Company Law*, para.46–06; and *Alexander v Alexander* (1896) 23 R. 724; *Tailby v Official Receiver* (1888) 13 App. Cas. 523; *Dawson v Isle* [1906] 1 Ch. 633; *Re George Inglefield Ltd* [1933] Ch. 1; *Re Kent and Sussex Sawmills Ltd* [1947] Ch. 177; *Independent Automatic Sales Ltd v Knowles & Foster* [1962] 1 W.L.R. 974; *Siebe Gorman & Co Ltd v Barclays Bank Ltd* [1979] 2 Lloyds Rep. 142; *Carreras Rothmans Ltd v Freeman Matthews Treasure Ltd* [1985] Ch. 207 (moneys in trust account not book debts); *Re Keenan Brothers Ltd* [1986] B.C.L.C. 242; *Re Brightlife Ltd* [1986] 3 All E.R. 673 (cash at bank not book debt).

[34] See s.396(1), as amended.

[35] Above.

[36] On the authority of *Re George Inglefield Ltd*, *supra*, and *Armour v Thyssen Edelstahlwerke A.G.*, *supra*. See paras 12–20 and 12–22.

hypothecs. A negative pledge is registrable under s.417(3)(c) of the Companies Act 1985. It is likely that this will continue to be the case when the 1989 provisions come into force, although s.415(2)(a) of the amended form of the 1985 Act merely permits negative pledges to be included among the prescribed particulars.[37]

(5) On the presentation of a petition for an administration order, no steps may be taken to enforce any security over the company's property without the leave of the court in terms of s.10(1)(b) of the Insolvency Act 1986. When an administration order has been made and for as long as it is in force, under s.11(3)(b) of the Act no steps may be taken to enforce any security over the company's property except with the consent of the administrator or leave of the court. Under ss.15 and 16, an administrator has extensive powers to deal with property of the company over which a security subsists.[38]

(6) In terms of s.62(4) of the Sale of Goods Act 1979, the provisions of the Act do not apply to a transaction in the form of a contract of sale which is intended to operate by way of pledge or other security.[39] It is essential that the transaction should have the form of a contract of sale. Otherwise the critical question is whether the transaction is intended to operate by way of security. The courts have generally adopted a substantive rather than formal approach.[40] A sale with a *pactum de retrovendendo* (an agreement to transfer the subjects back to the seller for an agreed price) has been held not to be intended to operate as a security, but in circumstances where there was no principal debt to be secured by the agreement.[41] In other circumstances such an agreement might amount to a substantive security.[42] If the transaction is intended to operate by way of security, the result is that the 1979 Act does not apply and the sale is governed by the common law. Consequently, in accordance with the common law rule, property passes on delivery, unless it is agreed that it should pass at a later time.[43] The transaction nevertheless remains a valid security, as long as property passes in accordance with the common law rule.

---

[37] Negative pledges undertaken by English companies are not at present registrable, although in practice they are often registered. As to notice of such provisions in respect of English companies, compare Palmer's *Company Law*, para.45–08, and Gore-Browne, *Companies*, para.18–14. The present English position causes difficulty in relation to securities created by English companies over Scottish property.

[38] See Chap.5, above.

[39] See Carey Miller, *Corporeal Moveables in Scots Law*, paras 11.10 and 11.11; Gloag and Henderson, *Introduction to the Law of Scotland* (9th ed., 1987), para.17.12. An extensive case law exists on the subsection, although the cases generally turn on their own facts and the interpretation of s.62(4), and there is little by way of statements of general principle. See *Robertson v Hall's Tr* (1896) 24 R. 120; *Jones & Co's Tr v Allan* (1901) 4 F. 374; *Hepburn v Law*, 1914 S.C. 918; *Gavin's Tr. v Fraser*, 1920 S.C. 674; *Newbigging v Morton*, 1930 S.C. 273; *Scottish Transit Trust v Scottish Land Cultivators*, 1955 S.C. 254; *G. & C. Finance Corp. v Brown*, 1961 S.L.T. 408; *Ladbroke Leasing (South West) Ltd v Reekie Plant Ltd*, 1983 S.L.T. 155.

[40] *Robertson v Hall's Tr., supra; Scottish Transit Trust v Scottish Land Cultivators, supra.* See para.13–05.

[41] *Gavin's Tr. v Fraser, supra.* See para.13–05.

[42] *Cf. Scottish Transit Trust v Scottish Land Cultivators, supra.*

[43] See Gloag and Irvine, pp.188–189; *Stair*, l, xiii, 14; Bell, *Comm.*, ii.11; Bell, *Prin.*, §1363.

Attempts to create preference by contract

13–08   Perhaps the most fundamental principle governing a Scottish insolvency is that the creditors rank equally in the assets that are available for distribution among them. The only creditors who receive a preference are those who have properly constituted securities of a form recognised by the law, those who have done diligence, and those whose debts receive a statutory preference under s.386 of, and Sch.6 to, the Insolvency Act 1986.[44] In relation to securities, the only form of security recognised by Scots law that involves purely personal rights is the guarantee or cautionary obligation,[45] where a third party incurs a personal accessory obligation. All other forms of security involve real, or trust, rights in particular items of property or, in the case of the floating charge, in a fluctuating fund of property. All such forms of security fall into nominate categories, and each has its own requirements for effective constitution, typically involving delivery, intimation or registration. On occasion attempts are made to confer the benefits of a real security through purely personal contractual arrangements. Such arrangements do not include the proper procedures for creation of any nominate security or form of diligence. Moreover, a mere contract is inherently incapable of creating anything more than personal rights.[46] Consequently any attempt to create rights similar to those of a real security, or of a trust, by merely contractual arrangements will be unsuccessful.

Typically such attempts involve an agreement which purports to vary the ranking which one of the parties will receive in the insolvency of the other. There is generally no objection to one party's agreeing not to enforce his debt until the ordinary creditors of the other have been paid in full,[47] but any attempt to obtain a preference will be struck down by the courts unless it amounts to a form of security or diligence recognised by the law and properly carried into effect.

In *Farmers' Mart Ltd v Milne*[48] the pursuers, a firm of auctioneers and valuers, employed the defender to act as their manager. A clause in his contract of employment provided that all fees that the defender might earn from any appointment as factor or trustee on an estate should be pooled with all fees and commissions earned by the pursuers on such estate, and the proceeds divided equally between the parties. The defender had in fact acted as a trustee in sequestration and a trustee for

---

[44] See Chap.13; certain categories of postponed debt also exist.
[45] See *Gloag and Irvine*, pp.642–669; *Gloag and Henderson*, Chap.21. It is possible to create a real third party security, as where one person grants a standard security in respect of the obligations of another; in such a case the granter of the security and the principal obligant stand in the relationship of cautioner and principal obligant, and are subject to the detailed rules relating to cautionary obligations. While a trust can be used as a security (see Chap.12), the rights of the beneficiary share important features with real rights, and cannot, in the context of insolvency be classified as purely personal.
[46] See *Bank of Scotland v Liquidators of Hutchison Main & Co Ltd*, 1914 S.C. (H.L.) 1; *Gibson v Hunter Home Designs Ltd*, 1976 S.C. 23.
[47] See Chap.16 on the subordination of debt.
[48] 1914 S.C. (H.L.) 84.

creditors[49], and the action related, *inter alia*, to his fees for these. It was held by the House of Lords that the agreement was illegal and accordingly unenforceable, in that it violated the fundamental principle of bankruptcy law providing for the equal distribution of assets among creditors. The objection to the pooling arrangement was described by Lord Dunedin as follows:

> "If the defender acted as a trustee in a sequestration he would in terms of this agreement be bound to put the fees that he got as remuneration as trustee into a pool with any fees which they, the pursuers, got for employment which he gave them as trustee, and then in the division there would not be absolutely equal division of those pooled fees, but before anything else the pursuers, if they were creditors on the estate on which he was a trustee, would receive such an allowance over and above the dividends which they would get in common with ordinary creditors as would give them 20s. in the £".[50]

Lord Atkinson considered the material clause to be:

> "[A] device between the pursuers and the defender, in fraud of the bankruptcy laws, to secure to the pursuers a larger dividend than the other creditors in that estate are receiving . . . In consideration that [the pursuers] would consent to the defender acting as trustee in certain bankruptcy matters in which they were creditors, he would allow part of his remuneration, which was paid out of the assets, to be applied in part to secure to the [pursuers] a larger dividend than the other creditors in those bankruptcy matters were receiving".[51]

In *British Eagle International Air Lines Ltd v Compagnie Nationale Air France*[52] various airline operators, including the plaintiffs (who were in liquidation) and the defendants, were parties to a clearing house arrangement set up by the International Air Transport Association for the monthly settlement of debits and credits which arose when members performed services for one another. The clearing house arrangement involved complex rules which prevented individual airlines from making claims against one another. It was held by the House of Lords, with Lords Morris and Simon dissenting, that the arrangements were contrary to public policy and unenforceable in that they contravened the principle[53] that the property of a company should be applied in satisfaction of its liabilities *pari passu*. Lord Cross expressed the reasoning of the majority as follows: **13–09**

> "It is true that if the respondents [the airline] are right the 'clearing house' creditors will be treated as though they were creditors with

---

[49] See 1914 S.C. 129 at 130.
[50] 1914 S.C. (H.L.) 84 at 85.
[51] *ibid.* at 88.
[52] [1975] 1 W.L.R. 758.
[53] Stated in relation to voluntary winding up in s.302 of the Companies Act 1948, now the Insolvency Act 1986, s.107.

valid charges on some of the book debts of British Eagle. But the parties to the 'clearing house' arrangements did not intend to give one another charges on some of each other's future book debts. The documents were not drawn so as to create charges but simply so as to set up by simple contract a method of settling each other's mutual indebtedness at monthly intervals. Moreover, if the documents had purported to create such charges, the charges would have been unenforceable against the liquidator for want of registration under section 95 of the Companies Act 1948. The 'clearing house' creditors are clearly not secured creditors. They are claiming nevertheless that they ought not to be treated in the liquidation as ordinary unsecured creditors but that they have achieved by the medium of the 'clearing house' agreement a position analogous to that of secured creditors without the need for the creation and registration of charges on the book debts in question. The respondents argue that the position which, according to them, the clearing house creditors have achieved, though it may be anomalous and unfair to the general body of unsecured creditors, is not forbidden by any provision in the Companies Act, and that the power of the court to go behind agreements, the results of which are repugnant to our insolvency legislation, is confined to cases in which the parties' dominant purpose was to evade its operation. I cannot accept this argument . . . What the respondents are saying here is that the parties to the 'clearing house' arrangements by agreeing that simple contract debts are to be satisfied in a particular way have succeeded in 'contracting out' of the provisions contained in section 302 for the payment of unsecured debts *'pari passu'*. In such a context it is to my mind irrelevant that the parties to the 'clearing house' arrangements had good business reasons for entering into them and did not direct their minds to the question how the arrangements might be affected by the insolvency of one or more of the parties. Such a 'contracting out' must, to my mind, be contrary to public policy. The question is, in essence, whether what was called in argument the 'mini liquidation' flowing from the clearing house arrangements is to yield to or to prevail over the general liquidation. I cannot doubt that on principle the rules of the general liquidation should prevail. I would therefore hold that notwithstanding the clearing house arrangements British Eagle on its liquidation became entitled to recover payment of the sums payable to it by other airlines for services rendered by it during that period and that airlines which had rendered services to it during that period became on the liquidation entitled to prove for the sums payable to them".[54]

13–10 The minority dissented on the ground that the insolvent company's claim against Air France was never part of its property; its property was limited to its entitlement under the clearing house arrangement.[55] While a provision designed to alter the contractual rights of the parties in the

---

[54] [1975] 1 W.L.R. 758 at 780 and 781.
[55] See Lord Morris at 765, 769–771.

event of insolvency[56] would be invalid, there was nothing in the clearing house arrangements that brought about any change on insolvency.

In applying the principle that the ranking of creditors cannot be altered by contract, it must be borne in mind that Scots law allows wide rights of retention on insolvency,[57] and contractual arrangements which do no more than reflect those rights will not offend against the basic principle. Thus the result in *Ex p. Mackay*,[58] the case principally relied on by the House of Lords in *British Eagle*, would probably have been different in Scotland. In that case one party sold a patent to another in exchange for payment of royalties. The second lent a sum to the first, and in consideration of the loan it was agreed that he would retain half of the royalties. It was further agreed that, in the event that the first party became bankrupt, the second could retain the whole of the royalties. The provision dealing with bankruptcy was held void. In Scotland, however, in the event of the insolvency of the first party owing money to the second, the second would have been entitled to retain all sums due by him to the first to the extent of the sum owed by the first. The contractual provision went no further than the common law.

In corporate banking arrangements, it is usual to find cross-guarantees from all of the companies in a group together with a contractual right of retention on the part of the bank in respect of any sums owed by the bank to companies in the group. Such arrangements do not contravene the principle that a preference cannot be conferred by contract, as the rights of retention involved go no further than the common law right of balancing accounts on insolvency as applied in a situation where companies have guaranteed one another's debts.[59] Contractual rights of retention will usually cover future and contingent debts, such as those arising under performance bonds, cautionary obligations and rights of relief. These are taken into account when the ordinary common law rules relating to the balancing of accounts in insolvency are applied.[60] Each such right is valued at the time of the

---

[56] As in *Ex p. Mackay* (1873) 8 Ch. App. 643.

[57] See Chap.17 and Wilson on *Debt* (2nd ed., 1991), para.13.10.

[58] Above.

[59] The principle that a bank may at any time, on giving notice, consolidate the accounts of one customer is also relevant. Because of the wide rights of retention which arise on insolvency in Scots law, the dictum of Millett J. in *Re Charge Card Services Ltd* [1987] Ch. 150, to the effect that, in England, a debtor cannot create a charge over funds in his own hands is not relevant in Scotland. In Scotland, a debtor is able to exercise a right of retention over such money at least in the event of the insolvency of his creditor, and the question of other rights in security is irrelevant. In the context of banking and clearing house arrangements, the exceptions to the general rules regarding retention in bankruptcy which are discussed in *Mycroft, Petr*, 1983 S.L.T. 352 will rarely be relevant. These relate to funds held on deposit, funds held for a person to whom the holder stands in a fiduciary relationship and funds appropriated to a specific purpose. The contract of deposit involves the delivery of property for safe custody only, and does not apply to the ordinary relationship of debtor and creditor which governs relations between banker and customer. It will apply only when valuables are handed to a banker for safe keeping. Where an account is appropriated for a special purpose, notably in the case of a trust account, it will not be available for the bank's general right of retention on insolvency.

[60] In relation to future and contingent debts, see *Borthwick v Scottish Widows' Fund* (1864) 2 M. 595, and Gloag and Irvine, pp.314–320. In the case of contingencies such as performance bonds, the bank may be able to obtain insurance to lessen the future risk.

insolvency, and the resulting value is taken into the accounting between the parties. Consequently, contractual rights of retention should provide for the valuation of future and contingent rights on insolvency in such a way that they do not go beyond the common law. If they do exceed the common law right they may be struck down on the basis that the equal ranking of creditors is altered.[61]

Trust rights, if properly constituted, will not be treated as an attempt to secure a preference by personal contract alone.[62] This accords with the basic treatment of such rights on insolvency—property held on trust does not fall under the insolvency.[63]

It should be noted that Pt VII (ss.154 to 191) of the Companies Act 1989 makes detailed provision for the recognition of the rules of certain investment exchanges and clearing houses, even where these differ from the usual rules governing the distribution of assets on insolvency. These provisions effectively override the effect of the *British Eagle* decision in relation to the insolvency of persons participating in recognised investment exchanges and clearing houses, and are designed to safeguard the operation of the financial markets concerned.

---

[61] The principal advantage of a bank's making specific contractual provision for retention rather than relying on the common law is that the rights of retention can be combined with cross-guarantees. That improves the bank's position significantly in a group insolvency.

[62] Carreras *Rothmans Ltd v Freeman Matthews Treasure Ltd* [1985] Ch. 207.

[63] See Chap.12.

CHAPTER 14

RETENTION OF TITLE

Introduction

When goods are sold and the seller gives credit to the purchaser, an **14–01** obvious means of protecting against the seller's insolvency is to stipulate that property in the goods will not pass until the price has been paid. This device has been in use for many years.[1] At common law, although it was presumed that property passed on delivery, a condition suspensive of the passing of property was recognised,[2] and thus the parties were apparently free between themselves to determine when property should pass, at least after delivery. Under the Sale of Goods Act 1979,[3] where there is a contract for the sale of specific or ascertained goods, parties are free to determine the time at which property is to be transferred to the buyer, which may be before or after delivery of the goods.[4] Further, where there is a contract for the sale of specific goods, or where goods are subsequently appropriated to the contract, the seller may, by contract, reserve the right of disposal of the goods until certain conditions are fulfilled, and in that event property in the goods will not pass until the conditions are fulfilled.[5] Both of these provisions clearly authorise retention of title to goods by a seller until such time as the price is paid in full, and the validity of clauses retaining title in that way was recognised in a number of cases.[6]

In certain cases attempts were made by suppliers of goods to retain property in the goods until all sums due by the purchaser to the seller had been paid. Such a provision prevents the passing of property until every debt due by the purchaser to the supplier has been paid, whatever the source of the debt may have been. Initially, clauses of retention of title of that nature were held invalid by the Scottish courts on the basis

---

[1] See Stair, I.xiv.4–5, Erskine, *Inst.*, III.iii.11; Bell, *Comm.*, 1.258; M.P. Brown, *Sale*, p.43; *Murdoch & Co Ltd v Greig* (1889) 16 R.396.

[2] *ibid.*

[3] S.17(1).

[4] For the common law, see Gloag and Irvine, pp.188–189; Stair, I.xiii.14; Bell, *Comm.*, 11.11; Bell, *Prin.*, §1363; *Pattern's Tr. v Liston* (1893) 20 R. 806.

[5] Sale of Goods Act 1979, s.19(1).

[6] *Michelin Tyre Co Ltd v Macfarlane (Glasgow) Ltd (in Liquidation)* (1917) 2 S.L.T. 205 (a contract of sale and return); *Archivent Sales and Development Ltd v Strathclyde Regional Council*, 1985 S.L.T. 154; *Glen v Gilbey Vintners Ltd*, 1986 S.L.T. 553. Such clauses merely suspend the time for performance of one party's obligation under the contract of sale, to transfer property, until such time as the other party's principal obligation, to pay the price, is itself performed; *cf. Johnston v Robertson* (1861) 23 D. 646 at 656, *per* LJ-C Inglis; *Turnbull v McLean & Co* (1874) 1 R. 730 at 738, *per* L.J.-C. Moncrieff.

that they were attempts to create a security over corporeal moveable property without possession of the security subject. Subject to a small number of specific exceptions, it is impossible to create a security right over corporeal moveable property in Scots law unless possession of the property is given to or retained by the holder of the security.[7] When the matter reached the House of Lords, however, in *Armour v Thyssen Edelstahlwerke A.G.*[8] it was held that such clauses were valid.

The decision in *Armour v Thyssen Edelstahlwerke A.G.*[9]

14–02   In *Armour v Thyssen Edelstahlwerke A.G.*[10] the retention of title clause under consideration was a very elaborate German provision, the first part of which was translated as follows:

> "All goods delivered by us remain our property (goods remaining in our ownership) until all debts owed to us, including any balances existing at relevant times—due to us on any legal grounds—are settled. This also holds good if payments are made for the purpose of settlement of specially designated claims. Debts owed to companies, being members of our combine, are deemed to be such debts."

There followed a series of sub-clauses which dealt with the consequences of the processing of the goods, the combination of the goods with other goods and the resale of the goods; these sub-clauses provided for co-ownership of products and the assignation of claims to the proceeds of sale in ways that are allowed by the German Civil Code but are not in accordance with the rules of Scots law relating to accession and specification (in respect of ownership of products) and the requirements of a valid assignation. The validity of the first part of the retention of title clause, quoted above, was the only question in issue by the time the case reached the House of Lords. That provision had been held ineffective in the Court of Session,[11] but its decision was reversed in the House of Lords. The critical reasoning in the speech of Lord Keith is as follows:

> "In the present case the appellants, the owners of the steel strip, transferred possession of it to Carron under what was unquestionably a contract of sale. There was no question of the appellants creating a right of security. They were not in the position of debtors

---

[7] *Emerald Stainless Steel Ltd v South Side Distribution Ltd*, 1982 S.C. 61; *Deutz Engines Ltd v Terex Ltd*, 1984 S.L.T. 273; *Hammer und Sohne v HWT Realisations Ltd*, 1985 S.L.T. (Sh. Ct) 21; *Tramp Oil and Marine Ltd v Captain Ros,*, unreported, January 1986; *Armour v Thyssen Edelstahlwerke AG* 1986 SLT 452 (Lord Mayfield); 1989 SLT 182 (Second Division). These cases, and the reasoning underlying them are discussed in detail in the first edition of this work. Essentially, the retention clause amounted to security in respect of all debts other than the price of the particular goods.

[8] 1990 S.L.T. 891.

[9] *ibid.*

[10] *ibid.*

[11] See n.1, above.

seeking to give a right of security to a creditor. They were themselves creditors of Carron for the price of the steel strip and it may be for other debts also. Carron obtained possession of the steel strip upon delivery, subject to a condition that it should not obtain the property until it had paid all debts due to the appellants. Can it be said that Carron somehow attempted to create a security over the goods in favour of the appellants? In order that it might do so it would require to have both the ownership and the possession, actual or constructive, of the goods. The essence of a right in security is that the debtor retains at least what *Gloag and Irvine* call the ultimate right to the goods. Can it be said that Carron obtained anything which gave it the capacity to retain an ultimate right to the goods? That could be so only if the contract of sale gave it the property in the goods, but the contract of sale said that the property in the goods was not to pass until all debts due to the appellants had been paid. We are here very far removed from the situation where a party in possession of corporeal moveables is seeking to create a subordinate right in favour of a creditor while retaining the ultimate right to himself. It is true that by entering into the contract of sale Carron agreed that it should receive possession of the goods on delivery but should not acquire the property until all debts due to the appellants had been paid, and thus agreed that the appellants would in effect have security over the goods after they had come into Carron's possession. But at that stage Carron had no interest of any kind whatever in any particular goods. Carron was never in a position to confer upon the appellants any subordinate right over the steel strip, nor did it ever seek to do so.

Section 17 of the Sale of Goods Act 1979 provides:

'(1) Where there is a contract for the sale of specific or ascertained goods the property in them is transferred to the buyer at such time as the parties to the contract intend it to be transferred. (2) For the purpose of ascertaining the intention of the parties regard shall be had to the terms of the contract, the conduct of the parties and the circumstances of the case.'

In the present case the parties in the contract of sale clearly express their intention that the property in the steel strip should not pass to Carron until all debts due by it to the appellants had been paid. In my opinion there are no grounds for refusing to give effect to that intention.

Further, s.19(1) of the same Act provides:

'Where there is a contract for the sale of specific goods or where goods are subsequently appropriated to the contract, the seller may, by the terms of the contract or appropriation, reserve the right of disposal of the goods until certain conditions are fulfilled; and in such a case, notwithstanding the delivery of the goods to the buyer, or to a carrier or other bailee or custodier for the purpose of transmission to the buyer, the property in the goods does not pass to the buyer until the conditions imposed by the seller are fulfilled.'

Here the appellants, by the terms of the contract of sale, have in effect reserved the right of disposal of the steel strip until fulfilment of the condition that all debts due to them by Carron have been paid. By virtue of this enactment, that has the effect that the property in the goods did not pass to Carron until that condition had been fulfilled. Counsel for Carron argued that the word "conditions" in s.19(1) must be read as excluding any condition which has the effect of creating a right of security over the goods. I am, however, unable to regard a provision reserving tide to the seller until payment of all debts due to him by the buyer as amounting to the creation by the buyer of a right of security in favour of the seller. Such a provision does, in a sense, give the seller security for the unpaid debts of the buyer. But it does so by way of a legitimate retention of title, not by virtue of any right over his own property conferred by the buyer.[12]"

It therefore appears that ss.17 and 19 of the Sale of Goods Act apply directly to a clause which reserves ownership until all debts owed by the purchaser to the seller have been paid. The argument which found favour in the Scottish courts was rejected because the "all debts" clause was not characterised as a security, but was rather considered a legitimate use of the contractual freedom conferred by ss.17 and 19.[13] That meant that "all sums" retention of title provisions were valid. It further indicates that a clause which retains property in goods until all sums due to the seller or to other companies in the seller's group[14] have been paid will be valid. If a retention of title is not a security because the purchaser never obtains the right of ownership or "ultimate right" to the goods that is necessary to constitute a security, such a clause cannot be a security either. In neither case does the purchaser ever obtain either property in the goods or the ultimate right to the goods.[15]

Seller's remedies on insolvency of purchaser

14–03   Lord Keith further considered the question of the seller's remedies in the event of the insolvency of the purchaser at a time when debts remain outstanding from the purchaser to the seller. On this point he stated:

"In all cases where a right of security is conferred the debtor retains an ultimate right over the subject matter in question. The creditor, having realised out of that subject matter a sufficient sum to meet the debt, is obliged to account to the debtor for any surplus. Where, however, the seller of goods retains title until some condition has been satisfied, and on failure of such satisfaction repossesses them,

---

[12] 1990 S.L.T. 391 at 894H—395B. See also Lord Jauncey at 895K—896G.

[13] See pp.250–252.

[14] Or, if adequately defined, associated in any other way with the seller.

[15] Such clauses have been common in German contracts, and an example is found in the contract between Thyssen and Carron. The evidence of German law at first instance in *Armour v Thyssen Edelstahlwerke AG* indicated that such clauses are now regarded as of doubtful validity in Germany, and that even "all sums" clauses are coming under challenge. The matter is discussed in the full version of Lord Mayfield's opinion, issued on February 4, 1986.

then he is not obliged to account to the buyer for any part of the value of the goods. Where the condition is to the effect that the price of the goods shall have been paid and it has not been paid, then in the situation where the market price of the goods has risen, so that they are worth more than the contract price, the extra value belongs to the unpaid seller. That is clearly the position where the condition relates to payment of the price of the actual goods, and goes to show that the retention of title provision is not one creating a right of security forming an exception to the general rule requiring possession by the creditor. The same is true, in my opinion, where the provision covers not only the price of the very goods which are the subject of the particular contract of sale, but also debts due to the seller under other contracts."[16]

The result of this reasoning seems to be that a seller who has the benefit of an all sums retention of title clause may repossess the whole of the goods supplied by him to the extent that property has not passed to the purchaser. That appears to be so even if the value of those goods is greater than the sum outstanding from the purchaser. In that case there will be an obligation on the seller to account to the purchaser for the difference between the value of the goods repossessed and the debt outstanding on insolvency from the purchaser to the seller. The basis for such an obligation is presumably the *condictio causa data causa non secuta*.[17]

A similar problem may arise in a case where property is retained **14–09** merely until payment of the price of the goods, but part of the price is paid before repossession. That situation was considered by the Court of Appeal in England in *Clough Mill Ltd v Martin*.[18] Robert Goff L.J. discussed it as follows:

"The difficulty with the present condition is that the retention of title applies to material, delivered and retained by the buyer, until payment in full for all the material delivered under the contract has been received by the seller. The effect is therefore that the seller may retain his title in material still held by the buyer, even if part of that material has been paid for. Furthermore, if in such circumstances the seller decides to exercise his rights and resell the material, questions can arise as to (1) whether account must be taken of the part payment already received in deciding how much the seller should be entitled to sell, and (2) whether, if he does resell, he is accountable to the buyer either in respect of the part payment already received, or in respect of any profit made on the resale by reason of a rise in the market value of the material.

Let me highlight these problems by taking a hypothetical example. Suppose that the seller agrees to sell 1,000 tons of material to the buyer at £10 a ton. He delivers 500 tons. Of those 500 tons, only

---

[16] 1990 S.L.T. 891 at 895C—E.
[17] See Gloag, *Contract*, pp.57–60. The basis of the *condictio* is failure of consideration.
[18] [1985] 1 W.L.R. 111.

250 tons are paid for by the buyer: so £2,500 have been paid, and another £2,500 are due and outstanding. The buyer becomes insolvent, and is unable further to perform the contract. The seller accepts the repudiation. Of the 500 tons delivered, 300 tons are still at the buyer's premises, unsold and unused, now worth £4,000 instead of £3,000 as they were at the time of the contract of sale. Can the seller resell the whole 300 tons? And, if he can and does so, does he have to account to the buyer for that part of the price already paid which cannot be appropriated to the 200 tons already used by the buyer in manufacture and so must be appropriated to part of the 300 tons, i.e. £500? And must the seller account to the buyer for the profit element of £1,000 obtainable on the resale, no doubt allowing for any expenses of the sale?

Now, if the contract was still subsisting, instead of having been determined by the seller's acceptance of the buyer's repudiation, it would be perfectly possible to conclude, on the basis of an implied term in the contract, that the seller could only resell so much of the material as was necessary to pay the outstanding part of the purchase price, the rest to remain available to the buyer for the purposes of the contract, and that if, contrary to that term, the seller were to sell more than was necessary to pay off the balance of the price, he must account for the surplus to the buyer. On that basis, any part payment would be taken into account, and there would be no question of the seller retaining any profits obtained on a resale. But, if the contract has been determined, such term could not be given effect to, unless it were to be held, on a true construction of the contract, that the term survived the determination of the contract upon the seller's accepting the buyer's repudiation, for which I can see no basis as a matter of construction. So the situation would simply be that the property in the 300 tons belonged to the seller who could exercise his rights as owner uninhibited by any contractual restrictions. He could therefore sell the material for his own account; though he would, I consider, be bound to repay any part of the purchase price already paid by the buyer which must be appropriated to the goods so sold, because such sum would be recoverable by the buyer on the ground of failure of consideration.

There is another possible solution to this problem. This is that the seller should be held to retain the title to the material as trustee, upon trust to sell the goods and apply the proceeds of sale, first in discharge of the outstanding balance of the purchase price, and then as to any surplus upon trust for the buyer. On that basis the seller, in my hypothetical example, would on selling the 300 tons hold the balance realised on the resale over and above the outstanding purchase price on trust for the buyer.

To me, the answer to these questions lies in giving effect to the condition in accordance with its terms, and on that approach I can discern no intention to create a trust. The condition provides that the plaintiff retains his ownership in the material. He therefore remains owner; but, during the subsistence of the contract, he can only exercise his power as owner consistently with the terms, express and implied, of the contract. On that basis in my judgment, he can during the subsistence of the contract only resell such amount of the material as is needed to discharge the balance of the outstanding purchase price; and if he sells more, he is accountable to the buyer for the surplus. However, once the contract has been determined, as it will be if the buyer repudiates the contract and the seller accepts the repudiation, the seller will have his rights as owner (including, of course, his right to sell the goods) uninhibited by any contractual restrictions; though any part of the purchase price received by him and attributable to the material so resold will be recoverable by the buyer on the ground of failure of consideration, subject to any set-off arising from a cross-claim by the plaintiff for damages for the buyer's repudiation."[19]

The foregoing views appear generally consonant with Scots law. The concept of a failure of consideration corresponds generally to the *condictio causa data causa non secuta*. The case for a trust would be considerably weaker in Scots law, on the basis that there appeared to be no intimation to the alleged beneficiary or other equivalent of delivery of the supposed trust fund.

In *Vale Sewing Machines Limited v Robb*[20] goods were sold by the pursuers to another company subject to a condition that "the property in the goods shall pass to the buyer only when the full purchase price and all additional charges relating to that item shall have been paid to the [pursuers] and until such time as payment in full has been made to the [pursuers], the buyer shall hold the goods to the order of the [pursuers] as bailee". The defender was appointed provisional liquidator of the purchasers therefore the goods had been fully paid for. It was accepted by both parties that property in the goods remained with the pursuers. The pursuers attempted to contract the defender by telephone, and had several conversations with his assistant during which they stated their claim to title to the goods. The defender ignored that claim and sold the goods to the principal shareholder of the purchasers at a price described by the sheriff as "grossly undervalued". The pursuers then raised an action against the defender for damages. A proof was held, and the defender stated in evidence that he had rejected the pursuers' claim to ownership of the goods as a matter of credibility. Sheriff Convery held that a liquidator faced with a claim to retention of title should not have adopted such a course. He observed that it was difficult to see how a liquidator could deal with that situation other than by a reference to the court in terms of s.112(1) of the Insolvency Act 1986. The court could then have decided the issue of ownership and could have made any necessary orders to regulate the storage or use of the goods and the payment of any costs that arose. In so doing, the court would have had regard both to the interests of creditors and to the interests of the party claiming ownership in. If, by contrast, a liquidator chose to reject a claim summarily and to dispose of the goods, he was liable to the party claiming ownership if the latter's claim ultimately proved to be valid. Consequently the pursuers were entitled to

---

[19] [1985] 1 W.L.R. 111 at 117–118.
[20] 1997 S.C.L.R. 797.

damages, which the sheriff assessed at as an equal to the unpaid balance of the purchase price. The sheriff further held that the defence found in s.234(3) and (4) of the Insolvency Act 1986 was not available. It is a requirement of that defence that a liquidator or other officeholder should both believe and have reasonable grounds for believing that he is entitled to seize or dispose of property which is not the property of the company. In the present case, the liquidator could not maintain that he had reasonable grounds for believing that he was entitled to dispose of the property because of the extract claims to ownership made by the pursuers. The pursuers in *Vale Sewing Machines* chose to base their action on the negligence of the liquidator in disposing of their goods. Sheriff Convery held that the delict committed by the defender was more than inadvertent carelessness in the performance of his duties of care as a liquidator, but that the pleadings were sufficient to cover a wilful failure in the defender's duties.

Practical consequences[21]

14–05   The main practical advantage of an all sums retention of title clause is that it is not necessary to determine whether the purchaser has made payment for each consignment of goods supplied. It is sufficient that the seller can establish in relation to any particular item supplied by him that, since the date of supply, there has always been a sum outstanding from the purchaser. That will usually be easier. Indeed, where goods are supplied at short intervals on a period of credit, used by the buyer, that is significantly longer than the intervals between supplies, sums will always be due by the buyer to the seller and property in goods will never pass until they have been used in manufacture or resold.[22] That result is somewhat anomalous, as it may mean that goods supplied will remain the seller's property even though the buyer never exceeds the allowed period of credit.

An all sums clause may provide that property will not pass until all debts due by the purchaser to the seller, at any time and from time to time, and whether before or after the date of the particular contract of sale, have been paid. It is thought that that was the intended effect of the clause under consideration in *Armour v Thyssen Edelstahlwerke AG*,[23] although the wording of the clause is not wholly clear. In some cases, however, as a matter of construction, the clause may mean that property will pass when all debts due to the seller by the purchaser at the date of the contract, including the price of the goods supplied under the contract, have been paid.

Ancillary provisions in retention of title clauses

14–06   If an all sums retention of title clause is to be effective, it is desirable that certain ancillary provisions should be added. The most important of these is a power to rescind the contract of sale in the event that payment

---

[21] See para.14–08.
[22] See pp.270–275.
[23] 1990 S.L.T. 891.

for any goods supplied is not made within the period of credit or in the event of the buyer's insolvency even if payment of the price has been made. Failure to make payment timeously is not generally a ground for rescission unless an ultimatum has been given making time of payment of the essence of the contract.[24] Likewise, insolvency by itself is not a ground for rescission (although consequential failure to perform may be).[25] If the analysis in *Clough Mill Ltd v Martin*[26] of the rights arising on repossession is followed, it is important that the contract should be rescinded, but if there is no express term allowing rescission an ultimatum procedure must be used, which entails considerable delay and uncertainty. Accordingly, an express power to rescind in the event of a failure to make timeous payment for any goods supplied is desirable. Such a provision will not help, however, in cases where it cannot readily be proved that the buyer has exceeded his period of credit in respect of particular goods, and to deal with such cases a power to rescind in the event of the buyer's insolvency[27] as advisable.

It is also desirable to include an express power to repossess goods supplied in the event of recission of the contract of sale. Such a power can be useful in an application for *interim* interdict, and may be worded in such a way as to give the seller a clear right to go on to the buyer's premises in order to search for and remove the goods.

Severance

In the law relating to restrictive covenants in restraint of trade[28] it is **14–07** recognised that, in some cases, it is possible to sever the invalid part of a covenant from the valid part and to uphold the latter.[29] There seems no reason why the same principle should not apply to any retention of title clause which is partly valid and partly invalid. An example would be a German clause which contained provisions which purported to alter the Scottish rules on specification and accession,[30] or to nullify the effect of s.25 of the Sale of Goods Act 1979.[31] If severance is to be effected, however, it is essential that it should be possible to separate physically the valid and invalid parts of the clause and to delete the invalid part without altering the meaning of the valid part. In addition, the provisions of the clause must not be so closely interconnected that the sense of the clause is destroyed by the excision of the offending provisions. In particular, if the deletion of the offending part alters the meaning of the remainder in any way, severance will not be permitted. In the restraint

---

[24] Gloag on *Contract*, pp.617–618. See also *Rodger (Builders) Ltd v Fawdry*, 1950 S.C. 483.

[25] Gloag on *Contract*, p.601.

[26] [1985] 1 W.L.R. 111.

[27] "Insolvency" should be defined in the contract, to cover at least insolvent winding up, administration and receivership. The grounds for apparent insolvency contained in the Bankruptcy (Scotland) Act 1985, s.7 might also be added to the definition.

[28] On which, see Gloag on *Contract*, pp.569–577; Walker on *Contracts*, paras 12.24–12.43, and McBryde on *Contract*, paras 25–55 to 25–109.

[29] See especially Gloag, *op. cit.*, p.574; Walker, *op. cit.*, para.12.42; McBryde, para.25–101; *Mulvein v Murray*, 1908 S.C. 528.

[30] See para.14–10.

[31] See para.14–09.

of trade cases, it is a general rule that the courts will not countenance the rewriting of a restrictive covenant[32], and if the meaning of the remaining sections of the clause is altered in any way, that is taken to amount to a rewriting.

In *Emerald Stainless Steel Ltd v South Side Distribution Ltd*[33] it was argued that the contractual term under consideration could be severed, with the earlier part receiving effect. This argument was rejected by Lord Ross[34], on the ground that the condition must be read as a whole and could not be broken down in that way. In *Deutz Engines Ltd v Terex Ltd*[35] severance was also argued. Lord Ross did not find it necessary to decide the question, because even if severance was effected, the clause was objectionable, according to the law as then understood, as an "all-sums" clause. The only reported case where severance has been permitted is *Glen v Gilbey Vintners Ltd.*[36] The clause there, so far as material, provided as follows:

> "(a) Unless otherwise agreed in writing between the Company and the Purchaser, property and title in Goods shall not pass to the Purchaser until the whole price therefor (each contract for the sale or supply of Goods being treated as a separate contract) has been received by the Company; and
> (b) Unless the Seller removes his claim to the property and title in the Goods by giving written notice to the Buyer the property and tide shall not pass to the Purchaser until all sums due by the Purchaser to the Company on any account whatsoever has been received by the Company; and in each case until the price or other sums due as the case may be has or have been received by the Company, the Purchaser shall hold such Goods in trust for the Company and shall not dispose of them save as Agent for the Company. Sub-clauses (a) and (b) above shall be construed and receive effect as a separate Clause and accordingly in the event of either of them being for any reason whatsoever unenforceable according to its terms, the other shall remain in full force and effect."

It was argued for the receivers of the purchaser that the clause was self-contradictory in that it purported both to reserve title in the seller and to impose a trust on the goods in the buyer's hands for behoof of the seller. This argument was rejected by Lord Clyde on the basis that the expression 'in trust for' was not to be construed as creating a strict relationship of trustee and beneficiary but rather an agency relationship. Lord Clyde further held that, although the seller admitted that sub-clause (b) was invalid as an all-sums clause, that provision could be severed from sub-clause (a), which involved simple retention of title. Lord Clyde said[37]:

---

[32] See *Walker*, para.12.43; and *Dumbarton Steam Boat Co v MacFarlane* (1899) 1 F. 993.
[33] 1982 S.C. 61.
[34] *ibid.* at 64.
[35] 1984 S.L.T. 273, discussed *supra*.
[36] 1986 S.L.T. 553.
[37] *ibid.* at 555.

"In my view this is a clear case where severance of what is recognised to be invalid can be made so as to preserve what is valid. The two provisions are set out separately from each other and there is an express provision whereby if the one is found to be unenforceable the other shall remain in full force and effect. Counsel for the [receivers] founded on the passage which immediately follows the two paragraphs. He argued that even if para (b) was deleted this passage would still stand in its entirety and accordingly the defect which was sought to be removed by a separation of para (b) still remained. On this approach, the passage in question would still refer to the price or other sums due as the case may be having been received by the company. In my view however if a separation is made then it is necessary to restrict the scope of the passage in question to such parts as apply to para (a). Such a restriction can be made without violence to the language or the grammar of the passage. The objectionable parts of the clause can then be wholly severed so as to leave a clear and enforceable provision."

Lord Clyde went on to distinguish the case from other cases where the good and bad parts of the clause were so woven together as to make separation impossible.

Identification of goods and payments

When a clause of retention of title is applied following insolvency, **14–08** practical problems can arise in identifying which articles in the insolvent company's possession have and have not been paid for. The issues involved are generally factual in nature but certain legal principles are relevant. In the case of a clause which only retains title until the price of the particular goods has been paid, it is important to consider whether the individual articles sold to the insolvent company can be identified, either through a serial number or through elements in their description. If they can be, it is a relatively straightforward accounting exercise to discover which articles have been paid for. In this connection, however, it is important to bear in mind the rules relating to the appropriation of payments.[38] The general rule is that the debtor, in this case the buyer, is entitled to appropriate payments to any particular debt owed by him to the seller. If, as is frequent, he fails to do so, the seller may appropriate the payment to any debt he pleases. If there is an account current, as will frequently be the case where credit is supplied by a seller to a buyer over a substantial period,[39] if no ascription is made, the rule in *Clayton*[40] applies, and payments are ascribed to the items in the account in chronological order.

If the articles in the insolvent company's possession cannot be individually identified, it must be discovered whether the company

---

[38] Discussed in detail in Gloag, *op. cit.*, pp.711–715; Walker, *op. cit.*, para.31.34; McBryde, *op. cit.*, paras 22–26 to 22–29.
[39] See *Thomas Montgomery & Sons v Gallacher*, 1982 S.L.T. 138.
[40] (1816) 1 Mer. 572.

operated a regular stock control system. The most common system is FIFO (first in first out), but in the case of heavy items, such as steel plates, which are regularly stacked on top of one another, LIFO (last in first out) may be used. If there is evidence of the regular use of such a system, it should be possible for the seller to establish, at least on a balance of probabilities, which of the goods in store have not been paid for and hence remain his property. On occasion, however, no stock control system is used and it is simply impossible to discover which individual articles have and have not been paid for. Such cases may raise difficult questions of balance of proof, but normally the burden of proving ownership is on the seller.

If the clause retains title until all sums owed by the purchaser to the seller have been paid, the first question is to identify when any particular item of property was supplied. That involves identifying the particular item of property, either by reference to a serial number or some other identifying mark or by reference to a regular stock control system. Once it has been discovered when an item of property was supplied, the next step is to examine the state of indebtedness between seller and purchaser during the intervening period. If the whole indebtedness of the purchaser to the seller was paid at any time during that period the retention of title will not operate; if it was never paid in full the retention will operate. If the retention applies to the whole debts owed by the purchaser to the seller's group, the investigation of the purchaser's indebtedness must be widened accordingly. In many cases, however, the purchaser's indebtedness will have subsisted continuously for a very long time. In such cases it may appear on a balance of probabilities that the goods in question are likely to have been supplied during the period of continuous indebtedness. In that event the seller will be able to prove his continuing ownership fairly readily. Such cases are likely to be frequent where goods are supplied at short intervals on a longer period of credit. Thus if supplies are made every week on 30 days' credit, and the purchaser makes use of the period of credit, it is inevitable that indebtedness will always be outstanding, even if the period of credit is never exceeded.

In most cases a seller who attempts to reclaim goods from an insolvent purchaser must, because he is pursuer in the resulting action, overcome the burden of proving on a balance of probabilities that he is the owner of the particular goods in question.

Subsales

14–09   Where a retention of title clause is effective, the buyer may want to resell goods subject to the clause to his own customers. In some cases, express authority to sell is given[41]. In most cases the seller will be aware

---

[41] As in *Emerald Stainless Ltd v South Side Distribution Ltd*, 1982 S.C. 61, where the power was restricted to sales in good faith and for full value in the normal course of the buyer's trading. Such restrictions do not oust s.25 of the Sale of Goods Act, which is designed essentially for the protection of third-party purchasers.

of the nature of the buyer's trade and that the buyer is likely to resell the goods in the course of that trade, and in such cases authority to resell the goods will almost certainly be implied. To withhold such authority would effectively destroy the whole purpose of the contract of sale containing the retention clause. Consideration of such implied terms will not usually be necessary, however, in view of the terms of s.25 of the Sale of Goods Act 1979. Section 25(1) provides as follows:

> "Where a person having bought or agreed to buy goods obtains, with the consent of the seller, possession of the goods or the documents of title to the goods, the delivery or transfer by that person . . . of the goods or documents of title, under any sale, pledge, or other disposition thereof to any person receiving the same in good faith and without notice of any lien or other right of the original seller in respect of the goods, has the same effect as if the person making the delivery or transfer were a mercantile agent in possession of the goods or documents of title with the consent of the owner."

The leading case in Scotland on s.25 is *Thomas Graham and Sons Ltd v Glenrothes Development Corporation*,[42] where the Lord President stated the requirements of what is now s.25(1) in the following terms[43]:

> "The first requirement of that subsection is that a person, having bought or agreed to buy goods, obtains, with the consent of the seller, possession of the goods. This requirement is admittedly satisfied in the present case . . .
>
> The second requirement of the subsection is the delivery or transfer by that person . . . of the goods under any sale of other disposition thereof to any person receiving the same in good faith and without notice or any right of the original seller in respect of the goods . . .
>
> The main attack, however, upon the relevancy of the defenders' averments was that they have not satisfied by averment the requirement of delivery or transfer by [the original buyer] under a sale or other disposition to the defenders [the buyers under the contract of resale]. But in my opinion, although with some hesitation, I consider that there is just enough in the averment . . . that, when the lorries arrived at the site, employees of the [original buyers] took delivery of the materials by unloading them and thereafter placed them on the defenders' site."

The Lord President went on[44] to state that the effect of the subsection is that the buyer under the original contract will have the ostensible authority of a mercantile agent to pass the property in the goods. The effects of s.25(1) in the context of retention of title were considered in *Archivent Sales and Development Ltd v Strathclyde Regional Council*,[45] where

---

[42] 1967 S.C. 284.
[43] *ibid.* at 293.
[44] *ibid.* at 294.
[45] 1985 S.L.T. 154.

a contract for the sale of ventilators to the main contractor acting under a building contract contained a simple retention of title clause. The building contract[46] contained a clause (cl.14(1)) in the following terms: "Where the value of any materials or goods has . . . been included in any interim Certificate under which the Contractor has received payment, such materials and goods shall become the property of the employer." The ventilators in question had undoubtedly been included in an interim certificate, and the question arose of whether property had passed to the employers under the building contract, thereby defeating the rights of the original supplier. Lord Mayfield[47] considered the requirements of s.25(1), as discussed in *Thomas Graham & Sons Ltd v Glenrothes Development Corporation*.[48] It was not disputed that the employer under the building contract acted in good faith and without notice of any right in the original seller in respect of the goods, as it was unaware of the provisions in the contract of sale which reserved title. The main contractor had, on the evidence, obtained possession of the ventilators.[49] Finally, delivery to the employers under the building contract took place when the ventilators, after they had been incorporated into the building, had been measured on the site by the employer's surveyor and not rejected. In these circumstances, Lord Mayfield held that the requirements of s.25(1) had been satisfied, with the result that property had been passed to the employer.

Section 25(1) is likely to be of fairly general application in cases where goods subject to a retention of title clause have been resold. It is clearly impossible for a seller and purchaser to contract out of the subsection in such a way as to bind a sub-purchaser. It is important, however, that the specific requirements of the subsection, as discussed by the Lord President in *Thomas Graham & Sons Ltd*, should be satisfied. A possible difficulty is that, as the use of retention of title clauses becomes virtually universal, the requirement that the sub-purchaser should be in good faith will not be satisfied, because he knows that there is at least a substantial possibility that the goods are subject to a retention of tide clause. It is suggested that the courts should not be anxious to construe the subsection in this way, for obvious practical reasons. In any event, as suggested above, it should be possible to imply authority to resell even before the passing of property in the great majority of contracts of sale incorporating retention of title clauses, and that would avoid any difficulty caused by the wording of s.25(1).

Accession and specification: fixtures

14–10   Goods subject to a retention of title clause will frequently be combined with other goods to create a new product. When a minor article is added to a major one in such a way as to form part of it, as when a plate is

---

[46] In the JCT Standard Form, Local Authorities Ed. with Quantities (1963 ed., July 1977 revision).

[47] 1985 S.L.T. 154 at 156–157.

[48] 1967 S.C. 284.

[49] Factors Act 1889, s.1(2), which provides that a person shall be deemed to be in possession of goods or documents of title to goods where the goods or documents are in his actual custody, was founded upon for this purpose.

welded to a ship under repair, the process is known as accession. When a wholly new article is created, as when a great diversity of components are combined to build a ship, the process is known as specification.[50] In such cases the question arises as to whether the owner of the goods that have been used can maintain his property in the goods, or whether property in the goods passes, either to the owner of the major component in the case of accession, or to the manufacturer in the case of specification. The rule followed in Scots law in cases of specification has been stated as follows[51]:

> "Where the new species can be again reduced to the mass or matter of which it was made, the law considers the former subject as still existing: therefore the new species continues to belong to the proprietor of that former subject, which still exists, though under another form; as in the case of plate made of bullion. But where the new species cannot be so reduced, there is no room for that *fictio juris*; as in wine, which, because it cannot be again turned into the grapes of which it was made, becomes the property, not of the owner of the grapes, but of the maker of the wine".[52]

With accession to moveables, the rule is similar except that ownership of the component passes to the owner of the major article to which it is attached. An example of the application of these rules is found in *International Banking Corporation v Ferguson, Shaw & Sons*,[53] where oil was used in the manufacture of lard. As it was impossible to restore the oil to its original state, property passed to the manufacturer of the lard.[54]

Accession (but not specification) also operates when moveable articles are attached to land or buildings. Components of a building, such as bricks or joists or windows, become part of the building. This applies even to components such as doors which can be removed without damage.[55] The same applies to articles such as pipes and cables which are buried in land. Although a wayleave or other servitude right may be reserved, that does not amount to ownership.[56] Other moveable objects may pass to the owner of the heritage as fixtures—these are articles which are necessary to the land and building but are so fixed to it as to become part of the heritage.[57] In determining whether an article has

---

[50] The law on these topics is discussed in Stair, *Inst.*, II, i, 39–41; Erskine, *Inst.*, II, i, 15–16; Bell, *Comm.*, I, 276–278; and Bell, *Prin.*, §§1296–1298.

[51] Erskine, *Inst.*, II, i, 16.

[52] Specification is equitable in nature, and it is essential that the manufacturer should have been in good faith if it is to obtain its advantages: *McDonald v Provan Ltd*, 1960 S.L.T. 231. This is not likely to be a problem in retention of title cases.

[53] 1910 S.C. 182; see also *Oliver & Boyd v Marr Typefounding Co Ltd* (1901) 9 S.L.T. 170.

[54] The owners of the oil were found entitled to its value.

[55] Stair, *Inst.*, II, i, 40; Erskine, *Inst.*, II, i, 16–17; Bell, *Comm.*, 1, 752, *et seq.*; Bell, *Prin.*, §1473.

[56] *Crichton v Turnbull*, 1946 S.C. 52.

[57] The leading case on fixtures is *Brand's Trs v Brand's Trs* (1876) 3 R. (HL) 16, where the question of whether an article of moveable property has been attached to land in such a way as to become a fixture is distinguished from the right that a limited owner such as a tenant may in exceptional circumstances have to remove the article. The latter question is unlikely to be relevant in retention of title cases.

become a fixture, it is not only the degree of physical attachment that is relevant.[58] The factors that are relevant have been described as follows:

> "The question whether a particular thing has become a fixture, that is, has become a part of the soil, or of some building attached to the soil, has not to be solved by the mere consideration whether it is, as a matter of fact affixed to the soil or building. That consideration, as well as the degree or extent of its attachment, is to be taken together with other elements. These elements are: whether it can be removed *integre, salve et commode*, ie without the destruction of itself as a separate thing, or of the soil or building to which it is attached; whether its annexation was of a permanent or *quasi*-permanent character; whether the building to which it was attached was specially adapted for its use; how far the use and enjoyment of the soil or building would be affected by its removal; the intention of the party attaching it. Intention, however, in this question means intention discoverable from the nature of the article and of the building, and the manner in which it is affixed, not intention proved by extrinsic evidence".[59]

14–11 The question of whether an article has become a fixture is the subject of a large number of judicial decisions; the principal cases will be found from the works undernoted.[60]

In cases involving accession or specification, a party who contributes materials or labour but loses or fails to obtain a right of property may have a remedy in recompense. Reference should be made to the standard works on this subject.[61]

The foregoing principles have important consequences for retention of title. It is generally considered impossible to contract out of the rules described above, as they involve methods of original acquisition of property which follow automatically if the particular requirements occur and are independent of the intention of the parties concerned. If goods are sold subject to a valid retention clause but are used to manufacture a new product, in such a way that they cannot be restored to their original state, property in the goods will pass to the manufacturer as a result of specification or accession. Similarly, if the goods are used in the construction of a building, or are attached to a building in such a way that they become a fixture, property will pass to the owner of the building. Thus a retention clause applying to goods which are intended

---

[58] *Scottish Discount Co Ltd v Blin*, 1986 S.L.T. 123.

[59] *Green's Encyclopaedia of the Laws of Scotland*, Vol.7, para.362, approved in *Scottish Discount Co Ltd v Blin*. See also *Howie's Trs v McLay* (1902) 5 F. 214, *per* Lord President Kinross.

[60] Article by Professor Gloag in *Green's Encyclopaedia of the Laws of Scotland*, vol 7, paras 361–385; Gloag and Henderson, *Introduction to the Law of Scotland* (9th ed.), pp.623–624. The most recent case in the Inner House, in which the general principles of the law are reviewed, is *Scottish Discount Co Ltd v Blin* (*supra*).

[61] Gloag on *Contract*, pp.319 *et seq.*; *Gloag and Henderson*, pp.161–164; Scot. Law Com, Memo. No. 28, *Corporeal Moveables, Mixing, Union and Creation*. The last-mentioned work is a useful discussion of accession and specification in general.

for use in manufacturing or construction is severely limited in its effectiveness, as it will not help the seller once the goods cannot be returned to their original state, or once they have become part of heritable property. This is of great practical importance, and difficult factual problems arise in determining whether goods can be restored to their original state on removal from a manufactured object, or whether goods have become a fixture.

Specification has been considered in three reported retention of title cases. In *Zahnrad Fabrik Passau GmbH v Terex Ltd*[62] axles and transmissions had been sold by the pursuers to the defenders and incorporated into finished or partly-finished earth-moving vehicles. It was averred that the axles had been attached to the main frame, painted and filled with oil. These averments were held irrelevant, in that they did not specify the mode of attachment to the main frame, and it was not averred that the axles could not be removed, or what damage or detriment would result if they could be removed. It was averred that the transmissions had been attached to the vehicles and painted and that alterations had been made in the pipes and plates attached to the transmissions. These averments were also held irrelevant; they did not indicate that the transmissions could not be removed from the vehicles without suffering damage. In reaching these conclusions, Lord Davidson stated the test that he applied as follows[63]:

> "I think that the appropriate test is not what is the diminution in the market value of the item once it has been separated from the vehicle, but rather what is the diminution, if any, in its efficiency as an axle or transmission."

In *Armour v Thyssen Edelstahlwerke AG*[64] steel strip was supplied to manufacturers of sinks. It was not contested that property in finished sinks, where the steel had been formed into shape, had passed by specification. The question arose, however, whether property had passed when the steel, which was supplied in long coils, had been cut into short lengths. Evidence was led that the cut steel was not readily saleable, and that it could not be re-welded to a saleable size and form. Melting down was not practicable because it caused a change in the composition of the material. Lord Mayfield concluded that specification operated, on the ground that once the steel was cut it was in a different form, and could not be returned to its original form. Lord Mayfield was influenced by the fact that, when the steel was cut it was saleable only in a different market; he held that the evidence on this matter was a recognition by the steel trade that the steel was in fact in a different form and thus in a manufacturing sense a new species. His decision on this point was reversed by the Second Division[65] although it did not affect their dismissal of the reclaiming motion. The Second Division held that the steel had not become a new species by being cut into strips.

---

[62] 1986 S.L.T. 84.
[63] *ibid.* at 88.
[64] 1986 S.L.T. 452.
[65] 1989 S.L.T. 182 at 188K-L, *per* LJ-C Ross and at 190I-J, *per* Lord McDonald. The matter was not argued in the House of Lords.

In *Kinloch Damph Ltd v Nordvik Salmon Farms Ltd*[66] the pursuers supplied two quantities of salmon smolts to the defenders. The parties' contracts contained a retention of title clause, which provided that until the price of the goods was paid in full the goods should, notwithstanding delivery, remain the property of the seller. The clause containing the retention of title further stated that, until property in the goods passed, the buyer should "rear the goods in accordance with good husbandry as applicable to the farming of salmon in Scotland". It concluded by stating that for the avoidance of doubt the buyer accepted that no amount of growth in the size of the fish should prevent the operation of the condition, nor should it permit the buyer to make any claim that title to the fish had passed to it by such fact alone. The contracts also stated that the pursuers' rights to repossession or recovery should in all cases be limited in value to an amount equivalent to any principal outstanding plus interest and the reasonable costs of recovery. Receivers were appointed to the buyer before the smolts had been paid for in full, and the seller brought an action against the buyer and its receivers for a range of remedies, including declarator that the "salmon smolts" supplied under the two contracts of sale were the property of the pursuers. The defenders presented two arguments against the declarator sought by the pursuers. First, they argued that the retention of title clauses constituted an effective attempt to create a security of goods which remained in the possession of the first defenders and which were not those which were the subject of the contract. Secondly, they argued that, by virtue of the feeding and husbandry that the first defenders had provided, the smolts that the pursuers had supplied had ceased to exist as such, and the salmon that were now in the defenders' possession had come into existence. By the operation of specificatio ownership of the *nova species*, the salmon, was vested in the first defenders. The defenders did not dispute that the smolts and the adult salmon were of the same biological species, *salmo salar*. Their argument was rather that the physiological changes undergone by smolts in becoming mature salmon are sufficient to render them a *nova species* in the legal sense.

Lord Macfadyen first considered the significance of the parties' contract in relation to the passing of title. He held that it was clear that they had agreed that title would not pass until the price had been paid. It was equally clear, and scarcely surprising, that the parties were aware of the fact that the fish would grow during the period when they remained the property of the pursuers. That explained the provisions dealing with the rearing of the fish and the acceptance that mere growth of the fish would not prevent the retention of title from operating. The defenders' argument based on *specificatio* could not be accepted in view of the latter provision. The provision that the pursuers' rights to repossession or recovery should be limited to an amount equivalent to the outstanding debt was to be characterised as a restriction on the extent to which the pursuers might vindicate their retained right of property in the fish. In that way the contracts mitigated the potential unfairness of the rule mentioned by Lord Keith in *Armour v Thyssen* that

---

[66] June 30, 1999.

any increase in value belongs to the unpaid seller who has retained title to the goods. In that way the parties had secured that the retention of title clause could not be operated oppressively. Once the pursuers had exercised their right of repossession up to the permitted limit and thus satisfy the outstanding debt, the price would be paid and the one repossessed stock would pass into the ownership of the buyer by virtue of the terms of the contract. Thus this case illustrates a manner in which a retention of title clause can be made to operate in a reasonable manner.

Lord Macfadyen went on to consider the defenders' contention that, **14–13** with the growth of the smolts into mature salmon, the doctrine of *specificatio* operated to vest ownership of the fish in the first defenders. He stated that he was not satisfied that any *nova species* had been created in respect of which the doctrine of *specificatio* could operate. What was disputed was the applicability of the doctrine to the natural growth of a living creature, albeit aided by nourishment and husbandry provided by man. While in a sense the smolts could be said no longer to exist, the proper scope of the doctrine of *specificatio* was in relation to inanimate objects or substances created by human effort out of materials which are used up and cease to exist in the process of creation. There was nothing in the authorities to suggest that the doctrine applied to the process of growth of living creatures. The lack of any such reference in the older writings was particularly significant because of the greater importance of animals in daily life in former times. It followed that the mature salmon in the first defenders' cages were, as objects of ownership, the same things as the smolts that the pursuers had supplied.

It cannot be claimed that the rules on specification and accession are particularly satisfactory. They are derived from Roman law,[67] and are perhaps better suited to an age of primitive technology. Even in such conditions, however, they suggest a rather imperfect compromise. It is not easy to see, for example, why a metal founder should be denied ownership when a woodworker is allowed it. The inadequacy of the rules is even more apparent when they are applied to modern manufacturing processes. When, for example, a vehicle is manufactured, components such as engines, gearboxes and wheels are usually bought by the manufacturer from outside suppliers. These are then built into the vehicle on the assembly line, but in such a way that they can be fairly easily removed; this is essential if repairs and replacements are to be possible during the working life of the vehicle. According to the established tests, such components are capable of being restored to substantially their original condition, and thus should remain the property of the supplier. If a component is removed, however, it will only have a second-hand value, and in some cases may even be almost unsaleable. In such circumstances, the usual practice is that the receiver or liquidator of the manufacturer agrees to make partial payment to the

---

[67] They are in fact the compromise that was reached in the *Digest* between the competing views of the Proculeians and the Sabinians; the former favoured the manufacturer and the latter the owner of the materials.

supplier and the supplier agrees that property should pass to the manufacturer, who alone can use the component effectively. A possible solution, although it is not one favourable to suppliers of goods, is to shift the emphasis in the basic test away from the question of whether the goods can be restored to their original state towards the question of whether the goods have retained substantially their original value. In other words, the economic status of the goods would be substituted for their physical status. This would allow the supplier to recover his goods in cases where they were as valuable to him as to the manufacturer, but not in cases where the goods have, through incorporation in the product, become much more valuable to the manufacturer than to the supplier. Nevertheless, this approach has been rejected by Lord Davidson and by the Second Division. It would undoubtedly represent a shift in the established law and can hardly be conceived without legislation.

In certain German clauses[68] it is provided that, if the goods sold are used in the manufacture of a new product, the seller is to become part-owner of the product. Specific provision for joint ownership in such circumstances is made in para.947(1) of the German Civil Code, and without such legislative provision it is difficult to see how such rights could be made effective. It seems clear that a Scottish retention of title clause could not effectually incorporate such a provision. An agreement to that effect would not amount to a sale of the product, at least under the Sale of Goods Act since there is no money consideration for the transfer of property in the product[69] and, except in the case of sales, under the Act the transfer of property in goods must generally be effected by delivery or its equivalent. The nearest that Scots law has come to such a concept is the decision in *Wylie & Lochhead v Mitchell*.[70] In that case, a manufacturer agreed to construct a hearse for a firm of undertakers to a design provided by them, the materials being supplied partly by each party. It was held that the parties became joint proprietors of the hearse, in proportion to the value of their contributions. The case is an unusual one, and it is significant that the contract was for the construction of the new article. There seems to be no justification for extending similar reasoning to sale of goods. The underlying commercial reality of a contract of sale of goods is that the seller passes property in goods to the buyer who is in turn obliged to pay the seller the price. If the contract of sale provided that the seller was to be entitled to a species of joint property in the manufactured product, the value of that right would usually be more than the price as it would include a share of the manufacturer's profit. That does not seem to accord with the commercial reality of sale. Moreover, practical difficulties would arise in realising the product, especially in cases where components from a large number of suppliers are combined to form one product. Calculating the value of the various part-owners' interests would be equally difficult, especially where some components are and others are not capable of removal.

---

[68] As in *Armour v Thyssen Edelstahlwerke AG* and *Zahnrad Fabrik Passau GmbH v Terex Ltd, supra.*
[69] *Cf.* Sale of Goods Act 1979, s.2(1).
[70] (1878) 8 M. 552.

Commixtion and confusion

Bulk goods such as grain or liquids such as whisky may be mixed in a **14–14** store with other similar products, in such a way that the constituents cannot be separated. This is referred to as commixtion in the case of solids and confusion in the case of liquids. In such cases, the owners of the constituents become *pro indiviso* proprietors of the new product, their shares being in proportion to the quantity and value of their contribution.[71] If the articles can be separated, property is not affected. Normally it is relatively simple to deal with cases where the various constituents are inseparable, as long as the combined product is still in existence. Problems can arise, however, when part or all of the combined product is drawn off and new ingredients are added, as happens in a grain store. In such cases the supplier faces difficulties of identification. Essentially he has to prove that some of his component is likely, on a balance of probabilities, to remain in the store, and thereafter he must prove the proportion that his component bears to the others in store. In appropriate cases, it may be possible to achieve this by means of the FIFO (first in first out) principle. This would apply, for example, to a grain store where grain was introduced at the top and drawn off at the bottom. Where, on the other hand, gram was introduced and drawn off at the top, the LIFO (last in first out) principle would be more appropriate. In either case, the supplier will be heavily dependent on the buyer's records relating to the store, and if these are inadequate the seller is likely to fail.

In cases where the goods are capable of physical separation, with the result that *pro indiviso* property does not arise, the problems of identification discussed at para.14–08 will be relevant.

Trusts

Purported retention of title clauses frequently attempt to make use of **14–15** the machinery of a trust.[72] There is no point in using a trust in relation to the goods themselves, because retention of title, as long as it is in appropriate terms, will suffice to protect the seller's position.[73] Attempts may be made, however, to create trust rights in favour of the seller over either the proceeds of sale of the goods or the products into which the goods have been incorporated. A clause designed to create a trust over proceeds of sale was discussed at length in *Clark Taylor & Co Ltd v Quality Site Development (Edinburgh) Ltd*, where its validity was decisively rejected. In view of the reasoning in that case, it appears extremely unlikely that valid trusts can be created over either proceeds of sale or manufactured products. The practical difficulties that would

---

[71] Erskine, II, i, 17; Bell, *Prin.*, §1298.

[72] As in *Clark Taylor & Co Ltd v Quality Site Development (Edinburgh) Ltd*, 1981 S.C. 111; *Emerald Stainless Steel Ltd v South Side Distribution Ltd*, 1982 S.C. 61; and *Deutz Engines Ltd v Terex Ltd*, 1984 S.L.T. 273.

[73] This did not prevent the sellers in *Emerald Stainless Steel* and *Deutz* from trying to incorporate trust provisions into their retention of title clauses; the clauses in these cases display a fundamental misunderstanding of what retention of title is designed to achieve.

arise if such trusts were accorded recognition are fully discussed in the Lord President's opinion, and because of these difficulties there are excellent reasons for simply holding that there is no underlying commercial reality of a trust in such cases. Apart from this consideration, the formal requirements for a person's declaring himself a trustee of his own property are likely to be difficult to satisfy in such cases, and this will normally form an additional reason for refusing validity. In the two later cases, *Emerald Stainless Steel Ltd v South Side Distribution Ltd* and *Deutz Engines Ltd v Terex Ltd*, *Clark Taylor* was treated as effectively precluding the use of trusts in retention of title clauses.[74]

Agency

14–16   A manufacturer or wholesaler who wants to distribute his goods to the public is not restricted to selling his goods to retailers who in turn resell them to the public. If he prefers, he can proceed by way of agency rather than sale. This enables him to retain the ownership of the goods until they reach the ultimate customer, with the result that he can reclaim them in the event of the agent's insolvency. Moreover, when goods are sold by an agent on his principal's behalf, the principal and agent may agree that the proceeds belong to the principal, not the agent, or are to be paid into a trust account for the principal.[75] The contract concluded by the agent is the principal's contract, and thus the price is *prima facie* the principal's. Moreover, agency is a fiduciary relationship,[76] and thus it is quite consistent with the agent's holding assets on trust for the principal; in some cases a constructive trust would be implied.[77]

Agency nevertheless has disadvantages for the principal. Because the principal is a party to the contract with the consumer, he is liable on any

---

[74] The court's approach in *Clark Taylor* is in complete contrast to the treatment of retention of title clauses in the leading English case, *Aluminium Industrie Vaasen BV v Romalpa Aluminium Ltd* [1976] 1 W.L.R. 676, where it was held that an "all-sums" clause created a fiduciary relationship (a relationship analogous to a trust) between the parties, which conferred upon the sellers equitable rights in the proceeds of sale of the goods supplied. The difference of approach is not surprising; the two systems are perhaps at their furthest apart in the law of moveable property, and English principles of equity frequently imply fiduciary relationships in situations where Scots law would not. What is surprising is that the *Romalpa* decision, and indeed subsequent English cases involving fiduciary relationships and rights in equity, such as *Borden (UK) Ltd v Scottish Timber Products Ltd* [1981] 1 Ch. 25, have been extensively cited in argument in Scottish cases. It is perhaps notable that none of those cases has been founded upon to any significant extent in Scottish judicial decisions. Scots law has its own distinctive approach to problems involving moveable property, and it has no need to invoke decisions which turn on highly technical concepts of English equity. It is most disappointing that the Government has seen fit to appoint an English lawyer, however eminent he may be in his own field, to review the law of securities over moveables in both jurisdictions. Indeed, especially in the field of retention of title, there is much to be said for review of the law on a European basis, since retention clauses drafted under the legal systems of other Member States of the European Communities are frequently encountered in practice. The European Commission had the matter under review for a time, but it is understood that its work has now been suspended.

[75] The agent will usually be entitled to deduct commission.

[76] See *Stair Memorial Encyclopaedia*, Vol.24, paras 170–188.

[77] *ibid.*, paras 170–188.

warranties as to the quality or fitness for purpose of the goods. Further, if the agency relationship is genuine, it is likely in practice that the manufacturer or wholesaler will be much more closely concerned with the distribution of his goods and relations with consumers than if he sells through retail distributors, using ordinary contracts of sale. That may be something that he wants to avoid.

It is essential to ensure that an alleged agency is genuine, and not a disguise for what is truly a contract of sale. The criteria for distinguishing agency from sale are discussed by Lord Dunedin in *Michelin Tyre Co Ltd v Macfarlane (Glasgow) Ltd (in Liquidation)*.[78] If the sums owed or paid by the ultimate customer to the alleged agent and by the alleged agent to the alleged principal appear in reality to be retail and wholesale prices respectively, it is likely that the relationship is sale, not agency. In particular, if an alleged agent appears to take the chance of profit and to bear the risk of loss on the goods, the relationship is likely to be sale; an agent is normally paid by commission, either fixed or related to the price for which the goods are sold.

Retention of title in the conflict of laws

Lex situs governs real rights

Retention of title clauses are extremely common in contracts which **14–17** involve the sale of goods by a seller in one jurisdiction to a buyer in another. In such cases, the question arises of which legal system is to determine the validity of the clause. The answer is, it is thought, quite straightforward. A retention of title clause purports to retain property in goods in the seller. The question in issue in any dispute about retention of title is whether the seller has been successful in retaining property, or whether property has in fact passed to the purchaser. Scots law has adopted the general rule that property rights, and indeed real rights for all sorts, in both moveable and immoveable (heritable) property, are governed by the *lex situs* (the law of the jurisdiction where the item of the property in question is situated for the time being). The reason for adopting this rule is that property rights, and real rights of every sort, affect third parties; a real right is good against the whole world. The persons most immediately affected by real rights in a particular item of property are those in the jurisdiction where it is situated, and from a practical standpoint the only sensible rule is that rights in any given item of property should be governed by the law of the jurisdiction where it is situated.

The leading Scottish case is *Inglis v Robertson and Baxter*,[79] which involved an attempted hypothecation of whisky which was said to have been created by the handing over of delivery warrants. The alleged hypothecation was effected by one Englishman in favour of another

---

[78] (1917) 2 S.L.T. 205 at 212.
[79] (1897) 24 R. 759; (1898) 25 R. (H.L.) 70.

Englishman, but the whisky was situated in a warehouse in Glasgow. Creditors of the alleged hypothecator subsequently arrested the whisky. Lord Watson held that the validity of the alleged hypothecation must be governed by Scots law. He said[80]:

> "The present question does not arise between two Englishmen, nor does it arise in relation to mercantile transactions which can reasonably be characterised as English. The *situs* of the goods was in Scotland. The Scottish creditors who claim their proceeds did not make any English contract; and in order to attach them they made use of the execution which the law of Scotland permits for converting their personal claim against the owner into a real charge upon the goods themselves. It would, in my opinion, be contrary to the elementary principles of international law, and so far as I know, without authority, to hold that the right of a Scottish creditor when so perfected can be defeated by a transaction between his debtor and the citizen of a foreign country which would be according to the law of that country, but is not according to the law of Scotland, sufficient to create a real right in the goods."

Lord Watson then referred to the question of whether the party who received the alleged hypothecation had a real right in the goods and continued:

> "That is a question which I have no hesitation in holding must, in the circumstances of this case, be solved by reference to the law of Scotland. The whisky was in Scotland, and was there held in actual possession by a custodier for [the alleged hypothecator] as the true owner. That state of the tide could not, so far as Scotland was concerned, be altered or overcome by a foreign transaction of pledge which had not, according to the rules of Scottish law, the effect of vesting the property of the whisky, or, in other words, a *jus in re*, in the pledgee."

It is further clear that the general rule that the *lex situs* governs real rights extends to security rights over moveable property. This was expressly held in the old case of *Mitchell v Burnet and Mouat*[81] and reaffirmed in the judgment of Lord Keith in *Carse v Coppen*.[82] The applicability of the *lex situs* did not arise on the approach taken by the Lord President, with whom Lord Russell agreed, and Lord Carmont, both of whom held that a Scottish company had no power to grant a floating charge, even over English assets.[83]

Application of lex situs *to sale of goods—governs real rights*

14–18   International contracts of sale of goods normally display one particular feature; namely that the goods move from one jurisdiction to another under the contract of sale. Thus, if a manufacturer in France sells to a

---

[80] (1898) 25 R. (H.L.) 70 at 73.
[81] (1746) Mor. 4468.
[82] 1958 S.C. 233 at 245–246.
[83] See also Anton on *Private International Law* (2nd ed.), pp.611–626.

customer in Scotland, the goods will usually be situated in France at the time when the contract is concluded, and in Scotland after the contract has been performed. The approach generally followed by the Scottish courts is that the legal system which should govern systems of proprietary right in the goods is that of the country where the goods are to end up. It is respectfully suggested that this is the only sensible solution. First, the parties' expectations throughout the transaction are that the goods will be delivered to and held in that jurisdiction. Consequently that is the jurisdiction where the goods are likely to be situated when any question of proprietary right arises. Second, the rationale of the choice of law rules relating to property rights, and especially those relating to securities and their validity, is largely the protection of those transacting with the possessor of goods. Such persons may deal with the goods themselves, as in the case of sub-purchasers or pledgees, or may want to do diligence or its foreign equivalents in relation to the goods. Persons who transact with the possessor of the goods are likely to be in the jurisdiction where the goods are situated, or at least to regard that jurisdiction as the one with which the goods are connected. Where, under a contract of sale, goods are delivered to premises in a particular jurisdiction with a view to being resold or worked upon on those premises, it is obvious that that jurisdiction is the one to which third parties transacting with the possessor will look. In the third place, in many cases considerable practical problems will arise if rules belonging to the legal system of one jurisdiction are applied to property situated in another jurisdiction. The rules of property law are generally highly specific to one legal system. Moreover, property law is normally conceived as an integrated system, where the rules are tailored to fit in with one another. Rules of this sort cannot readily be grafted on to another system. For example, the English system of equitable rights cannot readily be inserted among the rules of Scots property law and the elaborate German rules on co-ownership which correspond broadly to the Scots law of accession and specification cannot readily be integrated with the general conceptions and principles of Scots law. It is accordingly essential that one legal system should govern all real rights in any particular item of property. The only practical system for this purpose is the *lex situs* for the time being, and in an international sale, after delivery of the goods, the *situs* is clearly the jurisdiction where the goods have ended up. It is thought that the exact nature of the contract of sale, whether cif, fob, ex works or whatever, should not affect the question of the *lex situs* as long as the parties understand, as will nearly always be the case, that the goods are to end up in a particular jurisdiction. It is in that jurisdiction that the retention of title clause will have practical effect, and it is third parties in that jurisdiction who are most likely to be affected by it. Similarly, it should not matter in which country delivery is actually effected. The *situs* of the goods when they leave the seller's premises, and any intermediate *situs* that they acquire in the course of delivery, do not seem relevant to the choice of law for two reasons: first, the location of the goods in those *situs* is only transitory; and second, third parties who seek to acquire rights in the goods are much less likely to be situated in these intermediate jurisdictions. It would be possible to apply a rule that the validity of an attempt to retain title depends on the *lex situs* of the goods from time to time, but such a mechanical application of the *lex situs* could lead to arbitrary, and even bizarre, results. If, for example, a liquidator in Scotland wished to defeat an "all-sums" retention of title which was valid under Scots law, he could move the goods to a warehouse in France to invoke the local law, which is hostile to such provisions. Moreover, the ownership of goods could change repeatedly in the course of a journey. These results do not appear desirable,[84] and they can be avoided by adoption of the rule discussed in the last paragraph. The one exception to this, however, may be where there is no understanding between buyer and seller as to where the goods will end up.[85] In that case there is probably no alternative to the mechanical application of the *lex situs* from time to time.

Proper law of the contract of sale—affects personal rights

14–19   The other legal system that may have a bearing on retention of title clauses is the proper law of the contract containing the clause, but the scope of the proper law is strictly limited.[86] The application of the proper law is confined to the personal rights and obligations of the parties to the contract; that is, to the rights and obligations that bind the parties to the contract themselves but not outsiders. In particular, the proper law of the contract will determine the extent and interpretation of the parties' personal rights.[87] It will not govern the acquisition and transference of property, because that involves real rights and obligations, which are binding on third parties to the contract. Thus a third party may attempt to acquire the goods sold, or to do diligence against those goods. Whether he can do either of those things depends on property rights in the goods, and those property rights are governed, as explained above, by the *lex situs*.[88]

Apart from the above considerations, there are practical reasons for not applying the proper law of the contract to determine the validity of

---

[84] Although the first could be defeated by the application of public policy, and the second is more objectionable in theory than practice, as questions relating to real rights in the goods will hardly ever arise before they have reached the purchaser's premises.

[85] Although this will be highly unusual, since a seller will nearly always know where buyers from him carry on business, and will in any event see the shipping documents before the goods are despatched.

[86] For discussion of the meaning and application of the proper law, see Anton, *op. cit.*, pp.262–274. Where there is a choice of law clause in the contract, that will normally determine the proper law, although there are signs that the Scottish courts are prepared to disregard the parties' apparent choice if it appears to conflict with the true nature of the contract. If there is no choice of law clause, the proper law will be the system with which the contract appears to have its closest connection, in the light of its terms and all the surrounding circumstances. Generally speaking the place of performance is given primacy, but other elements may overrule that.

[87] This is subject, however, to the two important limitations laid down in *Hamlyn & Co v Talisker Distillery* (1894) R. (H.L.) 21 at 22–23, *per* the Lord Chancellor and at 25–26, *per* Lord Watson, namely that questions relating to the remedy sought are governed by the law of the forum and that Scots law will not apply rules of the proper law that are contrary to its own fundamental policy: see below, pp.283–284.

[88] Apart from the clear authorities on the application of the *lex situs*, it is obviously unreasonable that the legal system chosen by the parties to a contract of sale should affect the rights that third parties may acquire in the subjects of sale.

retention of title clauses. If unlimited scope were given to the parties to choose the proper law, it would be relatively easy to select a legal system which encourages retention of title. In practice, the choice of the proper law is rarely if ever discussed by parties, and the normal practice is that the seller imposes his legal system on the transaction. Thus a seller in France could choose a system such as German law in order to allow retention of title. The courts would probably have little difficulty in striking down a choice of legal system that had no genuine bearing on the contract, on public policy grounds. The second practical problem is more serious, however. Application of the proper law would mean that sellers resident in countries such as Scotland, England and Germany, where a favourable attitude has been taken to retention of title clauses, would obtain an advantage over sellers resident in countries such as France and Italy, where a much more restrictive attitude has been taken. That problem does not arise, however, if the *lex situs* governs the question of validity.

Cases on choice of law

In *Emerald Stainless Steel Ltd v South Side Distribution Ltd*[89] and *Deutz* **14–20** *Engines Ltd v Terex Ltd*[90] the contract of sale under consideration contained choice of law clauses which declared that the contract was to be governed by English law. In each case, Lord Ross found it unnecessary to determine whether English law was relevant because it was not averred in the pleadings, and he was accordingly bound to assume that it was the same as Scots law. The earliest case in which choice of law was a live issue was the decision of Sheriff Jardine in *Hammer und Sohne v HWT Realisations Ltd.*[91] Sheriff Jardine was prepared to concede that West German law was the proper law of the contract in that case, but held that the proper law was not the correct way to approach the question in issue. He pointed out[92] that the correct inquiry is not what law governs the contract but what law governs the particular question raised in the instant proceedings. The present case involved an order for delivery sought in a Scottish court in respect of goods situated in Scotland. The question at issue was whether a security had been created over those goods and, on the authority of *Mitchell v Burnet and Mouat*,[93] Sheriff Jardine held that the *lex situs* governed the creation of securities over moveables, and accordingly that Scots law governed the question at issue.

Sheriff Jardine referred to *Hamlyn & Co v Talisker Distillery*,[94] a leading case on the application of the proper law to questions of contractual right. In that case, the House of Lords held that questions of the construction of a contract are governed by its proper law,[95] but admitted

---

[89] 1982 S.C. 61.
[90] 1984 S.L.T. 273.
[91] 1985 S.L.T. (Sh. Ct.) 21.
[92] *ibid.* at 23.
[93] (1746) Mor. 4468.
[94] (1894) 21 R. (H.L.) 21.
[95] See the Lord Chancellor at 22–23 and Lord Watson at 25–26.

two important exceptions; namely questions relating to the remedy sought, which are governed by the law of the forum where the question is determined, and matters where recognition of the rule of the proper law would be contrary to the fundamental policy of Scots law. Sheriff Jardine held that the principle of Scots law that a security over moveables cannot generally be created without possession is such a fundamental principle and cannot be overcome by the application of the proper law of the contract.

In *Zahnrad Fabrik Passau GmbH v Terex Ltd*[96] goods were supplied by a German company to a Scottish company under the supplier's standard form of contract, which included a German choice of law clause and a German retention of title clause. It was argued for the Scottish company and its receivers that the validity of the retention of title clause must be tested against Scots law alone and not German law. This argument was rejected by Lord Davidson (although this part of his judgment was not necessary for his decision, and is accordingly *obiter*). He dealt with the matter as follows[97]:

> "If . . . the parties to a contract are entitled to agree when property is to pass, then I think it is wrong to regard the *lex situs* as being an inflexible corpus of law . . . In a contract regulating the rights and obligations *hinc inde* of two contracting parties, *prima facie* I see no reason why they should not incorporate into the contract one or more provisions of a foreign legal system. If the contracting parties choose to do that, then the condition relied upon may be open to challenge on, among others, the ground that it is opposed to a fundamental principle of the law of Scotland."

14-21 On this basis, he allowed the averments of German law to go to proof.

It is significant that Lord Davidson left open the possibility that the Scots rules governing the validity of retention clauses (which in this case were the rules relating to accession and specification) were so fundamental that any contrary foreign rule would be disregarded by Scots law. Nevertheless it is thought that any suggestion that the proper law of a contract can govern the creation of security and other property rights is not correct.

In *Armour v Thyssen Edelsahlwerke AG*[98] the question of choice of law arose at first instance, although the matter was not pursued on appeal by the sellers on the basis that the evidence of German law had been inadequate for their argument. The contract of sale by a German supplier to a Scottish customer included a German choice of law clause and a very elaborate German retention of title clause. Lord Mayfield held that the validity of the clause was governed exclusively by Scots law. He referred[99] to *Inglis v Robertson and Baxter*, and held that that case

---

[96] 1986 S.L.T. 84.
[97] *ibid.* at 88–89.
[98] 1986 S.L.T. 452.
[99] *ibid.* at 455.

was clear authority that the *lex situs* governs the creation of real rights in corporeal moveables. He stated[1]:

> "In my view . . . there is clear authority that the *lex situs* governs the creation of real rights in corporeal moveables. I consider it is also clear that whether or not a security has been created (or the effectiveness or otherwise) has to be determined by the law of the place where the goods are actually located. In my view that is supported by *Mitchell v Burnet and Mount*. Accordingly, it is my further view that if a security has been created then Scots law governs."

Lord Mayfield went on to consider the decisions of Lord Ross in *Emerald Stainless Steel* and *Deutz* and concluded that both those cases and the instant case raised questions about security rights, governed by the *lex situs*.

Lord Mayfield subsequently considered *Hamlyn & Co v Talisker Distillery*,[2] and on the basis of the statements of principle in that case advanced a further reason for rejecting the application of the proper law on the basis of the then prevalent view that an "all sums" retention of title clause was an attempt to create a security without possession. He pointed out[3] that the purpose of the rule that security over moveables cannot be created without possession is the protection of creditors. He regarded that as a fundamental principle of Scots law which must prevail against the proper law of any contract.

Although it was not necessary for his decision, Lord Mayfield went on to consider the evidence of German law that was led in the case at some length. He concluded that none of the three experts who gave evidence had complete confidence in his position, and that, accordingly, the averments of German law made by the defenders had not been proved. The case illustrates the extreme difficulty of proving foreign law in a field such as retention of title, and it may be that attempts to invoke foreign law fail simply because of the difficulty of adducing sufficient evidence. A further argument for the seller deserves notice. It was maintained that German law was the proper law of the contract and therefore governed its construction. Under German law, it was said, conditions of business might be applied to the extent that they were valid, even if they were in part invalid or ineffective; and consequently German law would treat the elaborate "all-sums" retention of title clause in the parties' contract as a clause of simple retention if that was all that Scots law, as the *lex situs*, would recognise.[4] Lord Mayfield did not require to deal with the substance of this issue because of his finding that the averments of German law had not been proved. It seems, however, that the seller's argument cannot be correct, on the basis of the

---

[1] *ibid.* at 456.
[2] (1894) 21 R. (H.L.) 21.
[3] 1986 S.L.T. 452 at 457.
[4] See 455F—I, 457G—H.

two exceptions recognised in *Hamlyn & Co v Talisker Distillery*.[5] In the first place, it is clear that the application of the alleged rule of German law founded on by the seller would involve the rewriting of the retention of title clause, and not the mere interpretation of its wording. The opening part of the clause provided that: "[a]ll goods delivered by us remain our property . . . until all debts owed to us . . . are settled". It is plain that that wording cannot be turned into a clause of simple retention by mere deletion. In any event, turning such wording into a simple retention clause would fundamentally alter the import of the clause. For these reasons, the rewriting involved would go well past the Scots rules allowing severance. That, it is submitted, would be contrary to a fundamental principle of Scots law, which has steadfastly set itself against the remaking of contracts. In the second place, the remaking or rewriting of a contractual provision, as against its mere interpretation, should not be governed by the proper law. It is rather a question of remedy and that, as *Hamlyn* makes clear, is a matter for the law of the forum.[6]

Procedural considerations

14–22   It remains to notice certain procedural matters that may be encountered in practice. As has been mentioned, goods subject to a valid retention clause may be recovered by the seller by virtue of his right of ownership. If court proceedings are required they will usually take the form of an action for delivery, or declarator and delivery. This is often combined with a conclusion for *interim* interdict, to prevent the receiver or liquidator or buyer from selling or disposing of goods in the buyer's possession. Motions for *interim* interdict are usually disposed of, if the retention clause appears *prima facie* valid, by the receiver or liquidators' granting an undertaking that (1) he will keep a detailed record, including serial numbers, if any, of all products obtained from the seller that are used or sold by him; and (2) he will account to the seller for the contract price of any article so used or sold in the event that the clause is eventually held to be (a) valid and (b) applicable to such article. The receiver's or liquidator's liability will be a debt of the receivership or liquidation, and thus payable in full. If such an undertaking is not given, *interim* interdict will normally be granted or refused according to the court's view of the validity of the retention clause in the particular instances of the case. The balance of convenience is rarely, if ever, the determining factor. Nevertheless, Lord Jauncey commented on the balance of convenience in *Goodyear Tyre and Rubber Co (Great Britain) Ltd v Hunter*.[7] In that case, Goodyear tyres had been supplied to the insolvent defenders both by the pursuers and by independent wholesalers. The tyres had no serial numbers, and it was doubtful if tyres supplied by the pursuers could be identified, as all the stock had been

---

[5] Above.
[6] An argument broadly similar to that in *Armour*, but based on English principles relating to severance, was rejected by Lord Jauncey, in *Goodyear Tyre and Rubber Co (Great Britain) Ltd v Hunter*, unreported, August 20, 1986, on the ground that the "all moneys" provision in the retention clause was simply not capable of severance.
[7] Above.

inmixed. Moreover, attempts were being or would be made to sell the shares in the insolvent defenders or their business, but if *interim* interdict were granted the defenders would be forced to cease trading. Further, if the trustee in sequestration or liquidator of the defenders sold tyres in which the property had not passed from the pursuers, they would remain liable in damages to the pursuers for the value of the tyres, or to account to the pursuers for their value. In these circumstances Lord Jauncey expressed the view that any prejudice suffered by the defenders if interdict were granted would probably be far greater than any prejudice suffered by the pursuers in the event of a refusal. He would accordingly have refused *interim* interdict on the balance of convenience alone had he not done so on the merits.

Care must be taken to ensure that a retention of title clause does not amount in reality to a floating charge. If it does, it is likely to be void either as not being in the form prescribed by s.462 of the Companies Act 1985 or as not being registered under s.410 of that Act.

Chapter 15

MANDATES AND POWERS OF ATTORNEY

Nature of rights

Mandate is the term traditionally used in Scots law for the relation- **15–01** ship of agency where the agent, or mandatory, is not remunerated as such. In modern commercial practice such a relationship usually arises as an ancillary part of a wider agreement, designed to aid the enforcement of the parties' rights and obligations. A power of attorney[1] is simply a written mandate, usually specifying the powers of the attorney, or mandatory, in considerable detail. The legal position of the attorney is exactly the same as that of a mandatory.

Mandate given in interests of mandatory

Where a mandate is given for the purposes of the mandatory, rather **15–02** than the mandant, it is irrevocable without the mandatory's consent.[2] It may, further, amount to an assignation, as where the mandatory is empowered to collect for his own purposes funds due to the mandant.[3] In such a case the mandate by itself will confer only personal rights on the mandatory, albeit of an irrevocable nature. In order to obtain a real right the mandatory must still intimate the assignation to the mandant's debtor. Both a cheque, at least if granted for the payee's own purposes,[4] and a bill of exchange operate as a mandate and assignation.[5] Presentation to the bank on which the cheque or bill is drawn operates as intimation to the debtor, completing the payee's real right in the funds assigned, to the extent that funds are available to meet the cheque or bill.[6]

---

[1] The expression is English in origin, but has been used in Scotland for many years. In older cases and textbooks "factory" is often used as a synonym.

[2] Bell, *Prin.*, 1.228; *Premier Briquette Co v Gray*, 1922 S.C. 329. Such a mandate is sometimes known as a procuratory *in rem suam*.

[3] *Carter v McIntosh* (1862) 24 D. 925, especially at 933, *per* L.J.-C. Inglis.

[4] It is thought that it is not essential that the cheque should be given for value, but that it will suffice if it is given for the payee's own purposes: *cf. British Linen Co Bank v Carruthers* (1883) 10 R. 923, where the criterion adopted is whether the cheque amounts to a procuratory *in rem suam*, for which value is not essential. For a further discussion of this issue, see McBryde, *Contract*, paras 17–64 to 17–72. The distinction between an ordinary mandate and a mandate for the mandatory's own purposes should be borne in mind in considering this issue, as it is only the latter that can amount to an assignation.

[5] *British Linen Co v Carruthers, supra.*

[6] Bills of Exchange Act 1882, s.53(2), re-enacting the common law, as amended by the Law Reform (Miscellaneous Provisions) (Scotland) Act 1985, s.11. Section 75A of the 1882 Act, introduced by s.11 of the 1985 Act, has the effect of making the assignation of a cheque subject to the resolutive condition that the drawer does not countermand payment; if he does, the bank is treated as having no funds available to meet the cheque.

A mandate not given in the mandatory's interests, but merely to serve the purposes of the mandant, is revocable by the mandant at any time.[7]

Effect of insolvency on mandate

15–03   If the mandate is not given in the mandatory's interests, it is treated as revoked by the insolvency of the mandant or the mandatory.[8] If it is given in the mandatory's interests, the effect of the mandant's insolvency varies according to the nature of the rights that the mandate is designed to enforce. If it is designed to facilitate the enforcement of real rights or trust rights or rights in security it will survive the mandant's insolvency, and can be enforced if necessary against the liquidator, administrator or receiver of the mandant. The critical point in such a case is that the rights that are to be enforced using the mandate are rights which prevail on the insolvency of the mandant,[9] and any procedure designed to enforce such rights will likewise prevail against the insolvency. If, on the other hand, the mandate is designed merely to facilitate the enforcement of personal rights that the mandatory has against the mandant, it will fall on the mandant's insolvency. If the rule were otherwise, the result would be that the mandatory was able to secure a preference in the mandant's insolvency in respect of purely personal rights, rather than ranking in the insolvency like all other personal creditors. That would contravene the fundamental principle of the law of insolvency that, apart from securities, diligence and statutory preferences, all personal creditors rank equally.[10]

Mandates to enforce real and trust rights and rights in security

15–04   In *Broughton v Stewart & Co*[11] one merchant had consigned goods to another firm of merchants as commission agents, and on the faith of those consignments the commission agents had made considerable advances to the consigner. As commission agents the consignees had a mandate to sell the goods, which remained the property of the consigner. They also enjoyed a factor's lien over those goods in security of the advances that they had made.[12] The consigner was sequestrated, and the trustee in his sequestration attempted to interdict the commission agents from selling any of the goods. Interdict was refused, on the basis that, after advances had been made on the faith of the security conferred by the lien, the mandate to sell became a mandate for the mandatory's own interests, designed to enforce his lien. The lien was a security right that prevailed against the sequestration, and the mandate accordingly survived along with the lien. Lord Meadowbank, who delivered the opinion of the court, said:

> "The mandate of a factor to sell is an ordinary mandate, revocable at pleasure; but if the consignee, on the faith of his lien, makes

---

[7] Erskine, *Inst.*, III.iii.32, 40.
[8] Bell, *Comm.* (5th ed.), i.488–496.
[9] For trust rights, see Chap.12.
[10] See paras 13–08—13–10.
[11] December 17, 1814, F.C.
[12] See Gloag and Irvine, *Rights in Security*, pp.363 *et seq.*

advances, he becomes *praepositus in rem suam* [a mandatory in his own interest] under the factory [mandate] to sell. He is entitled to say, 'Though I have a mandate revocable at pleasure, you must indemnify me *instanter* of any advances, or relieve me of the security I have come under for you.' If the trustee had said, 'There is money to relieve you, and I recall the order to sell,' he was entitled to do so, but it is only in that way that the mandate can be revoked, because *res non sunt integrae.* After advances are made, it is not enough to say that the lien over the goods is sufficient to secure the consignee; that is not the way in which the mercantile world goes on; the mandate becomes irrevocable, unless immediate means are taken to relieve the factor of his advances, and I have no doubt that such is the practice; for what man would engage in the business of a mercantile agent on other terms, or what can he do for all the bills he grants on the faith of the lien, unless he can bring the lien to market?"

In *Struthers v Commercial Bank of Scotland*[13] a bank letter of credit granted by Sir W. Forbes and Company was drawn in favour of Craig, payable on or after July 7. On July 2 it was indorsed in favour of the Commercial Bank by Craig's agent, full value less discount being given in exchange. It was presented for payment on July 6, July 7 being a Sunday, and payment was refused, on the basis that Craig's estates were then in the process of being sequestrated. Sequestration was awarded later the same day. In a competition between the trustee in sequestration and the Commercial Bank it was held that the Commercial Bank, as indorsee, was entitled to payment. Lord Fullerton, with whom the Lord President agreed, stated:

"A letter of credit of this kind is an order to honour the draft of the party to whom it is granted, and an authority to such party to draw. But it is perfectly understood in practice, that the power can only be exercised by the person with the document in his possession. The letter of credit . . . is given to the Commercial Bank indorsed; and they pay the amount minus the discount. . . I think that, by putting the letter of credit into the hands of the Commercial Bank for value, there was a mandate by Craig to the Commercial Bank to draw the money. And it was an effectual mandate, because no one could draw the money without being possessed of the letter of credit . . . If it were an ordinary gratuitous mandate to a third party, the mandant might put an end to it when he chose, and his creditors could compel him to do so. But it was not so. It was a mandate to draw for the mandatory's own behoof, he having in the meantime made the advance. He was mandatory *in rem suam,* and it is not in the power either of the bankrupt or of his creditors to revoke such a mandate . . . Whenever a mandatory has contracted an obligation on the faith of the mandate, it cannot be recalled".[14]

The critical point is that the letter of credit was for practical purposes equivalent to a negotiable instrument, and that the power in it could be

---

[13] (1842) 4 D. 460.
[14] At 468. See also Erskine, *Inst.,* iii.40.

only exercised by a person with the letter in his possession. Thus, once value had been given for it, possession of the document conferred a real right to the sum payable under the letter of credit,[15] and the mandate in favour of the Commercial Bank to claim payment from Sir W Forbes and Company was designed to permit enforcement of that real right.

Mandates to enforce purely personal rights

15–05   The case mentioned above should be contrasted with the case where a mandate is designed only to assist in the enforcement of personal rights. In such a case, it is a fundamental principle that a mandate cannot be used to alter the ranking of the personal creditors. Consequently any mandate which would have that effect will be revoked by the insolvency of the mandant. In *McKenzie v Campbell*,[16] Fraser, who had been charged with forgery, asked the defender, a law agent, to act for him in connection with the charge, and sent him a sum of money with authority to use it for the purposes of the defence to the charge. Shortly thereafter Fraser was sequestrated, but the defender continued to make use of the money for the purposes of the defence. The trustee in sequestration brought an action of accounting to recover the money, and was successful. On sequestration, the defender's employment as law agent was terminated, and the mandate, which was only designed to facilitate the performance of those services, was revoked with the employment. While the reasoning of the First Division is based on the fact that the mandate in favour of the solicitor was not granted for his purposes, and was therefore revocable on that account alone, it is clear that the result would have been the same if the mandate was for the solicitor's purposes but was only designed to assist enforcement of a personal right. Thus the Lord Ordinary (Kincairney) refers[17] to the relevance of the distinction between cases such as those under consideration, where the money remained the property of the bankrupt, and cases where it had become the property of the solicitor. Lord McLaren makes a similar point in his opinion.[18]

---

[15] See *Gloag and Irvine*, pp.577–578.
[16] (1894) 21 R. 904.
[17] At 907.
[18] At 911.

Chapter 16

DEBT SUBORDINATION AGREEMENTS

Introduction

In recent years there has been an increasing demand for a legal structure **16–01** which allows companies to issue subordinated debt. In its simplest form, subordinated debt is a transaction by which the lender of money to the company has his claim for repayment of the money subordinated to that of the other creditors. They have to be paid in full before he is entitled to any dividend out of the assets of the company. A second type of subordination is where one creditor agrees that he shall not be entitled to claim his full *pro rata* entitlement in the liquidation until one or more of the ordinary creditors in the liquidation have had their claims met beyond what would be otherwise their *pro rata* entitlement. Although these concepts are simple, their legal implications are complicated. Different legal devices and structures have been used in different jurisdictions to create enforceable legal instruments. They have been widely used in particular in relation to company buy-outs, intermediate financing arrangements and the issue of so-called "junk" bonds in takeovers. The issues involved, such as third party enforcement, the *pari passu* rules, and the *British Eagle* case,[1] have been the subject of much legal discussion in books and legal articles.[2]

Most debt subordination instruments as used in England, the United States and the Commonwealth are cumbersome and complex structures which do not always achieve their objectives with certainty.

It is proposed in this chapter:

(1) to look at the objectives of debt subordination instruments;
(2) to examine in the context of English law the type of debt subordination instruments most commonly used; and
(3) to examine the Scottish law in relation to debt subordination and to discuss the legal instruments which are effective under Scottish law to achieve the objectives of debt subordination.

---

[1] *British Eagle International Airlines Ltd v Compagnie Nationale Air France* [1975] 1 W.L.R. 758.

[2] See especially B. Johnston, "Debt Subordination: the Australian Perspective" [1987] Australian Business Law Review 80; P.R. Wood, *Law and Practice of International Finance* (1980), p.403; D.H. Calligar, "Subordination Agreements" (1961) 70 Yale Law Journal 376; B. Johnston, "Contractual Debt Subordination and Legislative Reform" [1991] The Journal of Business Law 225; G. McCormack, *Proprietary Claims and Insolvency* (Sweet and Maxwell, London, 1997), at 28035; and E. Ferran, *Company Law and Corporate Finance* (Oxford University Press, Oxford, 1999), Chap.16.

Objectives of debt subordination instruments

16–02   Although it is possible legally to bind a creditor of a solvent company in such a way that his debt is not paid before the payment of another debt, (which might be called "complete subordination"), subordination is usually only contracted to operate in the event of the bankruptcy or liquidation of the debtor. Where ordinary creditors, whether as a class or individually, lend to a company, the company's creditworthiness as far as they are concerned is significantly improved if money is lent to the company which is not to be paid in the event of the liquidation of the company before the ordinary creditors. This is because subordinated debt of that category is available to meet the claims of these creditors in the same way as share capital and reserves, *i.e.* equity. Indeed, for certain regulatory purposes subordinated debt is treated as share capital. In, for example, the *Report of July 1988 of the Basle Committee on Banking Regulations and Supervisory Practices on International Convergence of Capital Measurement and Capital Standards*, the banks concerned were required by 1992 to maintain capital of eight per cent of their assets and exposures. For this purpose capital was divided into two tiers comprising core capital (such as equity and disclosed reserves) and supplementary capital which could include certain categories of subordinated debt. Perpetual subordinated debt issues having the characteristics of equity, and subordinated term debt having a maturity of more than five years, could be included subject to detailed qualifications and limits. In this type of situation the subordinated debt, especially if it is perpetual debt, is intended to be the equivalent of permanent capital.

Just as regulators may insist on capital ratios in which they include subordinated debt as capital, to ensure the creditworthiness of companies regulated for the benefit of ordinary creditors, especially depositors, so also do private organisations lending large sums to companies where effectively they become in practice by far the largest creditor often insist that the holding company or owners or backers of the company provide finance at the same time which is to be subordinated to ordinary creditors. The main beneficiary of such an arrangement is the financing organisation. Although this purpose may also be achieved by the holding company or owner putting equity into the company, the equity solution is not always the preferable solution. That may be for a variety of reasons, including the following:

(1) dividends may be subject to a withholding tax whereas interest may not;

(2) capital duty may be payable on the issue of shares whereas not payable on the issue of loan capital, although this is no longer the case in the United Kingdom;

(3) a company may repay debt (which is acting as *de facto* capital) without triggering the possible need to reduce its share capital;

(4) the subordination agreement may be structured in such a way that the creditor receives a better financial result in the event of the liquidation of the company than if the holding company put the money in as equity; and

(5) the subordinated creditor may be given a favourable rate of interest to compensate him for his debt being locked into the

company, which would not be the case if share capital had to be issued.

English law and debt subordination instruments

The chief legal difficulty with debt subordination arises on the **16–03** insolvency of the debtor company. In terms of the Insolvency Act 1986 all distributions from a company upon the winding up of the company must be made *pari passu* amongst ordinary creditors.[3] The problem is that the *pari passu* rule is mandatory and there was a series of cases suggesting it might not be possible validly to contract out of the rule.

In *British Eagle International Airlines Ltd v Compagnie Nationale Air France*, Lord Cross said:

> "What the respondents are saying here is that the parties . . . by agreeing that simple contract debts are to be satisfied in a particular way have succeeded in 'contracting out' of [the *part passu* provisions] for the payment of unsecured debts *pari passu* . . . [S]uch 'contracting out' must, to my mind, be contrary to public policy . . . I cannot doubt that on principle the rules of general liquidation should prevail."[4]

The proposition that the statutory rules of *pari passu* distribution were mandatory and that creditors could not contract out was taken further in *Carreras Rothmans Ltd v Freeman Matthews Treasure Ltd,*[5] in which Peter Gibson J. summarised the principle in the *British Eagle* case as follows:

> "Where the effect of a contract is that an asset which is actually owned by a company at the commencement of its liquidation would be dealt with in a way other than in accordance with [the *pari passu* provisions], then to that extent the contract as a matter of public policy is avoided, whether or not the contract is entered into for consideration and for bona fide commercial reasons and whether or not the contractual provision affecting the asset is expressed to take effect only on insolvency."

There were several attempts to distinguish the *British Eagle* case.[6] In particular, in Australia in the Victoria Supreme Court in the case *of Horne v Chester & Fein Property Developments Pty Ltd,*[7] Southwell J. tried

---

[3] See Insolvency Act 1986, s.7 and Insolvency Rules 1986, r.4.181; and, in Scotland, Insolvency (Scotland) Rules 1986, r.4.66(4).

[4] [1975] 1 WLR 758 at 780–781; see also *National Westminster Bank Ltd v Halesowen Pressworks & Assemblies Ltd* [1972] A.C. 785 discussed in Chap.17.

[5] [1985] 1 ALL E.R. 155.

[6] See Johnston, "Debt Subordination: the Australian Perspective" [1987] *Australian Business Law Review* 80 at 102 ff.; R.B. Grantham, "Legal Imperialism and Debt Subordination" [1989] *New Zealand Law Journal* 224; *Re Malborough Concrete Constructions Pty Ltd* [1977] Qd R. 37; and *Re Industrial Welding Co Pty Ltd and the Companies Act* (1978) 3 A.C.L.R. 754.

[7] (1987) 5 A.C.L.C. 245.

to distinguish the *British Eagle* case in relation to a debt subordination agreement and gave a detailed review of the authorities. In that case the creditors of the company that had gone into liquidation had previously agreed to defer their claims to the claims of another creditor. Southwell J. stated, in trying to distinguish the House of Lords' decision in the *British Eagle* case:

> "The policy of the insolvency laws' . . . as it appears to me, was never intended to alter the rights and obligations of parties freely entering into a contract, unless the performance of the contract would upon insolvency adversely affect the rights of strangers to the contract . . . [T]he principle [of the *British Eagle* case] is, I believe, that in insolvency law, the whole of the debtor's estate should be available for distribution to all creditors, and no one creditor or group of creditors can lawfully contract in such a manner as to defeat other creditors not parties to the contract . . . When so examined, it may readily be seen that *British Eagle* is distinguishable from the present case, in which, as I have earlier said, the performance of the agreement between the three parties can in no way affect the entitlement of creditors not a party to that agreement."[8]

This narrow view as to the strictures entailed by *British Eagle* enunciated in the *Horne* case has not been widely accepted in England.[9]

In order to get round the problems perceived to be raised in the *British Eagle* case, English legal practitioners have used a variety of structures in framing debt subordination agreements. The two most usual instruments used are (1) contractual or "contingent debt" subordination agreements; and (2) subordination trusts.

Contractual or "contingent debt" subordination agreements

16–04   In a contingent debt subordination agreement, the subordinated debt is set up in such a way that the subordinated creditor has only a contingent or conditional right to repayment of the debt. This can apply conditionally either from the date of lending or, more usually, in the event of the insolvency or liquidation of the borrower. The debt is contingent or conditional in so far that the subordinated debt is either not to be repaid until the other creditors have been repaid in full, or the amount that is to be recovered by the subordinated creditor is stipulated to be only the amount that shareholders themselves would receive in a winding up. Under this scheme, a contingent or conditional debt will be admissible to proof in the winding up of the debtor company, but will only prove for a nominal or nil value.

---

[8] Above at 245, 248 and 250.
[9] See R.M. Goode, *Legal Problem of Credit and Security* (2nd ed., 1988), p.96.

An example of such a clause might be:

"(1) If the debtor becomes subject to any liquidation, dissolution or similar insolvency proceedings or to any assignment for the benefit of its creditors or any other distribution of its assets, the junior debt will be repayable only on condition that the senior debt has been or is capable of being paid in full. Accordingly in any such event the junior debt will be reduced to such amount down to zero as is necessary to ensure that the debtor is able to pay the senior debt in full.

(2) The reduction of the junior debt will be applied first to costs and expenses, secondly to interest, and thirdly to principal of the junior debt."[10]

Other methods provide that in the liquidation or dissolution proceedings, the subordinated debt is contingent on the debtor being solvent and that, accordingly, the subordinated debt is not payable except in so far that the debtor could pay it and still be solvent after the payment. It is stated that the debtor is solvent only if the company is able to pay its provable debts as they fall due, disregarding any debts which are subordinated. The subordinated debt, as a contingent debt, will be admissible to proof in the winding up of the debtor company, but will have only a nominal or nil value. That is because, the company being in liquidation, it is expected that the subordinated creditor will receive no dividend. If it is given a nominal value that is to reflect the market value of the subordinated debt on the basis of there being a gamble that something in the end of the day might be received. If as sometimes happens there is supervening solvency (*i.e.* repayment of ordinary creditors) the procedure in England is for the contingent claim to be amended to the face value of the subordinated debt with the subordinated creditor then entitled to prove for the full amount of the subordinated debt.[11]

Subordination trusts

In England, especially where there is a complex refinancing package **16–05** in relation to a company, it is often desired that the benefit of the subordination of the subordinated creditor is not extended to the body of creditors, *i.e.* all are not paid *pro rata* and in full before the

---

[10] See P Wood: "The Law of Subordinated Debt", p 12 for this example.

[11] See Andrew R. Keay, *McPherson's Law of Company Liquidation* (Sweet & Maxwell, 2001), p.679, where Keay states: "The timing for estimating the value of a contingent claim in a compulsory winding up is usually the date of the winding up order, and for a voluntary winding up the date of the resolution to wind up. If the contingency happens during the winding up [and it may in a debt subordination], the creditor is entitled to prove for the actual amount; if proof has already been lodged, the creditor will be permitted to withdraw and amend accordingly, though not so as to disturb dividends already paid [such as dividends already paid to the senior creditors]. The effect is not to convert the claim into a debt for the purposes of proof: it remains a contingent claim, but the happening of the contingency is treated as admissible evidence of the actual value at the time winding up started.".

subordinated creditor is entitled to a dividend. Usually the object is to structure the deal in such a way that another creditor obtains a distinct advantage in an insolvency over the body of ordinary creditors. Because of the *pari passu* rule, the highest right which an ordinary creditor could have in the liquidation is to a dividend as an ordinary creditor. Accordingly, if the object of the deal is to give the contractually preferred creditor the benefit of the subordinated creditor's dividend, it is sometimes contracted between the subordinated creditor and a preferred creditor that the subordinated creditor shall pay over all dividends received to the preferred creditor. This is, of course, not a real subordination (any more than the contingent debt structure was a real subordination), but it achieves, where it is effective, a result by which the preferred creditor is contractually entitled to obtain from the subordinated creditor all the subordinated creditor's dividends before the subordinated creditor is entitled to any payment. The weakness of this arrangement is that it is dependent on a contractual right of the preferred creditor against the subordinated creditor. It would obviously break down if the subordinated creditor was insolvent. In order to overcome this perceived risk the commonest structure is that the subordinated creditor agrees to hold dividends, proceeds and other payments on the subordinated debt received by the subordinated creditor on trust for the preferred creditor as property of the preferred creditor and in satisfaction of the preferred creditor's debt until the preferred creditor is paid in full. This type of device, although providing a legal structure which meets the objective of subordination, has a practical weakness. Trusts, as the Maxwell pension funds have shown in stark relief, may have their funds misappropriated if the trust is held by unscrupulous or negligent persons. Where a company is veering to insolvency, there is a risk that the funds intentionally or negligently may be treated as funds of the company and thereby lost.

The Vinelott J. cases

16–06   The first case, which considered debt subordination trusts, was *Re British & Commonwealth Holdings plc (No 3)*.[12] In that case there was a summons for directions by administrators who proposed a scheme of arrangement under s.425 of the Companies Act 1985 to enable them to make an interim distribution of the proceeds of assets realised in the administration. The company had issued convertible subordinated unsecured loan stock ("CULS"). In terms of the issue of the loan stock contained in a trust deed, the debt of the holders of the loan stock was subordinated to the claims of all other creditors in the event of a winding up. The administrators sought directions as to whether they could exclude the subordinated creditors from the scheme, and the trustee representing them from voting at the meeting to approve the scheme. The administrators argued that because there was an estimated deficiency for creditors whose debts were not subordinated, the subordinated creditors had no interest in the company and accordingly no right to vote at a meeting convened to consider the scheme. The trustee for

---

[12] [1992] B.C.C. 58.

the subordinated creditors did not concede that the proceeds of realisation would inevitably be insufficient to meet the claims of the scheme
creditors, and submitted that, unless and until there was a winding up,
the trustee was a creditor and had the same rights as any other creditor.
Alternatively, the trustee argued that the holders of CULS would not be
subordinated creditors in relation to any entitlement interest on any
surplus once the scheme creditors were paid in full.

In the course of his judgment, Vinelott J. detailed the main provisions
of the scheme as follows:

> "I must first say a little more about the terms of the trust deed.
> Clause 2 contains a covenant to pay to the trustee the principal
> moneys and premium (if any) owing on the CULS on 31 December
> 2000 and in the meantime interest at 7 3/4 per cent by half yearly
> payments. It also provides that payments to the holders of stock in
> respect of principal premium or interest are to be taken in satisfac-
> tion of the covenant with the trustee. That provision is, of course,
> permissive only and does not give the holders any right to call for
> payment.
>
> Clause 5, which provides for subordination, I must read in full:

> '(A) In the event of the winding up of the company the claims of the
>   stockholders will be subordinated in right of payment to the
>   claims of all other creditors of the company (other than
>   subordinated creditors) and any amounts payable to and
>   received by the trustee in respect of the stock will be received
>   by the trustee on trust to apply the same:
>
>> (i) first, in payment or satisfaction of the costs, charges,
>>   expenses and liabilities incurred by and any unpaid
>>   remuneration of, the trustee;
>> (ii) secondly, in payment of the claims of other creditors of
>>   the company (not being creditors who are, or are
>>   trustees for, subordinated creditors) to the extent that
>>   such claims are admitted to proof in the winding up and
>>   are not satisfied out of the other resources of the
>>   company; and
>> (iii) thirdly, as to the balance (if any) in or towards payment
>>   of the amounts owing on or in respect of the stock.
>
> (B) The trust secondly mentioned in subcl. (A) of this clause may
>   be performed by the trustee paying over to the liquidator for
>   the time being in the winding up of the company (the 'liquida-
>   tor') the amounts received by the trustee as aforesaid (less any
>   amounts thereof applied in the implementation of the trust first
>   mentioned in subcl. (a) of this clause) on terms that the
>   liquidator shall distribute the same accordingly and the receipt
>   of the liquidator for the same shall be a good discharge to the
>   trustee for the performance by it of the trust secondly men-
>   tioned in subcl. (A) of this clause.
>
> (C) The trustee shall be entitled and it is hereby authorised to call
>   for and to accept as conclusive evidence thereof a certificate
>   from the liquidator as to:

> (i) the amount of the claims of the other creditors referred to in subcl. (A)(ii) of this clause (except as therein mentioned); and
>
> (ii) the persons entitled thereto and their respective entitlements.

(D) The trustee is entitled (to the exclusion of the stockholders) to take proceedings for the winding up of the company in the event of the stock becoming immediately due and repayable to recover amounts owing in respect of the stock but no other remedy shall be available to the trustee or the stockholders to recover such amounts.'

Clause 10 gives the trustee power to determine that the CULS are immediately due and payable with accrued interest in specified events which include default in payment of principal and interest, the making of an order or the passing of a resolution for the winding up of the company or a subsidiary or the making of an administration order in relation to the company or a subsidiary. Notice has been duly given of a determination by the trustee.

Clause 12 provides that:

> 'The trustee shall (subject always to the provisions of cl. 5(A)) apply all monies received by it under these presents in respect of the stock at any time after the stock shall have become immediately due and repayable . . . '

. . . first, in paying its costs, charges, expenses and liabilities, and as to the residue towards payment of arrears of interest and then the principal and any premium due in respect of the stock. It is also provided that any payment to the stockholders is to be made *pari passu* in proportion to the amounts owing to them respectively.

Lastly clause 32 provides that:

> 'Each of the stockholders shall be entitled to sue for the performance and observance of the provisions of these presents so far as his stock is concerned save where the trustee has and exercises a discretion herein'."

He then concluded that the only way in which the sums due in respect of CULS could be enforced was by the presentation of a winding-up petition. He said further that the terms of the document of trust gave rise to issues of considerable complexity. He wondered whether, notwithstanding the decision of the House of Lords in *British Eagle International Airlines Ltd v Compagnie Nationale Air France* [1975] 1 W.L.R. 758, cl.5(A) took effect as a contract by the trustee on behalf of the holders of CULS not to claim any payment towards satisfaction of the CULS until the other creditors had been paid in full, or whether cl.5(1) operated by imposing a trust on any payment received in the winding up of the company. He said the resolution of this difficult and complex question might take years of court time to resolve. He held, however, that the effect of cl.5(A)(ii) was subordination. He stated:

> "The effect of clause 5(A)(ii) in my judgment is to subordinate the holders of CULS *to the claims* of other creditors, including claims to

interest prior to winding up and admitted to proof or under section 189(2) in respect of claims admitted to proof; it would otherwise conflict with the opening words of clause 5 (A) which provides that the claims of the holders of CULS are to be subordinated to '*the claims* of all other creditors of the company (other than subordinated creditors)'."

Finally he held that, if the subordinated creditors had had an interest in the company and to the extent that their interest was affected in a way which did not affect the other creditors, then *prima facie* they would have constituted a separate class. In so far as they had no interest in the assets of the company (and the case had been argued on the footing that "they do not stand to receive a share of the assets"), and equally to the extent that any interest they may have had was unaffected by the scheme, then whether considered as a single or as a separate class, they had no right to object to it.

The second important case decided by Vinelott J. was *Re Maxwell Communications Corp. (No.2).*[13] In that case Vinelott J. reviewed all the relevant authorities and concluded that the principle laid down in *Halesowen* applied only to those rules which, when infringed, would give one creditor an advantage denied to other creditors. A subordination agreement would not have this effect. In reviewing his own decision in the case of *British and Commonwealth Holdings plc*, Vinelott J. said there was one vital distinction between that case and the present case. In the previous case the subordination of the subordinated loan stock did not rest solely on the terms of a contract between the company and the trustee of the subordinated loan stock. The trust deed governing the issue of the subordinated loan stock provided that any moneys payable to the trustee would be held in trust to apply the same in payment of its own expenses and remuneration, and then towards payment of the claims of the other creditors submitted to proof in the winding-up. That machinery, which was a very common means of ensuring that debt is effectively subordinated was not available in the instant case, and accordingly he had to decide whether a contractual provision alone for subordination of a debt unsupported by a trust mechanism was effective under English law.

Vinelott J. decided that a contractual mechanism was effective to set up debt subordination. It would be very serious to deny such contractual effectiveness in England, if recognition of the efficacy of such agreements in insolvency was prevalent in foreign jurisdictions, including Scotland. The decision in this case may now have settled the uncertainty raised by *Halesowen*,[14] although a decision by a higher court would be welcomed.

---

[13] [1994] 1 B.C.L.C. 1.

[14] See R.M. Goode, *Principles of Corporate Insolvency Law* (Sweet & Maxwell Ltd, London, 1997) at p.46. As well as suggesting that Vinelott's decision was now the law, Professor Goode pointed out that to deny a debt subordination agreement validity could have the most serious consequences, particularly in view of the widespread recognition of such agreements in insolvencies in foreign jurisdictions, and of the fact that in many cases a company could not continue to trade and obtain credit unless some of the creditors were willing to subordinate their indebtedness. The commercial advantages of the use of debt subordination are given by Dr Ferran in *Company Law and Corporate Finance* (Oxford University Press, Oxford, 1999), at p.546.

The Court of Appeal in New South Wales in *United States Trust Co of New York v ANZ Banking Group Ltd*[15] adopted the same approach as Vinelott J., saying that there was no public policy of good sense which prohibited one creditor deferring payment of its debt in favour of the payment of a debt of another creditor, if the rights or entitlements of other creditors to payment remained unaffected. In Australia the matter has been put beyond doubt by the introduction of s.563C into the Corporations Law in 1992, which provides that a debt subordination agreement is not unenforceable except to the extent that subordination would disadvantage any creditor who was not a party to the subordination agreement.

Proposed reform of the English law on debt subordination

16–08   Because the devices described are complex, cumbersome and do not always achieve the type of debt subordination aimed for, the United Kingdom Review Committee on Insolvency Law and Practice advocated reform. They stated in 1982:

> "All unsecured debts must be paid, *pari passu* . . . It is therefore not open to a creditor to advance money on terms that the debt will be subordinated to other claims in the event of the borrower's insolvency . . . We can see no reason why a creditor who wishes to do so should not be permitted to subordinate his claim to those of all other creditors, or all other creditors except those of like degree. In this case the sophisticated conveyancing devices which have to be adopted to enable subordinated debt to be included will not be necessary. We therefore recommend the inclusion of an appropriate proviso to [the *pari passu* provisions] to allow effect to be given to subordination agreements."[16]

Despite the recommendation that a provision similar to s.501(a) of the United States Bankruptcy Code of 1978 (which expressly makes subordination agreements enforceable) be introduced in England and Wales, this proposal has not been adopted.

Application of *pari passu* rule in Scotland

16–09   In Scotland a simple agreement between a creditor and a debtor company by which the creditor agrees that his debt will be subordinated to ordinary creditors' claims is legally valid.[17] An undertaking to the debtor company that a secured creditor's debt will be subordinated to other secured creditors is called "preference by exclusion" by Bell. Bell states:

> "Rights of exclusion have in themselves no character of a Real Right, but operate merely in the way of Prohibition or Exclusion

---

[15] [1995] 13 A.C.L.C. 1225.

[16] *Report of the United Kingdom Review Committee on Insolvency Law.*

[17] This validity as regards Scotland was recognised by Vinelott J. in *Re Maxwell Communications Corp.* [1994] 1 B.C.L.C. 1 at 20.

against claims which otherwise would be entitled to a preference
. . . In consequence of a personal exception pleadable against a
creditor, or against a class of creditors as competitors with others; or
in consequence of a consent granted by one creditor to the preference of another—the order of preference, as it would stand according to the natural import and effect of the rival securities, may be
altered.

Exceptions pleadable to actions differ from objections in this, that
the latter are in the nature of negations to the action; the former,
positive allegiances which, admitting the action to be otherwise
good, exclude, or as our authors express it, elide the action. In
actions of competition, as ranking and sale, sequestration, or
multiple poinding which are each a congeries of all the reciprocal
actions necessary for determining on the rights and preferences of
the competitors, effect is given to the several exceptions by which,
on the one hand, the general body of creditors exclude a particular
creditor, or by which individual creditors exclude each other . . .

2. Sometimes the creditor related to the debtor, or particularly
interested in him, gives an express consent to his having a preference over the consenter. This has the effect of a personal exception
to exclude the consenter from entering into competition against the
person in whose favour he has yielded his rights; but that right as
against other creditors remains unimpaired, unless insofar as necessarily implied in the preference to which consent has been given . . .

4. The effect of personal exceptions can be available only to those
entitled to take benefit by them, but not so as to injure in other
respects the right of the creditor against whom they operate".[18]

This "preference by exclusion", or "negative pledge", operates also in
relation to ordinary creditors subordinating their claims over unsecured
estate to other ordinary creditors, although the cases do not refer to the
term expressly. The leading Scottish cases on the subordination of an
ordinary unsecured debt to claims of ordinary creditors are *Fair v
Hunter*[19] and *MacKinnon's Trustees v Dunlop*.[20] In *MacKinnon's Trustees v
Dunlop* Lord President Dunedin categorised the status of this type of
subordinated debt in Scots law and approved *Fair v Hunter*. He stated:

"Counsel for the respondents in a very able argument particularly
appealed to the case of *Fair v Hunter,* in which it was held that an
obligation to pay 'as soon as I have it in my power' was a proper
debt. Well, all depends on what one means by proper debt. The
truth is, there are three forms of obligations in such matters. There
is the form of an ordinary debt which you are bound to pay the
moment that you are sued upon it. It is not suggested that there is
such a debt here. Then, on the other hand, there is a form of *quasi*-
obligation which is truly no obligation at all, which simply says, 'I
promise to pay if I like to pay'; and I agree with the learned counsel

---

[18] Bell, *Comm.*, ii.132.
[19] (1861) 24 D. 1 (2nd Division).
[20] 1913 S.C. 232.

that the obligation here is not of that kind. But there is the third and intermediate case of which I think *Fair v Hunter* was an instance, in which a debtor may be bound in the sense that the obligation is good against him and yet it cannot come into competition with his ordinary and proper creditors, and that is just where the respondents' case fails, because there is no proper *jus crediti* which will destroy the father's power of disposal.

The circumstances in Fair's case were that Mr Hunter had a son through whom Fair had lost money, and the father was very anxious to make up to Fair the money which his son had lost. He was not in a condition at the time to do so. He had not any ready money, his money being locked up in Australia, and he was a member of a firm of Writers to the Signet in Edinburgh under a contract of copartnery by which he had become bound not to enter into any obligation, and he therefore did not wish to transgress the terms of his own copartnery. He entered into negotiations with Fair, and they came to an agreement by which Fair remitted a certain considerable portion of the son's debt, and the father gave an obligation that he would pay the rest when he could. And the father wrote a letter in which he said: 'I shall be most happy to pay to you, with interest, as soon as I have it in my power, by remittances from Australia or otherwise.' (24 D at 5). The father died, and an executor was appointed who proceeded to realise the estate, and the action was brought by Fair for constitution of the debt against the father's executor. The learned Judges held that it was a debt which could be constituted against the executry. But I think they clearly held that it was a debt of what I may call the intermediate kind, because the Lord Ordinary (Lord Kinloch), after giving his views, in which he said that this was not a mere promise which was no promise at all, namely, to pay if he chose, says this; 'Whether or not the pursuer shall be entitled to rank on the executry funds in competition with other creditors of the deceased, is not as the Lord Ordinary thinks, now the question. Those creditors are not here. No question is or can be raised in this process with them. It will be for the pursuer to consider, when he has got his decree, what he will do with it; and for other creditors of the deceased, and for the defender, to consider what effect is due to it, as respects any ranking on the estate of the deceased'."

In Scotland subordinated debt is not a "contingent" debt

16–10   In light of the dicta of Lord Dunedin in *MacKinnon's Trustees* it is clear that the type of subordinated debt referred to in *Fair v Hunter* is a "preference by exclusion". It does not rank as an ordinary debt and compete with ordinary creditors.[21] What a creditor is saying is that "my debt shall be subordinated to that of other creditors". The Scottish position is therefore essentially that as enunciated by Southwell J. in *Horne v Chester & Fein Property Developments Pty Ltd*.[22] It is therefore a

---

[21] Gloag on *Contract* (2nd ed., 1929), p.56.
[22] (1987) 5 A.C.L.C. 245.

true subordinated debt. The English device of structuring such a subordinated debt as a "contingent" debt is rather irrational. When claims are valued in a bankruptcy or liquidation, it is irrational to value, for the purposes of the bankruptcy or liquidation, a debt as having a nil or nominal value (if it is otherwise a valid and payable debt) merely because the funds in the bankruptcy or liquidation are very unlikely to be sufficient to meet it.[23] After all, ordinary debts are not given a nil or nominal value on the basis that the secured creditors and preferential creditors are likely to exhaust the funds. Similarly, postponed debts are valued at their face value. The internal availability of funds in a liquidation sufficient to meet a class of subordinated debts, is not a real contingency such as to make those debts "contingent" debts. In Scotland there may be a serious risk if a subordinated debt agreement is constituted as a contingent debt arrangement. Liquidations leading to "supervening solvency" are not uncommon; namely the liquidation of Rolls Royce. It is not certain that, if a subordinated debt agreement were constituted as a contingent debt agreement in Scotland, it would be simple to amend the valuation of the contingent debt at the later stage. Accordingly, it is suggested that, where the intention is to set up a subordinated debt agreement by which one creditor agrees to be subordinated to the general body of creditors, a clause along the following lines is agreed between the debtor company and the subordinated creditor:

> "If the debtor company becomes subject to any liquidation, dissolution, rehabilitation or insolvency proceeding or to any arrangement or composition for the benefit of its creditors or any other distribution of its assets, or any analogous event occurs, the subordinated creditor will rank subordinate to and after the prior payment of ordinary debts."

Subordination in Scotland by assignations in security

Although in England, where the subordinated creditor wishes to give **16–11** the preferred creditor the benefit of any dividend to which he may be entitled in a liquidation, a trust mechanism is sometimes used, this, as has been noted, has drawbacks. Although it is possible, where there is a trust, for there to be an independent trustee appointed (the international stock exchange in London requires the appointment of a trustee for domestic debt issues), there is no statutory requirement for a trustee. Accordingly, trust monies may become intermingled with non-trust monies or misappropriated if the recipient of the dividends is also acting as trustee for a third party creditor. Secondly, the courts in certain civilian countries have not received the trust or recognised equivalent instrument. Under certain regimes the trustee has been treated as the sole owner. Hence the beneficial ownership by the beneficiaries is simply not recognised and the beneficiaries are treated as having only a contractual right against the trustee, *i.e.* the beneficiary is treated as if he

---

[23] The contingent status of subordinated debt is doubted by Vinelott J. in *Re Maxwell Communications Corp.* [1994] 1 B.C.L.C. 1 at 18.

were in a creditor-debtor relationship with the trustee. Accordingly, the beneficiaries are exposed to the insolvency of the trustee because other creditors of the trustee will have claims on the purported trust assets. This exposure has been partially overcome recently, but the situation is unsafe. The Hague Convention on the Law Applicable to Trusts and on their Recognition, implemented in Britain by the Recognition of Trusts Act 1987, meets the problem in relation to trusts in countries which are a party to the Convention. In terms of Art.8, in the contracting states the validity of a voluntary written trust, its construction, effects and administration will be governed by the governing law of the trust. This may be expressly chosen by the settler. A trust created in accordance with that law is to be recognised as a trust in terms of Art.11. A third problem in relation to the trust device in Scotland is that there is not a developed law of "equitable estates" as in England.[24]

The most appropriate type of legal structure which is available in Scotland to achieve the purpose of having the preferred creditor receive the dividends of the subordinated creditor is a structure by which the subordinated creditor assigns his future dividends to the preferred creditor as security for an obligation undertaken by him in terms of which he is obliged to pay a sum equal to his dividends received to the preferred creditor. Such an agreement would usually limit the obligation to the extent of any shortfall on the preferred creditor's debt. The undertaking would also be limited to the amount of any dividends actually payable to the subordinated creditor. Finally it is advisable that the preferred creditor is given an irrevocable power of attorney by the subordinated creditor to lodge claims on behalf of the subordinated creditor in the event of the liquidation of the company. Only by that device can the preferred creditor force the subordinated creditor to lodge claims and hence make dividends payable which can be assigned in advance in security of the sums which may become payable. In Scotland it is open to a person in advance to assign future or contingent debts.[25] It is essential in Scotland that the assignation by the subordinated creditor to the preferred creditor of these future debts is intimated to the debtor company. This is best achieved by making the debtor company a party to the debt subordination agreement which includes the assignation in security. The following is the format for a common type of debt subordination agreement whereby a bank agrees to lend money to the subsidiary of a holding company, provided the holding company also puts money in as debt which is subordinated to the loan of the bank, entitling the bank to any dividends payable to the subordinated creditor in the event of the liquidation of its subsidiary.

That debts "assigned in security" by a company are not affected by its insolvency and are not attachable by others has been affirmed in England.[26]

---

[24] See *Stair Memorial Encyclopaedia*, "Trusts", vol.24, paras 7 *et seq.*
[25] *Flowerdew v Buchan* (1835) 13 S. 615; *Carter v McIntosh* (1862) 24 D. 925; *Allan & Son v Brown & Lightbody* (1890) 6 Sg Ct Rep. 278; and Wilson on Debt (2nd ed.) p.284.
[26] *Re Atlantic Computer Systems* [1991] B.C.L.C. 606 at 629.

CHAPTER 17

SET-OFF

Introduction

It is not within the scope of this work to give a detailed analysis of the **17–01** general working of set-off. Good descriptions are to be found in Gloag on *Contract*, pp.626, 644 to 654; Wilson on *Debt*, Chap.13; and McBryde on *Contract*, pp.531 to 540. An analysis will be attempted of the peculiar problems of set-off in insolvency. Like many other aspects of insolvency law, the courts have not always interpreted set-off in a clear and consistent manner.

Definition of set-off

Although set-off or "compensation" existed at common law,[1] the law **17–02** of set-off is for most purposes contained in the Compensation Act 1592. The effect of set-off is that one debt extinguishes another. The essential features of set-off under the Compensation Act are as follows:

(1) Liquid debts only

Debts must be both liquid or capable of immediate liquidation. A debt is liquid when it is actually due and the amount ascertained, unless the counterclaim can immediately be made liquid.[2] The dispute of a claim makes it illiquid, while an admission of a claim may make it liquid.[3]

(2) Debts due at the same time

Both debts must be due at the same time. A debt which is presently due may not be set off against a future debt or a contingent debt.[4]

(3) Concursus debiti et crediti

Each party must be debtor and creditor in the same capacity. A sum due to the defender as an executor may not be set off against a sum due to him personally.[5]

(4) Set-off must be pled

Set-off does not operate *ipso jure*. Set-off must be both pled and sustained by judgment before it has effect, unless there is an agreement

---

[1] See McBryde on *Contract*, para.22–24.
[2] *Munro v MacDonald's Exrs* (1866) 4 M. 687; *Niven v Clyde Fasteners Ltd*, 1986 S.L.T. 344.
[3] *Hamilton v Wright* (1839) 2 D. 86; *Thorns v Thorns* (1868) 6 M. 704; *Scottish NERy Co v Napier* (1859) 21 D. 700.
[4] Bell, *Comm.*, ii, 122; *Paul and Thain v Royal Bank* (1869) 7 M. 361.
[5] *Stuart v Stuart* (1869) 7 M. 366.

to set off.[6] If set-off is allowed, it has a retrospective effect with the result that interest may not be due on a debt after the date of concursus, even if one of the debts at that time was illiquid.[7] Not only must set-off be pled, it must be pled before decree is passed against a debtor.

(5) Debts of the same nature

The debts must be of the same nature. A money debt can be pleaded against a money debt. A demand for delivery of goods may be set off against a claim for similar goods, but a money debt may not be set off against a claim for delivery of goods.[8] If money is deposited and appropriated to a particular purpose, it cannot be set off against a separate debt due by the depositor.[9]

Balancing of accounts in bankruptcy

17–03   The statutory rules about set-off do not apply to insolvency. Rather the ordinary common law rules about set-off are widened so that:

(1) Liquid and illiquid claims

When one of the parties is insolvent, an illiquid claim may be set-off against a liquid claim.[10]

(2) Debts not of the same nature

When one of the parties is insolvent, set-off may be pleaded by the debtor to an insolvent company although the two claims are not of the same nature. For example, a claim for debt may be set off against a claim for delivery of goods.[11]

(3) Debts due at different times

The party who is sued on a claim which he admits to being payable may put forward in defence claims which are not yet due which involve only a contingent liability, or which are disputed and require to be established by proof.[12]

(4) Concursus debiti et crediti

The debtor and the creditor must be in the same capacity.[13]

Bankruptcy, liquidation, receivership, administration

(1) Bankruptcy and liquidation

17–04   The case law in relation to the "balancing of accounts in bankruptcy", which is the name given by Bell to the equitable right of retention or species of set-off available on insolvency, was developed in relation to

---

[6] *Cowan v Gowans* (1878) 5 R. 581.

[7] *Inch v Lee* (1903) 11 S.L.T. 374.

[8] Bell, *Comm.*, ii, 122.

[9] *Mycroft Petr*, 1983 S.L.T. 342.

[10] Bell, *Comm.*, ii, 122; *Scott's Tr. v Scott* (1887) 14 R. 1043 at 1051, *per* Lord President Inglis; *Clydesdale Bank Ltd v Gardiner* (1906) 14 S.L.T. 121.

[11] Bell, *Comm.*, ii, 122.

[12] *ibid.*; *Mill v Paul* (1825) 4 S. 219; *Hannay & Sons, Tr. v Armstrong Bros* (1875) 2 R. 399; *Borthwick v Scottish Widows Fund* (1864) 2 M. 595.

[13] *Cauvin v Robertson* (1773) Mor. 2581; *Taylor's Tr. v Paul* (1888) 15 R. 313.

the bankruptcy of individuals. Similar rules have been applied in the liquidation of companies.[14] The key fact which triggers the equitable right is the insolvency of the debtor. Liquidation, sequestration or a trust deed for creditors are equivalent to "bankruptcy".[15]

Attempts have been made to extend the equitable right of retention to cases of "near insolvency' but there would seem to be need of averments that the company is in financial difficulties and facing insolvency.[16] The Scottish law in this field is not statutory (whether this is an equitable right of retention or species of set-off available on insolvency is important where there is an international dimension to the insolvency).[17] Most jurisdictions have some form of set-off in this sort of situation. The jurisdictions in favour of insolvency set-off are the United States jurisdictions (except perhaps Louisiana), most, if not all, of the English-based jurisdictions, including Australia, New Zealand, Canada (including Quebec, where set-off is allowed by virtue of the Federal bankruptcy legislation which is overriding), Bahamas, Bermuda, the Cayman Islands, Hong Kong, India, Pakistan, Singapore, Zambia. Set-off on insolvency is also allowed in the Germanic and Scandinavian jurisdictions; in particular it is allowed in Austria (KO Art.19), Germany, Finland, Denmark, Japan, Korea, Netherlands, Norway, Sri Lanka and Switzerland. It has been allowed in Italy since 1942, and it is also allowed in Panama. China has enacted a bankruptcy law relating to enterprises which includes an insolvency set-off clause in terms of Art.33, although this is of limited application. Jurisdictions not allowing this species of set-off are France, Belgium, Egypt, Greece, Luxembourg, Spain, Chile, Brazil, Argentina, Columbia and South Africa.[18] It is important to note that none of the provisions in these jurisdictions, whether under statute or at common law, is totally equivalent. They are also subject to constant change. The Scottish courts will recognise set-off in certain insolvency situations where there is an international element.[19] This list should not be relied on except to give an initial impression. Liquidators must carefully check the position with a relevant jurisdiction before any decision whether to allow or disallow set-off is made.

In the case of *G & A (Hotels) Ltd v THB Marketing Services Ltd*[20] it was suggested by Lord Cowie, relying on *dicta* of Lord Fraser in the case of *Liquidators of Highland Engineering Ltd v Thomson*[21] that the right of retention was available in any liquidation and it was not necessary to aver that there was insolvency. Lord Cowie stated:

"This submission was based on the statement in Gloag on *Contract* at p 626 which is in the following terms: 'The rule that a demand for

---

[14] *Atlantic Engine Co (1920) Ltd v Lord Advocate*, 1955 S.L.T. 17.
[15] *G. and A. (Hotels) Ltd v THB Marketing Services Ltd*, 1983 S.L.T. 497; *Liquidators of Highland Engineering Ltd v Thomson*, 1972 S.C. 87.
[16] *Busby Spinning Co Ltd v BMK Ltd*, 1988 S.L.T. 246.
[17] See para.22–31.
[18] See P. Wood, *English and International Set-off* (1989).
[19] See para.22–31.
[20] Above.
[21] Above.

a liquid debt is not relevantly met by a defence founded on an illiquid or unascertained claim does not hold where the pursuer is bankrupt or where it is averred that he is insolvent'. Counsel for the pursuers founded strongly on the words 'where it is averred that he is insolvent', and argued that unless that was done, the exception did not apply, and the general rule must be enforced. I must confess that I was impressed by this argument since it seemed to me that it was for the defenders to bring themselves within the exception if they were going to found on it. Moreover it was explained to me by counsel for the pursuers that there was no question in the present case of the pursuers not being able to pay their debts in full. In these circumstances had it not been for an observation by Lord Fraser in the case *of Liquidators of Highland Engineering Ltd v Thomson* 1972 SC 87 at p 91,1 would have been inclined to give effect to this argument by counsel for the pursuers. The observation of Lord Fraser to which I refer comes in a passage where he is dealing with the general rule that retention or set-off cannot be pleaded unless both debts are liquid, but is pointing out that the general rule does not hold as to the balancing of accounts in bankruptcy. He then goes on: 'In the present case the respondents are debtors in a liquid debt, while their claim for remuneration is still illiquid, but as the matter arises in a liquidation (which for present purposes, I think is equivalent to bankruptcy) no difficulty arises on that account'.

In my opinion what Lord Fraser is saying in that passage, is that for the purposes of the exception to the general rule governing liquid and illiquid debts a liquidation is the equivalent of bankruptcy. If that is right then provided it is clear that the first pursuers are in liquidation it is not in my opinion necessary to aver that they are insolvent. It is perhaps of interest to note that in that case as in the present, Lord Fraser was informed that the company, although in members' voluntary liquidation, had an estimated surplus. I am not of course bound by the authority of Lord Fraser even assuming that I have interpreted his words correctly, but I would be slow to dissent from a judge of such eminence in the field of company law, and accordingly I have come to the conclusion that it is not necessary to make the specific averment of insolvency which counsel for the pursuers says the defenders must make to bring themselves within the exception, and I accordingly reject this submission also.''

17–05 It is thought that Lord Cowie did not properly understand the *dicta* of Lord Fraser. In the case of the *Liquidators of Highland Engineering v Thomson*[22] there indeed was a members' voluntary winding-up. However, there had been a petition for compulsory winding up and the company had been put into provisional compulsory winding up on a creditor's petition, *i.e.* provisional insolvent winding up. The provisional liquidator was claiming the right of retention in relation to sums owed to him as remuneration as provisional liquidator. The winding-up order

---

[22] Above.

as sought was eventually refused, but the set-off period was the period of the provisional compulsory winding-up. Indeed the company was still in provisional winding up when Lord Fraser held that set-off was open. It was only after allowing set-off that he moved on to deal with whether he should grant the petition. Accordingly it is thought that, when he stated "a liquidation (which for present purposes, I think is equivalent to bankruptcy)", he was referring to the specific circumstances of that case. It is thought that Gloag is right and that there has to be insolvency. The widening of the rules of set-off occurs in many countries, but only in the event of insolvency. Of course it may emerge that there is a supervening solvency, but the general principle would be that there had to be some form of finding of insolvency to start with. In the case of a provisional compulsory winding up, the Lord Ordinary would have had to be satisfied that there was a *prima facie* case on the creditor's petition for the compulsory winding-up order. Not only is there no previous suggestion in the authorities that there could be balancing of accounts in a non-insolvent liquidation, but Gloag states that it has to be averred that there is insolvency. Because the rights of retention in the balancing of accounts in bankruptcy are open both to the trustee and creditors, the extending of these rights to voluntary liquidations would open the way to persons voluntarily reconstructing companies in order to obtain the wider rights of retention if it suited them. It is not clear that these arguments were put to Lord Cowie. He says that Lord Fraser was informed that the company, although in members' voluntary liquidation, had an estimated surplus. This suggests that a clear picture was not given to Lord Cowie in argument because a members' voluntary liquidation requires an estimated surplus. It is hoped that, in the near future, the Inner House will clarify the position in relation to these cases.

(2) Receivership

In relation to receivership, it was suggested by Lord Ross in the case **17–06** of *Taylor, Petitioner*[23] that the rules of insolvency do not apply in receivership. He stated:

"In these circumstances, it does not appear to me . . . that receivership is so similar to bankruptcy or liquidation that the principles of law applicable to insolvency should be applied. Furthermore I am not satisfied that compensation should be disallowed for reasons of equity or public policy. The normal rules of compensation are plain (Gloag on *Contract* (2nd edn), pp 644–645). I see no ground for introducing into the law any fresh exception based on alleged public policy. There may well be reasons for certain exceptions in the case of bankruptcy or insolvency, but I see no ground for extending them to cases of receivership. As already pointed out, receivership is different to liquidation or bankruptcy, and there is no reason why the same rules should apply to these different situations."[24]

---

[23] 1982 S.L.T. 171 at 172.
[24] *ibid.*

However, in the subsequent case of *McPhail v Cunninghame District Council; William Louden & Son Ltd v Cunninghame District Council*,[25] Lord Kincraig accepted that the wider rules of set-off were available if the company was insolvent. He stated:

> "It is no objection to the right of set-off that the defenders' claim arises under a different contract from that out of which the debt to the pursuer arises. See Gloag on *Contract*, p 626. Here the defenders allege that the company was insolvent on 26 February 1975 and the principle stated in Gloag therefore applies."

The principle quoted in Gloag was that enunciated by Lord McLaren in *Ross v Ross*,[26] where he stated:

> "The doctrine [of retention] has received much extension in cases of bankruptcy and insolvency, where it is practically settled that anyone who has a claim against an insolvent estate is entitled to keep back money which he owes to the estate, and cannot be compelled to pay in full while he only receives a dividend."

Receivership does not itself entail insolvency. In terms of certain debentures, a receiver may be appointed if certain capital ratios are breached or where events of default not connected with solvency occur. Accordingly, receivership itself may not be relied on to invoke the wider rules of set-off. However, it is suggested that they may be invoked if insolvency accompanies the receivership.

(3) Administrations

17–07   It has not yet been judicially determined whether administration *per se* amounts to insolvency. In terms of s.245(5) of the Insolvency Act 1986, administration is defined as the onset of insolvency. An administration order is granted in terms of the Insolvency Act 1986 only if the court is satisfied that a company is or is likely to become unable to pay its debts. If a trust deed for creditors is equivalent to "bankruptcy", it is suggested that a voluntary arrangement involving remission of debts would also entail insolvency. If administration is just meant to be a more efficient method of gathering in assets prior to liquidation it will involve insolvency. It is thought therefore that, except in very exceptional circumstances, an administration order will be equivalent to insolvency.[27]

Debts prior to and post-insolvency

17–08   Although presently payable debts may be set off against unascertained and contingent debts, the obligations must exist at the date of insolvency. The presently payable debt may not be set off against an

---

[25] 1985 S.L.T. 149 at 152.
[26] (1885) 22 R. 461 at 465.
[27] Such a circumstance might be where an administrator was appointed by a holder of a floating charge because of a breach of the debenture not directly related to insolvency.

obligation incurred after the date of the insolvency. In *Asphaltic Lime-stone Co v Corporation of Glasgow*[28] the company, at the date of its liquidation, had two separate contracts with the corporation. One of these the liquidator declined to carry out. The other he implemented, and thereby acquired a claim for the contract price. The contention of the corporation that they were entitled to retain that price in security of their claim of damages for breach of the other contract was repelled on the ground that the damages were due by the company and the price was due to the liquidator, and that there could be no retention or compensation between a debt due before bankruptcy and a debt arising thereafter. Lord McLaren observed that the argument of the corporation in favour of set-off was:

"Founded on a complete misapprehension of the principle of retention in cases of bankruptcy or insolvency. In such cases, if the insolvent estate has a liquid claim against a solvent debtor, who again has a liquid claim against the insolvent estate, the principle of compensation is applied exactly as it would be if both parties were solvent. But if the claim of the solvent party is not liquid, eg, if the work has been done, but the time of payment has not arrived, then by an equitable extension of the principle of compensation he is allowed to retain the money which he owes against his claim on the insolvent estate, so that he may not suffer the injustice of having to pay his debt in full while only receiving a dividend on his own claim. But this principle of bankruptcy law presupposes reciprocal obligations which are both existing at the time of the declaration of insolvency, although only one of them is, it may be, immediately exigible. It has no application to the case of a new obligation arising after bankruptcy or declaration of insolvency when the rights of the parties are irrevocably fixed."

The situation in *Asphaltic Limestone Co Ltd* was reasonably straightforward. There was clearly a wholly new post-liquidation obligation on behalf of Glasgow Corporation to the company in liquidation. It will often be difficult to determine, where a claim arises after liquidation, whether the claim arose from obligations existing prior to the liquidation. For example, in the case of *Myles J. Callaghan Ltd (in Receivership) v City of Glasgow District Council*,[29] Lord Prosser held that a claim by a contractor for return of plant, which could be claimed only at the end of a contract which terminated after liquidation, could be set off against a claim by the employer for breach of contract occasioned by the contractor's going into receivership prior to liquidation. The use by the employer of the contractor's property was subject to rights vesting in the owners pending the date for return. Accordingly the claim for return,

---

[28] 1907 S.C. 463.
[29] 1988 S.L.T. 227; see also *Powdrill v Murrayhead Ltd*, 1997 S.L.T 1223, in which Lord Prosser held that a creditor in a liquid claim at the date of the insolvency is entitled, by the equitable extension of the principle of compensation, to invoke that pre-existing right to payment, as a defence in an action where he is sued for a debt, which is not wholly new and post-insolvency, but arises from the post-insolvency purification of a contingency, in respect of rights which were created by a pre-insolvency contract.

although it only became exigible after liquidation, had existed in the requisite sense prior to liquidation.

Lord McLaren in *Asphaltic Limestone Co* referred to "declaration of insolvency". It is not clear what precisely a "declaration of insolvency" is. In England in *Eros Films Ltd*[30] the court held that the giving of notice of a meeting for a creditors' voluntary winding up was analogous to the filing, by an individual, of a declaration of inability to pay debts. It is thought that "apparent insolvency", as defined by s.7 of the Bankruptcy (Scotland) Act 1985, would constitute a declaration of insolvency.

Debts incurred after insolvency

17–09   A debt which arises after insolvency may be set off against another debt which also arises after insolvency.[31]

Peculiar problems on receivership

Forth and Clyde Case

17–10   The effect of the crystallisation of a floating charge on debts owed to a company was clarified in the case of *Forth and Clyde Construction Co Ltd v Trinity Timber & Plywood Co Ltd*[32] by the First Division of the Scottish appeal court. The court examined the meaning of ss.13(7) and 31(1) of the Companies (Floating Charges and Receivers) (Scotland) Act 1972,[33] which read:

> "13.— . . . (7) On the appointment of a receiver under this section, the floating charge by virtue of which he was appointed shall, subject to sections 106A and 322 of the Act of 1948, attach to the property then subject to the charge; and such attachment shall have effect as if the charge were a fixed security over the property to which it has attached."

> "31.—(1) In this Act, unless the context otherwise requires, the following expressions shall have the following meanings respectively assigned to them, that is to say—'Act of 1948' means the Companies Act 1948; . . . 'fixed security', in relation to any property of a company, means any security, other than a floating charge or a charge having the nature of a floating charge, which on the winding up of the company in Scotland would be treated as an effective security over that property, and (without prejudice to that generality) includes a security over that property, being a heritable security within the meaning of section 9(8) of the Conveyancing and Feudal Reform (Scotland) Act 1970; "floating charge" has the meaning assigned to it by section 1 of this Act; . . . 'receiver' means

---

[30] [1963] Ch. 565.
[31] *Liquidators of Highland Engineering v Thomson*, 1972 S.C. 87.
[32] 1984 S.L.T. 94.
[33] 1988 S.L.T. 227.

a receiver of such part of the property of the company as is subject to the floating charge by virtue of which he has been appointed under section 11 of this Act."

The court held that the only type of "effective security" in relation to book debts was an assignation in security, duly intimated to the debtor. Lord Emslie stated:

"It is, of course, the case that the Act has not expressly provided that book debts shall be regarded as having been assigned in security to the holder of the floating charge on the date upon which it attaches to them but the language of s 13(7) makes it quite clear that the attachment is to have effect as if such an assignation in security had been granted and intimated by the company. From the date of the appointment of a receiver, the company, no doubt, retains the title to demand payment of the debt but no longer for its own behoof. The interest in the recovery of the debt is that of the holder of the floating charge, and a receiver who seeks recovery in the name of the company does so in order to secure the application of the recovered sum towards satisfaction of the company's debt due to the creditor in the floating charge."

Set-off to be pled against an assignee

When a debt is assigned, the debtor may plead against the assignee a **17–11** debt owed by the cedent provided that there was *concursus debiti et crediti* before the assignation was completed by intimation.[34] If, however, a debt is assigned, and the assignation intimated before the counter debt arises, there is no set-off. According to Bell, "the right to compensate passes against assignees if once vested against the cedent by a proper concourse before assignation. But if a debt be assigned, and the assignation intimated before the counter debt arises, the concourse is prevented, and there is no compensation".[35] Thus, if a debtor has a claim against a company, and the company has assigned a counterclaim to a third party, then the debtor may plead set-off against the assignee, provided that the right of set-off existed prior to the assignation duly intimated. Where a debtor acquires debts by purchase from other parties after the insolvency of a company, these debts may not be set off against any claims against the debtor assigned to a third party prior to insolvency, because the acquired debts would be post-insolvency debts.

Implications of Forth and Clyde case for set-off

Given that a receiver is to be treated, following the decision in the **17–12** *Forth and Clyde* case,[36] as if he were an assignee of any debts due to a company, and given that the ordinary principles of set-off entail that the

---

[34] Bell, *Comm.*, ii, 131; *Shiells v Fergusson, Davidson & Co* (1876) 4 R. 250; *Taylor, Petr*, 1982 S.L.T. 172 at 177, *per* Lord Ross.
[35] Bell, *Comm.*, i, 138.
[36] *Forth and Clyde Construction Co Ltd v Trinity Timber and Plywood Co Ltd*, 1984 S.L.T. 94.

receiver, as assignee, is subject to all pre-existing pleas of set-off pleadable against the cedent (the company) but is not subject to any such pleas manufactured by post-receivership purchase of creditors' claims against the company, it might be thought that the law was clear. Provided that receivership could be shown to be accompanied by insolvency no problem would arise.

Difficulties in case law in relation to set-off in receivership

17–13   The problem in the case law arises especially out of three cases, *McPhail v Lothian Regional Council*[38] ("the *Lothian Region* case"), *Taylor, Petr*[39] ("the *Typesetting* case') and *Myles J. Callaghan Ltd (in Receivership) v City of Glasgow District Council*[40] ("the *Myles Callaghan* case"). The first two cases were decided before the decision in the *Forth and Clyde* case and, in particular, before that case explained how the fixed security enforced by a receiver could be reconciled with the retention by a company of legal title to its assets such as its book debts. In the *Lothian Region* case, a debt owed to a company, which had granted an all-assets floating charge, was owed by a debtor who was, at the date of attachment, also a creditor of the company. When the receiver of the company raised an action against the debtor in his own name for payment of the debt, it was argued (1) that the debt should be set off against the debtor's counterclaim as creditor; and (2) that the receiver could have no title to sue in his own name for what was due to the company.

Lord Grieve dealt with the set-off argument on the basis that whether the receiver had a right to receive the charged debt free of a plea of set-off depended on whether the receiver took action in his own name or in that of the company. If he took action in his own name, set-off would not be available because mutuality would not exist, whereas if he took action in the name of the company, set-off could be pled. This distinction is now irrelevant in the light of the analysis given in the *Forth and Clyde* case of how a debt due to a company becomes, on crystallisation, due to the company for behoof of the floating charge creditor.

In the *Typesetting* case, Lord Ross proceeded on the basis that a receiver could not be treated as having the rights of an assignee of a company debt unless and until he obtained an actual assignation of the debt. On that basis, he decided that a debtor owing a charged debt could defeat a receiver's claim thereto by purchasing from other creditors a claim against the company in receivership and setting that claim off against the charged debt. Lord Ross also stated, as referred to above, that receivership was different from liquidation or bankruptcy, and rejected the idea that the rules relating to the balancing of accounts in bankruptcy should apply.

In the *Myles Callaghan* case, Lord Prosser (1) followed Lord Ross by agreeing that the company should sue in its own name for a debt after

---

[38] 1981 S.C.I. 19.
[39] 1982 S.L.T. 172.
[40] 1988 S.L.T. 227.

crystallisation of a floating charge; (2) held that, although the attachment of a floating charge "has effect as if the charge was a fixed security over the property to which it has attached", this did not imply that one must imagine some actual assignation with all the effects that that assignation would have upon title. The statutory provision was concerned with the effect of a security as a security. Title remained in the company (as it would not on assignation and intimation) but all the security effects of an assignation in security were to be regarded as available to the receiver; and (3) held that the receiver, having acquired the company's interest in a *jus crediti* (right to payment of a debt) for security purposes, did not acquire any right when suing in the company's name to deny the ordinary defences available to third parties against the company.

In the case of *McPhail v Cunninghame District Council* and *William Louden & Son Ltd v Cunninghame District Council* ("the *Louden* case"),[41] which preceded the *Forth and Clyde* case, Lord Kincraig took the view that the appointment of a receiver operated as an intimated assignation of the company's right to recover a debt due to the company and this right was subject to all the defences which could be pled against the cedent, *i.e.* the company, and if the company could be met successfully with a plea of set-off, the receiver's right must also be subject to the same set-off.

Effect of differences in case law

The different approaches taken by Lord Kincraig and Lord Prosser in **17–14** the *Louden* and *Myles Callaghan* cases have no real difference in effect, as was acknowledged by Lord Prosser.[42] The Scottish Law Commission, in their Consultative Memorandum No. 72 on "Floating Charges and Receivers" in October 1986, prior to Lord Prosser's judgment in the *Myles Callaghan* case, took the view that the route followed by Lord Kincraig in the *Louden* case was the correct approach; namely that the receiver was to be treated as an assignee subject to all pre-existing pleas of set-off pleadable against the cedent (the company). The Scottish Law Commission, however, suggested that the rule arrived at by Lord Kincraig and Lord Prosser be put into statutory form because of confusion in the past. Their working party suggested the following formulation:

> "The powers of a receiver to take possession of and realise the property of a company attached by a floating charge shall have effect subject to any rights of compensation or retention which have arisen prior to the attachment of the floating charge, but shall prevail over any such rights which may arise after such attachment."

This formulation puts into statutory form the effect of Lord Prosser's and Lord Kincraig's judgments in so far as set-off is available against a

---

[41] 1985 S.L.T. 149.
[42] *Myles J. Callaghan Ltd (in Receivership) v City of Glasgow D.C.*, 1988 S.L.T. 227.

receiver. However, it entails that rights which arise after the attachment of a floating charge may not be pled against debts owed to a company prior to the attachment of the floating charge.

It is thought that the Scottish Law Commission is correct in following Lord Kincraig in the *Louden* case where he held that receivership accompanied by insolvency opened the door to the general rules about the balancing of accounts in bankruptcy.

Set-off excluded by agreement

17–15 It is thought that, in Scotland, a party may, by agreement, exclude his right to claim a right of retention in the balancing of accounts in bankruptcy, as well as a right of compensation generally.[43] By contrast in England, set-off in insolvency, although procedural in the sense that it is part of the process of proof and requires the taking of an account, has been held to be mandatory by the House of Lords.[44] In England the parties may not exclude the statutory provisions by contract, and these override any prior agreement between the parties to keep the accounts separate. These statutory provisions in England are considered to regulate matters of public interest in the orderly administration of insolvent estates, and are not purely a source of private rights enacted for the benefit of individual debtors of the estate having cross-claims against it. The ruling in the *Halesowen* case prevents pre-bankruptcy waiving by creditors of their rights, and would appear to render unenforceable agreements thereby to subordinate unsecured debt on insolvency.[45] In contrast, in Scotland the right of retention has to be pled. It is therefore a private right and it is open to the parties to agree not to enforce such a right in the event of insolvency.

Proof of the claim giving rise to the right in the insolvency

17–16 It is thought that, because in Scotland the right of retention has to be pled and is, as it were, a defence to the action of a company for debt, the claim giving rise to the right does not have to be lodged in the liquidation. This has important implications. Generally in a liquidation a creditor is entitled to claim only the accumulated sum of principal and any interest which is due on the debt as at the date of the commencement of the winding up,[46] although where there is a surplus remaining after payment of the debts of a company proved in a winding up, the surplus is by statute now applied to paying interest on those debts in respect of the periods during which they have been outstanding since the company went into liquidation.[47] This means that interest running on any debt from the date of the commencement of the winding up is

---

[43] See McBryde, *Contract*, p.540.
[44] *National Westminster Bank Ltd v Halesowen Presswork & Assemblies Ltd* [1972] A.C. 785.
[45] See Chap.16.
[46] Bankruptcy (Scotland) Act 1985, Sch.1, para.1(1) as applied to liquidations by Insolvency (Scotland) Rules 1986, r.4.16(1).
[47] Insolvency Act 1986, s.189(2).

subordinated to all claims apart from those of shareholders in terms of s.189 of the Insolvency Act 1986. Because, however, the defence of set-off may fail if the debt being pled is a post-insolvency debt being claimed against a pre-insolvency debt,[48] it is important that the creditor also has a claim lodged in the liquidation. Although there is a provision in terms of s.52(9) of the Bankruptcy (Scotland) Act 1985 (as applied to liquidations by Insolvency (Scotland) Rules 1986, r.4.68(1)) for the late lodging of claims, this is not allowed to upset dividends already paid out.[49] It is suggested, therefore, where there is any doubt as to whether the plea of a right of retention will succeed, there should also be a claim lodged in the liquidation. Because, however, it is thought that the two could not be run simultaneously, the claim should be a contingent claim subject to the plea of the right of retention not being upheld. The liquidator will then be forced into a position of making a full provision for the claim so that there will be funds to meet its entitled *pro rata* payment, in the event that the contingent claim is upvalued on the plea of retention not succeeding.

Secured creditors and preferential creditors

A secured creditor is in a different position. He does not need to enter **17–17** the liquidation process at all, but may merely enforce his security. If he proves in the liquidation, he is entitled to the principal plus interest to the date of payment.[50] He also ranks only for non-secured debt.[51] In England, because set-off on insolvency is mandatory on debts proved in a liquidation, the secured creditor opens himself to a plea of set-off if he proves for the secured debt in the liquidation.[52] It is thought that, in England, if a secured debtor with also unsecured debt proves both debts in a liquidation, he runs the risk, given the mandatory set-off rules, that the liquidator could have set-off against the secured debt unsecured debt of the company leaving the creditor to rank for his unsecured debt. In terms of r.4.66(6) of the Insolvency (Scotland) Rules 1986, the order of priority in a liquidation must not affect the right of a secured creditor which is preferable to the rights of the liquidator. The secured creditors may redeem their securities without reference to the liquidator, or the liquidator may require them to discharge their securities by payment to them of the value of their securities.[53] It is thought that, because the secured element in the debt is not even classed as a claim, it will not be open to the liquidator to plead the right of retention against the secured debt to the prejudice of the secured creditor. It is thought that this argument would not apply in relation to a creditor who was both a preferential creditor and an ordinary creditor. In terms of s.248(b) of the Insolvency Act 1986, a security is widely defined to include "any

---

[48] In the case of *Myles J. Callaghan Ltd (in receivership) v City of Glasgow D.C.*, 1988 S.L.T. 227 on slightly different facts that type of situation could have arisen.

[49] See para.19–01.

[50] *National Commercial Bank of Scotland v Liquidators of Telford Grier McKay & Co*, 1969 S.C. 181.

[51] See para.19–06.

[52] *Re Norman Holding Co Ltd* [1990] 3 All E.R. 757.

[53] Bankruptcy (Scotland) Act 1985, Sch.1, para.5(2) as applied to liquidations by Insolvency (Scotland) Rules 1986, r.4.16(1).

security (whether heritable or moveable), any floating charge and any right of lien or preference and any right of retention (other than a right of compensation or set-off)". It may be argued that preference here would include a preferential creditor. However, it is difficult to see how the rights of a preferential creditor could be superior to the rights of a liquidator for his remuneration in the same way as a secured creditor having a lien or a standard security had superior rights. It is also not a "preference over property", and thought therefore not to be relevant. In the English case of *Re Unit 2 Windows Ltd*,[54] which preceded the Insolvency Act 1986, the court addressed itself to this sort of problem under the English legislation. Walton J. admitted that the case raised an austere point of law. He referred to a "fasciculus" of sections in the Companies Act which were not all that helpful. He thought that there was almost nothing to go on, and held that set-off should be apportioned rateably between preferential debts and non-preferential debts. It is thought that that case is not helpful. Walton J. acknowledged that his solution was a novel solution. He did not follow a previous case of *Re E.J. Morel (1934) Ltd*,[55] in which Buckley J. took a different and, it is thought, correct approach. He stated:

"On the one hand, counsel for the liquidator says that when the statutory set-off has been carried out, all the components have lost their identity, and the resulting balance cannot be said to consist either wholly or to any ascertainable extent of a debt which qualifies for preference, unless the credit which is to be set off against the debt is less than the debt in respect of advances for wages, in which case manifestly some part of the advance for wages must remain unsatisfied. He says that in those circumstances the person who is claiming preference cannot establish his claim to preference, because he cannot identify the character of any part of the resulting balance. In my view, the right solution for this problem is to treat the balance which results from the set-off as being non-preferential except to the extent that it can be demonstrated that the credit is insufficient to discharge the preferential claim in full. The result of a set-off is to give the creditor payment in full of his claim to the extent of the set-off, and in that way he is better off than creditors who merely have to rely on their right to prove and get a dividend. If he obtains, by set-off, payment in full, it seems reasonable that that payment in full should be treated as being in respect of that part of his debt which would rank first in priority. Moreover, the fact that if the preferential claim exceeds the amount of the credit to be set-off against it, there would be some part of the preferential claim which demonstrably had not been paid off, and could still claim preference, is a circumstance that seems to demonstrate that my method of approaching the solution is the right one."

Because in a "balancing of accounts in bankruptcy" the accounts of the different parties are run together and set-off may be pled in Scotland

[54] [1986] B.C.L.C. 31; [1985] 3 All E.R. 647.
[55] [1961] 1 All E.R. 796; [1962] Ch. 21.

against any other debt, it is thought by the authors that a trustee in bankruptcy or liquidator can plead in defence to a claim which happened to carry the preferential status, any counter debt. There is old authority to this effect in the case of *Maxwell v McCulloch's Creditors*,[56] a decision of the whole Court of Session, and in Bankton's *Institute*,[57] and the approach of these authorities was followed in Scotland in 1993 by the Outer House in the case of *Turner v Inland Revenue Commissioners*.[58]

Subordinated debt

A separate question arises where the liquidator owes subordinated **17–18** debt, *i.e.* the subordinated creditor is not entitled to payment except from a surplus after ordinary creditors have been paid in full. The question is whether the subordinated creditor is entitled to set off his subordinated claim against an ordinary claim or, if he is in liquidation, a preferential claim. Although it is thought that an ordinary creditor can set off his claim against a preferential claim or an ordinary claim and may choose to set off first against the preferential claim, a subordinated creditor is in a different position. He is not entitled to participate in the assets of a company until all debts, preferential and ordinary, are paid off. The position seems to the authors to be analogous to that of a contributory who is also a creditor of the company. In the leading case of *Cowan v Gowans*[59] the Inner House reviewed the English cases, which are still the main authorities, and held that set-off was not admissible in that type of relationship. It stated:

> "The name of Mr Gowans appears in the list of contributories made up by the liquidator as owner of 720 shares. The total amount of the calls payable on these shares is £7,200 . . . Mr Gowans objects to be put on the list of contributories on the ground that he is a creditor of the company for work done under his contract to a larger amount than the calls said to be due. In other words, he pleads compensation, founding upon the debts due by the company to him for the purpose of extinguishing the debt due by him for calls to the company. Now, one thing is clear, that if the claim of compensation be sustained the effect will be that Mr Gowans will receive payment in full of a part of his claim corresponding to the amount of calls due by him, and will thus secure a preference over the other creditors of the company . . . I think it would be strange if in a procedure, which has for its object the *pari passu* ranking of creditors, one creditor, because he also happens to be a contributory, should secure a preference over the other creditors of the company. Of course this question depends on the provisions of the Companies Acts, 1862 and 1867, and I am glad to be spared the necessity of examining these Acts in detail, because they have been made the subject of decision by the Court of Chancery in England

---

[56] (1738) Mor. 2550.
[57] Bankton, *Inst.*, I, 494.
[58] 1994 S.L.T. 811, *per* Lord Kirkwood.
[59] (1878) 5 R. 581.

in two cases. The first of these judgments was pronounced in a case of *Grissell* ([1866] 1 Ch App 528) by Lord Chelmsford with the assistance of the Lords Justice of Appeal, and the second in a case *of Black & Co* ([1872] 8 Ch App 254) by Lord Selborne with the same assistance. I will take the liberty of reading a passage from the opinion of Lord Selborne in the latter case, which is directly applicable here, and expresses exactly the view I take of the circumstances which have arisen. He says,—'The different sections of the Act,' ie the Act of 1862 'those which define the liability of limited companies, the 7th, 8th, 23d and 38th, those which deal with the administration of assets, the 98th 101st and 133d, those which give the power to make calls, not in the ordinary way, but specially for the purposes of this Act, the 102d and 133d, all have in view the payment *pari passu* and equally of the debts due to the creditors, and the liquidator who receives the calls necessarily receives them as a statutory trustee for the equal and rateable payment of all the creditors. The result of this contention, that one particular creditor may pay himself in full by retaining his own calls and not paying them, would in effect be to give him a preference, and to exonerate him from his obligation as a shareholder to contribute towards the payment of the debts of the other creditors. That appears to me to be utterly opposed to the whole principle of the law of set-off, and to all the provisions of the Act which bear on this subject' (8 Ch App 262). We find there not only the result of the consideration of the statutes by these Judges, but also a principle or reason on which the rule is founded, and which is perfectly satisfactory to my mind.''

It is thought that a subordinated creditor is in the same position as a shareholder. The shareholders claim to an entitlement from the company's assets is conditional on all the creditors being paid. Hence the claim of a contributory is in a different class to that of the creditors. It is very important when deciding whether a subordinated claim can be set off against an ordinary claim to examine the exact structure of the debt subordination agreement.[60] If the debt subordination agreement is structured so that the subordinated debt is claimable only after ordinary debts have all been collected and ordinary creditors paid off, then the subordinated creditor would be entitled to no set-off against an ordinary claim. If, however, the claim is exigible as soon as the debtor has paid ordinary creditors, it may be argued that the subordinated creditor could then set off his subordinated claim against any debt due by him to the debtor company still owing after sufficient of his ordinary debt has been paid to render the company sufficiently in funds to meet ordinary claims. In exercising that limited right of set off, the subordinated creditor who was also a debtor of the company could thereby improve his position as against the other subordinated creditors.

Letters of set-off

17–19   The balancing of accounts in bankruptcy or liquidation allows one party to set off or balance claims against another party on the insolvency of the other party. A banker therefore could combine the accounts of a

---

[60] See Chap.16.

customer in order to effect the balancing in the bankruptcy,[61] except where money is deposited and appropriated to a particular purpose.[62] Organisations extending credit, especially banks, often seek to rely on more than a bilateral right of retention between the organisation and its debtor. They will often try to set up letters of set-off whereby a sum due by one customer to the organisation can be retained against a sum due to the organisation by another customer. The latter feature does not appear to be objectionable. Nevertheless, the security conferred by letters of set-off amounts to a floating charge, unless a fixed sum is deposited with the organisation by the granter of the security. The criterion for determining whether a security is a floating charge is whether property can be taken out of the security without specific action on the part of the security holder, such as a partial discharge or retrocession. If it can, the security is a floating charge. With letters of set-off, the customer whose account is in credit normally decides whether money is to be withdrawn. The bank must comply with his instructions. It follows that the funds which constitute the security subjects can be withdrawn from the security without the consent of the security holder. Three consequences flow from the fact that the letters of set-off constitute a floating charge: first, such a security can only be created by a company; secondly, it must be registered under ss.410 to 424 of the Companies Act 1985; and thirdly, the bank's security will only rank on insolvency as a floating charge, after the preferential creditors.

Letters of set-off containing equitable charge

Banks sometimes have lending agreements with customers which talk **17–20** of a bank's "lien" on a customer's credit balance. In England it has been held that "a debtor cannot sensibly be said to have a lien on his own indebtedness to his creditor".[63] By that token he would not be able to grant an equitable charge over his indebtedness to his creditor, but could give such a charge to a third party. These principles were explicitly or by implication brought out in the case of *Re Charge Card Services Ltd*.[64] The facts of the *Charge Card* case were as follows:

Charge Card Services Ltd (the Company) entered into an invoice discounting agreement by which it agreed to factor its receivables to Commercial Credit Services Ltd (the Factor). Under cl.3(a) of the agreement the factor could require the company to repurchase any receivable in stated events, such as the debtor's dispute of liability, and under 3(c) the company guaranteed payment by every debtor and agreed to indemnify the factor against loss resulting from a debtor's failure to pay. Clause 4 provided that the purchase price payable by the factor for any receivable was to be the gross amount payable by the debtor less any discount allowable to him, unless the factor's discount

[61] Bell, *Comm.*, II, 122.
[62] *Mycroft, Petr*, 1983 S.L.T. 342.
[63] *National Westminster Bank Ltd v Halesowen Presswork and Assemblies Ltd* [1971] 1 Q.B. 1 at 46C, *per* Buckley L.J.
[64] [1986] 3 All E.R. 289.

charge was calculated in the manner prescribed by standard condition 3. Under cl.6 the factor's obligation to pay was made subject to the right of debits and rights of retention provided by standard condition 3. Standard condition 3(A) required the factor to maintain a current account to which would be credited sums including the purchase price of each receivable before deducting the discounting charge, and debited sums including certain contingent liabilities of the company under the agreement and the discounting charge. By standard condition 3(B) the factor was to remit to the company or its order any balance for the time being standing to the credit of the current account less any amount which the factor in its absolute discretion decided to retain as security for claims against the company, any risk of any non-payment by a debtor and any amount prospectively chargeable to the company as a debit under standard condition 3(A). Clause 10 (when read with cl.11) provided that if the company went into liquidation the factor could terminate the agreement and require the company to repurchase any outstanding receivables previously purchased by the factor. The repurchase price was not an item falling to be debited to the current account under standard 3(a).

The company went into insolvent liquidation and contended that the factor's right of retention under standard condition 3(B) was taken as security for rights of set-off and constituted a charge on book debts which was void against the liquidator for want of registration under the Companies Act.

It was held that the amount payable by the factor for a receivable was not the purchase price as such but the balance standing to the credit of the company's account after the relevant debits had been made, and subject to the right of retention. Accordingly, it was a case of accounting, not one of set-off, for there were no mutual but independent obligations capable of set-off. The question was merely a right of payment of a single balance remaining after the exercise of the right of retention. The consequence was that the right of retention was not a charge on money due to the company. The reason was because the amount that was due was arrived at after the deduction of the sum retained so that there was no relevant property capable of forming the subject matter of the charge.

As to the question of the factor's right to terminate the agreement and require the company to repurchase the outstanding receivables, that was not a case for debit to the current account. It constituted a true set-off. It was not able to be characterised as a charge because it was not possible for a charge to be given in favour of a debtor over his own indebtedness. In the course of the arguments it had been conceded that a debt could not be assigned back to the debtor by way of a mortgage, for that type of assignment would operate as a release of the debt. The same applied to an equitable charge. The court, however, affirmed that there was no objection to granting that type of equitable charge. It could not, however, be structured in that way. The court stated:

"The objection to a charge in these circumstances is not the process by which it is created, but to the result. A debt is a chose in action;

it is the right to sue the debtor. This can be assigned or made available to a third party, but not to the debtor, who cannot sue himself. Once any assignment or appropriation to the debtor becomes unconditional, the debt is wholly or partially released. The debtor cannot, and does not need to, resort to the creditor's claim against him in order to obtain the benefit of his security; his own liability to the creditor is automatically discharged or reduced."

It is thought that the principle enunciated in that case, that a debtor cannot give any form of security over his indebtedness to his creditor, is also the law of Scotland, but that the other principles relating to an equitable charge do not have any bearing on any Scottish form of security.

Letters of set-off containing an "assignation in security"

One method by which a debtor may give his creditor rights against **17–21** debts owed to the debtor by third parties is to grant the creditor an "assignation in security" of debts owed to the debtor by third parties. This means that the creditor could claim these assigned debts directly from the debtors without reference to the debtor himself. It is necessary in that type of arrangement that the debtors of the debtor have intimated to them that assignation is taking place. This can be done by notice from the debtor to these debtors, or by the debtors being made to sign the agreement containing the letters of set-off. Such a situation was considered in the case *Gallemos Ltd (in receivership) v Barratt Falkirk Ltd.*[65] In that case a company in receivership raised an action for payment against a construction company in respect of goods and services supplied. The pursuers had received goods and services from an associated company of the defenders. The defenders asserted that certain acknowledgment of order forms in respect of the goods and services supplied by their associated company to the pursuers constituted valid assignations in security to the associated company of the defenders' debts to the pursuers. On the forms the associated company reserved the right to *contra* any monies overdue by the pursuers against debts due to the pursuers, *inter alia*, the defenders, if payment was not made within 60 days. The court held that the assignation had to be in words that could be construed as effecting an immediate transference of rights from the debtor to the assignee, and the transfer became complete when intimation of the transfer was made to the debtor who then knew that the assignee had become creditor in the place of the assignor. It was vital that the document intimated to the debtor should inform the debtor of the extent of the right transferred to the assignee, because there could be no transfer of an undefined right, because the assignor's debtor must know the extent of his obligation to the assignee.

It is important, if "an assignation in security" is contained in so-called letters of set-off, that those handling the paperwork know what is happening. Otherwise a valid device may be undermined by actings.

---

[65] 1990 S.L.T. 98.

Letters of set-off containing guarantees

17–22   If it is not open to a party (not being a company) to give a floating charge over its receivables, and it is not desired that the party's debts are assigned to the creditor in security for his debt, there is another method of avoiding the difficulties. In place of the form of letters of set-off containing an English style equitable charge (not enforceable over debts situated in Scotland) or there being assignations in security, the credit extending organisation could take a guarantee from each of the third parties providing security in respect of debts due to the credit organisation by all persons on whose behalf the security is to be provided. The arrangement becomes a multipartite personal guarantee of a sort which is quite frequently used in Scotland. Under this arrangement each of the guarantors grants the bank or credit organisation a conventional right of retention in respect of all sums owing by the bank to the guarantor. The right of retention could be contained in the same document as the guarantee (usually the letters of set-off). The consequence of such an arrangement can be seen by considering guarantees and rights of retention granted by two associated companies. If both companies become insolvent, one owing money to the bank but the other having a credit balance in its account, the bank can demand payment from the second company under the guarantee. Thereafter the bank can exercise its right of retention in respect of the sums due by it to the second company. For this purpose it probably does not matter whether the right of retention is conventional or merely the common law right of balancing accounts in bankruptcy. The fact that the sum due under the guarantee is not payable until after insolvency (that being when the demand is made) does not matter. In *Asphaltic Limestone Co v Glasgow Corporation*,[66] Lord McLaren, discussing the common law right of balancing accounts in bankruptcy, said[67]: "[b]ut this principle of bankruptcy law presupposes reciprocal obligations which are both existing at the time of the declaration of insolvency, although only one of them is, it may be, immediately exigible."

This means that it does not matter whether the obligations can be enforced before insolvency. What matters is whether they have been created before insolvency.[68] It is thought by the authors that a similar principle would apply where the right of retention on insolvency was conventional.

Set-off and performance bonds

17–23   In some cases the obligation owed to or by a bank is not a money debt but a contingent liability. A common example would be where a performance bond has been granted. It is thought that a guarantee combined with a right of retention will be equally effective in such cases. Although the bank's obligation to pay money may be instantly

---

[66] 1907 S.C. 463.
[67] At 474.
[68] See para.17–08.

due, but the obligation owed to the bank contingent, the bank is entitled to retain the debt due by it in security of its contingent claim. It is a straightforward application of the principle of balancing accounts in bankruptcy.[69] Exactly the same result would occur where the right of retention is a conventional right designed to operate on insolvency, and it cannot make any difference that the liability owed to the bank arises under a guarantee as long as the liability was created before insolvency. The same rule applies when the obligation of the customer is to pay a money debt instantly due but the obligation owed by the institution is contingent. This is clear from the decision in *Borthwick v Scottish Widows' Fund*.[70] In that case, a bankrupt had effected three life assurance policies with the defenders, and was also indebted to the defenders in a substantial sum. It was held that the defenders, as debtors in the sums in the policies, were entitled to withhold payment of those sums so long as a debt of equal amount was due to them by the bankrupt. The case proceeded on the principle of balancing accounts in bankruptcy, and, although the decision was reached by a majority of five to two, must be unimpeachable authority for the proposition that a contingent debt may be retained against a liquid debt in cases of insolvency.[71]

Foreign currency debts

A right of retention is, in essence, a right to refuse to pay a debt or fulfil some other sort of obligation until the creditor performs an obligation due by him to the debtor. The obligation of either party can be an obligation to deliver goods, or to grant a disposition of land, or to do many other things apart from pay money. Consequently there can be no reason for refusing legal or conventional rights of retention when one obligation is to pay sterling and the other is to pay a foreign currency. The English case of *Re Dynamics Corporation of America*[72] suggests that the date for the conversion of the foreign currency debt should be the date of the winding up. It is thought that that case has no application to Scotland if set off is pled. As noted in para.19–08, the Scottish rule in the case of a creditor claiming in a foreign currency is that:

17–24

"A creditor may state the amount of his claim in a currency other than sterling where:

(a) his claim is constituted by decree or other order made by a court ordering the company to pay the creditor a sum expressed in a currency other than sterling, or

(b) where it is not so constituted, his claim arises from a contract or bill of exchange in terms of which payment is or may be required to be made by the company to the creditor in a currency other than sterling.

---

[69] See Gloag & Irvine on *Rights in Security*, pp.314–315.

[70] [1864] 2 M. 595.

[71] In the case all the other six judges of the Court of Session declined in consequence of being policy holders of the defender. It is also so treated in Gloag and Irvine on *Rights in Security*, pp.318–319.

[72] [1976] 2 All E.R. 669.

(2) Where a claim is stated in currency other than sterling for the purpose of the preceding paragraph, it shall be converted into sterling at the rate of exchange for that other currency at the mean of the buying and selling spot rates prevailing in the London market at the close of business on the date of commencement of winding-up."[73]

It is thought that the Scottish courts would apply the conversion rate as in the case of a claim but not have the date of the commencement of the winding up as the date of the establishment of the debt or the conversion date, unless a claim is lodged.[74] It is thought that, where compensation is pled, interest does not run after the date when the compensation is effected and compensation is effected *retro*.[75] However, in the case of the balancing of accounts in bankruptcy it is thought that the object of the equitable right is so that the retainer of the debt does not lose out against the claim from the insolvent estate. Because the debt of the insolvent estate keeps carrying interest, it would not be equitable for the claim of the person having the equitable right to be frozen as at the date of the commencement of the winding-up or the winding-up order if interest carried on being paid on the counter-debt. Bell states[76]: "[t]hus, the settlement of mutual debts may be referred to two distinct principles: The one is virtual payment in extinction; the other, retention till counter performance." It is thought that counter performance must mean the paying of the debt in full plus interest until payment. This is all the more so in the present financial markets, where debt instruments may be structured so that a very high interest rate may be payable to compensate for a poor deal on principal. Hence the person exercising the right of retention can hold out for principal, interest until payment and conversion at that date. He is, of course, sometimes advised also to lodge a contingent claim on a different basis.[77]

Set-off and the Crown

17–25   In relation to the balancing of accounts in bankruptcy and set-off generally, a party is not allowed by statute to claim set-off or retention in any proceedings brought by the Crown without leave of the court, unless the subject-matter of the counterclaim relates to the government department on whose behalf the proceedings are brought. By the same token, however, in any proceedings against a government department, the Crown may not take a plea of set-off or retention, without the leave of the court, if the subject-matter of the counterclaim does not relate to that department.[78] This is procedural because leave is normally given. Set-off is not open in a Crown claim for taxes, penalties, etc.[79]

---

[73] Insolvency (Scotland) Rules 1986, r.4.17.
[74] See para.17–16.
[75] *Inch v Lee* (1903) 11 S.L.T. 374.
[76] Bell, *Comm.*, II, 124.
[77] See para.17–16.
[78] Crown Proceedings Act 1947, s.50; *Atlantic Engine Co (1920) Ltd v Lord Advocate*, 1955 S.L.T. 17; *Laing v Lord Advocate*, 1973 S.L.T. (Notes) 81; *Smith v Lord Advocate (No 2)* 1981 S.L.T. 19.
[79] Crown Proceedings Act 1947, s.50.

Calls in liquidation

In a liquidation, a contributory may not set off amounts due by the **17–26**
company to him against calls unless all the creditors have been paid in
full.[80]

---

[80] Companies Act 1985, s.552; *Cowan v Gowans* (1878) 5 R. 581; *Property Investment Co of Scotland v Aikman* (1891) 28 S.L.R. 955; *Property Investment Co of Scotland v National Bank* (1891) 28 S.L.R. 884.

PART 5

PROCEDURE AND PRACTICE

CHAPTER 18

ACCOUNTING LAW AND PRACTICE

Introduction

Although the Companies Acts have laid down detailed rules about **18–01**
the preparation, auditing and publication of accounts of companies
registered under the Companies Acts (ss.221 to 262 of the Companies
Act 1985, as amended by ss.1 to 23 of the Companies Act 1989), there
had until the Cork reforms been little detailed legislation in relation to
the accounting and reporting of insolvent companies in Scotland. The
Cork legislation filled this gap although to a certain extent it merely
makes mandatory what was accounting convention or "best practice"
prior to December 29, 1986.

Statement of affairs

The main reform in the legislation was the introduction of a "state- **18–02**
ment of affairs" of the company, which is a statement giving a detailed
breakdown of all the assets and liabilities of the company as far as
ascertainable. A prescribed form of the statement of affairs is set out in
the Insolvency (Scotland) Rules 1986 for liquidations, administrations
and receiverships.[1] The only difference in the forms relates to whether it
is an administration, receivership or liquidation. Where there is a
"voluntary arrangement" the Rules list particulars to go into a statement
of affairs, but no form is prescribed.[2]

Administrators and receivers in Scotland are under a statutory duty to
require those connected with the company[3] to complete a statement of
affairs.[4] Liquidators, in cases where the court has made a winding-up
order, have a discretion whether to require those connected with the
company to complete a statement of affairs.[5] In the case of a creditors'
voluntary winding up, the directors of the company are under a
statutory duty to make out a statement of affairs of the company and
have that statement laid before the creditors' meeting.[6] It must then be
sent to the liquidator.[7] Similarly, where a members' voluntary winding

---

[1] The form in liquidations is Form 4.4 (Scot); in administrations it is Form 2.6 (Scot); and in receiverships it is Form 5 (Scot).

[2] Insolvency (Scotland) Rules 1986, r.1.5.

[3] See para.18–09.

[4] Insolvency Act 1986, para.47 of new Sch.B1.

[5] *ibid.*, s.131.

[6] *ibid.*, s.99(1) and (2).

[7] Insolvency (Scotland) Rules 1986, Sch.1, para.4.

up is converted into a creditors' voluntary winding up, the liquidator is under a statutory duty to make out a statement of affairs in the prescribed form and lay the statement before the creditors' meeting.[8] When the directors are proposing a "voluntary arrangement" under Pt 1 of the Insolvency Act 1986, they must deliver a statement of affairs to the "nominee" within seven days of the delivery of the proposal or such other time as he allows.[9] The statement must include all the details on the statutory forms used by administrators, liquidators and receivers since r.1.5 follows the format. In addition there must be included (a) particulars of debts owed by or to it by persons connected to it; (b) details of members and shareholdings; and (c) any other relevant particulars.[10] Similarly if the proposal is by the liquidator or administrator but he is not the nominee, a statement of affairs, as in the case of a directors' proposal, must be submitted to the nominee.[11]

In the case of a members' voluntary winding up, there is no statutory scope for a statement of affairs. Rather the directors make a statutory declaration of the company's solvency, *i.e.* that they have formed the opinion that the company will be able to pay its debts in full, together with interest at the full rate (*i.e.* the higher of the contracted rate or judicial rate), within a period of not more than 12 months from the date of the commencement of the winding up.[12] The declaration must be in the prescribed form.[13]

Function and format of statement of affairs

(1) Function

18–03   The function of the statement of affairs is: (a) to get as detailed a picture of the company's financial position as possible with the accounting format specially tailored to the accounting questions which arise on insolvency; and (b) to provide the "base accounts" which can be used to measure progress or movement in the liquidation, administration, receivership or voluntary arrangement.

(2) Format

18–04   The first page of the statement of affairs is a balance sheet detailing the total assets and liabilities of the company. It gives figures of the projected surplus/deficiency, based on estimated realisable values of assets less liabilities, available for distribution to the various categories of creditors, *i.e.* to (1) preferential creditors; (2) floating charge holders; (3) unsecured creditors; and (4) shareholders.

The totals of assets and liabilities are backed up by "lists". Lists A and B give respectively "assets which are not secured" and "assets which

---

[8] Insolvency Act 1986, s.95(3); and r.4.8, as applied to members' voluntary windings up by Sch.2 to the Rules.

[9] R.1.5(1).

[10] R.1.5.

[11] Insolvency Act 1986, s.2(3) and r.1.12(5).

[12] *ibid.*, s.89(1).

[13] Form 4.25 (Scot).

are secured". Lists C, D, E, F and G are lists of liabilities according to ranking and type of liability, as follows:

- Preferential creditors—List C
- Holders of floating charges—List D
  Unsecured creditors
- Trade accounts—List E
- Bills payable—List F
- Contingent liabilities—List G

> List A of "assets not specifically secured" has schedules I, II, III, IV and V giving details of:
> Schedule I—marketable securities;
> Schedule II—bills of exchange, promissory notes, etc.;
> Schedule III—trade debtors;
> Schedule IV—loans and advances; and
> Schedule V—unpaid calls.

The format of the statement of affairs must be followed "with such variations as circumstances require".[14] This is an important provision because the format is not comprehensive, as will be discussed later in this chapter.

Compilation and distribution of statement of affairs

The Insolvency Act 1986 and the Insolvency (Scotland) Rules 1986 **18–05** make provisions for the distribution of the statement of affairs by the: (a) administrator; (b) receiver; (c) liquidator; and (d) nominee in the case of proposed voluntary arrangements.

The provisions are similar but not the same. They are as follows:

(1) Administrator

Where an administration is entered into, the administrator is under a **18–06** statutory duty to require a statement of affairs to be compiled.[15] The procedure is for the administrator to serve a "notice requiring submission of administration statement of affairs" on certain persons connected with the company outlined in the statute.[16] The notice has to be in a prescribed form.[17] The persons required to compile the statement have 11 days beginning on the day they get the notice.[18] The persons making up the statement may be paid by the administrator out of his receipts.[19] The administrator is under a statutory obligation within three months of the administration to send a statement of his proposals to the Registrar of Companies and to all creditors and members.[20]

---

[14] Insolvency (Scotland) Rules 1986, r.7.30.
[15] Insolvency Act 1986, para.47(1) of new Sch.B1.
[16] See para.18–09.
[17] Form 2.5 (Scot).
[18] Insolvency Act 1986, para.48(1) of new Sch.B1.
[19] Insolvency (Scotland) Rules 1986, r.2.24(1), as substituted by SI 2003/2111.
[20] Insolvency Act 1986, paras 49(4) and (5) of new Sch.B1.

(2) Receiver

A receiver is also under a statutory duty to require a statement of affairs.[21] This he must do as soon as he is appointed.[22] As in the case of an administrator, the persons who are required to produce a statement of affairs[23] must do so within 21 days from the day after the notice of requirement of a statement of affairs is given to them by the receiver.[24] The form of notice of requirement to give a statement of affairs is Form 3.1 (Scot). As in the case of an administrator, the persons compiling the statement may be paid by the receiver, as expenses of the receivership, the reasonable costs of compiling the report.[25] The receiver is under a statutory duty within three months of his appointment to send to the registrar, to the holder of the floating charge, to any trustees for secured creditors and the creditors themselves, a report giving the background to the receivership and the amounts likely to be available for payment to preferential creditors and other creditors.[26] The receiver is also under a statutory duty to send a copy of the report to all unsecured creditors or to publish a notice stating an address to which unsecured creditors of the company should write for copies of the report to be sent to them free of charge.[27] A report must also be laid before a meeting of the company's unsecured creditors on not less than 14 days' notice.[28] Although the statement of affairs does not have to be sent to the various persons mentioned above, the receiver is under a statutory duty to include in the report a summary of the statement of affairs and his comments on it.[29] Section 67(6) of the Insolvency Act 1986 makes it clear that the receiver does not have to include in his report information which might seriously prejudice the carrying out of the receivership. This would include matters under negotiation with third parties, and would indicate why the statement of affairs itself would be too sensitive for publication. When the company is collecting in debts, it does not want to have to publish what the receiver thinks is the likely realisable value of the book debts.

(3) Liquidations

18–07 Where in the course of a members' voluntary winding up, the liquidator is of the opinion that the company will be unable to pay its debts in full, the liquidator is under a statutory obligation to compile a statement of affairs.[30] The statement of affairs shall be in a prescribed form.[31] In the case of a creditor's voluntary winding up, the directors of the company are under a statutory obligation to make out a statement of

---

[21] Insolvency Act 1986, s.66(1).
[22] *ibid.*, s.66(1).
[23] See para.18–09.
[24] Insolvency Act 1986, s.66(4).
[25] Insolvency (Scotland) Rules 1986, r.3.3(1).
[26] Insolvency Act 1986, s.67(1).
[27] *ibid.*, s.67(2).
[28] *ibid.*, s.67(2).
[29] *ibid.*, s.67(5).
[30] *ibid.*, s.95(3).
[31] Form 4.4(Scot).

affairs.[32] The statement of affairs shall be in a prescribed form.[33] In the case of a winding up by the court, the liquidator may require a statement of affairs from persons connected[34] with the company.[35] The procedure, as in receiverships and administrations, is for a notice to be served on the persons who are to draw up the statement of affairs. The notice has to be in a prescribed form.[36] Persons being required to draw up the statement of affairs have 21 days from the day after the serving of the notice to make up the statement of affairs.[37]

In the case of a creditors' voluntary winding up the liquidator is under a statutory duty to send a copy of the statement of affairs or a summary of it to all creditors and contributories within 28 days of the first meeting following the resolution for winding up of the company (Sch.1, para.6 of the Insolvency (Scotland) Rules 1986).[38] In the case of a winding up by the court, where there has been a statement of affairs, the liquidator has a discretion whether to send out a copy of the statement of affairs or summary to creditors and contributories.[39]

In addition, the liquidator, if required by the liquidation committee, shall send a written report to every member of the committee setting out the position generally as regards the progress of the winding up and matters arising in connection with it, to which the liquidator considers the committee's attention should be drawn.[40]

(4) Voluntary arrangements

Where the directors are making a proposal under s.1 of the Insolvency **18–08** Act 1986 and make up a statement of affairs under r.1.5, the nominee must give a report to the court within 28 days of getting notice of the proposal (subject to extension by the court).[41] This report must have lodged with it a copy or summary of the statement of affairs.[42] If the report is in favour of the proposal being considered, the nominee is duty bound to summon a meeting of the company and its creditors on at least 14 days' notice (not more than 28)[43] to consider the proposal.[44] The notice shall include a copy of the statement of affairs, or if he thinks fit, a summary of it, which must include a list of the creditors and the amount of their debts.[45]

Where an administrator or liquidator is making a proposal but is not the nominee, there is the same duty described above on a nominee, as

---

[32] Insolvency Act 1986, s.99(1).
[33] Form 4.4 (Scot).
[34] See para.18–09.
[35] Insolvency Act 1986, s.131(1).
[36] Form 4.3 (Scot).
[37] Insolvency Act 1986, s.131(4).
[38] Insolvency (Scotland) Rules 1986, r.4.10.
[39] *ibid.*, r.4.10.
[40] *ibid.*, r.4.56(1).
[41] Insolvency Act 1986, s.2(2).
[42] Insolvency (Scotland) Rules 1986, r.1.7(1).
[43] *ibid.*, r.1.9(1).
[44] Insolvency Act 1986, s.3(1).
[45] Insolvency (Scotland) Rules 1986, r.1.9(2).

there is when directors are making the proposal, about reporting to the court and summoning a meeting of the company and the creditors, with the same need to lodge with the court a copy or summary of the statement of affairs and attach a copy or summary of the statement of affairs and attach a copy or summary to the notice of the meeting.[46]

Where an administrator or liquidator is intending to make a proposal and is the nominee, he must call a meeting of the company and its creditors on at least 14 days' notice to consider the proposal[47] and, as above, include a copy or summary of the statement of affairs.[48]

Persons to compile statement of affairs

18–09   Where an administrator requires a statement of affairs in terms of para.47(1) of new Sch.B1 to the Insolvency Act 1986, a receiver requires a statement of affairs in terms of s.66(1) and a liquidator requires it in terms of s.131(1) of the Insolvency Act 1986, they may require the information from various people connected with the company. They can ask all of them or some of them. The people who may be required are:

(a) current or former officers of the company (*i.e.* directors, managers or secretaries)[49];

(b) anyone who has taken part in the formation of the company within one year before the administrationr, appointment of receiver or appointment of provisional liquidator (if no provisional liquidator the date of the winding-up order)[50];

(c) persons who are current employees of the company or who have been employees within the last year who, the administrator, receiver or liquidator is of the opinion, are capable of giving the requisite information[51];

(d) persons who have been directors, managers, secretary or employees of any company who is a director, manager or secretary of the company, or has been a director, manager or secretary of the company within a year.[52]

These statements of affairs must be verified by affidavit by the persons required to submit them.[53] The administrator, receiver or liquidator respectively may release any person from any requirement if they think fit.[54]

Abstract of receipts and payments

18–10   The Insolvency (Scotland) Rules lay down a prescribed form on which administrators, receivers and liquidators have to report what money they have received and what money they have paid out during the

---

[46] Insolvency Act 1986, ss.2(3) and 3(2), and r.1.12(6).
[47] *ibid.*, s.3(2), and r.1.11(1).
[48] Insolvency (Scotland) Rules 1986, r.1.11(2).
[49] Insolvency Act 1986, new Sch.B1, para.47(3), ss. 66(3) and 131(3).
[50] *ibid.*, new Sch.B1, para.47(3), 66(3) and 131(3).
[51] *ibid.*, new Sch.B1, para.47(3), 66(3) and 131(3).
[52] *ibid.*, new Sch.B1, para.47(3), 66(3) and 131(3).
[53] *ibid.*, new Sch.B1, para.47(2), 66(2) and 131(2).
[54] *ibid.*, new Sch.B1, para.48(3), 66(5), and 131(5).

course of their administrations, receiverships and liquidations, in accordance with their reporting duties set out in para.7.[55] The forms for administrators and receivers are the same and require details of receipts and payments and totals from the previous abstract carried forward and added to the receipts and payments within the period to which the current abstract relates. The form for liquidators has a similar style in relation to receipts and payments, but also has a section setting out an "Analysis of Balance", which breaks down the balance of receipts over payments in the hands of the liquidator into: (a) cash in the hands of the liquidator; (b) balances on current account or deposit receipt; and (c) investments made by the liquidator.

There is also a section headed "Progress Report". This merely sets out in brief the estimated assets and liabilities at the date of the commencement of the winding up in accordance with the statement of affairs, setting down the assets and inserting figures for secured creditors, debenture holders, preferential claims and services, and leads to the sum which should be available for unsecured creditors. There is then a third section which requires the following:

(a) total amount of the capital paid up at the commencement of the winding up;
(b) a description with relevant estimated financial figures of changes in the projected financial state of affairs of the company from that originally projected in the statement of affairs;
(c) a description and estimated value of outstanding unrealised assets of the company;
(d) causes which might delay the termination of the winding up; and
(e) the period which the liquidator projects that he will need to complete the winding up.

The reason for the "Analysis of Balance" and "Progress Report" in the case of liquidations is to give the creditors and contributories a running report of the likely dividend, if any, they are going to get in accord with their particular claim. Where there is a supervisor of a voluntary arrangement no style of abstract is prescribed, although the style of the return is prescribed.[56] The accounting date is the date of the supervisor's appointment or of the end day of his last abstract.[57] Most abstracts will be quite simple but, where a complicated scheme is involved, detail should be given of the scheme so that it is clear from the abstract whether the scheme is working.

Reporting requirements in relation to abstracts and progress reports

Administrators, receivers, liquidators and supervisors of voluntary **18–11** arrangements have slightly different reporting requirements. They are as follows:

---

[55] Administrations—Form 2.9 (Scot); receiverships—Form 3.2 (Scot); and liquidations—Form 4.5 (Scot).
[56] Form 1.3 (Scot).
[57] Insolvency (Scotland) Rules 1986, r.1.21(3).

(1) Administrators

The administrator is under a statutory duty to send to the court, to the Accountant in Bankruptcy,[58] and to each creditor a progress report.[59] The progress report must be sent within six weeks from the end of the six months after the date of his appointment and within six weeks of every subsequent period of six months. He must also send a progress report within six weeks after he ceases to act as an administrator.[60]

(2) Receivers

18–12 The receiver is under a statutory duty to send an abstract of his receipts and payments[61] to the Accountant in Bankruptcy, the holder of a floating charge by virtue of which he was appointed, and the members of the creditors' committee if there is one.[62] The receiver must send the abstract within two months from the end of 12 months after his appointment and thereafter at 12–monthly intervals. He must also send an abstract within two months after he ceases to act as a receiver.[63]

(3) Liquidators

18–13 The liquidator is under a statutory duty to send to the Accountant in Bankruptcy a statement if the winding up of a company is not concluded within one year after its commencement.[64] The first statement must be sent not more than 30 days after the end of that year, and subsequent statements must be sent not more than 30 days after the end of each accounting period after that year.[65] The statute lays down that the report must not only give particulars in relation to the proceedings in the liquidation but also the position of the liquidation. The prescribed form includes an abstract or statement as well as a progress report.

(4) Supervisors of voluntary arrangements

18–14 Where there is a supervisor of a voluntary arrangement he shall send, every 12 months, an abstract of receipts and payments to the court, the Registrar of Companies, the company, those creditors bound by the arrangement and, when the company is not in liquidation, to the company's auditors.[66]

Annual accounts

(1) Receivers

18–15 In addition to his duty to prepare an abstract of his receipts and payments, the receiver has a duty, as the company's agent, to keep sufficient accounting records to enable the company to comply with

---

[58] It is thought that the reference to the "registrar" in the rule is mistaken.
[59] Insolvency (Scotland) Rules 1986, r.2.38(1), as substituted by SI 2003/2111.
[60] *ibid.*, r.2.38(1), as substituted by SI 2003/2111.
[61] Form 3.2 (Scot).
[62] Insolvency (Scotland) Rules 1986, r.3.9(1).
[63] *ibid.*, r.3.9(1).
[64] Insolvency Act 1986, s.192(1).
[65] Insolvency (Scotland) Rules 1986, r.4.11, as amended by the Insolvency (Scotland) Amendment Rules 1987, Sch., art.13.
[66] *ibid.*, r.1.21(2).

s.221 of the Companies Act 1985, as amended by s.2 of the Companies Act 1989, in relation to accounting, *i.e.* sufficient to disclose with reasonable accuracy, at any time, the financial position of the company at that time.[67]

(2) Administrators

It is thought that administrators are under the same duty as receivers **18–16** in relation to the keeping of accounting records. An administrator, as deemed agent of the company, is under a duty to keep accounting records. (There is a provision in the Insolvency (Scotland) Rules 1986 that the requirement of a receiver to send abstracts of his receipts and payments is "without prejudice to the receiver's duty to render proper accounts required otherwise".[68] This is probably a reference to the generally accepted accounting duties of a receiver in terms of s.221 of the Companies Act 1985, as amended by s.2 of the Companies Act 1989. Surprisingly, there is no direct reference to this in relation to administrators.)

Final accounts

(1) Voluntary windings up

Only in the case of liquidations can one properly talk about a "final **18–17** account". In the case of a receivership and an administration, there is no final account, merely the last account after they cease to act.[69] In the case of a members' voluntary winding up and a creditors' voluntary winding up the liquidator is under a statutory duty to make up an account of the winding up, showing how it has been conducted and how the company's property has been disposed of.[70] In the case of a members' voluntary winding up, he must then call a general meeting of the company for the purpose of laying before it the account, and giving an explanation of it.[71] Similarly, in the case of a creditors' voluntary winding up, he must then call a general meeting of the company and a meeting of the creditors for the purpose of laying the account before the meeting and giving an explanation of it.[72] Within one week of the meeting/meetings, the liquidator is under an obligation to send to the Registrar of Companies a copy of the account. He must also make a return of the holding of the meeting/ meetings and of their dates.[73] There is a prescribed form for the liquidator's statement of account in members' and creditors' voluntary windings up, namely Form 4.26 (Scot). The statement of account in voluntary windings up briefly gives a statement of receipts taken in by the liquidator less his outgoings giving "net realisations". There is then a flow chart showing how the net realisations have been distributed in order of: (a) expenses of solicitor to

---

[67] *Smith Ltd v Middleton* [1979] 3 All E.R. 942.
[68] Insolvency (Scotland) Rules 1986, r.3.9(4).
[69] *ibid.*, rr.2.17(1) and 3.9(1).
[70] Insolvency Act 1986, ss.94(1) and 106(1).
[71] *ibid.*, s.94(1).
[72] *ibid.*, s.106(1).
[73] *ibid.*, ss.94(3) and 106(3).

liquidator; (b) other legal expenses; (c) liquidator's remuneration; (d) other liquidation expenses; (e) payments to debenture holders; (f) payments to preferential creditors; (g) payments to unsecured creditors (dividends in the £); and (h) returns to contributories with a division according to the type of shares.

(2) Winding up by the court

18–18   In a winding up by the court, the liquidator must submit a final liquidator's statement of receipts and payments but this is still in the form of previous statements; namely Form 4.5 (Scot). The final return should be sent immediately once the assets have been fully realised and distributed, notwithstanding that six months may not have elapsed since the previous return (returns have to be at six-monthly intervals).[74] The Form 4.26 (Scot) for voluntary windings up is a more extensive form than Form 4.5 (Scot) for windings up by the court when it is serving as a final return. (The format of Form 4.5 (Scot) makes no mention of distributions to contributories.) It is suggested that a schedule is attached to the liquidator's statement of receipts and payments in a final return to give a breakdown of the receipts, a breakdown of the statement of assets and liabilities and finally a breakdown of payments running through the items in the order that they are found in a statement of account in a voluntary winding up. Obviously, where there is no payment to contributories, the final section of the account can be omitted.

(3) Supervisor of voluntary arrangement

18–19   In terms of r.1.23 the supervisor must send to the members, creditors who are bound by the scheme and the Registrar of Companies, a copy of a report by him, summarising all receipts and payments made by him in pursuance of the arrangement, and explaining any difference in the actual implementation of it as compared with the proposal approved by the creditors' and company meetings. The report to the Registrar goes with Form 1.4 (Scot).

Reports under Company Directors Disqualification Act 1986

18–20   Liquidators, administrators and receivers are under a duty to make a report to the Secretary of State if it appears to them that a person who has been a director of the company which has become insolvent has conducted himself in a way which renders him unfit to be concerned in the management of a company.[75] The matters which are relevant in considering whether a director is unfit are listed in Pt II of Sch.I to the Company Directors Disqualification Act 1986. From an accounting point of view, the key parts are:

(a) para.6 of Sch.1: "the extent of the directors' responsibility for the causes of the company becoming insolvent";

---

[74] R.4.11.
[75] Company Directors Disqualification Act 1986, s.7(3).

(b) para.7 of Sch.1: "the extent of the directors' responsibility for any failure by the company to supply any goods or services which have been paid for (in whole or in part)".

The liquidator, administrator or receiver must form a view as to the accounting information which was available and should have been available to directors, and whether that should have put them on the alert. In determining whether a company was insolvent, the company is now deemed to be unable to pay its debts if it is proved to the satisfaction of the court that the value of the company's assets is less than the amount of its liabilities, taking into account its contingent and prospective liabilities.

General accounting matters in insolvency accounts

There are no accounting conventions in Scotland which specifically **18–21** govern the preparation of insolvency accounts, which are not now implicit in the legally prescribed forms. Although, if the business continues to trade, other conventions will be applicable to the trading accounts. There are also no Standard Statements of Accounting Practice (SSAPs). The following paragraphs give one or two points of practical guidance.

(1) Assets—realisable value

In the "statement of affairs", which is now the fundamental account- **18–22** ing document in insolvency, the figures which are being asked for are the sums which the various assets are estimated to produce. To highlight how this concept differs from a normal annual account, a separate column is given in list A for "book values". Apart from liquid assets like bills of exchange, promissory notes, stocks and shares and short-term loans, the estimated realisable value of assets is likely to differ from book value. Normally stock is put in at cost and "work in progress" is listed at cost. This means that, in a company healthily trading, its stock and work in progress has a book value less than the market value of those items. The liquidator will have to look very carefully to whether the "distress" element of an insolvency sale is going to reduce the value of these items or whether there is a sufficient market for there to be no "distress element".

In relation to heritable property, book value is normally historical cost. A liquidator should take appropriate steps to ascertain the present value of heritable property which might require him to commission an independent valuer's report. In relation to vehicles, they are probably being written down over five years and the book value may not reflect current market value. Plant and machinery is much more difficult to value, and valuation will depend on the type of machinery. If the machinery is specialised for a particular trade which is now redundant, there could be no market at all for the machinery.

(2) Patents, trade marks

Patents, trade marks and other intellectual property may not have a **18–23** book value in the last set of accounts. Trade marks and patents are dependent for their value on there being a demand for the goods for which they are patents or trade marks. If the market for these goods collapses (which often happens on insolvency), then the company has properly not ascribed them any book value. Great care should be taken not to dissipate the value of trade marks. The services of a trade mark agent should be taken for valuation purposes and guidance.

(3) Goodwill

18–24   As in the case of patents and trade marks, the last accounts will not normally have a figure for goodwill. Secondly, liquidation often leads to the dissipation of goodwill. However, this is not necessarily the case if parts of the business can be salvaged. Sometimes the goodwill is attached to a heritable property, in which case the goodwill will be valued under the estimated realisable value of the heritable property.

(4) Going concern

18–25   Assets will normally fetch more in the market place if they are sold as part of a going concern. Accordingly, the statement of affairs should list any part of the business which is likely to be able to be sold as a going concern. A trading account should be attached, as well as a balance sheet listing the assets of the going concern. This balance sheet could include the goodwill asset.

(5) Contingent liabilities

18–26   In normal accounts, a potential liability only has to be classed as a "contingent liability" if it is considered that there is a realistic possibility of the liability crystallising within the foreseeable future. In a liquidation account, however, it is important to list all liabilities, however contingent, with a detailed analysis of them.

(6) Deficiency account

18–27   The statement of affairs in an insolvent company is bound to show a deficiency. A deficiency account attempts to explain in financial terms how the deficiency has arisen under heads such as (a) the amount by which the assets have been written down for the purposes of the statement of affairs; (b) the liabilities arising as a result of the insolvency; and (c) the trading loss since the last accounts.

CHAPTER 19

PROOF AND RANKING OF CLAIMS

Proof and admissibility of claims

Creditors in a liquidation may prove in respect of all debts of the **19–01** company or claims against the company. The claims may be present or future, contingent, certain or uncertain, liquid or illiquid.

The creditor must submit his claim to the liquidator using a statutory style of form[1] (no oath required), and producing an account or voucher (according to the nature of the debt claimed) which constitutes *prima facie* evidence of the debt.[2] The liquidator may dispense with this requirement in respect of any debt or class of debt.[3] The liquidator, in order to satisfy himself as to the validity or amount of a claim submitted by a creditor, may require the creditor to produce further evidence, or require any other person who he believes can produce relevant evidence, to produce such evidence.[4] In order to vote at a meeting of the creditors, a claim must be submitted at or before the meeting.[5] In order to receive a dividend out of the assets of the company in respect of any accounting period, the claim must be submitted not later than eight weeks before the end of the accounting period.[6]

In a compulsory liquidation, in terms of s.153 of the Insolvency Act 1986: "The court may fix a time or times within which creditors are to prove their debt or claims or to be excluded from the benefit of any distribution made before those debts are proved". This rule would appear to be procedural and is subordinated to the general principle of *pari passu* treatment of all creditors applied by s.107 of the Insolvency Act 1986 to voluntary windings up, and by r.4.66(4) of the Insolvency (Scotland) Rules 1986 to compulsory windings up. Accordingly the creditor is entitled to prove late and have payments made to him in respect of dividends in which he has not participated. In terms of s.52(9) of the Bankruptcy (Scotland) Act 1985[7]:

"Where a creditor submits a claim to the liquidator later than 8 weeks before the end of an accounting period but more than 8

---

[1] Form 4.7 (Scot), as substituted by Insolvency (Scotland) Regulations 2003 (SI 2003/2109(S.8)).

[2] Insolvency (Scotland) Rules 1986, r.4.15(1).

[3] *ibid.*, r.4.15(2).

[4] Bankruptcy (Scotland) Act 1985, s.48(5) as applied to liquidations by Insolvency (Scotland) Rules 1986, r.4.16(1).

[5] *ibid.*, r.4.15(1).

[6] *ibid.*, r.4.15(1).

[7] As applied to liquidations by Insolvency (Scotland) Rules 1986, r.4.68(1).

weeks before the end of a subsequent accounting period in respect of which, after making allowance for contingencies, funds are available for the payment of a dividend, the liquidator shall, if he accepts the claim in whole or in part, pay to the creditor—

(a) the same dividend or dividends as has or have been paid to creditors of the same class in respect of any accounting period or periods; and

(b) whatever dividend may be payable to him in respect of the said subsequent accounting period:

Provided that paragraph (a) above shall be without prejudice to any dividend which has already been paid."

The effect of the above provision is to allow proving late, but not to allow any disturbance of dividends already paid. It would be difficult in practice to reclaim dividends already paid. A creditor must accordingly, at the very latest, submit his claim at least eight weeks before the end of the final accounting period, and then he runs the risk that there may not be sufficient funds to pay him the dividends in which he has not participated.

The presentation of a petition for liquidation or the concurrence in such a petition, or the submission of a claim in the liquidation interrupts prescription and bars the effect of any enactment or rule of law relating to the limitation of actions in any part of the United Kingdom.[8] A debt or any other liability arising out of a market contract which is the subject of default proceedings by an investment exchange or clearing house recognised under the Financial Services Act 1986 may not be claimed until the completion of those proceedings.[9]

Valuation of claims

(1) Amount which may be claimed generally

19–02   A creditor is entitled to claim the accumulated sum of principal and any interest which is due on the debt as at the date of the commencement of the winding up.[10]

(2) Discounts

19–03   In calculating the amount of his claim, a creditor must deduct any discount (other than any discount for payment in cash) which is allowable by contract or course of dealing between the creditor and the company or by the usage of trade.[11]

---

[8] Bankruptcy (Scotland) Act 1985, ss.8(5), 22(8), 73(5), as applied by the Insolvency (Scotland) Rules 1986, r.4.76.

[9] Companies Act 1989, s.159(4).

[10] Bankruptcy (Scotland) Act 1985, Sch.1, para.1(1) as applied to liquidations by Insolvency (Scotland) Rules 1986, r.4.16(1).

[11] *ibid.*, Sch.1, para.1(3) as applied to liquidations by Insolvency (Scotland) Rules 1986, r.4.16(1).

(3) Future debts

In terms of para.1(2) of Sch.1 to the Bankruptcy (Scotland) Act 1985[12]: **19–04**

> "If a debt does not depend on a contingency but would not be payable but for the liquidation until after the date of commencement of winding up, the amount of the claim shall be calculated as if the debt were payable on the date of commencement of winding up but subject to the deduction of interest at whichever is the greater of—
>
> (a) the prescribed rate at the date of commencement of the winding up; and
> (b) the rate applicable to that date apart from the liquidation— from the said date until the date for payment of the debt."

What the above provision aims at is a "discounting" of a future debt to give it its "net present value". The provision, however, does not result in "net present value" being arrived at. The "net present value" is meant to be that sum which, if interest were payable thereon from the present until the date when the future debt is due, would, together with the accumulated interest, equal the future debt (*e.g.* if the sum were put in the bank the future debt could be met by the banked sum with accumulated interest).

What the provision achieves is a very perverse result. If, for example, a debt of £1,000 was due to a bank five years from the date of winding up and overdraft interest was 20 per cent, the bank would have to deduct five times 20 per cent of £1,000 from the £1,000. This would result in the bank not being able to claim anything for its future debt.

(4) Contingent debts

A creditor is not entitled to vote or claim for a contingent debt. **19–05** However, he may apply to the liquidator or, if there is no liquidator, to the court to put a value on debt in so far as it is contingent.[13] The value which the liquidator or the court puts on the contingent debt is then the sum which the creditor is entitled to claim and no more. Where the debt subject to the contingency is an annuity, a cautioner for its payment is liable only for the value so determined. That is not the position, however, of cautioners in respect of debts other than annuities. Any interested person may appeal to the court against a valuation of a contingent debt and the court may affirm or vary that valuation.[14]

(5) Secured debts

The term "security" is widely defined by s.248(b) of the Insolvency **19–06** Act 1986 and includes "any security (whether heritable or moveable), any floating charge and any right of lien or preference and any right of

---

[12] As applied to liquidations by Insolvency (Scotland) Rules 1986, r.4.16(1).

[13] Bankruptcy (Scotland) Act 1985, Sch.1, para.3 as applied to liquidations by Insolvency (Scotland) Rules 1986, r.4.16(1).

[14] *ibid.*, Sch.1, para.3(3) as applied to liquidations by Insolvency (Scotland) Rules 1986, r.4.16(1).

retention (other than a right of compensation or set off)''. Inhibitions, arrestments in security and a right of retention over the future proceeds of insurance policies have been held to come within the meaning of that expression.[15]

In calculating the amount of his claim, a secured creditor must deduct the value of any security as estimated by him. He is, however, entitled to surrender the security. The liquidator may, at any time after the expiry of 12 weeks from the date of commencement of winding up, require a secured creditor, at the expense of the company's assets, to discharge the security or convey or assign to the liquidator on payment to the creditor of the value specified by the creditor; and the amount in respect of which the creditor shall then be entitled to claim shall be any balance of his debt remaining after receipt of such payment.[16] Where a creditor realises his security, he must deduct the amount realised (less the expenses of realisation) from the amount of his claim.[17] Where a liquidator requires a secured creditor to discharge a security, the creditor may not make a further claim specifying a different value for the security.[18]

In terms of s.56 of the Bankruptcy (Scotland) Act 1913 a creditor for voting purposes had to put a specified value on the obligation of any co-obligant who was liable to relief to the company and on any security which he held from an obligant liable in relief to the company or from whom the company had a right of relief. This provision is repealed.

(6) Co-obligant/Rule against double ranking

19–07   Where there is a co-obligant with the company and a creditor proceeds in the first instance against that co-obligant and secures payment of his debt, the co-obligant is subrogated to the creditor's claim and will obtain a ranking in place of the creditor.[19] The co-obligant who has paid the debt may require and obtain at his own expense from the creditor an assignation of the debt on payment of the debt, and thereafter may in respect of that debt submit a claim, and vote and draw a dividend.[20] Where there is a co-obligant to the company, and the creditor assents to a composition, the co-obligant is not freed or discharged from liability for the debt as a result.[21] If, however, a creditor draws a dividend from the liquidation and then obtains payment of the deficiency from a co-obligant, the co-obligant cannot rank in the liquidation because of the rule against double ranking.[22]

---

[15] *Goudy*, p.187.

[16] Bankruptcy (Scotland) Act 1985, Sch.1, para.5(2) as applied to liquidations by Insolvency (Scotland) Rules 1986, r.4.16(1).

[17] *ibid.*, Sch.1, para.5(3) as applied to liquidations by Insolvency (Scotland) Rules 1986, r.4.16(1).

[18] Insolvency (Scotland) Rules 1986, r.4.15(4).

[19] Gloag and Irvine, *Rights in Security*, pp.831–832.

[20] Bankruptcy (Scotland) Act 1985, s.60(3) as applied to liquidations by Insolvency (Scotland) Rules 1986, r.4.16(1).

[21] *ibid.*, s.60(1) as applied to liquidations by Insolvency (Scotland) Rules 1986, r.4.16(1).

[22] Bell, *Comm.*, ii, 420; *Mackinnon v Monkhouse* (1881) 9 R. 393.

A special problem arises where the co-obligant holds a security over any of the company's assets. The creditor may choose to claim in the first instance either against the co-obligant or against the company. At common law, if the creditor adopted the latter course, the loss to the company's assets would be considerably greater, since the co-obligant would not be required to account for his security. To avoid this mischief, it is provided by s.60(2) of the Bankruptcy (Scotland) Act 1985[23] that:

"Where

(a) a creditor has had a claim accepted in whole or in part; and

(b) a co-obligant holds a security over any part of the company's estate, the co-obligant shall account to the liquidator so as to put the company in the same position as if the co-obligant had paid the debt to the creditor and thereafter had had his claim accepted in whole or in part in the liquidation after deduction of the value of the security."

(7) Foreign currency claims

A creditor may state the amount of his claim in a currency other than **19–08** sterling where: (a) his claim is constituted by decree or other order made by a court ordering the company to pay to the creditor a sum expressed in a currency other than sterling; or (b) where it is not so constituted, his claim arises from a contract or bill of exchange in terms of which payment is or may be required to be made by the company to the creditor in a currency other than sterling.

Where a claim is stated in currency other than sterling, the rule is that it shall be converted into sterling at the rate of exchange for that other currency at the mean of the buying and selling spot rates prevailing in the London market at the close of business on the date of commencement of winding up.[24] This means that a creditor may suffer loss as a result of movements in exchange rates. The creditor does not have a claim for that loss. It does not rank *pari passu* with creditors claiming post-liquidation interest.[25] However, there are suggestions in the judgments in the case of *Re Lines Bros*[26] that, in the case of a liquidation which turns out to be solvent, if a foreign currency creditor has been paid less than his full contractual foreign currency debt, it is the duty of the liquidator to make good the shortfall before he pays anything to the shareholders. He has, in effect, a postponed ranking. Although such a debt is not now classed as "postponed", it is thought that it would rank now after "postponed" debts prior to payment to shareholders.

Adjudication of claims

(1) Voting at meetings

At the commencement of every meeting of creditors (other than a **19–09** statutory meeting) the liquidator must accept or reject the claim of each creditor for the purpose of voting at that meeting.[27]

---

[23] As applied to liquidations by Insolvency (Scotland) Rules 1986, r.4.16(1).

[24] *ibid.*, r.4.17.

[25] *Re Lines Bros Ltd (In Liquidation)* [1983] Ch. 1; [1982] 2 All E.R. 183.

[26] *ibid.*

[27] Bankruptcy (Scotland) Act 1985, s.49(1) as applied to liquidations by Insolvency (Scotland) Rules 1986, r.4.16(1).

(2) Adjudication for dividend payment

19–10   The liquidator must accept or reject every claim submitted to him at least four weeks before the end of every accounting period, if funds are going to be available for payment of a dividend.[28] If the claim is rejected, the liquidator must forthwith notify the creditor giving reasons for the rejection. In the case of both acceptance and rejection, the liquidator must record in the sederunt book his decision on the claim specifying: (1) the amount of the claim accepted by him; (2) the category of debt, and the value of any security, as decided by him; and (3) if he is rejecting the claim, his reasons therefor.[29]

The adjudication for voting purposes does not affect the adjudication made for the purpose of entitlement to a dividend. This is because it may be impracticable at the stage of a meeting to determine whether or not the debt truly subsists.

(3) Appeal from adjudication

19–11   The company or any creditor, may, if dissatisfied with the acceptance or rejection of any claim, appeal to the court in relation to the amount of the claim accepted, the categorisation of the debt, the valuing of a security, and in relation to reasons given for the rejection of a claim.[30] If the acceptance or rejection is in relation to voting, the appeal to the court must be within two weeks of the acceptance or rejection, and where the acceptance or rejection is in relation to dividend, the appeal must be not later than two weeks before the end of the accounting period.[31] If the deadline is missed, it is suggested that recourse should be had to the court's power to cure defects.[32]

APPLICATION OF ASSETS IN WINDING UP

(1) *Pari passu* principle

19–12   The assets of a company in voluntary liquidation are to be applied to the discharge of its liabilities. In terms of s.107 of the Insolvency Act 1986, a company's debts, subject to the provisions relating to preferential debts, must be paid *pari passu*. Preferential debts must also be paid *pari passu*.[33] By statutory instrument the *pari passu* principle has also been applied in Scotland to debts in a compulsory winding up.[34] A provision in a contract under which, in the event of a winding up, the company's assets are not to be distributed *pari passu* among creditors can be valid in

---

[28] Bankruptcy (Scotland) Act 1985, s.49(2) as applied to liquidations by Insolvency (Scotland) Rules 1986, r.4.16(1).

[29] *ibid.*, s.49(4) and (5) as applied to liquidations by Insolvency (Scotland) Rules 1986, r.4.16(1).

[30] *ibid.*, s.49(6) as applied to liquidations by Insolvency (Scotland) Rules 1986, r.4.16(1).

[31] *ibid.*, s.49(6) as applied to liquidations by Insolvency (Scotland) Rules 1986, r.4.16(1).

[32] See Chap.4.

[33] Insolvency Act 1986, s.175(2)(a).

[34] Insolvency (Scotland) Rules 1986, r.4.66(4).

Scotland. Provided the contract is between creditors in respect of their rights between themselves and no interfering with the rights of the general body of creditors.[35] Section 63(1) of the Insolvency Act 1986 enables the court to give directions to a receiver in respect of any matter arising in connection with "the performance by him of his functions". However, this does not entitle the court to impose a requirement, not only on the receiver, but on those who are making claims against the receiver when the effect would be to prevent the raising or continuance of an action in the court in terms of the relevant existing rules, unless that additional requirement had been satisfied. Nor would an appeal to the *nobile officium* be likely to be successful.[36] Exceptions to this rule are the netting agreements on certain recognised exchanges which are ring-fenced in terms of Pt VII of the Companies Act 1989 and subject to their own clearing before the general law takes effect.

(2) Subordinated debt

Just as the *pari passu* principle is invoked to avoid a creditor gaining **19–13** an advantage in a liquidation, it also entails that a creditor is not entitled to subordinate his debt in England. Subordinated debt is allowed in several countries and the Cork Committee[37] recommended that such an option be enforceable in Britain. This was not accepted. It is considered, however, that a term of a contract which made the payment of a debt subject to the contingency that other debts were paid would be enforceable in Scotland.[38]

Order of priority in liquidations

In terms of r.4.66(1) of the Insolvency (Scotland) Rules 1986: **19–14**

"The funds of the company's assets shall be distributed by the liquidator to meet the following expenses and debts in the order in which they are mentioned:

(a) the expenses of the liquidation;
(b) in the case of a winding up order, if there is a CVA in force, the expenses of the CVA;
(c) any preferential debts within the meaning of section 386 (excluding any interest which has been accrued thereon to the date of commencement of the winding up within the meaning of section 129);
(d) ordinary debts, that is to say a debt which is neither a secured debt nor a debt mentioned in any other subparagraph of this paragraph;

---

[35] See Chap.16. *British Eagle International Airlines Ltd v CIE Nationale Air France* [1975] 2 All E.R. 390; *Carreras Rothmans Ltd v Freeman Matthews Treasure Ltd (in Liquidation)* [1985] 1 All E.R. 155; [1984] B.C.L.C. 420.

[36] *Jamieson, Petrs*, 1997 S.L.C.R. 411; this decision means that the Scottish procedure available under s.63(1) of the Insolvency Act 1986 is more restricted than the court can make under the comparable s.35 of that Act in England.

[37] Report of the Review Committee on Insolvency Law and Practice, Cm.8558, paras 1448–1449.

[38] See Chap.16.

(e) interest at the official rate on—

    (i) the preferential debts, and
    (ii) the ordinary debts,

between the said date of commencement of the winding up and the date of payment of the debt; and

(f) any postponed debt."

Secured debts

19–1515   In terms of r.4.66(6), the order of priority must not affect the right of a secured creditor which is preferable to the rights of the liquidator. Accordingly, secured creditors may redeem their securities without reference to the liquidator, or the liquidator may require them to discharge the security by payment to him of the value of the security.[39] A problem arises in the case of a receiver being appointed after the commencement of the winding up. Following the ruling in *Manley, Petr*,[40] a holder of a floating charge may appoint a receiver after the commencement of winding up, and the receiver takes precedence over the liquidator. This means that the receiver is liable for the payment of the secured and preferential creditors of the company. This would give preferential creditors an interest in having a receiver appointed, and the receiver would have a statutory duty to pay the preferential creditors and then the holder of the floating charge. There is an unfortunate failure in the legislation to deal with the expenses of the liquidation, where a receiver is appointed after winding up.[41] The preferential creditors have priority in a winding up to the holder of the floating charge.[42]

Expenses of the liquidation

19–16   The court has a discretion in the event of the assets of a company being insufficient to satisfy the liabilities to make an order as to the payment out of the assets of the company of the expenses incurred in the winding up in such order of priority as the court thinks just.[43] (By r.4.66(1) of the Insolvency (Scotland) Rules 1986 as referred to above, expenses of a voluntary arrangement in force prior to a petition for winding up appear to rank immediately after the expenses of the liquidation. This is anomalous since the expenses of a prior insolvency procedure should rank before the expenses of the liquidation.) Subject to the court's discretion, there is a legal order of priority. The expenses of the liquidation have the following order of priority:

---

[39] Bankruptcy (Scotland) Act 1985, Sch.1, para.5(2) as applied to liquidations by Insolvency (Scotland) Rules 1986, r.4.16(1), see para.19–06.

[40] 1985 S.L.T. 42.

[41] See *Buchler v Talbot* [2004] All E.R. 1289, in which the House of Lords ruled that none of the expenses of winding up an English company were payable out of assets subject to a floating charge until principal and interest charged thereon had been paid.

[42] Insolvency Act 1986, s.175(2)(b).

[43] *ibid.*, ss.112 and 156.

(a) any outlays properly chargeable or incurred by the provisional liquidator in carrying out his functions in the liquidation, except those outlays specifically mentioned below;
(b) the cost, or proportionate cost, of any caution provided by a provisional liquidator, liquidator or special manager;
(c) the remuneration of the provisional liquidator (if any);
(d) the expenses of the petitioner in the liquidation, and of any person appearing in the liquidation whose expenses are allowed by the court;
(e) the remuneration of the special manager (if any);
(f) any allowance made by the liquidator for the cost of the preparation of a statement of affairs;
(g) the remuneration or emoluments of any person who has been employed by the liquidator to perform any services for the company, as required by law;
(h) the remuneration of the liquidator determined in accordance with the rules relating thereto; and
(i) the amount of any corporation tax on chargeable gains accruing on the realisation of any asset of the company (without regard to whether the realisation is effected by the liquidator, a secured creditor or otherwise).[44]

If there are no assets the liquidator is not entitled to receive any remuneration (unless an outside party is underwriting the costs of the liquidation) and he is personally liable for legal expenses incurred in the liquidation. He may be personally liable for other expenses of the liquidation if any contracting party has insisted on a personal guarantee from the liquidator.

Preferential debts

Demise of Crown Preferences

Section 386 of and Sch.6 to the Insolvency Act 1986 made major **19–17** changes to the previous categories of preferential debts in a liquidation and receivership. The main changes were as follows:

(1) direct taxes to the Inland Revenue ceased to be preferential debts;
(2) local rates ceased to be preferential debts;
(3) debts due to the Customs and Excise remained preferential debts but only in respect of a more limited period.

Enterprise Act

As of September 15, 2003, s.251(2) of the Enterprise Act 2002 provided **19–18** that debts due to the Inland Revenue, debts due to Customs and Excise and Social Security contributions shall cease to be preferential debts,

---

[44] Insolvency (Scotland) Rules 1986, r.4.67(1), as amended by para.32 of the Schedule to the Insolvency (Scotland) Amendment Rules 1987.

which of course may have the unintended consequence that these debts will be enforced more readily now that they no longer have preferential status.

Remaining preferences

Contributions to occupational pension schemes

19–19 Preference is given to any sum which is owed by the company and is a sum to which Sch.4 to the Pension Schemes Act 1993 applies (contributions to occupational pension schemes and state scheme premi5ms).[45]

Remuneration of employees

19–20 Preference is given to the wages or salary (whether payable for time or for piece work or earned wholly or partly by way of commission) of any person who is or has been an employee of the company in respect of services rendered to the company in respect of the whole or any part of the period of four months next before the *relevant*[46] date provided they do not exceed an amount which may be prescribed by regulations made by the Secretary of State.[47] Any remuneration payable by the company to a person in respect of a period of holiday or of absence from work through sickness or any other good cause is deemed to be wages or (as the case may be) salary in respect of services rendered to the company in that period, and includes any sums which, if they had been paid, would have been treated for the purposes of the enactments relating to social security as earnings in respect of that period.[48] Similarly the following payments are also deemed to be wages or salary:

(a) a guarantee payment under s.12(1) of the Employment Protection (Consolidation) Act 1978 (employee without work to do for a day or part of a day);

(b) remuneration on suspension on medical grounds under s.19 of the Employment Protection (Consolidation) Act 1978;

(c) any payment for time off under ss.31(3) (looking for work, etc.) or 31A(4) (antenatal care) of the Employment Protection (Consolidation) Act 1978, or under s.169 of the Trade Union and Labour Relations (Consolidation) Act 1992; or

(d) remuneration under a protective award made by an industrial tribunal under s.189 of the Trade Union and Labour Relations (Consolidation) Act 1992 (redundancy dismissal with compensation).[49]

---

[45] Insolvency (Scotland) Rules 1986, Sch.6, para.8.

[46] For the purposes of the provision the *relevant* date is defined by s.387(3) of the Insolvency Act 1986 as being, in the case of a company ordered to be wound up compulsorily, the date of the first appointment of a provisional liquidator, or, if none was appointed, the date of the holding up order, and in the creditors' winding up, the date of the passing of the resolution for winding up. If there had been a prior administration immediately before the winding up by the court the relevant date is the date that the company entered into administration.

[47] Insolvency (Scotland) Rules 1986, Sch.6, paras 9 and 13.

[48] *ibid.*, Sch.6, para.15.

[49] *ibid.*, Sch.6, para.13(2).

Accrued holiday remuneration

Preference is given to any sums owed by the company by way of **19–21** accrued holiday remuneration in respect of any period of employment before the relevant date[50] to a person whose employment by the company has been terminated, whether before, on or after that date. Where a person's employment has been terminated by or in consequence of his employer going into liquidation or (his employer being a company not in liquidation) by or in consequence of the appointment of a receiver under ss.53(6) or 54(5) of the Insolvency Act 1986, holiday remuneration is deemed to have accrued to that person in respect of any period of employment if, by virtue of his contract of employment or any enactment, that remuneration would have accrued in respect of that period if his employment had continued until he became entitled to be allowed the holiday.[51]

Payments by persons advancing money to the company for wages, etc.

Where third parties have advanced money to the company for the **19–22** purpose of the payment of wages or accrued holiday remuneration, which, if they had not been paid, would have been given priority as above, the persons who have advanced the moneys have priority for these advances.[52] A banker may obtain the maximum benefit under this provision by opening a separate "wages account" out of which advances are made for the payment of wages. The money must not only be advanced "for the purpose of paying the wages", but the money so advanced must have actually paid the wages, so reducing the employee's priority claims.[53] In addition, if loans are made by the bank to the company and these are secured, the bank may, on realising the security, appropriate the proceeds to paying off first the non-preferential part of the company's indebtedness, so that its preferential rights can be exercised in full in respect of any balance outstanding.[54] The bank faces a difficulty by the operation of the rule in *Clayton's Case*,[55] to the effect that any credit received must first be applied in discharging the earliest debit on the account which may have the effect of reducing its potential preferential claim. A further difficulty arises where a bank lends money on the "wages account" but at the same time, by some arrangement, money is lodged in another account by the company.[56] Briefly, it has been held that, where there were two interdependent accounts of which one was a wages account, and the bank would not have met the wages account unless the other account was maintained in sufficient credit to cover the wages account, the bank never did in fact make advances to meet wages. The company, when it drew on its wages account, was really drawing its own moneys standing to the credit of the other

---

[50] For "relevant" see para.19–20.
[51] Insolvency Act 1986, Sch.6, paras 10 and 14.
[52] *ibid.*, Sch.6, para.11.
[53] *Re E.J. Morel (1934) Ltd* [1962] Ch. 21; *Re Yeovil Glove Co Ltd* [1965] Ch. 148, CA.
[54] *Re William Hall (Contractors) Ltd* [1967] 1 W.L.R. 948.
[55] *Devaynes v Noble* (1816) 1 Mer. 572.
[56] For a discussion, see Greene and Fletcher, *Law and Practice of Receivership in Scotland* (2nd ed., 1992) paras 9.22–9.28.

account.[57] However, a preference has been held to be obtained for sums transferred to the wages account by debiting an overdrawn current account.[58]

Payments under Reserve Forces (Safeguard of Employment) Act 1985

19–23   Preference is given to any amount which is ordered (whether before or after the *relevant* date)[59] to be paid by the company under the Reserve Forces (Safeguard of Employment) Act 1985, and is so ordered in respect of a default made by the company at that date in the discharge of its obligations under that Act, provided that the amount does not exceed such amount as may be prescribed by regulation by the Secretary of State.[60] The same provisions in relation to wages and accrued holiday remuneration apply in relation to such orders.

Levies on coal and steel production

19–24   Preference is also given to debts comprising any sums due at the relevant date[61] from the company in respect of (1) the levies on the production of coal and steel referred to in Arts 49 and 50 of the ECSC Treaty; or (2) any surcharge for delay in payment of the levies.[62]

Prescribed Part/Special Status

19–25   A special type of preferential status is accorded to the "prescribed part" in terms of s.176A of the Insolvency Act 1986, as inserted by s.252 of the Enterprise Act 2002. This sum to be set aside for ordinary creditors is carved out of the net amount available for payment of a floating charge holder after payment of the preferential creditors (the company's "net property").[63] The prescribed part is 50 per cent of the company's net property on the first £10,000, and then 20 per cent of the rest up to a cap of £600, 000 of net property.[64] If the net property is less than £10,000, and the office holder thinks that the cost of making a distribution to ordinary creditors will be disproportionate to the benefits, he may apply to the court to disapply the provision.[65] There are provisions as to the averments in such an application.[66]

Ordinary debts

19–26   Ordinary debts are defined by r.4.66(1) of the Insolvency (Scotland) Rules 1986 as amended by Art.31 of the Schedule to the Insolvency (Scotland) Amendment Rules 1987 as all debts of a company which are

---

[57] *Re E.J. Morel (1934) Ltd* [1962] Ch. 21.

[58] *Re James R. Rutherford & Sons Ltd* [1964] 3 All E.R. 137.

[59] For "relevant" see para.19–20.

[60] Insolvency Act 1986, Sch.6, para.12. The prescribed amount at the date of publication of this book is £800 in terms of the Insolvency Proceedings (Monetary Limits) Order 1986 (SI 1986/1996).

[61] For "relevant" see para.19–20.

[62] Provided for in Art.50(3) of that Treaty and Art.6 of Decision 3/52 of the High Authority of the Coal and Steel Community; Insolvency Act 1986, Sch.6, para.15A (added by the Insolvency (ECSC Levy Debts) Regulations 1987 (SI 1987/1093). The regulations implement EC Commission Recommendation 86/198 (OJ L144, 29.8.56, p.40)).

[63] Insolvency Act 1986, s.176A(6).

[64] Art.3 of the Insolvency Act 1986 (Prescribed Part) Order 2003 (SI 2003/2097).

[65] Insolvency Act 1986, s.176A(5).

[66] Insolvency (Scotland) Rules 1986, r.7.13A, as inserted by the Enterprise Act 2002 (Consequential Amendments) (Prescribed Part) (Scotland) Order 2003 (SI 2003/2108(S.7)).

neither (1) the expenses of the liquidation and of the administration of any preceding voluntary arrangement; (2) preferential debts; (3) interest on preferential debts and ordinary debts between the date of commencement of the winding up and the payment of the debt; or (4) a postponed debt. They are usually the largest category of debt, but frequently receive no dividend.

Interest on claims

Where there is a surplus remaining after payment of the debts of a **19–27** company proved in a winding up, the surplus is by statute now applied to paying interest on those debts in respect of the periods during which they have been outstanding since the company went into liquidation.[67] In relation to this post-liquidation interest there is no ranking, and the preferred and ordinary creditors rank equally (s.189(3) of the Insolvency Act 1986). The rate of interest payable shall be the greater of the rate of interest specified in the debt contract or that prescribed under the Insolvency Rules.[68] The current "official rate" is 15 per cent.[69]

Postponed debt

Before the Cork reforms a claim which a loser on a foreign currency **19–28** conversion debt might have was treated as a "postponed" debt. Since then r.4.66(2) of the Insolvency (Scotland) Rules 1986 gives a statutory category of postponed debt. In terms of that rule, a postponed debt is also a creditor's right to any alienation which has been reduced or restored to the company's assets under s.242 of the Insolvency Act 1986 or to the proceeds of sale of such an alienation. This definition will apply where a gratuitous alienation has been reduced and the proceeds of the reduction are sufficient to pay the ordinary creditors in full. The alienee then ranks as a postponed creditor for any part of the proceeds of the reduction that is left. The statutory category will precede the creditor claiming a foreign currency loss.

In terms of s.178 of the Companies Act 1985, an obligation by a company to redeem or repurchase its shares, provided it is enforceable prior to winding up and the company could lawfully have made a distribution equal in value during the period between enforceability and winding up, is a debt on the company but postponed to all other debts including shareholders with prior rights.

A final type of debt which is dealt with by statute in so far as it is after a "postponed" debt, is a debt owed by the company as a dividend to the shareholders. It may be taken into account in adjusting the rights of contributories in terms of s.74(2)(f) of the Insolvency Act 1986.

---

[67] Insolvency Act 1986, s.189(2).
[68] *ibid.*, s.189(4) and (5).
[69] Insolvency (Scotland) Rules 1986, r.4.66(2)(b).

CHAPTER 20

CREDITORS' COMMITTEES

Introduction

Under the Insolvency Act 1986, there is provision for the establish- **20–01** ment of creditors' committees in all three legal régimes on insolvency, namely administrations,[1] receiverships,[2] and liquidations.[3] In the case of administrations and receiverships, the committee of creditors is to be known as "the creditors' committee".[4] In liquidations the committee of creditors is to be known as "the liquidation committee".[5] Creditors' committees in administrations and receiverships perform almost exactly the same functions. In liquidations, the liquidation committee has a larger role, although the reforms are not as large as the Cork Committee recommended.[6] It is proposed to treat the creditors' committees in administrations and receiverships together, and then to deal with the liquidation committee.

Creditors' committees in receiverships and administrations

(1) Establishment and membership

An administrator is required within 10 weeks of the company **20–02** entering administration to summon a meeting of the company's creditors.[7] At this meeting, the creditors may establish a creditors' committee.[8] Similarly, a receiver must, within three months (or such longer period as the court may allow) after his appointment, summon a meeting of the company's unsecured creditors in order to give them a report on the receivership.[9] That meeting of creditors may, if it thinks fit, establish a creditors' committee.[10] The committee must consist of at least three and not more than five creditors of the company elected at the meeting. Any creditor of the company who has lodged a claim is eligible

---

[1] Insolvency Act 1986, para.57 of new Sch.B1.
[2] *ibid.*, s.68(1).
[3] *ibid.*, ss.101 and 142(1).
[4] *ibid.*, para.57 of new Sch.B1, and s.68(1).
[5] *ibid.*, ss.101(1) and 142(1).
[6] Report of the Review Committee on Insolvency Law and Practice (Cmnd. 8558) at Chap.19.
[7] Insolvency Act 1986, para.51 of new Sch.B1.
[8] *ibid.*, para.57 of new Sch.B1.
[9] *ibid.*, s.68(1).
[10] *ibid.*, s.68(1).

to be a member of the committee, so long as his claim has not been rejected for the purpose of his entitlement to vote.[11] A body corporate or a partnership may be a member of the committee, but it cannot act as such otherwise than by a representative appointed.[12] The creditors' committee comes into existence when the administrator or receiver issues a certificate of due constitution.[13] If the chairman of the meeting which resolves to establish the committee is not the administrator or receiver, he must forthwith give notice of the resolution to the administrator or receiver and inform him of the names and addresses of the persons elected to be members of the committee.[14] No person may act as a member of the committee unless and until he has agreed to do so, and the administrator's or receiver's certificate of the committee's due constitution must not be issued until at least the minimum number of persons has agreed to act. The receiver or administrator then issues a certificate,[15] which he must send to the Accountant in Bankruptcy.[16] Any change in the establishment of the committee must be reported by the receiver or administrator to the Accountant in Bankruptcy.[17]

(2) Expenses of creditors' committees

20–03   The administrator or receiver must defray any reasonable travelling expenses directly incurred by members of the creditors' committee or their representatives in respect of their attendance at the committee's meetings, or otherwise on the committee's business as an expense of the administration or receivership.[18] This does not apply to any meeting of the committee held within three months of a previous meeting.[19]

(3) Duties, powers and functions of creditors' committee

20–04   The creditors' committee in relation to the administrator or receiver acts in such a manner as may be agreed from time to time with the administrator or receiver.[20] In addition, the creditors' committee in an administration must assist the administrator in discharging his functions.[21] In contrast, the creditors' committee in a receivership has no duty to assist the receiver, because their interests are usually not the same, but rather are under a legal duty to represent to the receiver the view of the unsecured creditors.[22] The creditors' committees may require the administrator or receiver to attend before them at any reasonable time on seven days' notice, and require the administrator or receiver to furnish them with such information relating to the carrying out of his

---

[11] Insolvency (Scotland) Rules 1986, r.2.36(1), as substituted by SI 2003/2111, and 3.4(2).
[12] *ibid.*, r.2.36(1), as substituted by SI 2003/2111, and 3.4(3).
[13] *ibid.*, r.2.36(1), as substituted by SI 2003/2111, 3.6(1) and 4.42(1).
[14] *ibid.*, r.2.36(1), as substituted by SI 2003/2111, 3.6(1), 4.42(2).
[15] Form 4.20 (Scot).
[16] Insolvency (Scotland) Rules 1986, r.2.36(1), as substituted by SI 2003/2111, 3.6(1) and 4.42(5).
[17] *ibid.*, r.2.36(1), as substituted by SI 2003/2111, 3.6(1) and 4.42(6).
[18] *ibid.*, r.2.36(1), as substituted by SI 2003/2111, 3.6(1) and (4) and 4.57(1).
[19] *ibid.*, r.2.36(1), as substituted by SI 2003/2111, 3.6(1) and 4.57(2).
[20] *ibid.*, r.2.36(4), as substituted by SI 2003/2111, and 3.5.
[21] *ibid.*, r.2.36(1), as substituted by SI 2003/2111.
[22] *ibid.*, r.3.5.

functions as they may reasonably require.[23] The committee in an administration is given the specific power on a vacancy occurring in the office of administrator in the absence of any continuing administrator to apply to the court to fill the vacancy.[24] The administrator or receiver must call a first meeting of the committee to take place within three months of his appointment or of the committee's establishment, whichever is the later, and after that he is under an obligation to call a meeting of the creditors' committee if he is requested by a creditor member of the committee. The meeting must then be held within 21 days of the request being received by the administrator or receiver.[25]

Liquidation committee

(1) Establishment and membership

At the first meeting of creditors, the creditors may establish a **20–05** liquidation committee.[26] In addition, in a compulsory winding up only, the liquidator may at any time, if he thinks fit, summon a general meeting of the company's creditors and contributors for the purpose of determining whether such a committee should be established, and if it is so determined, of establishing it.[27] He must also summon a meeting if he is requested, in accordance with the Rules, to do so by one-tenth in value of the company's creditors.[28] The liquidation committee in an insolvent liquidation consists of at least three and not more than five creditors of the company, elected by the meeting of creditors.[29] As in administrations and receiverships, the liquidation committee is constituted when the liquidator issues a certificate of its due constitution. The chairman of the meeting which resolved to establish the committee, if he is not the liquidator, must give notice of the resolution to the liquidator, and inform him of the names and addresses of the persons elected to be members of the committee.[30] The certificate must be sent by the liquidator to the Accountant in Bankruptcy.[31]

(2) Expenses of members of the liquidation committee

Members of the liquidation committee are entitled to reasonable **20–06** travelling expenses as an expense of the liquidation, unless the previous meeting was held less than three months before.[32] The members of the liquidation committee occupy a fiduciary position in relation to the company, and no conflict of interest should arise between their interests and their duty if this can be helped.[33] This is reinforced by the

---

[23] Insolvency Act 1986, para.57(2) of new Sch.B1, and s.68(2).
[24] *ibid.*, para.91(1)(a) of new Sch.B1.
[25] Insolvency (Scotland) Rules 1986, rr.2.36(1), as substituted by SI 2003/2111, 3.6(1) and 4.45.
[26] Insolvency Act 1986, ss.101 and 142.
[27] *ibid.*, s.142(2).
[28] *ibid.*, s.142(3).
[29] Insolvency (Scotland) Rules 1986, r.4.41(1).
[30] *ibid.*, r.4.42(2).
[31] *ibid.*, r.4.42(5), as amended by SI 2003/2111; Form 4.20 (Scot).
[32] Insolvency (Scotland) Rules 1986, r.4.57.
[33] *Re F.T. Hawkins & Co Ltd* [1952] Ch. 881.

Insolvency (Scotland) Rules 1986, which contain detailed provision relating to dealings by committee members. Briefly, a member of a committee is prohibited from receiving out of the company's assets any payment for services given or goods supplied in connection with the liquidation, or obtaining any profit from the liquidation, or acquiring any part of the company's assets.[34] This, however, is allowed (a) with the prior leave of the court; (b) if he does so as a matter of urgency; or (c) by performance of a contract in force before the date on which the company went into liquidation, if the committee member obtains the court's leave for the transaction, having applied for leave without undue delay.[35] Alternatively, he may enter into a transaction with the prior sanction of the liquidation committee, where it is satisfied (after full disclosure of the circumstances) that the transaction will be on normal commercial terms.[36]

(3) Powers of liquidation committee

20–07   The sanction of the committee or the court is necessary in a compulsory winding up, but not a creditors' voluntary winding up, to empower a liquidator to engage in legal proceedings.[37] Similarly, in a compulsory winding up, but not a creditors' winding up, the sanction of the liquidation committee or the court is necessary to enable a liquidator to carry on the business of the company for its beneficial winding up.[38] In addition, the sanction of the liquidation committee or the court is necessary for the liquidator to distribute the estate, shorten the accounting period, pay a class of creditors in full, make compromises and arrangements with creditors or compromises with debtors.[39]

(4) Relationship of liquidator to liquidation committee

20–08   The liquidator is under an obligation to report to the liquidation committee such matters as appear to him, or they have indicated are, of interest to them. In the latter case, the liquidator need not comply if (a) the request is frivolous or unreasonable; (b) the cost of compliance is out of proportion to the importance of the information; (c) there are insufficient assets.[40]

The liquidation committee meets when the liquidator decides, subject to two conditions:

    (a) the first meeting must be held within three months of the committee's establishment or the liquidator's appointment, whichever is later;

    (b) thereafter, meetings must be called if requested by a creditor member of the committee (the meeting to be held within 21

---

[34] Insolvency (Scotland) Rules 1986, r.4.58(2).
[35] *ibid.*, r.4.58(3).
[36] *ibid.*, r.4.58(3)(c); see *Re Gallard* [1896] 1 Q.B. 68.
[37] Insolvency Act 1986, ss.165 and 167 and Sch.4, para.4.
[38] *ibid.*, ss.165 and 167 and Sch.4, para.5.
[39] See "extraordinary powers of liquidators", Chap.4.
[40] Insolvency (Scotland) Rules 1986, r.4.44.

days of the request being received), and be set for a specified date if the committee has previously so resolved, with meetings held on seven days' notice.[41]

The liquidator must report to the liquidation committee in writing as directed by it (but not more often than once in any period of two months), setting out the position as regards the progress of the winding up and matters arising out of it.[42]

Meetings of creditors' committee and liquidation committee

The chairman of meetings is to be the administrator, receiver or **20–09** liquidator or a person nominated by him to act.[43] If he is acting through a nominee, the nominee must be a person who is qualified to act as an insolvency practitioner in relation to the company, or an employee of the administrator, receiver, or liquidator, or his firm, who is experienced in insolvency matters.[44] A meeting of the committee is duly constituted *if* due notice of it has been given to all the members, and at least two members are present or represented.[45] A member of the creditors' committee or liquidation committee may be represented by another person duly authorised by him for that purpose, provided that the person acting as a committee member's representative must hold a mandate entitling him to act (either generally, or specially) signed by or on behalf of the committee member.[46] A member of the creditors' or liquidation committee may resign by notice in writing delivered to the administrator, receiver or liquidator.[47] Membership of the creditors' or liquidation committee is automatically terminated if the member becomes bankrupt, does not attend three consecutive meetings of the committee (unless at the third of those meetings it is resolved that this rule should not apply), or the creditor ceases to be or is found never to have been a creditor.[48] A member of the committee may be removed by resolution at a meeting of the creditors.[49]

Liquidation committee where winding up follows administration

If a creditors' committee has been established in an administration, **20–10** and a liquidation follows on from the administration, the creditors' committee continues and is deemed to be a liquidation committee.[50]

---

[41] Insolvency (Scotland) Rules 1986, r.4.45.
[42] *ibid.*, r.4.56.
[43] *ibid.*, r.2.36(1), as substituted by SI 2003/2111, 3.6(1) and 4.46(1).
[44] *ibid.*, r.2.36(1), as substituted by SI 2003/2111, 3.6(1) and 4.46(2).
[45] *ibid.*, r.2.36(1), as substituted by SI 2003/2111, 3.6(1) and 4.47.
[46] *ibid.*, r.2.36(1), as substituted by SI 2003/2111, 3.6(1) and 4.48(1) and (2).
[47] *ibid.*, r.2.36(1), as substituted by SI 2003/2111, 3.6(1) and 4.49.
[48] *ibid.*, r.2.36(1), as substituted by SI 2003/2111, 3.6(1) and 4.50.
[49] *ibid.*, r.2.36(1), as substituted by SI 2003/2111, 3.6(1) and 4.51.
[50] *ibid.*, r.4.61(1), as amended by SI 2003/2111.

Chapter 21

MISCELLANEOUS ASPECTS OF CORPORATE INSOLVENCY LAW

Meetings

The Insolvency (Scotland) Rules 1986 lay down detailed provisions in **21–01** relation to meetings held in insolvency proceedings, other than meetings of creditors' committees in administrations or receiverships or of the liquidation committee. "Insolvency proceedings" is defined to mean any proceedings in relation to voluntary arrangements, administrations, receiverships and windings up.[1] There is therefore in place a general code for the conduct of meetings. In addition, given the special nature of the proceedings, where a voluntary arrangement is being considered, and where an administrator's proposals are being considered, there are special provisions.[2]

Most of the above-mentioned rules are of a procedural nature and should be consulted by those convening meetings, or attending meetings. However, the provisions are dealt with briefly from a legal point of view.

(1) Summoning of meetings

In fixing the date, time and place for a meeting, the person summon- **21–02** ing the meeting ("the convenor") must have regard to the convenience of the persons who are to attend, and meetings in all cases must be summoned for commencement between 10am and 4pm on a business day, unless the court otherwise directs.[3] The convenor must give not less than 21 days' notice of the date, time and place of the meeting to every person known to him as being entitled to attend the meeting except where the meeting is one of creditors to consider a directors' proposal for voluntary arrangement, or a meeting of creditors summoned to consider an administrator's proposals, or a meeting of unsecured creditors in receivership, under s.67(2) of the Insolvency Act 1986, or a meeting of creditors or contributories under s.138(3) or (4) of the Insolvency Act 1986, when the requisite notice is 14 days.[4] The notice must have a proxy form accompanying it.[5]

---

[1] Insolvency (Scotland) Rules 1986, r.0.2(1).
[2] *ibid.*, Pt I, Chap.5 and Pt II, Chap.3.
[3] *ibid.*, r.7.2. A "business day" is defined by r.0.2(1) to be any day other than a Saturday or Sunday, Christmas Day, Good Friday or a day which is a bank holiday in any part of Great Britain (i.e. bank holidays in Scotland and England, but not in Northern Ireland).
[4] *ibid.*, r.7.3(1) and (2), as amended by the Insolvency (Scotland) Amendment Rules 1987, Sch., art.35.
[5] *ibid.*, r.7.3(5).

(2) Quorum

21–03   The requisite quorum in a creditors' meeting is at least one creditor, and in the case of a meeting of contributories, at least two contributories, or all the contributories, if their number does not exceed two.[6] A quorum may be constituted by a proxy vote.[7]

(3) Entitlement to vote

21–04   At a creditors' meeting, a creditor is entitled to vote at any meeting if he has submitted his claim to "the responsible insolvency practitioner", which is defined to mean in relation to any insolvency proceedings the person acting as supervisor of a voluntary arrangement, the administrator, the receiver or liquidator, or provisional liquidator.[8] In relation to members of the company or contributories at their meetings, votes are according to the rights attaching to shares in accordance with the articles of association of the company.[9]

(4) Chairman of meetings

21–05   The chairman at any meeting of creditors in insolvency proceedings other than a meeting of creditors summoned under s.98 of the Insolvency Act 1986 must be the responsible insolvency practitioner, or a person nominated by him in writing, and if a person is nominated he must, except at a meeting of creditors summoned under s.95 of the Insolvency Act 1986, be either qualified to act as an insolvency practitioner or an employee of the firm of the insolvency practitioner who is experienced in insolvency matters.[10] The same provision applies to meetings of contributories in a liquidation.[11]

(5) Resolutions

21–06   At any meeting of creditors, contributories or members of a company, a resolution is passed when a majority in value of those voting, in person or by proxy, has voted in favour of it.[12] However, as previously referred to at para.21–01, there is an important exception in the case of a voluntary arrangement. At a creditors' meeting for any resolution to pass, approving any proposal or modification, there must be at least three-quarters in value of the creditors present or represented and voting, in person or by proxy, in favour of the resolution.[13] In the case of a resolution for the appointment of a liquidator, where there is more than one candidate the person with a majority in value of the votes is appointed, with progressive elimination of candidates until one candidate has a clear majority where there are several candidates.[14]

---

[6] Insolvency (Scotland) Rules 1986, r.7.7(1).

[7] *ibid.*, r.7.7(2).

[8] *ibid.*, rr 0.2(1) and 7.9(2).

[9] *ibid.*, r.7.10(1).

[10] *ibid.*, r.7.5(2).

[11] *ibid.*, r.7.5(3).

[12] *ibid.*, r.7.12(1).

[13] *ibid.*, r.7.12(2).

[14] *ibid.*, r.7.12(3).

(6) Voluntary arrangements

Where meetings of creditors and contributories are summoned under **21–07** s.3 of the Insolvency Act 1986 to consider a proposal for a voluntary arrangement, the meetings of creditors and contributories must be held on the same day and in the same place, but the creditors' meeting must be fixed for a time in advance of the company meeting.[15] The convenor may require directors of the company to attend or other officers of the company, past and present.[16] On the day on which the meetings are held, they may from time to time be adjourned, or may be held together if the chairman thinks that appropriate for the purpose of obtaining simultaneous agreement of the meetings to the proposal.[17] If the requisite majority is not obtained, the chairman may adjourn the meetings, and must adjourn the meetings if that is resolved.[18] If there are subsequent adjournments, the final adjournment may not be later than 14 days after the date on which the meetings were originally held, and if following any final adjournment of the meetings the proposal is not agreed by both meetings, it is deemed to be rejected.[19]

(7) Administrations

The administrator must give at least 14 days' notice to any directors or **21–08** officers that he requires them to attend a meeting of creditors summoned to consider his proposals.[20] If at the meeting there is not the requisite majority for approval of the administrator's proposals (with modifications, if any), the chairman may, and must if a resolution is passed to that effect, adjourn the meeting for not more than 14 days.[21]

Proxies and corporate representatives

A proxy may be given generally for all meetings in insolvency **21–09** proceedings or for a particular meeting or class of meetings.[22] Forms of proxy must be sent out with every notice summoning a meeting of creditors or contributories.[23] A proxy must be in the form sent out with the notice summoning the meeting or in a form substantially to the same effect.[24] A form of proxy must be filled out and signed by the principal, or by some person acting under his authority. Where it is signed by someone other than the principal, the nature of his authority must be stated on the form.[25] A proxy given for a particular meeting may be used at any adjournment of the meeting.[26] The proxy may be lodged at or before the meeting at which it is to be used.[27] Where the responsible

---

[15] Insolvency (Scotland) Rules 1986, r.1.14(2).
[16] *ibid.*, r.1.15.
[17] *ibid.*, r.1.16(1).
[18] *ibid.*, r.1.16(2).
[19] *ibid.*, r.1.16(5).
[20] *ibid.*, r.2.27(1) as substituted by SI 2003/2111.
[21] *ibid.*, r.2.27(2) as substituted by SI 2003/2111.
[22] *ibid.*, r.7.14(2).
[23] *ibid.*, r.7.15(1).
[24] *ibid.*, r.7.15(3).
[25] *ibid.*, r.7.15(4).
[26] *ibid.*, r.7.16(1).
[27] *ibid.*, r.7.16(2).

insolvency practitioner holds proxies to be used by him as chairman of the meeting and some other person then acts as chairman, the other person may use the insolvency practitioner's proxies as if he were himself proxy-holder.[28] Where a proxy directs a proxy-holder to vote for or against a resolution for the nomination or appointment of a person to be the responsible insolvency practitioner, the proxy-holder may, unless the proxy states otherwise, vote for or against (as he thinks fit) any resolution for the nomination or appointment of that person jointly with another or others.[29] A proxy-holder may propose any resolution which, if proposed by another, would be a resolution in favour of which he would be entitled to vote by virtue of the proxy.[30] Where a proxy gives specific directions as to voting, this does not, unless the proxy states otherwise, preclude the proxy-holder from voting at his discretion on resolutions put to the meeting which are not dealt with in the proxy.[31] The insolvency practitioner must retain all proxies in the sederunt book.[32] Creditors, members and contributories have a right to inspect proxies used at their respective meetings, and to take copies on paying the appropriate fee. The creditors are defined in the case of a company in liquidation as those creditors whose claims have been accepted in whole or in part and, in any other case, persons who have submitted in writing a claim to be creditors of the company concerned.[33] In neither case is a creditor included whose claim has been wholly rejected for purposes of voting, dividend or otherwise.[34] The rule allowing inspection is also available to the directors.[35] Any person attending a meeting is entitled to inspect proxies and claims, either immediately before or during the meeting, and whether they are to be used at the meeting or not.[36] A proxy-holder must not vote in favour of any resolution which would directly or indirectly place him, or any associate of his, in a position to receive any remuneration out of the insolvency state unless the proxy specifically directs him to vote in that way.[37] Where a person is authorised under s.375 of the Companies Act 1985 to represent a corporation at a meeting of creditors or contributories, he must produce to the chairman of the meeting a copy of the resolution from which he derives his authority.[38] The copy must be executed in accordance with what is now s.36B of the Companies Act 1985, as added by s.130(3) of the Companies Act 1989, but substituted by the Law Reform (Miscellaneous Provisions) (Scotland) Act 1990, or be certified by the secretary or a director of the corporation to be a true copy in terms of r.7.20(2) of the Insolvency (Scotland) Rules 1986.

---

[28] Insolvency (Scotland) Rules 1986, r.7.16(3).
[29] *ibid.*, r.7.16(4).
[30] *ibid.*, r.7.16(5).
[31] *ibid.*, r.7.16(6).
[32] *ibid.*, r.7.17(3).
[33] *ibid.*, r.7.18(2).
[34] *ibid.*, r.7.18(2).
[35] *ibid.*, r.7.18(3).
[36] *ibid.*, r.7.18(4).
[37] *ibid.*, r.7.19(1).
[38] *ibid.*, r.7.20(1).

Insurance companies/separate insolvency regimes

Insurance companies are treated in a different legal way from other **21–10** companies. Insurance companies are now regulated by the Financial Services Authority, and the provisions governing winding up in Scotland are contained in the Insurers (Winding Up (Scotland) Rules 2001[39] made under s.379 of the Financial Services and Markets Act 2000. Insurance companies may not be wound up voluntarily without the consent of the Financial Services Authority.[40] The authors know of no insurance company that has been wound up in Scotland in recent times, so that the law is wholly statutory.[41] It is beyond the scope of this book to go into much detail, and we therefore refer the reader to the key instruments.

Insurers (Winding Up)(Scotland) Rules 2001

Insurance companies in Scotland are governed by the Insurance **21–11** Companies Act 1982, and in relation to winding up by the Insurers (Winding Up)(Scotland) Rules 2001,[42] which supplement the Insolvency (Scotland) Rules 1986 in relation to the winding up of insurers in Scotland, revoking, and re-making with modifications, the Insurance Companies (Winding up) (Scotland) Rules 1986. Briefly, r.6 and Sch.1 provide for the valuation rules in relation to a company's general business policies. Rules 7 and 8 and Schs 2 to 5 provide for the valuation rules in relation to a company's long-term business policies. They introduce new requirements in relation to the valuation of unitised with profits policies, specify that the interest rate or rates used to calculate the present value of future payments must be fair and reasonable and change the basis of valuation from a modified net premium basis to a gross premium basis. Rules 9 and 10 make provision for the attribution of liabilities and assets to a company's long-term business in cases of doubt.

Rule 12 requires a liquidator to obtain actuarial advice before taking certain courses of action. Rule 14 allows the secretary of state to require that assets of a company, representing its long-term business, be held by a trustee. Rules 16 and 17 oblige the liquidator to comply with certain requirements imposed on him by the Secretary of State in relation, for example, to refraining from making certain investments and to the provision of information and accounts. Rule 20 allows a liquidator to accept late payment of premiums and to compensate policy holders whose policies have lapsed. Rule 25 stipulates various notice requirements where a stop order has been made.

The Insurers (Reorganisation and Winding Up) Regulations 2003

The Insurers (Reorganisation and Winding Up) Regulations 2003[43] **21–12** implement the Directive of the Parliament and the Council on the reorganisation and winding up of insurance undertakings (2001/17/EC)

---

[39] SI 2001/4040 (S.21).
[40] Financial Services and Markets Act 2000, s.366(1).
[41] In December 2003 a Dalkeith insurance company called Tribune went into liquidation.
[42] SI 2001/4040 (S.21).
[43] SI 2003/1102.

for all UK insurers except Lloyd's. These Regulations provide that, as from April 20, 2003, no winding up proceedings or voluntary arrangements in respect of EEA insurers can be undertaken in the UK except in the circumstances permitted by the Regulations. EEA reorganisation and winding up proceedings are to be recognised in the UK. Provisions are made for the exercise by EEA liquidators of their functions in the UK. Provision is made for the notification of reorganisation and winding up proceedings to competent authorities in other EEA Member States. Modifications are made to UK insolvency law in respect of notifications of various other matters, including important stages in the relevant procedures and forms in which creditors in other EEA States may enter claims, to the FSA, EEA authorities and creditors. The Regulations provide for the special order of priority for insurance debts created by the directive to apply to UK insurers and for the carrying through of the consequences of this in insolvency law. They make provision for application to insurers whose head office is outside the UK and the EEA. Provision is made for detailed amendment of existing secondary legislation, including the insolvency rules in all UK jurisdictions dealing with the reorganisation or winding up of insurers.[44]

Administration and insurance companies

21–13 The provisions in relation to administration contained in new Sch.B1 to the Insolvency Act 1986 do not apply to insurance companies, which—apart from Lloyd's—have their own administration procedure in terms of the Financial Services and Markets Act 2000 (Administration Orders Relating to Insurers) Order 2002 (SI 2002/1242), as amended by the Financial Services and Markets Act 2000 (Administration Orders Relating to Insurers) (Amendment) Order 2003 (SI 2003/2134).[45] Administration as regards insurers came into force on May 31, 2002.[46] This restriction, however, does not apply to companies which are exempt from the general prohibition in relation to effecting or carrying out contracts of insurance in terms of s.19 of the Financial Services and Markets Act 2000.[47] The restriction does not apply also to an authorised deposit taker effecting or carrying out contracts of insurance in the course of a banking business.[48] An "authorised deposit taker" means a person with permission under Pt IV of the Financial Services and Markets Act 2000 to accept deposits.

Remuneration of liquidators

21–14 The basis of remuneration which a liquidator may claim may be calculated by reference to the value of the company's estate. However, there has to be taken into account (a) the work which, having regard to

---

[44] For a useful guide to this complex area of law see Moss, Smith and Quirk, "Schemes for Insolvent Insurers and Reinsurers—the new legal provisions", *Insolvency Intelligence*, Vol.17, No.4 (April 2004), p.54.

[45] Insolvency Act 1986, para.9(2) of new Sch.B1.

[46] It is thought that the first case of an administration order on an insurance company was that of July 19, 2002, in respect of Folksam International Insurance Company (UK) Limited, an English registered company. Details of that administration are to be found in a web site dedicated to the administration by PriceWaterhouseCoopers. (It details also, *inter alia*, how US courts extended the protection available to the administrator in respect of US assets under section 304 of the United States Bankruptcy Code.)

[47] Insolvency Act 1986, para.9(3) of new Sch.B1.

[48] *ibid.*, para.9(3) of new Sch.B1.

that value, was reasonably undertaken by the liquidator; and (b) the extent of his responsibilities in administering the company's assets.[49] The liquidator may at any time before the end of an accounting period submit to the liquidation committee (if any) an interim claim in respect of that period for the outlays reasonably incurred by him, and for his remuneration; and the liquidation committee may make an interim determination in relation to the amount of the outlays and remuneration payable to the liquidator. Where they do so, the committee must take into account that interim determination when making their final determination.[50] If the liquidator considers that the remuneration fixed by the remuneration committee is insufficient, he may request that it be increased by a resolution of the creditors.[51] If the liquidator is still not satisfied, he may apply to the court for an order increasing the amount or rates. The liquidation committee may be heard at the hearing of the application or, if there is no such committee, the court may order that notice of the application be sent to one or more creditors, who may nominate one or more of their number to appear or be represented.[52] Any remuneration fixed by the liquidation committee or by resolution of creditors may be challenged on application by creditors representing 25 per cent or more in value of the creditors on the basis that the liquidator's remuneration is excessive.[53]

---

[49] Bankruptcy (Scotland) Act 1985, s.53 as applied to liquidators by Insolvency (Scotland) Rules 1986, r.4.32(1).
[50] Insolvency (Scotland) Rules 1986, r.4.32(2).
[51] *ibid.*, r.4.33.
[52] *ibid.*, r.4.34.
[53] *ibid.*, r.4.35.

Part 6

THE INTERNATIONAL DIMENSION

CHAPTER 22

CORPORATE INSOLVENCY—INTERNATIONAL DIMENSIONS

Introduction

The growth of international trade and with it firms with complex **22–01** interests and corporate structures straddling many jurisdictions inevitably means the rise in the number of corporate insolvencies with significant international elements. In the last decade the cases of *BCCI* and *Maxwell* were landmark insolvencies generating an enormous amount of case law in many jurisdictions. These two corporate insolvencies in particular highlighted how out of date the rules of private international law were. Many commentators saw the ideal solution as being a broad based international treaty to regulate cross-border insolvency and complement the rules of private international law. For example in *Re Bank of Credit and Commerce International S.A.*, Sir Nicolas Browne-Wilkinson V.-C. stated[1]:

> "It is a matter of profound regret to me that there is no international convention regulating international insolvency. This case, I hope, if it does nothing else may concentrate people's minds on the necessity for such a convention. What we do have are some rather dated rules of private international law which will regulate the disposal of the assets in the event that no rescue scheme is possible."

Although there is as yet no broad-based international convention or treaty, the jurisprudence in particular of the *BCCI* corporate banking empire insolvency has been very innovative in the interpretation of how British courts may co-operate under s.426 of the Insolvency Act 1986 with certain foreign courts in winding up interlocking corporate entities which have interests in many jurisdictions.[2] The same innovative approach to co-operation was demonstrated by the British courts in the insolvency of the *Maxwell* empire in developing co-operation between courts in different jurisdictions, although the assistance was outwith s.426 of the Insolvency Act 1986.[3]

Drive to uniformity of approach between Scottish courts and other courts in the UK in cases of cross-border insolvency

The classical position of the Scottish courts in the case of insolvencies **22–02** with an international dimension is quite clear. Where a Scottish company in winding up seeks to have its orders enforced in another

---

[1] [1992] B.C.L.C. 570 at 577.
[2] See I.F. Fletcher, *The Law of Insolvency* (3rd ed., Sweet and Maxwell, London, 2002) at p.824.
[3] *ibid.*, at p.828.

country, or where the equivalent of the liquidator of a company under a winding-up regime in a separate jurisdiction wishes to have his court order enforced in Scotland, these problems are settled by the Scots rules of private international law. Although the Treaty of Union 1707 united the kingdoms of England and Scotland "into one kingdom by the name of Great Britain" (Union with England Act 1706, Art.I), this did not mean that questions of private international law would no longer arise between England and Scotland. On the contrary, the Treaty of Union ensured that they would arise. Accordingly, for the purposes of Scots private international law, England remains a foreign country. Lord Chancellor Campbell stated in the case of *Stuart v Moore*[4]:

> "As to judicial jurisdiction, Scotland and England, although politi-cally under the same Crown, and under the supreme sway of one united legislature, are to be considered as independent countries, unconnected with one another. This case is of a judicial nature . . . and it is to be treated as if it had occurred in the reign of Queen Elizabeth."

Similarly the Isle of Man, the Channel Islands and, with qualifications dealt with in para.22–06, Northern Ireland are treated as foreign countries for the purposes of Scots private international law. That is, of course, true with the law of Ireland itself, as with all other countries.[5] This separate system of international law has been consistently recog-nised in England. In the case of *Queensland Mercantile and Agency Co, ex p. Australasian Investment Co*,[6] Lindley L.J. stated:

> "Are we to say that the Scotch court is wrong because it takes a different view of the application of international law than that which we should take? I think not. This part of the international law as recognised by the Scotch law becomes part of the Scotch law; and, to my mind, this court at all events is not at liberty to review international law so far as it becomes part of the Scotch law, and which Scotch lawyers say is Scotch law."

Accordingly, Scots private international law must be proved as a question of fact by evidence in the English courts when questions arise, as must English private international law in the Scottish courts. The Scottish courts may also refuse to follow English principles in the field of private international law, where these principles are regarded as unsound in Scotland.[7]

Although Scotland has a very different tradition in the field of private international law from England,[8] the infrequency of cases in Scotland in comparison to England, and the growing uniformity of commercial law,

---

[4] (1861) 4 Macq. 1.
[5] *Faulkner v Hill*, 1941 J.C. 20.
[6] [1892] 1 Ch. 219 at 226.
[7] *McElroy v McAllister*, 1949 S.C. 110 at 133.
[8] See Anton, *Private International Law* (2nd ed., 1990), pp.9–16.

have meant that the Scottish courts have looked increasingly to English authority for guidance when questions arise. For example in the case of *Inland Revenue v Highland Engineering Ltd*[9] Lord Grieve stated:

> "So far, I have considered the question apart from any authority which bears upon it, there being no Scottish authority that does. There are, however, two English authorities which do and I am happy to think that both support the view which I have taken regarding the suggested qualification of s 399 by s 444 (the Companies Act 1948). Had they not done so I would have felt constrained to reconsider my own opinion because it is clearly desirable that the construction of statutes which affect the United Kingdom should be the same both north and south of the border, particularly statutes such as the Companies Act."

In fact, in recent years the Scottish courts have turned more and more to English authorities for guidance and for understanding how this field of law was developing. A purely Scottish approach—if there ever was one—is no longer tenable. It makes no sense and this has been recognised at the highest judicial level. In the words of Anton,[10] "[i]t would be unrealistic to suppose that the House of Lords would sanction one solution in England and another in Scotland."

European and International Drive Towards Uniformity of Approach

This inter-UK drive to a uniform approach has been mirrored by a **22–03** similar drive at the European level. The reviews of the insolvency laws under Sir Kenneth Cork in the reports in 1976 and 1982[11] were indeed produced under the assumption that it would soon be necessary for the UK to implement a projected EC-wide draft Bankruptcy Convention. The motivation for the project of a European Bankruptcy Convention derived from a requirement imposed on the Member States of the Community by Art.220[12] of the Treaty of Rome. In terms of the fourth paragraph of that Article, there was an obligation on the Member States to conclude a convention to secure, for the benefit of nationals, "the simplification of formalities governing the reciprocal recognition and enforcement of judgments of courts or tribunals."

At an early stage, it was decided to separate the field of insolvency from the rest of the area of civil and commercial judgments covered by the remit in Art.220(4). The non-insolvency field became the subject of a separate convention which was concluded and came into force in February 1973. This Convention on Jurisdiction and Enforcement of Judgments in Civil and Commercial Matters ("the Brussels Convention") was incorporated into United Kingdom law by the Civil Jurisdic-

---

[9] 1975 S.L.T. 203 at 205.
[10] *Anton*, p.14.
[11] Cmnd 6602, and Cmnd 8558.
[12] Article 220 has now been renumbered as Art.293 in the consolidated version of the EC Treaty produced by the Amsterdam Treaty of 1997.

tion and Judgments Act 1982. The Brussels Convention attempts formally to exclude insolvency matters. However, the dividing line between what is an insolvency matter and what is not is complicated. It is also important in determining the scope of the Brussels Convention and hence what may be competent under the complementary insolvency regime.

The draft Bankruptcy Convention proved too difficult and complex for agreement of the Member States to be reached. The project was relaunched in April 1990 with the creation of an *ad hoc* working party inspired by the success of a Council of Europe Convention ("the Istanbul Convention"), which was open for signature on June 5, 1990.[13] This relaunch was remarkably successful and was nearly unanimously adopted in May 1996, until the UK Government withdrew at the last minute because of inter-EC arguments about beef. Three years later, with a doggedness typical of the European project, a German and Finnish initiative again revived the project and succeeded in achieving the adoption by the Council of the Regulation on Insolvency Proceedings ("the Regulation") on May 29, 2000. This Regulation has the advantage of being directly applicable to the Member States[14] according to the terms of Art.249 of the EC Treaty in its amended form. The key feature of the Regulation is that, where the centre of a company's main interests is in a Member State, it is that State which shall have jurisdiction to open main proceedings.[15] If the centre of main interests is outwith the EC this rule does not apply, and reliance can be placed on the traditional jurisprudence. This chapter much be qualified throughout to the effect that only statement is subject to possible exception if these rules of the Regulation apply.

Finally, on the international stage, in May 1997 the United Nations Commission on International Trade Law ("UNCITRAL") adopted a Model Law on Cross-Border Insolvency ("the Model Law"). The Model Law is a code which an enacting state ("ES") may incorporate in whole or in part into its own law, which may be invoked by any foreign representative whether or not its domestic law has similar provisions. Provision is made in s.14 of the Insolvency Act 2000 for the Model Law to be given effect in the UK by Regulations made by statutory instrument.[16] At the date of writing no Regulations have been made.

Format of chapter

22–04   Corporate insolvency law is unavoidably complex at the best of times, but cross-border corporate insolvency law with its extra dimensions makes "string theory"[17] appear absurdly simple. The authors have

---

[13] For references to the progress of these conventions see Fletcher, *op. cit.* at p.830.

[14] It is not applicable to Denmark.

[15] Article 3(1) of Regulation.

[16] In terms of s.16(2) of the Insolvency Act 2000, s.14 came into force on the day the Act was passed (November 30, 2000). The statutory instrument is subject to affirmative resolution of both Houses of Parliament as well as prior agreement of the Lord Chancellor and the Scottish Ministers.

[17] String theory tries to reconcile Newtonian physics with quantum theory, and is premised on there being eleven dimensions See B. Greene, *The Elegant Universe—Superstrings, Hidden Dimensions, and the Quest for the Ultimate Theory* (New York, W.W. Norton & Company, 1999).

decided to limit this chapter to the following four dimensions because other dimensions of this area of law are beyond the scope of this book.

- Part I—describes generally the problems of international corporate cross-border insolvencies in Scots law.
- Part II—describes enforcement of court orders under s.426 of the Insolvency Act 1986.
- Part III—describes the scope and application of the E.C. Regulation on Insolvency Proceedings[18] and the Scottish implementing Regulations.
- Part IV—describes the workings of the UNCITRAL Model Law on Cross-Border Insolvency.

PART I

CROSS-BORDER INSOLVENCIES

Jurisdiction of Scottish courts to wind up companies

The Court of Session has jurisdiction to wind up any company registered in Scotland.[19] Where the amount of a company's share capital paid up or credited as paid up does not exceed £120,000, the sheriff court of the sheriffdom in which the company's registered office is situated has concurrent jurisdiction with the Court of Session to wind up the company.[20] The Court of Session has power, having regard to the assets of the company, to remit a petition for winding up of a company whose issued capital does not exceed the limit to the sheriff court or to transfer the petition from one sheriff court to another.[21] The sheriff court does not have jurisdiction to wind up a company which does not have a share capital, either an unlimited company or a company limited by guarantee.[22] For the purposes of the Insolvency Act, the expression "registered office" means the place which has longest been the company's registered office during the six months immediately preceding the presentation of the petition for winding up.[23] A person bringing proceedings against a company may act on the assumption that the registered office as disclosed on the Registrar of Companies' official file is the registered office.[24] Formerly it was a matter of judicial construction that companies could not be wound-up under the Scottish bankruptcy legislation.[25] The Bankruptcy (Scotland) Act 1985 states that the estate

22–05

---

[18] Council Regulation (E.C.) No. 1346/2000, May 29, 2000; O.J L160/1, June 6, 2000.
[19] Insolvency Act 1986, s.120.
[20] *ibid.*, s.120(3).
[21] Insolvency Act 1986, s.120(3)(a) and (b), and Rules of the Court of Session, 74.23; *Chayney & Bull Ltd, Petrs*, 1930 S.C. 759; 1930 S.L.T. 623.
[22] *Pearce & Cannon, Petrs*, 1991 S.C.L.R. 861 (Sh.Ct.). The sheriff's statement that the sheriff court had no jurisdiction to wind up an unlimited company goes too far. The sheriff court has power to wind up an unlimited company provided it has a share capital.
[23] *ibid.*, s.120(4).
[24] *Ross v Invergordon Distillers Ltd*, 1961 S.L.T. 358; 1961 S.C. 286.
[25] *Standard Property Investments Co Ltd v Dunblane Hydropathic Co Ltd* (1884) 12 R. 328.

belonging to "a body corporate or an unincorporated body" may be sequestrated, but provides that it shall not be competent to sequestrate the estate of:

> "(a) the company registered under the Companies Act 1985 or under the former Companies Act (within the meaning of that Act); or
> (b) an entity in respect of which an enactment provides, expressly or by implication, that sequestration is incompetent."[26]

The Bankruptcy (Scotland) Act 1985 is silent about foreign corporations, but the reasoning in the *Dunblane Hydropathic* case[27] would suggest that a court might well infer that sequestration was not competent in relation to foreign or other companies which may be wound-up under the Insolvency Act 1986 as unregistered companies. Although sequestration is not apparently competent in relation to corporations, as an alternative to liquidation, the court may appoint a judicial factor.[28] It is thought that the court could appoint a judicial factor in the case of a foreign company, and it is perhaps sometimes a desirable option, especially if there is a winding up already in place in another country.

Scottish companies

22–06   The Court of Session and sheriff courts have jurisdiction to wind up companies registered in Scotland.[29] Similarly, the High Court and county courts have jurisdiction to wind up companies registered in England and Wales.[30] It is irrelevant where the registered office of a company is situated.[31] The sheriff may submit a stated case on any question of law for the opinion of the Court of Session.[32] In the case of unregistered UK companies, those companies are deemed to be registered in those parts of the UK where they have their principal places of business.[33] If the company has a principal place of business situated in both England and Wales, and Scotland, it is deemed to be registered in both countries and may be wound-up in either country.[34] An English court has no jurisdiction to wind up a company registered in Scotland.[35] The Court of Session has on some authority jurisdiction to wind up companies registered in Northern Ireland, but that is pursuant to s.220 of the Insolvency Act 1986, notwithstanding the terms of s.441 of that Act.[36]

---

[26] Bankruptcy (Scotland) Act 1985, s.6(2).
[27] (1884) 12 R. 328.
[28] *Fraser*, 1971 S.L.T. 146 and *McGuinness v Black (No 2)*, 1990 S.L.T. 461.
[29] Insolvency Act 1986, s.120.
[30] *ibid.*, s.117.
[31] *Re Baby Moon (United Kingdom)* (1985) P.C.C. 103.
[32] Insolvency Act 1986, s.120(3) (c).
[33] *ibid.*, s.221(2) and (3).
[34] *ibid.*, s.221(3).
[35] *ibid.*, s.120. *Re Scottish Joint Stock Trust Bank* [1900] W.N.114.
[36] *Re a Company (No. 007946 of 1993)* [1994] Ch. 198, *sub nom. The Normandy Marketing Ltd* [1993] B.C.C. 879; for full discussion see Smart, *Cross-Border Insolvency* (Butterworths, 1998), p.113–220; Dicey and Morris, *Conflict of Laws* (13th ed., 2000), pp.1129–1130. The authors agree with Smart, Dicey and Morris saying the case was wrongly decided.

The jurisdiction of the Scottish courts to wind up a company registered in Scotland is not in any way qualified by the nationality of its shareholders, the place where its business may be conducted or where its assets are situated. Lord Carmont in the case of *Carse v Coppen* stated[37]:

> "A company's domicile is created by registration; it is, so to say, born in Scotland and, however widespread its activities and contacts with other legal systems in the days of its vigour, to Scotland it must come to be laid to rest when its days are done, and according to Scots law should its affairs be wound-up."

For winding up purposes most other EC countries looked traditionally beyond the place of incorporation to determine the "nationality" of a company. The court looks at the *siège rélle*, the place where decisions are taken and orders given, the place of its central management. In Scotland and England the courts will not refuse to wind up under Scottish or English law even if all the business and assets of a company and its management are not in Scotland or England, and even if the liquidation in Scotland was not recognised in the country where the assets and business were.[38] The Civil Jurisdiction and Judgments Act 1982 did not affect the jurisdiction of the Scottish courts to wind up Scottish companies.[39] However, as stated in para.22–03, the Regulation on Insolvency Proceedings radically affects the traditional approach, if the company has its centre of main interests in a Member State other than the UK. The continental *siège rélle* rule has effectively entered UK law for corporate insolvencies where the company has its centre of main interests in the EU.

It is usual that a liquidator appointed by the Scottish court should reside within the jurisdiction and applications to appoint persons resident outwith Scotland have been refused.[40] However, it is not an inviolable rule that the liquidator in a Scottish winding up must reside in Scotland. As Lord President Robertson stated in the case of *The Barberton Development Syndicate*[41]:

> "I am not disposed to hold it incompetent to appoint a liquidator outside of our jurisdiction. But for manifest reasons it is preferable to have an officer within our jurisdiction, and residing at or near to the registered office, which is the headquarters of the company."

This opinion of Lord President Robertson was affirmed in the case of *The Liquidators of Bruce Peebles and Co Ltd v Shiells*[42] by Lord President Dunedin.

---

[37] 1951 S.C. 233 at 243–244.
[38] *Smyth & Co v The Salem (Oregon) Capital Flour Mills Co Ltd* (1887) 14 R. 441; and *A.-G. v Jewish Colonisation Association* [1990] 2 Q.B. 556; [1901] 1 Q.B. 123, CA.
[39] See the Civil Jurisdiction and Judgments Act 1982, s.43.
[40] *Brightwen & Co v City of Glasgow Bank* (1878) 6 R. 244; *The Barberton Development Syndicate* (1898) 25 R. 654; *Skinner (Hannan's Development and Finance Corp. Ltd)* (1899) 6 S.L.T. 388 (where a liquidator was removed from office as being in England and outwith the jurisdiction).
[41] Above.
[42] 1980 S.C. 692.

The position about the appointment of liquidators, who do not need to be resident in Scotland, is in contrast to the position of interim and permanent trustees in bankruptcy, who must reside within the jurisdiction of the Court of Session.[43] The creation of "insolvency practitioners" under the Insolvency Act 1986 would suggest that there is less desirability now for the liquidator to reside in Scotland. The main reason for the desirability of residing in Scotland was convenience. It may now be thought a restriction on the free movement of services under the Treaty of Rome if the Court of Session, for no good reasons, were to insist that liquidators be resident in Scotland. It is thought that Anton is incorrect in *Private International Law*[44] where he states that a liquidator appointed by the Scottish court must reside within the jurisdiction.

"Foreign" and "oversea" companies

22–07   A "foreign" company, *i.e.* one which was incorporated under the law of any country outside Great Britain, may be wound-up under s.221 of the Insolvency Act 1986 as an "unregistered company".[45] Such a company which establishes or has a place of business in Great Britain is known as an "oversea company",[46] and is subject to special provisions of the Companies Act 1985. That Act imposes a number of requirements upon the company in relation to registration of its presence, and the nomination of one or more resident persons authorised to accept service of process and other formal notices on the company's behalf. Such "oversea" companies are more clearly subject to the jurisdiction of the courts of Great Britain. In the following text, "foreign company" will denote all companies incorporated under some foreign law whether or not they happen to qualify as an "oversea company" under company law in Great Britain. It is worth remembering that, if an oversea company fails to notify the name and address of a person authorised to accept service of process, or where all such persons as have been so authorised are either dead, or for any reason cannot be served, a document may be served on the company at any place of business established by the company in Great Britain.[47]

In the case of foreign companies the jurisdiction of the British courts is not limited to those cases where a foreign company establishes a place of business in Great Britain. The reason is that the statutory definition of "unregistered company" in s.220 of the Insolvency Act 1986 is wide enough to comprehend any company, partnership or association formed under a foreign law. All these types of organisation are in principle able

---

[43] Bankruptcy (Scotland) Act 1985, ss.2(2) and 24(2).

[44] At p.722.

[45] Although jurisdiction in personal insolvencies is clearly spelt out in s.6 of the Bankruptcy (Scotland) Act 1985 the jurisdiction of the Scottish courts to wind up foreign companies is not made clear. Section 221 of the Insolvency Act 1986 does not expressly refer to foreign companies, but s.225 of the Insolvency Act 1986 rather implies this by stating that "a company incorporated outside Great Britain . . . may be wound-up as an unregistered company".

[46] Companies Act 1985, s.744.

[47] *ibid.*, s.695(2).

to be wound-up by the courts of Great Britain as "unregistered companies".[48] They may also be made subject to other insolvency regimes such as administration. In the case of *BRAC Rent-A-Car International Inc*,[49] a US company registered in Delaware, obtained an administration order in the UK in respect of the Delaware company, based on the ground that it's a main centre of interest was in the UK, and this gave the UK courts jurisdiction in terms of the EC Regulation on Insolvency Proceedings.

Although the definition in s.220 comprehends a large range of foreign entities, it does not comprehend certain international organisations. Municipal courts are not competent to adjudicate upon or to enforce their rights arising from transactions entered into by independent sovereign states on the international law planes. International organisations created by treaty are created by an exercise of the royal prerogative, and an organisation created by an exercise of the royal prerogative is not a corporation in terms of the Companies Acts unless it has been incorporated into law by Parliament.[50]

A partnership registered under the Limited Partnership Act 1907 is not able to be wound up as an unregistered company.[51]

Grounds for winding up a foreign company

Section 221(5) of the Insolvency Act 1986 lays down the circumstances **22–08** in which unregistered companies including foreign companies may be wound-up. It states:

"(5) The circumstances in which an unregistered company may be wound-up are as follows—[52]

(a) if the company is dissolved, or has ceased to carry on business, or is carrying on business only for the purpose of winding up its affairs;

(b) if the company is unable to pay its debts;

(c) if the court is of the opinion that it is just and equitable that the company should be wound-up."

What s.221(5) does essentially is to provide five independent free standing circumstances in which a court may wind up.[53]

The following examples show the type of situation where a winding-up order has been made of a foreign company relying on that section or its statutory predecessors.

---

[48] *Re Mercantile Bank of Australia* [1892] 2 Ch. 204.

[49] [2003] E.W.H.C. (Ch.) 128.

[50] *J.H. Rayner (Mincing Lane) Ltd v Department of Trade and Industry* [1990] 2 A.C. 418; see also *Re International Tin Council* [1987] 1 All E.R. 890; *Arab Monetary Fund v Hashim (No.3)* [1991] 2 A.C. 114.

[51] *Smith, Petr*, 1998 S.L.T. (Sh. Ct) 5.

[52] S.221(7) also provides a special case ground of winding up in Scotland applicable to unregistered companies, namely where the security of the creditor having a floating charge is in jeopardy.

[53] *Banque des Marchands de Moscou (Koupetschesky) v Kildersley* [1951] Ch. 112 at 125, *per* Evershed M.R.

Example 1

22–09   In the case of *Marshall, Petr*,[54] a petition was presented to the First Division of the Court of Session by the Reverend Theodore Marshall, 19 Coates Gardens, Edinburgh and other creditors of the Fidelity Loan and Trust Company under the 199th section of the Companies' Act, 1862,[55] praying the court, after intimation and service "to order that the said Fidelity Loan and Trust Company be wound-up by the court". The Fidelity Loan and Trust Company was a company incorporated under the laws of the State of Iowa, US, and had its principal place of business at Sioux City, Iowa. It also carried on business in England and Scotland. Its principal place of business in the UK was at 63 Castle Street, Edinburgh. It was not registered in the UK.

The business conducted at the Edinburgh branch office consisted in the borrowing of money on debentures of the company secured by mortgages on real estate in the US, deposited with and held by the Honourable Francis J. Moncrieff, CA, Robert Strahern, WS, and John P. Wright, WS, all of Edinburgh, as trustees under an agreement and deed of trust entered into between them and the company in October and November 1889.

It was provided that the agreement should be construed and interpreted, and the rights of parties determined by the Law of Scotland. The company became unable to meet its liabilities, and was obliged to suspend payment. It ceased to carry on business, and receivers were in the course of being appointed over the assets of the company by the US courts. The chief assets of the company in Scotland were mortgages lodged to secure the due payment of debentures and, in addition, the company held various bonds, stocks and other assets, although these were pledged, to a large extent, in security of advances made to the company in America.

In that case the Court of Session, in granting the prayer of the petition, expressed the view that the proceedings in Scotland should be ancillary to those in the US, which was the proper domicile of the company.

Example 2

22–10   In the case of *Inland Revenue v Highland Engineering Ltd*[56] a petition was presented by the Lord Advocate for and on behalf of the Commissioners of Inland Revenue for the compulsory winding up of a company called Industrial Estates 9New Zealand) Limited. the petitioner averred that Highland Engineering Ltd (which was in members' voluntary liquidation) was indebted to Industrial Estates (New Zealand) ltd to the sum of £12,223 and that that debt was the company's only remaining asset. He also averred that Highland Engineering Ltd, was indebted to

---

[54] (1895) 22 R. 697.
[55] The terms of s.199(3) are the same as the Insolvency Act 1986, s.221(5).
[56] 1975 S.L.T. 203.

the Inland Revenue in the sum of £7,969.91 as income tax. Highland Engineering Ltd denied that they were indebted to the company. The petitioner and the respondents agreed that the company was an unregistered company, that it had been struck off the New Zealand Register of Companies in 1973, and that it was now a dissolved company. The respondents pleaded that the court had no jurisdiction to wind up the company because, in order to comply with s.399(5)(a) of the Companies Act 1948,[57] an unregistered company must not only have been dissolved, but must also have carried on business in Great Britain. The petitioner had not averred that Industrial Estates (New Zealand) Ltd had carried on business in Great Britain. The prayer of the petition should therefore not be granted.

Lord Grieve held that the requirements necessary for a winding-up order had been met in as much as the company was unregistered and had been dissolved. Since it was not suggested that the company had assets in any country other than Scotland and all the interested parties were in Scotland, the winding up petition was granted.

Example 3

In the case of *Compania Merabello San Nicholas SA*,[58] referred to and **22–11** quoted with approval by Lord Grieve in *Inland Revenue v Highland Engineering Ltd*,[59] a Spanish company, Fertilisantes, made a claim for breach of a contract of carriage in respect of a cargo carried to Spain by a "one ship company" which had been incorporated in Panama. At all times the company's ship had been insured with a mutual insurance club called "Oceanus". Neither the company nor Oceanus had met the petitioners' judgment claim, and the only known asset of the company was its right against Oceanus. The English court made a winding-up order, the consequence of which was that the right of the company against Oceanus automatically vested in the petitioners in accordance with the Third Parties (Rights against Insurers) Act 1930. In his judgment, Megarry J.[60] stated:

> "I would accordingly attempt to summarise the essentials of the relevant law relating to the existence of jurisdiction to make a winding up order in normal cases in respect of a foreign company as follows—
>
> (1) There is no need to establish that the company ever had a place of business here.
> (2) There is no need to establish that the company ever carried on business here, unless perhaps the petition is based upon the company carrying on or having carried on business.
> (3) A proper connection with the jurisdiction must be established by sufficient evidence to show—

---

[57] Now Insolvency Act 1986, s.221 (5).
[58] [1973] Ch. 75.
[59] 1975 S.L.T. 203.
[60] Applies in *International Westminster Bank v Okeanos* [1987] 3 All E.R. 137, *sub nom. Re a Company (No 00359 of 1987)* [1988] Ch. 210.

   (a) that the company has some asset or assets within the
       jurisdiction; and
   (b) that there are one or more persons concerned in the
       proper distribution of the assets over whom the jurisdic-
       tion is exercisable.
   (4) It suffices if the assets of the company within the jurisdiction
       are of any nature; they need not be 'commercial' assets, or
       assets which indicate that the company formerly carried on
       business here.
   (5) The assets need not be assets which will be distributable to
       creditors by the liquidator in the winding up: it suffices if by
       the making of the winding up order they will be of benefit to
       the creditor or creditors in some other way.
   (6) If it is shown that there is no reasonable possibility of benefit
       accruing to creditors from making the winding up order, the
       jurisdiction is excluded."[61]

Jurisdictional problems caused by s.221 of the Insolvency Act 1986

22–12   Section 221 of the Insolvency Act 1986 has raised problems of
jurisdiction under English law. It is thought that Scottish law arrives at
the same answer as in England by the "exercise of a discretion once
jurisdiction is established by the statutory criteria"; as opposed to in
England having first the statutory criteria for jurisdiction followed by
further jurisdictional criteria. Briefly, s.221 sets down certain statutory
circumstances in which a foreign company may be wound-up. These are
very wide. In the case of *Banque des Marchands de Moscou (Koupetschesky)
v Kindersley*[62] the Master of the Rolls, Lord Evershed, doubted that the
statutory criteria for establishing jurisdiction were sufficient to establish
jurisdiction. He stated:

   "As a matter of principle, our courts would not assume, and
   Parliament should not be taken to have intended to confer, jurisdiction over matters which naturally and properly lie within the
   competence of the courts of other countries. There must be assets
   here to administer and persons subject, or at least submitting, to the
   jurisdiction who are concerned or interested in the property distribution of the assets. And when these conditions are present the
   exercise of the jurisdiction remains discretionary. *Prima facie* if the
   local law of the dissolved foreign corporation provided for the due
   administration of all the property and assets of the corporation
   wherever situate among the persons properly entitled to participate
   therein, the case would not be one for the interference by the
   machinery of the English courts. In the present case there are
   substantial assets standing in the name of the bank or its liquidator,
   and there are persons within the jurisdiction having claims to

---

[61] [1951] Ch. 112; see also *Re Titan International Inc* [1998] 1 B.C.L.C. 102 at 106, *per* Peter
Gibson L.J.
[62] *ibid.*

participate in the distribution of those assets. At the same time, by reason of the total extinction in Russia of the bank and the absence of any machinery under Russian law for the due distribution of the assets among the persons regarded as properly having claims upon them, there would be, unless the machinery of winding up under the Companies Act is available, no means of any kind existing for the administration of the English assets.''

In the case of *Re Lloyd Generate Italiano*[63] Pearson J. had held that the English court had no jurisdiction to wind up an Italian company that had carried on business through an agent in England and did not have a branch office or any assets in England. In the judgment in *Banque des Marchands de Moscou (Koupetschesky) v Kindersley*[64] the Master of the Rolls Lord Evershed stated that he regarded the case of *Re Lloyd Generate Italiano* as only authority for the proposition that there had to be assets in England, not for the view that proof of the existence of a "place" of business in England, whether established or otherwise, was a condition to the existence of jurisdiction in the English court. The views in *Banque des Marchands de Moscou (Koupetschesky) v Kindersley* have been generally approved including in Scotland.[65]

These cases would suggest that it is necessary that there be assets in England to establish jurisdiction (irrespective of the statutory criteria having been met). This test, however, has been superseded by recent cases. In the case of *Re Eloc Electro-Optieck and Communicatie BV*,[66] Nourse J. held that the English court had jurisdiction to wind up a Dutch company which had no assets within the English jurisdiction. In that case the Dutch company had traded in England but never had a place of business there. The petitioners were two employees whom the Dutch company dismissed. They recovered judgment against the company. The Dutch company ceased operating. On the hearing of the petition the Dutch company was not represented, but in a reserve judgment it was held that the court had jurisdiction to wind it up. Nourse J. referred to Megarry J.'s summary of the essentials in a normal case and to the fact that the petitioners had applied to the Department of Employment for payment out of the redundancy fund, but that, under the statutory provisions, no payment could be made until the company was wound up. He held that there was a reasonable possibility of benefit accruing to the petitioner from the making of a winding-up order. He stated:

"The benefit would consist of assets coming into the hands of the petitioners not from the company but from an outside source which can only be tapped if an order is made. In the light of that

---

[63] [1885] 29 Ch. D219.
[64] [1951] Ch. 112.
[65] *Tong Aik (Far East) Ltd v Eastern Minerals and Trading (1959) Ltd* (1965) 2 M.L.J. 149 (a Singapore case); *Re Kailis Groote Eylandt Fisheries Pty Ltd* (1977) 2 A.C.L.R. 574 (a South Australian case); *IRC v Highland Engineering Ltd* (1975) S.L.T. 203 and *Re Irish Shipping Ltd* [1985] H.K.L.R. 437 (a Hong Kong case).
[66] [1982] Ch. 43.

consideration and of the facts, first, that the company did carry on business in England and Wales, secondly, that it employed the petitioners in that business, and, thirdly, that the potential source of assets is directly related to that employment, there is, in my judgment, sufficient to found the jurisdiction of the court. To put it another way, it would, in my judgment, be a lamentable state of affairs if the court's jurisdiction was excluded by the mere technicality that the assets, in respect of which the reasonable possibility of benefit accruing to the petitioners derived, belonged not to the company but to an outside source. I think that support for this view is to be found in the fourth and fifth essentials in Megarry J's summary [1973] Ch 75, 92 . . . [and then he cites those essentials and continues] That shows, first, that the assets can be of any nature and, secondly, that the consequential benefit accruing to a creditor or creditors need not be channelled through the hands of the liquidator. To my mind that confirms that the ownership of the assets by the company is not a matter of crucial importance. I must again observe that Megarry J's summary of the essentials was directed to normal cases."[67]

22–13 The second case apparently reducing the non-statutory jurisdictional criteria in England is the case of *Re a Company (No 00359 of 1987)*.[68] In that case the business of a Liberian company Okeanos was managed in England by an associated company. The Liberian company contracted in 1984 for the building of a bulk carrier. About $13.5m of the total price of $18m was provided by the petitioner, an English bank, in return for a first secured mortgage on the vessel and the assignment to the petitioner of all the vessel's earnings. The company undertook that, for the duration of the facility, there would be no change in the ownership and control of the company, and that the vessel would be kept fully insured. The vessel was delivered to the company in January 1985 and the company drew on the whole of the facility. In 1986 the company was in financial difficulties, and in September defaulted in the interest payment. On November 17, the petitioner declared the whole of the company's indebtedness to be due in accordance with the provisions of the loan agreement. The petitioner obtained judgment for the amount of the debt in January 1987 and on February 3, presented a petition for the winding up of the company. On the question of whether the court had jurisdiction to wind up the company under s.221 of the Insolvency Act 1986, it was held that, since the company was unable to pay its debts and its only known asset was substantially less than its liabilities, the condition for the making of a winding-up order contained in s.221(5)(b) of the Insolvency Act 1986 was fulfilled. It was not necessary for the making of a winding-up order against a foreign company that the court be shown that the company had assets within the jurisdiction. A sufficiently close connection with the jurisdiction had to be established. Peter Gibson J. stated, referring to the *Eloc* case[69]:

---

[67] Approved in *Re a Company (No 00359 of 1987) International Westminster Bank plc v Okeanos Maritime Corp.* [1988] Ch. 210 at 223–224.

[68] [1988] Ch. 210.

[69] [1982] Ch. 43.

"In the circumstances, I am prepared consistently with the *Eloc* case [1982] Ch 43 to hold that the presence of assets in this country is not an essential condition for the court to have jurisdiction in relation to the winding up of a foreign company. In my judgment, provided a sufficient connection with the jurisdiction is shown, and there is a reasonable possibility of benefit for the creditors from the winding up, the court has jurisdiction to wind up the foreign company."

The fact that there is now no requirement for assets in the jurisdiction has been confirmed by a number of recent cases.[70] The Court of Appeal confirmed the above approach in the recent case of *Re Latreefers Inc. Stocznia Gdanska SA v Latreefers Inc.* that, to establish jurisdiction, only three core requirements had to be met; namely:

(1) there must be a sufficient connection with England and Wales which may, but does necessarily have to, consist of assets within the jurisdiction;

(2) there must be a reasonable possibility, if a winding-up order is made, of benefit to those applying for the winding-up order; and

(3) one or more persons interested in the distribution of assets of the company must be persons over whom the court can exercise the jurisdiction.

Interestingly the Court of Appeal also decided that there was nothing in the terms of ss.221(1), 229, 213 or 214 of the Insolvency Act 1986 to warrant the exclusion of the powers of the court under the latter two sections being exercisable in respect of a foreign company if an order for its winding up had been made in England and Wales. The court referred to the view of both Peter Gibson J. in *Okeanos*[71] and Chadwick J. in *Re Howard Holdings Inc.*[72]; though in each case without argument. The court accepted that this would involve applying to the directors of a foreign company English notions of commercial property. However, they agreed with Chadwick J. in *Re Howard Holdings Inc.*[73] that it was difficult to envisage any developed system of corporate law which does not impose some obligation on directors to consider whether the company is solvent and, if not, to consider what should be done about it. Moreover, both sections conferred on the court a discretion as to the amount (if any) which the director should contribute to the company's assets. Such a discretion seemed to them to be sufficient to enable account to be taken of any problems which might otherwise arise from the fact that the company was incorporated in a foreign jurisdiction. In summary, potential claims for misfeasance and wrongful and fraudulent trading provided a reasonable possibility of benefit to creditors and others so as to comply with the second core requirements.

---

[70] See the summary of the position set out by Knox J. in *Real Estate Development Co* [1991] B.C.L.C. 210 at 217; *Re Titan International Inc.* [1988] 1 B.C.L.C. 102 at 106; *Banco National De Cuba v Cosmos Trading Corp.* [2000] B.C.C. 910.

[71] [2001] B.C.C. 160; [1988] Ch. 210 at 227.

[72] [1988] B.C.C. 549 at 552.

[73] *ibid.* at 555.

Scottish position as regards assets

22–14   It is thought that in Scotland provided the statutory criteria are met, the court will have jurisdiction. In the case of *Inland Revenue v Highland Engineering Ltd*[74] Lord Grieve did not require proof of the existence of assets in Scotland to found jurisdiction, or any benefit to creditors. In narrow terms he stated:

> "It follows that, in my judgment, the requirements necessary for a winding up order being issued are met on averment, the company being unregistered and admittedly being dissolved."

In accepting the argument on behalf of the petitioners, he accepted a test for the discretionary exercise of the jurisdiction which is for all intents and purposes equivalent to the recently stated English test for the establishment of the jurisdiction once the statutory criteria are met namely that there is a case that the petitioners may benefit from a winding up.

Petitioner's connection to the jurisdiction

22–15   Item (3)(b) in the list made by Megarry J. in the *Okeanos* case, above, was that there were one or more persons concerned in the proper distribution of the assets over whom the jurisdiction is exercisable. This test was stated in 1950 by Evershed MR[75] and has been repeated at intervals.[76] This principle, however, is not absolute and the petitioning creditors need not be resident within the jurisdiction.[77]

Section 221(5)(b) company unable to pay its debts

22–16   The grounds for winding up a foreign company set out in s.221(5)(a) are very wide and require a careful study of the latest case law. The ground, on the other hand, in s.221(5)(b) is non-problematic, being identical to that set out in s.122(1)(f) of the Insolvency Act 1986 as one of the grounds on which a company registered under the Companies Act may be wound-up. As with s.122(1)(f), there are further provisions set out to determine whether the petitioner has established that the company is unable to pay its debts. Sections 222 and 224 of the Insolvency Act 1986 set out provisions which are similar to those set out in s.123 of that Act. The relevant provision in relation to Scotland is s.224(1)(b), which deems a foreign company unable to pay its debts if the *induciae* of a charitable payment on an extract decree, or an extract registered bond, or an extract registered protest, had expired without payment being made. The main catch-all provision, of course, is that a foreign company is deemed to be unable to pay its debts "if it is otherwise proved to the

---

[74] 1975 S.L.T. 203.
[75] *Banque des Marchands de Moscou (Koupetschesky) v Kindersley* [1951] Ch. 112 at 125; [1950] 2 All E.R. 549 at 556.
[76] *Re Real Estate Development Co* [1991] B.C.L.C. 210 at 218.
[77] In *Re Azoff-Don Commercial Bank* [1954] 1 Ch. 315.

satisfaction of the court that the company is unable to pay its debts as they fall due.[78]

Oversea companies

An "oversea company" in terms of s.744 of the Companies Act 1985 is **22–17** defined as:

> "(a) a company incorporated elsewhere than in Great Britain which, after commencement of this Act establishes a place of business in Great Britain; and
>
> (b) a company so incorporated which has, before that commencement, established a place of business and continues to have an established place of business in Great Britain at that commencement".

In terms of that section, "place of business" includes a share transfer or share registration office. A company has an established place of business in Great Britain if it has a specified or identifiable place at which it carries on business.[79] In the case of *Lord Advocate v Huron and Erie Loan and Savings Co*,[80] Lord Dunedin held that a Canadian company did not have a place of business in Scotland although it carried out business in Scotland by touting for loans and, in order to tout properly, had agents operating in Scotland.

In the case of "oversea companies" the Court of Session will always have jurisdiction to wind up if the place of business is in Scotland and is likely to exercise the rights to wind it up.

Winding up of foreign companies under section 225 of the Insolvency Act 1986

There is a slightly anomalous jurisdictional rule contained in s.225 of **22–18** the Insolvency Act 1986 which is supplemental to the winding up jurisdiction contained in s.221(5) of that Act. Section 225 of the Insolvency Act 1986 is in the following terms:

> "Where a company incorporated outside Great Britain which has been carrying on business in Great Britain ceases to carry on business in Great Britain, it may be wound-up as an unregistered company under this Act, notwithstanding that it has been dissolved or otherwise cease to exist as a company under or by virtue of the laws of the country under which it was incorporated."

The predecessor provision was designed to remove doubts about the jurisdiction of the English courts in relation to the winding up of

---

[78] S.224(1)(b).

[79] *Banque des Marchands de Moscou (Koupetschesky) v Kindersley* [1951] Ch. 112 at 126, 132, *per* Evershed M.R.

[80] 1911 S.C. 612 at 616.

companies originally formed under the laws of Tsarist Russia and subsequently dissolved at the time of the revolution in 1917. In fact the provision does not seem ever to have been expressly relied upon by a British court because cases invariably fall within the broader s.221. So, for example, in *IRC v Highland Engineering Ltd*,[81] a dissolved New Zealand company was wound-up under the terms of the predecessor provisions of ss.220 and 221. The provision is in fact anomalous and is entitled: "Oversea company may be wound-up though dissolved". Section 225 in fact deals with foreign companies that have been carrying on business in Great Britain, where the term "oversea company" is used to refer to a foreign company which has an established place of business in Great Britain.[82] Section 225 is narrower in its base than s.221 because it may only be used when a foreign company which has carried on business in Great Britain has ceased to carry on business. The Privy Council considered a Hong Kong provision almost identical to s.225 in the case of *Dairen Kisen Kabushiki Kaisha v Shiang Kee*,[83] with Lord Romer holding that a company had ceased to carry on business if it has been dissolved abroad. Accordingly, s.225 will be always applicable if the company has been wound up abroad.

Recognition of UK liquidations

22–19   Windings up in England and Wales, or Northern Ireland, will always be recognised by the Scottish courts.[84] Section 426(1) of the Insolvency Act 1986 provides:

> "An order made by a court in any part of the United Kingdom in the exercise of jurisdiction in relation to insolvency law shall be enforced in any other part of the United Kingdom as if it were made by a court exercising the corresponding jurisdiction in that other part".[85]

Subsections (2) and (3) of s.426 declare that nothing in subs.(1) requires a court in any part of the UK to enforce, in relation to properties situated in that part, any order made by a court in any other part of the UK.[86] The effect is that orders made in one of the constituent countries of the UK are not automatically enforced in another constituent country. Section 426(4) gives an obligation to assist, but s.426(5) makes it quite clear that the country receiving the request has a discretion as to how

---

[81] 1975 S.L.T. 203.

[82] Companies Act 1985, s.744.

[83] [1941] A.C. 373; s.313(2) of the Companies Ordinance 1932 now re-enacted as s.327A of the Companies Ordinance (C.32).

[84] *Queensland Mercantile & Agency Co Ltd v Australiasion Investment Co Ltd* (1888) 15 R. 935.

[85] See *Scottish Pacific Coast Mining Co Ltd v Walker* (1886) 13 R. 816 and [1886] W.N. 63 for an example of procedure under previous legislation. In those cases a Scottish order was enforced in England in relation to proceedings in California. Section 426(1) applies to corporate and personal insolvency.

[86] Section 426(3) of the Insolvency Act 1986 also empowers the Secretary of State by order to make the powers of a trustee or assignee effective throughout the UK. This order making power has not been used.

the assistance is given if assistance is to be given and that, in exercising the discretion, the court has regard to its own particular rules of private international law.

Recognition of Foreign companies: place of incorporation as basis for winding up

Since it is for the personal law of a company to indicate the person or **22–20** persons who are entitled to act on its behalf, the title of a liquidator appointed in accordance with the law of the place of incorporation will be recognised in Scotland.[87] In the case of *Dairen Kisen Kabushiki Kaisha v Shiang Kee*[88] a company incorporated under the laws of, and resident in, the Republic of China, and having one of its branches at Hong Kong where there were valuable assets belonging to it, was dissolved in China by decree of a Chinese court in accordance with the law of China. With reference to the dissolved Chinese company, Lord Romer stated:

> "The position therefore, is this. The company has ceased to exist by an act of the country by whose acts and under whose law it was made a juristic entity, and must, accordingly be treated as non-existent by all courts administering English law".

In fact, the recognition by the court of a liquidator appointed under the law of the place of incorporation is almost without exception.[89]

It is thought that in the case of foreign regimes analogous to liquidations, the same basis of recognition will be used.[90]

Multiple incorporation

A company formed under the Companies Act 1985 may only be **22–21** domiciled in England and Wales or Scotland. However, it is possible in certain jurisdictions, especially federal states, that a corporation may be formally incorporated in more than one state within the federal unit. There are, however, legal systems which permit a corporation to be incorporated locally as well as in some other foreign jurisdiction.[91]

---

[87] Anton, *Private International Law* at p.724; Stair, *Memorial Encyclopaedia*, vol.4, para.945 (Companies).

[88] [1941] A.C. 373.

[89] See *Baden, Delvaux and Lecuit v Société Générale pour Favoriser le Dévelopement du Commerce et de l'Industrie en France SA* [1983] B.C.L.C. 325, where four foreign liquidations were recognised.

[90] See *Schemmer v Property Resources Ltd* [1975] Ch. 273 for a discussion of the basis of recognition of foreign receivers and the necessary nexus between the receivership and any foreign property claimed; *Marshall, Petr* (1895) 22 R. 697 where Scottish liquidation is made ancillary to a receivership in Iowa. It was sufficient for the Scottish courts to recognise the Iowa receivership that the assets of the company were being administered by the Receivers appointed by the United States courts for the benefit of the debenture holders and other creditors.

[91] For a discussion of the resolution of conflicts as to the content of the laws where there are two corporate domiciles. See Smart, "Corporate Domicile" (1990) *Journal of Business Law* 126.

Where multiple incorporation is permitted under two legal systems, the company will be domiciled in each place of incorporation, and acts done validly, according to the law of either domicile, may be recognised in the Scottish and English courts.[92]

While a UK company cannot reincorporate abroad, it may register in a foreign country in order to do business there.[93] The only exception to this under the Insolvency Act 1986 would seem to be in the case of a foreign company which had a principal place of business in England and Wales, and in Scotland. In terms of s.221(3):

> "(3) For the purpose of determining a court's winding up jurisdiction, an unregistered company is deemed—
>
> (a) to be registered in England and Wales or Scotland, according as its principal place of business is situated in England and Wales or Scotland; or
>
> (b) if it has a principal place of business situated in both countries, to be registered in both countries,
>
> and the principal place of business situated in that part of Great Britain in which proceedings are being instituted is, for all purposes of the winding up, deemed to be the registered office of the company."

This would seem not to preclude the possibility of a foreign company being deemed to be registered in both England and Wales, and in Scotland. This would allow a winding up in England and a winding up in Scotland. There is an exception to the above jurisdiction rule—if the company is solvent but a winding-up order is nevertheless sought, an English court, for example, would have no jurisdiction to make the order if the central management and control of the company is not exercised in England and the company has its seat in a state which is a party to the 1968 Brussels Convention or the Lugano Convention. This is because, in those circumstances, the English court would not possess jurisdiction.[94] If the central management and control of the company were in Scotland or Northern Ireland but not in England, the court in England would have jurisdiction if the company also had a principal place of business in Scotland or Northern Ireland and in England, because the amended version of the 1968 Convention, applicable in intra-UK cases, does not apply to the winding up even of solvent companies unless, again, the company has its seat in a State which is a party to the 1968 Brussels Convention. In which case jurisdiction will not exist.[95]

No possibility of liquidation in the country of incorporation

22–22   The English courts have been reluctant to recognise liquidations except in the place of the incorporation of the company. An exception to this is where there is no likelihood of a liquidation in the country of

---

[92] *Hughes v Hannover* [1997] B.C.C. 921, above.

[93] *Tayside Floorcloth Co Ltd (Petrs)*, 1923 S.C. 590.

[94] See Civil Jurisdiction and Judgments Act 1982, ss.43(2)(b), 43(3)(b), 43(7)(a)—(b); Sch.1, arts 1(2), 16(2); Sch.3C, arts 1(2) and 16(2).

[95] See also Dicey & Morris, *The Conflict of Laws* (13th ed.), p.1131.

incorporation. The thinking would appear to be that, on the basis of "comity", it is defensible only to recognise a liquidation conducted in the country of incorporation, just as the English courts justify their own jurisdiction to make a liquidation order. Such concern is not shown where there is no likelihood of a liquidation in the country of incorporation.[96]

English and Commonwealth cases of recognition of liquidation not in place of incorporation

In the case of *Re Russo-Asiatic Bank*,[97] decided in Hong Kong, a **22–23** banking corporation established in Russia had branches in London, Shanghai and Hong Kong. The Hong Kong court denied effect to Soviet decrees dissolving the Russo-Asiatic Bank. Liquidations of the branch offices took place in London, Shanghai and Hong Kong, with a surplus resulting in the Hong Kong winding up. There was no liquidation in the place of incorporation. The liquidators in Shanghai applied for an order that they be given the surplus assets from the Hong Kong winding up. The London liquidator merely sought to represent the creditors in the English proceedings and to enter pleas in the Hong Kong winding up on behalf of those creditors. The Hong Kong court did not rule out recognition of the liquidations in London and Shanghai. Sir Henry Gollan C.J. stated:

"But the rule that the liquidation in Hong Kong of a branch of a foreign company should be ancillary to a liquidation in the country of its domicile can have no application in the circumstances of this case . . . as the ancillary to those in Russia, it follows that there is no court elsewhere which can . . . be regarded as the principal court to govern the liquidation.

There is no precedent to guide me in the exceptional circumstances of this case. But, it appears to me that, on principle, there is no reason why the London liquidator should not put in proofs on behalf of the creditors whom he represents, and I give him leave to do so. So far as the claim of the Shanghai liquidators for payment to them of the surplus is concerned, I dismiss it".[98]

In *Re a Company* (No 00359 of 1987),[99] a Liberian one-ship company had connections with England and Greece. Peter Gibson J., having determined that the English court had jurisdiction to make a winding-up order, turned to consider whether there was any more appropriate foreign jurisdiction. He stated:

"It is also appropriate for the court to consider whether any other jurisdiction is more appropriate for the winding up of this admit-

---

[96] Dicey & Morris, *The Conflict of Laws* (13th ed.), p.1151; *Re Azoff-Don Commercial Bank* [1954] Ch. 315; the passage in *Dicey & Morris* was cited with apparent approval in *Felixstowe Dock and Railway Co v United States Line Inc* [1989] Q.B. 360 at 374–375.
[97] [1930] H.K.L.R. 16.
[98] *ibid.* at 20–21.
[99] [1988] Ch. 210.

tedly insolvent company. In my judgment, there is none. Miss Heilborn accepts that Liberia is not a serious rival to this country for the purpose of jurisdiction. The Company seems to have had nothing to do with Liberia after its incorporation. But she suggested that Greece might be a more appropriate jurisdiction. I do not accept that. Apart from the fact that the vessel flies a Greek flag and that notices under the loan agreement and first preferred mortgage are required to be sent to the company care of Esperos in Greece I cannot see on what basis Greece would be a more appropriate jurisdiction to wind-up the company. In my judgment, for the reasons I have given, the company has a much closer connection with this jurisdiction."

Scotland—bases of recognition of liquidations not in place of incorporation

22–24   There would appear to be no doubt that it is open to the Scottish courts to recognise a liquidation not in the place of the incorporation of the company. In the case of *Queensland Mercantile and Agency Co Ltd v Australasian Investment Co Ltd*,[1] a Queensland company went into liquidation in Queensland and subsequently applied for and obtained a winding-up order in London, where it has assets and creditors. The winding-up order there was ordered to be ancillary to the proceedings in Australia.[2] In the course of the ancillary winding up in England the English liquidator obtained an order for a stay of proceedings already under way in Scotland. The Scottish court gave effect to the order of the English High Court and recognised a liquidation other than under the law of the place of recognition. Lord President Inglis stated:

> "The order which is sought to be enforced in the first petition before us is one issued by Mr Justice North in the liquidation of the Queensland Mercantile and Agency Co, Limited in England; and it has been contended by the respondents that that order ought not to be enforced, because the liquidation in which it was pronounced was not a statutory or valid liquidation. The company was in liquidation in Queensland before the application for the winding up order was made in London; and that, it is said, precluded the possibility of any such English winding up order being pronounced. I am in some doubt whether we ought to entertain that question, because we have before us an order of a competent court of jurisdiction, whose orders presumably, and upon the face of them, are to be enforced in this country; and I doubt whether it is right that we should enquire into the validity of these orders, unless there is something upon the face of them that shows that they are incompetent. But I think it right to say that I have no doubt whatever of the competency of the English liquidation, assuming the facts to be as stated—that is to say, that the Queensland

---

[1] (1888) 15 R. 935.
[2] (1888) 58 L.T. 878 at 879.

company had a branch business in London, that they had assets there and creditors there, and shareholders in the country also. It has been contended that the effect of the liquidation is the same as that of a sequestration in making the administration of the estate of the company one and indivisible; but that I think is a mistake. In a sequestration under our statute of 1856 the entire estate of the bankrupt is transferred to the trustee wherever situated and his title is of a very effective and strong kind; it makes him for the benefit of the creditors the absolute and exclusive proprietor of that estate, fortified by every kind of tide that a statute is capable of conferring upon him. And, therefore, in such a case as that, it is quite impossible to say that there can be a second sequestration either in the same country or in a different country from that in which the first has taken place; the whole estate is vested in one person, and it cannot, therefore, become *pro parte* vested in some other person by a subsequent proceeding. But a liquidation is followed by a very different state of affairs. The estate of the company is not transferred from the company to the liquidator, it remains vested in the company just as it was before the winding up order, and the liquidator is a mere administrator of the affairs of the company. He can do nothing in the way of using action or diligence except in the name of the company; and the company never becomes dissolved, and never is completely divested of its estate until the liquidation has come to an end. It may, therefore very well be, that although there is a winding up in the colony which would enable the liquidator there to ingather the whole assets of the company, if he can reach them, it may aid him very much in the performance of that duty that there should be another liquidation in England or elsewhere where also the company has been carrying on business. There seems to me to be nothing incompatible in the co-existence of the two. Therefore the suggestion that the English liquidation is invalid and cannot possibly co-exist with the Queensland liquidation I think is out of the case".[3]

In the case of *The Governor and Company of the Bank of England*[4] the Bank of Credit and Commerce International SA ("BCCI") was incorporated in Luxembourg and had branches in England and Scotland. A winding-up order of the bank was made in Luxembourg on January 3, 1992. The High Court in England ordered an "ancillary" winding up on January 14 1992. Parallel with the proceedings in England were two requests by the High Court in England under s.426 of the Insolvency Act for assistance of the Scottish courts. In terms of the first petition which was brought to the English court in the name of the Governor and Company of the Bank of England, the High Court in England requested the Scottish courts to appoint provisional liquidators on the branch of BCCI in Scotland. This was granted. Simultaneously with the hearing of the winding up order on January 14, 1992 in England, a request was made

[3] *Queensland Mercantile and Agency Co Ltd v Australasian Investment Co Ltd* (1888) 15 R. 935 at 939.
[4] Court of Session, unreported, 1991 and 1992.

by the High Court in England for the Court of Session to appoint liquidators in Scotland on BCCI. This the Court of Session did on January 15, after the making of the English winding up order. The Court of Session, accordingly, recognised the English "ancillary" winding-up order and winding up proceedings in England.

It is thought now that the English courts, given their experience in the BCCI case, will recognise liquidators although they are not in the place of incorporation. In contrast, in *Re IIT*,[5] Houlden J.A., having recognised a Luxembourg liquidation, stated: "[i]ndeed, I do not think that any other jurisdiction would have had authority to appoint liquidators for IIT."

This comment by a Canadian judge is obiter and was made without the relevant English authorities being cited, let alone the recent BCCI case. In addition, the evidence before the court in Ontario did not suggest that IIT had carried on business within, or submitted to, the jurisdiction of a court in any other country. This comment, therefore, can be ignored, especially in the light of the developments in the BCCI case, in assessing the attitude of the Scottish and English courts in the recognition of liquidations in other countries where a company has not been incorporated.

"Ancillary" liquidations

22–25   As a general rule matters affecting the affairs of a corporation are usually determined by the law of the state where the company was incorporated. Because, however, the Scottish courts may wind up a company in Scotland which is also being wound up in the country of its incorporation, it is usual that the Scottish court will regard its own proceedings as ancillary to the main liquidation taking place in the state in which the company is incorporated. So, for example, in the case of *Marshall, Petitioner*,[6] where a company was in receivership in the State of Iowa where it was incorporated, but there were assets and affairs in Scotland, the Court of Session ordered that the Scottish liquidation be ancillary to the liquidation in the country in which the company was being wound-up. In expressing the view that the Scottish liquidation should be "ancillary" to the liquidation in Iowa, the court relied, *inter alia*, on the English authority of *Re Commercial Bank of South Australia*.[7] In that case a banking company, incorporated and carrying on business in Australia, had a branch office in London but was not registered in England. The company, however, had English creditors, and assets in England. In granting a winding-up order Sir Ford North described how an ancillary winding up should operate. He stated:

"I think therefore, that the English creditors are entitled to have a winding up order made by this court. I do not think it would be

---

[5] (1975) 58 D.L.R. (3d) 55 at 58.
[6] (1895) 22 R. 697.
[7] [1886] 33 Ch. D 174; see also *Re BCCI S.A.* (No.10) [1997] Ch. 213 at 243.

right to insert any special directions in the order; this is not the proper time for giving such directions. But I will say this, that I think the winding up here will be ancillary to a winding up in Australia, and, if I have the control of the proceedings here, I will take care that there will be no conflict between the two courts, and I shall have regard to the interests of all the creditors and all the contributories, and shall endeavour to keep down the expenses of the winding up so far as is possible."

In the subsequent case of *Re English, Scottish & Australian Chartered Bank*,[8] Vaughan Williams J. set out the much quoted basis of an ancillary winding up:

"One knows that where there is a liquidation of one concern the general principle is . . . ascertain what is the domicile of the company in liquidation; let the court of the country of domicile act as the principal court to govern the liquidation; and let the other courts act as ancillary, as far as they can, to the principal liquidation."

An example of an ancillary winding up, which founded, *inter alia*, on the above mentioned English cases was *Re National Benefit Assurance Co*,[9] in which a company incorporated in England had also carried on business in Canada. The Canadian liabilities were far less than the English. The company was in liquidation in England and a liquidator had also been appointed in an ancillary winding up in the Canadian province of Manitoba. The Court of Appeal in Manitoba held that, because the duties of the Canadian liquidator were ancillary to the English winding up proceedings, assets collected by the Canadian liquidator had to be handed over to the English liquidator after payment of preferred creditors in Canada and the costs of the liquidation. After that the majority of creditors were left to bring their claims in the liquidation in England. In its judgment the Manitoba Court of Appeal stated:

"If, in the present liquidation, the Canadian assets were retained here it would only be for the purpose of paying the Canadian creditors *pari passu* with the English and other creditors . . . As there can be no apprehension that the Canadian creditors will not have equal treatment with all other creditors, there is no reason why the assets in the hands of the Canadian liquidator should not now be remitted to the English liquidator, less amount required to pay Canadian preferred creditors, and other amounts either approved by the court or by the English liquidator, and costs of the liquidation."

Co-ordination of proceedings through ancillary windings up

The reason for a liquidation being made ancillary to another liquida-   **22–26**
tion is to co-ordinate the insolvency proceedings, as well as to protect the assets in the ancillary jurisdiction or the rights of creditors there if

---

[8] [1893] 3 Ch. 385 at 394.
[9] (1927) 3 D.L.R. 289.

the main liquidation law is in conflict with that in the local jurisdiction. A good example of the way this co-ordination works is found in the insolvency of the *Queensland Mercantile and Agency Co Ltd*.[10] The facts were as follows.

Queensland Mercantile and Agency Co Ltd (the Queensland company) was incorporated in Queensland where it acted as agent for the Australasian Investment Co ("AIC"), a company registered in Scotland. In October 1887 the Queensland company was ordered to be wound up in the courts in Queensland. In January 1888 a winding-up order in respect of the Queensland company was made in England and the winding up there was directed to be ancillary to the proceedings in Australia. In February 1887 AIC commenced proceedings against the Queensland company in Scotland prior to the orders of the Australian and English courts. It alleged that the Queensland company had misappropriated investments belonging to AIC. In the Scottish proceedings AIC arrested certain assets belonging to the Queensland company in Scotland and thereby became a secured creditor on the arrested funds. The question before the English courts was whether the English should issue a restraining order on AIC from proceeding with the Scottish action. North J. stated:

> "It is true that there is a liquidation of the company also going on in Queensland, where the head office of the company was situate. To a certain extent I treat the winding up here as ancillary to the winding up there, but not to such an extent as to make this court an agent for the courts in Queensland, and I must investigate the matter as far as I can here."

North J. attempted to co-ordinate the two liquidations and the Scottish proceedings. He granted a stay of the Scottish proceedings and ordered that AIC's claim against the Queensland company was to be determined in Queensland, but with express reservation to AIC of the benefit of the arrestment.

Although a winding up may be described as "ancillary", the amount of work undertaken by the court where the ancillary winding up is taking place may expand and dwarf the proceedings in the court where the main winding up is held.

BCCI *case*

22–27   The most important case on ancillary windings-up was the case of *Re BCCI SA (No.10)*.[11] That case again concerned BCCI which was incorporated in Luxembourg and formed part of a group that carried on a

---

[10] *Re Queensland Mercantile and Agency Co Ltd* (1888) 58 L.T. 878; For subsequent proceedings see *Re Queensland Mercantile and Agency Co Ltd, ex p. Australasian Investment Co* [1892] 2 Ch. 536; *Queensland Mercantile and Agency Co Ltd v Australasian Investment Co* (1888) 15 R. 935; see also *Barclays Bank plc v Homan, Independent*, September 1, 1992, where Hoffman J. refused injunction in MCC case against examiner in proceedings in US under Bankruptcy Code ancillary to English administration from applying to US court for recovery of $30 million from Barclays as a preference, which would not have been recoverable under Insolvency Act 1986, s.239.

[11] [1997] Ch. 213.

banking business on an international scale. The group collapsed in the summer of 1991, and provisional liquidators of BCCI were appointed in England on July 5, 1991, on the application of the Bank of England. A similar action was taken by other regulators around the world with the intention and effect of closing down the operations of the BCCI group. In Luxembourg a *Commissaire de Surveillance* was appointed on July 8, 1991. Both the Court of Session in Scotland and the High Court of the Isle of Man appointed provisional liquidators of BCCI in their respective jurisdictions. On January 3, 1992, BCCI went into liquidation in Luxembourg, the country of its incorporation. Three liquidators were appointed. The Luxembourg winding-up order was followed by a winding-up order made in England on January 14, 1992, in terms of which BCCI was to be wound up under the provisions of the Insolvency Act 1986. On the same day as the English winding-up order was made, a winding-up order in respect of BCCI was made by the Court of Session in Scotland; and on January 15, 1992, the High Court in the Isle of Man also made a winding-up order. Both in Scotland and in the Isle of Man BCCI had carried on its banking business through branches.

It was subsequently agreed between the bank's liquidators in Luxembourg, in England and in various other jurisdictions, that 48.5 per cent of the global realisations of the banks' assets should be distributed by the English liquidators, who had at their disposal substantial proceeds of realisation of English assets. The liquidators also agreed that the liquidation worldwide should be a joint enterprise with all creditors, wherever situated, receiving the same level of dividend from a central pool. The English liquidators wished to release the funds at their disposal to the Luxembourg liquidators for a distribution among creditors worldwide *pari passu*, with the money, once transferred to Luxembourg, being distributed according to the principles of Luxembourg insolvency law. Luxembourg insolvency law disallowed set-off for a debtor who was simultaneously owed money by the insolvent company, whereas r.4.90 of the Insolvency Rules 1986 provided for mutual credit and set-off, permitting a creditor/debtor or creditor who was also a debtor to set-off his debt from the sum owed to him and prove any balance.

In the course of his judgment Sir Richard Scott analysed the nature of ancillary windings-up in England referring to all the important previous cases. Where a foreign company was in liquidation in its country of incorporation, any winding up in England would be ancillary to the foreign liquidation. If the company is incorporated abroad, English liquidators' ability to get in and realise the company's foreign assets will be very limited. It follows that, if a foreign company has a winding-up order made against it in its country of incorporation and a winding-up order made against it in England, the English liquidators' role is likely to be limited to getting in, realising and distributing the English assets.

Types of co-operation at common law in insolvency proceedings

There seems to be at common law no limit in principle to the type of **22–28** help which may be requested in the UK to aid a foreign court and vice versa, and to the type of co-operation between the courts that is possible.[12] A lot depends on the degree of trust between the jurisdictions and history of co-peration to achieve the best result for creditors and other stakeholders. English and American courts have, on occasions, shown a remarkable degree of co-operation. For example in January 16, 2003, Cenargo (a England registered company with a US Bond issue but no US assets or operations) filed for Chap.11. On January 28, 2003, Lombard, an English secured creditor, sought the appointment to Cenargo of provisional liquidators. Mr Justice Lightman acceded to this request, appointing Ernst & Young as provisional liquidators, and also granted the PLs an injunction against the directors of Cenargo from bringing contempt proceedings in the US. On the same day lawyers for the US Bondholders sought an order restraining Lombard and the PLs from taking further action. Although the traditional comity between the US and English courts appeared to have broken down, this was put right during a friendly conference call between Judge Drain and Mr Justice Lightman, with the result that Judge Drain effectively agreed that the UK was the most appropriate forum for a restructuring proceeding and the Chap.11 proceeding was stayed.

Maxwell type protocol

22–29   A particular problem arises where primary insolvency proceedings are initiated in more than one country. The case of Maxwell Communications Corporation is instructive of the type of co-operation that determination and ingenuity can produce. MCC was an English Holding company with more than 400 subsidiaries worldwide, of which the US subsidiaries comprised approximately 75 per cent of the value of the MCC corporate group. Because of this, MCC filed a voluntary Chap.11 petition in the United States Bankruptcy Court for the Southern District of New York.[13] One day later the High Court of Justice, Chancery Division, Companies Court in London put MCC into administration under the Insolvency Act 1986. Therefore the company was involved in two primary insolvency proceedings. It quickly became clear that jurisdictional complications and the potential for conflict between the laws of two sovereign countries would need to be expeditiously addressed. Chief United States Bankruptcy Judge Tina L. Brozman approved the appointment of an examiner to harmonize the proceedings. In this case, in an effort to reconcile potential conflict between the sovereign courts, and to facilitate and expedite the reorganization of MCC, the court found it necessary to expand the powers of the examiner[14] to include harmonization of the two countries' insolvency proceedings. Accordingly, the Examiner could, as a disinterested party, mediate between the administrator and the company as well as between the courts.

---

[12] See recent cases cited in relation to co-operation between courts in relation to s.426 of the Insolvency Act 1986 in para.22–38. It is thought the powers to co-operate are the same if the court is willing to exercise them.

[13] In 2002, Regus, a London listed company, also filed for Chap.11 protection and had its operations restructured in the New York District Court.

[14] Normally an examiner in a Chap.11 case is appointed to investigate, among other things, the acts, conduct, assets, liabilities, and financial condition of the debtor. Furthermore, s.1106(a)(3) of the Bankruptcy Code grants an examiner the right to investigate "any other matter relevant to the case or to the formulation of a plan."

The examiner and the UK administrators in the Maxwell bankruptcy case created a landmark framework approach to international insolvencies—the cross-border protocol. Protocols, entered into during bankruptcy proceedings, may cover any range of issues. The protocol developed in the *Maxwell* case (the "Maxwell Protocol") initiated the concept of a formalized, court-approved cross-border co-operation in the context of two plenary insolvency proceedings in the US and UK. The Maxwell Protocol was approved by both involved courts and initiated the concept of a formalized co-operation in order to achieve (1) maximization of the estate's value; and (2) harmonization of the two pending insolvency proceedings to minimize expense, waste and jurisdictional conflict. To accomplish these goals, the Maxwell Protocol instituted a framework to co-ordinate the functions of the UK administrators and the Examiner. Under this framework, the UK administrators were recognised as the corporate governance of the Maxwell estate, but major decisions concerning the estate such as borrowings and asset realisations would require consent of the US examiner or approval of the US Court. Moreover, the framework purposely left specific resolution of many issues open to determination during the course of the proceedings. In general, issues concerning the ultimate resolution of the proceedings and asset distribution were left to be addressed later in the proceedings. Ultimately, the Maxwell Protocol directed the parties to coordinate mutually interdependent plans of reorganisation and schemes of arrangement.

Order of priorities in an ancillary winding up

The general rule is that secured creditors, preferred creditors and the **22–30** expenses of the ancillary winding up are paid prior to funds being paid over to the lead liquidator to which we can also add set-off.[15] It was noted in the Canadian case of *Re National Benefit Assurance Co*,[16] that the Manitoba Court of Appeal ordered that assets in the hands of the Canadian liquidator should be remitted to the lead English liquidator "less amount required to pay Canadian preferred creditors, and other amounts either approved by the court or by the English liquidator, and costs of the liquidation". Also in the case of *Re Queensland Mercantile Agency Co Ltd*[17] North J. expressly reserved to Australasian Investment Co Ltd the benefit of the security it had allegedly obtained by arresting assets in Scotland. In the case of *Carron Iron Co v Maclaren*,[18] Lord St Leonards said that:

> "Nor will the rule operate to destroy any priority to which, from the nature of his security, a creditor in Scotland or Ireland is entitled against the assets in either country according to the law of the country, although they may come to be distributed here."

A similar ruling was made in *Re Standard Insurance Co Ltd*.[19] A New Zealand company was in liquidation in New Zealand but there was an

---

[15] See para.22–31.
[16] (1927) 3 D.L.R. 289.
[17] (1888) 58 L.T. 878 at 879.
[18] [1855] 5 H.L. Case 416 at 455.
[19] [1968] Qd R. 118.

ancillary winding up in Queensland and in each of the other Australian states. The court in Queensland held that, when a winding up was proceeding in different jurisdictions, the principle which had to be applied was that, subject to priorities secured by the local law, all creditors of the company were, as far as possible, to be treated equally wherever they were and wherever their debts were contracted.

It will be seen from a reading of the above mentioned cases that, where there is a lead liquidation, an ancillary liquidation and perhaps a second ancillary liquidation, the distribution of the assets in the second ancillary liquidation will be according to priorities and securities of the *lex situs*. The assets are then transmitted, as in the *Queensland Mercantile* case, to the first ancillary liquidation, where they are subject to any priorities in the first ancillary liquidation before being transmitted to the lead liquidator.

Set-off

22–31   The principle of set-off in Scots law is founded upon the Act of 1592,[20] which provides that:

> "Only debt de liquido ad liquidum instantile verefiet be wreit or aith of the partie before the geving of decreit be admittit be all Jugis withine this realme be way of exception."

The language suggests that the rule is one of procedure only. If so, it would be applied even in a Scottish liquidation with a foreign element. This does not mean that foreign rules of set-off may never be applied in Scotland. Under some systems of law the rules relating to set-off take effect by mere operation of the law and affect the substance of the obligation. If by applicable foreign law the obligation of one of the parties were so extinguished or reduced, the fact would be noticed by the Scottish courts.[21] Similarly in England, whether there may be set-off, or counterclaim has been regarded as a matter of procedure to be governed by English law.[22] The English courts, however, recognise the right of a Scottish debtor to plead set-off if it is available under the Scots law of the debt. In the case of *Macfarlane v Norris*[23] the plaintiff in England had been appointed in a Scottish sequestration as trustee. In the English action the defendant pleaded a Scottish set-off. The English court accepted that set-off was generally in England a matter of procedure. However, Blackburn J. was prepared to give effect to the Scots law of set-off. He stated:

> "The Plaintiff sues as trustee of a trader in Scotland, who became bankrupt; and the question, what passed under the transfer of the

---

[20] c.143.

[21] Anton, *Private International Law* (2nd ed., 1990), p.248.

[22] *Meyer v Dresser* [1864] 16 C.B. (NS) 646.

[23] [1862] 2 B. & S. 783; it is thought that the analysis in this case is not totally convincing unless the Scots rule is more than procedure.

bankrupt's goods and chattels to the trustee must be settled by the Scotch law, which must be averred on the pleadings . . . And I cannot reach the averment at the end of the plea otherwise than as averring that the property of the bankrupt, under such circumstances, came to the trustee with a right to deduct cross claims; . . . in other words, that the transfer in the Scotch law is a transfer of a balance of account after allowing for mutual credits."

Cockburn C.J. also stated:

"It is a true the pleader has adopted the form of the English plea of set-off and mutual credit; but we must take the plea as substantially amounting to this; . . . here are mutual credits, the effect of which, by Scotch law, is the discharge of the debtor from all excepting the balance."

The position in relation to set-off was subject to close scrutiny by Sir Richard Scott V.-C. in *Bank of Credit and Commerce International S.A. (No. 10)*.[24] He held that the ancillary nature of an English winding up did not relieve the English court of the obligation to apply English insolvency law to the resolution of any issue arising in the winding up in the English court including r.4.90 of the Insolvency Rules 1986 regarding set-off. In that case BCCI had been ordered in the ancillary winding up to be wound up under the Insolvency Act 1986, of which the Insolvency Rules 1986 were part of the statutory scheme. The set-off brought about by r.4.90 applied, under English law, to every creditor and every debtor whether or not the proper law of the debt was English law. The r.4.90 account, struck at the commencement of the winding up, would have the result that the creditor/debtor would be left either as a net creditor to prove for the balance or, as the case may be, as a net debtor to be sued for the balance, or, if the credits and debits were of exactly equal amounts, with no sum either owing or owed. The insolvency regimes in Scotland and in the Isle of Man had similar set-off rules as in r.4.90, and it would therefore in principle be right for net creditors in these two jurisdictions to be treated in the same way as net creditors who have proved in England.[25]

Discharge of debts under a foreign liquidation

Under Scottish law a foreign liquidation discharges only a company's **22–32** liabilities as are properly governed by the law of the country in which the liquidation takes place. They may not be discharged by a law of the country of the liquidation if that[26] is not the proper law of the liability.[27] In 1724, for example, the Scottish court held that a debt in terms of an English bond was regulated by English law and hence discharged upon the defender's bankruptcy in England.[28] Alternatively, if a creditor

---

[24] [19967] Ch. 213 at 236.
[25] In *Re BCCI S.A. (No.10)* [1997] Ch. 213 at 254.
[26] (1776) Mor. 4593 and App. No. (2) (foreign).
[27] *Adams v National Bank of Greece* [1961] A.C. 255, H.L.
[28] *Rochead v Scot* (1724) Mor. 4566.

participates in a foreign liquidation he is precluded from taking any separate measures in Scotland to obtain a preference. In the case of *Rhones v Parish*[29] a merchant had been bankrupted under the law of Bremen. The creditors, including the respondents, then elected certain of their number as members of the Senate of Bremen as trustees. The respondents meanwhile arrested moveables in Scotland belonging to the bankrupt, and also entered a proof in the proceedings in Bremen. The interlocutor of the Lord Ordinary, which was adhered to by the whole court, stated:

> "The respondents having given their vote for the choice of trustees, or having proved their debts before the trustees, and made a demand for payment, is sufficient evidence of their having acceded to the trust rights, which it seems by the law of Bremen is vested in certain members of the Senate, chosen by the creditors, and that accession precludes them from taking separate measures in this country in order to obtain a preference over the rest of the creditors."[30]

Grounds for non-enforcement of orders made in foreign liquidations

22–33 Although a Scottish court may recognise a foreign liquidation, that does not necessarily entail that the Scottish court will enforce the order of a foreign liquidation court. Generally the courts in the UK will not render assistance to a foreign insolvency proceedings which offended against some over-riding principle of public policy.[31] It is not sufficient that the foreign law is different from that in Scotland.[32]

The grounds for refusal to enforce a foreign judgment in a foreign liquidation are no different from the grounds for the non-enforcement of any other foreign judgment.[33] The main grounds can be summarised briefly as follows:

(1) revenue law;
(2) penal law;
(3) fraud;
(4) natural justice; and
(5) reciprocity.

---

[29] (1776) Mor. 4593 and App. No. (2) (foreign).

[30] See also *Glover v Vasie* (1776) Mor. 4562 and App. No. (3) (foreign) where a like determination was made with reference to an English bankruptcy. Vasie had received a dividend under an English commission but later arrested assets in Scotland. The court held that Vasie was barred from competing by arrestment with the English assignees; *Rose v McLeod* (1825) 4 S. 311. See also the important Privy Council case of *Wight v Eckhardt Marine GmbH* [2003] B.C.C. 702, where it was held that a discharge of a debt under the proper law of the debt entails that it cannot be proved in a liquidation, even if it was valid when the company went into liquidation.

[31] *Re a debtor, ex p. Viscount of the Royal Court of Jersey* [1981] Ch. 384 at 402.

[32] *Baden, Delvaux and Lecuit v Société Générale pour Favoriser le Dévelopement du Commerce et de l'Industrie en France SA* [1983] B.C.L.C. 325; *Connal & Co v Loder* (1868) 6 M. 1095.

[33] For detailed discussion see Anton, *Private International Law* (2nd ed., 1990), pp.99–106.

Revenue law

The UK courts and the Irish courts have firmly set themselves against **22-34** the enforcement of foreign revenue claims. In the case of *Government of India v Taylor*[34] the House of Lords unanimously held that a claim by or on behalf of a foreign state to recover taxes was unenforceable in the English courts. Lord Keith of Avenholm observed that "in no circumstances will the courts directly or indirectly enforce the revenue laws of another country".[35] This approach had been taken by the Irish courts in the case of *Peter Buchanan Ltd v McVey*[36] concerning a Scottish company in liquidation in Scotland at the instance of the Scottish Revenue. The liquidator brought an action in Ireland to recover assets of the company. Because it was shown that, after payment of the costs of the liquidation any money recovered would go to the Inland Revenue in Scotland, Kingsmill Moore J. held that essentially the action was an action to enforce a revenue debt of the Inland Revenue in Scotland and could not be enforced by the Irish court. He stated —

> "For the purpose of this case it is sufficient to say that when it appears to the court that the whole object of the suit is to collect tax for a foreign Revenue, and that this will be the sole result of a decision in favour of the plaintiff, then the court is entitled to reject the claim by refusing jurisdiction."

This case was upheld on appeal to the Supreme Court. The action was held to have the sole purpose of recovering taxes and was therefore not enforceable in Ireland. Maguire C.J. observed, however:

> "I agree that if the payment of a Revenue claim was only incidental and there had been other claims to be met, it would be difficult for our courts to refuse to lend assistance to bring assets of the company under the control of the liquidator."

This approach of the Irish courts[37] is exactly the approach taken by the Scottish courts. The leading Scottish case of *Scottish National Orchestra Ltd v Thomson's Exrs*[38] concerned a claim by the Swedish administrators of the estate of a person who had died domiciled in Sweden, but with assets in Scotland. The claim was, *inter alia*, for Swedish inheritance tax. Lord Robertson said that the administrators' claim would have failed if the only purpose had been to pay Swedish tax. However, after the tax had been paid, there were remaining assets which would be held for the beneficiaries in Sweden. Accordingly, as the enforcement of a foreign revenue debt was not the sole purpose of the action, the claim of the Swedish administrators would be upheld.

---

[34] [1955] A.C. 491.
[35] *ibid.* at 510.
[36] [1954] I.R. 89.
[37] See the comments also of Lord Mackay of Clashfern in *Williams & Humbert Ltd v W. & H. Trademarks (Jersey) Ltd* [1986] A.C. 368 at 440, which approve the analysis of Maguire C.J.
[38] 1969 S.L.T. 325; *A.G. of Canada v William Schulze & Co* (1901) 9 S.L.T. 4.

The enforcement of revenue law is widely construed and covers estate duty, rates, gambling dues, customs, state health insurance contributions. Although the EU Regulation on Insolvency Proceedings[39] does not expressly allow the enforcement of Revenue claims, it may mean in future that Member State claims will have to be enforced within the Member States. Already there is a high degree of co-operation and the public policy agreement is very thin when "partner" Member States are the claimants.[40]

Penal law

22–35   The Scottish courts will not uphold the criminal or penal law of a foreign country. It is not sufficient that there is a penal element.[41]

Fraud

22–36   The Scottish courts will deny recognition to a foreign decree by fraud. This is because under Scots law no judgment obtained by fraud could have any legal validity, and certainly not in any court of equity.[42] There is also some old authority for the proposition that foreign insolvency proceedings, even where they are conducted properly according to the foreign law, may in certain circumstances be a type of fraud upon the other creditors, and should not be upheld if resorted to merely to undermine or preclude Scottish insolvency proceedings. In the case of *Geddes v Mowat*[43] a debtor was domiciled, resident and carried on business in Scotland. On January 4, 1820, a commission of bankruptcy was issued in England. A week later the debtor's estate was sequestrated in Scotland. The English commission was later found to be invalid and a new commission was issued. The second commission was based upon the original act of bankruptcy. The English assignees petitioned the Scottish court, on the basis that the sequestration had been superseded by the English commission. This claim was rejected by the Court of Session. The House of Lords also held that the English commission was a nullity, and accordingly the sequestration had been the first in time. Lord Gifford suggested in his opinion that, where a person resorts to a foreign insolvency proceedings in order to undermine the general body of creditors, this could be a "fraud of the law of Scotland". He stated[44]:

> "There is another point to be observed upon; the bankrupt, as had already been stated, was a domiciled Scotsman . . . it is strongly to

---

[39] Council Regulation (E.C.) 1346/2000 of May 29, 2000 on insolvency proceedings [2000] O.J. L. 160/1.

[40] See para.22–58.

[41] *Huntington v Attrill* [1893] A.C. 150 at 157, where Lord Watson states: "proceedings, in order to come within the scope of the rule, must be in the nature of a suit in favour of the state whose law has been infringed"; *Re IIT* (1975) 58 D.L.R. 55, in which a Canadian court rejected the submission that a Luxembourg regulation was penal in nature on the grounds that, while it contained penal provisions, it was not penal in nature in the sense in which that term was interpreted in the conflict of laws; *Schemmer v Property-General of New Zealand v Ortiz* [1984] A.C. 1.

[42] *Boe v Anderson* (1857) 20 D. 11 at 32.

[43] [1824] 1 G1 & J 414; 2 Shaw's App Case 230.

[44] At 423.

be suspected, that finding himself in difficulties in Scotland, and foreseeing a sequestration, he removed to England, in order to commit an act of bankruptcy, and upon that the English commission was founded; . . . and I think it might admit of a serious question, independently of the point of priority, whether this commission of bankruptcy in England, under these circumstances, might not be considered as having been issued in fraud of the law of Scotland; issued as it was against a party, native of Scotland, then resident in Scotland, domiciled in Scotland for years, going to England, in December, and on 4 January committing an act of bankruptcy".[45]

Natural justice

A foreign judgment may be denied recognition if there has been a **22–37** breach of the rules of natural justice.[46] It is not necessary that every creditor must have received notice of the liquidation and been able to lodge a claim if there has been no unfairness.[47]

Reciprocity

There is some Commonwealth authority suggesting that courts sometimes consider whether recognition should be restricted in the case of a foreign insolvency where there is a lack of reciprocity.[48] In England, if anything, the courts seem to disregard the question of reciprocity, if perhaps on this fictional assumption that it exists.[49]

PART II

ENFORCEMENT OF COURT ORDERS UNDER SECTION 426 OF THE INSOLVENCY ACT 1986 WITHIN THE UNITED KINGDOM

AND

BETWEEN THE UNITED KINGDOM COURTS AND THE COURTS OF "DESIGNATED COUNTRIES AND TERRITORIES"

Section 426(4) of the Insolvency Act 1986 provides that: **22–38**

---

[45] See also in England *Re Henry Hooman* (1895) 1 L.T. 46; *Jet Holdings Inc v Patel* [1990] Q.B. 335; and *Adams v Cape Industries plc* [1990] 2 W.L.R. 657; and *Foster v Taylor* (1871) 31 U.C.R. 24.

[46] *Det Norske Bjergnings og Dykkercompagni v McLaren* (1885) 22 S.L.R. 861; *Price v Dewhurst* (1837) 8 Sim. 279; *Bergerem v Marsh* (1921) 91 L.J.K.B. 80, where a judgment based on *ex parte* proceedings with full notice was held to constitute a valid judgment in a Belgian insolvency; *Larkins v NUM* [1985] I.R. 671; *Bond Brewing Holding Ltd v Crawford* (1989) 92 A.L.R. 154.

[47] *Pattison v McVicar* (1886) 13 R. 550; *Southgate v Montgomerie* (1837) 15 S. 507; *Strike v Gleich* (1879) O.B. & F. 50.

[48] *William v Rice* (1926) 3 D.L.R. 225 at 250–251.

[49] *Employers' Liability Assurance Corpn v Sedgwick, Collins & Co* [1927] A.C. 95, in which the House of Lords treated as valid the liquidation of a company in Russia, although no provision had been made for English claims.

"The courts having jurisdiction in relation to insolvency law in any part of the United Kingdom shall assist the courts having the corresponding jurisdiction in any other part of the United Kingdom or any relevant country or territory."

The meaning of the expression "relevant country or territory" is given in subs.(11) and means:

"(a) any of the Channel Islands or the Isle of Man, or
(b) any country or territory designated for the purposes of this section by the Secretary of State by Order made by statutory instrument."

So far three orders have been made now, comprising 19 countries or territories so designated.[50] (The Republic of Ireland is no longer designated.)

Subsection (10) of s.426 gives the definition of the expression "insolvency law" for the purposes of the section, as it applies in each of the parts of the UK. In relation to Scotland, that amounts to:

"Provision extending to Scotland and made by or under this Act, section 6 to 10, 12, 15, 19(c) and 20 (with schedule 1) of the Company Directors Disqualification Act 1986, Part xviii of the Companies Act or the Bankruptcy (Scotland) Act 1985."

A key question in the interpretation of s.426 is how the expression "insolvency law" for the purposes of s.426(4) should be construed. In the case of *Hughes v Hannover Ruckversicherungs-Aktiengesellschasp*[51] Morritt L.J. held that in responding to a request for assistance made by an eligible court within the terms of that section, a court in England has available to it his own general jurisdiction and powers, and either:

(a) the insolvency law of England and Wales as defined by s.426(10)(a); or
(b) so much of the law of the relevant country as corresponds to that compromised in (a).[52]

On the above basis, the English court held that it could grant a Mareva junction in the *Hughes* case. The court is even able to grant a form of remedy available under the insolvency law of the requesting court,

---

[50] The Co-operation of Insolvency Court (Designation of Relevant Countries and Territories) Order 1986 (SI 1986/2123) together with subsequent orders made in 1996 and 1998: SI 1996/253; SI 1998/2766. The countries and territories so designated are: Anguilla, Australia, the Bahamas, Bermuda, Botswana, Brunei, Canada, Caanan Islands, Falkland Islands, Gibraltar, Hong Kong, Malaysia, Montserrat, New Zealand, St Helena, South Africa, Turks and Caicos Islands, Tuvalu, and the Virgin Islands. With modifications, the provisions of s.426 have also been extended to the Bailiwick of Guernsey and to Northern Ireland. See SI 1989/2409; and SI 1989/2405 (N.I. 19), Art.381 and Sch.9, para. 41(b).
[51] [1997] 1 B.C.L.C. 497; [1997] B.C.C. 921.
[52] For 426(10)(a) read 426(10)(b) for Scotland.

although unavailable either as part of the English insolvency law or under the general law of England.[53] However, although the court has those powers, it must bear in mind that the principles and practice of the law in the requesting jurisdiction are part of the law of that country, and these should be adhered to if possible.[54]

Section 426(4) appears to be mandatory with the words "shall assist", but this does not imply a lack of discretion in the way in which the courts may respond to the request from the relevant court. In the case of *Hughes v Hannover*[55] the court approved the words of Rattee J. in his judgment in *Re Bank of Credit and Commerce International S.A. (No. 9)* [1994] 1 ALL E.R. 764 at 785; [1993] B.C.C. 387 at 803 E.; namely:

"[The] court should exercise its discretion in favour of giving the particular assistance requested by the [foreign] court unless there is some good reason for not doing so."

An example of s.426 in operation is the case of *First Tokyo Index Trust Ltd, Petrs.*[56] In that case the joint liquidators of the Scottish company First Tokyo Index Trust plc, a company in the Maxwell group of companies, petitioned the Court of Session for orders under ss.236, 237 and 426 of the Insolvency Act 1986. Section 236 concerns the private examination of the office holder of a company. Section 237 concerns the production of evidence. The petition requested the court to order a private examination of Kevin Maxwell, who was a director of the petitioners, and Larry Trachtenburg, who had been the secretary of the petitioners. The petition also asked the Court of Session to issue to the High Court of Justice in England a request for assistance to examine the respondents in private and for documents to be produced before the court in England. The respondents consented to the granting of the orders, and the Court of Session made an order under s.236 for the respondents to be examined on oath in England. The Court of Session also ordered the respondents to produce property and documents, and issued a request to the High Court in England for assistance in the examination. **22–39**

That case shows that the courts may ask each other for examinations of persons and for documentation to be produced before either court. The case of *BCCI*[57] was a case where the English court asked the Court of Session to appoint certain persons as liquidators of BCCI in Scotland. The High Court in England had issued a winding-up order for the ancillary winding up of BCCI in England. This was after a winding-up order in Luxembourg. The Scottish court acceded to the request of the

[53] See also *Re Business City Express Ltd* [1997] B.C.C. 826; *Re Southern Equities Corp Ltd, England v Smith* [2001] Ch. 419; [2000] B.C.C. 123 (CA); *Re Duke Group Ltd* [2001] B.C.C. 144; and *Re Trading Partners Ltd, Akers* [2002] 1 B.C.L.C. 655.
[54] See *Re Southern Equities Corp Ltd, England v Smith* [2001] Ch. 419; [2000] B.C.C. 123 (CA); for commentary see Pugh, 2000 I.L.&P. 16(1)6–8 and Goldring and Perry, 2000 I.L.&P. 16(3)110–111.
[55] See *supra*.
[56] Unreported, February 21, 1992.
[57] Unreported, Court of Session, 1991 and 1992.

English court and appointed as joint liquidators of BCCI in Scotland one person resident in England and another resident in Scotland.

Section 426(1) relates to "insolvency law", which is defined in s.426(10) to cover bankruptcy and the various insolvency regimes. It accordingly allows administrators, receivers and supervisors of CVAs the equivalent access to the judicial co-operation machinery as a liquidator. In the *Goodman International* case[58] an application was made by the examiner (the Irish equivalent of a reporter to the court, under the Irish equivalent to an administration under the Irish Companies (Amendment) Act 1990, set up by that Act) to the High Court of Ireland asking it to request the assistance of the High Court in England pursuant to s.426 of the Insolvency Act 1986 to recognise the Irish regime as equivalent to administration, and to protect assets of the Goodman Group in England and Wales from creditor action with the same protection as the assets and companies in Ireland had under the Irish statute. The Republic of Ireland was a designated country pursuant to The Co-operation of Insolvency Courts (Designation of Relevant Countries and Territories) Order 1986. The reasoning behind this application was that, unless the creditors of the companies were restrained from proceeding against the companies and their assets in Ireland by the provisions of s.5 of the Companies (Amendment) Act 1990 of Ireland (which section is similar in essence to s.11 of the Insolvency Act 1986). An order was duly granted by the High Court of England and actions by creditors were stayed.

Scottish common law powers to strike down unfair preferences and gratuitous alienations survived the passing of the Insolvency Act 1986.[59] The definition of "insolvency law" only comprised provisions made by or under the Insolvency Act 1986.[60] This means that common law orders would not come under the provisions of s.426 for enforcement in the English courts, but rather would be enforceable under s.18(3) of the Civil Jurisdiction and Judgments Act 1982.[61]

PART III

EC REGULATION ON INSOLVENCY PROCEEDINGS

Introduction

22–40   The EC Regulation on insolvency proceedings ("the Regulation")[62] came into force on May 31, 2002 creating a Union-wide (with the exception of Denmark) set of rules for the orderly regulation of cross-

---

[58] Application to the Irish Courts—August 1990.
[59] See *Bank of Scotland v Pacific Shelf (Sixty Two) Ltd* (1988) 4 B.C.C. 457.
[60] See *Hughes v Hannover, supra.*
[61] For a commentary on this fine distinction see Smart, *Cross-Border Insolvency* (Butterworths, 1998), at pp.441–443.
[62] Council Regulation (E.C.) 1346/2000 of May 29, 2000 on insolvency proceedings [2000] O.J. L. 160/1.

Border insolvencies. The Regulation was made under Art.65 E.C., which authorises legislation on Justice and Home affairs for European Union states, with an opt-out for the UK, Ireland and Denmark. On this occasion the UK and Ireland opted in leaving Denmark as the only non-participating Member State.[63] The Regulation is directly applicable as part of the national laws of each Member State, except Denmark, without the need for national legislation to bring it into force.

The Regulation applies to collective insolvency proceedings which entail the partial or total divestment of a debtor and the appointment of a liquidator.[64] The Regulation is only one of a number of regulatory regimes which the E.C. has or is about to put in place to regulate the activities of undertakings which have cross-Border effects and to achieve judicial co-operation in civil matters within the meaning of Article 65 of the Treaty of Rome. For example, the Regulation does not apply to insolvency proceedings concerning insurance undertakings, credit institutions, investment undertakings which provide services involving the holding of funds or securities for third parties, or to collective investment undertakings.[65]

Article 2(a) defines "insolvency proceedings" as the proceedings listed in Annex A of the Regulation. In the case of the UK the relevant regimes are:

(a) winding up by or subject to the supervision of the court;
(b) creditors' voluntary winding up (with confirmation by the court);
(c) administration;
(d) voluntary arrangements under insolvency legislation; and
(e) bankruptcy or sequestration.

Article 3 of the Regulation provides that the courts of the Member State within the territory of which the centre of a debtor's main interests is situated shall have jurisdiction to open insolvency proceedings. In the case of a company or legal person, it is stated that the place of the registered office shall be presumed to be the centre of its main interests in the absence of proof to the contrary. Article 16 of the Regulation sets out the recognition principle. In terms of that Article any judgment opening insolvency proceedings handed down by a court of a Member State which has jurisdiction pursuant to Art.3 shall be recognised in all

---

[63] Recitals 32 and 33 of the Regulation deal with the position of the UK and Ireland, and Denmark respectively. Denmark also opted out of Council Regulation 44/2001, which replaced the Brussels Convention on Jurisdiction and enforcement of judgments from March 1, 2002.

[64] Art.1 of the Regulation.

[65] Art.1(2) of the Regulation. See Council Directive 2001/24 on the winding up of credit institutions [2001] O.J. L 125/15, which applies a separate regime to credit institutions etc., implemented by the Credit Institutions (Reorganisation and Winding up) Regulations 2004 (SI 2004/1045), made April 1, 2004, which came into force on May 5, 2004; see also Council Directive 2001/17 on the winding up of Insurance undertakings of March 19, 2001 and the Insurers (Reorganisation and Winding Up) Regulations 2003 (SI 2003/1102) implementing the Directive in the UK.

other Member States from the time that it becomes effective in the State on the opening of proceedings.

Article 25 of the Regulation sets out the regime for recognition and enforceability of other judgments. It states:

"1. Judgments handed down by a court whose judgment concerning the opening of proceedings is recognised in accordance with Article 16 and which concern the course and closure of insolvency proceedings, and compositions approved by that court shall also be recognised with no further formalities. Such judgments shall be enforced in accordance with Articles 31 to 51, with the exception of Article A34(2) of the Brussels Convention on Jurisdiction and the Enforcement of Judgments in Civil and Commercial Matters, as amended by the conventions of accession to this Convention.

The first sub-paragraph shall also apply to judgments deriving directly from the insolvency proceedings and which are closely linked with them, even if they were handed down by another court.

The first sub-paragraph shall also apply to judgments relating to preservation measures taken after the request for the opening of insolvency proceedings.

2. The recognition and enforcement of judgments other than those referred to in paragraph 1 shall be governed by the Convention referred to in paragraph 1, provided that that Convention is applicable.

3. The Member States shall not be obliged to recognise or enforce a judgment referred to in paragraph 1 which might result in a limitation of personal freedom or postal secrecy."

The Brussels Convention and the EC Regulation on Insolvency Proceedings

22–41   It was always understood during the extended part duration of the insolvency regime represented by the Regulation, that—outside the banking, insurance and investment sector—the Regulation would dovetail into the Brussels Convention of 1968,[66] which is referred to in Art.25 of the Regulation referred to in the previous paragraph. The terms of the Brussels Convention were set out in Sch.1 to the Civil Jurisdiction and Judgments Act 1982. Article 1, as amended, of the Convention provided:

"This Convention shall apply in civil and commercial matters whatever the nature of the court or tribunal. It shall not extend, in particular, to revenue, customs or administrative matters. The Convention shall not apply to—

1. The status or legal capacity of natural persons, rights and property arising out of matrimonial relationships, wills and succession.
2. Bankruptcy, proceedings relating to the winding up of insolvent companies or other legal persons, judicial arrangements, compositions and analogous proceedings."

---

[66] Now Council Regulation (E.C.) No. 44/2001 of December 22, 2000 [2001] O.J. L 12/1. It applies to proceedings started after March 21, 2002.

The leading case on the interpretation of that provision was *Gourdain v Nadler*,[67] in which the concept of bankruptcy was dealt with as follows:

> "As far as concerns bankruptcy, proceedings relating to the winding up of insolvent companies or other legal persons, judicial arrangements, compositions and analogous proceedings, according to the various laws of the Contracting Parties relating to debtors who have declared themselves unable to meet their liabilities, insolvency or the collapse of the debtor's credit worthiness, which involve the intervention of the courts culminating in the compulsory 'liquidation *des biens*' in the interest of the general body of creditors of the person, firm or company, or at least in supervision by the courts, it is necessary, if decisions relating to bankruptcy and winding up are to be excluded from the scope of the Convention, that they must derive directly from the bankruptcy or winding up and be closely connected with the proceedings for the 'liquidation *des biens*' or the '*réglement judiciaire*'."

Further light on the interpretation of Art.1 of the Convention is provided by the Jenard Report[68] which, in terms of s.3 of the Civil Jurisdiction and Judgments Act 1982, may be referred to for the interpretation of the Brussels Convention. Mr Jenard states:

> "However, matters falling outside the scope of the Convention do so only as they constitute the principal subject matter of the proceedings. They are thus not excluded when they come before the court as a subsidiary matter either in the main proceedings or in preliminary proceedings . . . Proceedings relating to a bankruptcy are not necessarily excluded from the Convention. Only proceedings arising directly from the bankruptcy and hence falling within the scope of the Bankruptcy Convention of the European Economic Community are excluded from the scope of the Convention."

It is suggested by the authors that this jurisprudence must be borne in mind when interpreting the Regulation and in deciding whether Scottish or English implementing legislation properly reflects the correct interpretation of the Regulation. It is also important to determine whether any types of action are in the anomalous position of not being covered by either the Brussels Convention (as amended) or by the Regulation.

International jurisdiction of the Regulation

Article 3 of the Regulation establishes a uniform set of jurisdictional **22–42** rules which are applicable to all the Member States covered by the Regulation. The Article envisages only two categories of proceedings. First the Regulation envisages main insolvency proceedings in the

---

[67] Case 133/78 [1979] E.C.R. 733. The jurisprudence in that case was accepted in the recent cases of *Re Hayward (Deceased)* [1997] 1 All E.R. 32 and *Ashurst v Pollard* [2000] 2 All E.R. Ch. D772.
[68] O.J. 1979 C.59, T.P. 10, 12.

country where the debtor, be it an individual or a company, has its "centre of main interests" and the territorial or secondary proceedings in other States where it has an "establishment".

Main proceedings (Article 3(1))

Where Art.3(1) entitles the courts of the Member State within whose territory the centre of the company's main interests is situated to open insolvency proceedings having the character of main proceedings, these proceedings have universal scope and are intended to encompass the company's assets on a world-wide basis and to affect all creditors, wherever situated.[69] It will not always be easy to determine the "centre of main interests" of a company. There is no definition of what the main interests are. Interests could include the location of assets, the corporate headquarters, the site where the board meets, or the country where the major part of its turnover is located. The Committee of the European Parliament, which approved the Regulation, cast some light on the definition, stating that "the centre of main interests is taken as meaning a place with which a debtor regularly has very close contacts, in which his manifold commercial interests are concentrated and in which the bulk of his assets is situated".[70] One assistance to interpretation is found in the Regulation in so far as Art.3(1) states that, in the case of a company or legal person, the place of the registered office shall be presumed to be the centre of its main interests in the absence of proof to the contrary. In order to avoid cross-border disputes about jurisdiction there is as a basic principle that there is to be automatic recognition of a prior order. Article 16(1) states that "[a]ny judgment opening insolvency proceedings handed down by a court of a Member State which has jurisdiction pursuant to Article 3 shall be recognised in all the other Member States from the time that it becomes effective in the State of the opening of proceedings."[71]

---

[69] See I.F. Fletcher, *Insolvency in Private International Law* (Clarendon Press, Oxford, 1999), p.260; the report on the Convention on Insolvency Proceedings, prepared by Professor M. Virgos and M.E. Schmidt, circulated as E.E.U. Council document 6500/96, DRS 8 (CFC), bearing the date May 3, 1996. Effect is given to Art.3 of the EC Regulation by an amendment of s.8 of the Insolvency Act 1986. In the Insolvency Act 1986 (Amendment) (No.2) Regulations 2002 (SI 2002/1240), para.5 (effective May 31, 2002), Art.2 and Annexes A—C of the EC Regulation apply to administration proceedings. In Scotland the EC Regulation on Insolvency Proceedings has been implemented by the Insolvency (Scotland) Regulations 2003 (SI 2003/2109 (S.8)). In the cases *Re BRAC Rent-A-Car Inc.*, *The Times*, February 24, 2003; [2003] E.W.H.C. 128; [2003] 1 W.L.R. 1421 and *Re The Salvage Association*, *The Times*, May 21, 2003; [2003] E.W.H.C. 1028; [2003] 3 All E.R. 246, *per* Blackburne J., it was held that, in terms of Art.3 of the EC Regulation, the English courts had jurisdiction to make an order in respect of a foreign company if it had its main centre of interests in the UK, although it was not an EC company—an obviously unintended knock on effect of the EC Regulation.

[70] European Parliament Legislative Observatory (May 29, 2000) final decision of the Committee on legal Affairs, internal market, reporter Kurt Lechner; see also Peter Burbridge, "Cross-Border insolvency within the European Union: Dawn of a New Era" (2002) 27 E.L.REV Octs 589 at 592.

[71] An important recent case on how centre of main interests is determined and on the automatic nature of recognition was that of *ISA Daisytek SAS*, at the Court of Appeal of Versailles, France, on September 4, 2003. It concerned an international group of companies which were put into administration in England on the basis that their main centres of

Secondary (Territorial) Proceedings (Article 3(2) to (4))

In terms of Art.3(2) of the Regulation, secondary proceedings may **22–43** only be open in circumstances where the centre of the debtor's main interests is situated within the territory of one of the Member States. If that condition is met, the courts of other Member States have jurisdiction to open insolvency proceedings against the debtor only if he possesses an establishment within the territory of the other Member State. In relation to the definition of secondary insolvency proceedings, the existence of an "establishment" belonging to the debtor is critical. Article 2(h) defines the term as meaning: "any place of operations where the debtor carries out a non-transitory economic activity with human means and goods."

The definition entails that there must be the presence of an activity, as opposed to merely the presence of assets. It also must be an economic activity of a non-transitory nature also, surprisingly, the requirement is that the economic activity is "with human means and goods." It is not yet clear what the definition of "establishment" entails. It is thought that the definition would include a "place of business" which included both personnel and assets. "Goods" cannot mean either the need for a manufacturing operation or the presence of physical stock which is

---

interests were in England, although only one was registered in England. A French court of first instance declared the administration order void as regards the French registered company, but the Versailles Court of Appeal quashed that order on the basis that the French court in terms of Arts 16 and 17 of the EC Regulation was required to recognise the English administration without further formality. The facts were that on May 16, 2003, the High Court in Leeds made administration orders in respect of English, German and French companies in the same Daisytek Group. These administration orders were made as main proceedings under the rules of international jurisdiction in the EC Regulation on Insolvency Proceedings 2000. It was held that the centre of main interests of each of the companies was in Bradford in West Yorkshire, England. The English company, Daisytek ISA Limited was a subsidiary of Daisytek International Corporation. That company and its subsidiaries had already on May 7, 2003 filed for Chap.11 bankruptcy protection in the USA. The English company was the holding company for the European group of companies, which were wholesale distributors of electronic office supplies, with the European activities co-ordinated from the head office in Bradford. In relation to three German companies, registered with premises in Germany, Judge McGonigal held on the evidence that Bradford was the place where each of the German companies conducted the administration of its interests on a regular basis, and placed particular emphasis on the ascertainability of the centre of main interest by third parties, following *Geveran Trading Co Limited v Skjevesland (No.3)* [2003] B.C.C. 209 at 223A, *per* Registrar Jacques. The Judge also made reference to para.75 of the Virgos-Schmidt Report on the original Convention. He considered that the most important "third parties" referred to in Recital (13) are potential creditors. In the case of a trading company the most important groups of potential creditors are likely to be financiers and trade suppliers. The financing of the business of the German companies was organised in Bradford and 70% of the goods supplied were supplied under contracts made in Bradford. A large majority of potential creditors by value knew that Bradford was where important functions of the German companies were carried out. With regard to the French company, ISA Daisytek SAS the Bradford group headquarters operated in relation to the French company in the same way that it operated in relation to the German companies. The French company was controlled from Bradford in the same way as the German companies. The decisions of the High Court and the French Court of Appeal show how quickly this complicated cross-border instrument is bedding down. (A fuller account of this case by Gabriel Moss Q.C.—as well as much additional valuable material on the EC Regulation—is to be found on the website of the International Insolvency Institute: *www.iiiglobal.org*).

being sold. The word "goods" is probably a translation of the French "Les Biens", which can mean assets as well as goods. A further key feature of secondary proceedings is that those proceedings must be restricted to the assets of the company situated in the territory of the secondary proceeding's jurisdiction (Art.3(2)). Further, where insolvency proceedings have already been opened at the place where the centre of the debtor's main interests is situated, any subsequent proceedings must be secondary proceedings (Art.3(3)). Another key point about secondary proceedings is that the secondary proceedings must be winding up proceedings (Art.3(3)). This narrows the range of proceedings available because the definition of "winding up proceedings" given in Art.2(c) is limited to "insolvency proceedings (within the meaning of para.(a)) involving realising the assets of the debtor", with the relevant procedures listed in Annex A and B to the Regulation. These procedures as listed in Annex B are fewer than those in Annex A.[72] A further restriction on the opening of secondary proceedings in Art. 3(4)(b) is that the opening of secondary proceedings may only be requested by a creditor who has his domicile, habitual residence or registered officer within the Member State in whose territory the establishment is situated, or whose claim arises from the operation of that establishment. A final point about independent territorial proceedings is that a liquidator in a subsequently opened main proceedings has the right to have the court convert those proceedings into a winding up if this proves to be in the interests of the creditors in the main proceedings (Art.37).

Choice of law code (Articles 4 to 15)

22–44   Articles 4 to 15 set up a uniform code of choice of law rules for cases covered by the Regulation. This takes the traditional discretionary freedom away from the Scottish and English courts, but with the counter-veiling benefit that there is now a predictability across the EU (excluding Denmark) as to what conflict rules will apply in any cross-Border insolvency. The predictability, of course, will not extend to situations where a State outwith the EU is party to the cross-border insolvency.

Basic principle (Article 4)

22–45   Article 4 sets out the basic principle that the law applicable to insolvency proceedings and their effects shall be that of the Member State within the territory of which such proceedings are open (referred to as the "State of the opening of proceedings"). The law of the State of the opening of proceedings shall determine the conditions for the opening of those proceedings, their conduct and their closure (Art.4(2)). Article 4(2) lists non-exhaustively the matters to be governed by the law of the State of opening of proceedings. These are set out in paras (a) to

---

[72] As regards the United Kingdom Annex B lists only (a) winding up by or subject to the supervision of the court; (b) creditors' voluntary winding up (with confirmation by the court); and (c) bankruptcy or sequestration, whereas Annex A lists (a) winding up by or subject to the supervision of the court; (b) creditors' voluntary winding up (with confirmation by the court); (c) administration; (d) voluntary arrangements under insolvency legislation; and (e) bankruptcy or sequestration.

(m) covering the effects of insolvency proceedings, both procedural and substantive, the persons and legal relationships concerns, and all the conditions for the opening, conduct and closure of the insolvency proceedings. These are:

(a) against which debtors insolvency proceedings may be brought on account of their capacity;
(b) the assets which form part of the estate and the treatment of assets acquired by or devolving on the debtor after the opening of insolvency proceedings;
(c) the respective powers of the debtor and the liquidator;
(d) the conditions under which set-offs may be invoked;
(e) the effects of insolvency proceedings on current contracts to which the debtor is party;
(f) the effects of the insolvency proceedings brought by individual creditors, with the exception of law suits pending;
(g) the claims which are to be lodged against the debtor's estate and the treatment of claims arising after the opening of insolvency proceedings;
(h) the rules governing the lodging, verification and admission of claims;
(i) the rules governing the distribution of proceeds from the realisation of assets, the ranking of claims and the rights of creditors who have obtained partial satisfaction after the opening of insolvency proceedings by virtue of a right *in rem* or through a set-off;
(j) the conditions for and the effects of closure of insolvency proceedings, in particular by composition;
(k) creditors' rights after the closure of insolvency proceedings;
(l) who is to bear the costs and expenses incurred in the insolvency proceedings;
(m) the rules relating to the voidness, voidability or enforceability of legal acts detrimental to all the creditors.

These matters are subject to certain qualifications set out in Arts 6, 8 and 15. Some of the provisions listed in Art.4(2) are directed at problems related to individual bankruptcies. Of overriding importance from the point of view of corporate insolvency are paras (g), (h) and (i). They result in the law of the State of opening of proceedings being determinative of each stage of the process of distribution of the assets, including the matter of what debts are, and are not, provable. The treatment of post-commencement claims against the assets, all aspects concerning proof and admission of claims; and the ranking of claims for the purposes of dividend, as well as how partly secured creditors are to be dealt with who have obtained partial satisfaction after the opening of insolvency proceedings by virtue of the enforcement of an *in rem* security or by set-off. Subject to Art6, set-off is primarily to be determined by reference to the law of the State of opening of proceedings. Article 4(2)(m) is also of key importance in establishing the basic principle that it is the law of the State of opening of proceedings which shall determine the rules relating to the voidness, voidability or unenforceability of legal acts detrimental to all the creditors. This would cover the striking down of all nature of preferences and gratuitous alienations or analogous transactions both before and after the commencement of insolvency. There is one qualification to Art.4(2)(m) in that, in terms of Art.13, Art.4(2)(m) is disapplied in certain circumstances in favour of the rule of some other Member State. Article 4(2)(m) is not to apply where the person benefited from an act detrimental to all the creditors provides proof that:

(a) the said act is subject to the law of a Member State other than that of the State of the opening of proceedings; and
(b) that the law does not allow any means of challenging that act in the relevant case.

In this way parties are protected who have reasonably relied upon the validity of a transaction whose governing law is that of a Member State, and which is valid according to both the insolvency law and the general law of that State.

Exception to the basic principle

22–46   Articles 5 to 15 set out several exceptions to the basic principle that the law of the State of opening of proceedings governs the insolvency. A brief analysis of these exceptions is given.

Third parties' rights in rem (Article 5)

22–47   The first major exception to the basic principle in Art.4 is contained in Art.5, which gives a rule to the effect that the rights *in rem* of creditors or third parties in respect of tangible or intangible, moveable or immovable assets belonging to the debtor which are situated within the territory of another Member State at the time of the opening of proceedings, shall continue to be determined by the law of where they are situated, and not be affected by the law of the State of opening of proceedings. The purpose of this provision is to safeguard the rights of parties to enter into transactions under which interests are created in favour of a creditor by way of security over assets. The provision is very widely drawn in so far as all types of property are capable of being affected including securities over book debts and receivables. The asset is only subject to the regime of Art.5 if it is situated within the territory of one of the Member States at the time of the opening of the insolvency proceedings. If the asset is situated outwith the territory of a Member State at the time of the opening of insolvency proceedings, Art.5 is not applicable, and it is then subject to the law of the State of opening of proceedings alone to decide to what extent the laws of the place where the asset is situated may be taken into account. Three rules are given for the identification of the Member State in which assets are situated. These rules are given in Art.2(g). In the case of tangible property, the physical location of the property is the Member State within the territory of which the property is situated. In the case of property and rights which are covered by a requirement for public registration, the situation of these assets is the Member State under whose authority the register is kept. Thirdly, in the case of "claims", *i.e.* debts due by parties to the insolvent debtor, these are situated within the territory of the Member State of which the third party required to meet them has the centre of his main interests, as determined by Art.A3(1). These rules supersede any contractual terms which have agreed the situation of the debts or claims to be some other jurisdiction. Article 5 is meant to protect pre-existing rights which were created before the insolvency proceedings were open. Article 5(2) gives a non-exhaustive list of the types of right covered by the expression *"in rem"*. Because this is a non-exhaustive definition and because different Member States adopt different approaches to rights *in rem*, it is thought that difficulties will arise in interpreting this exception.[73]

Set-off

Article 6(1) provides that the opening of insolvency proceedings shall **22–48** not affect the right of creditors to demand the set-off of their claims against the claims of the debtor, where such a set-off is permitted by the law applicable to the insolvent debtor's claim. This means that a choice of law rules of the State of opening of the proceedings must be applied to determine the governing law of that obligation which has given rise to a claim in favour of the insolvent debt. Only if set-off is permitted by the law applicable to that claim can the indebted party set-off that liability against the amount for which he stands in the role of creditor to the insolvent party. It may be noted that Art.6 does not insist that the claim should be governed by the law of one of the Member States, and could be the law of any other country outside the European Union. This provision deals with the intractable divide between the common law jurisdictions of the UK and Ireland, where set-off is allowed in an insolvency where there have been mutual dealings between the same parties in the same capacity and indeed is mandatory. In contrast, in States belonging to the civil law tradition, set-off is usually restricted to cases where debts and credits arise between the same parties in the context of a single transaction with any wider right to invoke set-off refused on the grounds that it would go against the principle of *pari passu* distribution of the company's assets.

Reservation of title

Reservation of title clauses within a contract to protect the unpaid **22–49** seller in the event of the buyer's insolvency are dealt with differently under the laws of the Member States.[74] Article 7 gives two rules to minimise the uncertainty which would otherwise arise in the case of cross-Border insolvency cases. These are exceptions to the basic principle that the law of the State of opening of the proceedings shall apply. The rules deal respectively with the opening of insolvency proceedings against the purchaser of an asset and the seller of the asset. In both cases the asset must be situated within the territory of a Member State other than the State of the opening of proceedings. The first rule in

---

[73] For a discussion of the complexities and difficulties of this provision see I.F. Fletcher, *Insolvency in Private International Law* (Clarendon Press, Oxford, 1999), pp.269–273.
[74] See G. McCormack, *Reservation of Title* (1990), pp.210–220.

Art.7(1) means that an unpaid seller is entitled to get his assets back in the case of the purchaser going into insolvency prior to the purchase price being paid, even though this is not allowed under the law of the State of the opening of the proceedings. Conversely, if it is the unpaid seller who goes into insolvency after the delivery of the asset, this is not grounds for the rescinding or terminating of the sale. In other words the purchaser acquires a title to the asset. It prevents a liquidator from repossessing an asset, leaving the purchaser with only a claim against the insolvency for breach of contract.

Contracts relating to immovable property

22–50   Article 8 provides that the effects of insolvency proceedings on a contract conferring the right to acquire or make use of immovable property shall be governed solely by the law of the Member State within the territory where the immovable property is situated. This means that an international contract for the sale or leasing of land will be governed by the law of the State where the immovable property is situated in the case of insolvency. The provision is not applicable where the property is situated in some third State.

Payment systems and financial markets

22–51   Article 9 provides that without prejudice to Art.5, the effects of insolvency proceedings on the rights and obligations of the parties to a payment or settlement system or to a financial market shall be governed solely by the law of the Member State applicable to that system or market. That provision, however, shall not preclude any action for voidness, voidability or unenforceability which may be taken to set aside payments or transactions under the law applicable to the relevant payment system or financial market. These provisions are designed to meet the need for special protection in the case of payment systems and financial markets. This applies, for example, to the position-closing agreements and netting agreements to be found in such systems as well as to the sale of securities and to the guarantees provided for such transactions as are governed in particular by Directive 98/26/EC of the European Parliament and of the Council of May 19, 1998, on settlement finality in payment and securities settlement systems.[75] For such transactions, the only law which is material should thus be that applicable to the system or market concerned. The rationale is given in recital 27 of the Regulation, which states that the provision is intended to prevent the possibility of mechanisms for the payment and settlement of transaction provided for in the payment and set-off systems are on the regulated financial markets of the Member States being altered in the case of insolvency of a business partner. Accordingly, Directive 98/26/EC contains special provisions which should taken precedence over the general rules in the Regulation.

Contracts of employment

22–52   Article 10 of the Regulation provides that the effects of insolvency proceedings on employment contracts and relationships shall be governed solely by the law of the Member State. Article 10 deals only with

---

[75] O.J. L 166/45, June 11, 1998.

the effect of insolvency upon the employment contract, such as whether the contract has been terminated by reason of insolvency. The ranking of employees' preferences for wages and other entitlements will be dealt with under the law of the State of the opening of proceedings. All Member States are, or are going to become, parties to the Rome Convention on the Law Applicable to Contractual Obligations of 19 June 1980, which has rules for determining the governing law of any contract. Article 6 of that Convention has choice of law rules applicable to individual employment contracts. If, by applying the Rome Convention Rules, the relevant applicable law is that of another Member State, Art.10 of the Regulation will apply and displace the law of the State of the opening of the proceedings.

Article 11 provides that the effects of insolvency proceedings on the **22–53** rights of the debtor in immovable property, a ship or an aircraft subject to registration in a public register shall be determined by the law of the Member State under the authority of which the register is kept. This Article deals with the effect of insolvency on high value assets which are subject to registration in a public register.

Community Patents and Trademarks

Article 12 provides that a Community Patent, a Community Trade- **22–54** mark or any other similar right established by Community law may be included only in the proceedings of the State of the opening of main proceedings. There are arrangements under EU law covering patents, trademarks and the rights of plant breeders in terms of which the Community right arising must be included in the first proceedings that are opened in a contracting State.[76] Because the main proceedings will not necessarily be the first proceedings to be opened, this meant that a special rule was needed to tie the determination of these various intellectual property rights to the law of the State of the opening of proceedings.

Protection of third party purchasers

Article 14 provides that where an asset, being immovable property, a **22–55** ship, or an aircraft subject to registration in a public register, is disposed of after the opening of insolvency proceedings, the validity of the Act is to be governed by the law of the State within in the territory of which the immovable asset is situated, or under the authority of which the register is kept. The disposal, however, must be for consideration for this rule to apply. Interestingly, Art.14 does not confine itself to assets situated in a Member State.

Effects of insolvency proceedings on law suits pending

Article 4(2)(f) excludes the law of the State of the opening of **22–56** proceedings from determining the effect of the opening of insolvency proceedings upon lawsuits pending. Article 15 provides a rule that the

---

[76] See Art.41 of the Community Patent Convention of December 15, 1975 (O.J. 1975 L 17/1), as modified by the Luxembourg Agreement of December 30, 1989 (O.J. 1989 L 401/10); Art.21 of Directive 89/104 of December 21, 1988 and Council Regulation (EC) 40/94 of December 20, 1993 on the Community Trademark; and Art.25 of Council Regulation (EC) 2100/94 of July 27, 1994 on Community Plant Variety Rights.

effects of insolvency proceedings on a law suit pending concerning an asset or a right of which the debtor has been divested shall be governed solely by the law of the Member State in which the lawsuit is pending.

Recognition of insolvency proceedings

22–57   Chapter II (Arts 16 to 26) set out the recognition regime across the EC in relation to insolvency proceedings. Also included are the powers exercisable by a liquidator in other Member States. The basic principle of automatic recognition is enshrined in Art.16(1) in terms of which "[a]ny judgment opening insolvency proceedings handed down by a court of a Member State which has jurisdiction pursuant to Article 3 shall be recognised in all the other Member States from the time that it becomes effective in the State of the opening of proceedings." This automatic recognition with immediate legal effect in all the Member States is a great advance on what went before, and effectively precludes the traditional "race of diligence" during the period between the commencement of insolvency proceedings in one country and the liquidator succeeding to obtain parallel powers in other jurisdictions. In terms of Art.2(f) the time of the opening of proceedings is the time at which the judgment opening proceedings becomes effective, irrespective of whether it is a final judgment. Recognition under Art.16 is only accorded to insolvency proceedings within the scope of the Regulation. A provisional liquidator is not included among the types of office holder listed in Annex AC, and hence the automatic recognition of his appointment is precluded. It may be however that use could be made of the provisions of Art.38, which would allow a provisional administrator appointed by a court to request help from the courts of another Member State. That of course would be a slower process than the automatic recognition.

Article 18(1) gives a liquidator appointed in the main proceedings power to act in all the Member States provided there are not a territorial or secondary insolvency proceedings opened. In particular he may raise court action in all the Member States and remove assets from other Member States. To facilitate this, Art.19 provides a uniform credential to prove his appointment. All that has to be produced is a certified copy of the original decision appointing him or any other certificate issued by the court which has jurisdiction. Articles 21 and 22 allow for the liquidator to request publication of the judgment opening the insolvency proceedings and to be registered in a public register. Conversely the Member States themselves may make mandatory such publicity or registration within public registers.

Public policy

22–58   Although there is automatic recognition and enforceability of judgments under Arts 16 and 25, Art.26 recognises that there may be situations where the enforcement of a judgment would be contrary to the public policy of the Member State. Refusal to enforce a judgment is acceptable but a high hurdle is set. The Member State may refuse to recognise insolvency proceedings opened in another Member State or to enforce a judgment handed down in the context of such proceedings where the effects of such recognition or enforcement would be manifestly contrary to the State's public policy, in particular its fundamental principles or the constitutional rights and liberties of the individual. Article 39 of the Regulation will perhaps lead to a test case on the scope for refusal to recognise a judgment as being manifestly contrary to public policy. In terms of Art.39 any creditor who has his habitual residence, domicile or registered office in a Member State other than the State of the opening of proceedings, including the tax authorities and social security authorities of Member States, shall have the right to launch claims in the insolvency proceedings in writing. As far as the UK is concerned, following the Scottish case of *Government of India v Taylor*,[77] foreign tax claims are not recognised on the basis that they are contrary to public policy. However, inroads have been made into this principle, especially by (a) Council Directive 76/308/EEC which provided for mutual assistance between Member States for the recovery of claims in relation to customs duties, VAT, agricultural levies, etc.; (b) Council Directive 2001/44/EC, which improved the then current arrangements for the recovery of VAT and extended the cross-border enforcement concept to direct taxes, providing that, if a request is made by a competent authority of another Member State, the Collector General shall collect the amount of the assessment specified, on behalf of the claiming Member State; and (c) Commission Directive 2002/94/EC, which set out how the competent authorities of the Member States must interact with each other in regard to requests for information, requests for recovery and the accompanying paperwork. It is thought, therefore, that all Revenue claims will be recoverable between the Member States.

Information for creditors and proving of claims

The Regulation's provisions in relation to the provision of information **22–59** to creditors and the proving of claims are generally straightforward but occasionally novel. Any creditor whose habitual residence, domicile or registered office is in an EU Member State is entitled to prove his claim in insolvency proceedings opened in another Member State (Art.39). Such creditors are to be given notice of the opening of proceedings and of any specific requirements or provisions of the particular Member State relating to the process of proving claims (Art.40). This notice has to be accompanied by a form indicating that it includes an invitation to lodge a claim and that there are time limits to be observed. That information is to be given in all the official languages of the institutions of the EU (see Sch.A). Creditors are required to provide appropriate information and documentation to support their claims (Art.41). Under Art.42, creditors are permitted to use their native language when proving their claims, but they can be required to provide a translation into the language of the State in which the proceedings were opened.

The novel aspect of the Regulation in relation to proving of claims is that, not only are liquidators in both main and secondary proceedings empowered to participate in other proceedings on the same basis as the creditor, they can also prove the claims which have been proved in

---

[77] [1955] A.C. 491 (HL).

proceedings for which they were appointed in other insolvency proceedings (Art.32).

Scottish secondary legislation implementing the Regulation

22–60   The Insolvency (Scotland) Regulations 2003[78] amend the Insolvency (Scotland) Rules 1986[79] to implement the Regulation.[80] New rr.1.46 to 1.48 and 2.22 to 2.44 of the Insolvency (Scotland) Rules 1986 provide for the conversion of, respectively, a voluntary arrangement and an administration into a winding up. These provisions implement Art.37 of the Regulation in terms of which the liquidator in the main proceedings may request that proceedings listed in Annex A previously opened in another Member State be converted into winding-up proceedings if this proves to be in the interests of the creditors in the main proceedings. In the case of Scotland the two types of proceedings which may be converted into winding up are voluntary arrangements and administrations. Administrative receivership is not a proceeding listed in Annex A.

Where a Member State liquidator proposes to apply to the court for the conversion under Art.37 of the EC Regulation of a voluntary arrangement/administration into a winding up, an affidavit must be prepared and sworn, and lodged in court in support of the application. The affidavit must state:

(a) that main proceedings have been opened in relation to the company in a member State other than the UK;

(b) the deponent's belief that the conversion of the voluntary arrangement/administration into a winding up would prove to be in the interests of the creditors in the main proceedings;

(c) the deponent's opinion as to whether the company ought to enter voluntary winding up or be wound up by the court; and

(d) all other matters that, in the opinion of the member State liquidator, would assist the court:

(i) in deciding whether to make such an order, and

(ii) if the court were to do so, in considering the need for any consequential provision that would be necessary or desirable.

Of critical importance is the provision (c) that the company may go into voluntary winding up or be wound up by the court in this type of conversion. If the court gives the go ahead for a creditors' voluntary winding up it is then necessary for the creditors' voluntary winding up to be confirmed by the court to bring such insolvency proceedings within the scope of Annex B of the Regulation. New r.4.84 of the Insolvency (Scotland) Rules 1986[81] prescribes a form in which the

---

[78] SI 2003/2109.

[79] SI 1986/1915, amended by SI 1987/1921 and SI 2002/2709 (S.10).

[80] Because the EC Regulation is directly applicable, only certain of its provisions are dealt with in the Insolvency (Scotland) Rules 1986, as amended.

[81] As inserted by SI 2003/2109.

member State liquidator must apply to the court, sets out what the affidavit must state, and gives the terms of the interlocutor. What is envisaged is that the court will merely confirm that the proceedings are creditors' voluntary winding up proceedings under Pt IV of the Insolvency Act 1986. The court is merely examining the documentation of the out of court winding up, and confirming that it corresponds to the provisions laid down in the Insolvency Act 1986 for the constitution of an out of court winding up. This may not be enough to set up the necessary nexus with the court.

In the leading case of *Gourdain v Nadler*[82] the Court of Justice envisaged that, for insolvency proceedings to be outwith the scope of the Brussels Convention, there would have to be intervention of the courts culminating in the compulsory "liquidation *des biens*" in the interest of the general body of creditors of the company, or at least in supervision by the courts. It may be wondered whether the type of confirmation set out in the Insolvency (Scotland) Regulations 2003 amounts to the type of supervision envisaged by the Court of Justice. Section 112 of the Insolvency Act 1986, which applies to compulsory and voluntary windings up, allows the liquidator, contributories and creditors to apply to the court to determine any question. In a sense this means that the court has supervisory powers over the voluntary winding up. However, whether these powers are exercised is dependent on an application being made to the court. It is thought, therefore, that the power under s.112 does not in itself amount to supervision.

This doubt in relation to whether voluntary windings up come within the Regulation extends also to out of court administrations.[83]

PART IV

IV. THE UNCITRAL MODEL LAW ON CROSS-BORDER INSOLVENCY

The United Nations Commission on International Trade Law **22–61** ("UNCITRAL") adopted a Model Law on cross-Border Insolvency ("the Model Law") in May 1997.[84] The text of the Model Law as adopted is included in that document as Annex I (pp.68—78). The Model Law is given as Appendix 2 in this book. Later a *Guide to Enactment of the Model Law on Cross-Border Insolvency* was issued by UNCITRAL as a resource for use by States which enact the Model Law and acts as an aid to interpretation of the Model Law's provisions.[85] Section 14 of the Insolvency Act 2000 for the Model Law provides for it to be given effect in the UK by Regulations made by statutory instrument, subject to affirmative resolution of both Houses of Parliament as well as requiring prior agreement by the Lord Chancellor and the Scottish Ministers. The

---

[82] Above at para.22–41.
[83] See para.5–12.
[84] UNCITRAL 30th Session, May 12–30, 1997: Official Records of the General Assembly of the United Nations, 52nd Session, Supplement No. 17 (A 152/17), Pt II, paras 12–225.
[85] UN General Assembly Document AICN, 9/442 (December 19, 1997).

enabling provision provides that it can be implemented with or without modification, and there is also provision for amendment of any of the terms of s.426 of the Insolvency Act 1986. It is expected that the UNCITRAL Model Law on cross-Border insolvency will be adopted by the UK (within a year from the date of writing of this book).

The beauty of a Model Law arrived at by international experts under the auspices of the United Nations Commission on International Trade is that it is not dependent on Treaty. Countries may adopt its provisions. Nor is the Model Law on Insolvency the first Model Law to be adopted in Scotland. The United Nation's Commission on International Trade (UNCITRAL) Model Law on International Commercial Arbitration has applied in Scotland since 1990, being enacted in Scotland by s.66 of and Sch.7 to the Law Reform (Miscellaneous Provisions) (Scotland) Act 1990 all international Arbitrations conducted in Scotland are now governed by the Model Law.

Scope of application of the Model Law on Cross-Border Insolvency

22–62   The Model Law consists of 32 Articles suitable for enactment into the existing laws of any State which desires to do so. A State which enacts any of the Model Law's provisions is referred to as an "Enacting State". The provisions become enforceable exclusively within the Enacting State, and there are no rules of direct jurisdiction or rules of choice of law. The Model Law is not dependent on a reciprocity[86] with other States and, once any provisions have been enacted, they may be invoked where they are applicable. The Model Law is strictly delimited in its application, and only applies in terms of Art.1 where:

(a) assistance is sought in the Enacting State by a foreign court or a foreign representative in connection with a foreign proceeding; or

(b) assistance is sought in a foreign State in connection with a proceeding under a law of the Enacting State relating to insolvency; or

(c) a foreign proceeding and a proceeding under a law of the Enacting State relating to insolvency in respect of the same debtor are taking place concurrently; or

(d) creditors or other interested persons in a foreign State have an interest in requesting the commencement of, or participating in, a proceeding under laws of the Enacting State relating to insolvency.

"Foreign proceeding" is defined in Art.2(a) of the Model Law to mean:

"A collective judicial or administrative proceeding in a foreign State, including an interim proceeding, pursuant to a law relating to

---

[86] It can, however, be modified to that effect. South Africa, for example, in enacting the model law, modified it so that it only applies to designated states, and the condition for designation is that the recognition afforded to South African proceedings in the state in question is such that designation is justified—not quite out-and-out reciprocity, but close.

insolvency in which proceeding the assets and affairs of the debtor are subject to control or supervision by a foreign court, for the purpose of reorganisation or liquidation."

This definition would certainly include compulsory winding up and administration, probably a CVA under the Insolvency Act 1986 and a CVA under s.425 of the Companies Act 1985, but would not include administrative receivership. It is thought that a creditor's voluntary winding up, unless the Regulations made under s.14 of the Insolvency Act 2000 make provision for some form of judicial intervention/ supervision of the creditor's voluntary winding up, would not be included because it is essentially a private exercise conducted according to public rules. However, the move to make all the insolvency regimes (especially now administration) less dependent on judicial intervention and bureaucratic supervision, means that "administrative proceeding" may be interpreted to mean the barest degree of state supervision.

Access and recognition under the Model Law on Insolvency

Access of foreign representatives and creditors to courts of the **22–63** Enacting State is covered by Arts 9 to 14, which comprise Chap.II of the Model Law and recognition of a foreign proceeding and relief is covered by Arts 15 to 24 (Chap.III). In terms of Art.9, a foreign representative is entitled to apply directly to a court of the Enacting State. A foreign representative is defined in Art.2(d) to mean "a person or body, including one appointed on an interim basis, authorised in a foreign proceeding to administer the reorganisation or the liquidation of the debtor's assets or affairs or to act as a representative of the foreign proceeding". An important provision is Art.10, which limits the jurisdiction of the Enacting State where an application is made. In terms of that Article, the sole fact that an application pursuant to the Model Law is made to a court in the enacting State by a foreign representative does not subject the foreign representative or the foreign assets and affairs of the debtor to the jurisdiction of the courts or the Enacting State for any purpose other than the application.

In order to obtain relief in the Enacting State, the foreign representative will need to have his local proceeding in the foreign court meet the criteria for international recognition which are contained in Arts 15 to 17 as with the EU Regulation on insolvency two categories of recognition exist. The foreign proceeding may qualify as a main or as a "non-main" proceeding dependent on the circumstances under which it was opened under the law of the foreign State. The definitions are given in Art.A2(b) and (c) as follows:

"(b) 'foreign main proceeding' means a foreign proceeding taking place in the State where the debtor has the centre of its main interest;

(c) "foreign non-main proceeding" means a foreign proceeding, other than a foreign main proceeding, taking place in a State where the debtor has an establishment within the meaning of sub-paragraph (f) of this Article."

The centre of main interests is not defined in the Model Law, although Art.16(3) provides a rebuttable presumption that in the case of a company it is where the registered office is. "Establishment" is defined in Art.2(f) as "any place of operations where the debtor carries out a non-transitory economic activity with human means and goods or services". This definition is almost the same as in the EU Regulation except for the inclusion of the words "or services". Where a foreign proceeding is recognised as a main proceeding, consequences flow automatically in terms of Art.20. They are:

> (a) a stay over the commencement or continuation of individual actions or proceedings concerning the debtor's assets, rights, obligations or liabilities;
> (b) a stay over any type of execution against the debtor's assets; and
> (c) a suspension of the debtor's right to transfer, encumber or otherwise dispose of any assets.

Article 21 applies to all cases whether a foreign proceeding is recognised, whether as a main or as a non-main proceeding, conferring a discretionary power on the court of the Enacting State to grant "any appropriate release including those specified in Art.A21(a) to (g). These types of relief are somewhat similar to those which apply automatically in terms of Art.20(1). Finally a consequence of recognition of a foreign proceeding is that the foreign representative may, provided the requirements of the law of the Enacting State are met, intervene in any proceedings in which the debtor is a party (Art.24).

Cross-Border co-operation between courts and co-ordination of concurrent proceedings

22–64   Articles 25, 26 and 27 (Chap.IV) provide for co-operation and direct communication between the court of the enacting State and foreign courts or foreign representatives, co-operation and direct communication between the administrator or liquidator under the law of the enacting State and foreign courts or foreign representatives. The forms of co-operation are listed in Art.27. These provisions set up a regime of co-operation similar to that found in the Anglo Saxon jurisdictions where there is a tradition of judicial intervention and co-operation between courts. In fact, one could say that the Model Law on Insolvency derives much of its classification jurisprudence from the continental systems, but its practical co-operation ethos from the Anglo Saxon jurisdictions.[87]

---

[87] For a full analysis and discussion of the Model Law from the point of view of an English lawyer, see I.F. Fletcher, *Insolvency in Private International Law* (Clarendon Press, Oxford, 1999), Chap.8: "A Global Initiative: UNCITRAL Model Law on Cross-Border Insolvency", pp.323–371.

INDEX